Leonardo da Vinci and the Pacioli Code. A nonfictional analysis of the science, mathematics, geometry, symbols, history and pictorial codes of the portraiture of the Franciscan friar and mathematician Luca Pacioli, the condottiero and jouster Galeazzo Sanseverino, and an enigmatic black fly, together with a cryptogram (IACO. B AR. VIGENNIS. P. 1495) describing the political intrigues in the Duchy of Milan during the time of Leonardo da Vinci. – Jerzy K. Kulski

The merit of painting lies in the exactness of reproduction. Painting is a science and all sciences are based on mathematics. No human enquiry can be a science unless it pursues its path through mathematical exposition and demonstration.

Whoever despises the supreme certainty of mathematics feeds on confusion and will never silence the contradictions of sophistical sciences, which lead to eternal quackery.

— *Leonardo da Vinci*

By the same author

China Heist (a crime novel)
Next Generation Sequencing: Advances, Applications, and Challenges (edited volume)
Leonardo da Vinci: The Melzi Chronicles (historical narrative)

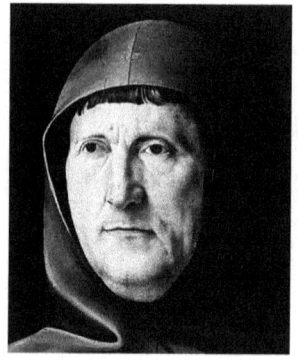

How many emperors and how many princes have passed of whom we have no recollection, and who sought to ensure their fame through power and riches?

O time, swift predator of created things, how many kings, how many people have you undone and how many changes and upheavals have followed?

— *Leonardo da Vinci*

Leonardo da Vinci & the Pacioli Code

Leonardo's mysterious portrait of Fra Luca Pacioli with patron, polyhedrons, drawing instruments and an encrypted cartouche accompanied by a sinister black fly

JERZY K. KULSKI

Non-fiction, science and art history.

Leonardo da Vinci & the Pacioli Code
Copyright © 2019 Jerzy K Kulski
All rights reserved.
ISBN: 978-0-6480653-3-3: softcover
ISBN: 978-0-6480653-4-0: e-book
A CiP catalogue record is available for this title from the National Library of Australia.

All rights reserved. No part of this book may be reproduced or transmitted in any form or by any means, electronic or mechanical, including photocopying, recording, or by any information storage and retrieval system, without permission in writing from the copyright owner.
First Edition: 2019v1.2
Published by Jerzy K. Kulski
www.jerzykulski.com

Cover design by Jerzy K. Kulski
Front cover image is *Fra Luca Pacioli and Student*, 1495 Oil, attributed to Jacopo de' Barbari. From the collection of the National Museum of Capodimonte in Naples. Image is in the Public Domain and it was obtain from Wikimedia Commons at:
https://commons.wikimedia.org/wiki/File:Pacioli.jpg

DEDICATION

The book is dedicated to Carla Glori who deciphered the enigmatic fly and the meaning of *IACO. B AR. VIGENNIS. P. 1495.*

ACKNOWLEDGEMENTS

I thank the following scholars for granting me permission to use their published figures and/or extensive quotes: Giovanni Barca, Javier Barrallo, Jennifer Bourn, Fritjof Capra, Argante Ciocci, Rachel Fletcher, Enrico Gamba, Dirk Haylebrouck, Siamak Khatibi, Stefaan Missinne, Vitor Murtinho, Philo, Klaus Schroer, Carlo Sequin, Christopher W. Tyler, Nicholas Wade and Susan Wardle. I also thank Carla Glori for her clarifications on the complex decryption of the cryptogram *IACO. B AR. VIGENNIS. P. 1495* written on the cartouche within the *Pacioli Portrait*. I especially acknowledge her permission to reproduce some of her copyrighted discoveries about the code that I included in Chapter 20.

I apologise to the following people who were deceased, retired or unable for whatever reason to reply to my emailed request for permission: Brenda Patione, Stephen Pepper, Hubert Weller and Tom Pastorello. I also thank Jan-Martin Wagner, Sarva Jagannadha Reddy, Pierre Deligne and the other mathematicians in their email club for discussions and debates about squaring the circle and transformations; and Sally Lloyd for pointing to some problems with my mathematical interpretations. I thank my good wife Tina for sustaining me during my research while writing this book and for help in proof reading some of the chapters. I am much obliged to retired clinical biochemist, colleague and friend Enrico Rossi for his precise editing and cogent comments. This book is not a fiction, nor an attempted reversion to Dan Brown's *The Da Vinci Code.*

In memory of Danker Hewton Purtle (27-11-1949 to 19-8-2017)

Table of Contents

PART 1. *Pacioli Portrait*
Chpt 1. Who was Fra Luca Pacioli?   1
Chpt 2. *Last Supper*, Betrayal & Old Men's Heads   17
Chpt 3. Unknown History of the *Pacioli Portrait*   27
Chpt 4. Barbari, Durer & Messina   41
Chpt 5. Duke of Urbino: A Most Unlikely Student of Luca Pacioli   64
Chpt 6. The Gallant Jouster, Galeazzo Sanseverino Sforza   71

PART 2. Phenomenological & Eidetic Analysis
Chpt 7. Visual Dialectics On Age, Nature & *Mona Lisa* Smiles   99
Chpt 8. Geometric Variations & Golden Ratios   116
Chpt 9. Euclid's Table: Drawing Tools, Numbers & Polyhedrons   141
Chpt 10. Spherical Triangles & Global Projections   184
Chpt 11. Squaring the Circle & Vitruvian Man   197
Chpt 12. Signature Rhombicuboctahedron & Meaningful Eyes   226
Chpt 13. Visual Pyramids of Light & Shadow   256
Chpt 14. Da Vinci Stereopsis: Depth Perception, Disparity & Shadows   278
Chpt 15. Vinci's Alphabetic Type Sets   304

PART 3. Colours, Dukes, Black Castle Rooms & Vinci's Academy
Chpt 16. Leonardo's Colours   313
Chpt 17. Il Moro & the Enigmatic Black Fly   321
Chpt 18. The Green Table: In Memory of Gian Galeazzo Sforza   344
Chpt 19. Sforza Castle, Black Rooms & Leonardo's Academy   361

PART 4. Cracking the Pacioli Code
Chpt 20. Carla Glori's Decryption With a Little Help From a Black Fly   387
Chpt 21. Leonardo Masterpiece? Misunderstood & Misattributed   405

About the Author   427

THE PACIOLI PORTRAIT: LEONARDO DA VINCI'S TRIBUTE TO ART, SCIENCE, MATHEMATICS, GEOMETRY & THE DIVINE PROPORTION (PHI – 1.618 …)

PART 1

Pacioli Portrait: Introduction and Deconstruction of the Mysterious Attribution

To come up against a 'dangerous ambiguity' that portends a 'besetting confusion' – this is hardly an unusual predicament for a philosopher to find himself in. – Robert Denoon Cumming, philosopher, 1992

FIG. 1. *Fra Luca Pacioli and Student*, 1495 Oil, attributed to Jacopo de' Barbari, from the collection of the National Museum of Capodimonte in Naples. Image is in the Public Domain and it was obtain from Wikimedia Commons at:
https://commons.wikimedia.org/wiki/File:Pacioli.jpg

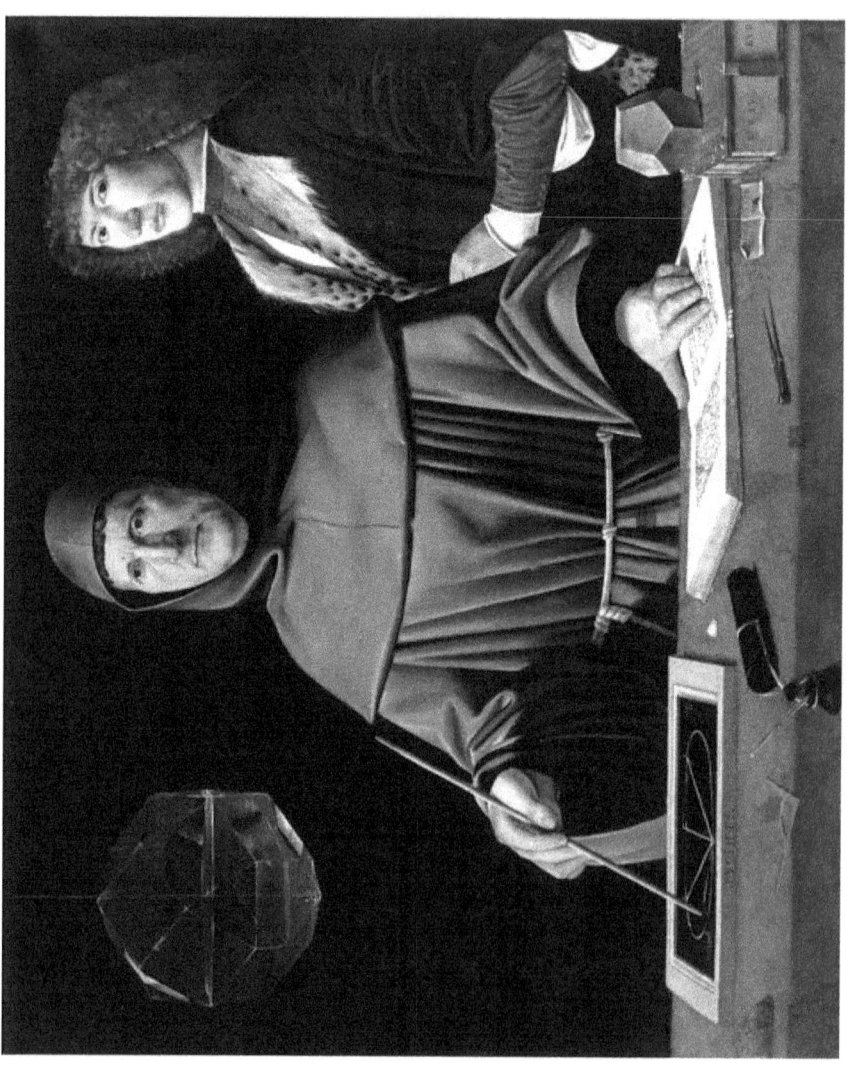

1

WHO WAS FRA LUCA PACIOLI?

The *Portrait of Luca Pacioli* at the National Museum of Capodimonte in Naples

There is a painting entitled *Fra Luca Pacioli and Student* attributed to Jacopo de' Barbari (accession number inv. Q 58) that has been exhibited at the National Museum of Capodimonte in Naples since 1957 (Fig. 1) and that still occupies a place of honour alongside works from the Farnese collection of statuary from Greco-Roman Antiquity. The painting is oil on panel that measures 98 x 108 cm (38.6 x 42.5 inches). It is one of the most evocative paintings of Renaissance Humanism, a masterpiece that honours the studies of mathematics and geometry. The reasoning and information gathered from these enlightening and revealing studies of mathematics and geometry throughout human history intrigued the Church intellectuals and many new studies and teachings were continuously sponsored by the main Italian courts of the fifteenth century. Another thing that is certain about the painting is that the central person providing the lesson on Euclidian geometry is Frà Luca Pacioli, a Franciscan monk and one of the most famous educators and mathematicians from the Renaissance period. Whenever I see an image of the painting, it evokes for me the hand and mind of a genius at work, a master painter of the Renaissance, somebody like Leonardo da Vinci who dedicated his entire life to teaching that painting was a science that was based on mathematics, geometry, perspective, light and vision, and human perception, the way of seeing properly with the eye and the mind. Moreover, Leonardo was a friend and mathematics student of Luca Pacioli and illustrator of the drawings of polyhedrons that accompanied Pacioli's thesis on *De Divina Proportione (Divine Proportion)*. And yet, the Museum has attributed the painting to the Venetian painter Jacopo de' Barbari who had never met or worked with Luca Pacioli. Here is what the Museum has posted on its website about the painting since 2016 in support of Jacopo de' Barbari (translated from Italian to English by Google translate):

The Portrait of Luca Pacioli *in Capodimonte*. *Published June 26, 2016*

At the Capodimonte Museum, the Portrait of Fra Luca Pacioli with a pupil, *is one of the most evocative paintings of Renaissance Humanism, and in particular of the studies on mathematics and geometry that animated the main Italian courts of the fifteenth century. The painting was purchased in 1903 by the Italian State, thus preventing its exportation abroad, and it was then donated to the then National Museum of Naples (current Archaeological Museum), before it was transferred to Capodimonte in 1957, where it occupies a place of honor alongside the works from the Farnese collection.*

The portrait depicts the Franciscan friar and distinguished mathematician Luca Pacioli (Borgo San Sepolcro, 1445-1517), a friend of Piero della Francesca and Leonardo, while, with his gaze focused, almost lost in front of him, demonstrates the eighth proposition from book XIII of the Elements of Euclid *to a disciple, dressed in the aristocratic fashion of the time, identified as the duke Guidobaldo da Montefeltro, who turns his eyes towards the spectator. The friar had dedicated to the young duke the* Summa de Arithmetica, *geometry, proportion and perspective, printed in Venice in 1494 and he depicted this in the painting right in front of the gentleman, with the inscription* Li [ber] R [egularum] Luc [ae] Bur [gensis]. *All around are scattered different objects for the study of mathematics and geometry (a quill pen with its case, a compass, a goniometer, a plaster and a sponge), but what particularly stand out are the two solid geometric shapes, widely studied by Luca Pacioli in his treatises: a dodecahedron, in wood, resting on the book, and a rhombicuboctahedron (semiregular polyhedron composed of eight equilateral triangles and eighteen squares) made of crystal, almost an apparition, half-filled with water, hanging from the ceiling by a thread not perfectly aligned. The inside of the hanging crystal reflects an image, perhaps the facade of the Palazzo Ducale di Urbino.*

The mysterious atmosphere and suspense that is breathed in the painting also is reflected in the enigma of the painter who managed to capture masterfully the educated and erudite climate that surrounded these figures of intellectuals, including Luca Pacioli. In fact, the signature that appears in the lower right corner (Iaco, Bar. Vigennis, 1495), *on a crumpled cartouche where a fly had just been laid, still arouses debate among the scholars about its interpretation: Is it Jacopo de' Barbari, Venetian artist and engraver who also worked in Germany and where he came into contact with Albrecht Dürer for his studies on human proportions, or rather, as recently proposed, by Jacometto Veneziano, another lagoon artist with exceptional qualities, among more loyal followers of Antonello da Messina?*

http://www.museocapodimonte.beniculturali.it/il-ritratto-di-luca-pacioli-a-capodimonte/

CHAPTER 1

Luca Pacioli, the Franciscan Friar and Holy Mathematician

Placed in the centre of the mysterious Capodimonte portrait, Luca Pacioli stands deep in thought behind a green-covered table in his Franciscan grey habit reminiscent of Jesus Christ in Leonardo da Vinci's painting of *The Last Supper*. Instead of Jesus pointing to a bible or nothing in particular as in *The Last Supper*, we see that the friar has drawn a geometric construction on a chalkboard with his right hand while his left hand rests on an opened book enlightening us about Euclidean Geometry. Various drawing and measuring instruments of mathematics rest on the table: a sponge, a protractor, a pen, a case, a piece of chalk, and compass. In the right corner of the table, a dodecahedron is placed upon a red book that bears Luca Pacioli's initials and so it might be his recently published *Summa*. The friar is not alone. He is in the presence of a mysterious disciple or patron, a well-dressed gentleman who stares out at us suspiciously and arrogantly from the right side of the painting as we look at him. On the opposite side of the painting, on the left side away from the disciple, a glass crystal half-filled with water is attached to a red line that is suspended from outside the top of the picture. The glass crystal is shaped like a rhombicuboctahedron, one of the thirteen semi-regular solids known among geometricists as Archimedean solids. Leonardo da Vinci had drawn and painted a similar rhombicuboctahedron image separately for Luca Pacioli's manuscript the *Divina Proportione* commissioned by the Duke of Milan, Ludovico Sforza and his son-in-law, Galeazzo Sanseverino, in 1496.

Today, the accountants and bookkeepers of the western world claim Fra Luca Pacioli to be their founding father, the saint of modern accounting and bookkeeping. He was the first person in Europe to publish a comprehensive book (*Summa*) on mathematics and the double-entry system of bookkeeping. He also is remembered as a Franciscan friar and an Italian mathematician who collaborated with Leonardo da Vinci in the publication of several treatises on mathematics, geometry and even wrote on the game of chess between 1496 and 1507.

Accounting is a profession involved in financial and business decisions in a system of audits, liabilities, tax returns, financial reports and bookkeeping that record and post routine transactions to clients, businesses and taxation authorities. Double-entry bookkeeping is part of the accounting system and, specifically, it is the practice of recording a business transaction in two equal parts, the debit (left column) and credit (right column) entries in an accounting journal. Some say this form of double-entry needs to be duplicated to be proper bookkeeping. Each transaction describes the object of the transaction (expenses, sales, fees, interests, and debts) and the source of payment (cash or credit). Evidence for basic accounting goes back 10,000 years with the use of writing and numbers emerging about 5,000 years ago. Luca Pacioli's description of the double-entry system of accounting that we still use today stems from his fifth book on mathematics *Summa de Arithmetica, Geometria, Proportioni et Proportionalita* (*Everything About Arithmetic, Geometry and Proportion*) published in the Italian vernacular by Paganino Paganini in Venice in 1494. The book contains little or no original mathematical work by Pacioli and it consists of ten chapters on a series of different mathematical topics, collectively covering essentially all of the knowledge of mathematics known during the Renaissance. It was intended to be a textbook for students of mathematics and business. The work was dedicated to Guidobaldo da Montefeltro (1472 to 1508), Duke of Urbino, a patron of the arts whom Luca Pacioli had met in Rome some years earlier in 1489.

Luca Pacioli also published other works on mathematics that Wikipedia lists as follows:

Tractatus mathematicus ad discipulos perusinos (Ms. Vatican Library, Lat. 3129), a nearly 600-page textbook dedicated to his students at the University of Perugia where Pacioli taught from 1477 to 1480. The manuscript was written between December 1477 and 29 April 1478. It contains 16 sections on merchant arithmetic, such as barter, exchange, profit, mixing metals, and algebra. One part of 25 pages is missing from the chapter on algebra.

De Viribus Quantitatis (Ms. Università degli Studi di Bologna, 1496–1508), a treatise on mathematics and magic. Written between 1496 and 1508, it contains the first reference to card tricks as well as guidance on how to juggle, eat fire, and make coins dance. It is the first work to note that Leonardo was left-handed while making reference to various other aspects of his life. *De Viribus Quantitatis* (*On the Power of Numbers*) is divided into three sections: mathematical problems, puzzles, and tricks, along with a collection of proverbs and verses. The book has been described as the 'foundation of modern magic and numerical puzzles', but it was never published and sat in the archives of the University of Bologna, where it was seen by only a small number of scholars during the Middle Ages. The book was rediscovered after David Singmaster, a mathematician, came across a reference to it in a 19th-century manuscript. An English translation was published for the first time in 2007.

Geometry (1509), a Latin translation of Euclid's *Elements*.

De Divina Proportione (written in Milan in 1496–98, published in Venice in 1509). Two versions of the original manuscript are extant, one in the Biblioteca Ambrosiana in Milan, the other in the Bibliothèque Publique et Universitaire in Geneva. The subject was mathematical and artistic proportion, especially the mathematics of the golden ratio, later to become known as *Phi* or the golden mean, the sacred proportion of 1:1.618 that was often applied as a design measure in architecture, drawing and painting.

CHAPTER 1

Two quantities are in the golden ratio if their ratio is the same as the ratio of their sum to the larger of the two quantities.

Leonardo da Vinci drew the illustrations of the regular solids in *De Divina Proportione* while he lived with and took mathematics lessons from Pacioli. Leonardo's drawings are probably the first illustrations of skeletonic solids, which allowed an easy distinction between front and back as a 3D representation. The work also discusses the use of perspective by painters such as Piero della Francesca, Melozzo da Forlì, and Marco Palmezzano. As a side note, the 'M' logo used by the Metropolitan Museum of Art in New York City is taken from *De Divina Proportione*.

At the beginning of *De Divina Proportione (Divine Proportion)* presented to the Duke of Milan on the 9th of February in 1498, Luca Pacioli inferred that the gentleman accompanying him in his portrait might be none other than his patron in Milan, Galeazzo Sanseverino, also know as Galeazzo Sforza Sanseverino, '[our] *own illustrious patron Signor Galeazzo Sforza, the powerful Vicar of Sanseverino and a general officer in the service of your Excellency, a captain of arms second to none today, and a diligent practitioner of our disciplines.*'

Leonardo da Vinci collaborated with Luca Pacioli in Milan between 1496 and 1499 on geometry, architecture and painting, and he provided for the *Divine Proportion* 60 illustrations of the regular solids that were used for the manuscripts (1498) and the 59 illustrations for the printed book (1509). The manuscripts and book consisted of three sections: *Compendium on the Divine Proportion* (twenty chapters) that discussed the golden ratio and polyhedrons from a mathematical perspective and their application in various arts; *Treatise on Architecture* (twenty chapters) that presented the ideas of Vitruvius on the application of mathematics in architecture; and a final section called *The Book is Divided into Three Parts*. This last section was mainly an Italian translation of Piero della Francesca's original Latin writings *On [the] Five Regular Solids* (*De quinque corporibus regularibus*) with mathematical examples.

In the foreward of the *Divine Proportion* manuscripts, Luca Pacioli dedicated the first copy to the Duke of Milan, Ludovico il Moro Sforza and the second copy to the Duke's son-in-law, Galeazzo da Sanseverino. The Duke's original manuscript copy is now in Switzerland at the Bibliothèque de Genève in Geneva, and Galeazzo Sanseverino's copy is now at the Biblioteca Ambrosiana in Milan. A third copy was passed on to Pier Soderini, the Gonfaloniere of Florence, when Leonardo da Vinci and Luca Pacioli were both back in Florence in 1501. This Florentine copy is now missing.

The following translated reprint of Luca Pacioli's dedication and tribute to Ludovico Sforza in Chapter One of the *Divine Proportion* is taken from the manuscript that is in Switzerland and that was given to the Duke of Milan.

To the very excellent Prince Ludovico Maria Sforza Anglo, Duke of Milan, ornament in times of peace as in times of war, this epistle of Brother Luca de Borgo San Sepolcro, of the Minor Orders, Professor of Sacred Theology:

On the Divine Proportion CHAPTER I

Today, Eminent Duke, the 9th day of February, the year of our Lord 1498, we are gathered in the impregnable citadel of your illustrious city of Milan, the most worthy place of your usual residence, in the presence of your majesty, and an assembly [dedicated to] praiseworthy scientific debate, composed of people of all ranks, famous and most wise, both religious and secular, with whom your magnificent court constantly abounds. Among whom, besides most reverend Lord Bishops, Protonotaries, and Abbots, there are present from our sacred seraphic Order, the reverend father and sublime theologian, Maestro Gometius; the most worthy preacher of the Sacred Scripture, friar Dominico, surnamed Ponzone; the reverend father Maestro Francesco Busti, presently acting regent in our worthy convent of Milan. And among the laymen present, first my own illustrious patron Signor Galeazzo Sforza, the powerful Vicar of Sanseverino and a general officer in the service of your Excellency, a captain of arms second to none today, and a diligent practitioner of our disciplines. And among the most perspicacious, powerful, and outstanding orators, supreme in medicine and astronomy: Ambroso Rosa, a most lucid and acute investigator of the works of Serapione and Avicenna, and of the heavenly bodies, and interpreter of things to come; the very learned Aluisi Marliano, capable of treating every illness; and most diligent observer of all aspects of medicine, Gabriel Pirovano – and much admired and venerated by all the aforesaid scholars, Nicolò Cusano, along with the expert in the same profession, Andrea Novarese, and other outstanding and often-consulted doctors of both civil and ecclesiastical law; and from your illustrious Magistracy, counselors, secretaries, chancellors. Among the company of most discerning architects, engineers and assiduous inventors of new things, Leonardo da Vinci, our Florentine compatriot, who, with every cast, sculpture and painting, confirms his surname. As with the admirable and stupendous equestrian statue, -- dedicated to the sacred memory of your glorious father --, whose height from the top of the head to the level ground is 12 braccia i.e., 36 times as much as the line AB given here in the margin [see Figure], and in all its enormous mass amounts to about 200,000 pounds, where each pound is made up of 12 common ounces which has nothing to envy from the work of Phidias and Praxiteles in Monte Cavallo; and of like excellence, the beautiful painting of the ardent desire of our Salvation, painted by his hand in the worthy and sacred refectory for receiving both bodily and spiritual nourishment, in the sacred temple of the Graces to whom today, Apelle, Miro, Policretus, and others, it is clear, must give the palm. And not satiated with all these, he expects to bring his invaluable work on locomotion, on percussion, weights, and all kinds of forces, that is, accidental weights, to a worthy conclusion -having already with all diligence finished his valuable book on painting and human motion. And [also present] his, so to speak, brother, Giacomo Andrea da Ferrara, a scrupulous disciple of Vitruvius, but not for

CHAPTER 1

that in any way diminished in remarkable military endeavours. Your Grace has said with mellifluous and gilded words, that person to be worthy of praise before God and man, who, having received some particular gift, communicates it voluntarily to others: because he awakens in them charity and merits praise and honour in making his, the sacred maxim:

Quod et sine figmento didici et sine invidia libenter comunico. *[The invention will be readily learned and do communal good.]*

... compiling the mathematical disciplines, a work dedicated to your magnanimous relative, <u>Guido Ubaldo, the Duke of Urbino</u>, and especially what is adduced in the fifth chapter of that book ... and prepared this compendium, ... to give the highest and most delightful flavor to all the aforesaid sciences and mathematical disciplines; and again for use by your Excellence and your reverent subjects, and to gild and ornament your most worthy library with its multitude of volumes on every subject, to put at your disposal this brief compendium and most useful treatise, entitled <u>De Divina Proportione</u>. ... With constant humility and due reverence, I commend myself continuously in the highest degree, to your Excellency the Duke, to whom I wish the greatest happiness.

Quae felicissime ad vota valeat *[The vows' values most happily served].*

The underlined parts in the translation highlight Luca Pacioli's dedication to the Duke Ludovico Maria Sforza, his patron Signor Galeazzo Sforza Sanseverino, Maestro Leonardo da Vinci and Duke Ludovico Maria Sforza's magnanimous relative, Guido Ubaldo, the Duke of Urbino, who was the son of Battista Sforza (died aged 25 years in 1472), the cousin of Lord Ludovico il Moro Sforza and the daughter of Alessandro Sforza, Lord of Pesaro. Thus, Ludovico Sforza was Guidobaldo da Montefeltro's uncle. Coincidently, Luca Pacioli's mathematics teacher, Piero della Francesca, had painted the diptych of Guidobaldo's mother and father. The Montefeltro family of Urbino was connected closely with the Sforza family, courtiers, artists and friends. So, let this heartfelt dedication by Luca Pacioli to Duke Ludovico Sforza resound loudly for this in part describes the subject of Leonardo da Vinci's painting of Luca Pacioli and Galeazzo Sforza Sanseverino in the *Pacioli Portrait*.

Most of the second volume of *Summa de arithmetica, geometria. proportioni et proportionalita* that was published in 1494 was only a slightly rewritten version of Piero della Francesca's work; and the third section of Pacioli's *De Divina Proportione* was an Italian translation of Piero della Francesca's Latin writings *On [the] Five Regular Solids*. In both cases, Pacioli omitted an attribution to Piero della Francesca. He was severely criticised for this and accused of plagiarism by the sixteenth-century art historian and biographer Giorgio Vasari. The accountant, writer and educator R. Emmett Taylor (1889–1956) wrote in his book *No Royal Road: Luca Pacioli and His Times* that Pacioli may have had nothing to do with the translated volume *De Divina Proportione*, and that it may just have been appended to his work because of his reputation as being a mathematician. However, no such defence can be presented concerning the inclusion of Piero della Francesca's material in Pacioli's *Summa*.

Luca Pacioli writings were mostly derivative – they were essentially textbooks – so by their very nature they were plagiarised – he passed on other people's ideas to the masses or more to the point, to those who were interested in gaining the knowledge of the past. Luca Pacioli was criticised as early as 1529 in a printed book entitled *Champ-fleury* by Geofroy Tory, a French humanist, writer and engraver who essentially accused the monk Luca Pacioli of stealing Leonardo's lettering (fonts) and not attributing the work and technique to him:

'Fra Luca Pacioli of Borgo San Sepolcro, of the Order of Friars Minor and theologian, who wrote in Italian vernacular a book titled Divine Proportion, and intended to depict the aforesaid Attic letters, has not described it or given explanation for it; and I am not surprised at all, because I heard from some Italians that he has deducted his letters and taken them from Maestro Leonardo Vinci, who died in Amboise and who was a very excellent philosopher and admirable painter and almost another Archimedes. It is said about Luca that he printed his letters as his own.'

Pacioli also wrote an unpublished treatise on chess, *De ludo scachorum* (*On the Game of Chess*). Long thought to have been lost, a surviving manuscript was rediscovered in 2006, in the 22,000-volume library of Count Guglielmo Coronini. A facsimile edition of the book was published in Pacioli's hometown of Sansepolcro in 2008. Based on Leonardo da Vinci's long association with the author and for having illustrated *De Divina Proportione*, some scholars speculated that Leonardo probably drew the chess problems that appear in the manuscript or that he at least designed the chess pieces used in the problems.

Short Biography and a Timeline of Luca Pacioli's Meetings with Leonardo da Vinci and Galeazzo Sanseverino Sforza

Luca Bartolomeo de Pacioli was born in about 1447 in Borgo Sansepolcro, near Arezzo, in the Republic of Florence, into a large and religious family. He had three older brothers, Antonio (died young), Ginepro and Ambrogio, and his father Bartolomeo was a small animal breeder and farmer. His mother was Maddalena di Francesco di Matteo Nuti from Villa Fariccio. Luca Pacioli's biographer Bernardino Baldi (1879) wrote that:

'The de Paciuoli family as far as I believe was ignoble and of little splendor.'

One of his brothers, Ambrogio, was a Franciscan friar and his other brother, Ginepro, was a guard at the Franciscan convent of Borgo

Sansepolcro. Also, his cousin, Niccolo, was a Camaldolese and prior monk in the church of S. Stefano di Farneto. Luca was destined to join them and become a man of the church. When his father died in 1459, Luca at 12 years of age was entrusted to the Folco family of Giovanni di Canti Bofolci who had two sons, Piergentile and Conte. While in their care he received an *abboco* (abacus) education intending to become a merchant.

After the Republic of Florence was founded in the year 1115 AD, there always was a strong emphasis by the ruling council (*Signoria*) elected by Florentine guild members to favour the merchant and trading classes in the city. The Italian abacus schools appeared more than a century after the publication of the *Book of Abacus* by Leonardo Fibonacci in 1202 and these schools placed great importance on mathematics as part of a commerce-directed curriculum. Fibonacci introduced the Hindu-Arabic numeral system that had originated in India in 400 BCE as a simpler and more practical way of calculating financial transactions than the old Roman numerical system that taxed the memory and produced too many computational errors. The Italian merchants and traders gradually adopted the Hindu-numeral and the Arabian algebraic mathematics to produce accountants, clerks and mathematical financiers. This further helped to establish abacus schools for students using salaried master instructors to teach a curriculum or independent teachers who tutored privately for a fee or salary from the homes of rich merchants, gentlemen and nobles. In between the eleventh and fourteenth centuries, the Italian city-states of Genoa, Florence and Venice and the kingdom of Naples were the leading European trade-centres that needed educated accountants. The oriental trade routes were extended during the crusades and they turned Venice and Genoa into competing world markets for oriental products such as spices, sugar, cotton, silk, perfumes, glasswork, exotic woods, ivory, animals, domestic slaves and ancient classical and scientific knowledge. It is likely that the travelling Italians gained knowledge of double-entry bookkeeping from the traders and bankers of Constantinople, Alexandria and Cyprus, and that some of the principles of double-entry bookkeeping already were practised in Florence by merchants and bankers in the late 13th century, long before the birth of Luca Pacioli.

Luca Pacioli's first teacher in Borgo Sansepolcro was the Florentine painter, mathematician and geometer Piero della Francesca (1415/1420-1492) who had interconnected mathematics and science with art. Indeed, some historians believe that Luca Pacioli had stolen the ideas about double-entry bookkeeping from his teacher Piero della Francesca who also was born in Borgo Sansepolcro. Although della Francesca lived and worked in Borgo Sansepolcro for most of his life, in the years between 1469 and 1486 he taught and worked in Urbino in the service of Federico III da Montefeltro who became the duke of Urbino in 1474. While in Urbino, he painted the monumental *Montefeltro Alterpiece* (now in the Brera Gallery, Milan) and added Luca Pacioli into the painting as one of the saintly figures. He also painted *The Flagellation of Christ* (Nazionale della Marche, Urbino), and a variety of official portraits of the duke of Urbino and his wife. Some of Piero della Francesca's other better-known works are *The Baptism of Christ* (National Gallery, London), *The Resurrection* (Museo Civico, Sansepolcro), *Paired Portrait of the Duke and Duchess of Urbino* (Uffizi, Florence), *Virgin and Child Enthroned with Four Angels* (Sterling and Francine Clark Art Institute, Williamstown), and the cycle of frescoes known as *The History of the True Cross* (Church of San Francesco, Arezzo). He used a distinctly original colour palette, geometric compositions and the rules of perspective that influenced Leonardo da Vinci and others who, like Piero della Francesca, believed that painting was a science.

In about 1465, when Luca Pacioli was about eighteen years of age, he moved to Venice to continue his education and to earn some money and board from the rich merchant Antonio de Rompiasi, both as his bookkeeper and the mathematics tutor of his three sons. While in Venice, he attended the lectures of the mathematician Domenico Bragadino at the *Scuolo di Rialto*, studied the history and philosophy of Aristotelianism and wrote a treatise on mathematics, which he dedicated to the Rompiasi family. In 1470, he stayed for a year in Rome at the house of the architect, philosopher and mathematician Leon Battista Alberti (born in Genoa in 1404-died in Rome in 1472), who, after his death, became a great influence on both Pacioli and Leonardo da Vinci and many others involved in architecture and design. Leon Battista Alberti was a humanist, artist, architect, poet, linguist, priest, philosopher and cryptographer, who was the main instigator of Renaissance art theory and the prototype Renaissance 'Universal Man' before the emergence of Leonardo da Vinci who subsequently inherited the title. Leon Battista Alberti wrote on beauty and the best ways to progress and excel in the arts.

> *Beauty: the adjustment of all parts proportionately so that one cannot add or subtract or change without impairing the harmony of the whole.*

Alberti believed in 'ideal' beauty. Leonardo filled his notebooks with Alberti's ideas, including page after page of observations on human proportions that finally resulted with his famous drawing of the *Vitruvian Man*, a human figure related to a square and a circle. Some of the titles of the influential treatises that Leon Battista Alberti wrote about were *De Re Aedificatoria (On the Art of Building in Ten Books), On Painting, On Sculpture* and *Family Life in Florence*. Leonardo da Vinci and Luca Pacioli would have read and studied all of Leon Battista Alberti's writings and they would have discussed and debated his ideas and contributions both in private and at

CHAPTER 1

public meetings, like when they were together at the gatherings and debates held by the Leonardo da Vinci Academy in Milan between 1496 and 1499. These gatherings involved writers, poets, artists, musicians, architects, engineers, mathematicians, astrologers, lawyers, physicians and patrons of the sciences and the arts and they evolved from Leonardo's lectures, debates and disputations on art, music, architecture, geometry, proportion and perspective.

In 1473, after his one-year stay in Rome, Luca Pacioli became a Franciscan Minor and then moved to Peruga in 1477 where he taught and tutored mathematics until 1480. Thereafter, he travelled again and visited the main courts and cities of Italy and lectured on mathematics at various Italian universities and military schools, including in Florence, Rome, Urbino and Naples. While in Rome in 1489, he met with Guidobaldo da Montefeltro, who became the Duke of Urbino in 1482 and was then already a leading patron of the arts and sciences. Luca Pacioli returned to Borgo Sansepolcro in 1491 and stayed there until 1493. After brief stays in Padua and Urbino, he returned to Venice in 1494 where he prepared his *opus magnum* the *Summa* for publication by Paganino de Paganini. There is no evidence to show that Luca Pacioli met with or befriended the Venetian painter Jacopo de' Barbari while he was in Venice at this time. And, if they did meet the question arises whether there was enough time available for Luca Pacioli to teach Jacopo de' Barbari all that he knew about the *Divine Proportion* and how to draw and paint a transparent rhombicuboctahedron that is depicted so brilliantly in the *Pacioli Portrait* at the Capodimonte National Museum. Given the extensive mathematical knowledge required and depicted about the *Divine Proportion* in the *Pacioli Portrait*, it seems improbable that Jacopo de' Barbari could have painted the *Pacioli Portrait* in 1494 or 1495.

After spending a year in Venice with his publisher, Pacioli returned to Florence in 1495. This is the same year that Leonardo left Milan for a brief visit to Florence where he acted as consultant to the architect Simone Pollaiolo il Cronaca in the building of the *Sala del Gran Consiglio* (the Grand Hall) on the main floor of the *Palazzo della Signoria*. While in Florence, he probably met with Luca Pacioli and elicited his interest about teaching mathematics at the Sforza court and schools in Milan. When Leonardo returned to Milan in 1495, he undoubtedly encouraged Ludovico Sforza and Galeazzo Sanseverino to invite the Franciscan monk officially to Milan. Luca Pacioli accepted Duke Ludovico Sforza's offer for the position of a professorship, an inaugural chair in mathematics at the University of Pavia.

By October of 1496, Luca Pacioli was in Milan teaching and collaborating with Leonardo da Vinci and living at the residence of Galeazzo Sanseverino. With the fall of Ludovico Sforza during the invasion of Milan by the French king Louis XII in October of 1499, Pacioli and da Vinci left Milan together in December and travelled to Mantua and Venice, before settling in Florence in the spring of 1500, each seeking patrons and commissions. Pacioli briefly moved to Pisa in 1500 to teach mathematics, but in the autumn of that same year, he returned to Florence where he stayed until 1507 before transferring from Florence to Pisa to teach at the university. During his Florentine stay, he also taught at the Bologna University from 1501-02 with assistance from Leonardo da Vinci's contacts at the university.

In the meantime, in the period between 1500 and 1507, Leonardo da Vinci was occupied by a variety of different painting, architectural and engineering projects sponsored in part by the *Gonfaloniere* Pietro Soderini and Niccolo Machiavelli representing the *Signoria* of the Republic of Florence. His stay in Florence was interrupted for a year when he accepted the position of Cesare Borgia's fortification engineer from July of 1502 to March of 1503 to reinforce the castles and defences that Cesare needed in his military campaign against the various opposing fiefs in the Romagna and Marche regions. Luca Pacioli must have been in attendance at one or more of the campaigns near Bologna because he wrote a note about Leonardo's bridge-building techniques for the Borgio troops.

'One day Cesare Valentino, Duke of Romagna and the present Lord of Piombino, found himself and his army at a river which was 24 paces wide, and could find no bridge, nor any material to make one except for a stack of wood all cut to length of 16 paces. And from this wood, using neither iron nor rope nor any other construction, his noble engineer made a bridge sufficiently strong for the army to pass over.'

Although undocumented, it seems likely that Leonardo maintained his close friendship with Luca Pacioli while they were in Florence together. Luca and Leonardo often resided at the Franciscan convent of Saint Croce where several Florentine artists had their permanent or temporary studios to undertake their artistry for the basilica and the convent. The Basilica of Santa Croce is a neo-Gothic Franciscan landmark, constructed in the year of 1294 and within walking distance of the Ponte alle Grazie. Today, it is known for its Giotto frescoes and the tombs of Michelangelo, Machiavelli and Galileo and commemorative plaques for Leonardo da Vinci and Dante who are buried elsewhere.

Eventually, Leonardo was tired and frustrated by his disputes with the *Signoria* about his obligations to them and those with his half-brothers in Florence about the inheritance that he was left after the death of his much beloved uncle. He returned to Milan in 1508 and worked for the next six years for the French governors of the Duchy of Milan with the French king, Louis XII as Milan's duke. About the time that Leonardo da Vinci left

Florence, Luca Pacioli visited Rome and Mantua and then returned to Venice in 1509 for a year to publish the printed version of the *Divine Proportion*. He dedicated the printed version to the *Gonfaloniere* of Florence, Pietro Soderini, who had supported many scholars and artists, including Leonardo da Vinci, Raphael, Michelangelo, and Machiavelli. After a year in Venice, Luca Pacioli moved to Perugia to teach mathematics at their university. Leonardo da Vinci and Luca Pacioli met again in Rome in 1514. Leonardo was there between 1513 and 1516 working for the Pope's younger brother, Giuliano de' Medici, the Duke of Nemours. Pope Leo X appointed Luca Pacioli as Professor of Mathematics in the Sapienza in Rome in 1514. However, after a year, Pacioli returned to Sansepolcro, and he died there on June 18, 1517.

Luca Pacioli was not an unusual friar in the sense that he was also a scientist and a clerical scholar. The study and teaching of natural sciences, astrology, mathematics and cosmology was a tradition of the Catholic Church. The missionaries sent out to the far-east and unknown places in the New World were encouraged to explore and report on the natural wonders and cultures of their new environment while simultaneously converting the heathens to the 'word of God'. The bible, canon law, sociology and politics were the main training and teaching subjects for the Catholic clerics, whereas science, cosmology and theology was more for the few intellectuals, well-healed, and influential in the Church. It also depended on what order or group you joined or were educated by and intended to follow. For example, the Jesuits who were founded as the Society of Jesus in Paris in 1534 by Ignatius of Loyola fifteen years after Leonardo da Vinci's death in Amboise in 1519 have had a long tradition as an order involved in the development of mathematics, science and astronomy while still preaching the 'wrath of God'.

The Middle Ages and Renaissance produced many clerics like Luca Pacioli who were theologians, astronomers, physicists, architects and mathematicians for these disciplines were important components of cosmology and for understanding the structure and design of God's heaven and heavenly bodies that shine brightly in the clear night's sky. Albertus Magnus, who lived from 1206 to 1280, was interested in biology, logic, metaphysics and psychology and he became the Patron Saint of natural sciences and biologists. Roger Bacon was a Franciscan friar who lived from 1214 to 1294 and contributed to mathematics and optics and the methodologies of scientific investigation. The principle of *Occam's razor* is recognised from the scholastic works of the Franciscan friar William of Ockham (1288 -1348) on logic, physics and theology. Some of the other better known scientist-clerics during the Renaissance period are Nicolaus Copernicus (mathematician and astronomer), Johannes Werner (mathematician, astronomer and geographer), Gabriele Falloppio (anatomist and physician), Marcin of Urzedow (physician, pharmacist and botanist), Francesco Maurolico (polymath), Maciej Miechowita (geographer), Nicholas of Cusa (astronomer, mathematician, polymath), and Nicole Oresme (mathematician, physicist, astronomer, polymath). Anthanasius Kircher observed microbes (little worms and animalcules) through a microscope and concluded that disease was caused by microorganisms in his *Scrutinium Pestis* of 1658.

Leonardo da Vinci, the scientist, philosopher, engineer and painter, was about seven years younger than Fra Luca Pacioli and he had a healthy disdain for the clerics and the priests of the Church. Leonardo believed the clergy and priests were the parasites of the people, living off the fear and insecurities of the uneducated working classes. He was anticlerical and antisacerdotal and liked to poke fun at silly religious beliefs and practices. He had an array of jokes and riddles about the clergy written out in his mirror writing in his notebooks. The following jest is taken from one of his notebooks:

A priest going the round of his parish on Saturday before Easter, sprinkling holy water in the houses as was his custom came to a painter's room and there sprinkled the water upon some of his pictures. The painter turned round, somewhat angered, and asked him why this sprinkling had been bestowed on his pictures; then the priest said that it was the custom and that it was his duty to do so, that he was doing good, and that whoever did a good deed might expect a return as good and better; for so God had promised that every good deed that was done on earth shall be rewarded a hundredfold from on high. Then the painter, having waited until the priest had walked out, stepped to the window above, and threw a large bucket of water on to his back, saying: Here is the reward a hundredfold from on high as you said would come from the good you did me with your holy water with which you have damaged half my pictures.

Because Leonardo da Vinci was no fan of the clerics and the priests, it seems curious that he befriended the friar Luca Pacioli. But, Luca was no ordinary cleric. Although he was a man of strong faith and fervently believed in God and Catholicism, he was more scientist and philosopher than cleric. He did little overall teaching in religious matters and spent more time in the instruction of mathematics and science. However, he saw that mathematics was part of God's design and he could easily bring in sacred numbers such as the number three into religious life and preaching:

'*There are three principal sins: Avarice, luxury and pride; three sorts of satisfaction for sin, fasting, almsgiving and prayer; three persons offended by sin, God, the sinner himself, and his neighbor; three witnesses in heaven,* Pater, verbum, *and* spiritus sanctus; *three degrees of penitence, contrition, confession and satisfaction…*'

CHAPTER 1

Luca Pacioli provided Leonardo da Vinci with the knowledge and beauty of mathematics, geometry, perspective and the golden ratio and together, they produced the epic and enlightening *Divine Proportion*. Pacioli also might have assisted Leonardo with the perspective and mathematical calculations for the *Last Supper* and suggested a mathematical design for his portrait together with Galeazzo Sanseverino Sforza and the polyhedrons.

Luca Pacioli's timeline:

1445. October. Born in Sansepolcro (at the time Borgo Sansepolcro), Tuscany, Republic of Florence.
1459. After the death of his father, he went to live with the Folco di Giovanni di Canti Bofolci family.
1460s. Moved to Venice and worked for Antonio Rompiasi, a merchant on Giudecca.
1470-1471. Was in Rome, met and lived with Leon Battista Alberti.
1477-1480. Worked at the *Studium* of Perugia.
1481. Moved to Zara.
1486. Stayed in Perugia.
1488 and 1489. Teaching '*in the worthy Middle School in Naples*'.
1489. Returned to teach in Rome, met Guidobaldo da Montefeltro, the Duke of Urbino.
1491-1493. Returned to Borgo Sansepolcro.
1494. Was in Venice to edit the *Summa* (dedicated to Guidobaldo da Montefeltro).
1495. Returned to Florence. Possibly met with Leonardo da Vinci who was briefly in Florence to consult on the building of the *Sala del Gran Consiglio* for the Palazzo della Signoria.
1496-1499. In Milan where he was Professor of Mathematics and frequented the cultured court of Ludovico Sforza. He lived with and was sponsored by Galeazzo Sanseverino, gentleman, soldier, jouster and the duke Ludovico's faithful son-in-law. Worked with Leonardo da Vinci on mathematical problems and the production of the illustrated manuscript and book *Divine Proportion*.
1498. Taught mathematics at the *Studium* of Pavia in the Duchy of Milan.
1500. Left Milan with Leonardo da Vinci and they travelled to Mantua and Venice before resettling in Florence.
1501-02. Taught at the *Studium* of Perugia and Bologna.
1501-1507. Taught in Florence.
1508. Taught in Rome and Mantua.
1509. Returned to Venice to advise on and see the printed version of the *Divine Proportion*.
1510. Taught mathematics in Perugia.
1514. Appointed by Pope Leo X to teach mathematics in Rome. Leonardo da Vinci was in Rome at the same time with Salai and Francesco Melzi (1513 to 1516).
1515. Returned to live and work in Borgo Sansepolcro.
18th June, 1517. He died in Borgo Sansepolcro.

The following inscription (translated from Italian) is written on the memorial stone that was placed in Luca Pacioli's house of birth in Borgo Sansepolcro in 1878.

'For Luca Pacioli, who had da Vinci and Alberti as friends and advisors, who turned algebra into a science, and applied it to geometry, who lectured in double-entry bookkeeping, whose work was the base and norm for later mathematical research; for this great fellow citizen, the people of San Sepulcro, ashamed of 370 years of silence, have placed this stone, 1878.'

References

Azzolini, Monica (2004). Anatomy of a Dispute: Leonardo, Pacioli, and Scientific Entertainment in Renaissance Milan. Early Science and Medicine 9:128–135.

Baldasso, R (2010). Portrait of Luca Pacioli and Disciple: A New, Mathematical Look. The Art Bulletin 92:83-102.

Bambach, Carmen (2002). Leonardo da Vinci (1452-1519). Essays, Heilbrunn Time Line of Art History. The MET.
https://www.metmuseum.org/toah/hd/leon/hd_leon.htm

Bambach CC, ed (2003). Documented Chronology of Leonardo's Life and Work. In, Leonardo da Vinci. Master Draftsman. The Metropolitan Museum Of Art, New York. New Haven and London. Yale University Press.

Barca GA. IACO. BAR. VIGENNIS P.1495. Enigma e Secretissima Scientia. *http://www.ritrattopacioli.it/Jacobarvigennis2.pdf (WWW site disconnected).*

Glori, Carla (2010). Il cartiglio di Leonardo. La Ricerca – 2010.
http://www.carlaglori.com/cartiglio/luca-pacioli/

Glori, Carla (2013). Il cartiglio di Leonardo. Decifrazioni e Soluzioni 2013.

Glori, Carla (2018). Il cartiglio di Leonardo. Il cartiglio. *http://www.carlaglori.com/mi-presento/, http://www.carlaglori.com/cartiglio/*

Kulski JK (2017). Leonardo da Vinci: The Melzi Chronicles. Published by Jerzy. K. Kulski. ISBN: 978-0-6480653-1-9

Mackinnon, Nick (1993). The Portrait of Fra Luca Pacioli. The Mathematical Gazette 77:130 - 219.

Museo di Capodimonte (2016). Il ritratto di Luca Pacioli a Capodimonte. *http://www.museocapodimonte.beniculturali.it/il-ritratto-di-luca-pacioli-a-capodimonte/*

Pacioli, Luca (1498). Divine Proportion (in English). 1498 edition. tennenbaum pacioli-divine-proportion.pdf. Uploaded by Israel Monroy Muñoz on Oct 22, 2014. *Full text of original edition (1498) in English.*

Sedgwick WT, Tyler HW, Bigelow RW (1939) A Short History of Science. New York: Macmillan Co.

Taylor RE (2018). No Royal Road: Luca Pacioli and His Times. Unc Press Enduring Editions.

Vasari, G. (1550). The Lives Of The Most Excellent Painters, Sculptors, and Architects. de Vere GdC, trans. New York, NY: The Modern Library; 2006.

2

LAST SUPPER, BETRAYAL & OLD MEN'S HEADS

Comparison Between the Portrait of Pacioli and Jesus in the *Last Supper*

Carmen Bambach from the Department of Drawings and Prints at The Metropolitan Museum of Art made the following observation about Leonardo da Vinci's painting of the *Last Supper* (ca. 1492/94–1498):

> 'Leonardo chose to capture the moment just after Christ tells his apostles that one of them will betray him, and at the institution of the Eucharist. The effect of his statement causes a visible response, in the form of a wave of emotion among the apostles. These reactions are quite specific to each apostle, expressing what Leonardo called the "motions of the mind." Despite the dramatic reaction of the apostles, Leonardo imposes a sense of order on the scene. Christ's head is at the centre of the composition, framed by a halo-like architectural opening. His head is also the vanishing point toward which all lines of the perspectival projection of the architectural setting converge. The apostles are arranged around him in four groups of three united by their posture and gesture. Judas, who was traditionally placed on the opposite side of the table, is here set apart from the other apostles by his shadowed face. Even in its current state, it is a masterpiece of dramatic narrative and subtle pictorial illusionism.'

After about five or six year's work, Leonardo finished his painting of the *Last Supper* in 1498 when Luca Pacioli was still in Milan as a mathematics teacher. A comparison between Jesus in the *Last Supper* and Luca Pacioli in his portrait reveals some strikingly similar features. Both Jesus and Pacioli are the central characters in their paintings. Both are contained within a distinct triangular shape with their arms and hands spread widely across the table. Jesus's left hand is turned up, whereas Luca Pacioli's left hand is turned down pointing to a sentence in an opened book. Luca Pacioli's right arm and hand are raised holding a long pointer, whereas a table supports Jesus's right hand and outstretched fingers. Luca Pacioli looks slightly to his right and out at a point directly ahead of him, whereas Jesus in the *Last Supper* looks slightly towards his left and at a bread roll that he is pointing at. Luca Pacioli's face is outlined by his hood and cowl, whereas Jesus's long hair outlines his face. Both men stand directly behind a table laden with various items. Luca Pacioli's table seems slightly lower than the table at Jesus's *Last Supper*. Both paintings are making a statement, rich in symbolism and with a message about betrayal. The message of betrayal is more obvious in the biblical story of the *Last Supper*. The wave of emotion among the apostles confirms Jesus has said that one of them will betray him. 'What, me? Impossible? Who is it?' Judas remains seated with a raised knife seen behind his back.

The message of betrayal in the *Pacioli Portrait* is much more subtle and hidden within the forgotten and changed Milanese history of that time, and it is incorporated in the painting's symbolism and cartouche or yellow notebook on the table with the anagram IACO. BAR. VIGENNIS P.1495. The secret story coded within the painting is the betrayal of the Duke of Milan, Gian Galeazzo Sforza, in 1494/5 by his guardian and uncle Ludovico Moro Sforza who stole the Duchy from his nephew and family. The green cloth in the foreground covers Gian Galeazzo Sforza's coffin, while the illuminated young man in the background beside Luca Pacioli stands accused as Ludovico Moro Sforza's ally complicit in the young duke's murder. This hidden betrayal to usurp the Duchy of Milan and the grand title of Duke of Milan is discussed in more detail in later chapters. But, this betrayal of Gian Galeazzo Sforza is one of the most important coded messages contained within Leonardo's painting of Luca Pacioli, the young man and the sinister black fly of Milan that represents the betrayer and usurper Ludovico Moro Sforza, the Duke of Bari, who became the 7th Duke of Milan by nefarious actions.

It is unlikely that the similarities between the *Last Supper* and the *Pacioli Portrait* are coincidental. It seems more likely that they are both the products of the same painter who produced them as a consequence of his observations and experiences with one long thought out and inspirational project that is intimately tied to the Milanese history and the political and Sforza family intrigues of the time.

In describing the triangular figure of Luca Pacioli, the Italian scholar, barrister and art historian Giovanni Barca pointed to the portrait's antithesis:

'... *first plane figure, basis of every other geometric figure and reference to squaring the circle, the triangular shape for the progressive height that tapers to induce the sense of ascending to the summit and peak, and the delimitation and proportion of the painting* poses the scientist and mathematician in contrast with the tetragonal and horizontal stability of the table, in symbolic meaning of sapiential excellence, of overcoming the level of the cultural and scientific context, in the antithesis and distinction between "dianoia" and "doxa", between "scientia" and "opinio", between idea and concept, between intellect and memory, between generating dynamic vision and rigid notion.' [Translated from Italian using Google translate].

FIG 2.1. *Luca Pacioli (left) and Jesus in the* Last Supper *(right) as triangular figures.*

These same thoughts on antithesis can be applied to Leonardo's painting of the *Last Supper* and his marvellous use of perspective, geometry and the divine proportions that he also alluded to in his *Portrait of Luca Pacioli*. In comparing the two paintings, Barca was impressed especially by the bright light that illuminates Pacioli and Jesus and the different show of hands by them and the apostles.

'*Likewise, in the two paintings, the hands stretch out, release and surrender in the rapture of the solemn moment, in the moment of proclamation and revelation, in the imminence of sublime events, of transcendence, of corresponding rational or mystical expansion. Even the bench from which the lesson is carried out by Pacioli is presented with solutions and descriptions that make themselves common, in the representation, to those of the table of the "Cenacolo" of S. Maria delle Grazie. If it is not a question of passive imitation, improbable and contrasting with the inspirational originality of both works, the homologies cannot be understood otherwise than as an expression of real reflections and mnemonic automatisms. In addition to the insertion of the central character in a triangular space, the perspective and level of the horizontal plane coincide, the diffusion from above the light, the vibrating shady shadings and precipices of the vertical falling direction of the canteen and the desk. ... A real coincidence and harmony between luminosity and psychic evidence is realised in the pictorial description, between concrete presence and mnestic, which, referring to the action and the experience of the characters, conveys the observer into subjective participation, inserted into their intimate inner vision, going beyond the realistic situational rendering towards a more extended*

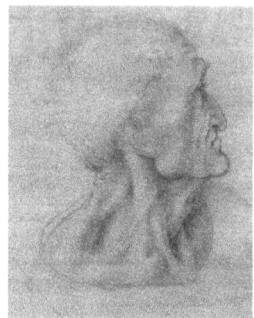

psychic and emotional adhesion. ... The light that illuminates the open book on the desk, explicit reference to attention and the ideational vision in formation, is reduced in the blackboard, removed from use...'

FIG. 2.2. *Leonardo's drawing of Judas (top) and his painting of the* Last Supper *(bottom).*

For Barca, the hand gestures in Leonardo's two paintings express the concepts of the soul:

'The transpositions in the narrative and descriptive context of very fine psychological notations also extend to reliefs and descriptions of psychomotor gestural reflexes and it can be seen how the left hand of Pacioli stands still, spread in the thumb, showing a residual tremulous tension in his fingers. The disposition of the hand shows a reactivity of expectation in the rapture and mental involvement of the intuitive vision, as a sign of a conserved vibrating and alert readiness to grasp the idea in progressive formation and the muscular reflex poses in semantic correlation between prearrangement and comprehension. Despite the diversity of the pathos of specific situations, the refinement of the notation, in relation to the reciprocal psychic and motor response, it relates to that of the hands of Christ in the "Last Supper" and the Madonna in the "Virgin of the Rocks", revealing the reflex gesture and the emotional reaction to happening events. The expressiveness shown by the hands, as a connotation of the reaction of the characters in the portrayed situation, is a characteristic feature of Leonardo and the "Last Supper" found in the variegated description of the hands of the Apostles and the dynamic shiver that runs through the entire painting, evoking at the same time sound diffusion, surprise and disbelief, dismay at Christ's announcement of imminent betrayal. ... "Who speak with the movements of the hands, eyes, eyelashes and the whole person, in wanting to express the concept of their soul."'

Leonardo's Drawings of Old Men like Luca Pacioli

When we look at a Leonardo drawing of Judas for his painting of the *Last Supper*, we can ask the following question: Did Leonardo draw a study of

Judas for the *Last Supper* based on his drawings of the facial features of Luca Pacioli and then disguise him with a beard?

Leonardo drew many mature and old men's heads in his notebooks and on paper expressively highlighting deformations left in the face through experiences, events, hardships, and disappointments with life (Fig. 2.3 to 2.8). These are the disfigurements, decay and degradation due to old age, illness, and regret and vice. Are some of the heads those of Luca Pacioli? If Leonardo befriended, lived and worked with Luca Pacioli from 1495 and then continued their friendship until at least into each other's old age, there is a very good chance that at some time during their friendship he sketched Luca's face and possibly even painted a number of portraits of him including the *Pacioli Portrait* that is currently and wrongfully attributed to de' Barbari.

The Italian art historian Giovanni Barca found at least three drawings by Leonardo da Vinci of heads of virile men that he compared to the *Pacioli Portrait* and concluded from these drawings that only Leonardo could be the author of the portrait. These three drawings are preserved at different locations; in Venice at the Gallerie dell'Accademia (Inv.264), the Royal Library of Turin (Inv.15575), and the Royal Collection of Windsor Castle (Inv.12556). The three heads have a strong likeness to the face in the *Pacioli Portrait*. All three drawings show a head and face in profile, each drawing shows a face with strong temperament, mental concentration, psychic firmness and meditative reflection. Each drawing is unique, and yet similar and comparable with the others. There are particular details and traits reproduced in each of the three drawings, such as the warts on the forehead and cheek that unite the three figures together and attest to the strong likelihood that the person was well known to Leonardo. According to Barca, the execution of these drawings constituted a study for a subsequent representative portrait for which there is no documentary evidence of conferment, or extemporaneous portraiture, only the face and head in the *Pacioli Portrait*. Barca has written in Italian that '*in this context there is an extraordinary resemblance between the character of the drawings and the Luca Pacioli of the painting, which is not only physiognomic, but in the choice of characterising inspiration in a conception directed at expressing the worthiness of high intellectual and moral meaning, caught in the instant in which the research and the mental reflection are condensed into an inner vision. The observation of the details reveals a precise confirmation of the hooked nose, the stretched lips, the enclosed and inquiring eyes, the swollen folds of the face, the massive forehead and the short fringe of the hair on the forehead.*' (Translated from Italian into English using Google Translate ©.)

In comparing the Venetian drawing with the *Pacioli Portrait* (Fig. 2.4), Barca noted the correspondences of chin, mouth, nose, orbital, eyebrows and forehead, warts on the forehead and right cheek, symmetry of the folds of the cheek, hump, nasal loop of the nostril, temporal cavity protruding supraciliary, arch and cheekbones, fringe of the hair on the forehead, and the clerical tonsure, which is the practice of cutting or shaving some or all of the hair on the scalp, as a sign of religious devotion or humility. If these comparisons were considered insufficient to prove the identity of the subject, then the signs and the disposition of the detected warts that are placed on the forehead and the right cheek, and that are present uniformly in the drawing and the painting are striking signatures or identifiers of the same person. Therefore, Barca concludes that the three drawings can be considered reliable representations of Luca Pacioli, documented and also historically proven by the painting. These putative drawings of Luca Pacioli by Leonardo da Vinci are not surprising, and their existence confirms their mutual interests in science, strong friendship and their well-documented long-lasting partnership and shared study activities with mathematics, geometry and puzzles as outlined in the *Divine Proportion* and possibly Luca Pacioli's books on chess and puzzles.

On reflection, it seems obvious that the three drawings of the 'old man's head' (and possibly others) are preparatory drawings for his painting of Luca Pacioli, trying to capture in the expression of the faces in red pencil, an exalted Eureka moment; that is, a stunning realisation that there is something beyond experimental science and beyond the intellectual values of speculative research and science, and closer to meditative insight and inspiration. In the *Pacioli Portrait*, Leonardo has provided Luca's face with that reserved, inner, rigorous and austere moment of inspired insight attached to research, investigation and understanding. The drawings of the heads explain and amplify Leonardo's intellectual and technical authority, his ability to synthesise foresight and awareness, and provide a celebratory vision of prestige and glory in the face of Luca Pacioli gazing out to space and towards the hanging rhombicuboctahedral crystal.

Could anybody else have painted Luca Pacioli's face – the exalted expression – even if they had access to Leonardo's secret drawings? Could Jacopo de' Barbari have painted Pacioli's old face with its wrinkles, lines, blemishes, jowls and shadows? No - not at all. It wasn't Barbari's style – it wasn't in his mind or thought processes – it was not within his capability or his technique or legacy to engender inspirational realistic expressions such as those portrayed by Leonardo da Vinci.

Leonardo's Drawings of Gian Giacomo Trivulzio (1440 – 1518) and Other Miserable Old Men's Heads

The drawings of old men's heads by Leonardo da Vinci are not only of those that resemble Luca Pacioli. There are many others. Some of them are drawings of his uncle and father, various friends and acquaintances, and possibly some are drawings of Gian Giacomo Trivulzio who was a

Condottiero and Governor of Milan in 1509 and a notable patron of Leonardo da Vinci. Indeed, some of the drawings by Leonardo resemble Gian Giacomo Trivulzio in his official portraits painted by others, but the main difference between him and Luca Pacioli is the hairstyle. Gian Giacomo Trivulzio wore his hair long and straight over his ears, whereas Luca Pacioli had short wavy hair above his ears. Gian Giacomo Trivulzio was an enemy and nemesis of Ludovico Moro Sforza and a great rival to Galeazzo Sanseverino and yet all three of them sponsored Leonardo da Vinci in his works. When Gian Giacomo Trivulzio was Governor of Milan in 1509 he commissioned Leonardo to construct an enormous equestrian monument to himself. But, before it even started, he fled Milan and retreated to France when the nineteen-year-old son of Ludovico Moro Sforza, Maximilian Sforza, who with a small army of Swiss troops backed by Pope Julius II had returned to take over the city on 29th December 1512.

Leonardo studied transitory facial effects and drew a series of one hundred grotesque and exaggerated heads possibly not as character types but as exercises in observation and understanding facial expressions and the male aging process. Of the roughly one hundred grotesque heads, half of them are in the Royal Collection at Windsor. The facial distortions first seen in his Florentine years mark the beginning of a string of similarly grotesque images that become more comic during the artist's Milanese periods. '*The images may be considered grotesque because they show something never seen in nature, yet something so accurately presented as to simulate a once-living sitter.*'

Gallery of Old Men's Heads by Leonardo da Vinci

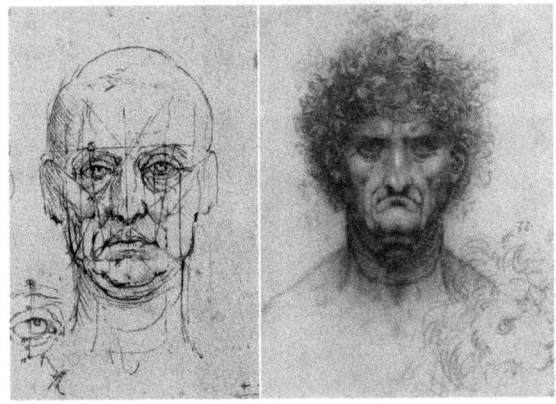

FIG. 2.3. *Old man with ivy and a lion (right). Pacioli or Trivulzio?*

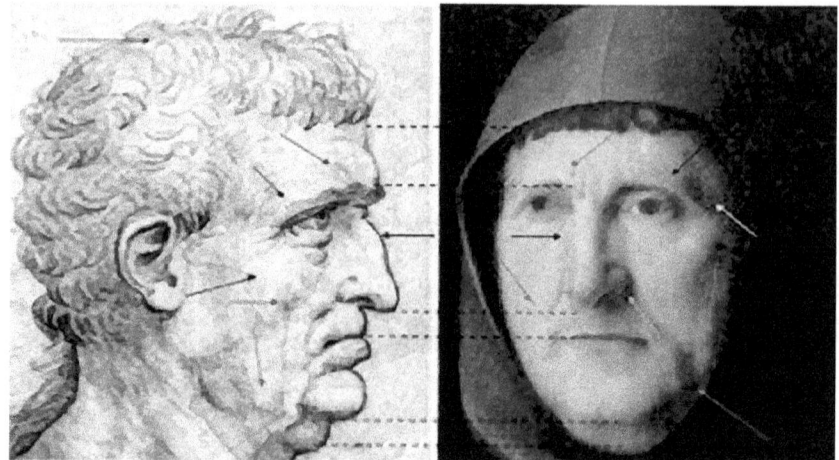

FIG. 2.4. *Possible drawing of Luca Pacioli (left) by Leonardo da Vinci preserved at the Royal Library of Turin (Inv.15575). Image taken from the essay by G.A. Barca with permission of the author.*

FIG. 2.5. *Luca Pacioli or Gian Giacomo Trivulzio? Is that a wart on the right cheek? Pacioli's drawings exposed his ears. Trivulzio's hair was long and straight and covered his ears.*

CHAPTER 2

FIG. 2.6. Left. Head of an old man. Red crayon. Unidentified artist - attributed to Leonardo da Vinci. In the Ruskin collection. Perhaps a portrait of Gian Giacomo Trivulzio, Governor of Milan in 1509. A character with long hair covering his ears, like other portraits of Gian Giacomo Trivulzio (see Fig. 2.8 below). Right. Oldish warrior (a Condottiero perhaps) with lion carved on his chest plate. A winged helmet. Perhaps he is a youngish version of the Condottiero, Gian Giacomo Trivulzio, or perhaps he is a soldier from Leonardo's the Battle of Anghiari.

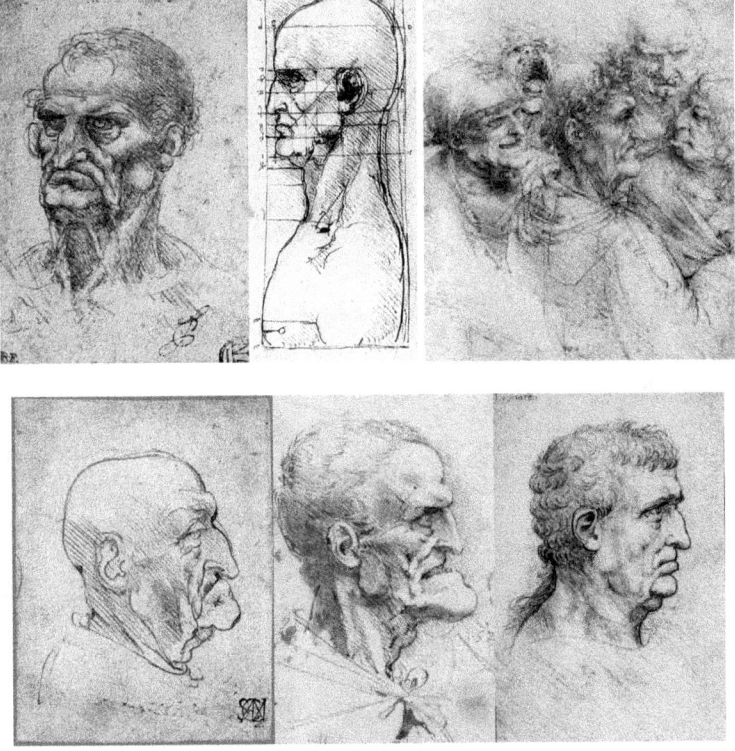

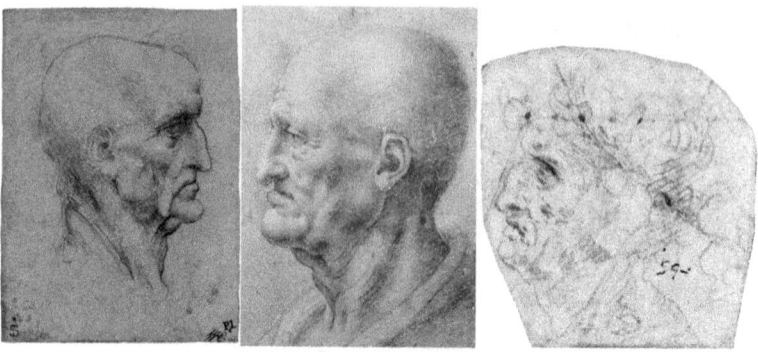

FIG. 2.7. *The profiles of Leonardo's old men show sharply aquiline noses, down-slanted mouths, and knotted brows, heads that are almost at the limits of the grotesque and deformity.*

FIG. 2.8. *A medal showing the profile of Gian Giacomo Trivulzio reveals a similarity to some of Leonardo's drawings of old men's profiles, especially in Fig. 2.6.*

References

Barca GA. IACO. BAR. VIGENNIS P.1495 Enigma e Secretissima Scientia. http://www.ritrattopacioli.it/Jacobarvigennis2.pdf *(WWW site disconnected).*

3

UNKNOWN HISTORY OF THE *PACIOLI PORTRAIT*

Renaissance Masterpiece and Dubious Attribution to Jacopo de' Barbari

The portrait of *Luca Pacioli and Student* painted during the Renaissance is like no other painting before or since. It is a revolutionary portrait of a man of the Catholic Church, a friar in his grey habit, revealing his message of reason and science in favour of the cultured and rational mind of geometry and mathematics as evidence for the Creator of All Things. The symbols of reason and architecture are boldly strewn across the canvas for the observer's eyes to look, marvel and ponder at the meaning of it all. There – stage right - on the left, as we look at it - a transparent rhombicuboctahedron hanging in space, attached to a thin line hanging from the top of the canvas. Below the rhombicuboctahedron is the beautifully crafted straight line of the pointer in the relaxed right hand of the friar pointing to the illustrated circle and the isosceles triangle within the circle on a chalkboard named *Euclides*. The pointer mysteriously rests on a line drawn from the apex of the triangle towards the circumference of the circle. The friar's left hand points to a printed passage within a blue-covered book of Euclidian geometry. There are geometric illustrations and written notes in the margins of the open pages. This is not the printed bible of the Christian Church, this is a book of science – physics, mathematics, geometry, scientific explanations – a printed book – something that can be readily placed and opened on a table to absorb the knowledge contained within its pages – to read and transmit the mysterious laws of nature to others. This is the time that the first printing presses in Gottenburg emerged from the darkness of the Middle Ages. Note also the other symbols of science, mathematics and measurements displayed across the green tablecloth – the projector, pen and ink to write down one's inspirations, observations, measurements and mathematical formulas. There, below the friar's left hand, is the all-important compass to measure and draw and point the way out of ignorance. And to the extreme right of the picture is a solid dodecahedron resting on a clasped red container or treasured book with the easily visible inscriptions of *H. R.LV* and *BVR* – separated by a red vertical clasp. Here the *V* probably represents our modern U. No such message about mathematics, geometry, science and the rational mind had ever been portrayed in portraiture before, not in the way that Luca Pacioli displays the message to us. The portrait of the lecturer and Man of God is telling us, 'look, the church can be rational and scientific and can provide us with good logical information and education and not just the clichéd fire and brimstone at the gates of hell that usually is delivered from the pulpit.'

And yet, the portrait in Capodimonte is a double portraiture and it has another person accompanying Luca Pacioli in the painting. This second figure is commonly referred to as a mysterious student or else, following the Museum's official line, he is referred to simply as Guidobaldo da Montefeltro, the Duke of Urbino. But, if he is the Duke of Urbino, the Feudal and Supreme Lord of his Duchy and respected Italian *condottiero*, then why is he not depicted as the central figure of the painting as tradition, authority and respect for his title and power of authority would demand in those times? Why does the Duke of Urbino not demonstrate his greater authority over Luca Pacioli and stand either in front of him or at least beside him? Instead, why does the illuminated younger man stand just behind and to the left side of the friar, staring out at us so meaningfully and contemptuously and yet so mysteriously? Why does he wear a green glove on his hand as if protecting his fingers from some dangerous substance? What are the interpretations of the painting's large array of symbolism really mean and why did the painter go to all the trouble of painting such an unusual and allegorical double portrait for its time? Was it for fame or money or some other reason? The painting oozes something strange - dark and sinister - and yet it is about enlightenment, science and mystical knowledge through the certainty of mathematics and the beauty of geometry. It is a deliberate and pristine presentation of enlightened symbolism and yet it is as dark as its black background with subliminal and coded historical messages waiting to be deciphered. What is the purpose of the dark and transparent polyhedron hanging in outer space that has transfixed the friar's gaze? It is fantastical. There seems to be more to the painting then meets the common untrained eye. It appears to present a puzzle that needs to be decoded and solved.

The evidence that Jacopo de' Barbari is the author of the painting is based solely on the encrypted inscription *Iaco. B ar. Vigennis. P. 1495.*

CHAPTER 3

Since the Museum has attributed Jacopo de' Barbari as the author of the painting, most scholars and art specialists generally accept uncritically that Barbari is indeed the creator of this masterpiece. However, it should be noted that attribution is not the same as authentication. **An attribution does not mean that the art is the work of the attributed artist, only that it could be by that artist.** In this regard, there is no provenance or documented evidence that has authenticated Jacopo de' Barbari as the creator of the *Pacioli Portrait*. In fact, most of the circumstantial and historical evidence and the paintings' pictorial cues suggest that Leonardo da Vinci and his assistants prepared and painted the *Pacioli Portrait* and that they added many hidden dimensions and messages to it that are not easily recognised or discerned by those without the proper code or background knowledge to decipher or understand it.

The big mystery is why, despite the overwhelming circumstantial evidence in favour of Leonardo da Vinci, the painting was never attributed officially to him. I can only surmise that the experts and official committees had insufficient evidence and background knowledge at the time of their considerations to favour Leonardo da Vinci as the rightful candidate, and therefore, they believed the cartouche and inscription was sufficient evidence for the Jacopo de' Barbari attribution.

The account presented in this book examines the evidence in the public domain and provides the arguments and rational that are overwhelmingly in favour of Leonardo da Vinci to be recognised as the real author of the painting.

Acquisition of the *Pacioli Portrait* by the National Museum of Capodimonte, Naples

The *Portrait of Luca Pacioli and Student* has been in the possession of Naples at least since 1903 and exhibited since 1957 in the art museum of the Palace of Capodimonte, a grand Bourbon *palazzo* on top of a hill just outside the old city limits of Naples. This palace was built in 1738 for Charles VII de Bourbon (1716-1788), king of Naples and Sicily (later to become Charles III, king of Spain) as his summer residence and to allow him to house the fabulous Farnese art collection which he had inherited from his mother, Elisabetta Farnese, last descendant of the sovereign ducal family of Parma. Over the next fifty years, the palace was enlarged and filled with more art, and in 1787, on the advice of Jacob Philipp Hackert, a laboratory for the restoration of paintings was created. After the end of the Bourbon monarchy in 1861, the palace eventually became part of the Italian State. It was transformed into a national museum in 1950, and, as one of the largest museums in Italy, it is now the prime repository of Neapolitan painting and decorative art, with several important works from other Italian schools of painting, and important ancient Roman sculptures. The Galleria Nazionale includes paintings from the 13th to the 18th centuries with major works by Raphael, Titian, Caravaggio, Giovanni Bellini, Giorgio Vasari, El Greco, Masaccio and many others, especially the paintings of the Neapolitan School with large holdings of Jusepe de Ribera, Luca Giordano and the followers of Caravaggio.

The *Pacioli Portrait* was reported in Naples in 1903 when the customs office of Naples confiscated it from an export agent who was attempting to send it to England, addressed to the English painter, collector and art dealer Charles Fairfax Murray (1849-1919). The customs officers were aware of the export agency acting on behalf of Sir Charles Fairfax Murray who was collecting major art treasures and antique books and manuscripts on art for little payment and they viewed these transactions as looting Italian art treasures. Sir Charles Fairfax Murray somehow knew about the portrait of *Luca Pacioli and Student* and its availability for purchase, and he intended to present it to the British Museum in London that already had numerous drawings by Leonardo da Vinci and several other paintings from his school of acolytes. Charles Fairfax Murray also had a large collection of rare books from the Renaissance about perspective drawing and painting, including the works of Durer, and he would have had a significant appreciation of the *Pacioli Portrait*. Some of the rare Italian books in his collection were the Luca Pacioli authored books (*Divina Proportione, Venetius,* 1509; *Arithmetica, Venetia,* 1484; *Summa de Arithmetica geometria Proportioni e Proportionalita, Venetiis,* 1494, folio, diagrams, vellum) and those by Leonardo Agostini (1521, 1557), Albertus Magnus (1474), Albertus de Saxonia (Tractatus Proportionum, Padua 1484), Alfraganus (*Rudimenta Astronomica, Ferrarie,* 1493), Antiquarie, Aristonenus (*Harmonicorum Elementorum, Venetiis,* 1562), Daniel Barbaro (*la Pratica della perspettiva, Venetia,* 1569), Pietro Bembo (*Venetia,* 1505, *Milano,* 1517), Vittoria Colonna, Dante, Erasmus, Euclides (1482), Hieronymus Fracastorius (*Syphilis, Romae,* 1531), Leonardo Ghaligaio (*Summa de Arithmetica,* 1521), and hundreds more, far too many to list here.

In 1872, Charles Fairfax Murray had left England to live and work in Italy where he married a 16-year-old Italian lass and settled in Florence. From there, he established an art agency network for the sale and purchase of artworks and he acted as an agent for Sir Federick Burton, Director of the National Gallery, London, which is the home for Leonardo da Vinci's second copy of *The Virgin of the Rocks*. Charles Fairfax Murray undoubtedly would have maintained his Italian network contacts on his return to England in 1882, and he possibly knew something about the provenance and attribution of the Luca Pacioli double portrait. Thus, he tried to snare it at a reasonable price for the National Gallery of London.

In 1903, the Naple's government officials who confiscated the *Pacioli*

Portrait from the export agent attempted to purchase it from the seller (thought to be a member of the Ottaviano-Medici family) on behalf of the Italian State using the antiquated and previous sequestration legislation of the Bourbon Kingdom that allowed them to take legal possession of an asset such as a historic painting in the Kingdom. In the context of taking legal possession of the painting from the unidentified owner and seller of the painting, two experts were brought in to estimate the commercial value for its purchase by the state. The two experts, Ricci and Venturi, had little or no knowledge as to who had produced the painting. There was no available documentation for them to evaluate the provenance of the painting. Nobody seemed to know much about the origins or execution of the painting. However, the experts discovered that there was an inscription on an unfolded note or cartouche in the painting that they believed indicated the painting's authorship. Magnifying the inscription on the cartouche, they deciphered it to be: IACO. BAR. VIGENNIS. P. 1495.

This was their 'hallelujah' moment. They believed the inscription revealed that the painting was by Jacopo de' Barbari as indicated by his supposed signature IACO BAR. Apart from the so-called signature, all the experts agreed that the central figure was Luca Pacioli, the Franciscan monk, presenting a lecture on Euclidian geometry. Luca Pacioli had been rediscovered by the Italian scholars before the turn of the century and he was well known by 1900 as a great Italian Renaissance mathematician that originated the techniques of double entry book-keeping.

Various art historians and experts who knew something about Renaissance art history suggested that, because the central figure in the painting was Luca Pacioli, it must have been painted by Leonardo da Vinci who studied and worked with the monk on mathematics in Milan between the years of 1496 and 1500. After some frantic discussions and disagreements, the Italian State agents decided that the *Pacioli Portrait* was not the work of Leonardo da Vinci. First of all, the painting technique didn't appear to have been done in his subtle hand. The agents thought that the portrait was too crude, bright and brash and didn't have the muted *sfumato* appearance of a *Mona Lisa* or *The Virgin on the Rocks*. The background of the painting was much too black and didn't have the natural airy background that might be expected in a Leonardo painting, e.g, mountains covered in cloud, a church steeple, birds, flowers, and such like. But, moreover, the State agents declared that they couldn't afford to buy this painting for Naples if it was a Leonardo da Vinci. His name would make it a priceless artwork and it would conjure up an incredibly bloody bun fight between the different states of Italy that the newly formed nation was not ready for.

Thus, to better serve the interests of the new Italian Federation, the lesser-known Venetian painter Jacopo de' Barbari was unanimously chosen by the experts and State agents to be the author of the painting based on a summary decipherment of the inscription on the cartouche. Furthermore, the sequestration of the painting by the State was made more affordable given that Jacopo de' Barbari was seen as a relatively minor painter compared to the maestro of the Renaissance, Leonardo da Vinci. Thus, the Italian State bought the painting at the cost of forty thousand lire instead of the eighteen thousand that was the pre-sale price of the unidentified painting and they soon moved it to the National Museum of Naples (currently the Archaeological Museum), before transferring it to the current museum location of Capodimonte in 1957.

By hurriedly attributing the painting to the Venetian painter Jacopo de' Barbari, nobody questioned how he could have painted such a mysterious masterpiece based on his output of mediocre portraits, mythological and religious paintings and still-lives. Jacopo de' Barbari was a moderately successful Italian painter of portraits and landscapes and he possessed a highly individual style, but he never had painted anything as highly imaginative or unusual like the *Pacioli Portrait* before or since 1500. He was largely derivative in his portraiture style, although he often added the scroll or cartouche as his signature spelling out his name, Barbari, in full. He occasionally painted dead game, partridges and rabbits, and he often left his signature visible on the picture as a combination of IA. D. BARBARI and a *caduceus*, that is, a symbol of a snake wrapped around a pitchfork – like the common, contemporary medical emblem. But mostly, he was a monochromatic printmaker, specialising in landscapes often filled with naked classical figures. He was greatly influenced by Leonardo da Vinci and Durer. There is no IA. D. BARBARI or a *caduceus* in the *Pacioli Portrait*, although there is the makings of a BAR, possibly representing the Duke of Bari, Ludovico Il Moro Sforza of Milan (see Chapters 17 and 20 for a full explanation).

Leonardo da Vinci and Luca Pacioli worked together on the production and illustration of Pacioli manuscript on geometry, known as the *Divine Proportion*. The *Pacioli Portrait* could only have been designed and influenced by Leonardo da Vinci and nobody else, for it also tells us the history and connection between them and the Sforza of the Duchy of Milan during the difficult and troubled times of their war with France and with themselves. So why does the painting continue to be attributed to Jacopo de' Barbari instead of to Leonardo da Vinci who was a friend and student of Pacioli during the years of 1496 to 1500 and beyond?

In the main, Jacopo de Barbari was a printmaker specialising in woodcut maps and printed black and white images of idyllic scenes of naked Grecian/Roman mythological figures or the slightly more tasteful religious scenes of various saints. There is no indications in Jacopo de Barbari's vast *oeuvre* that he could have been the author of the *Pacioli*

Portrait. Usually, Barbari added a *caduceus* as his signature emblem to his paintings and none was visible in the painting of *Luca Pacioli*. Besides, the experts of 1903 gave no significant explanation as to why a distinctive black fly was added to the end of the inscription on the cartouche. What was the particular meaning of this annoying insect in the painting? The black fly was like some evil intruder to the solemn scene of two eye-catching figures dominating the painting, with one of them a well-known historic Renaissance monk. What was the meaning of the black fly with the left side of its body covering the last digit of the date and concealing the actual year that shows a doubtful '5'? As a number of scholars in recent times have pointed out when questioning the attribution by the agents of 1903, why is it that they omitted to point out the significance of the fly and the real meaning of the inscription, and why did they deliberately exclude the cultural context and the scientific history that was directly linked to the acknowledged sponsorship by Luca Pacioli in his introductory chapters in the manuscript of the *Divine Proportion*? This significant omission, whether intentional or otherwise, missed the obvious connection between the *Pacioli Portrait* and the *Divine Proportion* manuscript and the strong inference that Leonardo da Vinci in a single painting had painted the portraits of his two highly contrasting friends, Fra Luca Pacioli, the Franciscan Friar, and Galeazzo Sanseverino, the Jouster, soldier of fortune, wealthy gentleman and son-in-law of the Duke of Milan, Ludovico il Moro Sforza. Leonardo da Vinci had painted their portraits at about the same time that Galeazzo Sanseverino commissioned Luca Pacioli to write and Leonardo da Vinci to illustrate the manuscript *Divine Proportion*. This was the real and actual provenance of the *Pacioli Portrait* – it began in Milan with Fra Luca Pacioli's appointment as the mathematics professor at the behest of Leonardo or his friend Galeazzo Sanseverino.

The Perceived Provenance of the *Pacioli Portrait* and its Possible Connection to the *Codex Vaticanus Urbinas*, Leonardo da Vinci's *Treatise on Painting*

The *Pacioli Portrait* was sequestered in Naples by the Italian State from a member of the cadet branch of the Ottaviano-Medici family who had arranged to sell it to agents who were preparing to send it to Charles Fairfax Murray in England. How a member of the House of Ottaviano in the region of Vesuvius came to be in the possession of the painting is not known, but a tentative history can be reconstructed if one traces the painting back three hundred and thirty years to the first documentary evidence of the painting's existence that was mentioned in an inventory of 1631. This inventory, and therefore the painting, was in the possession of the then-recently deceased Francesco Maria II della Rovere, Duke of

Urbino. The inventory provided no attribution or when or how it came into the possession of the Duke of Urbino in his lifetime. Included in a list of Della Rovere's Wardrobe goods, the first inventory only gives mere hypotheses on the author. Translated from Italian to English by Google translator the inventory simply stated:

Described. 1. 1631: "A portrait of a friar from S. Bernardino with a young man open dressed in antique fur, marked at the bottom, Divo Principi Guido in Tavola". 2. "A Friar, who is said to be the portrait of Fra Luca dal Borgo, who does not know whose hand is on the table, who teaches Euclid to the Duke Guido, from the Guardaroba d'Urbino". 3. 1654: "A painting on the table: a friar of S. Francesco with another figure of Ghirlandaio".

There is clear confusion in these inventories with the references to *Divo Principi Guido* and Duke Guido. Earlier inventories of 1582 and 1599 also identified the student as Guidobaldi, but this is because of an inscription that once ran along the bottom of the portrait *Divo Principi Guido*, which is a native expression indicating that the painting was dedicated to Guidobaldi, Pacioli's patron, as was the similar dedication in the *Summa Arithmetica* manuscript.

The subsequent documents revealed little, covering only the transfer of the painting in the middle of the seventeenth century from Urbino to Florence and the Urbinate dynasty to the Medici Florentine through the Rovere-Medici marriage. Some traces of the painting's whereabouts reappeared centuries later in Naples, always in the possession of the descendants of the family members of the cadet or minor branch of the Ottaviano-Medici, to arrive at the current museum destination following the state pre-emption of the sale destined abroad. The cadet branch of Ottaviano-Medici are distantly related to the Rovere-Medici families and today's ancestors believe that they should have inherited the Grand Duchy of Tuscany upon the death of the very last of the Medici Grand Dukes in 1737.

When Francesco Maria II della Rovere, the Duke of Urbino, died, he left most of his art collection to his grand-daughter, Vittoria Della Rovere, who was married to Ferdinando II de' Medici, Grand Duke of Tuscany, and she transferred her inherited art collection to Florence to the Uffizi Gallery. The duchy of Urbino was annexed by the Papal States and Pope Urban VIII left it in the control of his nephew Taddeo Barberini. The *Pacioli Portrait* appears to have been part of the art transferred to Florence. However, the House of Medici became extinct in 1737 with the death of the childless Grand Duke of Tuscany, Gian Gastone de' Medici and the Ottaviano-Medici branch might have inherited some of the Florentine or Uffizi paintings at this time as part of the different family branch disputes.

Coincidently, Leonardo da Vinci's translated *Treatise on Painting*, also known as the *Codex Urbinas,* was found to be in the possession of the deceased last Duke of Urbino, Francesco Maria II della Rovere, in 1631, and yet no connection has been made between the possible shared provenances of the Codex *Urbinas* and the *Pacioli Portrait* in the Duchy of Urbino. Although these two items indeed may have completely different provenances, it nevertheless is intriguing that they both have ended up in the possession of the Duke of Urbino and his family. It is possible that Leonardo's *Treatise on Painting* and his *Pacioli Portrait* had been bundled together as a gift or a sale to the Duke of Urbino after Leonardo's death in 1519 or that the *Pacioli Portrait* was presented to the Duke of Urbino when Leonardo and Luca Pacioli were in Florence together after 1500.

However, when the last Duke of Urbino, Francesco Maria II della Rovere, died without a son to inherit his possessions, the fief was annexed by the Pope. In 1658, Pope Alexander VII had all the manuscripts of the Urbino Library delivered to the Vatican Library, whereas the *Pacioli Portrait* was transferred to Florence by the dead duke's grand-daughter, Vittoria della Rovere.

Thus, let us consider the little that we know about the provenance of the '*Codex Urbinas*'. Leonardo da Vinci made numerous entries in his notebooks about painting and he wanted to publish these items under the general heading of *A Treatise on Painting*. His secretary and painting assistant Francesco Melzi (1491 to 1570) inherited all of Leonardo da Vinci's notebooks after his master had died in 1519. Then, sometime after 1524 and before 1542, Melzi gathered together all of the manuscripts on painting (the *Melzi Codex* or *Codex Urbinas*) and he set about to translate and publish them in Leonardo's name. He compiled the *Codex Urbinas* in Milan from which the abridged version of the Treatise originated. By 1542, Melzi had released various abridged handwritten translations to some collectors including Giovanni Berti of Florence. Copies of Leonardo's *Treatise on Painting* were likely circulating all over Italy wherever there was a school of painting before Francesco Melzi died in 1570. A copy of Leonardo's manuscript was recorded to be in the library of the Duke of Amalfi in Naples in 1655. However, the first abridged printed copies of *Treatise on Painting* were not published in French and Italian until 1651 (by Raffaelo du Fresne), long after Francesco Melzi's death. The printed copies of Leonardo's treatise were important because they showed to those who were interested that he treated painting as a science and not an art. Furthermore, the publications represented the only compilation of Leonardo's writings available to the public. Moreover, they preserved a large number of passages that would have been lost because they do not appear in any of the manuscripts in Leonardo's hand that have since been translated and published. Emil Ludwig eventually published the first, modern and up-dated edition of the *Codex Urbinas* in three volumes in 1882.

The *Codex Urbinas* was comprised of Leonardo da Vinci's translated manuscripts on painting that Francesco Melzi already had gathered together to translate and edit for his publication of a *Treatise on Painting*. The Codex (designated the number 1270) is now the property of the Vatican Library. It is a small folio volume, 20.4 x 15cm, with 331 numbered folios including blanks. The history of the *Codex Urbinas* from the time it left Melzi's hands to enter the library of the Duke Francesco della Rovere is still unknown. It is possible that Melzi had sent it to Urbino or elsewhere, such as Rome, in the hope of finding a publisher. Indeed, the publisher Emil Ludwig surmises that Melzi's codex came first from Rome to Urbino along with the whole library of cardinal Pietro Bembo (1470 to 1547) who had been the secretary to Pope Leo X. Bembo mainly lived and worked in Rome in his later years and he died there in his 77th year. Interestingly, Leonardo da Vinci, Francesco Melzi and Salai were all in Rome together between 1513 and 1516 in the service of the Pope's brother, Giuliano di Lorenzo de' Medici, Duke of Nemours. Fra Luca Pacioli also was in Rome at the time, specifically between 1514 and 1515. Pietro Bembo knew them all and Francesco Melzi is likely to have dealt with him officially on behalf of Leonardo da Vinci. Pietro Bembo's father, Bernardo Bembo, who was a Venetian ambassador to Florence, had formed a platonic relationship with Ginevra de' Benci who Leonardo da Vinci admired and painted her portrait between 1474 and 1476 when he was in Florence as a young painter. On the reverse side of the Benci portrait, Leonardo had painted the Latin motto *VIRTVTEM FORMA DECORAT* with a sprig of juniper to suggest Ginevra's name, encircled by laurel and palm. The motto and symbols are believed to represent Ginevra's intellectual and moral virtue as well as her physical beauty. Intriguingly, an infrared examination of the back of the painting also revealed Bembo' family motto *Virtue and Honour* beneath Ginevra's motto, suggesting that Bernardo Bembo was involved in the commission of the portrait. The Italian researcher and cryptographer Carla Glori supplemented Ginevra's Latin motto with the Latin word *Juniperus* (juniper sprig) and decoded the anagram into 50 Latin sentences signed VINCI that unequivocally refer to the portrait and the biography of Ginevra de Benci. Bernardo Bembo and Leonardo da Vinci died in the same month and the same year, May 1519, but in different parts of Europe, the former in the Republic of Venice and the later in Amboise, France.

Although Francesco Melzi appeared to procrastinate with the publication of the *Codex Urbina*, he hastened to try and publish the complete *Treatise on Painting* that he had prepared after he had heard that an anonymous painter had gone to Rome in the 1540s to arrange for the publication of a book on painting by Leonardo, apparently using the original manuscripts that Melzi had already translated from Leonardo's mirror writing. Unfortunately, the role of Pietro Bembo in transferring Leonardo's codex to Urbino is pure speculation because the first reliable records concerning the codex did not appear until 1640 when the manuscript was listed in the last catalogue of the Library at Urbino before it and the other codices of the Library were transferred to the Vatican Library in 1657. It is likely, although unconfirmed, that the *Codex Urbina* was in the same collection of manuscripts that had been previously donated to the Ambrosian Library in Milan. By the time, the art expert Abete Marini arranged to confirm their existence in 1809, Leonardo's manuscripts were no longer there; they had been stolen.

It should be noted that there are many critics of Francesco Melzi's organisation and preparation of the *Codex Urbinas*. Among the weaknesses, inadequacies and gaps cited concerning his compilation are those on the principles of perspective, and the passages on drawing and painting of the human figure. Many believe that he had not developed adequately many of Leonardo's ideas. This may well have contributed to his procrastination, a feeling that he had not fully absorbed many of Leonardo's original ideas and concepts as expected of an intelligent scientist. Also, he may have been intimidated by Leonardo's belief that the painter had to be an ideal person, a model of human dignity and compassion and with the proper ethics and sacrifices needed to occupy the highest position in the intellectual life of his society. Leonardo often stressed that painting like science was the search for complete knowledge, an exciting creative process and an exalted way of life, with similar characteristics to the divine proportions that he tried to illustrate in his painting of Luca Pacioli, Galeazzo Sanseverino and the polyhedrons.

After a seemingly long residency in the Duchy of Urbino, the *Pacioli Portrait* and the *Codex Urbinas* went their separate ways. The Codex was taken to the Vatican Library of the Pope, whereas the painting and the other art treasures became the property of the last Duke of Urbino's nine-year-old granddaughter, Vittoria della Rovere, daughter of Federico Ubaldo and Claudia de' Medici. These art treasures were moved to her properties in Florence when she was married in 1633 to her Medici first cousin Ferdinando II, Grand Duke of Tuscany. When Vittoria della Rovere died in 1694 some of her art treasures eventually became the property of Maria Caroline who became Queen consort and *de facto* ruler of Naples and Sicily when she married Ferdinand IV of Naples in 1768. However, it is not known whether the Grand Duchess Maria Caroline was responsible for bringing the *Pacioli Portrait* to Naples or whether it was a Medici friend or a relative who transferred the portrait before the paternal line of the House of Medici ended with the death of the childless Gian Gastone de' Medici, Grand Duke of Tuscany in 1737. Although the contents of the Medici properties and art treasures were willed to the Tuscan state in 1743, the *Pacioli Portrait* may have fallen into the hands of the Ottaviano Medici branch, the Neapolitan branch of the House of Medici, and taken to Ottajano (Ottaiano) located near Naples. Over the centuries, this remaining cadet branch of the House of Medici occupied leading positions in the aristocracy of the Kingdom of Two Sicilies. Among the members of the Ottaviano Medici dynasty, there were leaders of the Roman Catholic Church, ambassadors, cardinals, a pope, and Don Luigi de' Medici, who was representative of the Kingdom of Naples at the Congress of Vienna in 1860. Giuliano de' Medici di Toscana di Ottajano is the current living head of this cadet branch of the Medici and he holds the titles of 15th Prince of Ottajano (Ottaviano) and 12th Duke of Sarno.

The territory of Ottaviano is located in the Mt. Vesuvian area and the old Medici castle is now the headquarters of Vesuvius National Park. Bernadetto de' Medici, who was the cousin of the Grand Duke Cosimo de' Medici, inherited the fief of Ottaviano in 1567 and it remained in the Medici family until 1860, the year before the formation of the Kingdom of Italy. The separate kingdoms of Naples and Sicily were united into the New Kingdom of Two Sicilies in 1816 under the Bourbon king Ferdinand I, and it eventually was annexed by the Kingdom of Sardinia to end the Bourbon rule when the Kingdom of Italy was formed in 1861 and King Victor Emmanuel II of Sardinia was proclaimed King of Italy. The process of Italian unification was completed in 1871 when Rome became the capital of the Kingdom of Italy. Realpolitik continued to work against the new Italian nation until the Armistice of Villa Giusti completed the unification of Italy on the 4th November 1918. The Italian Republic replaced the Kingdom in June 1946 with 54% of the referendum vote.

The Kingdom of the Two Sicilies had been wealthy and 80 million ducats were taken from their banks as a contribution to assist the new Italian treasury, while other former states in the Italian unification paid far less. The economy of the area formerly known as Two Sicilies collapsed, leading to an unprecedented wave of emigration, with estimates of at least four million people leaving Naples or from regions near Naples for the north and abroad between 1876–1913. A member of the Ottaviano Medici branch may have been caught up in the Neapolitan austerity measures and tried to sell off some of their assets and artworks, including the attempted sale of the *Pacioli Portrait* to English interests. Of course, this is reasoned speculation because there is no documentary evidence to support this supposition. If Leonardo da Vinci was commissioned by Galeazzo Sforza Sanseverino or the Duke of Milan to paint the *Pacioli Portrait* in 1496 then the portrait had somehow left Milan and then during the next 400 years travelled mysteriously to Naples. If this painting could talk it would undoubtedly reveal an interesting tale about its ownerships, history and the identity of the subjects.

Conservation and Restoration of the *Pacioli Portrait*

In any discussion or analysis about the original appearance or technical aspects of the painting, we need to take into consideration whether it has been damaged, restored or changed in any way. We know very little about the restoration and conservation history of the ~510-year-old *Pacioli Portrait* or how it might have changed in appearance, size and structure. However, Renzo Baldasso, a fellow at the John W. Kluge Center of the Library of Congress, wrote a paper about the *Pacioli Portrait* and commented about the recent restoration and conservation of the painting, saying:

> *'Before the cleaning done in the early 1990s (referenced in the painting by the square just below the middle knot in the friar's rope belt), the 1956 restoration corrected overpainting and areas of paint loss, including the far-right section, the fur of the gentleman's coat, the area beneath the cartellino, and the LI of the inscription on the closed book, while also filling numerous wormholes. Noteworthily, the three ghosts in the suspended crystal are not afterthoughts or byproducts of restorations. These are the two shadows evident in the lower right square face (next to these, there is an indentation in the wood that has been retouched in a lighter tone) and the elongated horizontal presence of a greenish tone, which bends correctly at the adjacent face and represents the reflection of the green tablecloth. These reflections prove that despite the obliviousness of the friar and his companion to the suspended polyhedron, it actually exists in their space.'*

We need to remember these words and be aware that many other hands have attempted to restore parts of the painting and probably have changed it in ways that were unintended by the original painter or painters.

References

Baldasso R (2010). Portrait of Luca Pacioli and Disciple: A New, Mathematical Look. The Art Bulletin 92:83-102.
Glori, Carla. Il cartiglio. *http://www.carlaglori.com/mi-presento/*
Glori, Carla. The Story of Ginerva de' Benci. *Academia.*
https://www.academia.edu/34595891/LA_STORIA_DI_GINEVRA_BENCI_NELLE_CINQUANTA_FRASI_ANAGRAMMATE_DAL_MOTTO_VIRTUTEM_FORMA_DECORAT_LA_PAROLA-CHIAVE_IUNIPERUS. Retrieved November 16, 2017.

Gronau, Giorgio (2011). Documenti Artistici Urbinati. Accademia Raffaello Urbino.
Kulski JK (2017). Leonardo da Vinci: The Melzi Chronicles. Published by Jerzy. K. Kulski. ISBN: 978-0-6480653-1-9.
Lauwers, Luc & Willekens, Marleen (1994). Five Hundred Years of Bookkeeping: A Portrait of Luca Pacioli (Tijdschrift voor Economie en Management, Katholieke Universiteit Leuven, vol. XXXIX issue 3 p. 289–304).
Museo di Capodimonte (2016). Il ritratto di Luca Pacioli a Capodimonte. *http://www.museocapodimonte.beniculturali.it/il-ritratto-di-luca-pacioli-a-capodimonte/*
O'Malley CD (1969). Leonardo's Legacy. An international symposium. Berkeley and Los Angeles. University of California Press.
Pedretti, Carlo (1964). Leonardo da Vinci on painting. A lost book (Libro A). University of California Press, Berkeley and Los Angeles.
Wikipedia (2018). Portrait of Luca Pacioli.
https://en.wikipedia.org/wiki/Portrait_of_Luca_Pacioli

4

BARBARI, DURER & MESSINA: QUESTIONABLE ATTRIBUTIONS & INFLUENCES

Three Into One Won't Go

The National Museum of Capodimonte has attributed the *Pacioli Portrait* officially to Jacopo de' Barbari and this is generally accepted to be the correct attribution by those who write about the painting and Luca Pacioli. However, some critics believe that Barbari's authorship is a misattribution and two other painters, Albert Dürer and Leonardo da Vinci, are occasionally touted to be the actual painters. Before writing this book, I examined the history and the oeuvre of each of these Renaissance painters and concluded that Leonardo is the most likely author of the *Pacioli Portrait* based on the subjects and pictorial cues within the painting and the well-established historical connection between him and Luca Pacioli.

If anybody cares to examine the information available in the public domain on the history, life and works of the three main contenders, Leonardo da Vinci, Jacopo de' Barbari and Albrecht Durer, it seems incredible that they would still attribute the Campodimonte portrait of Luca Pacioli to the Venetian painter Jacopo de' Barbari or the German, Albrecht Durer. Is this because of bureaucratic and political inflexibility or for other reasons? It is difficult to fathom without asking those people who were responsible previously for the attribution and/or those who are currently in charge of the attribution.

Jacopo de' Barbari. A Short Biography

Did Luca Pacioli ever meet with Jacopo Barbari to discuss mathematics and geometry and his portrait either when he was in Venice in 1494 or at any other time or place? There is no evidence that they ever met. And if they had met, was there enough time for Pacioli to teach Barbari all that he knew about the *Divine Proportion* and how to draw and paint a transparent rhombicuboctahedron? Again, this seems most unlikely. Luca Pacioli left Venice in 1495 and soon after, he was planning to travel to Milan to meet with Leonardo da Vinci and to accept Duke Ludovico Sforza's inaugural chair in mathematics at the University of Pavia. Leonardo da Vinci and Galeazzo Sanseverino were among those encouraging the duke of Milan to offer him the chair. By early 1496 Pacioli was in Milan teaching and collaborating with Leonardo da Vinci and living at the residence of the Duke's son-in-law, Galeazzo Sanseverino.

Jacopo de' Barbari's surviving documents addressed to various Germans in Italian suggest that he was of Italian rather than of German descent. It is often suggested that he was born in Venice in 1460 and that he was eight years younger than Leonardo da Vinci. However, the place and date of Barbari's birth is unknown and his speculative birth dates range between 1450 and 1470. Thus, the birth year of 1460 is an average taken as a compromise of convenience. If he was born in 1460, then he was 40 years of age in 1500, when he supposedly completed the *Pacioli Portrait*. By 1511, his colleague and friend Albrecht Dürer described him as 'old and weak'.

Jacopo de' Barbari signed many of his engravings with a *caduceus*, the sign of Mercury (Figures 4.1.2, 4.1.3, 4.1.14, 4.1.16), and there is a Munich still-life of a dead-bird that has his name: *Jac.o de barbarj p 1504* painted on a piece of paper (Fig. 4.1.12). He left Venice for Germany in 1500, and worked for the Emperor Maximilian I in Nuremberg for a year, then in various other places for Frederick the Wise of Saxony between the years 1503-5, before moving to the court of the Elector Joachim I of Brandenburg from the year 1506 to 1508. By March 1510, he was working for Philip of Burgundy's successor, the Archduchess Margaret, in Brussels and Mechelen. In January 1511, he fell ill and made a will, and the Archduchess gave him a pension for life, on account of his old age and weakness. He died either in Brussels or Mechelen in 1516 and left twenty-three of his engraving plates in the possession of Archduchess Margaret. He died three years before Leonardo da Vinci's death in France.

The earliest and best-documented work by de' Barbari is his huge (1.345 x 2.818 metres, from six blocks) woodcut of the aerial view of Venice entitled *Map of Venice* and published in 1500 (Fig. 4.1.4). The work had taken him three years to complete, presumably when he also was supposed to have painted and completed the *Pacioli Portrait*. He produced two other woodcuts, both of men and satyrs, before 1500, which were the largest and most impressive figurative woodcuts yet produced. By the time the *Map of Venice* was published de' Barbari had already left for Germany where he met Dürer who later recorded in an introduction to a book on drawing that they had discussed human proportion:

> *'I find no one who has written anything about how to make canon of human proportions except for a man named Jacob, born in Venice and a charming painter. He showed me a man and a woman which he had made according to measure, so that I would now rather see what he meant than behold a new kingdom... Jacobus did not want to show his principles to me clearly, that I saw well.'*

Twenty years later, Dürer tried unsuccessfully to get the Archduchess Margaret, Habsburg Regent of the Netherlands, to give him a manuscript book that she had on the subject of human proportions by de' Barbari, who was dead; the book has not survived.

De' Barbari spent a year in Nuremberg, where Dürer lived, in 1500–1, and they developed a friendship and influenced each other for several years. None of his engravings are dated, but his best engravings were probably done after his move to Germany in 1500. His style was related to those of Alvise Vivarini and Giovanni Bellini, but he had a languorous quality of his own. Apart from Dürer, the influence of Mantegna's parallel hatching technique also appears in what are probably the earlier engravings done around the turn of the century. His engravings are mostly small, showing just a few figures. Truculent satyrs feature in several prints and there are many mythological subjects, including two versions of *Sacrifices to Priapus*. The earlier prints show figures with *'small heads and somewhat shapeless bodies, with sloping shoulders and thick torsos supported by slender legs'* — also seen in his paintings. Probably from his middle period came several nudes, the most famous being *Apollo and Diana*, *St. Sebastian* and the *Three Bound Captives*. He also painted mostly portraits or half-length groups of religious figures and a few 'still-lifes'; the best known being the *Sparrowhawk* (National Gallery, London), and the *Partridge, gauntlets, and crossbow bolt* (Alte Pinakothek, Munich). There is a *Portrait of a German Man,* a religious subject, a religious group, and a pair of figures. On seeing and comparing his collection of paintings, it is difficult to connect Barbari stylistically to the *Pacioli Portrait* in the Museo di Capodimonte in Naples.

There is no evidence that Leonardo da Vinci and Jacopo de' Barbari had ever met or even seen each other's paintings and drawings. The travel records of Jacopo de' Barbari within Italy are almost non-existent so it is impossible to know if at any time in his travels between 1495 and 1500 whether he had come across Leonardo da Vinci and Pacioli either in Milan or Venice. This possibility existed when they were all together in Venice in 1500, just before de' Barbari left for Germany. In December 1499 – shortly after the victorious entry of the French into Milan - Leonardo and Luca Pacioli left the city together to visit Mantua in late February and Venice in March where the Signoria had sought Leonardo's advice on how to defend themselves against the Turkish incursion in Friuli. Leonardo is known to have visited several different artists in Venice and de' Barbari may have been one of them. Pacioli, although a near-native of Florence, had studied, worked and preached in Venice before 1495 and he was well known among the Venetian artists for his famous mathematical text, the *Summa*. When Leonardo was in Venice, he was concentrating more on mathematical problems than painting. He also was known by now to have been the artist that illustrated Pacioli's manuscript, the *Divine Proportion,* with various geometric forms and drawings.

Since many of Leonardo's drawings and notebooks accompanied him in his travels he may well have shown de' Barbari his drawings of Pacioli's head and the more spectacular of his geometrical shapes such as the rhombicuboctahedron and his various pentagons. If de' Barbari had met Pacioli and Leonardo together in Venice in 1500 of March, he must have worked very quickly to finish the *Pacioli Portrait* in about the same year. If we need to attribute the *Pacioli Portrait* to Barbari, we could even fantasise that Leonardo spent a few weeks helping him design the picture with all the appropriate symbols and codes and possibly even helped him paint the face of Pacioli, letting de' Barbari paint the clothing, the student and the other trivial items. In this regard, the student in the background might be Leonardo da Vinci himself. Indeed, some have speculated this to be so. Jacopo de' Barbari is thought to have been a much faster painter than Leonardo and less inclined to get distracted with inconsequential matters or pay too much time and attention to the finer points and complicated details of a painting. If the *Pacioli Portrait* was painted solely by de' Barbari's hand then he must have quickly mastered the mathematics and the techniques of geometry to paint the exquisite hanging polyhedron and the masterful facial expression of Pacioli with all its immense subtleties that only a master could muster and execute. Looking at all of Jacopo's paintings there is not one that shows the subtlety and mastery that a painter had achieved with the polyhedron and Pacioli's face and the twisted mouth curled up and down at each corner. That is, because the painting is most likely by Leonardo and not Jacopo. No mention is made of Jacopo de' Barbari by Luca Pacioli in any of his writings. Pacioli always exalted the painters with whom he had significant philosophical relationships and especially those who had helped illustrate his works or had portrayed him. And they were Piero della Francesca and Leonardo da Vinci, not Jacopo de' Barbari.

The inscription on the cartouche of the *Pacioli Portrait* looks nothing like the stable signature normally adopted by Jacopo de' Barbari with the use of the abbreviation IA D.B. and with the symbol of the *caduceus*. Furthermore, this is not a Venetian painting as implied by many art experts, including by the Museum's attribution to de' Barbari. Based on the historic narrative deduced from the subject of the painting and the decoded cryptic message contained on the cartouche with influences and themes of the deepest ideological implications that were derived from the contemporary Platonism with a Florentine background, it was more a Milanese than a Venetian painting. Moreover, the painting is universal and outside the confinement of Venetian ideology both in its visions and dialectic of mood and infinite knowledge versus doubt and despair. Leonardo believed in unified dualism, that is, the balance of two opposites – the dialectic – and the science of mathematics and geometry to help spread beauty, cohesion, and contemplation to develop the methods that source the truth of being and the essence of a good life.

Should the Barbari attribution be removed from the *Pacioli Portrait* because of a historic misunderstanding and mismanagement? If the Barbari attribution remains will it be an obstacle to any further reasonable research on the origins and subjects of the painting? Would the elimination of Barbari's name from the record enliven a broader discussion and search for a more coherent confluence on a plurality of facts, quotations, themes, known data and a better understanding of personal events of historical figures associated with the creation of this painting? Documentation and verification of certain and incontrovertible historical data are essential to establish provenance or at least accurate attribution or credit for a proper basis towards progressing further or ongoing research.

Jacopo de' Barbari's timeline:
1450-1470. Place and date of birth unknown.
1494. May have met Luca Pacioli in Venice.
1500. May have met Luca Pacioli and Leonardo da Vinci in Venice.
1500. Left Venice. Met Albrecht Durer and worked for Emperor Maximilian I in Nuremberg, Germany.
1503-1505. Worked for Frederick the Wise of Saxony.
1506-1508. Worked in the court of the Elector Joachim I of Brandenburg in Germany.
1509. Worked in the Netherlands for Philip the Handsome of Burgundy.
1510. Worked in Brussels and Mechelen for Archduchess Margaret.
1511. Fell ill and Archduchess Margaret awarded him a pension for life.
1516. He died in Brussels.

Jacopo de' Barbari. Wikipedia.
https://en.wikipedia.org/wiki/Jacopo_de%27_Barbari#cite_note-NGA-2

Albrecht Durer: Short Biography

The German painter Albert Durer is another candidate that was proposed for the *Pacioli Portrait*, mainly because he was a friend of Jacopo de' Barbari and they influenced each other at least since 1500. He was 19 years younger than Leonardo da Vinci and 24 years younger than Luca Pacioli and he never met either of them. He was born on May 21, 1471 and made two trips to Italy, the first journey in 1494 to 1495 and the second journey in 1505 to 1507. Albert Durer was greatly influenced by Leonardo da Vinci and his teachings on art, drawing, painting and perspective, but it is unlikely that he painted the *Pacioli Portrait* in 1500 or earlier when Leonardo and Pacioli were working and living together in Milan.

Much more is known about Albrecht Dürer than Jacopo de' Barbari. He was born in Nuremberg in Germany on 21st of May in 1471 and he died there on the 6th of April in 1528. He was a painter, printmaker, and theorist of the German Renaissance and established his reputation and influence across Europe while he was still in his twenties because of his high-quality woodcut prints. He possibly was in communication with the major Italian artists of his time, including Raphael, Giovanni Bellini and perhaps even Leonardo da Vinci. The German Emperor Maximilian I was his patron from 1512 to 1519.

Dürer's vast body of work includes engravings, his preferred technique for making prints. He also produced many altarpieces, portraits and self-portraits (Figures 4.2.1, 4.2.2, and 4.2.3), watercolours and books on mathematics, geometry and art. The woodcuts, such as the *Apocalypse* series (1498), are more Gothic than the rest of his work. His best-known engravings include the *Knight, Death, and the Devil* (1513), *Saint Jerome in his Study* (1514) and *Melencolia I* (1514), which have been the subject of extensive analysis and interpretation. His watercolours also mark him as one of the first European landscape artists, while his ambitious woodcuts revolutionised the potential of that medium. He was obsessed by Leonardo da Vinci and tried to follow up on his theoretical treatises, which involved principles of mathematics, perspective, and ideal proportions.

Durer's city of birth, Nuremberg, was important and prosperous, and a centre for publishing and luxury trades. It had strong links with Italy, especially Venice, with a relatively short distance between them across the Alps. Durer made two journeys to Italy, the first between 1494 and 1495, and the second between 1505 and 1507. He was married in 1494 and within three months of his marriage, he left for Italy, alone, perhaps stimulated by an outbreak of plague in Nuremberg. He made watercolour sketches while travelling over the Alps to Venice where he intended to study its more advanced artistic world. He wrote that Giovanni Bellini was the oldest and still the best of the artists in Venice, and that Antonio Pollaiuolo, Andrea Mantegna, Lorenzo di Credi and others influenced him. On his return to Nuremberg in 1495, he opened his workshop, and over the next five years his style increasingly integrated Italian influences into an underlying Northern form. His famous series of sixteen great print designs for the *Apocalypse* is dated 1498, as is his engraving of *St. Michael Fighting the*

CHAPTER 4

Dragon. He made the first seven scenes of the *Great Passion* in the same year, and a little later, a series of eleven designs depicting the *Holy Family and Saints*. In 1500, Dürer and his assistants completed the *Seven Sorrows Polyptych* that was commissioned by Frederick III of Saxony in 1496. Between the years of 1503–1505, he produced the first seventeen of a set illustrating the *Life of the Virgin*, which took several years to complete. Jacopo de' Barbari visited Durer in Nuremberg in 1500 and taught him much about the new Italian developments in perspective, anatomy, and proportion. This became a lifelong preoccupation for Dürer and his experiments in human proportion produced his famous engraving of *Adam and Eve* (1504), which is the only existing engraving signed with his full name.

Durer's second journey to Italy was between 1505 and 1507, where he returned to painting, at first producing a series of works executed in tempera on linen. These included portraits and altarpieces, notably, the *Paumgartner* altarpiece and the *Adoration of the Magi*. In early 1506, he returned to Venice and stayed there until the spring of 1507, where he was given a valuable commission from the emigrant German community for the church of San Bartolomeo. This was the altarpiece known as the *Adoration of the Virgin* or the *Feast of Rose Garlands*. It included portraits of members of Venice's German community, but showed a strong Italian influence. It was subsequently acquired by the Emperor Rudolf II and taken to Prague. The other paintings that he produced in Venice include *The Virgin and Child with the Goldfinch*, *Christ among the Doctors*, and several smaller works.

Durer's 1506 painting *The Virgin and Child with the Goldfinch* (often named as a Siskin finch instead of a goldfinch) may have been influenced by Leonardo da Vinci's painting known as the *Madonna Litta* or *Madonna Lactans*, which may have been displayed in Venice when Durer was there between 1505 and 1507. Leonardo's extraordinary beautiful painting that was completed in Milan in about 1490 is tempera on canvas (transferred from panel) and is now displayed at the Hermitage Museum in Saint Petersburg. It shows the infant Christ suckling from his mother's breast while in his left hand, he holds a goldfinch, symbolic of his future Passion and Crucifixion. It has been speculated that Leonardo might have taken the *Madonna Litta* with him to Venice in March 1500, as the diarist Marcantonio Michiel recorded its presence in the Ca' Contarini in that city in 1543. Raphael, who probably had seen Leonardo da Vinci's *Madonna Lactans* when he was either in Venice or Leonardo's studio in Florence between 1504 and 1508, produced his painting on the same subject in about 1506. Durer made another drawing and painting on the same theme in 1515 where he has the Christ Child sitting on a cushion on the Virgin's knee while a small bird flies around his head, tied to a cord held in the Child's left hand. The goldfinch is a religious symbol because of the belief that it was splashed with Christ's blood on the road to Calvary, retaining a red spot around its beak. The ornithologist Herbert Friedmann wrote in his book *Symbolic Goldfinch* that this bird has four principal symbolic biblical meanings including the soul, sacrifice, death, and the Resurrection.

Although the Venetians held Dürer in high regard, he returned to Nuremberg by mid-1507 and remained in Germany until 1520. His reputation as a talented artist had spread throughout Europe and he was on friendly terms and in communication with most of the major artists including Raphael and Giovanni Bellini and possibly with Leonardo da Vinci because of Lorenzo di Credi. Between 1507 and 1511, Dürer worked on some of his most celebrated paintings: *Adam and Eve* (1507), *The Martyrdom of the Ten Thousand* (1508), *Virgin with the Iris* (1508), the altarpiece *Assumption of the Virgin* (1509), and *Adoration of the Trinity* (1511). During this period, he completed two woodcut series, the *Great Passion* and the *Life of the Virgin*, both published in 1511 together with a second edition of the *Apocalypse* series. The post-Venetian woodcuts show Dürer's development of *chiaroscuro* modelling effects that he may have learnt from Leonardo da Vinci to create a mid-tone throughout the print to which the highlights and shadows could be contrasted. During 1513 and 1514, Dürer created his three most famous engravings: *Knight, Death, and the Devil* (1513, probably based on Erasmus's treatise *Enchiridion militis Christiani*), *St. Jerome in his Study*, and the much-debated *Melencolia I* (both 1514).

In 1520, Dürer journeyed to the Netherlands and Brussels and stayed there until 1521. It was his fourth and last journey. Having secured his pension, Dürer finally returned home to Nuremberg in July 1521, caught an undetermined illness - perhaps malaria - which afflicted him for the rest of his life, and greatly reduced his rate of work. In his remaining seven years he produced a few paintings including a portrait of *Hieronymus Holtzschuher*, a *Madonna and Child* (1526), *Salvator Mundi* (1526), and two panels showing St. John with St. Peter in the background and St. Paul with St. Mark in the background. Dürer donated his last great work entitled the *Four Apostles* to the City of Nuremberg.

Dürer produced and published several books on mathematics and other subjects. *The Four Books on Measurement* that was published in Nuremberg in 1525 was the first book for adults on mathematics in German, and was even cited by Galileo and Kepler. Another book, a work on city fortifications, was published in 1527. *The Four Books on Human Proportion* were published posthumously, shortly after his death in 1528. Dürer exerted a huge influence on the artists of succeeding generations, especially in printmaking, the medium through which his contemporaries mostly experienced and admired his art, as his paintings were predominantly in private collections located in only a few cities. The generation of Italian engravers who soon followed in the shadow of Dürer trained themselves by copying either parts of his landscape backgrounds or his entire print. However, Dürer's influence became less dominant after 1515, when Marcantonio Raimondi perfected his new engraving style. Dürer's paintings had relatively little influence in Italy, although his intense and self-dramatising self-portraits continued to influence painters of the 19th and 20th century who desired a more dramatic portrait style. His work on geometry included the *Four Books on Measurement* and a book on two-dimensional geometry and the construction of regular polygons. Here, Dürer preferred the methods of Ptolemy over Euclid and his third book applied the principles of geometry to architecture, engineering and typography. In architecture, Durer cited Vitruvius and in typography, he depicted the geometric construction of the Latin alphabet relying on Italian precedent and the alphabets that Leonardo da Vinci had drawn for Luca Pacioli. Dürer's fourth book completed the progression of the first and second by moving to three-dimensional forms and the construction of polyhedra. He discussed the five Platonic solids, as well as seven Archimedean semi-regular solids, and several of his inventions. He was also familiar with the 'abbreviated construction' as described by Alberti and the geometrical construction of shadows, a technique of Leonardo da Vinci. Although Dürer made no innovations in these areas, he is noted to be the first Northern European outside of Italy to treat matters of visual representation in a scientific way, and with an understanding of Euclidean principles.

Albrecht Dürer never accomplished the same mastery of painting as Leonardo da Vinci, and it is most unlikely that he was the author of the *Pacioli Portrait* in the Museo di Capodimonte in Naples given his contrasting timeline, history and no evidence of a friendship with Luca Pacioli.

Albrecht Durer's time-line:
1471. Born 21st May in Nuremberg, Germany
1490. Finished his apprenticeship in drawing and goldsmithing.
1491-1494. Travelled in Germany and Netherlands.
1494-1495. Married Agnes Frey in Nuremberg and then travelled alone to Venice. May have met Jacopo de Barbari and Luca Pacioli in Venice in 1494.
1500. Met with Jacopo de Barbari in Nuremberg who introduced him to perspective, anatomy and proportion.
1495-1505. Opened his workshop in Nuremburg and worked there as an engraver and on woodcut prints.
1505-1507. Returned to Venice to develop his painting skills. May have met with Luca Pacioli and Leonardo da Vinci in Florence.

1507–1520. Returned to Nuremberg where he worked for 13 years as a master engraver and printer and occasional painter. In 1512 the Emperor Maximilian became his major patron until the emperor's death in 1519.
1520-1521. Travelled in the Netherlands and Brussels.
1521-1528. Back in Nuremberg engraving, painting and writing treatises on mathematics, proportion and painting. Died 6th April, 1528.

Nick Mackinnon: Speculation and Confusion in Favour of Albrecht Durer to be the Student in the *Pacioli Portrait*

Nick Mackinnon's oft-cited academic publication of 1993 in the *Mathematical Gazette* entitled *The Portrait of Fra Luca Pacioli* made a valiant but confused attempt to build a case for Albrecht Durer to be the 'student' standing beside Pacioli in the portrait. Mackinnon looked for connections between the lives of Durer and Pacioli and he attempted to connect them and their timelines often with highly confusing results and speculations. Here are his initial thoughts about the painting.

'While to a connoisseur the painting might be thought wooden and peripheral to the history of art, I believe that the artist has recorded the most important meeting of the Renaissance. Analysis of the mathematics of the picture, and that of Pacioli himself, allows one to decide the name of the artist; the date of the painting to within a month; the identity of the handsome student; the editions of the books on the table; and the number of the theorem, which Pacioli is demonstrating. Some may find my identification of the student to be "not proven", but the discussion of the portrait should be of interest nonetheless, as should my observations about the famous Melencolia I *of Albrecht Durer.'*

On the right hand side of the painting, a solid sculpture of dodecahedron stands on a red book, on which is written *LI.R.LVC.BVR*, translatable as *Liber Reverendi Luca Burgensis*. This identifies the work as the *Summa*, published in Venice in 1494, for no other work by Pacioli approaches this large size, not even the *Divine Proportion* that was illustrated by Leonardo da Vinci and published in Venice in 1509. Acknowledging the inscription *IACO. BAR. VIGENNIS. P. 1495*, Nick Mackinnon both questions and defends the attribution to Jacopo de' Barbari on several fronts:

'For opinion of many art historians that the painting is not by Jacopo Barbari, but by some other Venetian that they have to call Jacopo..... The only reason they have for doubting that Jacopo de' Barbari is the artist is that "Vigennis" might mean "twenty years old", and conventional art theory has it that Barbari was more like 40 in 1495, and by 1511 he was so old that he had to receive a pension from Margaret of the Netherlands. But can it really be that, with such a small area to work on, rather than

write out his full name, the artist prefers to risk confusion with Jacopo de' Barbari and give instead his age, a mere twenty? Is there any other example of an artist giving his own age in this manner? There is another example of Jacopo de Barbari's use of a cartellino to sign his pictures: Still life with partridge 1504 shown in Box 5, acknowledged as being influenced in its delicacy by Durer, of all people. Given that the mythical "Jacopo Bar." has shown such incredible mastery in one so young, especially in the painting of the crystal rhombicuboctahedron, surely it will be possible to find other works by him, since we know the year of his birth, the place where he worked, his Christian name, and the first portion of his surname. Where are the other signed works of Jacopo Bar. Born in Venice, 1475?'*

And later:

'Gilbert and Davis both concur that all the other possible candidates for authorship of this painting are ruled out, and Davis gives a (necessarily rather unconvincing) stylistic analysis of Barbari's works that indicate that Barbari is indeed the author of the Pacioli portrait. We come now to a complex twist in the story, as two red herrings are dragged across the trail. These involve the kind of documentation beloved by art historians, which seem to establish the provenance of the painting and also to demolish almost every theory advanced so far in this article. In fact they do no such thing.'

And in his notes:

'I have been rather scathing about this work [referring to M. D. Davis] in the text but it gave me the confidence to persist in my (already formed) view that Barbari is the author of the Pacioli portrait, and gave the crucial demolition of the Guidobaldi hypothesis.'

After momentarily excluding de' Barbari as the painter in favour of Albert Durer early on in the text, Nick Mackinnon suddenly comes out from left field and proposes that Leonardo da Vinci may have had a hand in some aspects of the painting:

The highlight of the portrait is the rhombicuboctahedron. And here we surely see the ineffable left hand of Leonardo da Vinci, who drew the superb pictures for De Divina Proportione, which, moreover, hang from a string in the originals. Pacioli left Venice for Milan in 1496 and was then with Leonardo for two years, during which time the illustrations for De Divina Proportione were made. Furthermore, Pacioli says in De Divina Proportione that a collection of crystal polyhedra is to be found in Milan. The rhombicuboctahedron could not be executed more exactly, and furthermore, the artist has complicated the task by showing it half full of water and showing the consequent reflections and refractions. By contrast, the (easier to depict) dodecahedron is at best a workmanlike job. We begin therefore to see the possibility that the portrait was not executed at one sitting, and in particular that the student need not have been painted from life. In fact, it is most unlikely that Pacioli would have included the almost unknown Durer in the portrait until such time as Durer had become famous, which might be as late as 1508, when Pacioli delivered the lecture on Elements V described in Box 6.'

And a little further on:

The rhombicuboctahedron, with both square and triangular faces, can therefore stand as a symbol of all four elements. By partially filling the solid with water, Leonardo contrives to make this symbol more concrete, for now the elements are represented by physical embodiments also: earth by the solidity of the glass, water and air are contained inside, and fire by the bright reflections. The fifth solid, the dodecahedron, given its place in a throwaway line in The Timeaus: "whereas a fifth figure yet alone remained, God used it for the universe in embellishing with signs". This remark was often misinterpreted as suggesting that twelve faces of the dodecahedron each contained one of the twelve signs of the zodiac, the belt of stars that extends a few degrees either side of the ecliptic, and we now recall that on the blackboard in the portrait construction used in antiquity to construct the angle of the plane of the ecliptic. So, not only does the portrait refer to the elements of geometry, but to the elements of nature as well. By painting in a water-filled rhombicuboctahedron, Leonardo, or another, has contrived a brilliant double reference to the Timeaeus.'

Having introduced Leonardo da Vinci as the most likely hand to have painted the transparent water-filled rhombicuboctahedron, Nick Mackinnon does not follow through to the most obvious conclusion that it was Leonardo, either with or without assistance, who was the actual author of the entire painting. Instead, he returns to implying that Durer is the painter and focuses in on Durer's second visit to Italy from 1505-1507 and speculates about a possible meeting between Durer and Pacioli and that Durer might have visited Florence before travelling on to Venice. He fails to mention that Leonardo da Vinci also was in Florence at this time and that Leonardo is far more likely to have painted the *Pacioli Portrait* than Durer. Furthermore, Durer was greatly influenced by Leonardo and many of his paintings, drawings and woodcarvings and his interest in the science of painting, perspective and the divine proportion reflects this influence. Nick Mackinnon acknowledges this to some small degree:

'Durer also makes a study of the semi-regular polyhedra, inventing the idea of a net to help him (figures 15 and 16). Again these polyhedra are first discussed by Piero in De quinque corporibus regularibus, *but here Durer could have been influenced by Piero by way of De Divina Proportione, rather than directly through a meeting with Pacioli. Pacioli is also a link between Durer and Leonardo da Vinci, whose studies of*

the proportions of horses were to influence Durer after his second visit to Italy. The drawing in figure 17 brings the proportions of the horse and the net of a polyhedron together.'

However, Mackinnon cannot completely ignore the much stronger relationship and the mathematical and geometrical co-interests between Leonardo and Pacioli pointing out in his reference section:

> *'Pacioli gives the same seven semi-regular divina proportione, but they are illustrated - Pacioli describes in the introductory letter as "supreme and very graceful figures of all the Platonic and mathematical regular bodies and dependants, which it would not be possible to make better in perspective drawing, even if Apelles, Myron or Polycleus and the others were to return among us, made and shaped by that ineffable left-hand, most fitted for all the mathematical disciplines, of the prince among the mortals of today, that first of Florentines, our Lionardo da Vinci, in that happy time when we were together in the most admirable city of Milan, working for the same patron" (2c, 2d). This was between 1496 and September 1499 when they left together for Florence in the face of the invading French.'*

> *"Leonardo wrote of their intellectual relationship:*
> *El dolci fructo, vago e si dilecto*
> *Costrinse gia philosophi cercare*
> *Causa de noi, che pasci l' intelletto."*
> *[Sweet desserts were vague and inappropriate for him.*
> *He already searched for a philosophy*
> *The cause of us grazed in his intellect].*

Luca Pacioli travelled widely and often about Italy as did Leonardo da Vinci and it is well documented that their paths interconnected significantly over many years particularly in the Duchy of Milan from 1496 to 1499, then during their travels to Venice in 1500, during their stay in Florence between 1500 and 1507, and then in Rome for at least one year in 1514. On the other hand, the interactions between Pacioli and de' Barbari or between Pacioli and Durer are undocumented, speculative and at best too fleeting to have produced the complex portraiture and design of the *Pacioli Portrait* that is exhibited in the Museo di Capodimonte in Naples.

Using maps and diagrams, Nick Mackinnon attempted to show the degree, nature, time and place of the connections between Pacioli, de' Barbari and Durer. He admits that the dates on the map are interpolated in places and sometimes based on the published conjectures of others. This is a seriously failed attempt because it is disingenuous to leave out Leonardo da Vinci from the equation and omit the important dates and places of the many meetings between him and Luca Pacioli. In contrast, Nick

Mackinnon preferred to speculate about an undocumented meeting that might have occurred between Barbari and Pacioli and Durer in Venice sometime between 1494 and 1496, and between Durer and Pacioli in Florence in November of 1505. While Durer and Barbari are likely to have met when living in Germany, there is no evidence that they met with Pacioli. Nevertheless, Nick Mackinnon hypothesises that Durer is the student in the *Pacioli Portrait*, and that he is there because he learned perspective from Pacioli. He cites and discusses the significance of the truncated polyhedron, a hanging gourd and the magic square in Durer's engraving *Melencolia I* (1514) as his *prima facie* evidence. His supporting evidence is Durer's engraving of *Knight, Death and Devil* (1513) and *St. Jerome in his Study* (1514). While these engravings are masterpieces and a clear tribute to the Italian masters who had influenced him, they in no way support the most unlikely possibility that he had anything to do with the *Pacioli Portrait*. Nick Mackinnon has drawn this extremely longbow in an attempt to connect the *Pacioli Portrait* to his essay on Albrecht Durer. This is like mixing cheese and chalk and calling it sugar. The title of his paper should have been '*Albrecht Durer's Perspective on Melencolia*', and as an aside, he still could have highlighted and discussed the various influences on Durer including those of Pacioli, Barbari and da Vinci. Albeit overly provocative, his paper is nevertheless informative and interesting. I found the following notes about Luca Pacioli and Barbari at the end of his paper enlightening for how the false meme was perpetuated that Jacopo de' Barbari is the author of the *Pacioli Portrait*:

271-299. Pacioli. The main biography is R.E. Taylor's No royal road, Amrno Press, 1980. Got hold of this book only after the text of this article had been typeset. Taylor says that a long time he believed that the student was Durer because of the striking likeness, but discards the hypothesis on the grounds of eye colour. I do not believe the argument from eye colour to be strong, and anyway Pacioli would not have permitted the unknown 1495 Durer to intrude on his portrait, if the student is Durer he cannot have been painted from life anyway. Taylor concurs with the Guidobaldi opinion, but no patron would be painted [in] such a subservient position: there would be a symmetry between a patron and Pacioli. Elsewhere Taylor claims a link between Durer and Pacioli as early as 1493, but he advances absolutely no evidence for this view. Taylor's discussion of the portrait is lengthy but superficial. He implies that he has actually seen it, but this makes all the more astonishing his claim that the open book is a manuscript of De Divina Proportione. I find the repeated failure of all who have studied this painting to correctly identify the perfectly rendered copy of Ratdolt's Euclid most revealing. Taylor also observes the fact that magic squares occur De viribus quantitatis and also in Melencolia I, but does not make the crucial observation that they are the very same square in both cases! ... 0. Benesch, "A new contribution to the problem of the

CHAPTER 4

Portrait of Fra Luca Pacioli" Essays in Honor of Hans Tietze (Paris 1958) is a good summary of the futile art-historical view of the portrait, with references to other studies.

I nevertheless remain bewildered that none of these experts and critics seriously considered or accepted that Leonardo da Vinci was the actual author of the *Pacioli Portrait*. Albrecht Durer's portraits were mainly self-portraits, and a few of his immediate family, German friends, merchants, clerics, and nobles including Emperor Maximilian I. There is no evidence of any drawings or painted portraits of Luca Pacioli or that he bothered with double portraiture.

Having accepted that Jacopo de' Barbari was the author of the *Pacioli Portrait*, Nick Mackinnon then argued in his published paper that the acolyte standing beside Luca Pacioli in the painting is the German engraver and painter Albrecht Durer:

I was convinced the moment I saw this picture that the student in the portrait of Pacioli was Durer, but at that instant the only evidence was the shock of recognition. Begin by observing the length, colour and style of the hair of the student, which would at this time have been most unusual in Italy. Compare the full lips, and the dimple in the top lips of the student and Durer. But it was the similar confident manner of the two men that I first noticed, for I was working from black-and-white reproductions, and spent a week on tenterhooks before establishing that Durer had ginger hair.

Mackinnon's statement that the length, colour and style of the hair of the student would have been unusual in Italy at this time is incorrect given that Leonardo's and/or his assistants in Milan had already painted similar hairstyles in the portraits of the *Musician* (1490), *Young Man with Ticker Tape* (1494) and *Young Man* (1495) as discussed later in Chapters 6 and 15. Mackinnon raises another two problems that he also needed to overcome to convince us that it is Albrecht Durer.

The beard is the first problem, and easily solved. A self-portrait of 1493 (Plate 3) shows Durer clean shaven. Taking the Pacioli portrait to be dated at 1495, we would expect the student to be between the ages of the two Durer self-portraits.

And later,

A second problem is the Alps. Durer spent most of his life in Germany: Pacioli spent all of his in Italy (apart from a short stay in Zara, now Zadar in the former Yugoslavia, which was then the territory of Venice). Between them are the Alps, crossed at the Brenner pass. Durer made two trips to Italy, in 1494-95 and in 1505.

And then later on,

Who did Durer meet in Venice in 1495? He spoke little Latin or Italian, and would naturally have met mainly people from the sizeable German colony, centred round the Fondaco dei Tedeschi near the Rialto. It is known through Durer's own words that he had contact with the Venetian painter of German origin, Jacopo de' Barbari, at some time between 1495 and 1500, either when Durer was in Venice or when Barbari was in Germany. The opinion of art historians is that the overwhelming likelihood is that their first meeting was in 1495, especially as Durer mentions him by name in a letter of 1507, saying that he has now seen the works of 'many painters much superior to Jacopo de' Barbari'.

This meeting between Durer and Barbari in Venice in 1494 or 1495 is an important requirement to support the Mackinnon narrative. The nail in the coffin is the following Mackinnon statement:

As there is no other artist who would be likely to include Durer in a painting, if Durer is the student then Barbari would have to be the artist.

The logical conclusion that follows from the above statement is that if Jacopo de' Barbari was not the artist then Durer was not the student. A stylistic analysis and history of Barbari's works and life in comparison to that of Leonardo da Vinci confirms that Barbari was not the author of the *Pacioli Portrait*.

The Sicilian Painter Antonello da Messina (1430-1479), Pioneer of Italian Portraiture

The National Museum of Capodimonte on their Web Page on the Internet briefly considered the influence of Sicilian painter Antonello da Messina on the *Pacioli Portrait*. The reference by the Museum to Antonello da Messina is interesting because he lived from 1430 to 1479, so the dates exclude him as the artist of the *Pacioli Portrait* because historically the painting must have been started and completed after 1495. However, judging from Messina's *oeuvre* it is evident that he had a major influence on the painting style of the author of the *Pacioli Portrait*. In short, the Museum informs us that the author of the portrait of Luca Pacioli at Capodimonte is Jacopo de' Barbari, a Venetian engraver and artist who also worked in Germany. This is their official version. Full stop. However, the evidence for Jacopo de' Barbari is tenuous and controversial. It depends almost entirely on the inscription written on a piece of unfolded paper, known as the cartouche. A black fly at the end of the inscription partially obscures the number 5 making it difficult to be sure that it is a five and not four or six. The inscription reads: *Iaco. B ar. Vigennis. P. 1495.*

Although Antonello da Messina died in 1479 and was no longer alive when the *Pacioli Portrait* was created, his style of painting portraiture is likely to have influenced Leonardo da Vinci and other Italian painters of the Renaissance and therefore, he should not be ignored. A glance through the portraiture of the early Renaissance reveals how much other painters including Leonardo da Vinci copied his style. Just seven paintings of the many in existence can illustrate his pioneering style that probably influenced Leonardo da Vinci greatly; the *Virgin Annunciate, Proud Man, St Jerome in his Study, Portrait of Trivulzio, ca. 1476, The Unknown Sailor, Il Condottiero and Salvator Mundi* (see Fig. 4.3).

Leonardo's yellowed and unfolded notepaper with the cryptic message in the *Pacioli Portrait* appears to have been taken directly from Messina's paintings of the *Salvator Mundi* and the *Portrait of Trivulzio, ca. 1476*. Even Messina's painting of *St Jerome in His Study* has an unfolded notepaper with an undecipherable message attached to his study wall.

While in Venice in 1475, Antonello da Messina was offered the opportunity to travel to Milan and become the court portrait painter to the Duke of Milan, Galeazzo Maria Sforza, but he declined the offer. Instead, he returned to Sicily by September of 1476 and died there a few years later in Messina in 1479. The Sforza Court was well aware of his portraiture style and they would have encouraged the Milanese painters to try and mimic his style. It appears that nobody took up a similar style until Leonardo da Vinci arrived in Milan in about 1481. It is the Messina style that Leonardo da Vinci used for the *Pacioli Portrait*.

Antonello da Messina was born in the town of Messina in Sicily, but he trained in Naples to paint in the Flemish style with guidance from his teacher Niccolo Colantonio and a few examples of Netherlandish paintings by Rogier van der Weyden and Jan van Eyck that belonged to their patron, Alfonso of Aragon, who was the King of Naples from 1442 to 1458. After completing his training, Antonello spent most of his time in Messina in Sicily with occasional travel and work in Calabria and Naples and at least one year in Venice. Isabella of Aragon, the young princess who married her cousin, the young duke of Milan, Gian Galeazzo Sforza, would have seen many of Antonello da Messina's paintings in the court of Naples and encouraged Leonardo da Vinci to paint his portraits in a similar style. Hence, if you look at the Antonello da Messina's portraits known as the *Virgin Annunciate* in the Palazzo Abetellis in Palermo and the *Unknown Sailor* in the Mandralisca Museum of Cefalù in Sicily you will see an uncanny resemblance to the style of the *Mona Lisa*.

Galleries of Barbari, Durer and Messina

The following picture galleries show a selection of paintings attributed to

Jacopo de' Barbari, Albrecht Durer and Antonello da Messina. All images of the paintings were sourced from Web Gallery of Art (WGA): https://www.wga.hu; and Wikimedia commons: https://commons.wikimedia.org/wiki/Main_Page.

Jacopo de' Barbari: The following 20 images are a selected collection of Barbari's paintings, woodcuts and engravings.

CHAPTER 4

FIG. 4.1. *Jacopo de' Barbari (1460-1516) picture gallery.*

1, Virgin and Child Flanked by St John the Baptist and St Anthony Abbot: 1490s, oil on canvas, 47 x 55 cm, Musée du Louvre, Paris; image from WGA. **2,** Victory Reclining Amid Trophies: 1500-1503, engraving and ink, 13.8 × 19.4 cm, National Gallery of Art, Washington D.C; image from Artsy online or Wikimedia Commons. **3,** Triton and Nereid: 1495-1516: engraving, sheet 12.8 x 19.2 cm, Private collection, Bridgeman Art Library; image (lot 14) from Christie's online. **4,** Perspective Plan of Venice: 1500, woodcut produced with six blocks, 135 x 282 cm, Museo Correr, Venice; image from WGA. **5,** Triumph of Men Over Satyrs:

1495-1497. Woodcut finished with pen and brown ink, 42.8 x 30 cm, Musei Civici di Pavia; image from Lombardia Beni Culturali online. **6,** An Old Man and a Young Woman: 1503, oil on panel, 40.3 x 32.4 cm, Philadelphia Museum of Art. image from Wikimedia Commons. **7,** Christ: 1503, oil on panel, 31 x 25 cm, Schlossmuseum, Weimar; image from WGA. **8,** Salvator Mundi: oil on panel, 41.9 x 30.5 cm, Private collection; image from Wikimedia Commons. **9,** Portrait of a Man: 1505-06 oil on linden panel, 38 x 30 cm, Kunsthistorisches Museum, Vienna; Image from WGA. **10,** Portrait of a Man (verso of Man & Woman nude): 1497-1500, oil on poplar panel, 61 x 46 cm, Staatliche Museen, Berlin; image from WGA. **11,** Man & Woman nude (verso of the Portrait of a Man): 1497-1500, oil on poplar panel, 61 x 46 cm, Staatliche Museen, Berlin; image from WGA. **12,** Still-Life with Partridge and Gauntlet: 1504, wood, 52 x 42.5 cm, Alte Pinakothek, Munich; image from WGA. **13,** Sacrifice to Priapus: 1499-1501, engraving and ink print, 28.7 x 39.1 cm, Metropolitan Museum of Art, New York, USA; image from Wikimedia Commons. **14,** Nude Woman Holding a Mirror: 1503-04, engraving, 85 x 60 mm, National Gallery of Art, Washington; image from WGA. **15,** Sparrowhawk: 1510, oil on oak, 17.8 cm x 10.8 cm, National Gallery, London: image from Wikimedia Commons. **16,** Judith with the Head of Holofernes: 17.7 x 10.3 cm, Fine Arts Museums of San Francisco; image from Wikimedia Commons. **17,** Portrait of Henri V., of Mecklenburg. 1507, oil on panel, 59.3 x 37.5 cm., Mauritshuis, The Hague, Netherlands; image from Wikimedia Commons. **18,** Portrait of Young Man: 1505, oil on panel, 28 x 23 cm, National Gallery of Art (NGA) - Washington DC; image from NGA online. **19,** Mars and Venus: 1510-1512, Engraving with additions in graphite, ink, and wash, 29.2 x 17.5 cm., Minneapolis Institute of Art: image from Wikimedia Commons. **20,** Cleopatra, 1495-1516, engraving, 18.1 x 11.7 cm, British Museum, London; image from WGA.

Albrecht Durer: The following 9 images are a few selected examples.

(continued)

FIG. 4.2. Albrecht Durer (1471-1528) picture gallery.

1, Self-portrait: 1493s, oil on parchment mounted on canvas, 56.5 x 45.5 cm, Musée du Louvre, Paris. **2**, Self-portrait: 1498, oil on panel, 52 × 41 cm, Prado Museum, Madrid. **3**, Self-portrait: 1500: oil on panel 67.1 x 48.9 cm, Alte Pinakothek, Munich. **4**, Self-portrait, detail Feast of the Rosary: 1506: oil on panel 162 x 194.5 cm, National Gallery, Prague. **5**, Barbara Durer (mother): 1490-1493, oil on fir, 47 x 35.8 cm, Germanisches Nationalmuseum. **6**, Albrecht Durer Senior (father): 1490, oil on panel, 47.5 x 39.5 cm, Uffizi Gallery, Florence. **7,** Albrecht Durer Senior (father): 1497, oil on linden wood, 51 x 40.3 cm, National Gallery, London. **8,** Portrait of Oswolt Krel: 1499, oil on panel, 50 x 39 cm, Alte Pinakothek, Munich. **9,** Portrait of a Young Man: 1500 oil on lime, 25.4 x 29.1 cm, Alte Pinakothek, Munich.

Antonello da Messina: The following 12 images are a selected collection of da Messina's religious and portrait painting.

(continued)

FIG. 4.3. Antonello da Messina (1430-1479) picture gallery.

1, Portrait of a Man: 1474, oil on wood, 32 x 26 cm, Gemaldegalerie Berlin. **2,** Il Condottiere: 1475, oil on panel, 36.2 × 30 cm, Louvre Museum, Paris. **3,** Portrait of a Man: 1476, oil on poplar, 35.6 x 25.4 cm, National Gallery, London. **4,** Trivulzio of Milan: 1476: oil on panel 35.5 x 28 cm, Civico d'Arte, Turin. **5,** Portrait of a Young Man: 1478, oil on walnut, 20.4 x 14.5 cm, Gemaldegalerie, Berlin. 1490-1493, oil on fir, 47 x 35.8 cm, Germanisches Nationalmuseum. **6,** Madonna Reading: 1475, oil on panel, 45 x 34.5 cm, Galleria Regionale della Sicilia, Palermo. **7,** Salvator Mundi: 1465, oil on panel, 38.7 x 29.8 cm, National Gallery, London. **8,** Ecce Homo: 1473, oil on panel, 48.5 x 38 cm, Colliegio Alberoni, Piacenza. **9,** St. Jerome in his Study: 1475, oil on lime, 45.7 x 36.2 cm, National Gallery, London. **10,** Throned Madonna, detail from polyptych: 1473, painting, 129 cm x 76 cm, Museo Nazionale, Messina. **11,** St Jerome: 1460-1465, tempura, 40 x 30.5 cm, Museo della Magna Grecia. **12,** Calvary: 1475, oil on panel, 52.5 x 42.5 cm, Royal Museum of Fine Arts, Antwerp, Belgium.

References

Brown, David Alan (2001). *Virtue and Beauty*, Princeton, N.J.; Chichester: Princeton University Press.
Friedmann, Herbert (2019). Symbolic Goldfinch. Princeton University Press, Google Books.
Mackinnon, Nick (1993). The Portrait of Fra Luca Pacioli. The Mathematical Gazette 77:130 - 219.
Wikipedia (2018). Jacopo de' Barbari.
  https://en.wikipedia.org/wiki/Jacopo_de%27_Barbari#cite_note-NGA-2
Wikipedia (2018). Albrecht Durer. https://en.wikipedia.org/wiki/Albrecht_Dürer
Wikipedia (2018). Antonello da Messina.
  https://en.wikipedia.org/wiki/Antonello_da_Messina
Wikipedia (2018). Luca Pacioli. https://en.wikipedia.org/wiki/Luca_Pacioli
Wikipedia (2018). Portrait of Luca Pacioli.
  https://en.wikipedia.org/wiki/Portrait_of_Luca_Pacioli

5

DUKE OF URBINO: A MOST UNLIKELY STUDENT OF LUCA PACIOLI

Guidobaldo I da Montefeltro (1472-1508), Duke of Urbino (1482-1508) and Cultured Mercenary Military Leader of the Renaissance

According to the consensus view, Guidobaldo I da Montefeltro is the student in the *Pacioli Portrait*. This is also the view of the Capodimonte Museum as stated on their web page at:
http://www.museocapodimonte.beniculturali.it/il-ritratto-di-luca-pacioli-a-capodimonte/

'The portrait depicts the Franciscan friar and distinguished mathematician Luca Pacioli (Borgo San Sepolcro, 1445-1517), a friend of Piero della Francesca and Leonardo, while, with his gaze focused, almost lost in front of him, demonstrates the eighth proposition from book XIII of the Elements of Euclid to a disciple, dressed in the aristocratic fashion of the time, identified with the duke Guidobaldo da Montefeltro, who turns his eyes towards the spectator. The friar had dedicated to the young duke the Summa de Arithmetica, geometry, proportioni et proportionality, printed in Venice in 1494 and he depicted this in the painting right in front of the gentleman, with the inscription Li [ber] R [egularum] Luc [ae] Bur [gensis].'

In 1494, Pacioli was in Venice to publish a printed version of his great encyclopaedia of the knowledge of the schools of abacus, the *Summa de arithmetica, geometry, proportioni et proportionalita*, which was published by Paganino de' Paganini, a printer with whom Pacioli continued a long-term collaboration. The work was dedicated to Guidobaldo I di Montefeltro, Duke of Urbino, whom Pacioli had met in Rome in 1489, but there is no evidence that they met again after Rome. The publication of the *Summa*, the courses that he held in major cultural centres of the time and the attendance of eminent characters at his lectures turned Fra Luca into a well-known celebrity and one of the most successful scholars of mathematics in the latter half of his life. His fame brought Pacioli to Milan between 1496 and 1499 where the duke, Ludovico Sforza, appointed him as a public mathematics teacher at the Palatine Schools.

Nick Mackinnon in his published article entitled *The Portrait of Fra Luca Pacioli* pointed out that Guidobaldo is supposed to have been Pacioli's pupil, but this legend is based solely on the misidentification of the student in the *Pacioli Portrait* at the Capodimonte Museum. There is no record of Pacioli ever visiting Urbino, although he could have been in Urbino whenever he was at Sansepolcro because a short mountain road connects Sansepolcro with Urbino. Pacioli's *Summa* is dedicated to Guidobaldo, as is Piero's *De corporibus*, and the competing 1505 and 1509 editions of *Euclid*. These dedications probably led to the Museum's belief that Guidobaldo is the student and sponsor in the *Pacioli Portrait*.

Mackinnon further states that, '*This belief stems from the misinterpretation of an inventory, but there should never have been any doubt about the matter, for any amount of documentation cannot make the handsome ambitious red-head of the Pacioli portrait into the gifted but sickly Guidobaldo whose portrait appears in Box 3.*' Here, Mackinnon has referred us to Raphael's official portrait of Guidobaldo, Duke of Urbino that reveals a pasty, pale and sickly fellow (Fig. 5.1) who looks nothing like the full-blooded bull of a gentleman in the *Pacioli Portrait*. It is not surprising that Guidobaldo looked pale and sickly because he is believed to have suffered from gout and pellagra, a disease due to a deficiency in niacin or tryptophan and the inability to produce niacin or nicotinic acid properly from the essential amino acids in the diet. Without proper treatment, pellagra can result in death in four or five years. Guidobaldo lived for 36 years and died heirless in Fossombrone in 1508. He was succeeded by his nephew Francesco Maria della Rovere who was the son of Giovanni della Rovere, and of Giovanna da Montefeltro, the sister of Guidobaldo. Francesco was also the nephew of Giuliano della Rovere who became Pope Julius II in 1503.

Mackinnon also believes that no patron like Guidobaldo would allow himself to be painted in such a subservient position and that he would need to be in the front or central position as the main focus of attention or at least in symmetry with Pacioli. Apart from Raphael's portrait showing that Guidobaldo looked nothing like the Gentleman in the *Pacioli Portrait*, Mackinnon believes that the following three inventories found by Gronau in 1631 on the death of the last duke of Urbino are responsible for the misinterpretation.

1. *1631:* "*Un ritratto di un frate di S. Bernardino con un giovene apresso vestito di peliccia all' antica segnato al basso. Divo Principi Guido in Tavola*".

2. "*Un Frate, che si dice sia il ritratto di Fra Luca dal Borgo, che non si sa di chi*

sia mano in tavola, che insegna Euclide al Duca Guido, della Guardaroba d'Urbino".

3. *1654: "Un quadro in tavola. Un Frate di' S. Francesco con altra figura del Ghirlandaio.*

These and other inventories of 1582 and 1599 with dedications to Guidobaldo are misleading. The dedications in these three unrelated inventories were extrapolated wrongfully across to the *Pacioli Portrait*. That is, the student in the *Pacioli Portrait* should not be identified as Guidobaldo, Duke of Urbino just because Luca Pacioli dedicated his *Summa* book to him in 1494. Besides, Luca Pacioli dedicated his books and manuscripts to others as well, including Ludovico Sforza, the Duke Milan, and his son-in-law Galeazzo Sanseverino-Sforza. While Guidobaldo is the most unlikely student and patron in the *Pacioli Portrait*, he is nevertheless, of interest to our story because of his blood connection to the House of Sforza.

FIG. 5.1. *Portrait of Guidobaldo da Montefeltro by Raphael. Detail.Oil on panel. Uffizi Gallery. Wikimedia Commons. Public Domain.*
https://commons.wikimedia.org/wiki/File:Guidobaldo_montefeltro.jpg

The duchy of Urbino was one of the many small states or fiefdoms in Renaissance Italy, but despite its location in the mountains and the relatively small population of 150,000 people, it was one of the greatest centres of culture because of the dedicated sponsorship to the arts by their lords and dukes emanating from Frederigo da Montefeltro (1422 to 1482). Some of the dukes also were tough military men and leaders of the papal mercenary armies. While the dukes supported the Pope they were allowed to keep hold of their duchy that all the popes believed belonged to them. Frederigo da Montefeltro had his team of scribes in his scriptorium and he commissioned the construction of a great library, only second in size and wealth to the Vatican library that was the largest in Italy. As a *condottiero*, a soldier of fortune, Frederigo da Montefeltro served Francesco I Sforza and his son Galeazzo Sforza on several occasions including when they were the dukes of Milan. After the death of his wife, Gentile Brancaleoni, he married Battista Sforza (1446-1472), the daughter of Elisabetta Malatesta and Alessandro Sforza (1409-1473), lord of Pesaro and Parma and the brother of Francesco Sforza, Duke of Milan. Together they produced six daughters before Battista gave birth to their first son and heir Guidobaldo da Montefeltro on 24th January 1472. Battista never fully recovered from her last pregnancy and delivery and she fell ill and died at the age of 26 years in July of the same year. Her husband who called her *'the delight of both my public and private hours'* was devastated by her death and retired from public life. So, his heir, Guidobaldo da Montefeltro, was a Sforza on his mother's side.

Guidobaldo da Montefeltro was only ten years old when he succeeded his father Frederigo who died in 1482. He officially assumed his father's command of the armies of Naples, Milan and Florence in defence of Ferrara during the Salt Wars against Venice, but his cousin, Ottaviano Ubaldini, was the *de facto* commander. As a child, Guidobaldo was an excellent scholar and studied Latin, Greek, philosophy, literature, art, and history under the tutorship of the humanist Ludovico Odasio from Padua and the painter and mathematician Piero dalla Francesca. With the help of his wife Elisabetta Gonzaga, who he married in 1489, Guidobaldo became a man of great learning and he led his court at Urbino to even greater heights of cultural splendour where men of letters such as Pietro Bembo and Bernardo Accolti often met and where his library and castles accumulated great books, precious objects, paintings and sculptures. Both Piero dalla Francesca and Luca Pacioli dedicated their mathematical works to Guidobaldo to honour his interests and sponsorships towards the humanities. The poet and playwright Baldassare Castiglione later described the etiquette, behaviour and morals of Guidobaldo's court in his popular publication *Il Cortegiano* or *The Book of the Courtier*. Although Guidobaldo was a poor military commander, he was an able administrator and ruler and much loved and respected by his subjects.

Because Guidobaldo's mother Battista was a Sforza, the niece of Francesco Sforza and cousin of Ludovico, they were political allies until Ludovico Sforza became the duke of Milan in 1496 and was overthrown and exiled from Milan by the French in 1500. Guidobaldo was paid as a military commander in the service of various other States on many occasions. In 1494, he was a captain in Pope Alexander VI's army alongside the French troops of King Charles VIII of France during the latter's invasion of southern Italy. In 1495, he changed sides and joined the Republic of Venice and the Papal States as part of the League of Venice in their fight against Charles VIII. In January of 1497, while fighting for the Pope against the Orsini near Bracciano, he was wounded and taken prisoner and held at the castle of Soriano until he raised the ransom to pay the Orsini brothers and the *condottiero* Vitellozzo Vitelli, who freed him the following year. In 1498 while serving Venice in their fight against Florence, he and his troops were surrounded in Bibbiena and trapped in the mountains until the *condottiero* Paolo Vitelli allowed the ailing Guidobaldo to return to Urbino. While recovering from his wounds in Urbino, Guidobaldo was placed on alert by Venice and the Pope to be ready to assist them and the French King Louis XII with their attack against Duke Ludovico Sforza and invasion of Milan.

In contrast to the reasonable and intelligent nature of Guidobaldo, many of the other *condottieri* were violent and cunning men who often outsmarted themselves and met with unpleasant and violent ends. For example, the *condottiero* Paolo Vitelli was accused of treason and put to death by Florence in 1499; and his brother Vitellozzo Vitelli was strangled by Cesare Borgia's troops for treason when Cesare was waging war in the fiefdoms of Romagna and Marche. Because of a treacherous plot against him, Cesare also killed the Orsini brothers and Oliverotto da Fermo in Senigallia in 1502. After a few years of peace in Urbino, Guidobaldo was forced to flee to Mantua and Venice in 1502 to escape the armies of Cesare Borgia, who now wanted Urbino for himself and his father Pope Alexander VI. Coincidently, Leonardo da Vinci was in Urbino with Cesare Borgia as his fortifications engineer. Guidobaldo returned to Urbino in 1504 soon after the death of Pope Alexander VI and he continued to sponsor the arts and sciences until his death in 1508. His widowed wife, Elisabetta Gonzaga lived in Urbino and was the Regent to the underage heir, Francesco Maria I della Rovere, until June 1516. Pope Leo X, a Medici, expelled her from Urbino in 1516 so that he could give the duchy to his nephew Lorenzo II di Piero de' Medici, the new Duke of Urbino. The Duchy of Urbino reverted to the Della Rovere family after Lorenzo's death in 1519. Leonardo da Vinci oversaw the marriage celebrations of Lorenzo de' Medici to Madeleine de la Tour in Amboise in France on 13 June 1518. Before their deaths in 1519, Lorenzo and Madeleine produced a daughter, Catherine de' Medici, who went on to become the Queen of France after she married king Henry II of France.

Since Guidobaldo was involved in many military conflicts between 1494 and 1500, it is hard to imagine when he might have found the time to pose for his portrait with Luca Pacioli by Jacopo de Barbari. When he was absent for long periods from the court of Urbino, his good and loyal wife Elizabetta Gonzaga ruled fairly and intelligently on his behalf. Because of their sophisticated culture and scholarship, love of learning and intelligent conversation, their court at Urbino was a model for Renaissance Europe and the envy of the Italian nobility including the vindictive Cesare Borgia.

Student or Self-portrait of Leonardo da Vinci?

It has been suggested by a few scholars and Renaissance aficionados that the student is Leonardo da Vinci's self-portrait. However, it is unlikely to be Leonardo da Vinci because the student does not look anything like the portrait in profile of Leonardo da Vinci by Francesco Melzi, the only known portrait of Leonardo (Fig. 5.2). We can see that the face in Melzi's drawing is far too refined and sensitive to be the same person in the *Pacioli Portrait*. Leonardo was already 43 years of age in 1495 with the hair on his head possibly receding from his forehead and temples as indicated in the Melzi drawing. The unidentified man in the *Pacioli Portrait* looks much younger than 43 years of age. Perhaps he is in his late twenties or early thirties, with a full and thick crop of hair hanging low over his forehead. Based on the comparison with the Melzi drawing, we can exclude Leonardo da Vinci to be the young man in the *Pacioli Portrait*.

FIG. 5.2. *Francesco Melzi. Portrait of Leonardo, 1515-1518. RCIN 912726. Royal Collection Trust / © Her Majesty Queen Elizabeth II 2017.*

Who is the Student in the *Pacioli Portrait*?

The four main candidates who were suggested to be the student, painter or sponsor in the *Pacioli Portrait* are Guidobaldo da Montefeltro, Galeazzo Sanseverino, Albrecht Durer and Leonardo da Vinci. We previously dismissed Durer as a possibility because he didn't have the proper credentials nor did he know Pacioli, and therefore did not have any reason to be the model for the painting. The suggestion that it is Leonardo da Vinci can be dismissed because the student looks nothing like Francesco Melzi's portrait of Leonardo da Vinci with a beard (Fig. 5.2). Also, we know that the student is not Guidobaldo because the person next to Pacioli looks nothing like the portrait of Guidobaldo by Raphael (Fig. 5.1). This then leaves us with Galeazzo Sanseverino. He was six years younger than Leonardo and would have been 37 years old in 1495 in the prime of his life as a soldier, jouster and Ludovico Sforza's son-in-law, bodyguard and secret agent. He is considered and described in greater detail in the following chapter.

References

Barca GA. IACO. BAR. VIGENNIS P.1495. Enigma e "Secretissima Scientia. http://www.ritrattopacioli.it/Jacobarvigennis2.pdf (site disconnected).

Mackinnon, Nick (1993). The Portrait of Fra Luca Pacioli. The Mathematical Gazette 77:130 - 219.

6

THE GALLANT JOUSTER, GALEAZZO SANSEVERINO SFORZA

Galeazzo Sanseverino Sforza, Illustrious Patron of Luca Pacioli and Leonardo da Vinci

In his manuscript and printed book entitled *Divine Proportion,* Luca Pacioli revealed the identity of the most likely student in Leonardo da Vinci's *Pacioli Portrait* at the Capodimonte Museum in Naples to be their illustrious patron Galeazzo Sanseverino. In the first and last chapter of the *Divine Proportion,* Luca Pacioli wrote the following dedication about his eminent sponsor, Signor Galeazzo Sanseverino, the man that paid his living wages and provided him with food and board while in Milan:

'And among the laymen present, first my own illustrious patron Signor Galeazzo Sforza, the powerful Vicar of Sanseverino and a general officer in the service of your Excellency, a captain of arms second to none today, and a diligent practitioner of our disciplines.'

At the end of the last chapter:

'It is here in your illustrious, great city of Milan, with not ordinary efforts and long vigils, under the protective shade of your Excellency, and of your, as if son, my, unworthy that I am, personal and singular patron, his eminent lordship Galeazzo Sanseverino de Aragon, second to none in the military arts, and a great lover of our disciplines, especially in the day's work of his assiduous studies, where he tastes of the most useful and sweet fruit.

And let the conclusion of our discussion be the humble supplication and due reverence by the perpetual servant of your Excellency, to whom, infinitely and in every manner, [this work] is commended. Quae iterum atque iterum ad vota felicissime valeat, once again with all the best wishes.'

Although Luca Pacioli referred to his own illustrious patron as Signor Galeazzo Sforza, the powerful Vicar of Sanseverino, I simply refer to him as Galeazzo Sanseverino, occasionally addressing him as Galeazzo Sanseverino Sforza, the son-in-law of Ludovico Sforza who was the Governor (before 1495) or Duke of Milan (1495 to 1500). Note that Luca Pacioli highlights his illustrious patron to be a general officer in the service of his Excellency, the Duke of Milan, and a captain of arms second to none, and a diligent practitioner of our disciplines, for Galeazzo Sanseverino was interested in the sciences, mathematics, architecture and music. He was a gentleman of the Duke's ruling court and a nobleman of Milan, and you can see this by his clothes and proud stature as portrayed in the *Pacioli Portrait*.

Like Leonardo, Galeazzo Sanseverino appreciated the importance of mathematics and particularly its application in warfare and fortifications, as Luca Pacioli acknowledged in his *Divine Proportion*:

'If one looks carefully at artillery in general, take whatever he will, such as bastions, and other redoubts, mortars, armour, pitfalls, mangonels, flame throwers, ballistics, catapults, different kinds of rams, with all other innumerable ingenious machines and instruments, they will always be found to be fabricated and formed with the strength of numbers, measure and their proportions. What else are fortresses, towers, moats, walls, ante-walls, ditches, bridges, fortified battle towers, embrasures, mantles, and other strong points in the boroughs, cities and castles, then all geometry and proportion, all balanced and put into order with levels and plumb bobs? For no other reason were the ancient Romans so victorious, as written by Vegetio Frontino and other outstanding authors, if not by the great care and diligent preparations of their engineers and other admirals of the land and the sea, who could not possibly manage without the mathematical disciplines, that is Arithmetic, Geometry, and Proportion.'

These words undoubtedly echoed from those between Galeazzo Sanseverino and Leonardo da Vinci during their many discussions on how mathematics can impact on assessing sieges, strength of fortifications that they both knew about from the previous publications on the art and the science of warfare. The earlier formative relationship between Leonardo da Vinci and Galeazzo Sanseverino had grown into the very best of friendships. Galeazzo was not only Leonardo's official patron, but he was also his landlord, providing him with rooms for his accommodation and studios for his painting and science, and allowing him full access to all the other parts of the Sanseverino palaces inside and outside the western gates of the city. This included the valuable books and historical documents in their extensive private libraries as well as the surrounding stables where some of the best-bred horses in Lombardy could be seen. On most nights Galeazzo and Leonardo would drink red wine and talk, for Galeazzo, like

CHAPTER 6

Leonardo, was interested in many things, especially mathematics, philosophy, the sciences, and the arts. Galeazzo was an expert on warfare and the arts of combat, a subject that Leonardo wanted to learn more about, for although he was handy with a knife and a short sword, he knew full well that he was no master in a fight to the death, and up to now he had never killed anybody.

> '*Galeazzo's tutor was Pietro Monte, an Italian knight who was regarded by many to be the best swordman in Italy and beyond. At that time, Monte was travelling in Spain, but Leonardo would meet him soon enough, and he would be taught by Monte the game of darts and how to best fight with a sword or a lance while sitting on horseback. These lessons were valuable for Leonardo in his later years for preparing jousts for court festivities. Monte and Sanseverino advised him on selecting mounts and saddles for war and the joust, gave details on preparing jousting armour and equipment, and provided directions on how to handle the lance (including targeting the opponent's horse) and on the correct posture to gain advantage in reaching over the opponent. Both Galeazzo Sanseverino and Pietro Monte also taught Leonardo the art of constructing battle armour for foot soldiers, and horsemen and horses, and for festivals.*' (Kulski 2017).

When Leonardo arrived in Milan from Florence in 1481/3, it is likely that he immediately looked for suitable patrons and supporters for employment and for commissioning and purchasing his works. Not much is known about Leonardo's first four or five years in Milan. We know that his first major project in Milan was to paint the *Virgin of the Rocks* for the Confraternity of Immaculate Conception in collaboration with the de Predis brothers Ambrogio and Evangelista. The painting was to be an altarpiece in the Chapel of the Conception in the Church of San Francesco Grande and the contract eventually led to many legal problems with the Confraternity. Leonardo signed the contract for the *Virgin of the Rocks* on 25th April 1483 and it still exists in the State Archives of Milan. The Church of San Francesco Grande, which no longer exists (demolished in 1806 and replaced by army barracks), was close to Porta Vercellina (Vercellina Gate) and close to the home and workshop of the Predis brothers where Leonardo stayed. This also was close to the property of the Sanseverino brothers and their stable of horses where Leonardo probably visited during his early years in Milan and met with Galeazzo Sanseverino who already was a courtier of influence in the court of the young Duke, Gian Galeazzo Sforza, and his uncle, Ludovico Sforza. Leonardo was interested in weapons of war and fortifications at the time and he intended to inform the Sforza court and the courtiers and senators of his interest in fortifications. In Leonardo's translated notebooks there are various references to Galeazzo Sanseverino and his horses, masquerades and the construction of his equestrian state.

716. Messer Galeazzo's big genet.

717. Messer Galeazzo's Sicilian horse.

718. Measurement of the Sicilian horse the leg from behind, seen in front, lifted and extended.

719. Again, the bronze horse may be taken in hand, which is to be to the immortal glory and eternal honour of the happy memory of the prince your father, and of the illustrious house of Sforza.

720. On the 23rd of April 1490, I began this book, and recommenced the horse.

721. There is to be seen, in the mountains of Parma and Piacenza, a multitude of shells and corals full of holes, still sticking to the rocks, and when I was at work on the great horse for Milan, a large sackful of them, which were found thereabout, was brought to me into my workshop, by certain peasants.

722. Believe me, Leonardo the Florentine, who has to do the equestrian bronze statue of the Duke Francesco that he does not need to care about it, because he has worked for all his lifetime, and, being so great a work, I doubt whether he can ever finish it.

723. Of the horse, I will say nothing because I know the times.

724. During ten years the works on the marbles have been going on I will not wait for my payment beyond the time when my works are finished.

Item: on the 26th January following, I, being in the house of Messer Galeazzo da San Severino, was arranging the festival for his jousting, and certain footmen having undressed to try on some costumes of wild men for the said festival, Giacomo went to the purse of one of them which lay on the bed with other clothes, 2 lire 4 S, and took out such money as was in it.

Leonardo did not provide any personal opinions or criticisms about Galeazzo Sanseverino in his notebooks. He only mentioned that he visited his house and used his horses as models for his drawings and his equestrian statue in honour of the first Sforza duke, Francesco Maria Sforza. Although Galeazzo Sanseverino was six years younger than Leonardo, they became life-long friends soon after Leonardo arrived in Milan. They shared many interests, adventures and philosophical debates in those years until Sanseverino loyally backed Ludovico Sforza and was defeated by the French king Louis XII in 1500. In that same year, Leonardo moved to Florence and Sanseverino was exiled to Germany in the service of Maximilian I until the French king pardoned him. In 1504, Sanseverino moved to France where he was appointed firstly as a councillor of the state, then as king Louis XII's chamberlain, and finally as the Grand Ecuyer de France. Sanseverino, like Leonardo, also served King Francois I of France. Sanseverino died in 1525 when he was killed while defending his French king in the Battle of Pavia. His death was six years after Leonardo da Vinci had died in the French king's arms in Amboise, France in 1519.

CHAPTER 6

Galeazzo Sanseverino's Pedigree as a *Condottiero*

Galeazzo Sanseverino was born in Naples in 1458 to Giovanna da Correggio and he was the third son of Roberto Sanseverino who was in Naples at the time to serve king Ferdinand of Aragon as his military advisor. When Galeazzo was born, his father Roberto was away from Naples on a pilgrimage to the Holy Land. Galeazzo Sanseverino was the brother of Gianfrancesco (1450-1501), Gaspare (1455-1519), Antonio Maria (1460-1509); half-brother of Giulio (born 1475), Federico (born 1476), Ugo, and Giorgio. Galeazzo and his three brothers, Gianfrancesco, Gaspare and Antonio Maria would become *condottieri* in the service of the duke Gian Galeazzo Sforza and Ludovico Sforza and the duchy of Milan, and then later for the kings of France, Louis XII and Francois I. One of Galeazzo's half brothers, Frederico, joined the church in 1481 and in 1492 was appointed a cardinal of Rome where he died in 1516. He and his seven brothers and five sisters were related to the Sforza, for their grandmother was Elisa Sforza, the sister of Francesco Sforza, the first Sforza Duke of Milan after the reign of the Visconti dukes.

Galeazzo's father, Roberto, was born in Milan in 1418, and he was a highly successful *condottiero* who had served various masters including three Dukes of Milan (1440 to 1481), the King of Naples (1458 to 1463), the Republic of Florence (1467), the Duchy of Savoy (1476), the Republic of Genoa (1478), and the Republic of Venice (1482 to 1487). When Roberto served the King of Naples, Ferdinand of Aragon, from 1458 to 1462, the King granted him the titled surname of Aragona. Roberto named two of his eight sons, Gian Francesco and Galeazzo, after the previous two Sforza dukes; Francesco whom he had served loyally in the 1440s and 1450s, and Galeazzo Maria whom he served from 1471 until the duke's assassination in 1476. When Galeazzo Maria Sforza's six-year-old son Gian Galeazzo Sforza inherited the Duchy of Milan from his father, his mother Bona of Savoy became Regent of the Duchy of Milan and appointed Cicco Simonetta as her Chief counsellor and Governor of Milan. However, Roberto Sanseverino opposed the appointment of Cicco Simonetta and so he and Ludovico Sforza were forced into exile. Roberto was condemned to death by beheading in absentia and his goods were confiscated and given to Ercole d'Este. He then became captain-general of the Republic of Genoa, fighting against Milan in 1478. However, in 1479, he was pardoned and permitted to return to Milan following the reconciliation of Ludovico Sforza with Bona of Savoy, the regent mother of the young duke. Soon after his pardon, Ludovico Sforza rallied his supporters and arrested and executed Cicco Simonetta, exiled Bona of Savoy and was appointed the Governor of Milan and the ward of the young duke Galeazzo Maria Sforza.

He betrayed Roberto Sanseverino who was forced to flee from Milan and look for support elsewhere.

Roberto was hired by Venice in 1482 and he fought against Milan in the War of Ferrara. On the other hand, Roberto Sanseverino's four sons, who also were *condottieri*, chose to stay in Milan in the service of Ludovico Sforza. With the Bagnolo peace treaty of 7 August 1484, Roberto Sanseverino was elected captain-general of the Italian League; but, in October 1485, he was given leave by the Venetians to fight the Aragonese and their allies in the service of the Holy See. This military campaign failed, and so the Pope dismissed Roberto who returned to Venice where he was given a new command of the Venetian troops against Sigismund of Habsburg. In the Calliano Battle of 10 August 1487, Roberto Sanseverino was wounded, fell into the river and drowned. His body was recovered, taken to the autonomous province of Trento in Northern Italy and buried in the cathedral crypt. His sons later transferred his body to the church of San Francesco in Milan. Roberto had fought in wars, battles and skirmishes for most of his life and still lived to a relatively ripe age of 69 years. Although he was a Sforza, he fell out with them and four of his sons who had stayed in Milan to support Ludovico and his nephew the Duke of Milan, Gian Galeazzo Sforza.

Galeazzo Sanseverino and his two elder brothers had the pedigree of the *condottieri* – rich and influential patrons of the arts, sciences, agriculture, entertainments and weapons of war. The *condottieri* were Italian soldiers of fortune, men who could amass and command an army of mercenaries for battles, wars and sieges. *Condottiere* (singular) is derived from the word '*condatta*' or 'contract', by which the *condottieri* (plural) accepted as their reward a substantial payment for services rendered for a city or a lord. They were contracted by the dukes, lords and councilors of the Italian city-states and the Papacy throughout the Middle Ages, the Renaissance and until the mid-17th century. Roberto Sanseverino was one such successful *condottieri*, a leader of professional mercenaries, who benefitted from serving various lords, councils (*Signoria*) and cities. The sons of his first wife followed in his footsteps, and Galeazzo Sanseverino, like his father, lived and died by the sword, jousting and fighting into his old age (1458-1525) until his eventual death on the battlefield. Some of the famous Italian *condottieri* in the times of Leonardo da Vinci (1452 to 1519), as remembered by Niccolo Machiavelli in his *History of Florence*, were Francesco Sforza (1401-1466) who served Filippo Maria Visconti of the Duchy of Milan; Bartolomeo Colleoni (c. 1400–1475) immortalised by Leonardo da Vinci's teacher, Andrea del Verrocchio with his equestrian bronze at Campo dei Santi Giovanni e Paolo, Venice; Sigismondo Pandolfo Malatesta (1417–1468), lord of Rimini, hired by the Venetians to fight against the Turks, patron of the architect and engineer, Leone Battista Alberti; Federico III da

Montefeltro (1422–1482), lord of Urbino and distinguished patron of the arts, architecture and science; Gian Giacomo Trivulzio (c. 1441–1518) who sponsored Leonardo da Vinci, but was an enemy of Galeazzo Sanseverino and Ludovico Sforza, was one of the most experienced commanders during the Italian Wars supporting King Louis XII of France; Prospero Colonna (1452–1523) fought in the service of the Papal States and then served the Holy Roman Empire and Spain during the Italian Wars; Francesco II of Gonzaga (1466-1519), the Marquess of Mantua, married to Isabella d'Este, commanded the Italian armies at the Battle of Fornovo; Cesare Borgia (1475–1507), Duke of Valentino, the illegitimate son of Pope Alexander VI (Rodrigo Borgia) and brother of Lucrezia Borgia. Cesare also was an ally of the French king Louis XII and commander of the papal armies for whom Leonardo da Vinci worked for as his engineer of fortifications during the Romagna campaign of 1502 to 1503. Most of these *condottieri* were wealthy, influential, enthusiastic and generous patrons of the arts and sciences. Leonardo da Vinci in pursuing his career in the courts and on the periphery of the rich and powerful class knew his success largely depended on them. The *condottieri* sponsored him because of his knowledge and understanding of weapons and fortification engineering as well as the art of painting, theatre and designing monuments and palaces.

When Leonardo first arrived in Milan at some time between 1481 and 1483, Galeazzo Sanseverino may have helped him draft his famous letter of application to his illustrious Lord Ludovico Sforza for the position of a fortification engineer. The original copy of this letter is not in Leonardo's hand, but possibly by a professional scribe or by one or other of his sponsors like Galeazzo Sanseverino who knew of the vacancy in the court and helped Leonardo to draft the letter. Although the letter shows that Leonardo had a strong interest in military engineering, he wasn't appointed to Ludovico's court until about 1488, and it was in the position of Advisor on Fortifications and Master of Entertainments and Festivities. Leonardo resided in Milan for five to seven years before the Sforza were willing to appoint him to their court.

Galeazzo Sanseverino. Chivalrous and Loyal Courtier of Ludovico Sforza

Julia Mary Cartwright Ady (nee Cartwright), the English art critic, author and historian of the Italian Renaissance who lived from 1851 to 1924, wrote two historical accounts that incorporated the times, letters and characters of Milan during the Renaissance. One was entitled *Beatrice d'Este, Duchess of Milan, 1475-1497, a study of the Renaissance* (published 1899), and the other was *Isabella d'Este, Marchioness of Mantua, 1474-1539; a study of the Renaissance* (published 1903). In both books, she highlights the charm of

Ludovico Sforza's army commander and courtier Galeazzo Sanseverino. It is evident from her writing that she greatly admired the dashing Galeazzo. In the *Beatrice d"Este* publication she summarised him in the following way:

'But the most famous and popular of all the brothers was Galeazzo. This brilliant and accomplished cavalier, who was to play so great a part at the Milanese court, early attracted the notice of Lodovico by his personal charm and rare skill in knightly exercises. As a rider and jouster, he was without a rival. Wherever he entered the lists, at Milan or Venice, at Ferrara or Urbino, he invariably carried off the prize, and was proclaimed victor in the games. And to this prowess in courtly exercises, he joined a love of art and learning which especially commended him to the Moro. Unlike his brother Captain Fracassa, who refused Caterina Sforza's invitation to join in dance and song, saying that war was his trade and he sought no other, Galeazzo was a model of courtesy and grace. All fair ladies had a smile for him. Isabella d'Este and Elisabetta Gonzaga honoured him with their friendship, and Beatrice d'Este found in him the truest of friends and best of servants. Three kings of France, Charles VIII., Louis XII., and Francis I., singled him out for special distinction, and after enjoying the highest honour at Lodovico Sforza's court, he lived to become Grand Ecuyer of France in the next century. French Italian chroniclers alike own the fascination of his handsome presence and extol the "gentilezza" of this very perfect knight. Leonardo da Vinci and Luca Pacioli the mathematician had in him a noble, generous patron, and Baldassare Castiglione, who knew him in his youth at Milan, has enshrined his memory in the pages of his "Cortigiano." It was this rare union of qualities which endeared the young Sanseverino to the Moro, who chose him for his intimate friend and companion. On his return from his successful campaign against the Forli rebels, Lodovico appointed him Captain-general of the Milanese armies, a step which naturally excited great jealousy among his rivals, and mortally wounded the pride of Messer Gian Giacomo Trivulzio, an older captain in the same service. Short of stature and rude of speech, with the big nose and rugged features that are familiar to us in Caradosso's medal, this able soldier presented a curious contrast to the brilliant and courtly Messer Galeazzo, whose rival he remained to the end of his life. Yet he knew how to appreciate genius, and after his triumphant return to Milan in 1499, employed Leonardo to paint his portrait and design his tomb. Although a Guelph by birth, Trivulzio, up to this time, had been one of Lodovico's most active supporters. But when he saw a younger rival preferred to him, he left Milan in disgust and retired to Naples, where he entered King Ferrante's service, and became from that time a bitter enemy of the Sforza's. Meanwhile, the Moro loaded his favourite Galeazzo with honours and rewards. He gave him the fine estate of Castelnuovo in the Tortonese, which had once belonged to his father, the great Condottiere Roberto, as well as a house in Pavia near the church of San Francesco and a palace in Milan, near the Porta Vercellina, and allowed him to build a villa and extensive stables in the park of the Castello. As a last and crowning honour, he bestowed upon this fortunate youth the hand of his illegitimate daughter Bianca, a beautiful and attractive child to whom he was fondly attached. Of her mother, we have no certain knowledge, but she is generally

CHAPTER 6

supposed to have been some mistress of low origin, and Bianca herself is described by a contemporary writer as "figlia ex pellice nata." The wedding was solemnised with great splendour in the chapel of the Castello di Pavia, on the last day of the year 1489, but the young princess was still a child, and Galeazzo had to wait five years before he took home his bride. After his marriage he adopted the name of Sforza Visconti, and was treated by Lodovico as a member of his family.'

Later Julia Mary Cartwright wrote of him as a gallant ladies companion:

'The regent himself was too deeply engaged in state affairs, and devoted too much time and attention to the details of administration, to be able to accompany his wife as a rule. But she had a devoted comrade in her husband's son-in-law, whom he deputed to escort the duchess on her more distant expeditions. Since his betrothal to Lodovico's daughter, Galeazzo had enjoyed all the privileges of a son, and was already, what the Moro had promised to make him, the first man in the state. He assisted at all state audiences, and was the only person present when Lodovico received foreign ambassadors. He shared the Moro's private life, and always dined alone with the duke and duchess when there were no other guests at their table. His letters to Isabella d'Este give lively accounts of the expeditions which he took in Beatrice's company during the first few months of her married life.'

In her book about the life of Beatrice d"Este, Julia Cartwright used the letters written between Isabella d'Este, Beatrice d'Este, Ludovico Sforza and Galeazzo Sanseverino to highlight the close connection that Galeazzo had with Ludovico and his wife and other members of their family. The following is a letter that Galeazzo Sanseverino wrote to Ludovico Sforza's sister-in-law, the Marchesa of Mantua, Isabella d'Este, on the 13th of February 1491 to describe the pleasant day in which he and the duchess spent at Cussago, one of Lodovico Sforza's favourite villas on the sunny slopes of the Brianza, six miles from Milan, on the way to Como.

'Having reached Cussago, we had a grand fishing expedition in the river, and caught an immense quantity of large pike, trout, lampreys, crabs, and several other good sorts of smaller fish, and proceeded to dine off them until we could eat no more. Then, to make our meal digest the better, directly after dinner we began to play at ball with great vigour and energy, and after we had played for some time we went over to the palace, which is really very beautiful, and, among other things, contains a doorway of carved marble, as fine as the new works at the Certosa. Next, we examined the result of our sport, which had been laid out in front of the place, and took back as many of the lampreys and crabs as we could eat with us, and sent some of the lampreys to his Highness the Duke. When this was done, we went to another palace and caught more than a thousand large trout, and after choosing out the best for presents and for our own holy throats, we had the rest thrown back into the water. And then we mounted our horses again, and began to let fly *some of those good falcons of mine, which you saw at Pavia, along the river-side, and they killed several birds. By this time it was already four o'clock. We rode out to hunt stags and fawns, and after giving chase to twenty-two and killing two stags and two fawns, we returned home and reached Milan an hour after dark, and presented the result of our day's sport to my lord the Duke of Bari. My illustrious lord took the greatest possible pleasure in hearing all we had done, far more, indeed, than if he had been there in person, and I believe that my duchess will in the end reap the greatest benefit, and that Signor Lodovico will give her Cussago, which is a place of rare beauty and worth. But I have cut my boots to pieces and torn my clothes, and played the fool into the bargain, and these are the rewards one gains in the service of ladies. However, I will have patience, since it is all for the sake of my duchess, whom I never mean to fail in life or death.'*

Beatrice d'Este revealed in many letters to her sister Isabella d'Este of Galeazzo Sanseverino's knightly valour and love for her and her husband Ludovico in his role as her companion and entertainer whenever her husband was not available to her. Sanseverino showed her the affection that she craved from her husband knowing that he was a philanderer. She wrote many lively accounts of her country life in the company of her husband and Galeazzo Sanseverino during the Spring of 1491 when harmony was restored temporarily between the married couple, and her husband's philandering was temporarily suspended.

Julia Cartwright also highlighted the continuing literary debate and correspondence that Galeazzo Sanseverino had with the d'Este sisters about the virtue and valour of the two knights Roland (Orlando) and Rinaldo in the unfinished poem *Orlando Inamorato* [Orlando in Love] written by Matteo Maria Boiardo and first published in 1482. The correspondence was mostly between Galeazzo Sanseverino and Isabella d'Este where Galeazzo had taken the side of Roland while Isabella defended the actions of Rinaldo in the battle between these two good paladins in their quest for the heart and life of the beautiful Angelica, the daughter of the King of Cathay (China) who was beleaguered by the Tartars and Mongols. The banter about romantic love lingered on between them as a coquettish tease and play between a man and a woman until it was finally resolved when Beatrice asked her court poet Bellincioni to write and finish off the unfinished conclusion to Boiardo's poem and end the debate.

Despite the obvious dangers, boar and stag hunting was a favourite pastime for Beatrice d'Este during her first few years of marriage to Ludovico. One of the letters in Julie Cartwright's collection reveals how during an organised hunt Galeazzo Sanseverino gallantly saved Beatrice from an attack and possible death by a wild boar. Ludovico Sforza in a letter to his sister-in-law Isabella d'Este informed her that he and Beatrice were staying at Cuzzago and while on long hunting expeditions they encountered a savage boar that had already wounded several greyhounds.

CHAPTER 6

'My wife came suddenly face to face with this furious beast, and herself gave it the first wound, after which Messer Galeazzo and I followed suit, so that the boar must have had great pleasure in feeling how much trouble it had given us and to what dangers its hunters had been exposed.'

As a consequence of the fatigue associated with the dangerous hunt, Beatrice fell seriously ill and Isabella d'Este hurried back to assist her sister with her convalescence during the next few weeks. Messer Galeazzo Sanseverino was by their side to assist loyally in the recovery of the Duchess of Bari with his witty dialogue, repartee and practical jokes. Julie Cartwright writes much more about the illustrious Galeazzo Sanseverino for she truly admired him as many had during his life time and thereafter, like Baldassare Castiglione who wrote *The Book of the Courtier* about him and his exploits. However, the excerpts that I have taken from Julie Cartwright's book about the life of Beatrice d'Este are sufficient to illustrate Galeazzo Sanseverino's magnificence and why he stands so proudly and intimidatingly behind and to the side of Luca Pacioli in Leonardo's portrait that perhaps should be entitled *The Portraits of Fra Luca Pacioli and his Milanese Sponsor Messer Galeazzo Sanseverino*.

While Galeazzo Sanseverino chivalrously attended to the needs and caprices of Beatrice d'Este, the Duchess of Bari, he fell out with Isabella Aragon, the young Duchess of Milan, falsely accusing her of trying to poison him with sugar. Before Galeazzo Sanseverino had married Ludovico Sforza's illegitimate daughter Bianca in 1491, he was the bodyguard of the young duke of Milan, Gian Galeazzo Sforza, and he had instructed him in horse-riding, hunting, jousting and various other manly endeavours. After the young duke married Isabella Aragon of Naples in 1489, Galeazzo Sanseverino drifted closer to support his father-in-law Ludovico in his intrigues against the young duke and his wife Isabella Aragon Sforza who was the legitimate Duchess of Milan. The hostility towards the Duke and Duchess of Milan by their uncle Ludovico Sforza and cousin Galeazzo Sanseverino probably upset Leonardo because he liked them both and did not want them to be upset or distressed by unwarranted and sinister political ambitions. Nevertheless, the power lay with Ludovico and Leonardo had to be careful not to upset him and become his enemy. Ludovico thought that Leonardo had become too close to the young duke and his wife after the successful festivals and celebrations to honour them and their princely marriage and so he set about to put a wedge between them by moving them to Pavia away from Leonardo and Galeazzo Sanseverino who he demanded focus their duties on him in Milan and elsewhere.

A Jouster's Spirit

In a joust at a carousel or tournament, two fully armoured horsemen in colourful costumes gallop towards each other wielding heavy lances with blunted tips for the sole purpose of one of them successfully striking the other's shield or armour to win the bout. A strike is deemed a 'hit' and therefore a win. To snap the lance and knock the opponent off his horse is a spectacular bonus for all to see except for the victim sitting or laying on the ground with wounded pride. The two charging jousters are separated from each other by a 'tilt' – a wooden barrier or fence – to prevent the horses from colliding and also to allow the angle of the strike to be optimised for the lance to break or snap for maximum visual and auditory effect. The horses are covered with brightly decorated cloth to display the colours of the jouster's family name or their sponsor or supporters. If the two jousters fail to strike one or the other in the first pass they will repeat the attempts a set number of times before accepting a draw and standing down for the next competitors.

Jousting is a dangerous sport – many riders have died from broken necks as a result of their fall or permanently disabled by splinters from a breaking lance piercing their eyes and blinding them. For example, the father of Guidobaldo, Federico da Montefeltro (1422-1482), the duke of Urbino from 1444 until his death, was a successful *condottiero* who lost his nasal bridge and right eye at a jousting tournament accident. Jousting was originally designed for military training, but quickly developed into a popular formal entertainment. The tournaments were highly regulated and ritualistic in keeping with the courtly ideals of chivalry. It was dishonourable to exploit an opponent's disadvantage or fight unfairly in any way. The stands were always full of courtly and rich spectators and members of the nobility who were attracted to the jousting tournaments to see the jousters show off their courage, skill and talents. The tournaments were merged with magnificent pageants and became state occasions following distinguished marriages or treaties between states.

Leonardo may have first heard of Galeazzo Sanseverino when they were in Florence for the Jousting tournament (*Giostra*) in Santa Croce in front of the Franciscan church on 28th January 1475. The tournament and festivities were staged by the Medici to celebrate a political alliance between Florence, Milan and Venice. Participants were there from Milan, Pesaro, Rimini, Urbino, Arezzo, Mantova and Naples. Galeazzo Sanseverino was there as a 17-year-old to attend to the famous Sanseverino–Milanese horses for the tournament and to participate as a beginner in the spectacular jousts. Leonardo was there at the age of 23 years to assist Verrocchio to prepare the banners for the various Florentine participants and decorate the winning standard for the eventual winner, Giuliano de Medici.

CHAPTER 6

According to an anonymous chronicler, Giuliano broke a total of 59 lances with seventeen hits on the helmet, two *in fractura*, one on the eye-piece, thirty on the breast-plate, eleven on the arm-guard and two hits on the pauldron. Giuliano dedicated his win to the Queen of the Joust, Simonetta Vespucci, a celebrity and great beauty of her time. Poets wrote about the *Giostra*, the *Stanze* by Angelo Poliziano and *Carmen de Ludicro Certamine* by Naldo Naldi. One year later, in the Spring of 1476, the Queen of the Joust died due to ill health – probably from tuberculosis. Her open coffin was paraded through the streets of Florence for huge crowds of mourners to see her beauty for one last time. She was buried in the Church of Ognissanti, the parish Church of the Vespucci. Three years later, on 26th April, 1478, her platonic lover and greatest admirer Giuliano de Medici was murdered by the Pazzi family bankers in the presence of hundreds of worshippers while he and his brother attended mass at the cathedral. Lorenzo de Medici survived the failed attempt to overthrow the Medici rule. Nevertheless, these deaths, among various other events and issues, led Leonardo to leave Florence and move to Milan in 1481 to find the good grace of Fortune and to meet with Galeazzo Sanseverino as his patron and sponsor.

On the 17th of January 1491 Ludovico Sforza, Duke of Bari, married Beatrice d'Este in the chapel of the Castello of Pavia. The new bride moved to Milan on the 22nd of January. To celebrate the marriage and the arrival of Ludovico's bride in Milan, tournaments and festivities were held for the next few days in the city of Milan and at the Sforzia Castle. Julie Cartwright, in her book *Beatrice d'Este,* describes the festivities and Jousting tournament (*Giostra*) as follows:

'On the 26th, the Giostra, which was to be the crowning event of the week's festivities, began. At the tournament held in Pavia in honour of Giangaleazzo's wedding, the knights had for the most part, appeared in their ordinary attire; but this time, to add greater splendour to the occasion, they entered the lists in companies, clad in fancy costumes and bearing symbolical devices after the fashion of the day. First of all came the Mantuan troop of twenty horsemen clad in green velvet and gold lace, bearing golden lances and olive boughs in their hand, with Isabella's kinsman, Alfonso Gonzaga, at their head. Then came Annibale Bentivoglio, the young husband of Lucrezia d'Este, with the Bologna knights, riding on a triumphal car drawn by stags and unicorns, the badge of the House of Este. These were followed by Gaspare di Sanseverino, with a band of twelve riders in black and gold Moorish dress, bearing Lodovico's device of the Moor's head on their helmets and white doves on their black armour. Last of all came a troop of wild Scythians, mounted on Barbary steeds, who galloped across the piazza, and then, halting in front of the ducal party, suddenly threw off their disguise and appeared in magnificent array, with the captain of the Milanese armies, Galeazzo di Sanseverino, at their head. He planted his golden lance in the

ground, and at this sign, a giant Moor, advancing to the front, recited a poem in honour of Duchess Beatrice.'

These pageants and masques formed an important feature of Renaissance fetes, and were evidently regarded as such by the chroniclers of these wedding festivities, but for us the chief interest of this tournament lies in the knowledge that the Scythian disguise assumed by Galeazzo di Sanseverino and his companions was designed by no less a personage than Leonardo da Vinci. Some of the drawings of savages and masks which we see today on the stray leaves of his sketch-books probably relate to these figures, but we know for certain from Leonardo's note that he was employed by Messer Galeazzo to arrange the masquerade of 26th January in 1491. Julie Cartwright elaborates further:

'In a note in his own handwriting, on the margin of the Codex Atlanticus, we read, "Item, 26 of January, being in the house of Messer Galeazzo di San Sev^o, ordering the Festa of his Giostra, certain men-at-arms took off their vests to try on some clothes of savages, upon which Giacomo" ... *(the apprentice whom he had already caught thieving at Pavia)* ... *"took up a purse which lay on the bed with their other clothes, and took the money that was inside it." The actual share which the great Florentine took in the preparation of the wedding festivities has often been discussed, and we are never likely to know how much of the duchess's cabinet he painted, or what part he took in the decoration of the city, but at least this characteristic note on the lad whose honesty he had reason to suspect, proves that he was present in Milan at the time, and was the authority to whom Lodovico's son-in-law naturally turned for advice in planning this masquerade. Incidents of this kind help us to realise how many and varied were the offices Leonardo was called upon to discharge in his master's service, and how frequent were the interruptions which interfered with the painting of his pictures or the modelling of his great horse.'*

After the initial pageant, the serious business of the *Giostra* began, and the tilting-matches lasted during three whole days.

'Among the foremost knights who distinguished themselves on this occasion, the chronicler and court poet mention the Marquis of Mantua, who entered the lists in disguise; young Annibale Bentivoglio, who wounded his hand badly, but refused to leave the ground; the Marchesino Girolamo Stanga, one of Isabella d'Este's special friends and of Beatrice's most devoted servants; and Niccolo da Correggio, who was universally admired in his suit of gold brocade. All four Sanseverini brothers fought in the lists with their wonted skill and valour, but once more Messer Galeazzo, 'Gentis columen', came off the victor and proved himself unrivalled in courtly exercises, both as jouster and swordsman. On the last day of the tournament the prizes were given away, and Messer Galeazzo was conducted triumphantly to the Rocca, and there received the "pallium" of

gold brocade from the bride's own hand. As soon as Lodovico recognised the Marquis of Mantua, he sent him a pressing invitation to take his place with the ducal party; and Gianfrancesco, unable to refuse so courteous a request, joined his wife and sat down with the rest of his kinsfolk to the family banquet, which was held that night in the Castello. And thus, soon after, the festivities were brought to a close.'

We know from various historical documents and people's writings and letters including Leonardo's notebooks that Leonardo and Galeazzo Sanseverino knew each other well and that Leonardo worked for the Sforza court to help Galeazzo Sanseverino with celebratory festivals, the jousts, masquerades and various other theatrical displays involving mock battles and horses. Galeazzo Sanseverino was commander of the Sforza armies and a successful horse breeder and he provided the best of horse breeds as gifts to various dignitaries and lords and put them on display at the jousts and festivals and parades.

Galeazzo Sanseverino lived for over 66 years from 12th June 1458 until 25th February 1525 when he died in the battle of Pavia in Lombardy defending the life of King Francois I of France. His full name at the time of his death was Galeazzo Sanseverino Aragon Visconti Sforza and he had accumulated a string of titles and privileges including Count of Caiazzo, Grand Squire of France, Knight of the Order of San Michele, Lord of Voghera, Colomo, Cittadella, Meunsur-Yevre, Silvano d'Orba, Castelnuovo Scrivia, Zavattarello, Pianello Val Tidone, and Romagnese. Moreover, he was notorious for being the son-in-law and loyal supporter of Ludovico Sforza, the black fly of Milan. Galeazzo Sanseverino was a much-admired Italian *condottiere*, a famous jouster, and a captain-general in the Milanese army and a Chivalrous Courtier and Gentleman in Ludovico Sforza's ruling government and court before the latter's capture, imprisonment, and death in France in 1508. After the French army captured Galeazzo Sanseverino in 1500, King Louis XII pardoned him because, in 1494, he had been awarded a knighthood of the Order of Saint Michael by the then living king of France, Charles VIII. So, Galeazzo Sanseverino became a chivalrous and loyal servant of the French kings, and he was one of many advisors who favoured Leonardo's appointment to the French court as King Francois's chief architect, painter, and philosopher.

Leonardo's *Portrait of a Musician*. Is it Galeazzo Sanseverino?

The *Portrait of a Musician* (Fig. 6.1), owned by the Pinacoteca Ambrosiana in Milan, was attributed officially to Leonardo da Vinci in about 2010 by the art historian and researcher Professor Pietro Cesere Marani of the Politecnico Milano. There is no original documentation for the *Portrait of a Musician* so the attribution was based on chronology, subject, comparative style and the influence of the Sicilian painter Antonello da Messina. The portrait hung in the Louvre from 1796 to 1815 when it was attributed to Bernadino Luini, a Leonardo acolyte. It was in the possession of the Biblioteca Ambrosiana in 1671 and was catalogued as *Portrait of Ludovico il Moro* until it was cleaned and the piece of sheet music was revealed in the figure's hand. The letters 'CANT...ANG...' were discernable and the abbreviation was suggested to be *'Canticum Angelicum'* or *'Cantor Angelo'*. From this it was concluded that the portrait was of a musician, and the names put forward were Josquin des Prez who was a visiting composer and choirmaster from France; Franchino Gaffario, choirmaster of the Milan cathedral who composed the *'Canticum Angelicum'*; Attalante Miglioretti, poet and minstrel who travelled to Milan from Florence with Leonardo; and Angelo Testagrossa, singer and singing master who might be the *'Cantor Angelo'*. Angelo Testagrossa was also the Duchess Isabella Aragon Sforza's singing teacher who Leonardo knew well. And then many others later noticed the similarity between the portrait of the musician and the gentleman in the *Pacioli Portrait* and concluded that it is Galeazzo Sanseverino in both portraits.

FIG. 6.1. Leonardo da Vinci. Portrait of a Young Man (The Musician). 1490. Pinacoteca Ambrosiana, Milan. Web Gallery of Art. Public domain. PD-Art.

The *Portrait of the Musician* is still variously attributed to Leonardo da Vinci, Bernardino Luini, Ambrogio de Predis, Antonio Boltraffio and the German Albrecht Durer. If the accepted date of the portrait is 1489, then it is unlikely to be a de Predis portrait because he preferred painting profiles even up to 1496 when he painted the wedding portraits of Emperor

CHAPTER 6

Maximilian I and his Milanese wife Bianca Sforza. Albrecht Durer didn't take up portrait painting until about 1493 and especially not until after his visit to Venice in 1494 and 1495, and, therefore, the *Musician* is unlikely to be his portrait. This rightfully leaves Leonardo or one of his assistants as the most likely author of the portrait. The deniers and sceptics suggest that it isn't a Leonardo because it doesn't show his usual skills, talents and professionalism. The colours are too muted and the background lacks the usual Leonardo deference to nature. While these objections seem reasonable, it is a portrait of a person, a courtier, and hence, Leonardo probably decided to keep things simple, focus on the sitter and leave out all the fancy allegories about man's connection to nature. The *Musician* is much like his other portraits such as the *Woman with the Ermine* and *La Belle Ferronnière* that are influenced by the style of Antonello da Messina.

The *Musician* looks unfinished (Fig. 6.1), but it shows the general characteristics of Leonardo's portraits of courtiers and/or their mistresses:

- Backgrounds left in shadow, black or another dark monocolour.
- Figures shown at half-length or slightly more.
- The sitter might look directly at the viewer or slightly out to the side of the viewer.
- Subjects positioned at three-quarter turn for improved identification of the sitter.
- One or more hands visible, usually holding a clue or script or paper puzzle to help identify the sitter or their personality.

The characteristics visible in the portraits of the *Lady with an Ermine* and *La Belle Ferronnière* are the same that Leonardo suggested for painting portraits in poor light. The sitter is usually positioned against a black background to bring out the personality of the sitter. Leonardo's portraits of Cecilia Gallerani (*Lady with an Ermine*) and his *Portrait of a Musician* are perfect examples of him putting his theories into practice. Here, he is influenced greatly by the portraits of the great Sicilian painter, Antonello da Messina (Fig. 4.3). The portrayed figures seem to emerge from a rather dark, gloomy or black background, almost larger than life and full of character. Even Leonardo's later works including the *Virgin of the Rocks* and his *Mona Lisa* demonstrate a similar approach. Moreover, if they are identified as Leonardo's subjects, the identification is based usually on a referral to a similar Leonardo painting in somebody's letter or as seen and eulogised by a poet from his times. Despite the occasional obvious clues, Leonardo's portraits and subjects remain largely unidentified.

The *Portrait of the Musician* has certain additional characteristics of a Leonardo painting: the emphasised bone structure, the relaxed pose, exquisitely curling hair, elegant or rough fingers, the expressive eyes and mouth, and the fact that the painting is at an advanced state, but looks unfinished. The features of the hand are almost identical to that of Cecilia Gallerani in Leonardo's famous portrait commonly known as the *Lady with an Ermine* (painted around 1483, now in Krakow). The musician's eyes resemble those of the angel Gabriel in the *Virgin of the Rocks*. The orange tunic appears unfinished and the hand seems to need more work. The painting has been heavily restored and repainted and infrared and UV investigations have revealed that the black garment was originally painted red, similar to the figure of the patron in the *Luca Portrait*. Although the painting of the musician might be unfinished and immobile, Leonardo already has captured some kind of energy within the musician – a tension – a concentration – similar to the *Luca Pacioli* portrait. Leonardo has used light and dark to capture strong shading effects on the musician's face; who seems to be concentrating hard on his music, perhaps using his mind and memory to learn this piece. The musician's middle distance fixed stare is lost in space similar to that of *Luca Pacioli* and the *Lady with the Ermine*. Leonardo's finished product of the *Portrait of the Musician* would have been just as stunning as the *Lady with the Ermine*. It is generally assumed that the *Portrait of the Musician* belongs to Leonardo's early years in Milan and it is often dated around 1485, although it could be as late as the 1490s.

Can we say that the *Portrait of the Musician* is Galeazzo Sanseverino? It is possible if we accept that Galeazzo Sanseverino was Leonardo's patron in the late 1480s and that he was an active courtier, entertainer, singer and musician in his own right. Did Galeazzo Sanseverino commission the portrait for his nuptials wedding engagement to Bianca Sforza, the illegitimate daughter of Ludovico Sforza? Possibly. But then, why is it unfinished? Why did not Galeazzo Sanseverino convince Leonardo to finish it or accept it as it is? The mystery and questions will remain until some documentation is found that might point towards a convincing answer.

It is worth quoting an extract from a letter by Galeazzo Sanseverino to Isabella d'Este, the sister of Ludovico Sforza's recently wedded-wife, Beatrice d'Este that Julie Cartwright published in her book on the life of *Beatrice d'Este* revealing what Galeazzo Sanseverino thought of his own singing abilities.

'This morning, being Friday I started at ten o'clock with the duchess and all of her ladies on horseback to go to Cussago, and in order to let your Highness enter fully into our pleasures, I must tell you that first of all I had to do was to ride in a chariot with the duchess and Dioda, and as we drove we sang more than twenty-five songs, arranged for three voices. That is to say, Dioda took the tenor part, and the duchess the soprano, whilst I sang sometimes bass and sometimes soprano, and played so many foolish tricks that I really think I may claim to be more of a fool than Dioda! And now farewell for

to-night, and I will try to improve still further, so as to afford your Highness the more pleasure when you come here in the summer.'

FIG. 6.2. *Comparison between the young man in the* Pacioli Portrait *at the Capodimonte Museum, Naples (left) and in the* Portrait of a Young Man (The Musician) *at the Pinacoteca Ambrosiana, Milan. Web Gallery of Art. Public domain.*

When we compare the *Portrait of the Musician* with Galeazzo Sanseverino in the *Pacioli Portrait* we see two men side by side who look similar, but not identical (Fig. 6.2). Galeazzo turns his gaze towards us whereas the musician looks out to the side; Galeazzo's left hand is covered in a green glove while the musician's left hand holds the musical notes; Galeazzo has a much thicker and fuller crop of hair with his black cap set back while the musician's hair is curlier, lighter and his red cap set forward on his head; and Galeazzo has a red shirt while the musician has a black shirt (previous under colour was red). They both have a white feather or spear (head) in front of their shirt, and they both have long straight noses – but with different shapes, thick fleshy lips and a solid square jaw. They look similar, and yet with enough differences to cast some doubt as to whether these two pictures are of the same person. Are they the same person – at different times – in different clothes, but similar fashion – in different settings – or are they simply different people? For me, the face in the *Pacioli Portrait* looks longer and more rectangular than the more triangular and wider face of the musician. They are not identical.

By the end of 1494, Leonardo's positive view of Galeazzo Sanseverino may have changed considerably as a consequence of the suspicious death of the Duke of Milan, Gian Galeazzo Sforza, aged 25 years, just before he became the rightful and sole ruler of Milan. It was at a time when Ludovico

Sforza would have had to step aside because Gian Galeazzo Sforza and his wife Isabella Aragon were of legal age to rule the Duchy of Milan in their own right. It seems that Ludovico Sforza could not let go of the power that he coveted and already held and wanted even more. He desired to be the rightful and sole ruler of Milan with no interference from anybody else, especially not from his nephew and niece. And he achieved this easily by convincing the ruling council to vote for him and oust Gian Galeazzo Sforza's son, Francesco II who was the next in line to inherit the title of Duke of Milan. Leonardo watched all this in dismay and may have sided with the moral rights of the duke's widow who should have become the Regent of Milan and the governor overseeing her son's entitlements, similar to the Regency of Bona of Savoy when Gian Galeazzo Sforza was a boy. However, Ludovico Sforza, the sinister black fly and unscrupulous usurper would not allow a legitimate takeover. After all, he overthrew Bona of Savoy, exiled her, and usurped the power and guardianship of the young duke Gian Galeazzo. This time around he would simply usurp all the entitlements of Gian Galeazzo Sforza and his son Francesco. After-all, Gian Galeazzo Sforza's son was only three years old and the widowed Duchess of Milan, Isabella Aragon Sforza, wielded no power. Leonardo would have felt Isabella's injustice, and he secretly expressed this perceived wrong in the coded messages of the *Pacioli Portrait*, with Galeazzo Sanseverino wearing the green glove of poison half concealed by Luca Pacioli friar's habit.

The Inscription IACO.BAR.VIGEN/N I S. P and the Dark Side of Galeazzo Sanseverino

The inscription IACO.BAR.VIGEN/N I S on the cartouche in the *Pacioli Portrait* contains all the necessary letters to spell out the names SANSEVERINO or VINCI – try it and see. The name Luca Pacioli is presented as an abbreviation on the red book and therefore, could be separated from the inscription on the cartouche.

Furthermore, the letters VIGENNIS plus the obscured number five at the end of 1495 is decoded simply to mean twenty (plus) 5 (25) - the age of the Duke Gian (GEN) Galeazzo who was murdered in Pavia (P) on the 20th or 21st of October of 1494 by the black fly – his uncle – the Duke of BARI (BAR.).

The critics and scholars, trying to interpret what VIGENNIS (twenty years old) had to do with Jacopo de' Barbari, scratched their heads, looked for various explanations other than his age, or just gave up and then speculated that may be he was in his twenties for this work. Here is what Nick Mackinnon had to write about VIGENNIS in his 1993 paper on the *Pacioli Portrait*:

CHAPTER 6

'The only reason they have for doubting that Jacopo de' Barbari is the artist is that "Vigennis" might mean "twenty years old", and conventional art theory has it that Barbari was more like 40 in 1495, and by 1511 he was so old that he had to receive a pension from Margaret of the Netherlands. But can it really be that, with such a small area to work on, rather than write out his full name, the artist prefers to risk confusion with Jacopo de' Barbari and give instead his age, a mere twenty? Is there any other example of an artist giving his own age in this manner?'

Leonardo possibly has provided a clue about the number 20 to suggest that somebody who is or was twenty-something years of age is missing from the painting. Does the poisonous black fly point to an obscured number 5 and suggest that we look up and across at the coded message VIGEN NIS. P.? Does the P. at the end of the code mean *Perdidit* (destroyed) in Latin with the full stop as added emphasis for terminated or the end of somebody's life aged twenty? If so, could the code be referring directly to the untimely and suspicious death of the young duke Gian Galeazzo Sforza in Pavia [P] on 23rd or 24th of October in 1494/5 when he was only 24 or 25 years of age? Does this coded message suggest that Luca Pacioli is, in fact, administering the last rites over the covered coffin of the dead young duke of Milan, Gian Galeazzo Sforza, who was assassinated and extinguished by his contemptuous uncle Ludovico Sforza? These serious questions are tackled in much greater detail in the later chapters of this book and the da Vinci code as decrypted by Carla Glori is presented in the penultimate chapter.

Galeazzo Sanseverino may not have been as chivalrous as he was often portrayed in the letters of the d'Este sisters. Soon after the death of the young duke of Milan, he and his stepfather, Ludovico Sforza, were involved in sexual intrigues at the Milanese court that may have led to the deaths of their wives, Giovanna Bianca Sforza on 23rd of November in 1496 and Beatrice d'Este on 2nd of January in 1497, respectively. The deaths of their wives may have eventuated from the long-standing feud between Ludovico Sforza and the Dal Verme family of Bobbio, a fortress town located strategically in the Trebbia River valley between Genoa and/or Piacenza and Pavia south of Milan. In 1436, the ruling Visconti family presented the Dal Verme family, the heirs of the *condottiero* Jacopo Dal Verme, with the small village, castle and fief of Zavattarello, located about 20 km from Bobbio. In 1485, Ludovico Sforza ordered the murder by poison of Count Pietro Dal Verme, who had no male heirs, in order to take possession of the castle of Zavattarello and the town of Bobbio. Later, Ludovico gave the castle and the surrounding lands to his son-in-law Galeazzo Sanseverino. Francesca, the daughter of Count Pietro Dal Verme was placed in the care of Clara Sforza, but she hated the Sforza for murdering her father and stealing her families' wealth and properties. On her deathbed, Francesca confessed to poisoning Ludovico Sforza's wife, Beatrice d'Este, the Duchess of Milan, at the instigation of Galeazzo Sanseverino. This admission of murder from the mouth of Francesca Dal Verme was reported by the Italian historian Ludovico Muratori (1672-1750) in his *Enstensi Antiquities* and later embellished by Carla Glori in her historical reconstruction of Giovanna Bianca Sforza as the original model for *Mona Lisa* with Bobbio as her background. The suspicious death of Giovanna Bianca Sforza, known as Bianca, seven weeks before the death of Beatrice d'Este, seemed to imply that her death was due to murder as well. The deaths of Bianca and Beatrice seemed like revenge for the murder of Gian Galeazzo Sforza in October of 1494, and the Ludovico Sforza/Galeazzo Sanseverino family rule began to unravel a few years after the death of their wives. In 1499, Ludovico Sforza and Galeazzo Sanseverino fled to Germany when the invading French army captained by the Milanese *condottiero* Gian Giacomo Trivulzio captured Milan. Bernardino Della Corte, to whom had been given custody of the castle of Milan, surrendered to the French for money and was rewarded with the fief of Zavattarello and other properties that belonged to the Dal Verme family. But, the Dal Verme continued claiming their rights and the bitter feud between them and Sanseverino finally ended with the death of Galeazzo Sanseverino during the battle of Pavia in 1525. From that moment, the Dal Verme remained uncontested rulers of Zavattarello.

The biography of Giovanna Bianca Sforza suggests that she might have been the victim of political and sexual intrigues during Ludovico Sforza's tenure, first when he was the regent and then when he was the Duke of Milan in the late 1490s. She was born in 1482, her mother was Bernardina de Corradis, the wife of the Count Palatine Antonio de' Gentili from Tortona. Ludovico legitimised his illegitimate daughter by ordering his nephew, the young duke Gian Galeazzo Sforza, to legally grant her legitimacy with a signed diploma dated on 8th of November 1489 at the castle of Vigevano, naming the husband of Bernardina de Corradis to be her legitimate father. Simultaneously, Ludovico promised the betrothal of his illegitimate daughter Bianca to Galeazzo Sanseverino and gave him the prestigious counties of Bobbio, Voghera and the lordship of Castel San Giovanni. A few months later, back in Milan, Galeazzo Sanseverino celebrated his nuptials with the little, 7-year-old Bianca. Six years later, on 20th June 1496, Ludovico permitted Bianca the *'trasductio ad maritum'*, the definitive deed of matrimonial practices with her husband Galeazzo Sanseverino. Ludovico decision was seen to be about his self-interest, his desire to please his favourite Galeazzo and at the same time to expand and unify his feudal domains over the entire territory that he stole from the Dal Verme family. Bianca and Galeazzo were given Bobbio and Voghera, the Castel San Giovanni and the fertile green lands of the Oltrepò and the Val

Tidone (Zavattarello), Rocca d' Olgisio, Pianello Val Tidone, Romagnese, Pecorara and its valley and other fiefdoms. It was essential for Ludovico Sforza that Galeazzo, as commander of the Ducal Army, remain loyal to him and his family and not transgress elsewhere. Therefore, was Francesca Dal Verme's rumoured confession a lie to fuel suspicion and break the tight bond between Galeazzo Sanseverino and Ludovico Sforza or was it the truth? I suspect it was the former, an attempt to wreak vengeance with a lie to further fuel Ludovico's paranoia with his coming troubles from a looming French invasion.

Beatrice and Bianca, despite a six-year difference in age, were greatly attached and were regular companions at court parties, official functions and festivals. The Duchess Beatrice d'Este was devastated by the death of her friend Bianca and by the infidelities of her husband Ludovico Sforza. During their six-year marriage, he had maintained sexual relationships with at least two of his powerful courtesans and lovers, Cecilia Gallerani and Lucrezia Crivelli. Cecilia gave birth to Ludovico's son, Cesare, in May of 1491, and Lucrezia produced his son Giovanni in 1497. Galeazzo Sanseverino was complicit in Ludovico's sexual adventures while trying to protect his wife from the courtly intrigues. However, neither Galeazzo nor Ludovico, nor their loyal physician Ambrogio da Rosate, could protect Bianca from a death of unknown cause; a widespread malaise and stomach pains that accompanied her demise, symptoms that were similar to those of the dying Gian Galeazzo Sforza two years before her death.

Luca Pacioli arrived in Milan in 1496 at the invitation of Ludovico Sforza to teach mathematics and was there at the time of the deaths of Bianca and Beatrice. In deciphering the coded inscription IACO.BAR. VIGEN/NIS on the cartouche in the *Pacioli Portrait*, Carla Glori believes that it alludes to Bianca and Beatrice as the wives of Galeazzo Sanseverino and Ludovico Sforza respectively, but not concerning their deaths, which happened after the year written on the cartouche.

Sanseverino Picture Gallery

FIG. 6.3. *Sanseverino clan praying to and worshipping Ludovico Il Moro Sforza, the 7th Duke of Milan. Giovan Pietro Birago. Detail from the Sforziada Frontispiece. Warsaw, Biblioteka Naradowa, Inc. F. 1347. Public domain.*

FIG. 6.4. *Two possible images of Galeazzo Sanseverino, portrait by Albrecht Durer (left), and a detail from the painting of Battle of Pavia (1525) where he lost his life.*
http://www.kleio.org/en/history/famtree/vip/317a/?gallery#7455

FIG. 6.5. Left: *Coat of Arms of the Sanseverino featuring the emblematic House Colours of red and white.* https://wikivividly.com/langit/wiki/File:Stemma_sanseverino_grande.jpg
Right: 'What us?' *A detail from Leonardo's* Last Supper *depicting Galeazzo Sanseverino as an apostle with a beard (middle). Note the hand in the lower right pointing the blade of a knife towards him and the other apostle at the end of the table possibly accusing them of Milanese political treachery and betrayal.*
http://www.kleio.org/en/history/famtree/vip/317a/?gallery#7455

References

Ady CM (1907). A history of Milan, under the House of Sforza. Edward Armstrong (editor). New York: G. P. Putnam's Sons. London: Methuen & Co. 1907.
https://archive.org/stream/historyofmilanun017956mbp/historyofmilanun017956mbp_djvu.txt

Cartwright, Julia Mary (1899). Isabella d' Este, Marchioness of Mantua 1474-1539.

CHAPTER 6

A Study of the Renaissance. Dent & Co (1899). J. Murray, London 1903, 1919.

Cartwright, Julia Mary (1908). Beatrice d'Este, Duchess of Milan, 1475-1479. J. M. Dent amp Co. Online:

http://readcentral.com/massappealnews/chapters/Julia-MaryCartwright/Beatrice-dEste-Duchess-of-Milan-1475-1497/003.

https://books.google.com.au/books?id=EHFHnl7mYg4C.

Damiani, Roberto (2014). Condottieri di ventura. Galeazzo da san Severino marquis of Castelnuovo.

https://condottieridiventura.it/galeazzo-da-san-severino-marchese-di-castelnuovo/

Giulini A (1912). Bianca Sanseverino Sforza, Archivio Storico Lombardo serie IV, volume XVIII, anno XXXIX, Libreria Bocca, Milano.

Cook, Herbert (1907). A Portrait of a Musician, by Leonardo da Vinci. The Burlington Magazine for Connoisseurs 12 (56) 91-93 (+103).

Glori C (2011). Cappello U, Enigma Leonardo: decifrazioni e scoperte - La Gioconda. In memoria di Bianca, Savona, 2011-2012.

Kulski JK (2017). Leonardo da Vinci: The Melzi Chronicles. Published by Jerzy. K. Kulski. ISBN: 978-0-6480653-1-9

Marani, Pietro Cesare, editor (2010). Leonardo da Vinci - Il Musico, Cataloghi di mostre. Silvana Italy.Muratori L (1717). Delle Antichità Estensi, in Modena, nella Stamperia Ducale, 1717.

Pacioli, Luca (1498). Divine Proportion (in English). 1498 edition. tennenbaum pacioli-divine-proportion.pdf. Uploaded by Israel Monroy Muñoz on Oct 22, 2014. *Full text of original edition (1498) in English.*

Richter JP (1880). The Notebooks of Leonardo da Vinci.

http://www.fromoldbooks.org/RichterNotebooksOfLeonardo/

http://www.gutenberg.org/ebooks/5000

PART 2

Phenomenological & Eidetic Analysis of the *Pacioli Portrait:* Hidden Eclecticism, Geometry, and Science

Everything in the phenomenal universe is a straight line and circle. The horizon, our heads, arms, electrons, the oceans, planets and stars. Their principle function is to radiate. The task of the human being is also to radiate. – Alonzo King, choreographer, 2018.
Eidetic reduction, in phenomenology, a method by which the philosopher moves from the consciousness of individual and concrete objects to the transempirical realm of pure essences and thus achieves an intuition of the eidos (Greek: "shape") of a thing—i.e., of what it is in its invariable and essential structure, apart from all that is contingent or accidental to it. The eidos is thus the principle or necessary structure of the thing. – The Editors of Encyclopedia Britannica, 1998

7

VISUAL DIALECTICS ON AGE, NATURE & *MONA LISA* SMILES

Leonardo's *Contrapposto* & Dialectic Vision

The dialectic is the theory of opposites that swings like a pendulum between thesis and antithesis and makes up the whole. It is what we know as the yin and yang, happiness and sadness, youth and age, light and dark, green and red, pleasure and pain, and the colours at the opposite ends of a spectrum that when joined together with those in between are an unifying metaphysical process that helps to explain the apparent diversity of the world and human nature. We see the dualism of opposites pulsating in Leonardo's painting of Luca Pacioli with his depictions of youth (the student/jouster), age (Pacioli), the crooked smile, the uneven eyes, light and dark, shadow and brightness, the menacing black background (death) and the green tablecloth (growth), and the mysterious rhombicuboctahedron hanging from the heavens providing contradictory, riddle-laid dialectic tensions and questions to the whole scene. The *Pacioli Portrait* represents Leonardo's dialectic perspective in his overall philosophy and visualisation of painting and art and how the various layers of encrypted dimensions add life and movement to the overall creation and point of the painting. The two energies (forces), yin (black) and yang (white), and the gradations (colours) in between produce a painting pulsating with enormous tension and vibrancy in its contradictory two-dimensional passivity. Leonardo's portrait of Luca Pacioli (old man), the Jouster (young man), and the sinister black fly of Milan (a hidden dark history) is ironic. It shows observers a range of pictorial clues to unravel the camouflaged mysteries of the universe and human behaviour, mysteries that often are revealed to us only by science, art, mathematics, experience, history, education (teaching) and experiment (measured activity).

The Chinese philosophers advanced dialectical perspectives and thinking some 3,000 years ago culminating in the ancient symbol of Yin-Yang, the interlocking black and white shapes within the circle that represent the interaction of the two energies or forces – the yin (black) and the yang (white). The yin signifies the dark, passive, downward, cold, contracting and weak forces, whereas the yang signifies bright, active, upward, hot, expanding and strong forces. These energies and forces are in continual, simultaneous movements and interconnections; they shape various outcomes that in turn are shaped by them. The representations of Yin-Yang are similar to Leonardo da Vinci's use of contrasting painting techniques; on one hand, the use of *contrapposto* (counterpoise) that sets opposites against one another, and on the other hand, the use of *sfumato* (softening transitions or outlines) to allow tones and colours to shade into one another and gradually soften outlines as *'without lines or border, in the manner of smoke or beyond the picture plane.'*

The Ancient Greeks including Plato and Socrates knew the concepts of Yin-Yang as the philosophy of dialectics. Plato believed that the human soul possesses latent knowledge, which could be brought out and elucidated by a specific type of philosophical discourse that he called the dialèctic: a bringing to birth of enlightenment from the depths of a person's higher being. He believed that a higher consciousness was needed to do this, and the result would bring forth a literal enlightenment and a furthered understanding of human nature. According to Plato in *The Commonwealth (VII, 533d)*:

'Dialectic is the only philosophical process which seeks for wisdom by anagogically uplifting our Intellectual foundations so that our Higher Self ascends to the Origin.'

The German philosopher Immanuel Kant who lived in the 18th century believed that the ancient Greeks used dialectic to signify the logic of false appearance or semblance. Socrates believed the process of dialectic in Plato's works was to bring out the ideas of others and act as a guide for the soul to lead reason along the proper pathway (known as a psychagogue). On the other hand, Aristotelian Dialectic is commonly defined simply as a dialogue (argument) between two people holding different or opposite points of view about a subject and wishing to establish the truth through reasoned arguments. According to Aristotle in the *Topics*, dialectic was just two of the four types of reasoning or inference that illuminated the broad scope of dialectic reasoning. The four types of Aristotelian reasoning are known as demonstrative inference, dialectical inference, contentious inference, and an inference that dialectically ends in a contradiction. Inferences are the steps in deductive and inductive reasoning, moving from premises to logical consequences or conclusions. Although Aristotle identified four types of inference, the modern interpretation is that there are only two modes of inference: demonstrative and dialectical. The former is causal reasoning and the latter is non-causal (or contingent) reasoning. However, dialectical reasoning (as a mode of inquiry rather than as a method of disputation) operates in both instances because, in the final analysis, the human mind works by demonstrative and dialectic inference, something of which Leonardo was aware of and practised skillfully in his own particular way.

Leonardo used the dialectic in his writing and in his rhetorical debates such as at the Leonardo Academy, which was a gathering of the poets, artists, scientists and various intellectuals that were in Milan at the time of Leonardo da Vinci. He also used dialectic logic and argument in his art with the science of painting and his experiments with mathematics. He married the dialectic with the antithesis, that is, he contrasted the opposites of like elements, such as good and bad, pain and pleasure, etc. Simply put, he used the dialectic as a method to explore the unity of opposites (duality), their balance (stasis) and tensions, and explored how opposing conditions prevail, one over the other, and how an element undergoes change or transformation as it persists through opposite properties. The dialectic method explores the fundamental role and nature of complementary opposites in the ongoing self-organising process of creation. According to the ancients and Leonardo, a unity of opposites is present in the universe as difference and sameness, as expressed by Heraclitus's aphorism:

The road up and the road down are the same thing.

Leonardo's dialectic is similar to the Hegelian dialectic that the German philosopher Georg Wilhelm Friedrich Hegel developed during the turn of the 18th and 19th centuries to describe a contradiction of ideas to resolve the determining factor in their interaction by providing a thesis (propositions giving rise to the ideas), an antithesis (the counter-propositions which counter or negate the thesis), and the solution that resolves the tension between the opposing or different ideas by refutation, synthesis, combination, or qualitative improvement. Hegel described various cases of 'unity of opposites', including the concepts of Finite and Infinite, Force and Matter, Identity and Difference, Positive and Negative, Form and Content, Chance and Necessity, Cause and Effect, Subject and Object and many other concepts that Leonardo also touched on in his own writings in his notebooks.

Although Leonardo uses both dualism and dialectic in his writings, paintings and drawings, the two concepts are distinct. Dualism is characterised as mutually antagonistic realities that cannot co-exist together. They are binary opposites characterised by an either/or relationship and no assumption is made about interdependence, simultaneity or possible unification of opposing forces. In contrast, a dialectic focuses on simultaneous existence of each force or element and the tensions that exist between them as opposites and to think of them as 'both/and' instead of 'either/or'.

Modern dialectics consists of four separate concepts: contradiction, motion, totality and *praxis* (practice, doing or custom, not theory). Contradiction is the co-existence of oppositional forces, motion is the shift or movement between the competing poles of action and totality is the interconnection and reciprocal influence of multiple individual and social factors that may operate together with each shaping and being shaped by the other. *Praxis* is the process by which a theory, lesson, or skill is enacted, embodied, or realised as well as the political action and education along with all of its consequences by the human communicator. The Ancient Greek's referred to *praxis* as the activity engaged in by all people, such as Aristotelian *theoria* (thinking), *poiesis* (making) and *praxis* (doing). The social philosopher Karl Marx engaged in *praxis* as a practice to separate theory (inaction) and action from each other so that *praxis* (doing) involved political analyses (thinking about conflicts, imbalances, and contradictions in the world) and activities to change the world in order to contribute to a social organisation in which people could live with one another free from all forms of domination.

Michael Gelb in his 1998 book *How to Think Like Leonardo da Vinci* reminded us of Leonardo's dialectic vision of art. He suggested that da Vinci's genius stemmed from his insatiable curiosity (*curiosita*), the unrelenting quest for learning, and his ability to test ideas and hypotheses through deductive and inductive reasoning, experience and experiment (*dimostrazione*) and a willingness to learn from mistakes. Essentially, this is the modern scientific method on how to gain knowledge and test hypotheses. He embraced the ambiguity, paradox, uncertainty and contradictory impulses through the dialectic and his study and use of *sfumato* (literally 'going up in smoke'), and his willingness and ability to explore and gain clarity by comparing and contrasting from opposite points of view (*contrapposta*). His search for beauty led him to explore ugliness and old age, and he carefully explored the ugly as much as the beautiful, sketching and drawing their facial shapes and expressions and body movements and contortions. To understand joy, you must know sorrow; to understand change you must have constancy. Dialectic thinking and method embodied Leonardo's work and thoughts because multiple and opposing perspectives yield deeper understanding of any phenomenon. Academically, this also is known as the dialectic method in a phenomenological research design.

CHAPTER 7

Leonardo's Spirituality, Science and Creative Action

Karel Vereycken in his article *The Key to a New Renaissance* that was published in *Fidelio* (vol 9, number 1) in the Spring of 2000 writes that Leonardo da Vinci is an example of a humble and great self-teacher in the service of action:

> '*Leonardo is the test-tube baby of the great laboratory of the Renaissance, a humble and gigantic self-teacher, in the image of Nicolaus of Cusa's* Layman, *where theologian meets craftsman. Because, for Cusa, God's act of love cannot take place outside knowledge in the service of action. So, far from seeing science and creative action as what alienates the man of faith, it is precisely their growth that brings man closer to the Absolute. In the spirit of the coincidence of opposites, it is the most metaphysical speculation that will bear the most fruit in terms of earthly discoveries.*'

Accordingly, the Renaissance revolution began with the philosophical ideas and dialectical mysticism and political action of Nicolaus of Cusa (1401-1464) and ended with Leonardo da Vinci's contribution when he left Italy for France during the winter of 1516. Nicolaus of Cusa wrote about squaring the circle, regular polyhedra and that the earth was not the centre of the universe nor was it at rest. These same ideas were contemplated and progressed on to various degrees by Leonardo who revealed a participatory transcendence, a Theo-philosophy that generated scientific discoveries, and an understanding of the individualistic and the voluntaristic transformation of the world. Thus, the mystical or spiritual lessons that Leonardo provides us within the *Pacioli Portrait* is that science and creative action (teaching, building, painting) strengthens a man's faith and brings him closer to the *Creator of All Things* and *Absolute Knowledge*; which is represented allegorically by the rhombicuboctahedron 'floating' in space. We can see some of Leonardo's concept of opposites or antithesis in the painting where these philosophical dilemmas are expressed by contrasting age and wisdom (Pacioli and the student), the half-smile and diverging eyes of Pacioli's exalted expression, and the way the items are distributed across the green table.

Leonardo da Vinci believed in the Nicolaus of Cusa creative spirit and the Buddha awareness to do good things and serve his fellow man to the best of his abilities. His life and conduct were unfailingly governed by lofty principles and aims, and he often reminded his friends and acolytes about the importance of mindfulness to live in the present and to prevent our minds from wandering too much all over the place. Leonardo extolled those virtues in his reverse writing when he wrote:

'The average human looks without seeing, listens without hearing, touches without feeling, eats without tasting, moves without physical awareness, inhales without awareness of odour or fragrance, and talks without thinking. Finally, a life dedicated to seeing and understanding the world around us, doing what we can to help those less fortunate than ourselves, and sharing love and joy and knowledge, is a life well-lived.'

Young Man and Old Man

If Leonardo da Vinci painted the double portrait of Luca Pacioli and Galeazzo Sanseverino in 1496 then Galeazzo Sanseverino was 38 years old, Leonardo was 44 years old, and Luca Pacioli was 51 years old. The portrait seems to depict a much younger looking Galeazzo Sanseverino, somebody in their late twenties or early thirties, whereas Luca Pacioli's lined face looks much older than 51 years, closer to 60. Was this an age discrepancy? Is this how they looked or has Leonardo taken liberties with their appearance? Perhaps he has made Galeazzo look younger and Luca much older to highlight the dialectic difference in age between an enlightened older teacher and an arrogant younger student. This difference between the looks of a young and old man and their contrasting relationships was an ongoing topic of interest for Leonardo and a subject of a number of his drawings of old and young men together, and his fascination with physiognomy and the contrasts between youth and old age and between beauty and ugliness. Leonardo wrote the following about painting ugly faces:

'It seems to me to be no small charm in a painter when he gives his figures a pleasing air, and this grace, if he have it not by nature, he may acquire by incidental study in this way: Look about you and take the best parts of many beautiful faces, of which the beauty is confirmed rather by public fame than by your own judgment; for you might be mistaken and choose faces which have some resemblance to your own. For it would seem that such resemblances often please us; and if you should be ugly, you would select faces that were not beautiful and you would then make ugly faces, as many painters do. For often a master's work resembles himself. So select beauties as I tell you, and fix them in your mind.'

Thus, Leonardo may have modified the look of Pacioli and Sanseverino to provide an iconic rather than an accurate or factual look.

In his allegorical image of the dialectic of pleasure and pain, Leonardo drew the young man (pleasure) and the old man (pain) emerging out of the lower half of the same body (Fig. 7.1).

CHAPTER 7

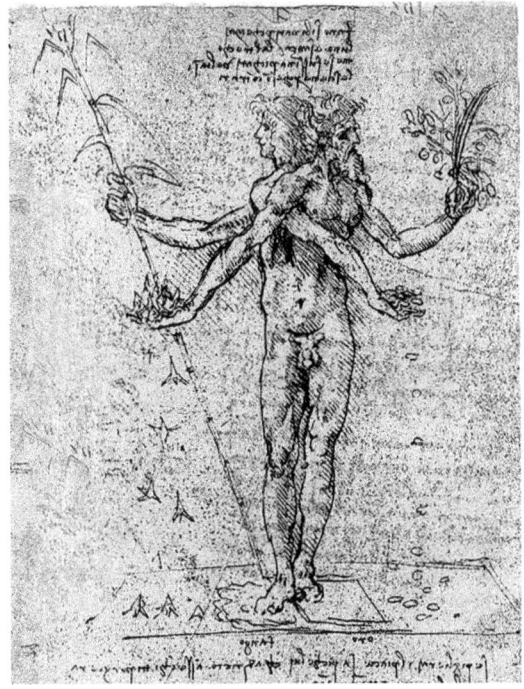

FIG. 7.1. Leonardo's allegorical drawing of Pleasure and Pain.

He accompanied his drawing with the following notes:

Pleasure and Pain represent as twins, since there never is one without the other; and as if they were united back to back, since they are contrary to each other. (Clay, gold). If you take Pleasure know that he has behind him one who will deal you Tribulation and Repentance. This represents Pleasure together with Pain and shows them as twins because one is never apart from the other. They are back to back because they are opposed to each other; and they exist as contraries in the same body, because they have the same basis, inasmuch as the origin of pleasure is labour and pain, and the various forms of evil pleasure are the origin of pain. Therefore it is here represented with a reed in his right hand, which is useless and without strength, and the wounds it inflicts are poisoned. In Tuscany they are put to support beds, to signify that it is here that vain dreams come, and here a great part of life is consumed. It is here that much precious time is wasted, that is, in the morning, when the mind is composed and rested, and the body is made fit to begin new labours; there again many vain pleasures are enjoyed; both by the mind in imagining impossible things, and by the body in taking those pleasures that are often the cause of the failing of life. And for these reasons the reed is held as their support. In contrast to the smiling and beautiful youthful face of Pleasure, Displeasure is a mournful, bearded old man who with wounded heart drops painful spiked caltrops from his right hand while his left hand holds a bush of thorned roses where worldly pleasures like its flowers wilt and the sharp and painful thorns are retained. The right leg of the body of pleasure rests weakly on a sheet of soft clay while the left leg of pain stands strong and hard on a firm tablet of gold. There is pleasure and pain in the one body, which cannot exist one without the other.'

In another drawing dated December 1478, now at the Uffizi in Florence, Leonardo drew the figure of an old man in profile, which appears to be an early example of Leonardo's interest in grotesque heads. He has exaggerated the man's nose and chin to the point that they appear almost to touch one another, a strange and purposeful arrangement like drawing the crescent moon. The youth opposite the old man has an ideal and youthful physiognomy. This drawing shows Leonardo's early interest of juxtaposing the old against the young or the ugly against the beautiful to invoke his concept of *contrapposto*, the contrast of movements of the body and flexion of its parts, an antithesis by setting opposites against one another to heighten vividness, that is, vividness achieved through opposition and variety. In the *Codice Urbino (61 rv)* Leonardo wrote:

'I say that in narrative paintings you should closely intermingle direct opposites, because they offer a great contrast to each other, and the more so the more they are adjacent. Thus, have the ugly one next to the beautiful, the large next to the small, the old next to the young.'

By placing an attentive younger man next to the older man in the *Pacioli Portrait*, Leonardo offers a meditation on aging and the passage of time. He considered the metamorphosis of all things through age and aging, whether in relation to the earth and his interest in fossils in the *Codex Leicester* or the human body in his dissection drawings and his speculations about arterial sclerosis and the death of an old man (*RL 19005r*) to his philosophical musings on death as an eternal sleep (*Codex Atlanticus 207v/76v-a*). Leonardo approached the subject of aging and mortality from many angles. In the *Pacioli Portrait*, the proximity of a wrinkled old man's face next to a handsome, smooth-skinned younger man creates a psychological tension without clearly defining the relationship of the two figures beyond the contrast in physical appearance. The facial distortion also constitutes an ingenious subversion of the Renaissance conventions of portraiture that delight as inventive creations. John Garton in his article entitled *Leonardo's early grotesque head* pointed out that Leon Battista Alberti described portraiture as an art form that overcomes death by preserving the living, but that the wrinkled, grotesque heads of Leonardo appear to wryly subvert that classical ideal. In this regard, Leonardo's *Pacioli Portrait* does subvert the Renaissance conventions and classical ideal by engaging in the broader themes of science, wisdom, antithesis, aging, and wry invention.

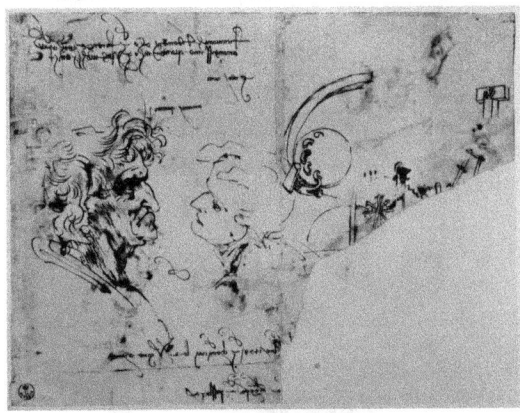

FIG. 7.2. *Leonardo da Vinci, Two heads with inscriptions in notarial script, 20.2 × 26.6 cm, inv. no. 446E, Gabinetto Disegni e Stampi degli Uffizi, Florence.*

Leonardo also drew many old men's heads as complete oddities, exaggerated grotesque heads, that when assembled as a continuous corpus is almost iconic in their completeness. There are approximately one hundred drawings of grotesque heads, half of which belong to the Royal Collection at Windsor, that are too diverse to fit nicely into a few categorical types. They need to be published into a single volume to demonstrate Leonardo's propensity for accepting portraiture's outward conventions of format while subverting its emphasis on beauty and reverence. They demonstrate Leonardo's appreciation of human individuality by the 'look' of faces, especially old faces, and the biological diversity within the same species. Also, when choosing the heads and faces that Leonardo needed to remember for his *Last Supper* painting, he recommended the following method of keeping in mind the form of a face:

'If you want to acquire facility for bearing in mind the expression of a face, first make yourself familiar with a variety of [forms of] several heads, eyes, noses, mouths, chins and cheeks and necks and shoulders: And to put a case: Noses are of 10 types: straight, bulbous, hollow, prominent above or below the middle, aquiline, regular, flat, round or pointed. These hold good as to profile. In full-face they are of 11 types; these are equal thick in the middle, thin in the middle, with the tip thick and the root narrow, or narrow at the tip and wide at the root; with the nostrils wide or narrow, high or low, and the openings wide or hidden by the point; and you will find an equal variety in the other details; which things you must draw from nature and fix them in your mind. Or else, when you have to draw a face by heart, carry with you a little book in which you have

noted such features; and when you have cast a glance at the face of the person you wish to draw, you can look, in private, which nose or mouth is most like, or there make a little mark to recognise it again at home. Of grotesque faces, I need say nothing, because they are kept in mind without difficulty.'

FIG. 7.3. *Leonardo da Vinci. Old Man and Youth. Red chalk on paper. Uffizi Gallery, Florence, Web Gallery of Art. Wikimedia Commons. PD-Art.*

Presumably, in the Renaissance, a few knew about or saw Leonardo's repertoire of strange heads and perhaps even celebrated their oddity as a sign of his ingenuity. In his *Idea del Tempio della Pittura* of 1590, the painter and writer Giovan Paolo Lomazzo wrote about the marvellous in Leonardo's works that is especially evident in his ugly and monstrous creations of human heads. Leonardo's Uffizi drawing of 1478 (Fig. 7.3) survives as an early example of how such visual oddities became a leitmotiv of creativity. Other 'young man – old man' drawings by Leonardo demonstrate that it was a subject he enjoyed to ponder and illustrate as part of his dialectic or synthesis of visual opposites.

Contrapposto. Luca Pacioli and *Mona Lisa's* Crooked Smile

Leonardo da Vinci is famous for having painted *Mona Lisa* with her enigmatic smile. In contrast to *Mona Lisa*, Leonardo gave Luca Pacioli a crooked smile that should be every bit as famous as *Mona Lisa's* enigmatic smile. Just look at Luca Pacioli's crooked smile – one side is a smile, and the other side is sadness – pure *contrapposto* by Leonardo da Vinci. How could this genius, this masterful use of *contrapposto* be attributed to Jacopo de' Barbari? Where in Jacopo de' Barbari's portraits is there any hint of *contrapposto* or the genius of the crooked smile invented by Leonardo da Vinci? Nowhere. Jacopo de' Barbari may have seen Leonardo's *Pacioli Portrait* in Venice in 1500 and copied the young Student, Galeazzo Sanseverino, staring out at us. But, where is the masterful expression in the mouth of an old man in any of his works? There is none.

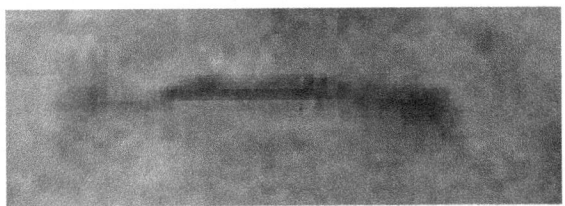

FIG. 7.4. Detail. Luca Pacioli's crooked smile.

Leonardo would have enjoyed painting the sense of irony and dualism in Luca's happy/sad smile. What was he smiling about? Was it because he was a scientist or a friar? What was he sad about? We have a very good idea what Leonardo thought about the clergy and the sad turn of the lip probably reflects this duplicitous and fraudulent nature of the church. The turned-up lip probably reflects Leonardo and Luca's love of science that made them happy to ponder the sunny side of God's creation of the beautiful natural world. Leonardo was a master of capturing facial microexpressions and painting them in such a way as to reveal feelings as he saw them or how he wanted us to see them.

Microexpressions are those very short or fleeting unintentional expressions that often betray the underlying hidden feelings that we mask with our false face – the false facemask that we present to the world. These false facemasks are controlled or manipulated expressions that we have learnt to manufacture according to display rules. We have learnt these display rules from infancy to give out deliberate messages or what we want to reveal. The intentional expressions are part of our socialisation over many years of self-study of self-control. On the other hand, the microexpressions, the unhappy face, the grimace, that are displayed unintentionally for milliseconds or a few seconds contradict the dominant, but false smiling face that we attempt to show to the world. Often, as people grow old, they can or want no longer to hide their microexpressions and so they develop the asymmetrical face where one side shows a happy smiling face and the other side is an unhappy sad face, with a frown and the lip turned down as we see in Luca Pacioli's face.

In the book entitled *The Classroom X-Factor: The Power of Body Language and Non-verbal Communication in Teaching,* John White and John Gardner define a closed-mouth smiling expression as a facial expression characterised by an upward curving of the corners of the mouth indicating pleasure, amusement, or derision. In a crooked smile, the lips turn up in a smile on one side while the lips on the other side remain horizontal or turn slightly down, in a frown or grimace. Modern-day lawyers and criminal investigators study the closed-mouth facial expressions of their clients and suspects in an attempt to judge their true feelings and assess the purpose of the smile. Is it a false or crooked smile or a genuine or empathetic one? The two rules of thumb (that may be right or wrong) that lawyers and facial expression analysts use are that (1) a fixed smile that lasts longer than is appropriate might reveal deception and a lie, and (2) a fixed smile masks other feelings. Whereas the natural smile disappears as the situation changes, the fixed, false smile lingers, the type that you often see on a politician's face.

A crooked or twisted smile is bent, angled or winding, and not straight. It means one corner of the mouth goes up higher than the other. This is because the muscles are stronger on one side. If a smile is twisted intentionally then it might be called a smirk. The crooked smile where one side of the smile lifts up and while the other side of the smile stays relatively flat or points downward is also known as the asymmetrical smile. Generally few people over a certain age (e.g., over 50 years of age) are able to maintain a perfectly symmetrical smile that doesn't turn into a grimace or asymmetry. John White and John Gardner also commented on the asymmetry of *Mona Lisa's* smile:

'If you look closely at the Mona Lisa *painting, you will notice that her smile is not perfectly symmetrical. It seems a little bigger on the left side than the right. A quick glance at 'expert analyses' of this smile throws up a plethora of theories, but one theory concerns left and right brain thinking……*

As the left side of a person's face is controlled by the right side of their brain, it means the left side tends to be more emotionally expressive. But this really only takes effect when one engages in posed expressions. Hence, if we consider the Mona Lisa *smile, it could be that she is actually 'posing the smile' as it is bigger on the left side of her face. When one engages in more genuine and spontaneous expressions, then the face puts on a more symmetrical display – in this case, with both sides of the face presenting the smile in a balanced manner….'*

The famous 'Mona Lisa smile' is an excellent example of applying subtle asymmetry to a face. For Sigmund Freud, the smile of *Mona Lisa 'lies on the cusp of good and evil, compassion and cruelty, seduction and innocence, the fleeting and the eternal'.*

What about Luca Pacioli's left and right brain? Why was the right side of his mouth up and the left side down? Was it because of a mild stroke?

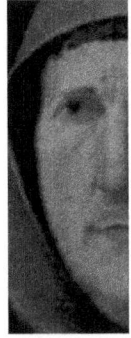

FIG. 7.5. *The two halves of Pacioli's face; the right side and the left side accentuate the crooked smile. Right side of face: curiosity, satisfaction. Left side of face: weariness, sadness, unhappiness.*

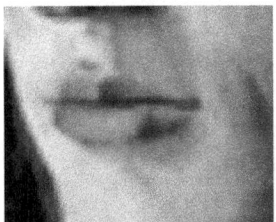

FIG. 7.6. *The student's smile as a straight line.*

FIG. 7.7. *Mona Lisa's smile has a hint of asymmetry.*

Leonardo did not provide an anatomical explanation for a smile in any of his notebooks. On the other hand, Jeffrey T. Frederick (2004), in his book on *Mastering Voir Dire and Jury Selection*, says:

> *'Today we believe that there are over 20 muscles in the face that can produce in over a 1000 distinct expressions although only eight basic emotions in the face are easily recognised – sadness, anger, fear, disgust, surprise, happiness, contempt and disinterest.*

To understand more, we need to look for other body language cues and especially the auditory cues. There are at least eight auditory clues that can indicate anxiety or deception, such as speech disturbance, hesitancy, pitch, amount and speed of speech, tone, false or tense laughter, and word choice.'

Many of these auditory cues cannot be depicted pictorially, although a skilled draughtsman or a genius can portray anxiety, hesitancy, false or tense laughter and deception with a pen or a brush.

So, on closer inspection, we can see that Pacioli's crooked smile splits his face into two contrasting looks like the yin and yang, a contented right side and an unhappy left side. Since Leonardo da Vinci invented the expressive asymmetric smile in portraiture it is more likely that the *Pacioli Portrait* was painted by him and not by Jacopo de' Barbari who was a relatively symmetrical and conservative portraiture painter. There is no evidence that Barbari painted asymmetrical features (mouth, nose, eyes, right and left side of the face) or that he even was aware of facial asymmetry.

A Comparison of Facial Shadows

Leonardo advised on the qualities of light in portrait painting:

'A very high degree of grace in the light and shadow is added to the faces of those who sit in the doorways of rooms that are dark, where the eyes of the observer see the shadowed part of the face obscured by the shadows of the room, and see the lighted part of the face with the greater brilliance which the air gives it. Through this increase in the shadows and the lights, the face is given greater relief.'

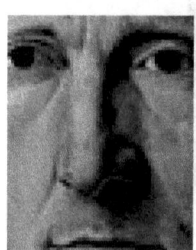 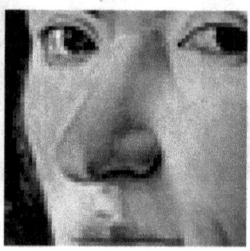 

FIG. 7.8. *Shadows on the nose indicate the direction of the light source somewhere above and to the right of the two figures. More light is on Galeazzo Sanseverino that produces softer shadows than on Luca Pacioli.* Mona Lisa *is added for comparison.*

Perhaps, Luca Pacioli is much darker than Galeazzo Sanseverino because Leonardo is showing the viewer that the younger man is more energetically lit up than the older man. Leonardo writes the following comment on painting [Item 599, Richter]:

'Make your work carry out your purpose and meaning. That is, when you draw a figure consider well who it is and what you wish it to be doing. With regard to any action, which you give in a picture to an old man or to a young one, you must make it more energetic in the young man in proportion as he is stronger than the old one; and in the same way with a young man and an infant.'

The Comparison Between *Luca Pacioli's* and *Mona Lisa's* Face, Warts and All

The angle of *Mona Lisa's* head is positioned midway between that of Luca Pacioli and the young man. *Mona Lisa's* hair and veil are like Luca Pacioli's hood and habit highlighting the oval-shaped face and aquiline nose. *Mona Lisa* has a distinctive wart at the corner of her left eye at the top edge of the bridge of her nose (Fig. 7.8). You can see the warts on Luca Pacioli's forehead above the right eye near the bridge of his nose in Fig. 7.9. These medical and facial blemishes (disfigurements) are unique features in Leonardo's paintings. For example, Leonardo also painted a youthful blemish (pimple) to the lower left of his sitter's lower lip in a painting known as the *La Belle Ferronniere's*. This blemish that was seen in photographed copies of the painting before 2015 seems to have been painted out (airbrushed) from her face in a recent restoration by the restorers at the Louvre in 2015.

During the Renaissance, the Florentine and Milanese nobility, in particular, wanted more realistic representations of themselves. And so, the court painters were challenged to create more convincing portraits than the usual profile and it stimulated experimentation and innovation. Piero della Francesca, Domenico Ghirlandaio, Lorenzo di Credi, Sandro Botticelli and Leonardo da Vinci as well as other artists expanded their technique accordingly, adding three-quarter portraiture to the traditional religious and classical subjects. Leonardo da Vinci and Botticelli were among the first Italian artists to add allegorical symbols to their secular portraits. For instance, *Mona Lisa's* radical portraiture departs from the conventional profiles painted often by the likes of Ambrogio de Predis with the introduction of the three-quarter pose with the head and eyes turned towards the viewer that increases the sense of connection between the sitter and the viewer while her enigmatic smile adds a new dimension not seen elsewhere. The settings of the *Mona Lisa* and *Luca Pacioli* portraits are different as are their props because they have different narratives, but they also have some striking similarities that suggest that Leonardo da Vinci authored both portraits. The similarities between the heads of Luca,

Galeazzo, and *Mona Lisa* are evident also with the heads in Leonardo's other portraits such as the *Lady With the Ermine, La Belle Ferronniere, The Musician, Young Man at 20 Years*, and *Portrait of a Young Man*.

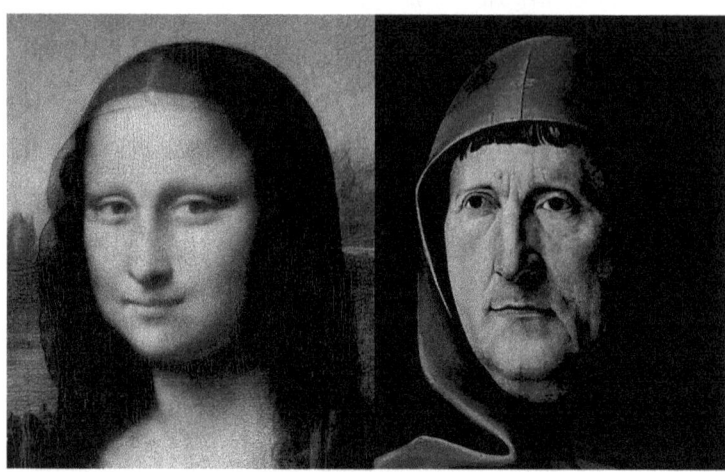

FIG. 7.9. *Luca looks like an older and crustier version of* Mona Lisa. *The contrast is evident, but there is also a haunting similarity.*

There are contrasting differences or *contrapposto* that we can see also in the eyes, mouths and noses of *Mona Lisa* and *Galeazzo Sanseverino* in Fig. 7.10. These and other features display the differences that are set among the similarities that intrigue the viewer's eye and mind.

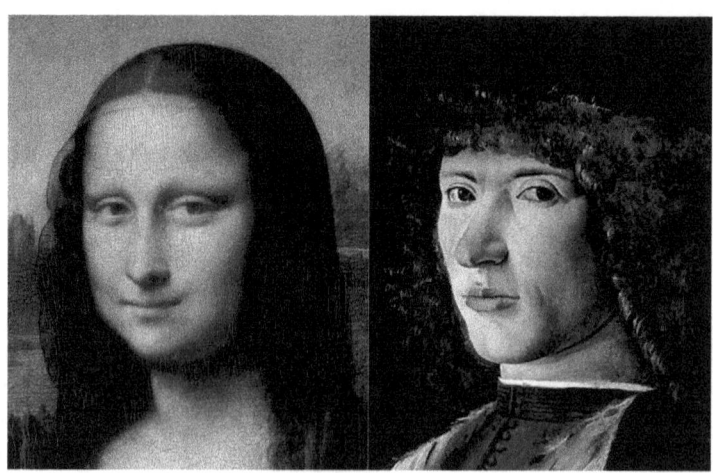

FIG. 7.10. *The contrasting eyes and mouths of Mona Lisa & Galeazzo Sanseverino convey different messages to us.*

References

Azzolini, Monica (2004). Anatomy of a Dispute: Leonardo, Pacioli, and Scientific Entertainment in Renaissance Milan', Early Science and Medicine 9.2:128–135 and notes.

Frederick, Jeffery T (2004). Mastering Voir Dire and Jury Selection, page 46, Second Edition, Published by General Practice, Solo and Small Firm Section, American Bar association, Chicago, Illinois).

Garton, John (2014). Leonardo's early grotesque head. Leonardo da Vinci. Between Art and Science. Eds., Francesca Fiorani and Anna Marazeula Kim (2014). McIntire Department of Art, University of Virginia, Charlottesville, VA, USA. *http://faculty.virginia.edu/Fiorani/NEH-Institute/essays/garton/*

Hope-Hennessy, John (1966). The Portrait in the Renaissance, Bollingen Foundation, New York, pp. 71-72.

Pederson, Jill (2008). The Academia Leonardi Vinci: Visualizing dialectic in Renaissance Milan, 1480–1499. Ph.D. Thesis, The Johns Hopkins University, 2008, 428; 3288613

White, John and Gardner, John (2013). The Classroom X-Factor: The Power of Body Language and Non-verbal Communication in Teaching. Routledge, London and New York, page 119.

8

GEOMETRIC VARIATIONS & GOLDEN RATIOS

Leonardo's Basic and Transformed Geometry

The *Pacioli Portrait* is clearly about arithmetic, geometry and geometric perspective. It is a marvellous celebration and a dedication to the universality of mathematics and the basic geometric shapes that are presented to us in the lecture by Luca Pacioli who stands there with a pointer in hand over a chalk drawing of two right-angled triangles that form an isosceles triangle inscribed in a circle. He is caught frozen at the moment that he is drawing another chord within the circle on his way to creating a circular segment (curved triangle) as part of a pentagon within a circle. Drawing and measuring instruments are scattered across the table and Euclid's book on geometry, *Elements*, is open at the page that shows a similar drawing. Leonardo da Vinci was interested in Euclidian and non-Euclidian geometry, hyperbolic geometry (drawing meridians on a globe), the divine proportion (golden ratio), knot theory, geometric topology and transformations, and especially deformed rectangles, triangles and circles. He called the deformed triangles (circular segments) falcates. Knowing Leonardo's passion for geometry we can see in the *Pacioli Portrait* how he has presented and emphasised points, lines, triangles, squares, rectangles, solids (pyramids and cylinders), polyhedrons (cube, dodecahedron, rhombicuboctahedron, e.t.c.,), circular segments and all kinds of Euclidean and non-Euclidian perspectives. He looked at painting and nature from the perspective of a geometer who believed that nature and the universe were built and evolved from God's laws of geometry.

Leonardo's notebooks are full of geometrical drawings and notes about geometry. He especially delighted in circular segments and the patterns that they made. He filled entire pages with these circular segments in full circles and semi-circles. He also wrote down lessons about geometry starting with the basics of the point, the line, triangle and circle (Figs. 8.1 and 8.2).

The Basic Shapes: Points, Lines, Triangles, Squares and Circles

The *Pacioli Portrait* practically, symbolically and philosophically presents six basic shapes within its design; (1) the point, (2) a straight line like |, curved lines like the C, S and many others, (3) two lines meeting at a point like V, L and T or two straight lines crossing over each other like X and +, (4) the circle and spheres, (5) triangle, and (6) rectangle (or square). These basic shapes are distributed throughout nature and the universe in various forms and are used widely in painting, architecture and design. According to Leonardo all the problems of perspective begin and end with the point:

'The elements of perspective--Of the Point (item 42). All the problems of perspective are made clear by the five terms of mathematicians, which are: - the point, the line, the angle, the superficies and the solid. The point is unique of its kind. And the point has neither height, breadth, length, nor depth, whence it is to be regarded as indivisible and as having no dimensions in space. The line is of three kinds, straight, curved and sinuous and it has neither breadth, height, nor depth. Hence it is indivisible, excepting in its length, and its ends are two points. The angle is the junction of two lines in a point.'

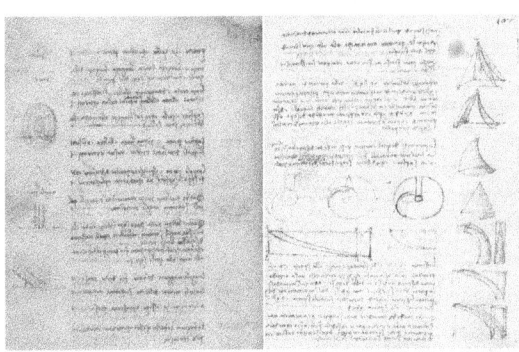

FIG. 8.1. *(A), left, folio from Leonardo da Vinci's Codice Madrid II, F.140v., copy of text and figures in Euclid's Elements. (B), right, folio from Leonardo da Vinci's catalogue of transformations in Codice Madrid II, F.107r (depicted by Fritjof Capra as Fig. 7-6 in* The Science of Leonardo (2008).

The elements of perspective--Of the Point (item 45).
1, the superficies is a limitation of the body. 2, and the limitation of a body is no part of that body. 3, and the limitation of one body is that which begins another. 4, that which is not part of any body is nothing. Nothing is that which fills no space.

If one single point placed in a circle may be the starting point of an infinite number of lines, and the termination of an infinite number of lines, there must be an infinite number of points separable from this point, and these when reunited become one again; whence it follows that the part may be equal to the whole.

The point, being indivisible, occupies no space. That which occupies no space is nothing. The limiting surface of one thing is the beginning of another. 1. That which has no limitations, has no form. 2. That which is no part of any body is called nothing. The limitations of two conterminous bodies are interchangeably the surface of each. All the surfaces of a body are not parts of that body.'

'Of the line (item 47). DEFINITION OF THE NATURE OF THE LINE. *The line has in itself neither matter nor substance and may rather be called an imaginary idea than a real object; and this being its nature it occupies no space. Therefore an infinite number of lines may be conceived of as intersecting each other at a point, which has no dimensions and is only of the thickness (if thickness it may be called) of one single line.'*

'HOW WE MAY CONCLUDE THAT A SUPERFICIES TERMINATES IN A POINT? *An angular surface is reduced to a point where it terminates in an angle. Or, if the sides of that angle are produced in a straight line, then—beyond that angle—another surface is generated, smaller, or equal to, or larger than the first.'*

FIG. 8.2. *Dots, circles, bisecting lines and triangles.*

What is the Point of the Point?

According to Leonardo:

WHAT'S THE POINT? *Therefore the end of nothingness and the beginning of the line are in contact with one another, but they are not joined together, and in such contact is the point, which divides the continuation of nothingness and the line. It follows that the point is less than nothing, and if all the parts of nothingness are equal to one we may the more conclude that all the points also are equal to one single point and one point is equal to all. And from this it follows that many points imagined in continuous contact do not constitute the line, and as a consequence many lines in continuous contact as regards their sides do not make a surface, nor do many surfaces in continuous contact make a body, because among us bodies are not formed of incorporeal things. The point is that which has no centre because it is all centre, and nothing can be less. The contact of the liquid with*

CHAPTER 8

the solid is a surface common to the liquid and to the solid, and the lighter liquids with the heavier have the same. All the points are equal to one and one to all. Write of the nature of time as distinct from its geometry.

OF TIME AS A CONTINUOUS QUANTITY: Although time is numbered among continuous quantities yet through its being invisible and without substance it does not altogether fall under the category of geometrical terms, which are divided in figures and bodies of infinite variety, as may constantly be seen to be the case with things visible and things of substance; but it harmonises with these only as regards its first principles, namely as to the point and the line. The point as viewed in terms of time is to be compared with the instant, and the line resembles the length of a quantity of time. And just as points are the beginning and end of the said line so instants form the end and the beginning of a certain given space of time. And if a line be divisible to infinity it is not impossible for a space of time to be so divided. And if the divided parts of a line may bear a certain proportion of one to another so also may the parts of time.

Five hundred years after Leonardo da Vinci's death in 1519, some physicists and cosmologist still see the universe expansion as many varied points from within a single moving point. This has been described variously as the Standard Model of particle physics depending on the particular theories of quantum and particle physics and whether the universe is taken to be a single-particle universe or a multi-particle universe. Generally, the Standard Model describes twelve fundamental building blocks or fermions that makeup matter and twelve bosons that transmit the four fundamental forces, gravity, electromagnetism, and weak and strong nuclear forces. During the past few decades, however, physicists have developed string theory in an attempt to provide a more complete, unified, and consistent description of the fundamental structure of our universe known as the Theory of Everything. One-dimensional objects called strings replace all of the point-like particles of a multi-particle universe. For example, an electron is not a moving point, but instead it is a tiny loop of a string that can oscillate in different ways. If it oscillates a certain way, then we see the string as an electron. If it oscillates some other way, then we see it as a photon, or a quark, and so on. In this way, the entire world is made of strings. This description of strings reminds me of the intricate entangled knots that Leonardo loved to draw from a single piece of string (Fig. 8.3).

Whether a particle or string-like Universe is the correct description of Nature, neither has yet been proven. Leonardo da Vinci's concept about the point, the line and Nature still resonates favourably as a basic explanation of the fundamentals of the Universe.

Therefore the end of nothingness and the beginning of the line are in contact with one another, but they are not joined together, and in such contact is the point, which divides the continuation of nothingness and the line. It follows that the point is less than nothing, and if all the parts of nothingness are equal to one we may the more conclude that all the points also are equal to one single point and one point is equal to all.'

FIG. 8.3. *One of Leonardo's knotted strings advertising the Leonardo da Vinci Academy.*

Surprisingly, some of Leonardo's expressed ideas about points and *'the end of nothingness and the beginning of the line'* seem to have been developed in recent times into unified field theories by amateur physicists like Nassim Haramein and Bob Bryanton. Many would label Haramein's Unified Field Theory as pseudoscience, and yet it echoes some of Leonardo's concepts about the point, the line and the Universe. Haramein posits that the fractal nature of our reality shows that everything is constructed from points, each point recursively/infinitely embedded within all other points, and therefore all points are connected to form a fractal universe. The YouTube video maker Rob Bryanton has expressed similar views on his blog about the dimensions of the Universe, *Imagining the Tenth Dimension*, saying that the point is something of indeterminate size that is responsible for the existence of ten dimensions. The point has no size, no dimension, it is infinitely large, or infinitesimally small, and therefore, it can grow into a circle (2-D), sphere (3-D) or hypersphere (4-D) between the infinitely large and the infinitely small and move through 10 imagined dimensions. According to Bryanton, zero is the zeroth dimension, or the starting point of indeterminate size that takes us way up to the tenth dimension, a timeless ultimate ensemble of everything. This lowly starting point of indeterminate size at the zeroth dimension is infinitely large and encompasses everything that is within the information that becomes reality. Like zero, a point is without time, without process, a geometric structure rather than a simple mathematic of infinite values.

The prevailing concept of the creation of an expanding universe from a Big Bang singularity (a single point) was developed about sixty-years ago, long after Leonardo da Vinci's time, but he already knew that we live in a moving universe. The current belief that expansion of the universe creates the progression of time and the energy of particles is consistent with Leonardo's view that all existence is in motion. He especially would appreciate the following explanation by Gerard Bassols about the interconnecting points in the universe:

'If we roll back the expanding universe it would collapse into a single point, every point in the current universe would become one single point, the big bang. And from the big bang to now it is opposite, the big bang point has become every point in the current universe, and we cannot single any of them as being "where the big bang happened"'. https://www.quora.com/We-say-the-universe-was-formed-from-a-single-point-what-was-outside-that-point.

Rectilinear Planer Figures and Solid Bodies

There are many continuous and interconnecting points of rectilinear planer figures and solid bodies in the *Pacioli Portrait*. There are lines, straight lines, curves, circles, triangles, squares, and rectangles, as well as cubes, cylinders, pyramids and a dodecahedron. The hanging rhombicuboctahedron alone has 24 points (identical vertices), 48 straight lines (edges), 44 triangles and 18 squares – that is, there are 8 equilateral triangles and 18 square faces consisting of 36 triangles. Johannes Kepler gave this polyhedron its name in 1618 in his book *'Harmonices Mundi'*. The term *rhombi* relates to the bands of squares (*rhombi*) that lie in the face planes of a cube and in between 8 equilateral triangles of the polyhedron. Leonardo 's model of the hanging rhombicuboctahedron in the *Pacioli Portrait* is made up of glass plates half-filled with water and he allowed it to capture the reflections and refractions of light in an examination of image transformation through transparent substances like glass, air and water. The cylindrical shapes in the painting are the black pen case and the student's and Pacioli's arms. The inkwell is shaped like a triangular flask or flat-bottom cone hanging from the cylindrical pen case. The cylinder and triangular shapes (pyramids and cones) are reminders that Leonardo was absorbed in experimental drawings on how to bend rectilinear planar figures and solid bodies as part of his interest in the theoretical and practical problems of topical transformations. These transformations were catalogued in the pages of his notebook known as Codex Madrid II, folio 107r and shown in Fig. 8.1b. These drawings were part of his investigations into curvilinear transformations where he contemplated how to turn the rectilinear planar figures and solid bodies such as cones, flasks, pyramids, and cylinders into curvilinear ones that remain conserved in area or volume. In the painting of the pencil case and the ink well he is pointing out to the viewer that he is interested in topological transformations and shapes that can be arbitrarily stretched, expanded or shrank and yet preserve some general geometric properties (curvilinear shape and continuous linear surface) and colour (black).

Topology and Transformations

In his book *The Science of Leonardo*, Fritjof Capra wrote the following:

'As soon as Leonardo achieved sufficient confidence and facility with transformations of rectilinear figures, he turned to the main topic of his mathematical explorations—the transformations of curvilinear figures. In an interesting "transitional" example, he draws a square with an inscribed circle and then transforms the square into a parallelogram, thereby turning the circle into an ellipse. On the same folio, he transforms the square into a rectangle, which elongates the circle into a different ellipse. Leonardo explains that the relationship of the figura ovale (ellipse) with respect to the parallelogram is the same as that of the circle with respect to the square, and he asserts that the area of an ellipse can easily be obtained if the right equivalent circle is found.'

By extension, Fritjof Capra's comments provide additional insights into the *Pacioli Portrait*. First, let's look at the slate blackboard. A triangle is drawn within the circle contained within a rectangle of the blackboard, but the line drawn through the centre of the circle divides the rectangle into two equal squares just as it divides the circle into semicircles and two equal triangles. Thus, by adding just one line through the centre of the circle Leonardo has transformed three different shapes, the rectangle, the triangle and the circle into six mirrored shapes. This is pure Leonardesque style and trickery. Furthermore, the circle on the blackboard is not what it seems to be – it is an optical illusion created by Leonardo for our eye and brain to transform and reinterpret the actual ellipse to be seen as an imaginary circle. Trace the perimeter with your finger or a pen and you will see that it is not a circle; it is an ellipse. In other words, Leonardo has drawn an ellipse within a rectangle and then transformed the rectangle into a parallelogram outlined by the borders of the slate, turning the ellipse into an illusionary circle.

This illusionary mapping is an alternative to Leonardo's transformation of a circle into an ellipse, in which the points of one curve are mapped onto those of another together with the mapping of all other corresponding points from the square onto the parallelogram. And yet, it is a continuous transformation—a gradual movement, or *'flow, of one figure into the other—which was how Leonardo understood his "geometry done with motion."'*

A parallelogram is a quadrilateral flat shape with parallel opposite sides. Special cases include rectangles (which also have right angles), rhombuses (whose sides are all the same length), and squares (with same-length sides and right angles). In mathematics, an ellipse is a curve in a plane surrounding two focal points such that the sum of the distances to the two focal points is constant for every point on the curve. A circle is a special case of an ellipse, where both foci are at the same point, the centre (Fig. 8.2). The circle can be transformed into a non-circular ellipse by calculating and changing its parameters in the process of orderly topological transformation or deformation (stretching, bending, crumpling). In isometric 3D drawings, the circle is drawn as an ellipse, and it is difficult to calculate and draw the shape of an ellipse especially within a parallelogram. It is even more difficult to then calculate and inscribe an equilateral triangle into the ellipse and give the impression that the equilateral triangle is inscribed in a properly shaped circle. This is further proof that this painting was produced by Leonardo because the equilateral triangle inscribed into the ellipse is one of Leonardo's calculated geometric tricks illustrated in his notebooks that only he could have accomplished easily in his lifetime. Pure mastery by Leonardo that was most probably beyond the capabilities of Barbari and most other painters of the Renaissance to play these geometric games and riddles about transformations.

Now, let us compare the blackboard and slate to the open book that Pacioli's hand is placed on. Like the blackboard, the book is essentially a parallelogram. The blackboard and the open book are essentially the same size and shape (width and length) and technically they can be said to be congruent because they could be transformed into each other by isometry. However, compared to the blackboard, the open book is long and slanty with its long side slanted and angled away from the horizontal. We know that the long side is slanted away from the horizontal because we can see that its orientation is different from the horizontal plane of the table and the blackboard beside it. If it was not slanted away from the vertical and horizontal planes it would be a mirror image of the blackboard. Leonardo has given us a marvellous and subtle lesson in geometric isometry in this painting where he has changed a few parameters in the orderly process of topological transformation. These isometries include the modern techniques of rotation, translation (offset), reflection, glides, tags and identity mapping. Also, each page of the open book is a parallelogram in its own right, but the text on each page divides it approximately into a 'golden rectangle' with the ratio of 0.68 (black border) and 1.0 (text), a ratio that is known as the divine proportion.

According to Fritjof Capra, Leonardo's geometric transformations of planar figures and solid bodies are examples of topological, continuous transformations. There is a one-to-one correspondence between the points of the original figure and the points of the transformed figure, and that the transformation carries nearby points into other nearby points. There are three types of curvilinear transformations that Leonardo uses repeatedly in various combinations; these are transformations by translation, detachment (cutting) and reattachment (repasting), and gradual deformation (Fig. 8.4). In the first type, a given figure with one curvilinear side is translated into a new position in such a way that the two figures overlap. The second type of transformation is creating a curvilinear triangle (*falcate*) by cutting out a segment from a triangle and then reattaching it on the other side. The third type of transformation involves gradual deformations rather than movements of rigid figures by moving divisions into different positions. Leonardo also created an immense variety of geometric forms from intersecting circles, triangles, and squares based upon topological principles. These semicircular shapes were always built on the basis of a circle with an inscribed square resulting either with a rectangle or a triangle inside the semicircle.

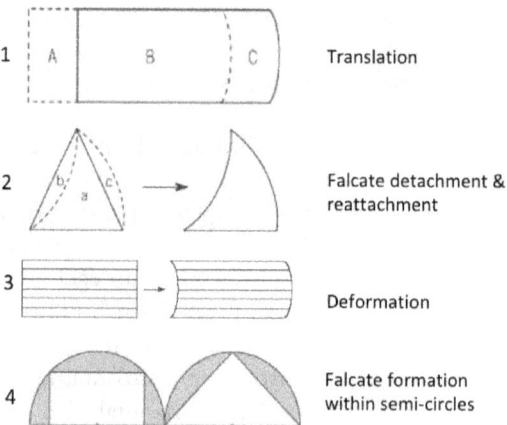

FIG 8.4. *Leonardo's curvilinear transformations as depicted by Fritjof Capra (Figs. A-2, A-3, A-4) in* The Science of Leonardo (2008).

The pages of Leonardo's *Codex Atlanticus* show a great variety of geometric shapes built from intersecting circles, triangles, and squares filled with a great variety of shaded segments that he called *falcates* (curvilinear triangles).

In all of them, the ratio between the shaded areas (also called 'empty') and the white areas (also called 'full') is always the same, because the white areas - no matter how fragmented they maybe - are always equal to the original inscribed half square (rectangle or triangle), and the shaded areas are equal to the original shaded areas outside the half square. The infinite variations of geometric forms in which an area or volume was always conserved were meant to mirror the inexhaustible transmutations in the living forms of nature within limited and unchanging quantities of matter. Some of these transmutations are revisited in chapters 10 to 13.

Hidden Geometric Dimensions and Divine Proportions within the *Pacioli Portrait*

The geometric design and symmetry of the *Pacioli Portrait* is based on basic shapes built from hidden points, curved and straight lines, triangles, squares, rectangles, intersecting circles and a great variety of other shapes and forms. The *Divine Proportion* is the golden ratio, a golden pattern that Luca Pacioli wrote about and that Leonardo da Vinci illustrated in the manuscript for the Duke of Milan in 1498. It is a recurring feature in the *Pacioli Portrait* that is analysed in the following sections.

Euclid provided the first known definition of the divine proportion in his book the *Elements* in 300 BCE: '*A straight line is said to have been cut in extreme and mean ratio when, as the whole line is to the greater segment, so is the greater to the lesser.*' Today Euclid's mean and extreme ratio is also known as the divine section, golden ratio, golden mean, golden number and divine proportion. All of these refer to the act of cutting a line at one uniquely important point that produces the golden ratio. Luca Pacioli and Leonardo da Vinci illustrated the golden ratio on the straight line in the *Divine Proportion* in both their hand-prepared version of 1498 and the printed book version of 1509.

The golden proportion is the number 1.618 (recurring) or Phi for quantities 'a' and 'b' where if a >b>0 then 'a + b' is to 'a' as 'a' is to 'b'. This irrational number is known also as the golden mean. The algebraic expression with fives alone is possible: let Phi equal $0.5 \times 5^{0.5} + 0.5 = 1.6180339$ recurring. The inverse of Phi (1/Phi) = $0.5 \times 5^{0.5} - 0.5 = 0.6180339$. The divine proportion is present in every pentagon and pentagram and in the wooden model of the dodecahedron that stands in clear view on Luca Pacioli's book, the *Summa*, in the *Pacioli Portrait*. A dodecahedron consists of twelve pentagons, and the pentagon connects all the points to form a 5-pointed star with the ratios of the lengths of the resulting line segments that are all based on Phi or 1.618 (Fig. 8.5). It is also represented by the formulae ratio of 1 to $1/2$ ($\sqrt{5} + 1$), which is $1:1/2(2.2360679775+1) = 1:1/2(3.2360679775) = 1:1.61803398875$.

FIG. 8.5. A detail in the Pacioli Portrait *of the dodecahedron structure that consists of 12 pentagons. The author has drawn a 5-pointed star on the face of the pentagon with the line segments that are based on Phi or 1.618 shown as arrows.*

The divine proportion is not the same as the rule of thirds that is a compositional aid used by photographers. The divine proportion creates divisions into 38.2% and 61.8% (or ratios of 0.382 and 0.618) whereas dividing in thirds produces divisions of 33.3% and 66.7%, which results in subtle differences and implications. The basic golden rectangle is in a ratio of 1:1.618, which is about the size of a postcard whether in portrait or landscape mode. However, the rectangular shape of the *Pacioli Portrait* lacks the golden dimension; instead, it is 98 x 108 cm at a ratio of 1:1.102. This is squarer than the golden rectangle of 1:1.618, possibly because somebody had cropped it after it had been painted.

The golden sections of any picture can be found by using the horizontal and vertical lines across a painting and subdividing the divine proportion into rectangles or triangles at points 0, 0.382, 0.612 and 1.0 (Fig. 8.6). The same golden ratios are contained within the golden rectangles of the two faces. The subdivisions of the picture into nine golden rectangles helps to highlight the items in each rectangle and connects the points of interest between each of the sections. For example, highlighting the lower and middle regions brings attention to the items on the table and the arms and hands of the two figures. On the other hand, highlighting the upper region brings greater attention to the rhombicuboctahedron and the two figures, Luca Pacioli and Galeazzo Sanseverino.

CHAPTER 8

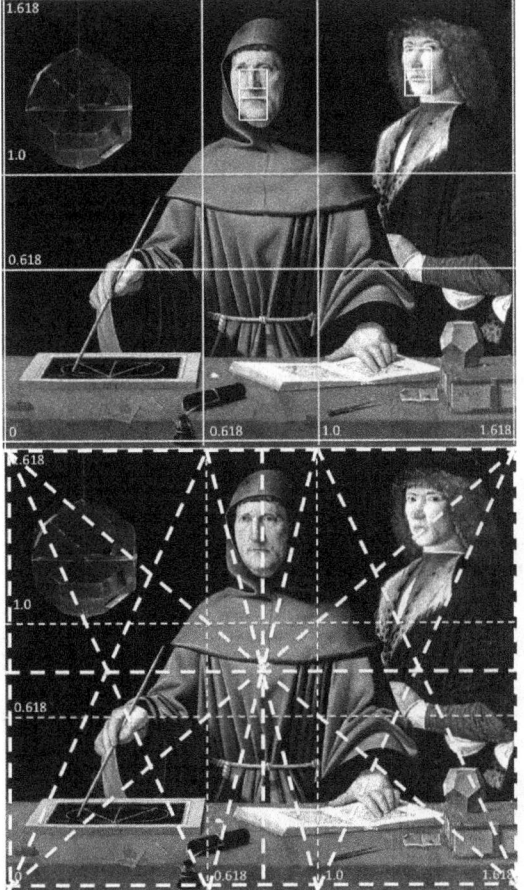

FIG. 8.6. Golden proportions. Top, solid lines divide the Pacioli Portrait *into 9 golden sections, and bottom, the dashed lines divide the portrait into golden and harmonious triangles.*

Based on the analysis of Kevin Frank posted on the Internet (http://lucapaciolipainting.blogspot.com.au/), we can see that the symmetrical composition of the *Pacioli Portrait* was derived in part with the use of the golden rectangle based on the two right-angled triangles that Luca Pacioli has drawn in his portrait. Fig. 8.7 shows two golden rectangles ABCD and BEFC each with a single diagonal BD and BF, respectively, that have been joined to form the equilateral triangle BDF within a larger rectangle AEFD connecting Luca Pacioli and Galeazzo Sanseverino with the rhombicuboctahedron and particular items on the table below them. Luca Pacioli remains the dominant figure within the equilateral triangle and the main rectangle. The bisected triangle is similar to the one on the drawing slate. Pacioli's pointer, the piece of chalk and his forefinger all touch the base of the triangle and the chalk lies exactly on the golden mean of the baseline. Kevin Frank deduced from his geometrical analysis that the top portion of the portrait had been cropped because the rectangle is equidistant to all the sides except the top. When he extended the top by the estimated correct amount and applied the horizontal golden rectangle to the top and sides of the painting he found that the bottom side rested exactly on Pacioli's belt and the top of the dodecahedron. The knot on the left side of Pacioli's waist lies on the golden mean of the line along the belt to the dodecahedron, a structure that also is based on Phi.

The use of golden rectangles in the composition of the painting have infused it with vibrancy and organic energy and when joined together they form the triangle that outline Pacioli's physical shape and his teachings using a blackboard and the book *Elements* by Euclid.

FIG. 8.7. *Compositional pyramid, triangles, circles, rectangles, and golden sectors within* the Pacioli Portrait.

Kevin Frank pointed out the following allegories and additional characteristics of the painting. The student's eyes are at the exact level of Pacioli's third eye (thoughts/teaching) at point B and the top of the suspended polyhedron at point A. Pacioli absorbs the knowledge of his blackboard and the opened book through the rays of light directed into his brain by way of his eyes. The line of the triangle from his right eye to the blackboard bisects the triangle within the circle shown on the drawing slate. In his blog, Kevin Frank suggests that the student in the background is Leonardo da Vinci, although he still attributed the painting to Jacopo de' Barbari.

Following on from Kevin Frank's analysis, I have made a drawing that has retained his equilateral triangle ABC, but replaced his golden rectangle with a circle so that it looks more like the drawing on the chalkboard in the *Pacioli Portrait* (Fig. 8.8, top). However, I complicated the image somewhat by also adding an inverted equilateral triangle DEF to create a hexagram (Fig. 8.8, top). The tips of the hexagram highlight different elements and objects within the painting. One of the tips, at point D, falls outside of the picture. Moreover, I calculated the golden ratio within the circle using the midpoints of the sides of the triangle ABC. So, in this figure, a circle was drawn around the triangle ABC and the golden ratios determined for the line XY. The ratio is golden from LM (0.62) to XL or MY (0.38).

The calculation for Phi using a triangle and a circle was taken from the Internet online page *Cut the Circle: The Geometry of the Golden Ratio*. In the figure, let L and M be the midpoints of the sides AB and AC of a triangle ABC. Let X and Y be the intersections of LM extended with the circumcircle of the triangle ABC. Then LM/MY=ϕ.

If 2a is the side length of the triangle ABC, then AM=MC=LM=a, and XL=MY=b. By the *Intersecting Chords Theorem* MX·MY=AM·MC. This corresponds to (a+b)·b=a·a. Denoting a/b=x, then 1+x=x2, and x=ϕ. Similarly, a golden rectangle can be drawn in the circle and the golden ratio determined for the diameter of the circle as shown in Fig. 8.8, bottom. In this figure, a circle has been drawn around the triangle and the golden ratios determined for the diameter AD. The ratio of BC (0.618) to AB or CD (0.382) is golden.

The eye-centring principle in portraiture painting is that the compositional pyramid rising from the bottom of the frame to a centre of consciousness high on the midline finds its expression in the configuration of many portrait paintings (Fig. 8.7 & 8.8). The analyses by Christopher W. Tyler revealed a dominant positioning principle for one eye in a portrait to lie on the vertical axis with an unbiased accuracy of the order of +/-5%. Analysis of the vertical location showed that the dominant height is at or above the Golden Section level on the vertical axis (Fig. 8.8, bottom). In general, the layout of the portrait follows the principle of the compositional pyramid, with a centre of consciousness at its apex.

In another variation taken from Kevin Frank's triangle within a rectangle, an equilateral triangle can be placed within the circle where the entire circle is drawn inside the borders of the *Pacioli Portrait* as if it were the surface of the chalkboard in the painting (Fig. 8.9). Alternatively, an isosceles triangle can be drawn where the sides of the triangle follow Luca Pacioli's pointer exactly on one side and along the outside of his left arm on the other side to the apex of the dashed triangle. The base of the triangle, which is a chord of a circle, runs along one side of the blackboard and the edge of the table across the apex of the V formed by Luca Pacioli's left thumb and forefinger, and across to the edge of the dodecahedron. In this figure, the sides of the dashed rectangle drawn within the circle include an edge that runs up from the base of the isosceles triangle through the centre of the rhombicuboctahedron to meet the edge across the tip of Luca's nose that contacts the other edge that runs down from the side of Galeazzo's jaw across his arm to the dodecahedron (Fig. 8.9, left).

FIG. 8.8. *Compositional hexagram (top) and triangle and rectangle (bottom) within a circle with golden sectors (0.38, 0.68) within* the **Pacioli Portrait**.

So what is Pacioli transforming or doing by drawing another line within the circle? At one level he is creating a circular segment. Perhaps it is the beginning of a rectangle within a circle. At another level he might be contemplating how to draw a polygon within the circle as a means to calculate the circumference of the circle. Alternatively, his contemplation of the circular segment may have conjured up Nicholas Cusa's revelation that the polygon can never fully coincide with the circle just as our reasoning (science) will never be able to grasp the totality of the Absolute.

Luca is enclosed by a perfect isosceles triangle like Jesus in Leonardo's *Last Supper* (Fig. 8.9). This similarity could not be a simple coincidence, but must have been intentional, filling Leonardo's mind when he painted the *Pacioli Portrait* at about the same time that he was adding the finishing touches to his painting of the *Last Supper* at the Convent of Santa Maria delle Grazie in Milan.

FIG. 8.9. *Luca Pacioli enclosed within a circle and an equilateral triangle (solid lines) and isosceles triangle (dashed lines) compared to Jesus within an isosceles triangle in Leonardo's painting of the* Last Supper.

On returning to the golden ratio, we can find the golden means within the *Pacioli Portrait* using various approaches. One simple way is to draw vertical and horizontal lines through the golden ratios or objects of interest in the painting and see what is connected. Thus, the line AA' and circle 1 in Fig. 8.10 shows the position of the golden mean along that line. The positions of the golden mean are also shown as circles 2 and 3 for the lines BB' and CC', respectively. Also, a straight dotted line can be seen to pass through the centre of the circles to provide a different perspective that are mirror images of the dissecting line passing through circle 1. The knots on Pacioli's belt along the line A to A' symbolise poverty, chastity and obedience and Leonardo has painted them to resemble hangmen knots. This analysis demonstrates the complexity that exists within Leonardo's simple designs using the mathematical and philosophical concepts of the divine proportion and geometry. Could anybody else other than Leonardo da Vinci have produced this painting of Pacioli and Sanseverino. Certainly not de' Barbari; he did not have Leonardo's skill nor was he with Pacioli in Milan at this time. Perhaps Albrecht Durer, who copied Leonardo and took up his lessons on perspective, might have accomplished something similar, although there is no comparable painting by him.

FIG. 8.10. *Measuring golden ratios along horizontal lines A, B and C.*

There are at least eight easily discernible golden lines (A to H) with the divine ratio of 1:1.62 in the *Pacioli Portrait*. These are shown in Fig. 8.11. Line A shows the width of the painting with the golden mean present at two different points along the line, at 'a1' after the inkwell, and in the reverse direction at 'a2' before the head of the compass. Vertical lines drawn through 'a1' and' a2' create a rectangle incorporating Luca Pacioli's waist, chest, shoulders and head. The vertical line at 'a1' passes by the rim of the pen case, the end of the slate board and the edge of the rope around Pacioli's waist. The vertical line at 'a2' edges the tip of Pacioli's left thumb and the other side of the rope around Pacioli's waist. Line B shows the different points where the golden means are distributed on the line between the sponge and the notepaper. Line C shows the golden ratio across Luca's book and the position of the golden mean near the vertical clasp. Line D connects the bisected circle on the chalkboard at the end of the pointer with the book by Euclid opened at a page describing the theorem how to bisect the circle with an equilateral triangle. The golden mean highlights the chalk on the table and the string tied around the cylindrical pen case. Line E connects Pacioli's knotted waistband with the dodecahedron placed on Luca Pacioli's book of arithmetic, called the *Summa*. Golden lines F, G and H show that Luca Pacioli is connected with

Galeazzo Sanseverino and the rhombicuboctahedron at different levels and with different ratios. These are but a few examples of how Leonardo used mathematics and the divine proportion to interconnect objects and people in various ways to give them added intrinsic meaning.

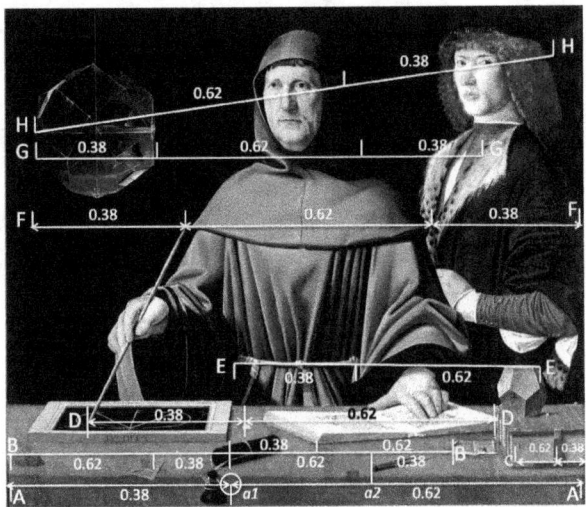

FIG. 8.11. *Eight easily discernable golden lines (A to H) and golden means between 0.38 and 0.62 on the lines between selected anchor points in the* Pacioli Portrait.

The golden spirals depicting Leonardo da Vinci and Luca Pacioli's lessons on the *Divine Proportion* are shown in Fig. 8.12. The spiral in Fig. 8.12 (left) is a little distorted and not exactly in the shape of the classical golden spiral that have been elucidated in many of Leonardo's other paintings, but I was impressed by its lovely flow starting above the wrist of Luca Pacioli's fingers and curving its way through the centre of the book of *Euclidian Elements* around the projector, past the cartouche and fly, through Pacioli's book on mathematics, onward through the student's arm and face peaking at the top of the vertical line and the passing back down over Pacioli's head, through Leonardo's rhombicuboctahedron and down to the eraser (sponge) next to the drawing slate labelled with Euclid's name. The spiral starting from the top of Pacioli's left hand and finishing below the sponge completely envelopes Luca Pacioli in all his contemplative and spiritual glory. Rays of golden lines can also be projected between the opposing corners of the rectangles to visualise the connections between various objects in the painting and the proportion of differentiation between them. The vertical line of the golden rectangles passes through the left hanging knot of Luca's belt past his left thumb and down to the projector pointing towards the yellow notepaper. The template of the golden spiral can be moved about and drawn from various regions of the painting. Fig. 8.12 (right) shows the mirror image of the pattern of the golden spiral if drawn from below Luca Pacioli's right palm.

FIG. 8.12. Mirror images of a distorted golden spiral and rays overlaid on the Luca Pacioli portrait, *using Matic Jurglic's online Golden Ratio Generator.*

Apart from the harmonious golden triangles, golden sections, and golden proportions, the painting is highly symmetrical because it is composed of a multitude of squares (Fig. 8.13). This gives the painting its solidity and stability, despite the rhombicuboctahedron creating a slight misbalance or tension while hanging in its own space at about the same level as the heads of Luca Pacioli and Galeazzo Sanseverino. The basic geometric perspective can be divided into squares (or rectangles) to highlight various elements within the painting. The square is at the basic core of the divine proportion and the golden rectangle. In the portrait, we can see that many squares can be used as the contents of a matrix within the rectangular shape of the painting (Fig. 8.13). The squares numbered one to four make up the larger square that contains the hanging rhombicuboctahedron. The squares 5 to 18 in the painting were drawn based on the midpoint of the line labelled m, which is the shorter portion (as b=0.382) of the line A' to A" with unit length of one and a golden ratio. Squares 19 and 20 are shown at a slightly different size to the others, where the distorted square 19 has the bloodied red arm and green glove and rectangle 20 contains the dodecahedron and Pacioli's book the *Summa* that displays the golden rectangle (A+B) along the side with the author's name. Placing squares within a matrix is essentially like designing and examining shapes using graph paper or straight lines drawn vertically and horizontally to make up a regular grid. It is the most basic of forms to examine perspective space within a painting and drawing. As Rosalind Krauss has said of Renaissance painters in general, they drew '*perspective lattice on the depicted world as the armature of its organisation.*' My perspective lattice with its array of large squares highlights

Pacioli's face (square 9) and the student's face (square 17) for comparison and contrast, and it shows the harmony provided by the other parts of Pacioli's figure (squares 6, 11, 12, 13, 14) that shape the overall balance of the picture. Seeing how certain squares fit together and connect with the different elements and themes reveals the basic composition and structure of the picture.

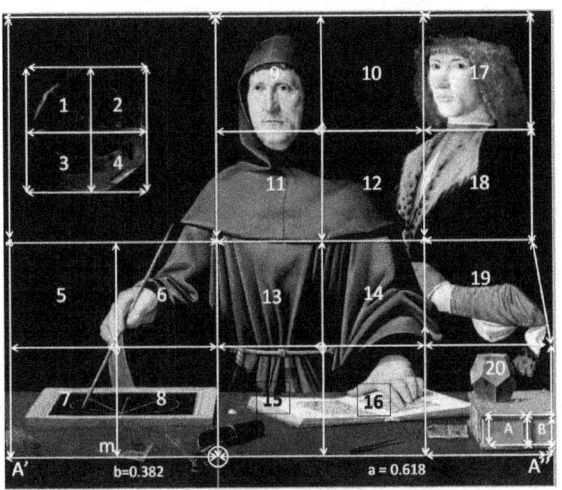

FIG. 8.13. *The rectangular and square structure of the* Pacioli Portrait *that provides the painting its strength and stability.*

FIG. 8.14. *Luca Pacioli and Galeazzo Sanseverino outlined in square, rectangular and triangular shapes.*

Whereas the *Pacioli Portrait* is almost a square in its compositional structure, Luca Pacioli and Galeazzo Sanseverino are shaped differently. Fig. 8.14 shows that Pacioli was drawn more as a Rectangular Man with a few upper and lower internal triangles, while Galeazzo Sanseverino is much more of a Triangular Man with fewer rectangles. Pacioli also is shaped more like a rhombicuboctahedron than Sanseverino. And on the table, there are many V for Vinci. The painting provides the interested viewer with numerous geometric and topological shapes to identify and play with.

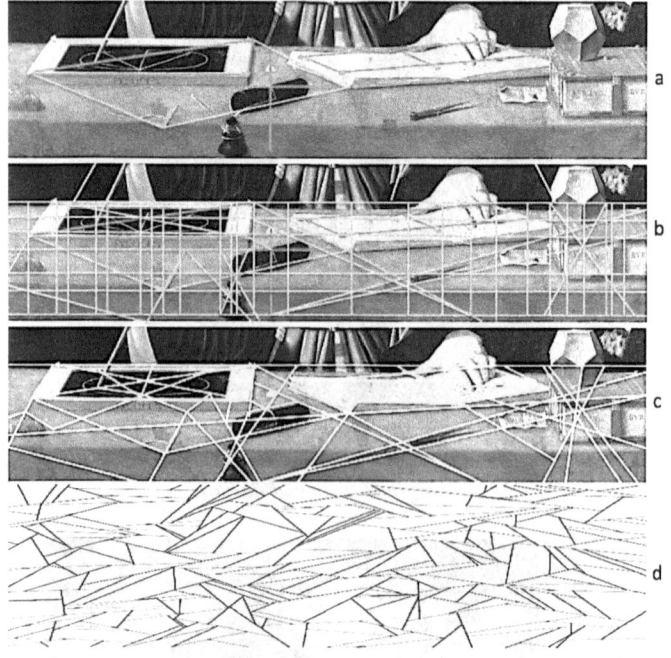

FIG. 8.15. *Orthogonal, rectangular and triangular perspective shapes on the Luca Pacioli display table (a to c). Drawing of Gilbert tessellation, bottom panel (d).*

We discern that the intrinsic geometry of the *Pacioli Portrait* is embedded with harmonious golden triangles, golden sections, and golden proportions, squares within squares, triangles within triangles, circles, rectangles, polyhedrons and various strange shapes interwoven in the clothing. Points and straight lines or curved lines are the basis of the triangles, squares and other shapes. This is one of the main lessons of this painting. There are also irregular cracks and patterns on the display table, just like those that develop on the ice or mud (Fig. 8.15). The items and books on the display table look normal and simple in their distribution as the objects that they represent. The different utensils required for geometric measurements and drawing are cleverly distributed across the table in a linear, but angled perspective to provide a mysterious narrative and attract attention to each item in a way that the eye might scan from one neighbouring object to the other, backwards and forwards and then on to next set of neighbouring items. However, the perspective underneath the orderly array of the items and books on the table is a complex, chaotic pattern resembling what is known today as Gilbert tessellation. The hidden dimension here is the random crack dimension composed of irregular patterns of triangles, rectangles, parallelograms, and pentagrams.

The table and its objects make up such a complexity of regular and irregular tiling of triangles, squares and rectangles that it becomes a chaotic geometric pattern that requires a professional topologist to sort out (Fig. 8.15). For the amateur, the pattern on the table might resemble a Gilbert tessellation or random crack network that is a mathematical model for the formation of mud-cracks, needle-like crystals, and similar structures. This network of cracks is named after Edgar Gilbert, who studied this model in 1967 and found that the cracks begin to develop at a set of points randomly spread throughout the plane according to a Poisson distribution. Then, each crack spreads in two opposite directions along a line through the initiation point, with the slope of the line chosen uniformly at random. The cracks continue spreading at uniform speed until they reach another crack, at which point they stop, forming a T-junction. The result is a tessellation of the plane by irregular convex polygons. A variant of the model that also has been studied restricts the orientations of the cracks to be axis-parallel, resulting in a random tessellation of the plane by rectangles. In comparison to alternative models in which cracks may cross each other or in which cracks are formed one at a time rather than simultaneously, the mud crack patterns in nature topologically resemble the Gilbert model ((Fig. 8.15d). Once again Leonardo was well ahead of his time with his designed abstraction. Within these complex patterns, Leonardo would have seen and discerned the regular and irregular shapes and perspectives for the objects that he laid on the display table.

Creating Pictorial Space with the Golden Ratio and Rectangle

Leonardo was not the only artist to use perspective and the divine proportions in his paintings during his time. He may have acquired some of this knowledge from his friend Sandro Botticelli who had used the divine perspective in a number of his paintings including the *'The Birth of Venice'* (1482 to 1485) and the *'Annunciation.'*

The dimensions of the canvas (172.5 cm x 278.5 cm) of the *'The Birth of Venus'* are close to the golden ratio (width to height) of 1.618 and there are other golden ratios within the composition as discussed by Gary Meisner in his online blog about the Golden Number. For example, the lower horizontal line is the golden ratio at the top of the seashell, whereas the upper horizontal line is the golden ratio directly through Venus's navel and where the land on the horizon meets the sea. Also, the vertical lines on the left side and the right side centralise Venus, and the right-sided vertical line crosses the painting exactly at the point of the golden ratio where Hora's right thumb and finger are touching, as though she is grasping the Golden Ratio proportion and reaching for something Divine. The gold ratio proportions even apply to Venus herself with the golden ratio crossing at her navel between her head and feet.

FIG. 8.16. *The golden ratio lines applied to Sandro Botticelli's painting of* The Birth of Venus *based on the analysis of Gary Meisner (2014) at https://www.goldennumber.net/botticelli-birth-venus-golden-ratio-art/*.

Although Michelangelo was younger than his rival Leonardo da Vinci by 23 years, he also used the golden ratio in his art and design. We see this on the ceiling of the Sistine Chapel in his *'The creation of Adam'* where the fingers of God and Adam touch. Michelangelo painted on the ceiling of the Sistine Chapel between the years of 1508 and 1512 and Gary Meisner has written extensively about his analysis of the extensive use of the golden ratio by Michelangelo in the Sistine Chapel.

However, long before Botticelli and Michelangelo, Leonardo had already used the golden ratio perspective in his first painting, the *Annunciation* of 1472, when he was 20 years of age and then later on in a number of his iconic finished and unfinished paintings including *Ginevra de' Benci* (1474), *St. Jerome* (1482), *Last Supper* (1497), *Salvator Mundi* (1500), and

Mona Lisa (1497 to 1504). So Botticelli and Michelangelo probably adopted the technique of using the perspective of the golden ratio in painting from Leonardo who was advocating and teaching golden ratio perspective in his lessons to his pupils.

Looking at Leonardo's *Annunciation* (Fig. 8.17), his first known painting, I am guided by Gary Meisner's 2014 article on the Internet entitled '*Home / Design/ Art / Da Vinci and the Divine Proportion in Art Composition*'.

FIG. 8.17. *The golden rectangles and golden spirals applied to Leonardo's painting of the* Annunciation *at different anchor points, the mountain and the Virgin's face (top), and the angel's and Virgin's face (bottom); using Matic Jurglic's online Golden Ratio Generator.*

Gary Meisner showed the following divine proportions within the *Annunciation* that are not necessarily depicted or recreated in Fig. 8.17:

    1. Alignment of vertical walls and courtyard entry separating the angel from the Virgin Mary.

    2. The alignment of the vertical lines of the left side with the mountain peak and the positioning of the angel wing and face with the trees.

    3. The positioning of the horizontal line relative to the angel's fingers of his right hand and the Virgin Mary's breasts and lower palm of her left hand.

4. The positioning of the lower horizontal line relative to the angel's left arm and knee with the top of the bench and the Virgin Mary's knees.

5. The width of the table ornaments has the golden mean.

6. The mountain peaks at the top of the canvas are in golden ratio proportion.

Gary Meisner performed a similar analysis for the golden means in *The Last Supper* and *Mona Lisa* and I refer the interested reader to his web pages to see the clear evidence of the repeated use of the Phi proportion by Leonardo da Vinci.

References

Atalay, Bulent (2014). Math and the Mona Lisa: the art and science of Leonardo da Vinci. Smithsonian Books, Washington.

Bogomolny, Alexander (1996). Golden Ratio in Geometry. *https://www.cut-the-knot.org/do_you_know/GoldenRatio.shtml*

Bryanton, Robert (2010). Imagining the Tenth Dimension. *http://imaginingthetenthdimension.blogspot.com/2010/05/our-universe-as-point.html*.

Capra F (2008). The Science of Leonardo: Inside the Mind of the Great Genius of the Renaissance. Anchor Books Edition, New York. *https://erenow.com/biographies/the-science-of-leonardo-inside-the-mind-of-the-great-genius-of-the-renaissance/*

Golden Ratio Calculator at *https://www.omnicalculator.com/math/golden-ratio#golden-rectangle*.

Jurglic, Matic. Golden Ratio Generator: *http://golden-ratio.club*.

Krauss, Rosalind (1985). The Originality of the Avant-Garde and Other Modernist Myths, Cambridge, Mass. and London.

Meisner, Gary (2014). Home / Design/Art / Da Vinci and the Divine Proportion in Art Composition. *https://www.goldennumber.net/art-composition-design/*

Meisner, Gary (2018). The golden ratio. The divine beauty of mathematics. Race Point Publishing.

Onstott, Scott (2015). Secrets in Plain Sight. Leonardo da Vinci. SIPS Productions Inc. Middletown, DE., USA. *http://www.secretsinplainsight.com*

Pepper S (2001). Leonardo da Vinci and the Perspective of Light. Fidelio 10 (1):33-53.

Tyler CW (2007). Some principles of spatial organisation in art. Spatial Vision 20:509-530.

9

EUCLID'S TABLE: DRAWING TOOLS, NUMBERS, PROPORTIONS & POLYHEDRONS

Drawing Instruments, a Black Fly and Three Books on Mathematics

Metaphorically, the portrait of Luca Pacioli shows him to be like Christ in Leonardo's painting of the *Last Supper*. Instead of the 12 apostles at the table as in the *Last Supper*, 12 distinct inanimate items accompany Luca Pacioli at his table (Fig. 9.1). Like Jesus, Luca Pacioli is the central figure in the painting. He stands upright behind the table, his left hand on the open pages of a book and the pointer held in his opened right hand. The 12 inanimate items on the table are the sponge, slate, acute angle protractor, inkwell, pen, pen-case, chalk, Euclid's open book, compass, folded paper or notebook with black fly, Pacioli's closed book, and a dodecahedron on top of it. If we look carefully, we notice that there are only 10 inanimate items lying directly on the surface of the table, the inkwell hangs off the string attached to the pen-case and the dodecahedron lies on the closed book. Also, only 6 of the 12 inanimate items are for drawing and measuring, the other items seem to be necessary for the study of mathematics and geometry. The folded paper, fly and dodecahedron are obscure references to Luca Pacioli's time in Milan and his construction of the three hand-written manuscripts entitled the *Divine Proportion* that were commissioned for Galeazzo Sanseverino and his father-in-law, the Duke of Milan, Ludovico il Moro Sforza. In regard to the six drawing instruments, the sponge is to remove the chalk drawings from the blackboard, the chalk is to draw on the blackboard, the acute angle protractor is to draw lines, angles, triangles, squares and so on, the quill pen and ink are to draw or take notes on paper or print coded messages on the yellow notepaper, and the compass is to take measurements and draw the circumference of a circle. The two books provide the information about the theorems and how to draw basic geometric shapes and design solid polyhedrons.

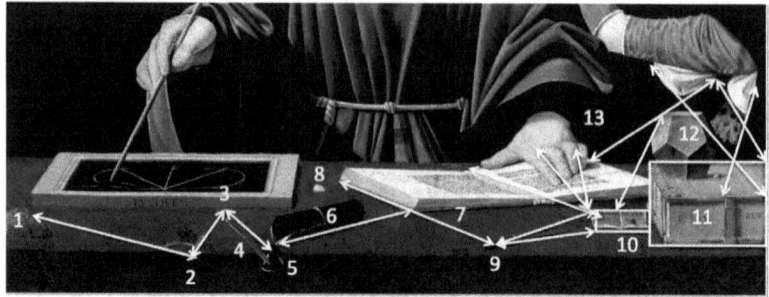

FIG. 9.1. *The 12 inanimate items on Luca Pacioli's table starting from the sponge (1) and ending with dodecahedron (12); and Luca's four fingers and a thumb (13) resting on the open book of Euclid's geometry (7). Detail of the* Pacioli Portrait.

The different utensils required for geometric measurements and drawing are cleverly distributed across the table in a linear, but angled perspective to provide a mysterious narrative and attract attention to each item in a way that the eye might scan from one neighbouring object to the other, backwards and forwards and then on to next set of neighbouring items (Fig. 9.1). Although one may start to scan from anywhere on the table and possibly at the open book (7) or the drawing slate (3) near the tip of the pointer, I have numbered the items of interest in relative order from numbers 1 to 13 starting with the eraser or moist sponge (1), protractor (2), slate (3), the pen (4) in the inkwell (5), along the pen holder (6) to the open book (7) and along the side of the book to the chalk (8), back down to the measuring compass (9) and along its two arms that are slightly spread out pointing directly to the cartouche with the cryptic message and black fly (10) next to Pacioli's bound book the *Summa de Arithmetica* boxed in red leather (11) on which sits a solid dodecahedron (12) displaying its pentagonic structure and subtly pointing us back to Pacioli's four fingers (13) that direct us back to the cartouche with the cryptic message and black fly (10). This linear display of drawing and measuring instruments across the table ending in a looped repeating message is such an amazingly simple compositional organisation that it has held me spell-bound in meditative circular contemplation for hours on end. After much pondering over the mysteries of the items on the green table, I am grateful to Carla Glori for decrypting the incredibly powerful message sent to us from long ago that is contained in the cartouche or notebook labelled by Leonardo da Vinci as IACO.B AR. VIGEN NIS. P. 1495 (or 1496) (see Chapter 20 for details).

The sponge (item 1 in Fig. 9.1), other than simply wiping off chalk writing or drawing, possibly represents other things as well. In one way, its shape, colour and look contrasts with the bread rolls on the table in Leonardo's painting of the *Last Supper*, and in this context it conjures up images of the wet sponge at the end of a spear that was offered up to Jesus on the cross by a Roman soldier.

Leonardo's Acute Angle Protractor, White Chalk and the Cylindrical Pen Holder

The V of the protractor at the edge of the table is an obvious clue that Leonardo da Vinci produced the *Portrait*. He stands in front of the painting as a V for Vinci (Fig. 9.2) and not a B for Barbari. The V's are everywhere, seen as items 2 to 5, 9 and 13 in Fig. 9.1. Leonardo's notebooks also are scattered with drawings of similar shaped compasses and drawing instruments (Fig. 9.3).

Leonardo's bronze protractor in the foreground of the painting directly beneath the chalkboard (item 2 in Fig. 9.1) might have been an intentional addition as his signature. If you look closely you can see that it has the shape of his initials, the L for Leonardo, the d for da and the V for Vinci – LdV – Leonardo da Vinci (Fig. 9.2). Interestingly, it is also the main symbol or emblem of the Freemasons. Although we should not accuse Leonardo of being a freemason – he often exhibited the thoughts and characteristics of a freemason or freemasonry. Freemasonry describes itself as a system of morality, veiled in allegory and illustrated by symbols. The symbolism is mainly, but not exclusively, drawn from the manual tools of stonemasons – the square and compass, the level and plumb rule, the trowel and hammer. A moral lesson is attached to each of these tools, although the assignment is by no means consistent. The meaning of the symbolism is taught and explored through ritual. One entire sheet in Leonardo's notebooks is devoted to these drawing instruments, some designed like an A with an O on top (Fig. 9.3).

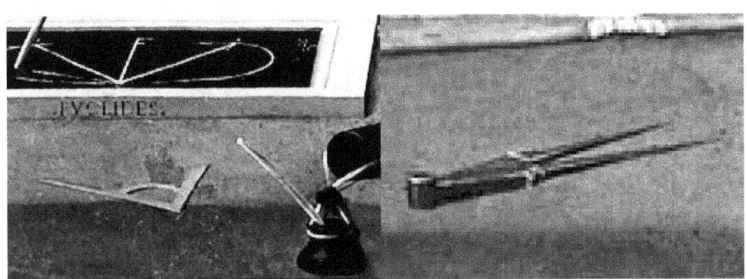

FIG. 9.2. The symbolic V for Vinci with the bronze protractor, the triangles on the blackboard (left), and the compass on the table (right).

The white chalk marker sparkles like a pyramidal shaped pearl on the table (item 8 in Fig. 9.1); and it is there for arithmetic and constructing the circles and triangles on the *'Euclides'* blackboard (item 3 in Fig. 9.1). Leonardo also used charcoal and brown chalk for a number of his drawings; the so-called self-portrait of himself as an old man was drawn with brown-chalk.

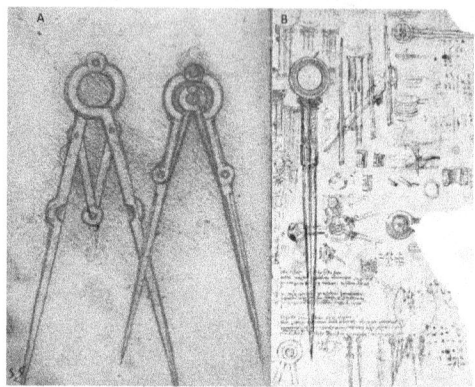

FIG. 9.3. Leonardo's drawings of compasses and measuring instruments with the A and the O on top. Madrid Codex.

The penholder (item 3) to which the inkwell (item 5) is attached (Fig. 9.1) is shaped like a cylinder or round column (Fig. 9.4). The inkwell is shaped like a truncated cone, its top representing a removable dome. I point this out because Luca Pacioli has given a whole lesson about the shape, design and measurement of cylindrical shaped columns and cones in his manuscript of the *Divine Proportion* for Galeazzo Sanseverino and Ludovico Sforza, the Duke of Milan. He provided figures of cylinders (circular columns in his Figs. 16 and 26) and cones (*corta rotunda* in his Fig. 32A) to make his points clearer for his audience (Fig. 9.4).

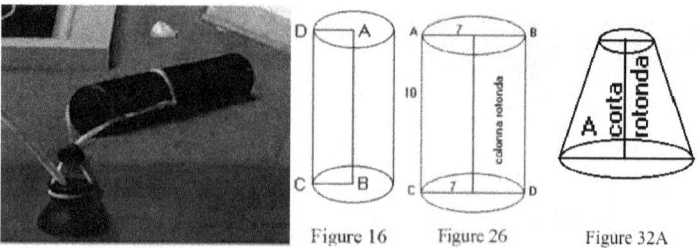

FIG. 9.4. Leonardo's painting of the cylindrical pen-case and the conical inkwell in the Pacioli Portrait *compared to Luca's drawings of cylinders and conical inkwells in the 1498 edition of the* Divine Proportion *(in English, Tennenbaum translation).*

CHAPTER 9

Here is a part of Pacioli's lesson on the round columns in *Chapter LVIII* under the subheading of *'On the oblong solids, that is, longer or higher than wide'*:

The columns are of two constructions, that is round and lateral. Just as with plane figures, some are curvilinear, and are those that are contained by curved or bent lines, and others are called rectilinear, and are those that are contained between two straight lines. The round column [see Plate XLII] is a solid contained between two equal circular bases, which are equidistant between them. The which is defined by our philosopher, in the [21st definition of the] XIth, as follows, that is: the round corporeal figure of which the bases are two plane circles at the extremities and equal in crassitudine, that is height (or thickness), made by the tracing of the rectangular parallelogram, with the side which contains the right angle being fixed, and the said surface rotated until it returns to its original place. And this figure is called the round column. Whence, of the round column, the sphere and the circle, there is one same centre.'

Pacioli then goes on to provide examples of measurements and geometric constructions including his *Figure 16* shown in Fig. 9.4. He then follows this up with a few chapters about lateral, quadrilateral and pentagonal columns before he gets to his *Figure 26* in *Chapter LXII* under the subheading of *'On the method of measuring all kinds of columns, and first the round ones'*, and he writes:

'For example, to better understand it, let the round column be ABCD, whose height AC or BD is 10, and the diameters of each one of the bases - the one AB and the other CD - is 7 [see Figure 26]. I say that to square this 70 and every other one similarly, you take one of the said diameters, whichever it may be, AB or CD, which makes no difference, they being equal, that is, 7; and this 7 must be multiplied by itself. That will make 49, and of this I say one takes 11/14ths, which is 38 1/2. And this I say is multiplied by the height or length, of the entire column, that is, by BD or AC, which we put at 10. That will make 385, and this much we will say to be the capacity or volume of that entire column. And this case, excellent Duke, means that if these numbers represent Braccia of whatever sort one wishes, in that measure there will be 385 small square cubes, that is, like dice of one braccio each way, that is, one braccio in length, one braccio in width and one braccio in height, as the figure here shows [see Fig...].'

He treats Leonardo's inkwell shape as a truncated cone in his *Fig. 32A* in *Chapter LXV*, *'On the lateral pyramids and their diversity'* and says in part:

'There are some others [lateral pyramids] called short or truncated, and they are those which do not arrive at a point to a cone, but lack the peak, and are called truncated or cut. And there are as many of these as there are their respective whole ones, and likewise in name, whether round or lateral, as appears here in outline (Fig.), the round truncated A, the short triangular B, the cut quadrangular C. And this seems to me to be sufficient for their knowledge. And next at hand, we will speak of their elegant measurement.'

Leonardo has shown the round truncated cone as *Fig. 32A* in the *Divine Proportion* and as an inkwell in his *Pacioli Portrait* (Fig. 9.4). And yet, it must be repeated and remembered here that Leonardo also provided drawings and paintings of these three-dimensional shapes of cylinders and cones as well as 57 other shapes of solids as separate plates that accompanied the manuscript of the *Divine Proportion*. We see these as his *Plate XLII* (*Columna Rotunda Solida*) and *Plate L* (*Pyramis Rotunda Solida*) of the 59 that were drawn for the 1498 first edition of *De Divina Proportione* and the woodcut prints *LVII* and *LVIII* of his additional illustrations for the printed edition of 1509 (Fig. 9.5). Leonardo's inkwell is a truncated version of his cone in *Plate L* first edition and *Plate LVIII* of the printed edition.

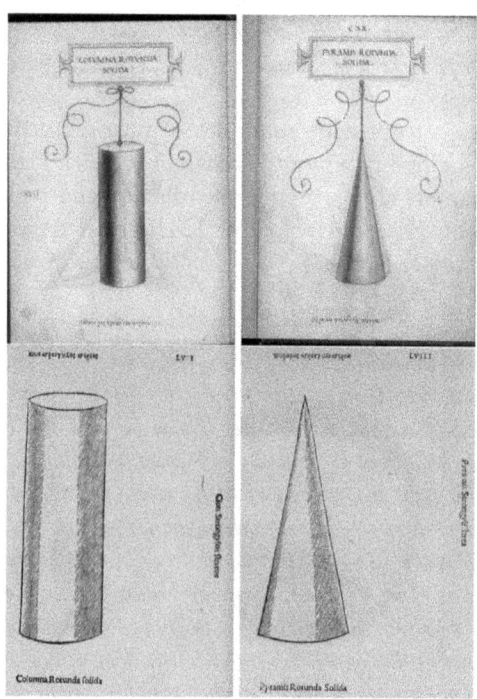

FIG. 9.5. *Leonardo da Vinci's drawings of the cylinder and the cone for Luca Pacioli's* Divine Proportion *for the 1498 edition (top) and 1509 print edition (bottom)*.

Only Leonardo had the knowledge and technical expertise to paint the different polygonal solids in the *Pacioli Portrait*. It seems absurd to think that Jacopo de' Barbari had the same knowledge and the technical drawing experience to be able to add the perfectly drawn prisms, cone, cylinder, cube, pyramid, dodecahedron and the rhombicuboctahedron to the *Pacioli Portrait* disguised as items such as the triangular prism sponge, rectangular pyramidal chalk, cylindrical penholder, truncated round pyramidal inkwell, windows reflected onto the rhombicuboctahedron, quadrangular or rectangular books and blackboard, variously shaped body parts and the dodecahedron on Pacioli's book shaped like a rectangular prism (Fig. 1.1).

Interestingly, the cord around the penholder in the *Portrait* looks like it is dividing the cylindrical penholder at a position corresponding to a third of its length or possibly at the golden section (Fig. 9.4).

Three Books of Mathematical and Historical Knowledge

There are three books on the green table of the *Pacioli Portrait*; Euclid's *Elements*, Pacioli's *Summa*, and Leonardo's miniature notebook with the cryptic message '*IACO.BAR.VIGEN / NIS P. 1495*', a message that is barely visible in the painting. Euclid's book is open on a page with a geometric proposition about a triangle in a circle, while Pacioli's book, the *Summa*, is closed. Between the two books is Leonardo da Vinci small yellow notebook that contains secrets and the skeleton key to decipher the hidden messages about a privileged and tyrannical ruler of the Duchy of Milan. This yellow notebook is Leonardo's self-deprecating joke, about himself and his secret notebooks, the notebooks written in code that were easy to decode if you knew how or where to look (mirror writing). Despite tens of thousands of pages of written notes in his Codices and notebooks, there is surprisingly little personal information about himself, his friends and acquaintances. For some reason, he chose not to use his notebooks as diaries or reminders to himself about his day-to-day emotions, feelings, disappointments or joys. Instead, they were his working notes, thoughts, drawings, ideas and plans that occupied his intellectual rather than his personal and emotional mind about human relationships. Although Euclid's *Elements* and Pacioli's *Summa* have been analysed and written about in detail by a large number of different authors in academic and non-academic journals, only one person, Carla Glori, has tackled, deciphered and written about the third book, Leonardo's cryptic miniature notebook, that is, the cartouche with the fly sitting on top of it; and this is the main subject of Chapter 20.

The Franciscan friar Luca Pacioli is illustrating the 8th proposition of the 13th book of the *Elements* of Euclid. The index finger of his left hand points to the Euclidean text while his right hand draws on the blackboard; a triangle is inscribed in the circle and this is related to the theorem that he is concentrating on in the book. Beside him on the table, there is a weighty volume of the *Summa de arithmetica, geometry, proportioni et proportionality,* a mathematical textbook that Luca Pacioli had authored; the first edition was printed in Venice in 1494. On top of Luca Pacioli's book is a model of a regular wooden dodecahedron. The book that Luca Pacioli is pointing to with his left hand is the first edition of Euclid's *Elementa in artem geometriae et*

Campani commentations, simply known as *Euclid's Elements* and first published in Latin in Venice by Erhard Ratdolt twelve years earlier in 1482. It is believed to be the first book with a known date of publication to contain printed diagrams, hundreds of which were used to illustrate Euclid's theorems. Adelardus Bathoniensis translated it from Arabic into Latin sometime between 1116 and 1142, and then in 1296, Campanus Novariensis added revisions and commentary to the translated manuscript.

Missing from the *Pacioli Portrait* is an image of the *Divina Proportione*, the third book or manuscript that Luca Pacioli prepared and presented to his two Milanese patrons, Galeazzo Sanseverino and Ludovico Sforza, the Duke of Milan in 1498. The first printed edition of *Divina Proportione* was published in Venice in 1509. Leonardo da Vinci provided 60 drawings for each of the three manuscript copies and the printed published version. The fact that the printed version of the *Divina Proportione* is absent from the painting suggests that the *Pacioli Portrait* was finished before 1509. The central idea that recurs with a certain insistence in the painting and both in the *Summa* and in the *Divina Proportione* is the centrality of the Euclidean theory of the proportions in mathematical knowledge as well as in the arts and sciences. This idea is the core of the mathematical program of the arts and sciences undertaken by Friar Luca in his tireless work of teaching and disseminating mathematical culture among his contemporaries, *litterati* and *practical vulgaris*, and it is the meeting ground between the holy mathematician of Sansepolcro and the Florentine painter and scientist, Leonardo da Vinci. For both Luca and Leonardo, the mathematics contained within the *Summa* (1494) and *Divina Proportione* (1498) was a reflection of the Creator, and Nature's instruments used to shape the universe and order it in numbers, *pondere et mensura*. They both believed that mathematics was the universal language of the sciences and the arts extrapolated from God's wisdom to be discovered and expanded by man in a never-ending contemplation of reason and logic. The mathematical process of knowledge that Luca Pacioli presented to his audience was linked to his metaphysical assumptions and beliefs, and the glory to God was foremost in his mind when he dedicated his two major works to different heads of state, one to the Duke of Urbino (1494) and the other to the Duke of Milan (1498). Because the Duke of Milan was captured by the French and imprisoned in 1500 in France where he died in Loches in 1508, the first printed edition of the *Divina proportione,* published in 1509, was instead dedicated to Piero Soderini, the perpetual *gonfaloniere* of Florence. Luca Pacioli seemed forever to be the opportunist with his dedications.

Mathematics was presented by Luca Pacioli as the foundation of the sciences and the arts and was therefore applied to all fields of knowledge: to astronomy, to music, to commercial practice, to medicine, to sculpture, to civil and military architecture, to the art of war, the *perspectiva artificialis* and painting, medicine, jurisprudence, the arts of the *trivium* (grammar, rhetoric, dialectic), philosophy, theology as well as esoteric speculations on the divine proportion and on the five regular bodies of the universe. Luca Pacioli devoted much of his life to the study and teaching of this universal discipline, convinced that he could pay homage to the glory of God and to the well-being of merchants, artisans, land surveyors, masters of abacus, engineers, plumbers, cartographers, artillery masters, and technicians who might have used his books on mathematics.

(a) Summa, the Closed Red Book

The closed volume placed on the table bears the abbreviation *LI. R. LUC.BUR.* - which, when written in full, is *LIBER REVERENDI LUCAE BURGENSIS*. Luca Pacioli was referred to as Fra Luca dal Borgo (*Reverendi Lucae Burgensis*), the friar from Borgo San Sepolcro, or the friar from Sansepolcro for he was born in Borgo Sansepolcro in 1445. This closed volume represents his *Summa de Aritmetica*, a mathematical compendium that he published in Venice in 1494. Therefore, the *Portrait of Pacioli* was painted after 1494, probably after Pacioli moved to Milan in 1496 at the age of fifty years when he was recruited by Ludovico il Moro to teach mathematics at the University of Pavia. He remained in the Duchy of Milan until the French invasion and fall of the Sforza in 1499. It should be noted that the painting of the triangle within the circle bears testament, commemorative evidence that the representation on the blackboard is a precise reference to the illustration of the sheet in the *Divine Proportion* pertaining to the construction of the pentagon or hexagon within the circle. Published in Venice only in 1509, but elaborated and already completed in Milan, as attested by the effusive dedication to Ludovico Il Moro in a manuscript codex bearing the date of 1498, the Milanese period or soon thereafter appears as the most probable time and place for the realisation of the *Pacioli Portrait*, when the painter, Leonardo, while painting the *Last Supper* was at least present in the same area and period as Luca Pacioli. If the prevailing reading of the title of the scroll (1495) is to be assumed to mark the date of the start or completion of the painting, then one might have to suppose that Pacioli had arrived in Milan the year before 1496. However, the faded wing of the fly covers the last number of the presumed year, which may be different from the number 5 and therefore bring the painting back to 1496. However, the hypothesis that the painting was completed in Venice before 1496 seems improbable, although completion of the painting after 1500 either in Venice or Florence is a slight possibility based on Luca Pacioli and Leonardo's overlapping timelines.

Much has been written about the *Summa* and there is no need to go over it in any great detail. However, understanding the context of this book provides a better background to the painting and why Luca Pacioli is the key figure in it. The *Summa* was a work of central importance in the history of Italian mathematics since many of the branches of the discipline cultivated before and during the Middle Ages are brought together in the publication. The numerous references to the *Summa* in the works of the great mathematicians of the sixteenth century attest to the importance and diffusion of the book that was an indispensable reference point not only for Renaissance technicians and merchants but also for theoretical mathematicians. The *Summa* is composed of 308 short sections. The first eight are not numbered and contain, in addition to the dedicatory epistle to Guidobaldo da Montefeltro, a summary of the work and a detailed index of the subjects. The sections numbered from 1 to 150 present speculative and practical arithmetic, and operations with radicals and algebra. The last 158 sections contain a treatise on commercial mathematics, a tariff and a geometry treatise. The work covers four distinct fields of mathematics: arithmetic, algebra, accounting and geometry. Only trigonometry is missing. Pacioli declared that the purpose of the *Summa* was purely didactic. He collected '*many different and very necessary parts of Arithmetica, Geometry, Proportion and Proportionality*', with a twofold aim: to offer the reader a '*summa*' of the known rules of practical mathematics; and to illustrate '*of each operative act its foundations according to the ancient and still modern philosophi*'. Since only a few learned people were able to understand Latin at the end of the fifteenth century, Pacioli choose to write the *Summa* in the common tongue, the '*materna*' and '*vernacula lengua*'. He believed that while Latin was the language of the cultured and the learned, the availability of the *Summa* in the vulgar language of the technicians satisfied the need of mathematics in both the mechanical and liberal arts. Whatever the art, the profession or the '*facultà*' of the reader, the *Summa* will still be useful, given that mathematics is '*to be able to apply to all things*'. Pacioli completed his book with an explanation that his motivation to publish the *Summa* was to spread the idea that God created the world through numbers, geometric figures and proportions. He preached that mathematics was the mind of God.

In this regard, Luca Pacioli's project in Milan to produce a *Compendium De Divina Proportione* with drawings and paintings by Leonardo da Vinci was an extension of the *Summa*. For Luca Pacioli, Leonardo was the '*prince today between mortals*' and a worthy heir of Piero della Francesca, the '*monarch*' of painting, as he had described Piero in the *Summa*. Leonardo created numerous panels of the polyhedra that Pacioli in *De Divina Proportione* acknowledged, '*in perspective design, it is not possible in the world to make them better*'. The relationship between Luca Pacioli and Leonardo da Vinci was a typical case of convergence of the interests of mathematical scholarship within the culture of the practice of mathematics. Leonardo da Vinci bought a copy of the *Summa* for 119 soldi (Atl 228r, already 104r.), and he jotted down a note to himself, '*Learn the multiplication of the roots of maestro Luca*' (Atl.331r, already 120r). Leonardo was now over forty years of age and the ideal mature student for Pacioli who taught him the theory of proportions, which is the foundation of all the arts and all knowledge. The *Pacioli Portrait* is a lesson by Luca Pacioli on Euclidian geometry and his *Summa* for the benefit of Leonardo da Vinci. Galeazzo Sanseverino is in the portrait because he is their very wealthy patron who oversees the lessons, but also for his intellectual enlightenment.

(b) Leonardo's miniature notebook with the cryptic message IACO.BAR.VIGEN / NIS P. 1495

Leonardo produced many notebooks with his secretive mirror writing and at last count about ten have survived to this day. In this regard, the cryptic message on the notebook or the folded note is almost a personal joke or self-parody of his secret notebooks. Although this mini-notebook or folded cartouche is supposed to be the signature pictorial clue of Jacopo de' Barbari, the irony is that neither he nor Leonardo invented this artifice. Other artists such as Bellini and Antonello da Messena (see Fig. 4.3), and the Flemish painters Rogier van der Weyden and Jan van Eyck had already employed the use of the informative cartouche, book or letter before them. The message on the note in the *Pacioli* portrait says: IACO.BAR.VIGEN/ NIS P. 1495.

The message has nothing to do with Jacopo de' Barbari. We know that it is about Leonardo da Vinci and his time in Milan because Carla Glori decrypted the message gloriously and some of her decryptions are presented in Chapter 20.

[c] Euclid's Elements

Euclid was an ancient Greek mathematician who resided in Alexandria, Hellenistic Egypt and the Ptolemaic Kingdom during the time of Ptolemy I, the Macedonian Greek general who ruled Egypt from 323-263 BC. Euclid died in 285 BC; in comparison, the Greek mathematician, scientist and philosopher, Pythagoras (570-495 BC), preceded him by about 300 years and Archimedes (287-212 BC) followed him a generation later. The Pythagorean theorem that all school children at one time or another have attempted to commit to memory is fundamental to Euclidean geometry. The theorem states that the square of the hypotenuse (the side opposite the right angle) is equal to the sum of the squares of the other two sides, and that it can be written as the following equation: $a^2 + b^2 = c^2$, where the c represents the length of the hypotenuse and a and b the lengths of the triangle's other two sides that are at a right angle (90 degrees) to each other.

This fundamental theorem is displayed on the chalkboard in the *Portrait*.

Luca Pacioli's mathematical education, in addition to learning the tradition of the abacus, would have been from his readings and studies of the *Elements* of Euclid, translated into Latin from Arabic in an edition of the XIII century dating back to Giovanni Campano, and from the works of Fibonacci, *Liber abaci* (1202) and *Practica geometriae* (1220), also in Latin. He undoubtedly learnt much from the mathematician, geometer and painter Pietro della Francesca (1416-1492) who also lived in Sansepolcro. Luca, the friar of Sansepolcro, thus spread the mathematical teachings of Pietro della Francesca when he became a mathematics teacher who was recruited by universities and courts throughout Italy and taught in the cities of Perugia, Zara, Florence, Rome, Sansepolcro, Naples, Assisi, Urbino, and Venice - where he published the *Summa* (1494) - and in Milan where he met and worked with Leonardo da Vinci and they spent three years (1496-1499) together in great intellectual fervour to produce the *Compendium De Divina Proportione* (1498) dedicated to Ludovico il Moro Sforza. Leonardo da Vinci produced the drawings on perspective and the regular polyhedral for his manuscripts and the printed book. For his part, Leonardo learned a lot more about algebra and geometry from Luca, and developed a greater interest in mathematical issues. After the expulsion of the Moor, il Moro Sforza, from Milan by the French king, Pacioli moved to Florence for a few years and taught mathematics in the Pisan colleges. He also taught the *Elements* of Euclid to students in Bologna, and then again in Venice in 1508.

It is evident from the portrait that Luca Pacioli is giving a lecture on Euclidian geometry, probably to Ludovico Sforza and his court of intellectuals and gentlemen. There is even a pen in an inkwell to use for writing down notes. It seems Luca is busily going through each of the Euclidean propositions in the *Elements*. He uses the arithmetic and algebraic language of *Book XIII* of the *Elements of Euclid* to describe the Euclidean propositions concerning the divine proportion, showing how these properties compete in the genesis of the 5 regular bodies starting from the diameter of the sphere that contains them. The second part of Euclid's text is arithmetic with metaphysical explanations that end with a compendium in which the proportions between volumes and surfaces of regular polyhedra are shown. Pacioli, recapitulating the relationship between the squared diameter of the sphere and the squared sides (length of the edges) of the inscribed polyhedral, reminded his students of Euclid's proposition 18 that the tetrahedron has the proportion 3:2, the cube 3:1, the octahedron 2:1, and that the proportions for the icosahedron and the dodecahedron are irrational, since in both cases the ratio between the diameter and the corner, due to the *divine proportion*, are 'incommunicable' quantities with precisely one minor line for the icosahedron and a residue for the dodecahedron. He demonstrates that the polyhedron of 20 triangular bases can be inscribed in a sphere and that the dodecahedron seen in the portrait can be constructed by the use of the divine proportion; the reciprocal relations between polyhedra are attributable to the proportions that bind the edges of the 5 regular bodies with the diameter of the sphere in which they are inscribed. The proportions not only constitute the generative principle of the polyhedral, but also their principle of order. Leonardo da Vinci's drawings and coloured paintings of these mathematical abstractions described by Pacioli help to demonstrate the concrete reality of the polyhedrons as three-dimensional material objects for all to see. Pacioli prides himself on presenting these beautifully drawn and painted images as objects of reality to the eyes of Ludovico il Moro Sforza, the Duke of Milan. Leonardo da Vinci drew and painted at least sixty of these solid objects for Ludovico to see them as decorative shapes hanging from a complex and varied system of small rings and knots tied to a fixed label with the Latin names for each of the polyhedra.

Leonardo produced the same impression of concreteness for the two solid bodies in his *Pacioli Portrait*, the wooden dodecahedron placed on the left of the friar and the body of 26 bases, hanging by a thread, like the solids of Leonardo's illustrations for the *Divine Proportion*. The rhombicuboctahedron, half full of water, refracts the Ducal palace of Ludovico il Moro Sforza three times on its crystal surface. The optical virtuosity with which Leonardo depicts the palace of Sforza reflects on the character of Galeazzo Sanseverino to whom Pacioli dedicates the *Divine Proportion* that was built from the contents of the *Summa* below him. The collaboration between the mathematician and Leonardo da Vinci took place through the lessons contained within the book of Euclid, which Luca Pacioli translated and published in 1508 into the vernacular of his 'Tuscan countrymen'.

Geometric Deconstruction and Reconstruction of the Dodecahedron

In the *Pacioli Portrait*, on the opposite side to the hanging rhombicuboctahedron, a dodecahedron sits solidly on top of a book, shaped like a cube. In contrast to the rhombicuboctahedron, the pentagonal dodecahedron is composed of twelve regular pentagonal faces with three of them meeting at each vertex. It has 30 edges (lines) and twenty vertices (points) and is one of the five Platonic solids. Each of its 12 pentagonal faces can be divided into five triangles to provide 60 triangles within the dodecahedron. Leonardo has added the dodecahedron to the painting because it incorporates the Golden Ratio that shapes the universe. This was not an absurd idea by Leonardo and the ancients, including

Euclid, because atomic physicists now know that the radius of hydrogen is the Golden Ratio that is embedded into the Planck length (field coupling to make gravity) and plays a quantitative role in atomic physics and operates in a variety of natural phenomena.

Because a dodecahedron consists of twelve pentagons and each pentagon connects all the points (vertices) to form a five-pointed star, the ratios of the lengths of the resulting line segments are all based on phi or 1.618 (see Fig. 8.5). Leonardo understood this relationship between dodecahedrons and the Golden Ratio and therefore added it to his painting and placed it on Pacioli's book, the *Summa*. It is unlikely that Barbari had undertaken the same intensive geometric and mathematical studies as Leonardo to understand these mathematical connections of polygons to nature and the universe, although there is no evidence available to say that he did not. However, Leonardo was unique in that he demonstrated in one of his drawings that a dodecahedron can be transformed into a cube and then easily reconstructed back into a dodecahedron from the shape of a cube (Fig. 9.6). He used three-dimensional geometry to transform a dodecahedron into a cube by using four clear and easy steps that he illustrated on a page of his Codex Forster I, folio 7r (also see Fig. 7-5, page 202 of Fritjof Capra's *The Science of Leonardo*). First, he cut the dodecahedron into 12 equal pyramids with pentagons at their base. Next, he cut each of the 12 pyramids into five smaller pyramids with triangular bases to produce 60 pyramids of equal size. Then, the triangular base of each pyramid was used to form a rectangle of equal area. Finally, he stacked the 30 rectangular pyramids into a cube that had the same volume of the dodecahedron (Fig. 9.6). Then, he reversed the process by starting with a cube and returning it to a dodecahedron. In this way, Leonardo had transformed one body shape into another body shape without either diminution or increase of matter, and he demonstrated the principle of conservation of area and/or volume. The cube, rectangle, triangular base, pentagonal base, dodecahedron, and pyramid are all shown in the painting of his geometric elements that depicts the theme of transformation of forms. Even the rhombicuboctahedron hanging in front of Luca Pacioli is composed of triangles and squares that can be deconstructed and reconstructed into basic components or even transformed into a pyramid with a rectangular base or a cube.

In *Divine Proportion*, first published in Milan in December of 1497, Luca Pacioli's writes:

'It is possible to arrogate the fifth quality not unworthily to the aforementioned: that is, just as God confers Being to Heavenly Virtue, by another name called Fifth Essence, and by its mediation, to the other four simple bodies, that is, to the four elements earth, water, air and fire, and, through these, to every other thing in nature, so this our sacred

proportion gives the formal being - according to the ancient Plato in his Timaeus - attributing to heaven the figure of the solid called dodecahedron, otherwise the solid of 12 pentagons, which, as will be shown below, is not possible to make without our proportion. And similarly, to each one of the other elements, he assigned its own, absolutely distinct form; that is, to fire, the pyramidal figure called tetrahedron, to earth the cubic figure called hexahedron, to air, the figure called octahedron, and to water that called icosahedron. And these such forms and figures are called by scholars the regular solids, as we will discuss each of them individually below.'

FIG. 9.6. *Transformation of a dodecahedron into a cube. Leonardo da Vinci* Codex Forster I, folio 7r. *Reproduced from F. Capra's Fig. 7-5 in* The Science of Leonardo (2008).

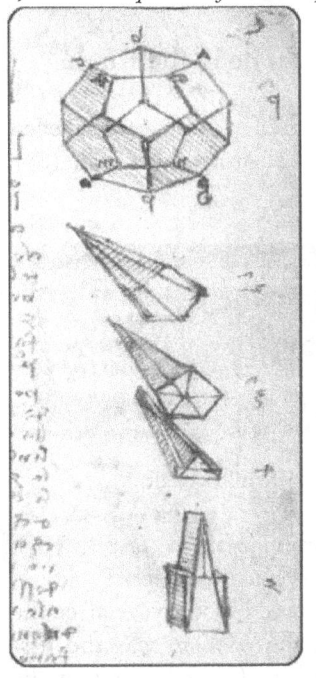

'*And then, by means of these, we will speak of the infinite other solids called dependents. Nor is it possible to relate the 5 regular solids to one another, nor to understand their circumscriptions by the sphere, without our said proportion. Without that pentagon, as will be shown, it is not possible either to form or imagine the solid, most noble above all the other regulars,* **called dodecahedron**, *that is, the solid with twelve equilateral and equiangular pentagons, by another name called the solid with twelve pentagonal faces, whose form, as will be shown, the divine Plato attributed to the* Quint Essence, *that is, to Heaven, and rightly so. But it is manifest that the 3 angles of the equilateral and equiangular pentagon, are less than 4 right angles, and 4 of them are more than 4 right angles. Whence, of the 3 angles of an equilateral and equiangular pentagon, it is possible to form the solid angle, but of 4 of its angles or more, it is not possible to form a solid angle. And so, only one solid of equilateral and equiangular pentagons is formed, the which is called by the philosophers', a dodecahedron, or otherwise solid of 12 pentagons, in which the angles of the pentagons three by three, form and contain all the solid angles of the said solid.*'

In *CHAPTER XLVI* of the *Divine Proportion*, Luca Pacioli informs the Duke of Milan how Leonardo da Vinci showed that a dodecahedron can be transformed into a cube and then easily reconstructed from a cube (Fig. 9.6).

'*Whence, excellent Duke, from the things we have discussed, it is manifest that, there being 5 regular solids, if it were possible, as one might suppose, to inscribe each one in the other, it would follow that each one of them should receive 4, and consequently, there would be 20 inscriptions, that is, 4 times 5. But, because each one does not receive each one, as was said, there are but 12 inscriptions. That is, only one in the tetrahedron, the octahedron; and two in the cube, that is, the tetrahedron and the octahedron; and two also in the octahedron, that is, the cube and the tetrahedron. And there are three of them in the icosahedron, that is, the dodecahedron, the cube and the tetrahedron; and there are four in the dodecahedron, that is, the icosahedron, the cube, the octahedron and the fourth, the tetrahedron. And all these add up to twelve. But the dodecahedron is, of all of them, endowed with the singular prerogative, as receptacle to all, of not prohibiting or forbidding lodging to any. And for that reason also, the ancient Plato along with others mentioned, attributed it to the Universe.'*

Blackboard Diagram of the Euclidian Triangle in the Circle

In the *Pacioli Portrait*, Leonardo da Vinci has painted a blackboard labelled *'Euclides'* that has a drawing of a circle circumscribed around a triangle (Fig. 9.7).

FIG. 9.7. *Detail of Euclides Blackboard in the* Pacioli Portrait.

In his 1993 published paper entitled *The Portrait of Luca Pacioli*, Nick Mackinnon identified the edition of *Euclid's Elements* to which Pacioli is pointing. He assumed the date of the painting was 1495, a year after the publication of the *Summa*, and concluded that the *Elements* was the first printed Venetian edition of 1482. If so, then the *Elements* book in the painting is 13 years old, and Leonardo probably obtained many of his lessons about geometry from this particular book. Nick Mackinnon also noticed that the diagram on the blackboard is not an exact copy of the one in the text, although it is similar. The diagram in the middle of *Euclid's Elements* is depicted in the *Portrait* with such accuracy that this detail must be more than merely of iconic significance. Mackinnon believed that the painter was reminding us of the mathematician Pappus of Alexandria (290-350 BC) and his compendium of mathematics called the *Collection*, in which Pappus presented his *hexagon theorem* in projective geometry. In this regard, it is noteworthy that Leonardo became fascinated and absorbed in projective and transformational geometry as well as in recreational mathematics (puzzles), doubling the cube, polygons and polyhedrons that are covered in the *Collection*. According to Mackinnon, Pacioli in the painting is expositing a proposition from *Book XIV* of the *Elements*, which also is used extensively in Pacioli's *De Divina Proportione* (Fig. 9.8). This is *Proposition 2: The same circle circumscribes both the pentagon of the dodecahedron and the triangle of the icosahedron inscribed in the same sphere*. This is logically close to Pappus's proposition *III.58* in the *Collection* where he also inscribed the icosahedron in a sphere with the same latitudinal circles as those for the dodecahedron, and observed *Elements XIV.2* as a corollary. He also gave an independent proof in *Collection V.48*.

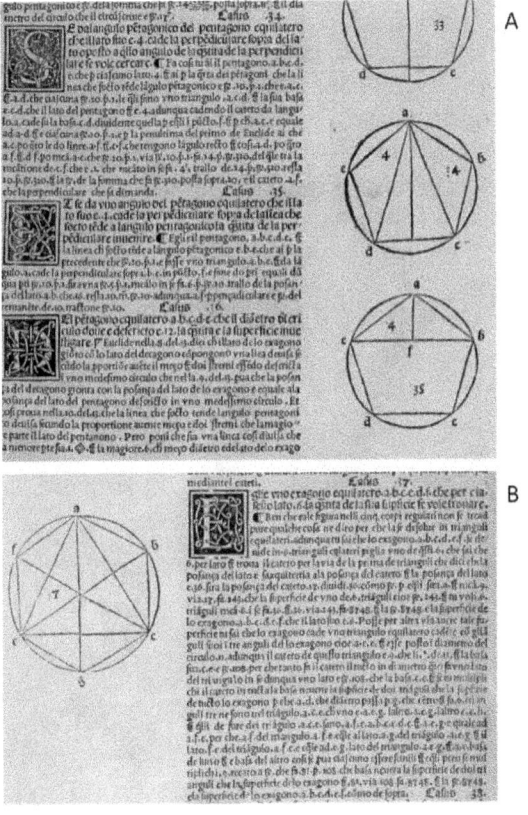

FIG. 9.8. *Drawings of (A) the Pentagon (Figure 34) and (B) the Hexagon (Figure 37) in the printed edition (1509) of the* Divine Proportion. *Images taken from Pacioli, Luca (1509),* De Divine Proportione. *Printed edition (Italian). Getty Research Institute.* https://archive.org/details/divinaproportion00paci/page/n3.

To test his hypothesis, Nick Mackinnon recreated Pacioli's drawings on a chalkboard and concluded that the portrait did indeed show Pacioli in the act of expositing *Elements XIV.8*. Thus, in the *Pacioli Portrait*, the 1482 edition of *Euclid* is open at *Book XIII.12*, which is required in the proof of *XIV.8*. However, the disturbing issue for Mackinnon was that the book is shown open halfway, whereas *Book XIII* is located towards the end of the book. To account for this apparent pictorial discrepancy, Mackinnon suggested that the portrait was painted with a blank book open near the middle where it would lie flat and the painter then simply added a copy of the text exactly from *Book XIII.12*. This was painted by somebody who knew the contents of the book and who could cheekily introduce this pictorial discrepancy with full confidence that the puzzle that he painted would be solved one day by somebody who had read the 'same' book and was aware of the 'error'. This somebody may have turned out to be Nick Mackinnon who came along five hundred years later to solve the pictorial puzzle of what Luca Pacioli's lesson was in *Euclid's Elements*.

While both Argante Ciocci and Enrico Gamba seem to be in agreement with Mackinnon that the text is open to a specific page of Euclid's *Elements*, they believe that the specific page is the one with the proposition *VIII* and *VIIII* of the book *XIII*: the square of the side of the equilateral triangle inscribed in a circumference is three times the square of the semidiameter of the circumference. Argante Ciocci even provides a photograph of what he believed is the specific page of *Euclid's Elements* (Fig. 9.9).

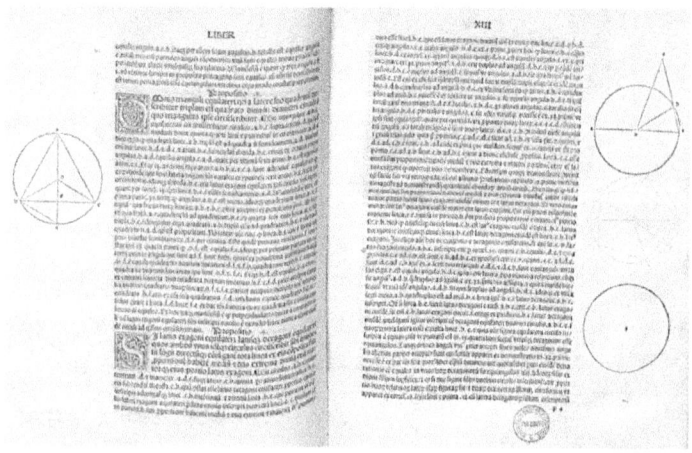

FIG. 9.9. *Photographed pages of proposition VIII and VIIII of the book XIII in Euclid's Elements (1482 edition). Image taken from Argante Ciocci (2015): The double portrait of the polyhedral Luca Pacioli. Spanish Journal of Accounting History. No.15, 107-130.*
http://www.e-theca.net/emiliopanella/hospes/ciocci.htm

It is difficult to judge from Leonardo's depiction of the page whether it is the same, but it looks similar. However, the drawing of the triangle in the circle on Pacioli's blackboard looks different to the drawing in the photograph of the page in Euclid's book. It seems that Luca Pacioli is about to solve a different problem and he is challenging the viewers to anticipate him and solve the geometric puzzle themselves. In this regard, Nick Mackinnon might be right. Luca Pacioli is challenging us to show that the same circle circumscribes both the pentagon of the dodecahedron and the triangle of the icosahedron inscribed in the same sphere. On the other hand, Luca might have decided to show us that the same circle circumscribes both the pentagon of the dodecahedron and the triangle of the hexagon that was illustrated later in his Figures number 34 and 37, respectively (Fig. 9.8) in the printed 1509 edition of the *Divine Proportion*, but not in the handwritten manuscripts of 1498. Luca Pacioli provided the solutions for those two figures in the printed edition in the third part *Libellus in tres partials divisus (Book in three parts)* that was a translation of Piero della Francesca's Latin writings *On Five Regular Solids* with mathematical examples.

Comparison of Leonardo's Handwritten Blackboard and Notebook Numbers

According to Argante Ciocci in his paper '*The double portraiture of the polyhedral Luca Pacioli*,' there is a set of numbers in the lower left of the blackboard in the *Pacioli Portrait* that represents a sum: 478+935+621=2034 (Fig. 9.7 and 9.10). The handwritten blackboard numbers 1 to 9 look similar to Leonardo's handwritten numbers in the pages of his notebooks (Fig. 9.10). This is additional evidence to support the theory that Leonardo da Vinci painted the *Pacioli Portrait* that is exhibited at the Capodimonte Museum in Naples. Handwriting is like a fingerprint or DNA evidence presented in the Court of Justice and it helps to demonstrate that Leonardo is the author of the *Portrait*. The numbers 2, 3, 4, 5, 6, 7 and 8 on the blackboard and the numbers on a page taken from one of his notebooks are demonstratively similar. The number 2 topples slightly to the left and has an elongated base. The number 3 has a distinctive hanging tail or slight hook. His 4 is a cross slightly hooded and his 8 is straight and proud. The 5 and 6 lean a little to the right. The top of the 5 has an elongated peak to the right and the bottom has a small compact hook to the left. The 7 is an arrow head >. The 9 has an extended hanging tail. The Leonardo da Vinci numbers are different to those written by Albrecht Durer, but there were too few numbers in the Jacopo de' Barbari's paintings to allow for a conclusive comparison. The number 1504 on the note with de' Barbari's signature seems insufficient for a direct comparison with Leonardo's numbers, although the dot over the 1 is like an 'i' and the slight flourish on the top of the 4 seems different to Leonardo's numbers 1 or 4. Barbari's 5 is more of an elongated S than Leonardo's compacted five. Handwriting is unique and identifiable and an expert could determine if the numbers on Pacioli's blackboard are in Leonardo's distinctive hand or that of Jacopo de' Barbari. This might require an extensive examination of official handwritten letters or documents containing examples of their style of writing numbers. There is additional handwriting that is difficult to decipher on Pacioli's blackboard, but might reveal information about ownership (propriety) after careful microscopic examination.

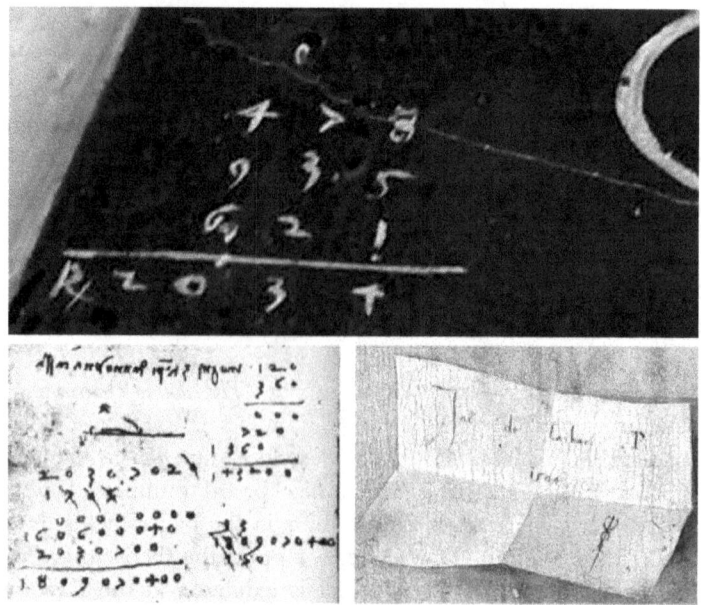

FIG. 9.10. Top, the sum of 478+935+621=2034 on Luca Pacioli's blackboard (Detail of the Pacioli Portrait). Bottom left, Leonardo da Vinci's handwritten numbers on a page of one of his notebooks (Paris Manuscript L, folio 79v-80r, acoustics) and bottom right, a detail of Jacopo de' Barbari's note with the number i504 from his painting Still-Life with Partridge and Gauntlet: 1504, Alte Pinakothek, Munich; image from WGA.

Blackboard Calculations: Ratios and Formulae

In the opinion of Argante Ciocci, the numbers 478+935+621=2034 on the blackboard (Fig. 9.10) refer to the three segments drawn in the upper left corner of the blackboard and to the figure of the rhombicuboctahedron hanging from the ceiling because the number 2034 includes the symbol R of the square root that might refer to the three squared numbers preceding it. He asks the following question - does Pacioli refer to the calculations to establish the relationship between the diameter of a sphere and the side of the rhombicuboctahedron inscribed in it? I'm not convinced that this is the

CHAPTER 9

sole purpose of the arithmetic example. Enrico Gamba has provided a different interpretation:

'I think that one of the aims of the painting is to launch a challenge: with the left hand Pacioli indicates a well defined and identifiable theorem of Euclid's Elements, with a wand in the right hand pointing on the slate an unfinished geometric figure, there is a triangle inscribed in a circumference and there is a segment that floats, which does not end up anywhere. Pacioli challenges us to solve a problem, he wants us to complete the figure, he wants us to say what it is. In addition to the geometric figure, on the slate, we find below the sum 478+935+621=2034. What interpretation to give these numbers? Are they randomly chosen? Knowing Pacioli it is difficult to do so.'

The copy of the Elements placed on the table corresponds to the first printed edition, Venice 1482, the text is open to a specific page, the one with the proposition VIII of the book XIII: the square of the side of the equilateral triangle inscribed in a circumference is three times the square of the semidiameter of the circumference. Below the proposition IX: the golden section of the semidiameter of a circumference is the side of the regular decagon inscribed in it. The Pacioli index is aimed at the beginning of proposition VIII. It seems that this is the proposition in question. What does that have to do with the figure left incomplete on the blackboard, and has anything to do with the four numbers? One possible answer may be the following. Proposition VIII, book XIII - the square of the side of the triangle is three times the square of the semidiameter - it relates the semidiameter to the side of the inscribed triangle. Continuing along the same line one can think of a relationship between the semidiameter and the side of the square inscribed in the same circumference. In this case, the incomplete segment would be the side of the inscribed square, which would be completed at point X. The relationship between the sides of the triangle and the square inscribed in the same circumference is thus obtained: if the square of the side of the square is equal to double the square of the semidiameter, then there is a relation between the square and the triangle that the square of the side of the square is 2/3 of the square of the side of the equilateral triangle.'

Gamba illustrates his last point about *'the sides of the triangle and the square inscribed in the same circumference'* with Fig. 9.11. He then says:

The hypothesis can find an indirect confirmation from the numerical calculation: 478+935+621=2034. At a first examination, it is not about particular numbers, friendly numbers, perfect, etc., you immediately notice that in the three numbers added there are not repeated figures. The only one we say harmony that I found is the following: if 621 is the perimeter of an equilateral triangle of side 207, then 478 is the perimeter of the square built on the radius of the circumscribed circumference. Or in proposition VIII, in the book XIII Euclid surveyor relates the surfaces, while Pacioli which is also arithmetic and algebraic, relates the perimeters according to the use of the environment of practical mathematics, or abkistic mathematics, of always dealing with numerical cases. Even the three segments drawn in the upper corner of the blackboard gain a sense, representing the three dimensions in play: the half-diameter, the side of the square and the side of the inscribed equilateral triangle. One last clue in favour of this hypothesis is that the hanging rhombicuboctahedron is made up of squares and equilateral triangles. But again, hypotheses are all to deny, my intent is only to arouse new interest in this work.'

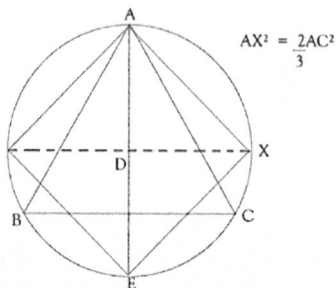

FIG. 9.11. *Shows the relation between the square and the triangle and that the square of the side of the square is 2/3 of the square of the side of the equilateral triangle. Taken from Enrico Gamba (2011). Proviamo a rileggere il "Doppio ritratto" di Luca Pacioli. Online at Hevelius' webzine. http://www.hevelius.it/webzine/leggi.php?codice=242*

Gamba's hypothesis is reasonable, but it seems to me that Leonardo provided his viewers with a greater challenge than just solving the puzzle about the ratio of 2:3 or 3:2 with the triangle, square and circle as examples. It is also about the magic of the numbers 1, 3, 6, and 9 in its series of 9 numbers from 1 to 9. More about that later. For now, let us continue with the consideration of the ratio 3:2 and Leonardo's collaboration with Luca Pacioli in the publication of the *Divine Proportion*. Leonardo preempts Luca Pacioli's example in the *Divine Proportion* with his own more complicated mathematical example on the blackboard. Let us now look at Pacioli's simple example in the *Divine Proportion* using a different example of the 3:2 or 1.5 to 1 ratio (Fig. 9.12) that he calls the *sexquialtera* (Latin). This Latin term is still used today, (*sesquialtera* with a slightly different spelling), and it is defined in the Latin dictionary as *'in ratio of 3 to 2'* or *'one-and-a-half times as much'*. In choral music, the *sexquialtera* proportion implies the ratio of 3:2 when three musical notes are to be sung in the time of two. Now let us see what Luca Pacioli has to say about the *sesquialtera* in his lecture to the duke of Milan, Ludovico Sforza. But, first, we must remember that the *Divine Proportion* is based mostly on *Euclid's Elements*; Pacioli tells us that this is so under the following heading:

'*About those things, which the reader needs to make note of, in order to understand this book, and about the symbols used. Next, to make things easier, note the following conventions we have adopted: whenever we cite the 1st of the first, and the 4th of the second, the 10th of the fifth, the 20th of the sixth, and so on, to the fifteenth, we always mean by the first notation, the number of the conclusion [proposition] and by the second, the number of the books of our philosopher Euclid, whom everyone imitates, as the archimandrite of this discipline. In other words, saying "by the fifth of the first" signifies, "by the 5th conclusion of his first book", and likewise of the other sections of his whole book on the Elements and first principles of Arithmetic and Geometry. But when we cite the authority of another of his works, or of another author, we will name such a book and such an author.'*

Pacioli's acknowledgement of Euclid is clear enough. The definitions, propositions and 15 books in the edition used by Pacioli was the 1482 printing, translated from the Arabic and annotated in the late 1200's by Johannes Campanus (Campano da Novara). Leonardo da Vinci included this edition in his *Pacioli Portrait* of the Franciscan friar who in *Chapter VII* of the *Divine Proportion* goes on to tell us about the **sexqualtera:**

'On the first effect of a line divided according to our proportion. When a straight line be divided according to the proportion having the mean and two extremes -- for this was another name given by scholars to our admirable proportion -- if to its larger part is added the half of the entire line so proportionally divided, it will follow of necessity that the square of their sum always is the quintuple, that is, 5 times as much, of the square of the said half of the whole. Before proceeding to other things, we must clarify how the said proportion is to be understood and interposed among the quantities, and what it is called in the works of the greatest scholars. That is why I say it is called proportio habens medium et duo extremi, *that is, "the proportion having a mean and two extremes," to which every* **ternary** *[a quantity composed of three items, values, etc] must be subjected; no matter what the* **ternary** *might be, it will always consist of a mean and two extremes, since the mean without the extremes is not possible to conceive. It is thus that we were taught to divide a quantity in the 29th [30th] of the VIth, having first described in the 3rd Definition of the VIth how one must understand this division; even though in his IInd, by the 11th, he demonstrates how to divide the line with the same quality and force, without naming the proportion until the end of the Vth book. And by Campanus, it is adduced from the numbers in the 16th [18th] of the IXth. And this much on the subject of its name.'*

How its mean and its extremes are to be understood. Once we understand how our proportion came to be called by its particular name, we still have to clear up how the cited mean and extremes, in whatever quantity you will, must be understood and how they must be arranged, so that among them one might find the said divine proportion. For example, let there be three quantities of the same type, whose proportions among them otherwise are not known. Let the first be A and let its number be 9; the second B and its number 6; the third C and 4 [see Figure 2, Fig. 9.12 in this book]. I say that among them there are two proportions, **one between A and B, that is, of 9 to 6,** *all which congruent proportions we call in our work the* **sexqualtera**, *and is* *obtained when the larger term contains the smaller, **one and one-half times**. Since 9 contains 6 and still 3 more, which is the half of 6, so it also is called a* **sexquialtera**. *But since we do not here intend to discuss proportions generally, having extensively treated and clarified them, together with proportionalities, in our work cited above, I will not elaborate on them further here, but we should always take as presupposed, what is generally said of them, with their definitions and divisions. **And we will speak here only of this one proportion, since we have not found it treated in such a very useful way, by anyone else before this.***'

'Now turning to the purpose with which we began, of the three quantities, let the second, B, be to the third, C, as 6 is to 4, also a **sexquialtera** proportion. For now, we do not care whether the proportions are equal or unequal: but our intent is only to make clear how among the three terms of similar type, there are by necessity two proportions. Similarly, I say that our divine proportion observes the same conditions; that is, **that always between its three terms, that is, the mean and two extremes, it invariably contains two proportions always of one same denomination**. This, which with other proportions, whether they be continuous or discontinuous, can occur in infinitely various ways, because sometimes between their three terms it will be double, sometimes triple, et sic in ceteris for all the common species. But there is no possible variation between the mean and the extremes of this our proportion, as will be shown.'

'Whence, I rightfully make this [invariance], the fourth property that our proportion shares with the Supreme Architect; and because it is counted among the other proportions, without any difference in species or of any other kind, in being subject to the conditions established by their definitions, in this we can compare it to Our Saviour, who came not to dissolve the Law, but rather to fulfil it, and conversed with men, and made himself subject and obedient to Mary and Joseph. Thus, this our proportion, sent by heaven, dwells with the other proportions in definition and conditions, and does not degrade them, rather, makes them more magnificent, maintaining the principle of unity among all quantities indifferently, itself never changing, as our Saint Severino says of the great God, videlicet: Stabilisque manens dat cuncta moveri ["That is, while remaining stable, he gives motion to everything."]. From this we can know how to distinguish our proportion from others that might occur: that we will always find the three terms disposed in the same proportion as follows: namely, that the product of the smaller extreme and the sum of the smaller and mean, will be equal to the square of the mean, and consequently, by the 10th Definition of the Vth, this sum, of necessity, will be its larger extreme. And when 3 quantities of whatever type find themselves ordered thus, they are said to be according to the proportion having the mean and two extremes. And its larger extreme always equals the sum of the smaller and the mean, so that we are able to say that the said larger extreme is the entire quantity divided into those two such parts, that is, the smaller extreme and the mean in that way. The reason why we must note, that the given proportion cannot be rational, nor is it ever possible, if the larger extreme be rational, for either the smaller extreme or the mean to be denominated by any number, since it will always be irrational, will be made clear below. And in this, it agrees in the 3rd manner with God, as above.'

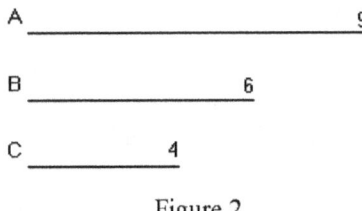

Figure 2

FIG. 9.12. *Luca Pacioli's illustration of the* sesqualtera *proportion in Fig. 2, in the 1498 edition of the* Divine Proportion *(in English, Tennenbaum translation).*

The Luca Pacioli's example shown in Fig. 9.12 has three lines consisting of the lengths, 4, 6 and 9 units, and their relative ratios as presented for his *sexquialtera* proportions are the following:

9:4=2.25:1
9:6=1.5:1
6:4=1.5:1

In comparison, the ternary (a quantity composed of three items, values, e.t.c.) that Leonardo presents in his painting is more complex, it is 9 numbers (1 to 9) divided into three rows of three columns; 478, 935, 621. When we examine their relative ratios we find that they do not follow Luca Pacioli's results precisely. Nevertheless, there is an imperfect *sexquialtera* proportion of 1.506:1 between 935 and 621:

935:478=1.956:1 or 2:1
935:621=1.506:1 or 1.5:1
621:478=1.299:1 or 1.3:1

Leonardo was a friend of the choirmaster of the *Duomo* of Milan whose paean to choral singing was '*Harmonia est Discordia Concors*', translated as '*Harmony is Discord Rendered Concordant*'. Leonardo was a highly competent musician and composer so he knew about *duble (double)*, *tripla (triple)* and *sesquialtera (3;2)* proportions because it was the tempo and mensural proportion in the music of his time. For example, three semibreves (three whole musical notes shaped as an open oval equal to four beats in 4/4 time) were used in triple proportion (*tripla*) either in all choral voices or in one voice in a 3:1 ratio of note duration before a change into *sesquialtera* and a 3:2 (1.5:1) ratio of note duration. In one extraordinary sense Leonardo's numbers have provided us with a tempo of ternary proportions like those that he painted as musical symbols on his note for the unfinished painting of the *Musician* (Fig. 9.13). To contrast choral sections in triple time with those in double time was one of the most common means of achieving compositional contrast within a movement or section of a given work. The circle O or half circle C with or without a vertical stroke | was used as a sign of tempo in a written musical score as were the figures of 3 and 3/2. So, is the drawing of circle/sphere a double connotation or pictorial allusion to musical symbols and tempos in the drawing on Luca Pacioli's blackboard? Is he drawing musical notations for choral works? We can find Leonardo's *sesquialtera* notations (#) in a number of his short musical scores in his notebooks and other places (Fig. 9.13). However, numerous musical sources suggest that there was often a lack of distinction between the *tripla* and *sesquialtera* in practice because of the absence of proper notation in the writing of vocal works. Soon after Leonardo's death in 1519, the binary signatures (the *duble* beat) became the standard for most pieces and the ternary passage within them were still noted as *sesquialtera* or triple proportions.

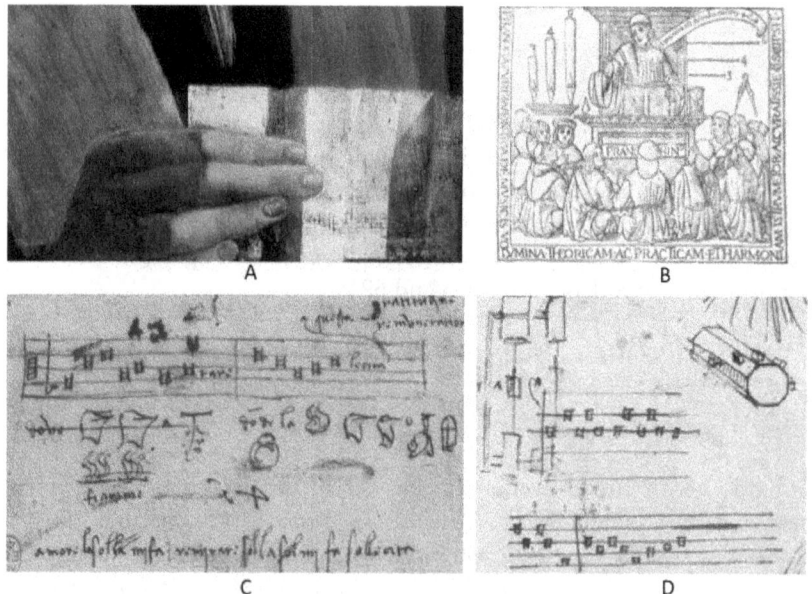

FIG. 9.13. (A), detail of a musical score in Leonardo's unfinished Portrait of the Musician, Ambrosiana, Milan. (B), woodcut showing Gaffurius (aka Franchino) teaching music, from his treatise Angelicum Opus Musice (Milan, 1508). (C) and (D), Leonardo's sesquialtera notations (#) in a number of his short musical scores in his folios.

CHAPTER 9

Blackboard Calculation: A Game of Numbers - Three Sets of Three with 1 to 9 Summed to 2034

Leonardo da Vinci loved mathematical games and puzzles to entertain himself, his friends and the Sforza court of Milan. He even helped Luca Pacioli prepare a compendium of card tricks, number puzzles and illusions that was called the *De Viiribus Quantitatis (On The Power of Numbers)*. The manuscript was rediscovered in the archives of the University library of Bologna in about 1994 and has been translated into English and studied in detail by several scholars since about 2007. The Compendium is divided into three parts, mathematical problems, puzzles and tricks, along with a collection of proverbs and verse. Leonardo da Vinci probably invented many of these puzzles, card tricks and fables for Luca Pacioli to write about. So, it is no surprise that he has written down one of these mathematical puzzles on the corner of Luca Pacioli's blackboard with the drawing of the triangle in the circle. It is noteworthy that Albrecht Durer introduced a 4 x 4 magic square into his woodcut, *Melancholia I* (1514) that seems to be the same one illustrated in Pacioli's *De Viribus Quantitatis*.

Leonardo's box of 9 digits distributed as a 3x3 box of 1 to 9 is like a 3x3 Magic Square and similar to a simpler version of the modern game of Sukudo where one of 9 boxes has to be filled out with the numbers 1 to 9 in a mixed-up series of three. In the magic square that Luca Pacioli described and illustrated in the *De Viiribus Quantitatis,* the numbers 1 to 9 are aligned in a way that 5 is located in the central position of the matrix and that each of the vertical and horizontal columns of the matrix must add up to 15. Luca Pacioli's example of the 3x3 Magic Square named 'Saturn' in the *De Viiribus Quantitatis* is the following:

816
357
492

There are only 8 possible unique Magic Squares. Leonardo's 3x3 box is not a typical Magic Square because the number 5 is not in the central location and each of the vertical and horizontal columns do not add up to 15. Instead, Leonardo's central number is 3. Also, if his numbers were meant to show a Magic Square then he probably would not have summed the numbers to 2034.

Regarding Leonardo's numbers on the blackboard, the 9 numbers chosen for the sum of the three numbers of three (478+935+621) are taken from a series of consecutive numbers 123456789 that add up to four numbers 2034. However, when these four numbers are summed together as individual numbers 0+2+3+4 then they add up to nine. In other words, this mathematical addition of three numbers of three starts with 9 numbers with 3 sets of three (3x3=9) and finishes with one four-digit number 2034 that adds up to 9. So, by removing the zero from the summed number 2034, the series of 4 numbers becomes a series of 3 numbers, 234, that sums to 9; where 3 is the midpoint between 2 and 4; and when the midpoint is squared (3^2) it also becomes 9; which is a weird lesson about mathematical proportions. Perhaps, this example is in support of Luca Pacioli's statement in *Divine Proportion:*

'For now, we do not care whether the proportions are equal or unequal: but our intent is only to make clear how among the three terms of similar type, there are by necessity two proportions.'

Leonardo is telling us something about the number 9 and its 1/3 ratios of 3 and 6. In a basic divisibility test add up the digits in the number and see if 3, 6 or 9 can divide the sum without a remainder.

The number 9 today is believed by some to be an *'angel number'* often connected with universal spiritual laws and enlightenment, karma, and spiritual healing. Nine is the symbol of enlightenment. It is revered in Hinduism and considered a complete, perfect and divine number; and in the bible it is used 49 times and symbolises completeness or finality. The number 9 has other mathematical attributes. When you multiply any number by 9, then add the resulting digits and reduce them to a single digit, it transforms back to a 9. For example, 6x9=54, reduce 54 to a single digit by adding them together: 5+4=9. Similarly, 8x9=72, 7+2=9; 23x9=207, 2+0+7=9; and so forth. Also, if you add 9 to any other number, then reduce that number to a single digit, it always comes back to itself, as if the 9 had not been added in the first instance. For example, 5+9=14, 1+4=5; 7+9=16, 1+6=7; or 24 (2+4 reduces to 6)+9=33, 3+3=6.

If you double 9, it will always result in 9 (36+36=72, 7+2 is 9, 18+18=36, 3+6=9 and so on. Also, 6x9=54 and 5+4=9, e.t.c); and 6+3=9, 3+6=9, where 9 unites both sides of 3 and 6. The sequence of numbers from 1 to 9 adds up to 45, but it can also equal 100 if a multiplication operator is inserted between the 8 and the 9 such that 1+2+3+4+5+6+7+8x9=100.

If we bisect a circle, the resulting angles always reduce to the number nine.

Circle=360 degrees=3+6=9
180 degrees=1+8=9
90 degrees=9
45 degrees=4+5=9
270 degrees=2+7=9
22.5 degrees=2+2+5=9

11.25 degrees=1+1+2+5=9
5.625 degrees is (5+6+2+5=18) is (1+8=9).
2.8125 (2+8+1+2+5=18) is (1+8=9)
The resulting angle always reduces to 9.

The pattern of 9 always develops with the sum of the angles in regular polygons in a circle.
Triangle =60+60+60=180 (1+8+0)=(1+8=9)
Square=90+90+90+90=90 x4=360 =(3+6+0=9)
Pentagon=108+108+108+108+108=540=(5+4+0=9)
Hexagon=120 x 6=720=(7+2+0=9)
Octagon=135x8=1080=(1+0+8+0=9)
Nonagon=140 x9=1260=(1+2+6+0=9)
Decagon=144x10=1440=(1+4+4+0=9)
Icosagon=162x20=3240=(3+2+4+0=9)

Therefore, the resulting angles of the bisected circle always reduce to the number nine, ultimately converging into a singularity. Conversely, the polygons reveal the exact opposite. Their vectors result in an outward divergence. Thus, the number nine reveals a linear duality. It is both singularity and a vacuum. Nine models everything and nothing simultaneously.

The summation of 1 to 9 is 45 and 4+5=9. The sum of all digits excluding nine is 36. 1+2+3+4+5+6+7+8=36 (3+6=9). However, the summation of all the digits in decreasing numbers does not always add up to 9 as in the previous examples. For example, 1 to 3=6, 1 to 4=10, 1 to 5=15 (1+5=6), 1 to 6=21 (1+2=3), and 1 to 7=28 (2+8=10). And yet subtracting the five products from each other in the following series of 6-10-15-21-28 yields the consecutive four numbers 4567.

Paradoxically, nine added to any single digit returns the same digit, i.e., 9+5=14 (1+4=5). So nine quite literally equals all the digits (3^) and nothing (0) as in 2034 (9 & 0). Why was 6 afraid of 7? Because 7, 8, 9.

There are 9 out of 12 items lying on the Pacioli table, [9x12=108 (1+0+8=9)], below the three features, the rhombicuboctahedron, Luca Pacioli and Galeazzo Sanseverino, that are at the level of our eye line. Compare these sacred numbers, 3, 6, 9, in the *Pacioli Portrait* to those in Leonardo's *Last Supper* where he has painted the twelve apostles and Jesus, placing the apostles in 2 groups of 3 (6 apostles) on either side of Jesus (12 apostles). This correspondence of numbers between the two paintings is not surprising if Leonardo da Vinci had designed and painted the *Pacioli Portrait* at about the same time that he painted the *Last Supper*. The numbers of 3, 6, 9, and 12 were vibrating in Leonardo's mind because of their biblical and geometric connotations especially for the angles of bisections or polygons in a circle. This correspondence of numbers between the *Last Supper* and the *Pacioli Portrait* is most unlikely to have entered the mind/eye of Jacopo de' Barbari. These are the hidden and unique dimensions of Leonardo da Vinci and his paintings – the mystery and secrets that only he could have added to his portraiture. And yet, most who have known the *Pacioli Portrait* throughout history somehow were unable to decipher it and attribute the painting to Leonardo da Vinci. Even in Luca Pacioli's *Divine Proportion* there is little or no suggestion of the sacredness of the series of 3, 6, 9 and 12, and that they increase by increments of three, the number of the Holy Trinity. The numbers 3, 6 and 9 is what makes the 3-sided equilateral triangle with the three angles of 60 degrees (3x60=180 [1+8+0=9]) a highly spiritual symbol for Luca Pacioli. Perhaps, it had an essence of symbolism that reminded him of Jesus's suffering and sacrifice to humanity; the crucifixion on the cross appearing as an inverted triangle with Jesus's arms stretched out to form a Y on the T at the base of the triangle and his overlapping feet nailed together at the apex, the point of affinity, the end and the beginning of Christianity.

And what can we see in Leonardo's four-digit number 2034 other than that it also adds up to 9, the skeleton key to the universe? It is a composite number with a positive integer that can be formed by multiplying two smaller positive integers. Equivalently, it is a positive integer that has at least one divisor other than 1 and itself (2034) and it is divisible by 2 (1017), by 3 (=678), by 6 (=378), by 9 (=226) and by 113 (=18) to produce whole numbers with no remainder, but not by 4, 5, 7, 8 or 12. Hence, there are only 9 items on Pacioli's table and not twelve. The Prime Factors of 2034 are 2•3²•113=2x3x3x113=2x9x113=9x226=2034, and 2034 is the number of self-avoiding walks of length 9 (with 226 points). A self-avoiding walk is a path from one point to another, which never intersects itself when the steps are only allowed in a discrete number of directions and of certain lengths. Therefore, does this number have anything to do with Leonardo's drawings and designs of his overlapping knots? And, although Leonardo did not know it, the number 0432 Hz (after reordering 2034) is the harmonic of light frequency that speaks or resonates directly with humans. However, in Leonardo's words:

'Let proportion be found not only in numbers, but also in sounds, weights, times and positions, and what ever force there is.'

Leonardo's Bifurcating Proportion Tree

Leonardo grappled with proportions and irrational numbers contained in the tenth book of the *Elements* and he transcribed his version of the ways that natural numbers came together regularly and/or diverged into subsets according to Luca Pacioli's proportion tree of mathematics presented at the end of *De Divina Proportione*. He illustrated a multifurcating proportion tree or pathway in one of his notebooks (Fig. 9.14). It is an arithmetic progression or growth function in terms of a branching pathway with circled stops or nodes that grow numerically and exponentially along the way. The arithmetic progression on the path between two circled numbers is two numbers less than the circled number ahead of it. So the number subtracted between the circled 2 and the circled 8 is 6, between the circled 8 and the circled 9 is 7, between the circled 8 and the circled 10 is 8, and so on. There is always a difference of 2 between the path number and the circled number preceding it. The numbers along the path are an arithmetic progression of natural numbers that have been calculated by subtracting the numbers between two adjoining numbers (e.g., 14-9=5) and adding it to the path number before it (e.g., 7+5=12), for example, to produce the number 12 along the pathway between the two nodes, that is, the circled numbers 9 and 14 in Fig. 9.14A. Thus, [2] 6 [8] 7 [9] 12 [14] 15 [17] 16 [18] 21 [23] to 29 [31], and so on, are a proportional, arithmetic progression of numbers where the bracketed numbers are seen within the circles of Leonardo's drawing, but the non-bracketed pathway numbers between the nodes are not presented in Leonardo's drawing (Fig. 9.14A).

Essentially, the proportional growth of numbers in Leonardo's pathway of numbers or proportion tree (Fig. 9.14A) starts with $n1$ and then subtracts $n1$ from any following number whatever it might be in the natural progression. Thus, if we let $n1=3$, then any number before 6 is 3 numbers less such as for the following series of numbers, (3) 6, (4) 7, (5) 8, (6) 9, and so on. However, if $n1=2$, then the progression is similar to the numbers in Leonardo's drawing in Fig. 9.14A; (2) 4, (3) 5, (4) 6, (5) 7, (6) 8, and so on, where the numbers in brackets are the pathway numbers shown in Fig. 9.14B and the numbers without brackets are Leonardo's numbers within each node (circle) in Fig. 9.14A. In this way, all the path numbers (seen in Fig. 9.14B, but not 9.14A), like the circled numbers (seen in Fig. 9.14A), are unique in a series or a set of regular numbers from 1 to 38 along each of the paths between the nodes, and between 2 and 40 in each of the circles or nodes.

Multifurcation is a special feature of Leonardo's tree, that is, the ancestral branch splits or forks into more than two branches at particular internal nodes. Leonardo shows a tree in Fig. 9.14A with trichotomous branching stemming from seven different nodes; (2), (22), (24), (30), (31), (33) and (36). He probably observed and copied this type of trichotomous branching in flowering plants like the *Edgeworthia chrysantha*.

Another feature of Leonardo's Proportion Tree is that it takes 9 steps from the first position or root to reach the terminal position of any of his 5 trichotomous terminal nodes (19, 20, 21), (25, 26, 27), (28, 29, 32), (34, 35,

40) or (37, 38, 39). These 9 steps are a fortuitous number given that the number of self-avoiding walks of length 9 stems from the number 2034 on Pacioli's chalkboard. The 9-step number and the trichotomy (division into three categories) are the most telling connections between Leonardo's Proportion Tree and his 'magic numbers' calculation on the chalkboard in the *Pacioli Portrait*.

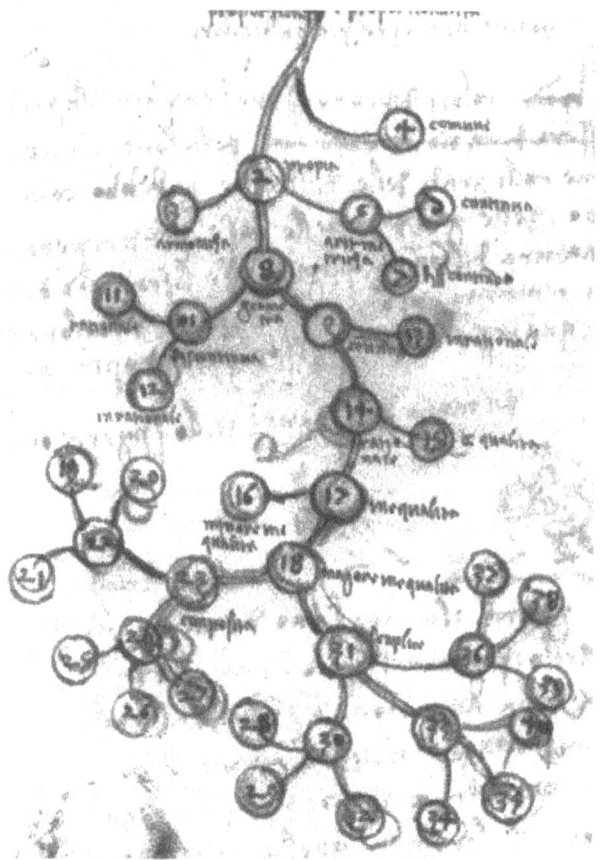

FIG. 9.14A. *Leonardo da Vinci's Proportion Tree*.

For no discernible reason, there are 24 terminal nodes with 14 terminal nodes on the right and 10 terminal nodes on the left. There are five single-node terminations (3, 4, 13, 15, 16), two 2-node terminations (6 & 7, 11 & 12), and five three-node terminations (19, 20, 21; 25, 26, 27; 28, 29, 32; 34, 35, 40; 37, 38, 39) resulting in 12 families, groups or ancestral connections. The terminal clusters stem from 12 nodes, assuming that node 4 stems from an invisible or unmarked node.

CHAPTER 9

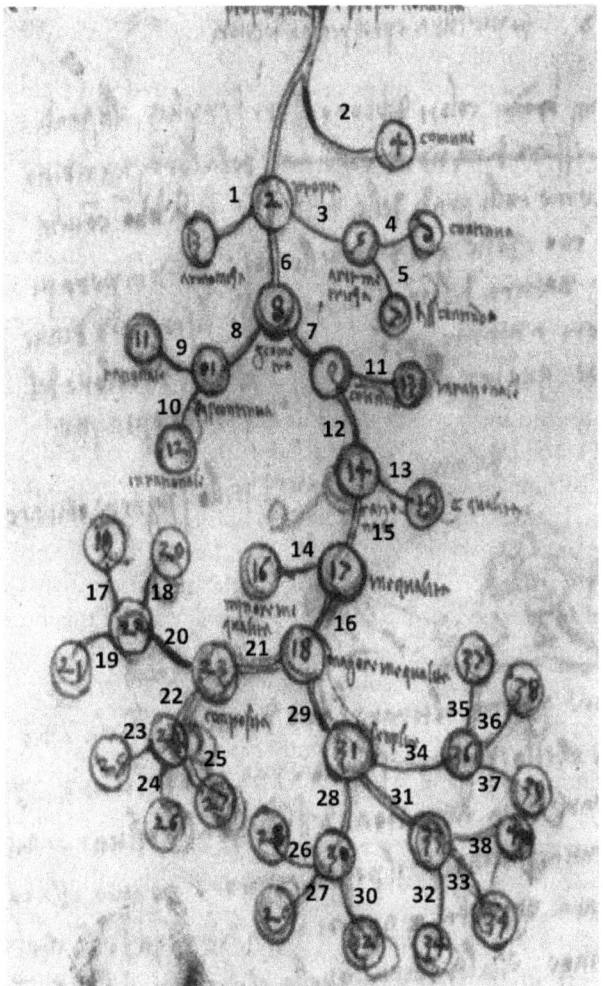

FIG. 9.14B. *Leonardo da Vinci's Proportion Tree. Jerzy Kulski has added numbers 1 to 38 on the branches between Leonardo's circled numbers (2 to 40) based on calculations of relative proportional differences between the circled numbers that are discussed in the text.*

[a] A pattern of threes in the number sequence of 2 to 40 nodes

In a progression of the numbers from branch to node in Fig. 9.14B that is formulated as 1 to 3 (6), 2 to 4 (9), 3 to 5 (12), 4 to 6 (15) and so on, ending at 38 to 40 (117), the number in brackets is the sum of the progression of numbers between the branch number and the node number and it is always divisible initially by 3. For example, in the first progression 1 to 3, the sum of the progression of numbers between 1 on the branch and 3 on the node is 1+2+3=6, and the sum 6 is placed in brackets. Similarly, in the last progression of 38 to 40, the sum of the progression of numbers between 38 on the branch and 40 on the node is 38+39+40=117, and the sum 117 is placed in brackets. In this way, each transition from branch number to node number in Fig. 9.14B produces a number that is divisible by three when the progression of numbers between the branch number and the node number is summed and the middle number between the branch and node number is added to the formulae. This produces an arithmetic progression of 39 numbers from 3 to 117 that are separated from each other by 3 (3, 6, 12, 15 ...117). The branch to node number progression of 1 to 39 (x3) is one number above the author's branch number progression of 1 to 38 and Leonardo's node numbers of 2 to 40 in Fig.9.14B. The 39 is divisible by 3 whereas 38 and 40 are not. Thus, each node is separated symbolically and mathematically from its connecting branch by the number one (God's power), two (the Father and the Son [man and woman]) and a hidden third number (the Holy Ghost [life and resurrection]) that produces a pattern of threes (the Holy Triangle or Holy Trilogy) in a progression of the nodes from 2 to 40 in Fig. 9.14A. Was Leonardo aware of the different number patterns (1, 2, 3) separating his branches from his nodes in his arithmetic progression of 2 to 40? He probably shared this number game of progressive patterns with Fra Luca Pacioli as a holy joke about the Holy Trinity and the mysteries of life, creation and the universe.

On this basis, three is the unseen number that transitions between the branch number and the node number on Leonardo's Proportion Tree. Whether intentional or not Leonardo is showing us how numbers can be easily transitioned into other numbers or patterns and still be maintained within a logical framework. This kind of reasoning led him to produce his coded message IACO.B AR. VIGEN NIS. P. 149(5?) in the *Pacioli Portrait* that is discussed in detail in Chapter 20. Incidentally, the year in the coded message is divisible by 3 if it is **1494** (sum of 18, with 18/3=6) or **1497** (sum of 21, with 21/3=7), but not if it is 1495 (19/3), 1496 (20/3), 1498 (22/3) or 1499 (23/3)

In a previous section, I discussed the 'angel number' 9 that is divisible by 3 to the whole number 3. In this section, I have revealed Leonardo's hidden 'angel number' 3 that can be found between the 'hidden' branch numbers and the visible node numbers in Fig. 9.14A. This game of three by three in Leonardo's Proportion Tree connects him tangentially to his three numbers of three on Pacioli's blackboard (Fig. 9.10).

[b] Why did Leonardo finish his tree nodes with the number 40?

Leonardo's polytomous branching tree is an illustration of the progression of numbers from 2 to 40 that sum (2+3+4+5...40) to 819, which in turn sum (8+1+9) to 18, and then (1+8) to 9, a number that is divisible by 3.

This number game with 3, 6 or 9 where 2 to 40 are 39 numbers, where 3+(3x3=9)=12 (1+2=3) takes us back to the number 2034 on Pacioli's chalkboard (Fig. 9.10) where 2+0+3+4=9, a number that is divisible by 3. This connection between the *Pacioli Portrait* and Leonardo's Proportion Tree is more than a simple coincidence. This link is synchronous. It shows us Leonardo's interest in 3+3+3=9 and that the sum of digits in a number divisible by three always reduces to 3. And yet, despite this simplicity, it seems that Leonardo liked to discover the different ways that arithmetic numbers can be brought together to reduce down to 3 or add up to 9.

The terminal number 40 is an octagonal number and part of a sequence of generalised pentagonal numbers, that is, it is the sum of the first four pentagonal numbers, and it is a pentagonal pyramidal number. It is also a repeated digit of 4 numbers in base 3 (1111, $3^0+3^1+3^2+3^3$). The number 40 in the bible is mentioned 146 times in the Scriptures that generally symbolises a period of trial, tribulations or testing (for Mosses, Noah, Jonah, Ezekiel. Elijah, children of Israel), the generation of man (wandering the wilderness for forty years) and rebirth (e.g., after God flooded the earth with rain for 40 days and nights).

Fundamentally, the number 40 represents the square and circle in Leonardo's mind. He started his tree from a point (represented by zero or 1) from which he drew his lines (represented by 2) with 39 branches ending in the number 40 in one of the terminal nodes. The 4 in 40 is the smallest squared prime and it represents the 4-sided (quadrilateral) plane figure, which includes the rhombi, rectangles and squares, while the 0 in 40 represents the circle, ellipse or curve in his paintings, drawings and writings. The point, line, circle and square are the fundamental shapes in all art. The square and the circle are distinctly represented in his *Vitruvian Man* (Chapter 11), whereas the squares and curved shapes are transformed and more subtly distributed throughout the *Pacioli Portrait*. If the circle that is drawn on the Pacioli blackboard is divided by 4, then it makes right angles and four quadrants (Fig. 8.2), which is the basis of the base number of a mathematic plane, the cardinal directions, four seasons, and the duodecimal and the vigesimal systems. Leonardo da Vinci claimed that he squared the circle; the *Vitruvian Man* may be proof that he succeeded (See Chapter 11 for a detailed discussion). In the same spirit, we must consider then that the numbers in his sum 2034 in Fig. 9.10 are ultimately the numbers 0, 2, 3, and 4 that he used symbolically to represent a point, a line between two points, a triangle and a square or rhombi, respectively, in his *Pacioli Portrait* as previously discussed in Chapter 8. However, the numbers 0 or 1, 2, 3 and 4 are also spiritual symbols, where 4 represents God's righteousness, truth and moral virtue, and His creation of the Universe on the 4th day. In this sense, Leonardo's Tree represents Creation starting with God's power

(0 and 1), Man and Woman (2), the mysterious Holy Trinity (3), and ending in God's creation of the sun, moon, stars and life on the fourth day (4).

[c] Categorical and Biological Trees

The handwritten labels associated with certain numbers in Leonardo's proportion tree (Fig. 9.14) represent different types of mathematical categories (*coiter, continua, arithmetica, proprietdicta, armonica, discontinua, geometrica, irrationalis, continua, discontinuua,* e.t.c.,) that Luca Pacioli included in his tree of mathematical categories and that he presented in the appendix of *De Divina Proportione* (Fig. 9.15). In this context, both Leonardo and Luca's trees are a metaphor for the evolution of human mathematical and scientific knowledge stemming from a seed (origin) and then branching out into various categories.

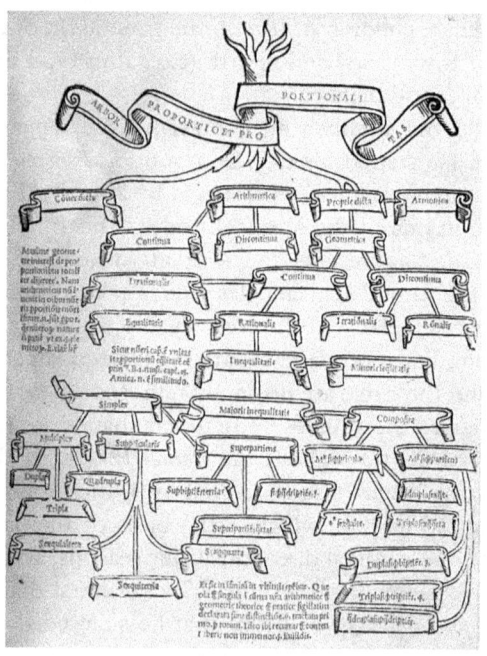

FIG. 9.15. *Luca Pacioli's Tree of Proportions and Proportionality from* De Divina Proportione *published in 1509.*

Why Leonardo calculated and drew the proportionality tree of natural numbers with differences of 2 and 3 in Fig. 9.14A is a mystery, but it is probably the result of his study of the growth and development of plants. It resembles the evolutionary tree of life and appears to be the precursor to the modern science and bioinformatics of evolutionary pathways, tree building and branching, and drawing phylogenetic networks and distance matrices. In fact, for Leonardo, mathematical principles and geometry conditioned the growth patterns and forms of plants. In the folio 78V of the Paris Manuscript M with an accompanying drawing, Leonardo formulated that when the branches of plants matured each year, the sum total of their cross-section is equal to the cross-section of the trunk (Fig. 9.16). In the modern plant sciences, this is *The Leonardo da Vinci Rule* expressed as '*the sum of the cross-sectional area of all tree branches above a branching point at any height is equal to the cross-sectional area of the trunk or the branch immediately below the branching point.*' This rule was tested as recently as 2014 by two Japanese scientists, Ryoko Minamino and Masaki Tateno, using simulations based on biomechanical models, and they concluded in their published paper, entitled *Tree Branching: Leonardo da Vinci's Rule versus Biomechanical Models*, that *The Leonardo da Vinci Rule* is valid under realistic measurement conditions.

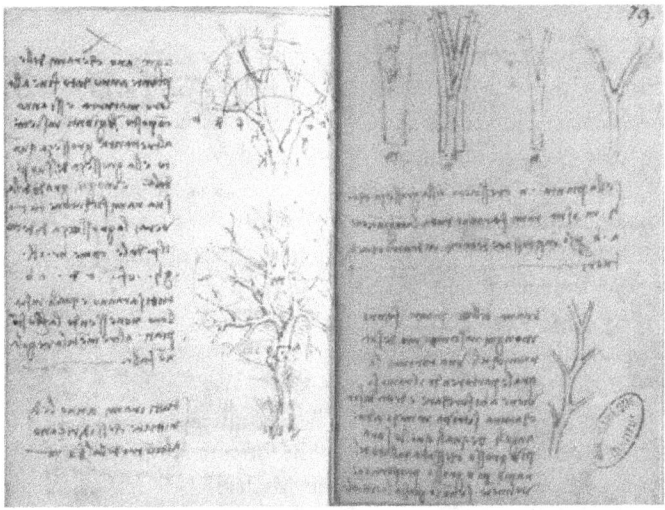

FIG. 9.16. Leonardo da Vinci's tree growth rule illustrated in Folio 78v-79r of Paris Manuscript M.

Leonardo's Mathematical Acculturation by Luca Pacioli

The studies of Augusto Marinoni on the mathematics of Leonardo have demonstrated that his arithmetic and geometric knowledge was proficient, but limited before the arrival of Luca Pacioli in Milan. This coincided with a process of mathematical acculturation of Leonardo that is demonstrated in the Forster II (1st), Madrid II, and in the manuscripts M, I, L and K (I and II) of the Institut de France, dating from the period of attendance of the two Tuscans in Milan and the writing of the *Divine Proportion*. The careful and precise analysis of the mathematical writings contained in Leonardo da Vinci notebooks led Marinoni to the following conclusion:

'*From 1496 until about 1504 Leonardo is in continuous or occasional contact, direct or indirect (through the books of maestro Luca) with Pacioli. In these years, his love for geometry is ignited and developed, both in his drawings for* Divina Proportione *and in the systematic study of Euclid, clearly demonstrated for the first six books and part of the tenth. The presence of the latter from the first "lessons" means that Leonardo immediately faced the problem of irrational numbers, or the relationship between incommensurable segments, such as the side and the diagonal of the square, the radius and the circumference and the problem of so-called "deaf roots". In this fervent initiation of Leonardo to the problems of geometry he undoubtedly depended on Pacioli, as his inspirer, advisor, teacher and translator. Between the meaningless letters and the difficult Latin of the Elements, the mediation of a mathematical scholar who was also his friend was indispensable, and so he called his teacher, Luca, a compatriot.*'

In Leonardo's manuscript K, dotted with numerous references to the propositions of the *Elements* of Euclid, (f.49r) is written: '*The proportion not only in numbers and measures found, but also in sounds, weights, times and sites and any empower you both*'. This phrase was copied word by word by Leonardo from Luca Pacioli's *Summa* and it testifies to the universality of the application of the theory contained in the fifth book of Euclid's *Elements*. Pacioli, in turn, translated and copied it from the commentary of Campano in the work of Euclid and probably used it to assist Leonardo in his translation of numerical propositions into a pictorial formulation. Other clues consist of the numerous drawings by Leonardo when he transcribed many of the propositions of the first six books of the *Elements* into his visual language and mirror writing. These drawings further testify to the lessons given on Euclid by Pacioli for the benefit of the artist. In a list of written works cited by Leonardo in the Madrid code 8936, the first three books that he listed were by Luca Pacioli who had introduced him to the study of the *Elements*.

The public lectures by Fra Luca Pacioli in Milan concerned the work of Euclid and these are repeated in the first ten chapters of the *Divine Proportion* that was completed by 1498. The discussion of the irrationals contained in the tenth chapter of the *Elements,* was undoubtedly a difficult subject for most of the students who attended the friar's Milanese lessons. However, the different propositions in chapter ten appear in graphic form in Leonardo's notebooks and in particular in the *Madrid* codice at the Institut de France. Marinoni noted that the tenth chapter is the least read and the most difficult of the books of the *Elements*, but that it has a practical application for the construction of polyhedra. So when Pacioli arrived in Milan and became friends with Leonardo he would have asked him to design and illustrate polyhedra for his *De Divina Proportione*. To do this properly, Leonardo must have read the *Elements* and the *Summa* to assimilate the theory of proportions (Manuscript Forster II). Neither Leonardo nor Barbari (if he indeed was the author of the *Pacioli Portrait*) could have developed such complex geometric constructions as those of the rhombicuboctahedron, dodecahedron or the icosahedron *planus, vacuus, abscissus, elevatus,* without profoundly understanding and improving on the previously scant knowledge about dimensions, surface area and volume, symmetry, rotation, the three-dimensional properties and the pictorial geometry of these complex solids (Fig. 9.17).

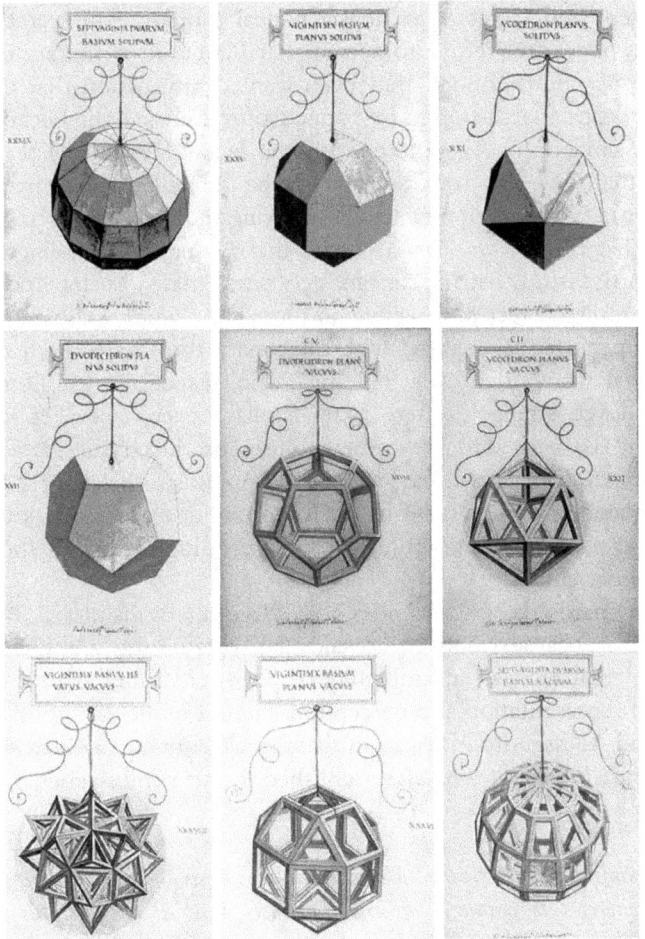

FIG. 9.17. *An example of 9 of the 60 paintings of geometric shapes and solids that Leonardo da Vinci provided for Luca Pacioli's 1498 edition of* Divine Proportion.

We have some insights from Leonardo's history and notebooks on how he gained and developed this knowledge, but how Jacopo de Barbari could have become an expert on the design of polyhedrons remains a total mystery and is beyond any reasonable credence given what we already know about the intellectual relationship between Leonardo and Luca Pacioli.

The mathematical acculturation of Leonardo da Vinci as the self proclaimed *'man without letters'* after the meeting with Fra Luca Pacioli in 1496 is undeniable. Is there any such evidence that Jacopo de' Barbari underwent similar mathematical acculturation under the auspices of Luca Pacioli? None. On the other hand, we know that Leonardo is the author of the geometric drawings for the *Divina Proportione* (Fig. 9.17) and that he was an exponent and collector of mathematical puzzles. And yet the critics remain sceptical and refuse to accept that Leonardo is the author of the *Pacioli Portrait*. Furthermore, they even wanted affirmation that the panels of polyhedrons that he drew or painted only came about because of his gradual assimilation to geometry with the help of Pacioli. They want to ascertain that the geometric drawings for the *Divina Proportione* are the result of science rather than simple art and copying models constructed by Luca Pacioli. That is, they want to ascertain that Leonardo's drawings matured following the study of Euclidean geometry that was transposed in a mathematically correct perspective and were not simply the product of an empirical perspective, realised with illusionary tools and based on three-dimensional wooden models built by Pacioli especially for Leonardo to copy. And yet, strangely, there is no similar concern or skepticism that Jacopo de' Barbari somehow miraculously produced the *Pacioli Portrait* without ever having met Luca Pacioli or ever studied the shapes, structures and mathematics of polyhedrons (well, not as far as anybody knows; it is strange, how the collective mind works in creating bizarre mythologies in the art history circles).

The Leonardo da Vinci sceptics have forgotten or dismissed that he was first and foremost a scientist who said that painting was a science and not an art and that art was an ambiguity of perspective understood to be the science of representation and perception. Here, I quote the words of Fabio Frosini and Allessandro Nova from their article entitled *Leonardo da Vinci on nature: knowledge and representation*, published in the Venice series S. 11-31 of 2015.

The ambiguity of perspective, which he understood as the science of representation, which is connected to painting but simultaneously returned to its status as natural philosophy and returned to the theory of vision, constantly keeps both levels in play: nature understood in its most profound reality, almost as a fact that affirms its power in relation to the observer, and art as interaction with this profound reality, but also emulation, competition and, in some respects, its reduction on the basis of precise conventions, i.e. a "language", which is verified by the effects it produces in the audience of the visual show staged in the painting.'

Sylvie Duvernoy, an architect in Florence, in her article entitled '*Leonardo and Theoretical Mathematics*' for the *Nexus Network Journal* in 2008, explored and highlighted Leonardo da Vinci's study of mathematics late in life and his attempts to rise above planar geometry and reach the realm of the third dimension, only to be defeated by the limited possibilities of his period to calculate quantities. However, she made the following conclusion about his drawings for Luca Pacioli:

'On a more general level, we may conclude that Leonardo contributed to mathematical and scientific research in the Renaissance period by demonstrating the power of the tool of three-dimensional representation as a research device as well as a persuasive instrument. The well-known series of drawings of the Platonic solids and non-solids that he made as illustrations for the book of his friend Luca Pacioli is simply one of the many examples of this.'

Sylvie Duvernoy noted that when Leonardo da Vinci first met Luca Pacioli, he started a systematic study of theoretical mathematics, going from recent and contemporary publications back to classical sources and textbooks. There is ample evidence in his notebooks that he tackled two galling and taxing geometric problems still occupying the scientists of his time: the duplication of the cube and the squaring of the circle. Although he put in an enormous and an ingenious effort using graphical, geometric, arithmetic and stereometric approaches in an attempt to solve these problems, Sylvie Duvernoy believes that there is no evidence that he ever succeeded. He did make some geometric discoveries along the way, which were mostly empirical (by chance) than by explanatory theory; and he achieved his greatest mathematical result using a mechanical approach in the realm of three-dimensional geometry by determining the location of the centre of gravity of a pyramid. The generalization of this discovery led to the statement in the *codex Arundel, folio 218* that, '*the centre of gravity of any pyramid – round, triangular, square, or of any number of sides – is in the fourth part of its axis near the base.*' He had an additional theorem in his *Codex Arundel folio 123v* concerning the tetrahedron, which might have been an unique finding by him:

'The pyramid with triangular base has the centre of its natural gravity in the segment which extends from the middle of the base [that is the midpoint of one edge] to the middle of the side [that is, edge] opposite the base; and it is located on the segment equally distant of the line joining the base with the aforesaid side.'

References

Atalay, Bulent (2014). Math and the Mona Lisa: the art and science of Leonardo da Vinci. Smithsonian Books, Washington.

Baldasso R (2010). The Portrait of Luca Pacioli and Disciple: a new mathematical look. Art Bulletin, Vol. XCII, n°. 1-2, pp. 83-102.

Bryanton, Robert (2010). Our Universe as a Dodecahedron.
https://www.youtube.com/watch?v=Qu1GD_AifpM

Capra, Fritjof (2008). The Science of Leonardo: Inside the Mind of the Great Genius of the Renaissance. Anchor Books Edition, New York.
https://erenow.net/biographies/the-science-of-leonardo-inside-the-mind-of-the-great-genius-of-the-renaissance/

Ciocci, Argante. Luca Pacioli, Leonardo da Vinci and the divine proportion.
http://www.e-theca.net/emiliopanella/hospes/ciocci.htm

Ciocci, Argante (2015): The double portrait of the polyhedral Luca Pacioli. Spanish Journal of Accounting History. No.15, 107-130.
http://www.e-theca.net/emiliopanella/hospes/ciocci.htm

DeFord, Ruth I (2015). Tactus, mensuration and rhythm in the Renaissance music. Cambridge, United Kingdom. Cambridge University Press.

Duvernoy, Sylvia (2008). Leonardo and theoretical mathematics. Nexus Network Journal 10: 39-50.

Euclid (1956). The Thirteen Books of The Elements. Sir Thomas L. Heath, trans. Vol 2. New York: Dover Publications.

Frosini, Fabio and Nova, Allessandro (2015). Leonardo da Vinci on nature: knowledge and representation, published in the Venice series S. 11-31.

Gamba, Enrico (2010): Proviamo a rileggere il "Doppio ritratto" di Luca Pacioli. In F.M. Cesaroni, M. Ciambotti, E. Gamba, V. Montebelli, *Le tre facce del poliedrico Luca Pacioli*, Quaderni del Centro Internazionale di Studi Uribo e la Prospettiva, Urbino Age.

Gamba, Enrico (2011). Proviamo a rileggere il *"Doppio ritratto"* di Luca Pacioli. Online at Hevelius' webzine. Matematica e Cultura. Speciale Venezia marzo.
http://www.hevelius.it/webzine/leggi.php?codice=242

Hedges, Joe (2010). Leonardo da Vinci the Musician.
http://www.joehedges.com/2010/03/leonardo-da-vinci-the-musician/?fbclid=IwAR3zDyGTS3u5I4OgEEkAbWykHdfs5kGdzSKRivK35MFydpcciOSFWZcltrs

Hill, Michael Lee (2018). 432 Hz – Unlocking The Magnificence Of The 3, 6 and 9, The Key To The Universe!
https://michaelleehill.net/blogs/news/432-hz-unlocking-the-magnificence-of-the-3-6-and-9-the-key-to-the-universehttps://www.youtube.com/watch?v=-3gLxPdamK8

Iwamoto A, Matsumura Y, Ohba H, Murata J, Imaichi R (2005). Development and structure of trichotomous branching in *Edgeworthia chrysantha* (Thymelaeaceae). American Journal Botany 92:1350-1358.

Kingsbury, Stephen A. (2002). Tempo and Mensural Proportion in the music of the Sixteenth Century. Choral Journal 42 (9):25-33.

Lite, Gary: The Secret Behind Numbers 369. Tesla Code Is Finally REVEALED!
https://www.youtube.com/watch?v=GnEWOYKgI4o

Mackinnon, Nick (1993). The Portrait of Fra Luca Pacioli. The Mathematical Gazette 77:130-219.
Marani, Pietro C (2016). Leonardo's *Cartonetti* for Luca Pacioli's Platonic Bodies. In: Illuminating Leonardo. A Festschrift for Carlo Pedretti Celebrating His 70 Years of Scholarship (1944-2014). Leonardo studies, Volume 1. Brill. ISBN: 9789004304130.
Marinoni, Augusto (1982). La matematica di Leonardo da Vinci. Arcadia.
Minamino R, Tateno M (2014). Tree Branching: Leonardo da Vinci's Rule versus Biomechanical Models. PLoS ONE 9(4): e93535.
 https://doi.org/10.1371/journal.pone.0093535
Pacioli, Luca (1509). De Divine Proportione. Printed edition (Italian). Getty Research Institute. *https://archive.org/details/divinaproportion00paci/page/n3*
Pacioli, Luca (1509). De Divine Proportione. Printed edition (Italian) De Divina Proportione. Published on Aug 23, 2011, Stevens Institute of Technology.
 https://issuu.com/s.c.williams-library/docs/de_divina_proportione
Pacioli, Luca (1498). Divine Proportion (in English). 1498 edition. *Tennenbaum pacioli-divine-proportion.pdf.* Uploaded by Israel Monroy Muñoz on Oct 22, 2014. Full text of original edition (1498) in English.
 https://www.scribd.com/document/244035060/tennenbaum-pacioli-divine-proportion-pdf
Robert, Vesna Petresin (2008). Perception of order and ambiguity in Leonardo's design concepts. Nexus Network Journal 10:101-128.
Swetz FJ. Leonardo da Vinci's Geometric Sketches.
 https://www.maa.org/book/export/html/116816
Hirth TWNDS (2015). Luca Pacioli and his 1500 book De Viribus Quantitatis. Thesis. Master in the History and Philosophy of Sciences. Autonomous Section of History and Philosophy of Science, Faculty of Sciences, University of Lisbon, Lisbon, Portugal. Fig 20 shows Luca Pacioli's Magic Square.
Talwalker, Presh (2015). 3x3 magic squares.
 https://mindyourdecisions.com/blog/2015/11/08/how-many-3x3-magic-squares-are-there-sunday-puzzle/
 https://www.youtube.com/watch?v=zPnN046OM34
Winternitz, Emanual (1982). Leonardo da Vinci as a Musician. New Haven and London. Yale University Press.
Zollner, Frank (2013). A double Leonardo. On two exhibitions (and their catalogues) in London and Paris. Zeitschrift fur Kunstgeschichte 76:417-427.
 https://www.gko.unileipzig.de/fileadmin/user_upload/kunstgeschichte/pdf/zoellner/Publikationen/unselbst_Publi/Zoellner-A_Double_Leonardo.pdf
Zollner, Frank (2015). Leonardo. Basic Art 2.0. Taschen Art, Reprint Edition, Amazon.

10

SPHERICAL TRIANGLES & GLOBAL PROJECTIONS

Vesica Piscis, Global Projections and a Perspectograph for Drawing an Armillary Sphere

Leonardo da Vinci had a great interest in the ways that he could project images onto different shaped surfaces and objects. There is evidence that Leonardo designed and constructed isometric global projections of world maps (Fig. 10.1, top) and projected images of them onto polyhedrons or spherical structures (Fig. 10.2). This might have been his version of the thoroughly modern 'philospheres'. Essentially, Leonardo da Vinci was drawing and displaying spherical geometrical triangles approximately four hundred years before Franz Reuleaux published his book on the importance of these triangles in the design of machines rotating in a square. Drill bits for drilling square holes are one such example of the use of the shape of the Reuleaux triangle in machinery, and many guitarists use the Reuleaux triangle as a guitar pick. These triangles are widely used in design and architecture, as rolling cylinders and as parts in engineering mechanical linkages and for reciprocating motion.

Leonardo showed how to create these spherical triangles with a compass from the arcs of three circles with their centres at the apices of the triangle. He also constructed the Reuleaux triangle within a pentagon within a circle (Fig. 10.1, lower left) as if this was a precursor to or an afterthought of his *Vitruvian Man* (Chapter 11). These spherical or Reuleaux triangles resemble the shapes of some petals and leaves of plants that Leonardo was interested in. Also, they are related to the *Vesica Piscis* or 'fishes bladder' that were crude representations of the vagina or vulva in prehistoric art and as symbols of fish since the birth of Christianity. Barrallo and colleagues, in a 2015 journal publication illustrated how the *Vesica Piscis* was drawn geometrically from two intersecting circles or by

CHAPTER 10

circumventing a diamond constructed of two equilateral triangles (Fig. 10.3). Leonardo da Vinci was fascinated by these curvilinear triangles seen in nature and he used them in his design of trefoil knots, heptagon shapes and even added them to the bodice of his painting of *Mona Lisa* to show that she was connected to Milan's Sforza family and not to the Florentine del Giocondo family, a myth that continues to be propagated to this day. These trefoil knots form the basis of the Borromean Rings gifted by Francesco Sforza, the 4th Duke of Milan, as a symbol to the Borromeo family in recognition for the support they gave him in defence of Milan.

The design of the eight-spherical-geometrical triangles that made up the isometric octant world maps known as the *Mappamundi* (Fig. 10.1, top) could be projected on to the surface of a sphere to produce the globe of the world or the universe that are displayed in the hand of the *Salvator Mundi* in some Renaissance versions painted by Leonardo da Vinci, his assistants and others (Fig. 10.2, right). There is even a drawing by Michelangelo of a philosopher with a human skull in his hands (Fig. 10.2, left) that might be Leonardo da Vinci giving a lecture in Rome when they were both there between 1513 and 1516. Again, Leonardo da Vinci seems to have been way ahead of his time in the different ways of constructing and displaying images.

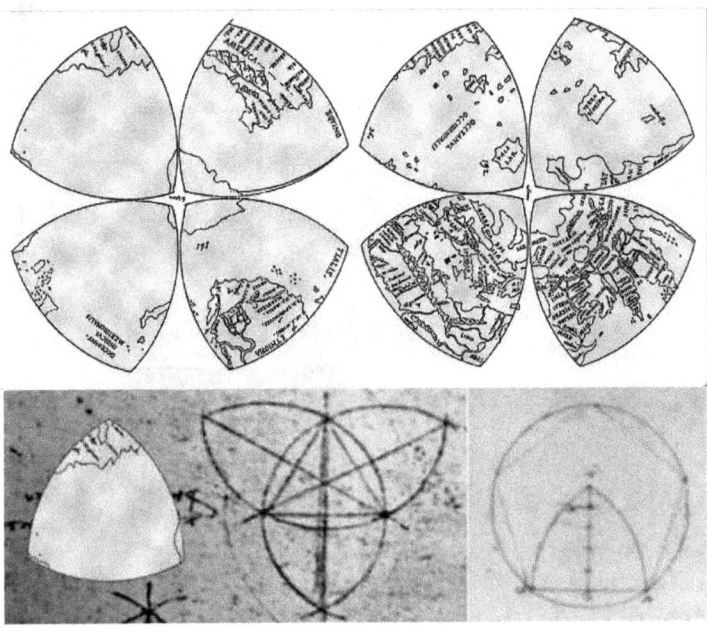

FIG. 10.1. Leonardo's octant world map using 'equidistant triangular globe gores' (above) and drawings of curvilinear triangles (below) inspired by similar shapes seen in nature. Tyler (2017).

FIG. 10.2. Left, Michelangelo's drawing of an old man with a human skull. Right, Leonardo's painting of the Salvator Mundi *with a glass orb with 3 points in a triangular shape.*

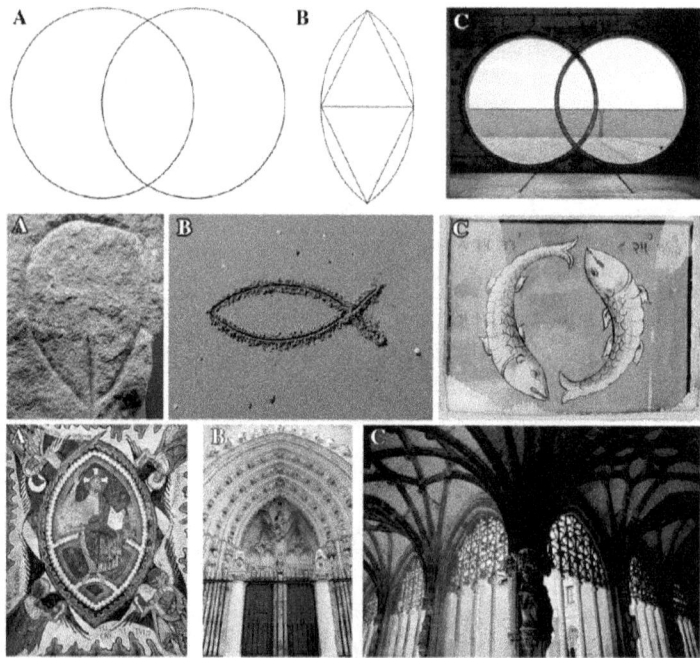

FIG. 10.3. Vesica Piscis. Top (A, B, C), diagrams and architectural constructs of the Vesica Piscis *or Reuleaux Triangle. Middle, A, prehistoric engraving; and B and C, Christian symbols of the* Vesica Piscis. *Bottom (A, B, C), artistic and architectural shapes of the* Vesica Piscis *like constructs. For more information see Barrallo et al., (2015).*

Leonardo's interest in perspective and measuring spheres and polygons is depicted in his drawing of an armillary sphere (or spherical astrolabe) using a perspective window (perspectograph) for drawing perspective correctly of three-dimensional objects (Fig. 10.4). The spherical astrolabe that da Vinci chose to depict in his drawing of the perspectograph is an analytic device of adjustable rings that models objects in the sky centred on the Earth or the Sun. This drawing probably dates back to his Florentine period before 1481. Leonardo's perspectograph for obtaining and transferring the points and outlines of a scence or picture was a clear pane of glass placed into a frame on a stand in front of a viewing slot. The painter placed the perspectograph in front of the scene to be painted, and then while looking through the viewing slot with one eye, he outlined the scene onto the glass. The drawing could be easily transferred onto canvas as an outline and then the details drawn or painted in as required.

FIG. 10.4. *Drawing of a man using a perspectograph to draw an armillary sphere. Leonardo da Vinci (Codex Atlanticus I, 5r; ~1480).*

The modern perspectograph is used today mainly for learning how to draw and as a copying tool. It is better known as the View Frame and it can be purchased on the Internet, advertised as a tool for teaching the artist to understand and translate linear perspective, measure proportions, foreshorten, scaling, composition, tilts, angles and the rule of thirds.

The armillary sphere is used to create stereographic projections or maps onto a flat plane, some of which are illustrated in Leonardo's notebooks. Stereographical mapping is accomplished by drawing straight lines from the North Pole of the sphere or the polygon to the plane on a flat surface. Lines drawn from one point pierce the spheres surface to connect to the plane tangent at the point's antipode (Fig. 10.5). The Greek astronomer Ptolemy (c. AD 100-170) knew the principles of stereographic projection in antiquity. Modern European scholars learnt these principles largely from Arabic writers. A major source of these principles in the 17th century was the French Jesuit Francois de Aguilon's long account of stereographic projection in his publication the *Opticorum* (1613). This account was accompanied by an image of a literal projection of the heavens, with a light being shone through an armillary held by Atlas and the spheres and circles of the armillary projected as shadows on the ground (Fig. 10.6). The image was a print from the engravings made by Peter Paul Rubens (1577-1640) and it shows how projection works. It is very different from the method of Vitruvius (1st Century BC) and the drawings of the position of the Sun in the sky (*analemma*) featured in the *De Architectura* that Leonardo would have studied.

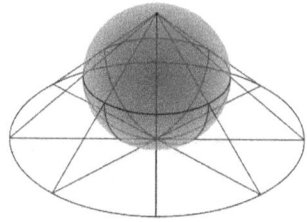

FIG. 10.5. *A 3D stereographical projection from the north pole onto a plane below the sphere. CheChe version adapted from Mark Howison at English Wikipedia. File licensed under Creative Commons Attribution-Share Alike 4.0 international.*
https://commons.wikimedia.org/wiki/File:Stereographic_projection_in_3D.svg

FIG. 10.6. *Illustration by Rubens for 'Opticorum libri sex philosophis juxta ac mathematicis utiles', by François d'Aguilon. It demonstrates the principle of a general perspective projection, of which the stereographic projection is a special case. Public Domain. Wikipedia.*
https://en.wikipedia.org/wiki/Stereographic_projection#/media/File:RubensAguilonStereographic.jpg

The Da Vinci Globe: the World Map on an Ostrich Egg

In 2012 an engraved ostrich egg was found at a London map fair that showed a detailed map of the world cartographed during the Renaissance geographical explorations (Fig. 10.7, left). It soon became known as the Da Vinci Globe. The investigations of Professor Carlo Pedretti, the famed art historian and expert on the works of Leonardo da Vinci, revealed that the world map on the ostrich egg was designed and constructed by Leonardo dating from 1504. Moreover, irrefutable evidence published by Professor Stefaan J. Missinne in 2018 showed that the Da Vinci Globe was the first constructed globe to show the map of the world after Christopher Columbus's four voyages between 1492 and 1502, and the prototype for the Lenox Globe, a copper globe dating from 1504 (Fig. 10.7, right) and that is exhibited at the New York Public Library (NYPL). The surface details of this copper globe can be accessed and seen in detail on the Internet as the *Hunt-Lenox Globe* at the NYPL collections. Recent extensive studies of the pictograph of the ostrich egg (the Da Vinci Globe) by Geert J. Verhoeven and Stefaan J. Missinne (2019), referenced at the end of this chapter, confirmed beyond reasonable doubt that the artist of both globes was Leonardo da Vinci. The provenance of the egg-shells used for the da Vinci Globe was traced back to ostriches that were kept in an enclosure (the Struzzeria) in the castle garden of the Viscount of Milan in Pavia.

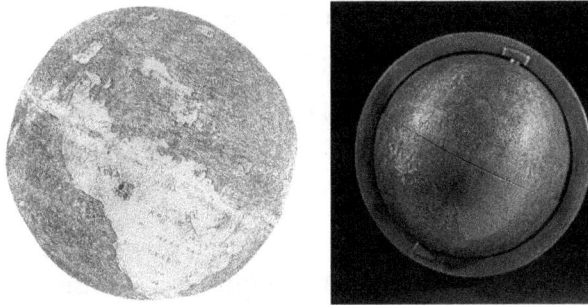

FIG. 10.7. *The Da Vinci Globe (left) and the Hunt-Lenox Globe shown in the paper by Verhoeven and Missinne (2017) and obtained with permission from Stefaan J. Missinne.*

Nicholas of Cusa's Paradox of the Polygon and the Nonmatching Circle

The German cardinal and theologian Nicholas of Cusa (1401-1464) wrote many essays on philosophy, science and mathematics entitled *Of Learned Ignorance, On the Vision of God, The Layman on Mind, On Conjectures* and other titles that influenced Piero della Francesca, Luca Pacioli and Leonardo da Vinci. In his essay *On the Vision of God*, Nicholas of Cusa wrote that man was unable to access the divine directly and in order to illustrate his point he used a metaphor of monks walking along a segment of a semi-circle to look at a painting hanging on the wall of the face of Christ looking back at them. He told the monks that the Son of God is looking at them and following them everywhere:

'He even looks at you when you turn your back on him. But, God looks at everyone at the same time, even while He has a personal relationship with each... It is the icon of You, but with mental and intellectual eyes. This Truth is signified by this contracted shadow-like image. But Your true Face is free of all contraction. For it is neither quantitative nor qualitative nor temporal nor spatial. For it is Absolute Form, which is also the Face of faces.'

To further illustrate his point of man's inability to access the divine directly, Nicholas of Cusa adopted the following mathematical metaphor in *On Learned Ignorance*:

'The more angles the inscribed polygon has, the more similar it is to the circle. However, even if the number of its angles is increased ad infinitum, the polygon never becomes equal, unless it is resolved into an identity with the circle.'

This is because the two objects are of fundamentally different species and natures. Paradoxically, the more successfully you multiply the number of sides and angles (singularities) of the polygon, the further away you get from the circle, which is characterised by having no angles at all.

'All rational and conceptual thought must be renounced, for, just as in the image of a polygon inscribed within a circle, where the multiplication of angles will never allow the polygon to coincide with the circle, so our reasoning will never be able to grasp the totality of the Absolute.'

Curving Triangles and Circular Segments within Circles and Squares

Leonardo da Vinci was fully aware of Cusa's Paradox and he explored various geometric models that transitioned between the triangle, polygons, circle and various other shapes in his drawings and paintings. In his notebooks, da Vinci developed the idea of having the triangle in the square that is in the octagon that is in the circle that is in a square and that is in a rhombus in which the circle, semicircle, quadrant, octant and sector all fill the same area relative to the enclosing square rhombus (Fig. 10.8). A rhombus (a quadrilateral with all sides equal in length and shaped like a diamond) is not a square unless the angles are all right angles, but a square is a rhombus. It is noteworthy, that Leonardo's drawings of the relationship between the circle and its circumscribing square and the diagonals drawn through the circle are represented in the geometry of his famous drawing of the *Vitruvian Man* (Chapter 11). Christopher W. Tyler in his paper on *Leonardo da Vinci's World Map* in 2017 provided a further detailed mathematical analysis of Leonardo's circle in a square rhombus (Fig. 10.8):

'At lower left, he develops an octagonal analysis of the area of a circle inscribed in a square rhombus (regular diamond shape) by approximating it with the eight triangles making up an inscribed octagon, reconfigured as an 'accordion' figure of eight isosceles triangles (or, actually, seven isosceles triangles and two right triangles making up the eighth, labeled abcdefghi) together with a lenticular segment labeled K to account for the eight missing lenticular elements in the octagonal approximation to the circle. This large lenticular segment K should have an area eight times larger than that of each of the eight segments in the circular figure, giving it a linear extent of sqrt(8), or 2*sqrt(2). Deriving this ratio seems to be the motivation for the scaled figures of the semicircle, quadrant, octant and sector, which all fill the same area relative to the original circle, making it clear that the lenticular segment is in the correct ratio of sqrt(8)/4 = 0.707 to the width of the eight triangle figure abcdefghi.'

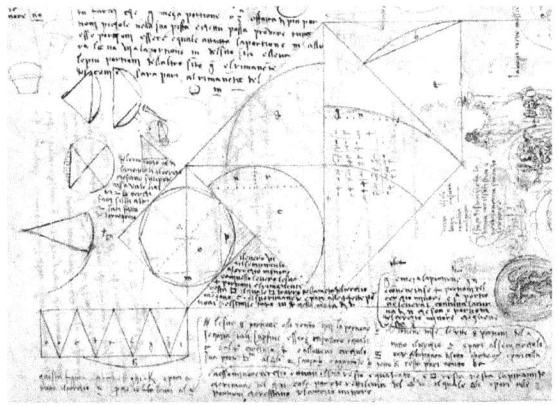

FIG. 10.8. *Octagonal analysis of the area of a circle inscribed in a square rhombus (left-right reversed) in which Da Vinci is developing the idea that the circle, semicircle, quadrant, octant and sector all fill the same area relative to the enclosing rhombic square. (Leonardo da Vinci, Royal Library, Windsor, 12700v; detail).*

Tyler then provided the following observations about squaring the circle:

'This analysis of the area of the circle does not solve the problem of squaring the circle because there is apparently no indication how to derive the area of the lenticular segment, but it does show da Vinci thinking about the progressive fractional subdivisions of circles in a way that can be readily generalised to the solid geometry of spheres. It also links da Vinci directly with Toscanelli in the analysis of the problem of squaring the circle, which at one point he thought he had actually achieved: "On the night of St Andrew I reached the end [i.e., the goal] of squaring the circle and at the end of candlelight, of the night and of the paper on which I was writing, it was completed." (Madrid Manuscript II, 112a).'

'A further analysis in which he took a similar approach to the spherical geometry per se is found in the Paris Manuscript (... [see Fig. 10.9, below]). Here da Vinci subdivides *a sphere into octants and explores different ways of segmenting (or digitizing!) the volume of an octant to quantify its volume. Indeed, this analysis may be considered a precursor to the differential calculus developed formally by Newton and Leibniz nearly two centuries later. Moreover, some of the approaches on these pages involve explicit visualization of the spherical octant as a Reuleaux-like spherical triangle, which may well have been what suggested the Reuleaux triangle approach to Da Vinci for his world map'*

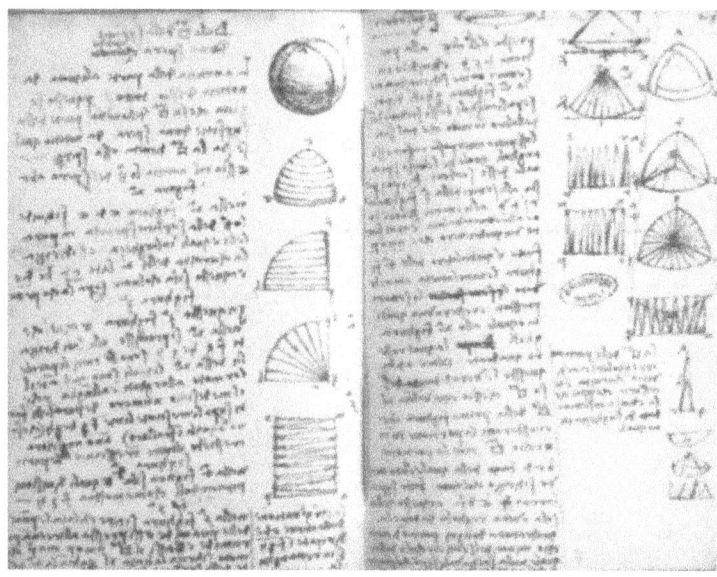

FIG. 10.9. *Octahedral analysis of the volume of a sphere with various forms of segmentation (Leonardo da Vinci, Paris Manuscript E 24v,25r).*

Spherical Triangles in *Salvator Mundi*, the *Pacioli Portrait* and Modern Architecture

In the *Salvator Mundi* painting (Fig. 10.2) Leonardo has placed three dots in a triangular shape on the transparent orb in the hand of Christ (Fig. 10.10). According to Messine and Verhoeven in their recent paper entitled *Leonardo Depicted America: Misread as the Moon* published in Advances in Historical Studies (2019) these three dots form a right-angled triangle that represent the three bright stars of the Southern Cross described by the explorer Amerigo Vespucci in his letter to Lorenzo di Pierfrancesco de' Medici about the *Mundus Novus*. They say the following about the rendition of the three bright stars on Christ's orb of the universe:

'The angle formed by the painted three stars seems to be larger than ninety degrees, but this rendering is entirely normal. It results from the perspective distortion characteristic for

a two-dimensional painting when portraying a right-angled constellation that follows the three-dimensional curvature of the orb, a topic that Leonardo understood and mastered in this painting.'

Given the spherical shape of the orb, these three dots may take on a spherical triangular shape as seen in Fig. 10.9 and depicted in Fig. 10.10. There is also the triangular spherical shape of Christ's palm seen through the transparent orb. This is another example of how Leonardo has taken a conventional geometrical shape like the triangle (3 bright dots) or the rectangle (palm of hand) and changed it into an 'illusionary' spherical triangle in 2D space using the transparent orb as his 3D prop in the *Salvator Mundi* painting.

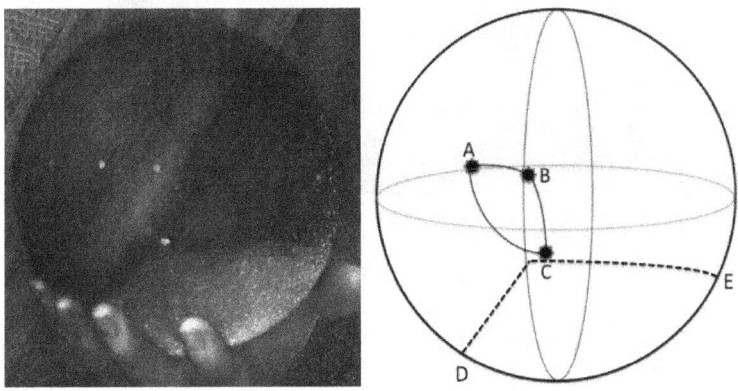

Fig. 10.10. The spherical triangle shaped by the three stars A, B and C (right) on Christ's Orb of the Universe (left). The dashed lines D to C to E closed by the solid line E to D (right) represent the spherical triangular shape of Christ's palm seen through the transparent orb (left).

Some of the spherical triangles drawn in Leonardo da Vinci's notebooks (Fig. 10.9) also can be seen in the *Pacioli Portrait* where parts of Galeazzo Sanseverino's white shirt hang out like transformed triangles from the lower half of his bent left arm (Fig. 10.11). In the *Pacioli Portrait*, the triangular space between the student's arm and the dodecahedron on the red book represent Leonardo's brilliant topological transformations and continuous mapping either as point-set topology or combinatorial topology. These transformations are the white curvilinear triangles where one of them continues at right angles and transforms into a distorted rectangular shape of frayed leopard-skinned cloth. Given the placement of these topologies beside and on top of the dodecahedron, the effect is startling and mysterious. The imaginary dashed line (a, a') from the arm to the closed book points the viewer's eye directly to the raised circular button (a') on the cover of the red book labelled with the inscription *H. R.LV* and *BVR* separated by a red clasp. What was Leonardo thinking?

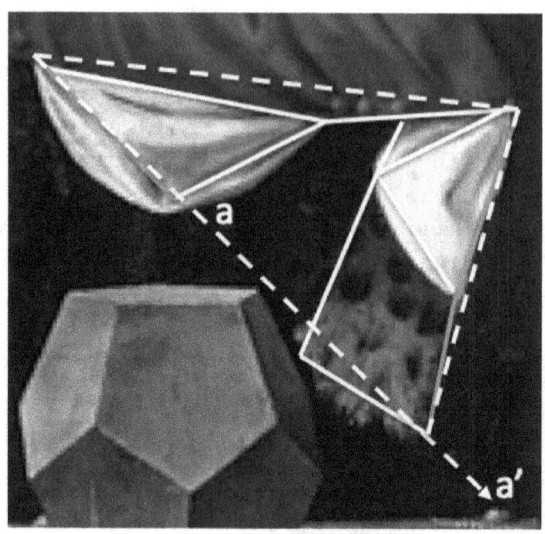

FIG. 10.11. *Leonardo's semi-circular triangles or circular segments hanging from the arm of the student in the* Pacioli Portrait.

Apart from the white sleeves of Galeazzo Sanseverino's undershirt (Fig. 10.11), Leonardo has given the portion of Luca Pacioli's cowl that covers his shoulders and upper chest a distinct semi-spherical shape (Fig. 10.12). This curved triangular shape of the cape depicted as the circular segment ABC has been transformed from a circle within a square. The shadowed folds at the ends of Luca's sleeves on his left arm also depict semi-circular triangles (Fig. 10.13). In addition, the golden ratio intervals of 0.382 and 0.618 occur across various parts of the portrait such as on a straight line between the setsquare and the vertical clasp of the red book on the table as well as on an imaginary line drawn between the outside edges of the rhombicuboctahedron and Galeazzo Sanseverino's head (Fig. 10.12). The interval of 0.618 connects Luca Pacioli with the rhombicuboctahedron and separates them from Galeazzo Sanseverino who is positioned in the other interval of 0.382. The clasp of the book seems to divide the width of the book also into a golden ratio interval. There are other golden ratio intervals distributed throughout the picture (see Chapter 8) and there seem to be more of them than the transformed semi-circular triangles (Fig. 10.13).

The semi-circular triangles in Leonardo's *Pacioli Portrait* (Fig. 10.12 & 10.13) resemble the spherical sections on the roof of the iconic Sydney Opera House designed by Jorn Utzon or Norman Foster's architecture of The Armadillo (The Clyde Auditorium) in Glasgow (Fig. 10.14).

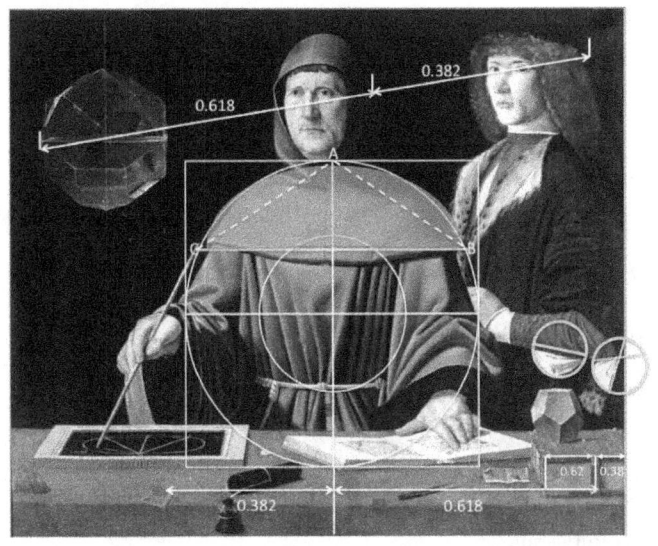

FIG. 10.12. *The top of Luca Pacioli's cape forms the circular segment ABC comparable to the circular segments and sectors on Galeazzo Sanseverino's arm.*

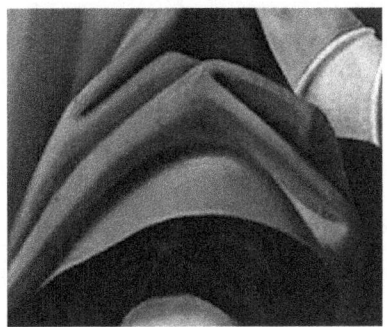

FIG. 10.13. *Detail of* Pacioli Portrait. *Folds on the left arm of Luca Pacioli's cape in the form of circular segments.*

FIG. 10.14. *Spherical triangular shapes (sails) as the roof of the Sydney Opera House (left), and the architectural structure of the Clyde Auditorium in Glasgow (right). Photos of Barrallo et al., (2015).*

References

Barrallo J, Gonzalez-Quintial F, Sanchez-Beitia S (2015). An Introduction to the Vesica Piscis, the Reuleaux Triangle and Related Geometric Constructions in Modern Architecture. Nexus Netw J 17:671–684. DOI 10.1007/s00004-015-0253-9

Capra F (2008). The Science of Leonardo: Inside the Mind of the Great Genius of the Renaissance. Anchor Books Edition, New York.
https://erenow.com/biographies/the-science-of-leonardo-inside-the-mind-of-the-great-genius-of-the-renaissance/

Hoy J, Millett KC (2015). A Mathematical Analysis of Knotting and Linking in Leonardo da Vinci's Cartelle of the Accademia Vinciana. Journal of Mathematics and the Arts.
http://web.math.ucsb.edu/~millett/Papers/Millett2014Leonardov5.pdf

Mackinnon, Nick (1993). The Portrait of Fra Luca Pacioli. The Mathematical Gazette 77:130-219.

Missinne S (2018). The Da Vinci Globe. Newcastle upon Tyne: Cambridge Scholars Publishing.

Missinne S, Verhoeven G (2019). Leonardo Depicted America: Misread as the Moon. Advances in Historical Studies 8:139-147.

Reuleaux F (1876) The Kinematics of Machinery: Outlines of a Theory of Machines. London: Macmillan.

Richter JP, editor (1880). The Notebooks of Leonardo da Vinci.
http://www.fromoldbooks.org/Richter-NotebooksOfLeonardo/

Sigmund, Paul, E., ed. (1991). Nicholas of Cusa and The Catholic Concordance. Cambridge: Cambridge University Press.

Tyler CW (2017). Leonardo da Vinci's World Map. In Cosmos and History: The Journal of Natural and Social Philosophy 13 (2):261-280.
https://www.cosmosandhistory.org/index.php/journal/article/viewFile/594/1030

Verhoeven GJ, Missinne S (2017). Unfolding Leonardo Da Vinci's Globe (Ad 1504) to Reveal its Historical World Map. ISPRS Annals of the Photogrammetry, Remote Sensing and Spatial Information Sciences, Volume IV-2/W2, 2017 26th International CIPA Symposium 2017, 28 August–01 September 2017, Ottawa, Canada. doi:10.5194/isprs-annals-IV-2-W2-303-2017.

Da Vinci Globe. https://en.wikipedia.org/wiki/Da_Vinci_Globe

Lennox Globe: Northern hemisphere:
http://digitalcollections.nypl.org/items/16891d60-66fc-0133-fbd6-00505686a51c

Mappamundi online: Flickr Photo of Leonardo's Octant Map, the Mappamundi, showing the world in Reuleaux triangles.
https://www.flickr.com/photos/lloydb/529393602

Mappamundi from ODT: Leonardo da Vinci Flickr Group:
https://www.flickr.com/groups/leonardo-da-vinci/

Southern hemisphere: http://digitalcollections.nypl.org/items/f7a0eb50-66fb-0133-9c56-00505686a51c

11

SQUARING THE CIRCLE AND *VITRUVIAN MAN*

Squaring the Circle or Circling the Square

Leonardo's *Pacioli Portrait* (Fig. 1.1) seems to have Luca Pacioli contemplating the age-old problem of how to square the circle or circle the square. The construction of a square with the same area as a circle by using only a finite number of steps with compass and straightedge has challenged geometers since at least the ancient Babylonian times in 540 BC. The great minds challenged to square the circle using geometry include Anaxagoras, Hippocrates of Chios, Eudemus, Archimedes, and Euclid in ancient times, Leonardo da Vinci and Luca Pacioli in the Renaissance and Srinivasa Ramanujan (1913), Martin Gardner (1966), Benjamin Bold (1982), Robert Dixon (1991) and Sarva Jagannadha Reddy (2018) in modern times. Today, mathematicians know that 'circling the square' or 'squaring the circle' is impossible theoretically because only the transcendence number Pi (3.14159) can construct the circle, whereas rational numbers normally are used to construct a square. Therefore, it is impossible to construct circles and squares of equal areas or perimeters precisely. For example, in Fig. 12.1, if the area of the circle equals the area of the square, each with 3.142 square units, then the circumference of the circle is 6.286 units and the perimeter of the square is 7.091 units, which are not equal. In other words, if the area of the square equals the area of the circle then the perimeter of the square is larger than the circle, and the two can never fit into each other precisely. On the other hand, if the perimeter of the circle and square are the same at 2 x *Pi* (6.286 units), then their areas are different; circle=3.143 units, and square=2.469 units.

The expression 'squaring the circle' is sometimes used as a metaphor for trying to do the impossible. The Italian poet Dante (1265 to 1321) wrote about the problem of squaring the circle in his *The Divine Comedy* in the *Paradise* Canto *XXXIII lines 133–135*:

As the geometer his mind applies
To square the circle, nor for all his wit
Finds the right formula, howe'er he tries.

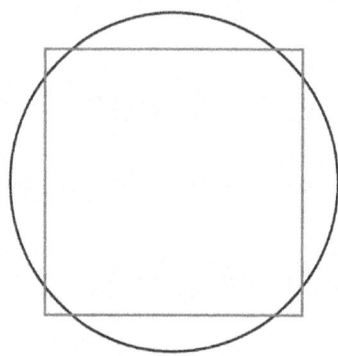
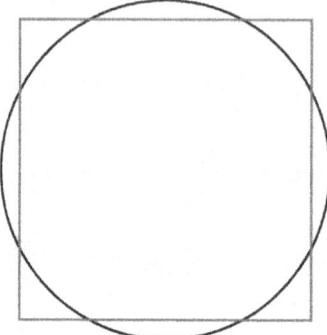

CIRCLE OF RADIUS 1.
SQUARE OF SIDE π/2.
PERIMETERS OF CIRCLE AND SQUARE = 2π.
V–1a

CIRCLE OF RADIUS 1.
SQUARE OF SIDE √π.
AREAS OF CIRCLE AND SQUARE = π.
V–1b

FIG. 11.1. Squaring the circle for equal parameters or for equal areas and the dimensions required for squaring a unit circle. Left, a circle of radius 1 is equal in perimeter to square of side of Π/2, where each perimeter = 2Π. Right, a circle of radius 1 is equal in area to a square of side √Π, where each area = Π. Image obtained from Rachel Fletcher (2013).

For Dante, squaring the circle represented a task beyond human comprehension and he compared it to his inability to comprehend *Paradise*. Leonardo da Vinci wanted to prove Dante wrong and set about to find the geometric solution to squaring the circle. He knew a little about the history of squaring the circle and called it the ancient problem of the quadrature of the circle. He seemed a little ambivalent about whether or not Archimedes had found the quadrature of the circle and wrote down the following comments in his notebooks:

Archimedes gave the quadrature of a polygonal figure, but not of the circle. Hence Archimedes never squared any figure with curved sides. He squared the circle minus the smallest portion that the intellect can conceive, that is the smallest point visible.

OF *SQUARING THE CIRCLE, AND WHO IT WAS THAT FIRST DISCOVERED IT BY ACCIDENT. Vitruvius, measuring miles by means of the*

CHAPTER 11

repeated revolutions of the wheels, which move vehicles, extended over many Stadia the lines of the circumferences of the circles of these wheels. He became aware of them by the animals that moved the vehicles. But he did not discern that this was a means of finding a square equal to a circle. This was first done by Archimedes of Syracuse, who by multiplying the second diameter of a circle by half its circumference produced a rectangular quadrilateral equal figure to the circle.

In comparison, Luca Pacioli thought that it was easy to square the circle (Fig. 11.2) and he described it in his manuscript the *Divine Proportion* for the Duke of Milan, Ludovico Moro Sforza, in this way:

The reason the said 11/14ths is taken, that is, of the 14 parts of the multiplication of the diameter by itself in each circle, is because, it was found, with many approximations by Archimedes that the circle in comparison with the square of its diameter, is as 11 to 14. That is, if the square of the diameter were 14, the circle would be 11, even though it is still not known with precision by any scientist. But it is off by little, as here, to the eye, it appears in the figure, that the circle is less than the said square by as much as are the angles [corners] of the said square [see Figure 28], which area is lost by the circle; the which corners of the entire square are the 3/14ths, that is, 3 of the 14 parts. And the 11 comes to be contained by the circular space, as it appears in the square ABCD, whose sides are equal to the diameter of the circle, that is, to the line EF, which divides it in half, passing through the point G, called the center of the said circle, as our philosopher tells us at the beginning of his first book.'

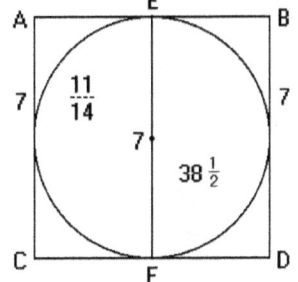

FIG. 11.2. *The square and circle, Figure 28, illustrated in the* Divine Proportion *(1498) by Luca Pacioli.*

However, when we calculate the areas or the circumference/perimeter of Luca Pacioli's circle and square (Fig. 11.2) we find no equivalence because they are different. The area of circle is 38.5 units sq., and the area of the square is 49 units sq., whereas the circumference of circle is 22 units and the perimeter of the square is 28 units. So, Luca Pacioli has not squared the circle.

In her paper entitled '*Leonardo and Theoretical Mathematics*', Sylvie Duvernoy points out that Leonardo was absorbed with squaring the circle all of his life, but ultimately failed because the problem is unsolvable. She wrote the following:

'Leonardo also spent a lot of time trying to solve a second classical problem: the squaring

of the circle. One day he even claims to have reached a solution: on *Codex Madrid II*, folio 112r we read, "*the night of St Andrew, I finally found the quadrature of the circle; and as the light of the candle and the night and the paper on which I wrote were coming to an end, it was completed; at the end of the hour.*" But the solution is not there...'

She then showed his graphical approach with his drawings from folio 471 of the *Codex Atlanticus* (Fig. 11.3). Interestingly, these are comparable, but contrasting shapes and drawings of sectors and sections within semicircles in folio 167r,a-b of *Codex Atlanticus* (Fig. 11.4) that Shellagh and Jonathan Routh reproduced in their book, *Leonardo's Kitchen Note Books*, mockingly describing them as his designs for folding table napkins for the Sforza banquets. Jokes aside, Sylvie Duvernoy was more serious when she wrote:

> *In any case, he remained unsatisfied with the approximate ratio between the circumference and the diameter as 22/7. Therefore he tries to take this approximation beyond the 96-sided polygon in an attempt to bring the difference of areas between circle and polygon to be as small as the "mathematical point", which has no quantity. This research generates an enormous quantity of sketches that show an infinite variety of decorative shapes (Codex Atlanticus, fol. 471, fig. 9).*

And she concluded:

> *This methodology does not lead to a satisfactory solution, or even to any progress towards a result, but the value of his effort lies in this attempt at extension* ad infinitum.

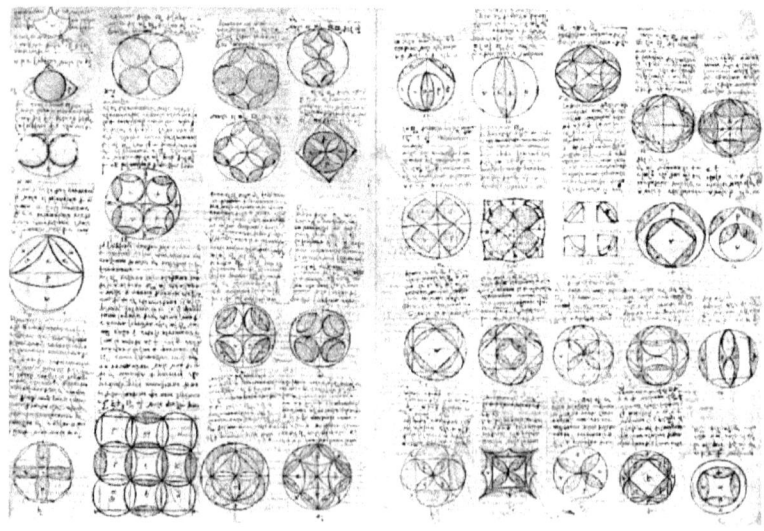

FIG. 11.3. *Squaring the circle. Leonardo da Vinci, Codex Atlanticus, folio 471.*

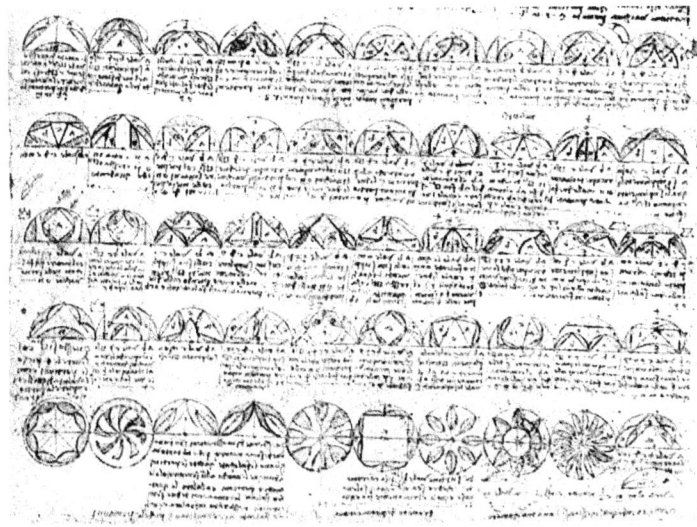

FIG. 11.4. Squaring the semicircle. Some of Leonardo's semicircle arrays with geometric drawings, designs and calculations of segments, sectors, lunes, lenses, circles, squares and triangles within the semicircles. Details within folio 167r,a-b of Codex Atlanticus.

Yet, beneath the arrays of circles and semicircles with the bewildering variety of geometric forms drawn by Leonardo in his notebooks is his accompanying text with explanations such as, '*If one removes equal parts from equal figures, the remainder must be equal*' and '*To square, fill in the empty parts.*' This was Leonardo's '*game of geometry*' that Fritjof Capra explained in his book *The Science of Leonardo*. '*In all of Leonardo's drawings of the circular and semicircular arrays, the ratio between the shaded areas (also called "empty") and the white areas (also called "full") is always the same, because the white areas—no matter how fragmented they maybe—are always equal to the original inscribed half square (rectangle or triangle), and the shaded areas are equal to the original shaded areas outside the half square.*'

Fritjof Capra, in the appendix of his book, reproduced one of Leonardo's figures for us to show how Leonardo squared these circular and semicircular figures.

'*In Figure A-6, I have selected a specific diagram from the double folio to illustrate Leonardo's technique. The text under the diagram reads: "To square, fill in the triangle with the four falcates outside." I have redrawn the diagram in Figures A-7 a and b so as to make its geometry explicit. Inside the large half circle with radius R, Leonardo has generated eight shaded segments B by drawing four smaller half circles with half the radius, $r = R/2$ (see Fig. A-7 a). The falcates he mentions are the white areas marked F.*'

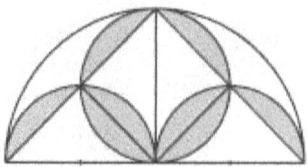

FIG. 11.5. Capra Figure A-6: Sample diagram (number 7 in row 7, Codex Atlanticus, folio 455).

'By specifying that the four "empty" (shaded) areas inside the triangle are to be "filled in" with the four falcates, Leonardo indicates that the areas F and B are equal. Here is how he might have reasoned. Since he knew that the area of a circle is proportional to the square of its radius, he could show that the area of the large half circle is four times that of each small half circle, and that consequently the area of the large segment A is four times that of the small segment B (see Fig. A-7b). This means that, if two small segments are subtracted from the large segment, the area of the remaining curved figure (composed of two falcates) will be equal to the area subtracted, and hence the area of the falcate F is equal to that of the small segment B.'

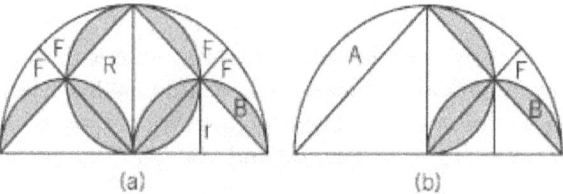

FIG. 11.6. Capra Figure A-7: Geometry of the sample diagram.

'For the other figures, the squaring procedure can be more elaborate, but eventually the original diagrams are always recovered. This is Leonardo's "game of geometry." Each diagram represents a geometric—or, rather, topological—equation, and the accompanying instruction describes how the equation is to be solved to square the curvilinear figure.'

Leonardo's failure to square the circle nevertheless is the prevailing view because we believe that modern mathematics has proven beyond reasonable doubt that the value of *Pi* cannot be obtained from an algebraic equation – which, by definition, also means that a circle cannot be squared by simple geometric means (straight-edge and compass). *Pi* is an irrational and transcendental number equivalent to 3.14159, and the area of a circle might be irrational because it is $Pi.r^2$. In contrast, the area of the square is the product of the square of the length of one side; which produces a simple rational algebraic number. An irrational number cannot equal a rational number. Consequently, all related algebraic 'proofs' to square the circle are flawed; and therefore, Leonardo da Vinci could not have squared the circle. However, because transcendental numbers were unknown to Leonardo da Vinci and Luca Pacioli, then they are irrelevant to what we are trying to understand about them historically. In this context, we can separate the transcendental impossibility from the algebraic and geometric approximation and the proximate possibility of squaring the circle. While modern mathematics might be right, and despite the uncertainty principle, this mathematical abstraction might be a little like comparing quantum physics with classical physics and saying classical physics is wrong. Most people understand the old version of classical physics and its relevance in the world, whereas quantum physics, the proven modern reality, seems to be far beyond the reach of most people's comprehension. Leonardo had a far different understanding about squaring the circle than the modern mathematician, one that stemmed from his geometric perspective and real numbers and not from Lindemann's German proof of 1882 that *Pi* is a transcendental number, a value derived from Euler's irrational equation. Although it is impossible to square the circle based on *Pi* as a transcendental number, perhaps it still can be viewed in a real number system and extended to geometry as in eigenvalues, periodicity and proportions to square the circle with compass and straightedge to a reasonable approximation.

There is also squaring the circle at a symbolic level that Rachel Fletcher described in her 2007 Nexus Network Journal article entitled '*Squaring the Circle: Marriage of Heaven and Earth.*'

> *'But "squaring the circle"—drawing circles and squares of equal areas or perimeters by means of a compass or rule—has eluded geometers from early times. The problem cannot be solved with absolute precision, for circles are measured by the incommensurable value pi (= 3.1415927...), which cannot be accurately expressed in finite whole numbers by which we measure squares. At the symbolic level, however, the quest to obtain circles and squares of equal measure is equivalent to seeking the union of transcendent and finite qualities, or the marriage of heaven and earth. Various pursuits draw from the properties of music, geometry and even astronomical measures and distances. Each attempt offers new insight into the wonder of mathematical order. In this column, we consider methods for achieving circles and squares of equal perimeters, focusing on geometric approaches conducive to design applications and setting aside for now the problem of achieving circles and squares of equal areas.'*

For many modern representations, the starting point to squaring the circle is the square. It seems that Leonardo constructed the square and triangles mainly from circles and semicircles rather than the other way around. This can be seen in his folio 471 in the *Codex Atlanticus*. Therefore, contained within one of Leonardo da Vinci's drawings of his decorated circle and semicircle designs is the proximate solution to the problem achieved by squaring a segment of a circle with the help of other circles. In his world, during the Renaissance, Leonardo da Vinci was probably right when he wrote in his notebook that on one particular night of St. Andrew he had squared the circle. The possibility and impossibility of squaring the circle or circling the square rages on today as before and the arguments for and against can been seen in the articles by Hubert Weller (1999), Gernot Hoffmann (2005), Rachel Fletcher (2004, 2007, 2013), Tom Pastorello (2013), Sarva Jagannadha Reddy (2015), Vitor Murtinho (2015), Leno Mascia (2016), and Klaus Schroer (2017, 2018) referenced at the end of this chapter.

Vitruvian Man and Squaring the Circle

Ultimately, at the symbolic level, Leonardo da Vinci squared the circle by combining the square and the circle in his drawing of the proportions of the human male body, known as the *Vitruvian Man*. In this regard, he succeeded in his quest to obtain circles and squares of equal measure that are equivalent to the finite size of the human body and he demonstrated the union of transcendent and finite qualities, and therefore, he married heaven with earth.

Marcus Vitruvius Pollio (probably lived 80 BC to 15 BC), better known as Vitruvius, was a Roman author, architect and civil and military engineer who produced a major work entitled *De Architectura* that greatly influenced Leonardo da Vinci. In *Book III, Chapter 1, Paragraph 3*, Vitruvius wrote about the proportions of man:

'Just so the parts of Temples should correspond with each other, and with the whole. The navel is naturally placed in the centre of the human body, and, if in a man lying with his face upward, and his hands and feet extended, from his navel as the centre, a circle be described, it will touch his fingers and toes. It is not alone by a circle, that the human body is thus circumscribed, as may be seen by placing it within a square. For measuring from the feet to the crown of the head, and then across the arms fully extended, we find the latter measure equal to the former; so that lines at right angles to each other, enclosing the figure, will form a square.'

Using Vitruvius's description, Leonardo Da Vinci produced his famous drawing of the *Vitruvian Man*, in one case where he stands upright within a square with legs together and arms stretched horizontally, and in the other case, he stands upright within a circle with raised arms and legs spread apart. He is one man, with four arms and four legs (Fig. 11.7). This representation, which objectively reflects the human body's proportions, also illustrates the Renaissance idea of man as a symbolic microcosm, thus praising his role for being the centre of the universe. This idea of man at the centre of the universe is displayed in the *Vitruvian Man* by his dynamic movement between and contained within the square (earth) and the circle (heaven or the universe).

Man's attempts to develop practical measurement units probably began at least 10,000 years BC as seen in the depths of the Pech Merle cave in France with the depiction of the palm and five-fingers of the hand as a potential unit of measure and as a measuring instrument. Since then, man has developed various measurement units (a scale) based on the human body including the finger, palm, foot and cubit that are referred to by Vitruvius in his book *De Architectura*. Based on the total number of fingers or toes, like the ancient Greeks and other ancient civilisations, we have the number ten as our established, archaic metric system including what we sometimes consider are the more modern decimal (base 10) number system and the decimal computation systems used by computers.

Nowhere in the Vitruvian treatise of *De Architectura* is there a clarification on the proportional system that establishes a relationship between the square and the circle. This has led to immense and symbolic speculation in regard to what geometric rules and methods guided Leonardo to construct the drawing of his *Vitruvian Man* within a square of the length of one hundred and eighty-one millimetres and a half (181.5 mm) and a circle with the circumference's radius of one hundred and ten millimetres (110 mm). Based on these measurements, the area of the square is 3,2942.3 sq. mm and the area of the circle is 3,8013.2 sq mm with 86% similarity. On the other hand, the perimeter of the square is 726 mm and the circumference of the circle is 691 mm, with 95% similarity between the two numbers. The areas and circumferences of Leonardo's circle and square are approaching equivalence with the length of circumference and perimeter almost the same at 95%.

Also, the square's vertical sides are slightly skewed, by about 1 mm, and the circumference is built from successive arcs, which consequently correspond to slightly different central points. The sheet containing Leonardo's drawing is 246 by 345 mm and this intentionally or unintentionally corresponds to a root 2 proportion and in paper size is in-between the modern A4 (210 by 297 mm) and A3 (297 by 420) printing paper. On the same sheet as his drawing of *Vitruvian Man*, Leonardo wrote some text in his neat hand of reverse or mirror writing. Above the drawing of the circle is written:

Vitruvius, the architect, says in his work on architecture that the measurements of the human body are distributed by Nature as follows: that is that 4 fingers make one palm and 4 palms make a foot, 6 palms is a cubit; 4 cubits is a man's height. And 4 cubits makes one pace and 24 palms make a man's height; and these measures he used in his building. If you spread your legs as much as to decrease your height by 1/14 and spread and raise your arms until your middle fingers touch the same level as the top of your head you must know that the centre of the outspread limbs will be in the navel and the space between the legs will be an equilateral triangle.

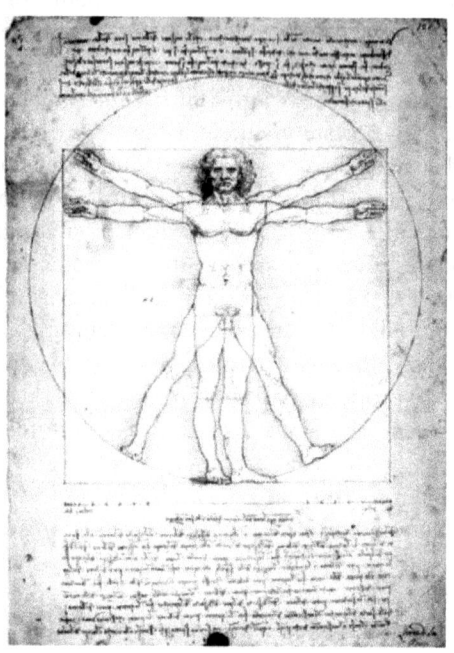

FIG. 11.7. *Leonardo da Vinci, study of human proportions in the manner of Vitruvius (c. 1490), Gallerie dell'Accademia, Gabinetto dei Disegno e Stampe, n. 228, Venice.*

The sentence below the square and the ruler that measures the width of the square with marked units, Leonardo has written:

The length of the man's outspread arms is equal to his height.

And then below this centralised sentence, Leonardo in a single paragraph has listed the following proportional measurements of a man.

From the hairline to the bottom of the chin is 1/10 of the height of a man; from the bottom of the chin to the top of the head is 1/8 of his height; from the top of the chest to the top of the head is 1/6 of the height of a man. From the top of the chest to the hairline is 1/7 of the height of a man. The maximum width of the shoulders is ¼ of the height of a man. From the nipples to the top of the head is ¼ of the height of a man.

CHAPTER 11

The greatest width of the shoulders contains itself ¼ of the height of a man.
From the elbow to the tip of the hand is 1/5 of the height of a man;
from the elbow to the angle of the armpit is 1/8 of the height of a man.
The whole length of the hand is 1/10 of the height of a man;
the root of the penis is the middle or the height of ½ a man.
The foot is 1/7 of the height of a man.
From the sole of the foot to below the knee is ¼ of height of a man.
From below the knee to the root of the penis is ¼ of the height of a man.
The distances from the bottom of the chin to the nose and from the eyebrows to the hairline is in each case the same, and like the ear equal to 1/3 of the face.

Elsewhere, he has written:

If nature has composed the human body so that in its proportions the separate individual elements answer to the total form, then the Ancients seem to have had reason to decide that bringing their creations to full completion likewise required a correspondence between the measure of individual elements and the appearance of the work as a whole.

The quality of a person's life is in direct proportion to their commitment to excellence, regardless of their chosen field of endeavour. We will receive not what we idly wish for but what we justly earn. Our rewards will always be in exact proportion to our service.

In Leonardo's drawing, the man in the square stands still, his feet together at the base of the square and his arms stretched out horizontally touching the opposite sides of the square while his head touches the upper side of the square. The two diagonals of the square cross over his genitals (symbolic of procreation), with the upper and lower triangles meeting at the base of his penis. In the square, the centres of his body and the square are located at his genitals and symbolically he is anchored to the physical world. In contrast, the man in the circle has moved from the static position in the square to a dynamic position along the circumference of the circle by simply moving his feet apart and by raising his arms and hands to touch the edge of the circle, head-high and along the upper edge of the square. He has moved in a way that the centre of his body has moved up from his genitals to his navel, that is, to the centre of the circle. The navel is the umbilical cord that links him directly to his mother and to successive generations and Adam and Eve and the origin of humans. In the *Vitruvian Man*, man is bound as one (the square) and the other (the circle), and thus, Leonardo da Vinci had squared the circle. The human body has not one, but two procreative centres, the navel and the genitals (Fig. 11.8).

Another way to square the circle metaphorically is to produce an ellipse (or in the case of Leonardo da Vinci, a rhombicuboctahedron) that could fit into either a square or a circle. Elliptic philosophy can be seen in the circle and square, an attempt at depicting the material and spiritual nature of life. If one were to merge these two geometric shapes into one, the result would be an ellipse. When humankind views the spiritual and material separately, the result is a distortion of true reality. Science cannot provide evidence of the spiritual, whereas religion cannot manipulate the material. True art can merge the two.

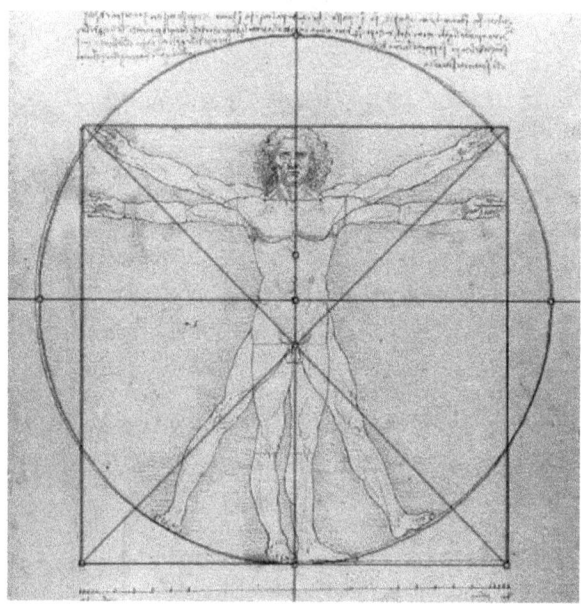

FIG. 11.8. *The centre of the square is represented by Vitruvian Man's genitalia (male) and the centre of the circle is represented by Vitruvian Man's navel-umbilical cord (female).*

On closer inspection of the measurements of the square and circle in *Vitruvian Man*, it is possible that Leonardo has put the man in an ever-expanding cube as well as in an ever-expanding sphere and that is why they do not measure up exactly as a square and a circle in the actual drawing.

Aikido is a Japanese martial art founded by Morihei Ueshiba who lived for 86 years between 1883-1969. The film actor and action hero Steven Seagal was a student, exponent, instructor and teacher of Aikido. Philippe Voarino, an Aikido student and master, in September 2013 revealed a number of interesting points about the *Vitruvian Man* that most other commentators seem to have missed, that is, the position of the feet of the *Vitruvian Man* are those of a martial art exponent.

Generally, Leonardo's drawing is seen simply as illustrating human proportions defined by Vitruvius as quoted above. Thus, the foot being a sixth of the body height is well illustrated by the foot in a static position. However, changing the feet to a dynamic position leads to a different interpretation. The Vitruvian man moves exactly as one should in Aikido and this pledges for an interpretation of the drawing linked with the movement and the 'hito e mi' position as follows:

The feet position is, in a very remarkable way, the very specific and peculiar feet position, which must be used in Aikido, it is a perfect 'hito e mi':

"The feet in that position form a right angle triangle which hypotenuse is located at the back of the body (which is why it is called 'ushiro sankaku' in Japanese). Morihiro Saito explains:

The back triangle stance, in the posture of right 'hanmi', forms a triangle alongside the outside of the right foot with the inside of the left foot. The Founder called this stance 'hito-e-mi'. — Traditional Aikido vol. 1, p.19

That feet position is the crucial originality of Aikido among all other martial arts.'

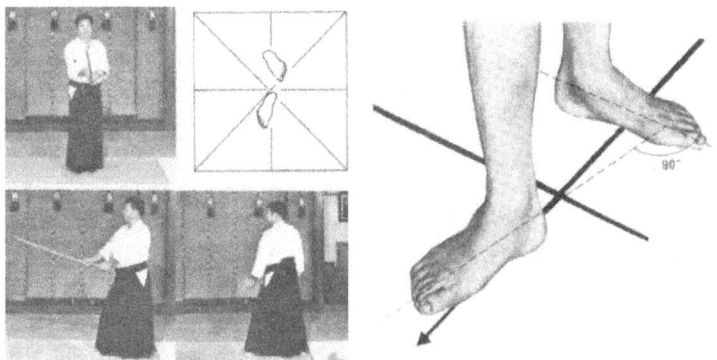

FIG. 11.9. The Vitruvian Man footwork used in Aikido martial arts. The feet form a right angle triangle with the hypotenuse located at the back of the body ('ushiro sankura' in Japanese). Taken from Phillipe Voarino at http://www.aikidotakemusu.org/en/articles/aikido-and-vitruvian-man-2.

Philippe Voarino added the following observations:

'Through the nature of his physical body, man belongs to earth and its elements, therefore to the square. It is only within this frame, between birth and death, that he has the ability to move (as it can be checked in the drawing, the man fits in both the square and the circle). He therefore belongs to the square by nature and to the circle by his movement. He belongs to both these geometrical figures. However moving up from the square to the circle is impossible without a corporal principle. That principle is clearly shown in the drawing whether in the static or the dynamic representation: in the triangle and more precisely the right angle triangle formed by the man's feet when he moves according to the laws which determined Vitruvius' harmonious proportions as illustrated by Leonardo.

The Founder of Aikido tells us the same in a perfectly clear and concrete manner:

"From a material point of view, TRIANGLE is the Sky/Heaven (Ten). The Sky/heaven is the principle and the corporal principle. — see Morihei Ueshiba, Takemusu Aiki, vol.1, p153, Ed Cénacle de France"

For O sensei (Ueshiba) and Leonardo da Vinci, the corporal principle, which governs the physical movement is without ambiguity the triangle.

In the same text, O sensei defines the movement as:

"Ka CIRCLE Sui, the harmonious union of Fire and Water through which the balance between Heaven and Earth is reached (matsuri)."

And he adds that in the circle, the role of the Fire is to *"completely fuse the principle"* (i.e., the triangle) to the Water channeling the action of Fire (what he calls politeness). For the Founder of Aikido, the harmonious movement is born out of the fusion of triangle to the circle; an idea clearly expressed by the triangular position within the circle in Leonardo's drawing.

Eventually, according to O sensei, the place where this balance between Heaven and Earth is not to be found somewhere far. This *"place"* where Heaven acts is earth (Chi)

SQUARE: *"Earth is the place where the Power of Heaven appears — p.154"*

and: *"People think that Heaven is a transcendental place but in reality Heaven and Earth are just one. — Morihei Ueshiba, Takemusu Aiki, vol.3, p 48, Ed Cénacle de France"*

That specific point is precisely the teaching of Leonardo's drawing, which shows that the triangle-man (heaven) acts in the circle without leaving the square (Earth)."

These observations by Philippe Voarino that connect *Vitruvian Man* to a Japanese Martial Art are similar to what Luca Pacioli might have said about Leonardo's *Vitruvian Man*, except that he probably would have interpreted Leonardo's *Vitruvian Man* in the square as being the corporal man on the Earth (material existence), and the man in circle as the spiritual existence of man in the Universe (Heaven). Hence, we see the same drawing, and yet we can have similar or slightly different interpretations across various cultures and periods.

A different point of view about *Vitruvian Man's* feet is presented by Leno Mascia of Loughborough University in the United Kingdom, who also paid attention to the 'oddity' of the posture of the legs. He believed the open legs posture was added to illustrate the human proportion in a dynamic situation and the tangential disposition of the muscles for the upper delineation of the left leg allowed Leonardo to emphasise the rotation of the left foot from the original right-angle position. Leno Mascia used vector analysis and diagrams to interpret the right-angle position of the left foot in the square and the angulated posture of the left foot in the circle as a way to alleviate the unbalance created by the angular dissymmetry by spreading the legs. This can be inferred from the observation that when the legs are spread, the uppermost protrusion of the toes on the two sides of the circle have been placed at about the same attitude. However, a line drawn from the middle of the right foot on the edge of the circle to the bottom of the heel of the left foot results in the inclination of the base of the equilateral triangle dipping down from the right foot to the left foot with a measured height ratio of 1/14 for the right foot to between 1/16 and 1/18 for the left foot.

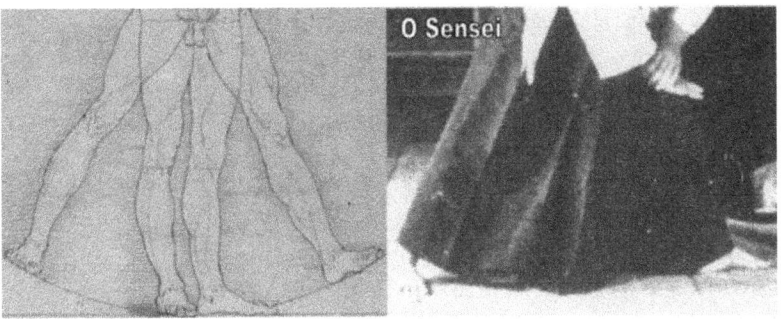

FIG. 11.10. *The Vitruvian Man footwork used in Aikido martial arts. The feet form a right angle triangle with the hypotenuse located at the back of the body for stability and balance. Taken from Phillipe Voarino at http://www.aikidotakemusu.org/en/articles/aikido-and-vitruvian-man-2.*

Divine Proportion (Golden Ratio) and the *Vitruvian Man*

Many scholars have presupposed that the relation between the square and the circle in Leonardo's drawing of the *Vitruvian Man* was established by applying the Golden ratio that corresponds to proposition number thirty in Book *VI* of *Euclid's Elements*: 'To cut a given finite straight line in extreme and mean ratio'.

The other presupposition is that Luca Pacioli taught Leonardo the Golden ratio. Indeed, Pacioli would come to name the particular proportion of the Golden ratio as *De Divina Proportione* and this was the topic of the manuscript that he completed in Milan in December 1498, with the first edition printed in Florence in 1509. Various scholars purport to have found the use of the Golden ratio in two of Leonardo's paintings before he met Luca Pacioli, but it seems to have been more prevalent in his later paintings.

The general recognition of the Golden ratio's importance in art and nature due to its geometrical commonality is often associated with the assumption that Leonardo knew and mastered this harmonious proportion and used it to construct his square and circle in drawing the *Vitruvian Man*. However, this assumption seems to be wrong because if we remove a Golden square from a Golden rectangle that was constructed by the divine proportion (Golden ratio) where the side length of the removed square is equal to the rectangle's smaller side then we will again obtain a new Golden rectangle. It is this particularity of the Golden ratio that turns this proportion into a popular method for geometric drawings. However, the Golden ratio is missing from Leonardo's drawing of the *Vitruvian Man* because it is precisely about a square and a circle and not a rectangle. Therefore, using the golden ratio to try and reconstruct Leonardo's drawing can only result in discrepancies and errors such as those produced by Rocco Sinisgalli who achieved a difference of 4.5 mm in the circumference diameter from that in Leonardo's drawing.

On the other hand, Takashi Ida from the Nagoya Institute of Technology in Japan in his article online entitled *Vitruvian Man by Leonardo da Vinci and the Golden ratio* concluded that *'the ratio of the radius of the circle to the side length of the square was intended to be $137/225 = 0.6088\cdots$; but not the golden ratio $(1 / r) = (5^{1/2} - 1) / 2 = 0.6180\cdots$.'* Leno Mascia, on reading Ida's conclusion, commented that the ratio of H/R (height and side of the square/radius of the circle) in Leonardo's drawing is 1.70 – 1.72 and greater than golden ratio value of 1.618; and that if the radius of the circle were to be increased to reach an H/R ratio equal to 1.618, the position of the fingers of the raised arms would no longer be able to maintain the dual contact with the square and the circle. His own conclusion makes the additional interesting point that the theory underlying Leonardo's drawing is that, 'the *'ideal man'* (*homo bene figuratus*) will fit simultaneously in a circle and square when the arms are stretched out, so that the middle fingers are aligned with the crown of the head, and the legs are opened to an extent to form an equilateral triangle. Therefore, Leonardo's theory contained within the *Vitruvian Man* is that the proportions of the human body are adjustable parameters to satisfy the conditions imposed by the design of the drawing.

Geometric Construction of the *Vitruvian Man*

How did Leonardo construct the square and the circle in his drawing of the *Vitruvian Man*? Leonardo never described how he did it, so this has intrigued many scholars and geometers over the centuries. Many believe it is based on the divine proportion (Golden ratio) that Leonardo learnt from Luca Pacioli. There are many different interpretations and solutions other than using the Golden ratio to reconstruct the drawing; and I have listed some of them in the references at the end of the chapter. The most elegant of the solutions and the simplest way to construct Leonardo's square and circle as seen in the *Vitruvian Man* was posted anonymously as a *World Mysteries* blog on the Internet and I recreate it here starting with two squares (Fig. 11.11). First draw a square (solid lines), duplicate it and rotate it 45 degrees (large dashed lines) through the central point 'P' where the solid diagonal lines intersect. The diameter of the circle is the diagonal line 'a' from the apex of the rotated square to position 'b' on the baseline of the basic square. The radius of the circle is 'a' to 'O' or 'b' to 'O' where 'O' is the origin of the circle. The point 'P' between the solid lines represents the top of *Vitruvian Man's* genitals and the point 'O' between the dashed lines is his navel. And that is it, Fig. 11.11 without the man corresponds to Fig. 11.8 with the *Vitruvian Man*. Whether Leonardo used this method with a compass and a ruler I do not know, but for me it was the easiest way to understand and recreate the square and the circle in the *Vitruvian Man* using the Microsoft PowerPoint software on a computer starting with a square.

Although there have been many attempts to recreate Leonardo da Vinci's drawing of the *Vitruvian Man* in the circle and square using the divine proportion, some recent publications have pointed out that Leonardo's drawing is not based on the divine proportion and that he finished the drawing in 1490 at least six years before he had met with Luca Pacioli in Milan. In this regard, we may cite the following five five authors; Rachel Fletcher (2007, 2013), Victor Murtinho (2015), **Sarva Jagannadha Reddy** (2018), **Klaus Schröer** (1998) and Tom Pastorello (2013) for the different ways that they attempted to square the circle for the *Vitruvian Man*.

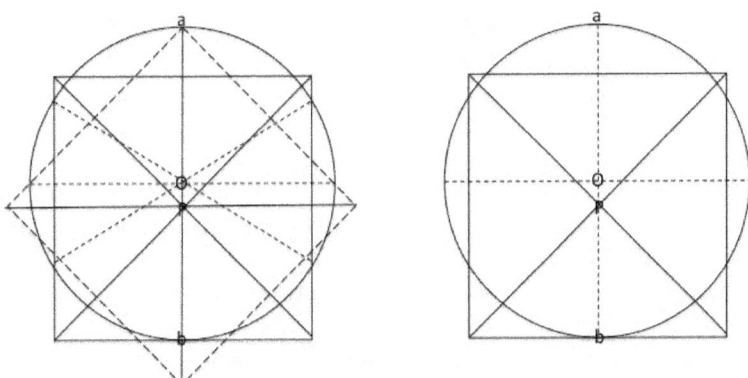

FIG. 11.11. Reconstructing Leonardo's Circle and Square in the Vitruvian Man *by starting with 2 overlapping squares at 45 degrees to each other (solid lines and dashed lines) and drawing a circle from its origin that is the midpoint O of line ab. The figure on the right can be superimposed on* Vitruvian Man *in Fig. 11.8. O=1/2(a to b).*

(a) *Rachel Fletcher*

In her 2007 paper, Rachel Fletcher provided a history of squaring the circle and seven techniques for drawing a circle and square of equal perimeter; a *vesica piscis*, a double *vesica piscis*, golden section, the great pyramid, relative measure of earth and moon, the heptagon, and the Danish Engineer Tons Brunes's Sacred Cut. The circle and square were equal in perimeter within 1.4% for the *vesica piscis* method, 4.8% for the a double *vesica piscis*, 0.1% for the golden section, precisely at 8 *Pi* for the great pyramid method, and within 0.6% for the Brunes's Sacred Cut. She concludes that, *'If geometry is the art of reconciling diverse spatial elements, the quest to square the circle is an art of the highest order.'*

(b) Vitor Murtinho and others

The Portuguese architect Vitor Murtinho analysed five published reconstructions by others and generated his own drawing using a double *vesica piscis* construction (Fig. 11.12) that was the closest to the measurements of the square and the circle in Leonardo's drawing of *Vitruvian Man*. The shape of a *vesica piscis* is like a convex lens and it is an area formed by two equilateral triangles and four equal circular segments. The *vesica piscis* is depicted in Euclid's Elements and seen as the intersection of two congruent disks each centred on the perimeter of the other and where an equilateral triangle and a segment together form a sector of one-sixth of the circle (60°).

Murtinho says, *'... if we take the circumference and not the square as a starting point and represent two orthogonal axes going through the centre of the figure, we obtain four noticeable points in the circumference (A, B, D and E) that would conceptually enable the representation of a skewed square (Fig. 13). If centred in each of these points (vertices of the imaginary square) we represent a circumference with a radius equal to the diameter (e.g. AB or DE) of the given circumference, and so tangent to it, we will obtain a set of four circumferences that allow us to, in pairs and on opposing situations, draw two vesica piscis, one with a vertical and the other with a horizontal axis. Within this construction, each auxiliary circumference pair will originate an intersection point. These four intersection points will make it possible to draw a square (F, G, H and J) that sections the original circumference (centre C) in eight different points. This square's side length is one hundred and eighty-one point one millimetres (181.1 mm). If the construction is made from the Leonardian square, we will obtain a circumference diameter of two hundred and twenty point seven millimetres (220.7 mm).'*

In Leonardo's drawing, the square side is 181.5 mm and the circumference diameter is 220 mm. By reconstructing Leonardo's drawing using a double *vesica piscis* construction, Murtinho achieved the circle diameter of 220.7 mm resulting in a discrepancy of +0.7 mm. Based on the measurements of *Vitruvius*, and using the same measure of length for the square (181.5 mm), the circumference diameter is about two hundred and twenty-six point eight millimetres (226.8 mm), which represented the greatest deviation of 6.8 mm from Leonardo's drawing. Rocco Sinisgalli's reconstruction based on the divine proportion (Golden ratio) produced a difference of 4.5 mm

CHAPTER 11

in the circumference diameter from Leonardo's drawing. Otto Helbing's reconstruction based on the use of a heptagon as an approximation of the circle (e.g., Leonardo's hanging rhombicuboctahedron) also resulted in a deviation of 3.6 mm from the circumference diameter of Leonardo's drawing. The smallest deviation noted by Murtinho, other than his own, was -0.9 mm by Lionel March using a regular octagon as his starting point. In March's reconstruction a side length of the octagon is equal to the side of the square and the distance between the centre of the octagon and one of its sides' midpoints corresponds to the diameter of the circumference in Leonardo's drawing. However, there is no similar drawing in Leonardo's notebooks, so it is unlikely that he used the octagon as his starting point. According to Murtinho, there are only three points in Leonardo's drawing of *Vitruvian Man* that belong to the reference circumference and that enable finding the circumference's centre for the final geometric construction; these are the symmetrical points at the corners (right angle points) of the upper side of the square and the mid-point of the length of the lower square.

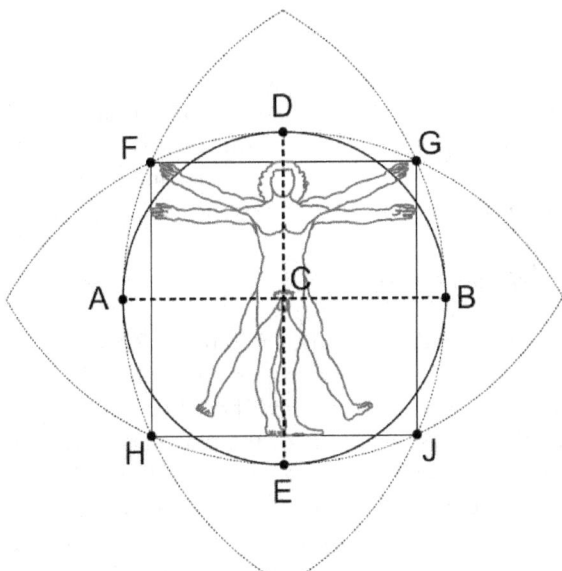

FIG. 11.12. *A double* vesica piscis *construction. With permission of Vitor Murtinho (2015). Leonardo's Vitruvian Man Drawing: A New Interpretation Looking at Leonardo's Geometric Constructions. Nexus Netw J (2015) 17:507–524.*

The drawing by Vitor Murtinho using a double *vesica piscis* construction seems to be a reasonable reconstruction because Leonardo is known to have drawn *vesicas* oriented in orthogonal axes. The *vesicas* or convex lenses are partly visible in the *Pacioli Portrait*, those curved triangles of white cloth hanging from Galeazzo Sanseverino's arm (Fig. 10.10) and the grey curved triangle of Luca Pacioli's cloak across his chest (Fig. 10.11). Also, Leonardo drew many *vesicas* in his notebooks. For Leonardo, the drawing of the *Vitruvian Man* was an attempt to show graphically that, for better or for worse, man is the centre of the universe. To accomplish this, he took the circle and not the square as his starting point. And the transformation of the square into a circle takes place by the *Vitruvian Man* shifting the position of his arms from the horizontal to the oblique and spreading his legs so that the body's shape changes from the T to the X shape, the crucifixion cross of Jesus Christ and St. Andrew, respectively. Thus, Leonardo wrote in his notes one night in 1486 after working on a project to paint the fresco of St. Andrew on the diagonal cross (X) for the Sforza of the Duchy of Milan in the Church of St. Andrew in Melzo:

'... *the morning (crossed through and replaced by night) of St. Andrews, after the candles and the paper I was writing on were consumed, I finally squared the circle.*' and later, '*could you give me a place to be kept secret, like the church of S. Andrea in Melzo.*'

In celebration, Leonardo painted the squared circle logo and the four-leafed clover within a circle on two walls of the apse of St. Andrew in Melzo, near Milan. They are still there on the wall of the church. He later went on to use the four-leafed clover in overlaying the square as part of the embroidery in the dress of his painting of the *Lady with the Ermine*.

(c) Sarva Jagannadha Reddy

Mr. Sarva Jagannadha Reddy, a retired Zoology lecturer turned mathematician, showed in his 2015 paper '*Leonardo da Vinci's ingenious way of carving one-fourth area of a segment in a circle*' how Leonardo might have squared the circle. Mr. Reddy has taken one of the drawings of Leonardo da Vinci's four-leafed clover within the square and circle (Fig. 11.3) and he squared the circle by subtracting the area of the petals (or convex lenses) from the circle (Fig. 11.5) and demonstrated algebraically that the remainder of the circle's area equals the entire area of the square (Fig. 11.13). In another reconstruction, Mr. Reddy showed that Leonardo da Vinci could have squared a segment of a circle with the help of using four other adjoining circles. Mr. Reddy has long argued that there is no difference between the square and the circle, both are one, and that *Pi* exists in a circle and a square as the same thing. However, Mr. Reddy, unlike Leonardo da Vinci before him, claims to have found that the true value of Cosmic Pi is 3.1464466... and not the conventional transcendental value of 3.1415926.

He claims that the true value of Cosmic *Pi*, which is derived from 14 minus the square root of two divided by four, permits the squaring of the circle, whereas the transcendental value makes it impossible to square the circle.

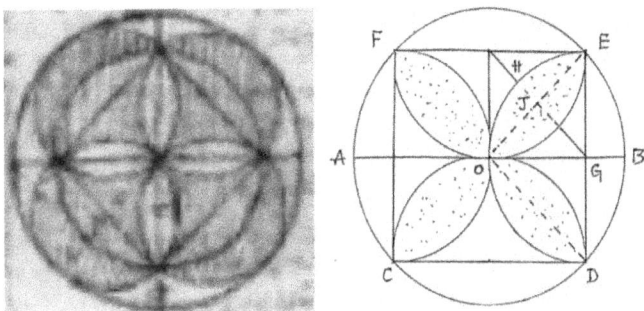

FIG. 11.13. *(Left) A detail of one of Leonardo's drawings of a square derived from four intersecting circles with a circle taken from folio 471 (Fig. 11.3) and showing the 4 petals within the square that Mr Reddy used (right) to prove algebraically that Leonardo had squared the circle.*

(d) Klaus Schröer and Hubert Weller

Klaus Schröer in his publication *Das Geheimnes der Proportionsstudie* (Waxmann Publisher, Germany, 1998) used Leonardo's drawing of *Vitruvian Man* to demonstrate how a square and circle of equal area can be created by extending numerous (infinite) sets of squares and circles of unequal area from Leonardo's initial unequal square and circle until their area ratios converge to 1.00037. He did this by using the ratio of 0.453 (starting from 0.4 to 0.5 in various preliminary experiments) as the radius for each of the circles drawn from starting points on *Vitruvian Man's* shoulder that are the centres for the rotation of the arms to obtain the contact of the middle finger with the square and both the square and the circle. Leonardo had left two distinct contact points marked on his drawing for placing the point of the compass on the left and right side of *Vitruvian Man's* shoulders to construct more circles and squares (Fig. 11.14). So by using the ratio, $x = 0.436$, of the edge length of the starting square ($a = 1$) as the radius of the arm movements, Schröer drew more and more pairs of circles and squares so that the ratios of areas of the following pairs converged together to the value of 1.00037 (Fig. 11.15). In this way, the new circles and squares eventually converged so that the area of the circle is almost always the same as the area of the square. Although the Klaus Schröer approach is interesting, it seems to violate the restriction of constructing a square with the same area as a circle by using only a finite number of steps with compass and straightedge. However, Schröer claims that this sequence of convergence was meant as a solution of the squaring of the circle in an infinite number of steps that Leonardo claimed to possess. In his drawing Leonardo only showed the construction of two consecutive sequences based on two successive generations, generation n and generation n+1 that were already close to the state of convergence where both pairs were almost of equal areas. Leonardo was not interested in a construction limited to a small number of steps – he was interested in the construction of an infinite number of steps that are continually convergent to a limit, the equal area of the circle and the square.

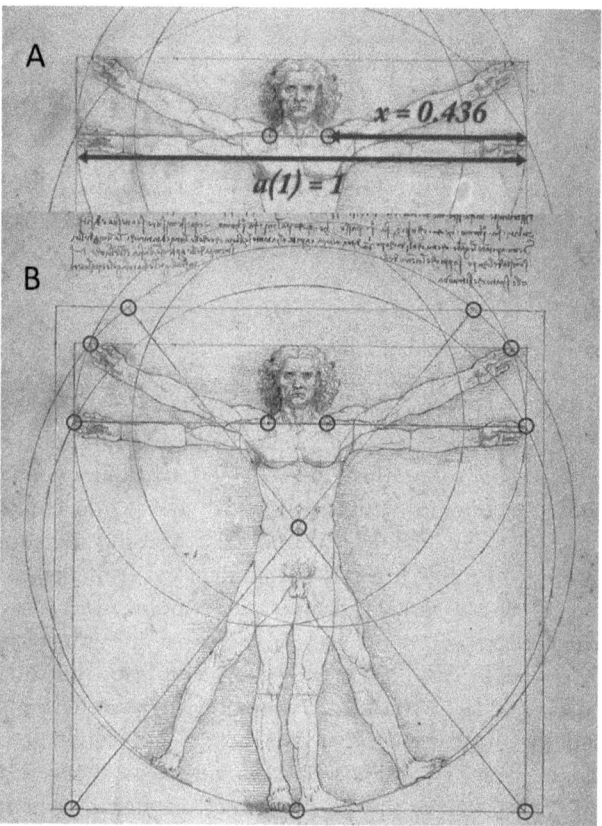

FIG. 11.14. *Klaus Schröer's procedure for infinite squaring of the circle. Images taken from Klaus Schröer online at http://www.klaus-schroer.com/leonardo*

Hubert Weller and his students published a paper on the Internet that explains Klaus Schröer's findings and procedure. Comparing areas of the square and circle in Leonardo's drawing, Weller's students calculated the area of circle to be 176.72 cm² and the area of the square to be 153.51 cm² with 14% difference. However, redrawing a new circle using Schröer's ratio of 0.436 based on the ratio of the length of the arm to length of Leonardo's square (Fig. 11.15), the new Schröer's circle yielded an area of 153.94 cm² with only 0.28% of difference to the area of Leonardo's square (Fig. 11.14). And then, when a new larger square was constructed from the centre of the new circle (Fig. 11.15), the area of the second square was 176.89 cm² and almost the same as the area of Leonardo's circle of 176.72 cm² with only 0.1% of difference. This procedure can be repeated over and over as shown in Fig. 11.16, creating multiple circles and squares with areas that progressively converge towards 100% equivalence. Hubert Weller's conclusion about the mathematics and the drawing is that the *'real fascination is not answering the question of the problem of squaring the circle, but the convergence of that sequence generated by Leonardo's procedure! That's the real secret of this drawing!'*

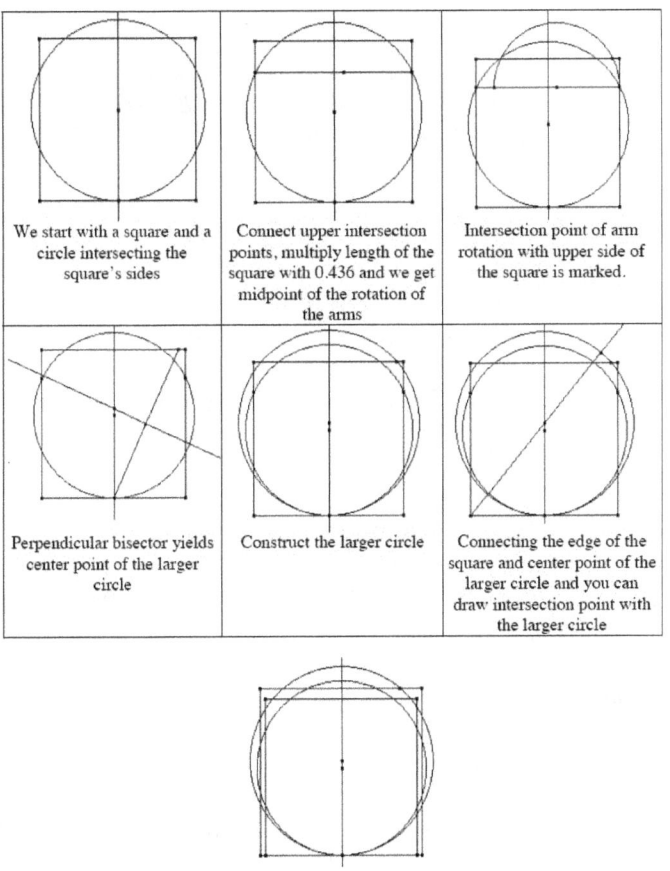

FIG. 11.15. *Klaus Schröer's procedure for infinite squaring of the circle published by Hubert Weller online at http://www.acdca.ac.at/kongress/1999goesing/g_weller.pdf*

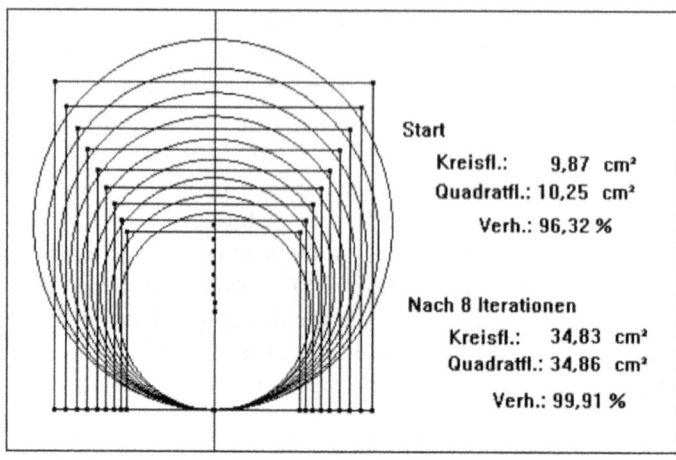

FIG. 11.16. Image of repeated circles and squares using the Klaus Schröer procedure for infinite squaring of the circle published by Hubert Weller online at: http://www.acdca.ac.at/kongress/1999goesing/g_weller.pdf

(e) Tom Pastorello

Tom Pastorello, Professor Emeritus of Syracuse University in New York, used the same dots on the ends of the neckline of the *Vitruvian Man* as Klaus Schröer to circle the square or square the circle in his construction, but with only two additional geometric steps using the compass and straightedge. Professor Pastrello provided measurements on the areas of the circle and the square to support his claim, and he wrote on his webpage that:

'The equality of Leonardo's square and the circle drawn according to my instructions can be proven to greater than 99% accuracy. Use any proportional copy of Leonardo's Vitruvian Man, including a printout of the file copy of the accompanying illustration, to measure one side of Leonardo's square and the radius of the circle drawn according to my instructions. Using the formula $pr^2 = s^2$, that expresses the equality of circle and square areas; substitute the length of Leonardo's square for s, the radius length of my circle for r and 3.14 for p. No matter what specific lengths or consistent metrics you use, the equality will be accurate to a degree greater than 99%.'

Pastorello's following description provides the solution for circling the square:

'Use a straight edge to draw a radius line from one of the dots on the neckline through the centre of the man's arm to the hand tip on the circumference of the circle. From which neckline dot to what rotated hand does one draw a radius? Leonardo is

trying to reconcile the opposites of square and circle. I took this as a hint from Leonardo to set a compass point on one dot of the neckline, extend the compass marker to the fingertip on the opposite side of the neckline dot and draw a circle, as shown in the second illustration. The circle's circumference is adjacent to the square on the square's inside right side. The astounding result is that the circle so drawn is equal in area to Leonardo's square!"

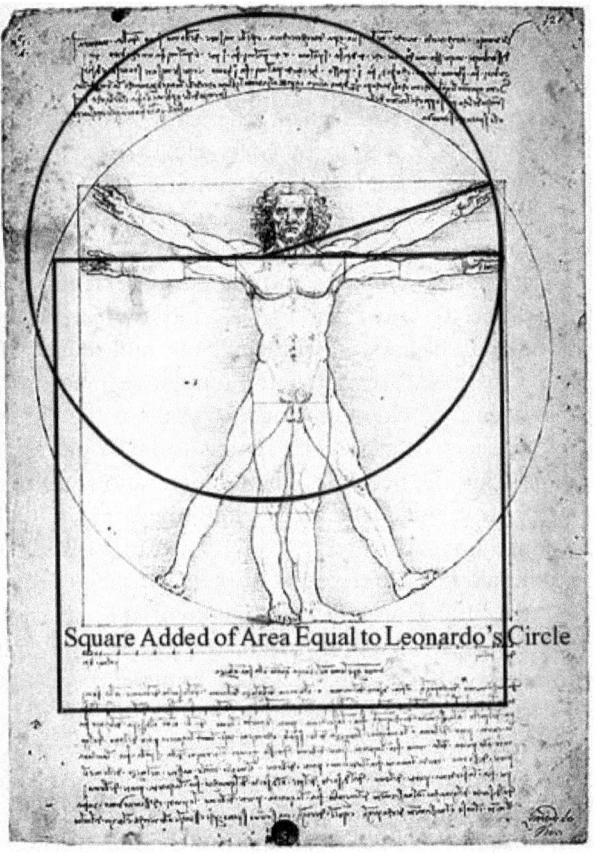

FIG. 11.17. The Pastorello solution. Radius and circle added (bold lines) of area equal to Leonardo's square followed by square added (bold lines) of area equal to Leonardo's circle. See Pastorello (2013) in the Reference section at the end of the chapter.

Pastorello found the length of Leonardo's square to be 3.875 inches and the length of a straight edge line from the left dot on the neckline to the tip of the right hand (the radius of the new circle) to be 2.1875 inches (Fig. 11.17). Using the standard equations for area, he calculated that the area of the square was 15.0156 sq. inches and the area of the circle was 15.025 sq. inches, an equivalence of 99.94%, despite using an imprecise straight edge ruler and compass to draw his square or circle. However, Pastorello made no mention about the lengths of the circumference and perimeter of his circle and square with an equivalent area. Using Pastorello's measurements of the length of Leonardo's square and the radius of his circle as before, then (1) the perimeter of the square is 15.5 cm, and (2) the circumference of the circle is 13.8 cm. The perimeter and the circumference are not the same with only 88.7% similarity. Therefore, if the area of the circle and the square is the same then the circumference and perimeters are different, and vice versa. So Pastorello could only equal the area of the circle and the square, but not their circumference and perimeters. However, he did go on and show that he could also square the circle by adding one other geometric step using only a straight edge. He drew a line through the neckline that extends from the left-side circumference of Leonardo's circle to the right-side circumference of his own new circle and extended it down into the shape of a square (Fig. 11.17).

Why did Leonardo use the arms and the neckline of the *Vitruvian Man* as his starting point to draw new circles and triangles? According to Pastorello, the procedure can start with any circle and square whose side is the line of which the circle's radius is the longest segment of the Golden ratio (square side equals circle radius plus 0.618 times the circle radius). In the *Vitruvian Man*, the starting point happens to be in the top half of the circle and square along the neckline. The Golden ratio is the starting point of a sector of the new radius and circle along the neckline that will equal the area of Leonardo's square (Fig. 11.17). Instead of using Pastorello's Golden ratio point along the horizontal diameter of the new circle, Schröer preferred the ratio of 0.436 along the length of the square to find the midpoint of the rotation of the arms and the intersection points for the construction of a larger circle (Fig. 11.14). In contrast, Leno Mascia (2018) found the same starting point as Pastorello and Schröer at the edge of the neckline by first drawing the lines of a triangle from the mid-collarbone point along the raised and horizontal arms to the tip of second finger of each arm. This again simply highlights the different geometric procedures for finding the same or different starting points of interest within Leonardo's drawings of the circle and square that contain the image of the *Vitruvian Man*.

Conclusion

The starting point for the construction of the circle and the square can be either from the circle or the square. Judging from Leonardo's drawings in his notebooks, his starting points were mostly with the circle that produced a square. The painter, draftsman and teacher Anthony Panzera summed up Leonardo's drawing in his article *Learning From Leonardo's The Vitruvian Man*

CHAPTER 11

when he concluded:

'Using his own language—the visual language of drawing—Leonardo was able to do what others had failed to do. By visually combining in one drawing the figure in the square and the figure in the circle, he gave movement and meaning to Vitruvius' words. The poetic synthesis linking the combined figures of the circle and the square creates a harmony of such universal proportion that the visual image allows for instant recognition and clear comprehension of the meaning behind the words.'

When I look at the *Vitruvian Man* (Fig. 11.8), I see a man with a free-will standing proudly naked and upright with his arms spread out ready to fly before he is transformed cruelly by Fate to a position of suffering on a crucifix, like Jesus nailed to the T-shaped cross or St. Andrew tied to the X-shaped cross. On the other hand, if we look at the *Vitruvian Man* as a semaphore, he is signalling letters of the alphabet, rotating between R and U when waving his arms or between T and X shapes when using his arms and legs. RUTX – are you T-shaped or X-shaped, *Vitruvian Man*?

I have long considered that Leonardo da Vinci was a great admirer of St. John the Baptist and preferred him over the other saints, but it never crossed my mind that the drawing of *Vitruvian Man* might represent St. John. This is not too surprising because St. John the Baptist was the patron saint and protector of Florence and many Florentine painters introduced St. John into their paintings, and none more so than Leonardo da Vinci. St. John was the prophet who recognised Jesus as the Messiah and baptised him. But, it was probably St. John's intrepidness and courage against the despot Herod that impressed Leonardo the most. St. John features in at least five of Leonardo's paintings; *The Baptism of Christ*, *Virgin of the Rocks*, *The Virgin and Child with St. Anne and St. John*, *Bacchus* and *John the Baptist*. Many of Leonardo's acolytes, such as Bernardino Luini and Andrea Solario painted the decapitated head of John the Baptist on Salome's platter to present to King Herod. Therefore, it was interesting to read the following opinion from Professor Pastorello:

'Some suggest that his Vitruvian Man *is Jesus. I suggest that the neckline may be symbolic of John the Baptist's beheading and that, therefore, the* Vitruvian Man *is an allusion to John the Baptist. To understand his need for secrecy, I suggest further that one read about Leonardo's heretical beliefs involving the supremacy of John the Baptist over Jesus and the consequences that such a belief would have had were it known to church officials. (A good starting point for literature on this topic is The Templar Revelation by L. Picknett and C. Prince, Touchstone Books, NY, NY, 1997.) Leonardo's secret encoding, within his* Vitruvian Man, *of his astounding solution to the squaring of the circle, may have merely masked the more explosive beliefs of his heresy.'*

How does all this relate to the circle in the *Pacioli Portrait*? Apart from the possible hidden squaring of the circle in the painting (Fig. 1.1), the *Portrait* contains many other encoded secrets that hide Leonardo's heretical and treasonous political beliefs.

References

Capra, Fritjof (2008). The Science of Leonardo: Inside the Mind of the Great Genius of the Renaissance. Anchor Books Edition, New York.
https://erenow.com/biographies/the-science-of-leonardo-inside-the-mind-of-the-great-genius-of-the-renaissance?. Retrieved 9 Aug., 2019.

Euclid (1956). The Thirteen Books of The Elements. Sir Thomas L. Heath, trans. Vol 2. New York: Dover Publications.

Fletcher, Rachel (2004). Musings on the Vesica Piscis. Nexus Network Journal 6(2): 95–110, *doi:10.1007/s00004-004-0021-8.*

Fletcher, Rachel (2007). Geometer's Angle, Squaring the Circle: Marriage of Heaven and Earth. Nexus Network Journal 9(1):119–143.

Fletcher, Rachel (2013). Infinite Measure: Learning to Design in Geometric Harmony with Art, Architecture and Nature. Staunton, Virginia: GFT Publishing. *https://infinitemeasure.com/publications/*

Helbing, Mario Otto (2005). Il Poli'gono Reietto. Chiasso: Edizioni Leggere.

Hoffmann, Gernot (2005). Circle a square.
http://docs-hoffmann.de/circsqua22042005.pdf. Retrieved 9 Aug., 2019.

Ida, Takashi. Vitruvian Man by Leonardo da Vinci and the Golden ratio.
http://www.crl.nitech.ac.jp/~ida/education/VitruvianMan/. Retrieved 9 Aug., 2019.

Lindemann F (1882). Über die Zahl π. Mathematische Annalen 20: 213–225.

March, Lionel (1998). Architectonics of Humanism: Essays on Number in Architecture. Chichester: Academy Editions.

Mascia, Leono Liberato (2016). A Vitruvius inspired criterion for the construction of polygons. Nexus Netw J 18:533–545. *DOI 10.1007/s00004-015-0258-4.*

Mascia, Leno (2018). Observation on the geometry behind the design of the 'Vitruvian man' by Leonardo da Vinci. *Down-loaded from ResearchGate.*
https://www.researchgate.net/publication/325908788. Retrieved 9 Aug., 2019.

Murtinho, Vitor (2015). Leonardo's Vitruvian Man Drawing: A New Interpretation Looking at Leonardo's Geometric Constructions. Nexus Netw J 17:507–524. *DOI 10.1007/s00004-015-0247-7.*

Pacioli, Luca (1498). Divine Proportion (in English). 1498 edition. *Tennenbaum pacioli-divine-proportion.pdf.* Uploaded by Israel Monroy Muñoz on Oct 22, 2014. Full text of original edition (1498) in English.
https://www.scribd.com/document/244035060/tennenbaum-pacioli-divine-proportion-pdf. Retrieved 9 Aug., 2019.

Panzera, Anthony (2009). Learning From Leonardo's The Vitruvian Man. Excerpt in Drawing pages 34 to 41. Reprinted from Drawing Winter: Copyright © 2009 by Interweave Press, LLC. Pdf. *Retrieved 9 Aug., 2019.*
http://anthonypanzeraart.com/AP_PDF/VitruvianMan.pdf.
https://www.artistsnetwork.com/art-mediums/drawing/drawing-winter-2009/

Pastorello, Tom (2013). Leonardo squared the circle! Da Vinci's secret solution in the Vitruvian Man decoded. *https://web.archive.org/web/20130403044351/http://arthistory.about.com/library/weekly/bl_leo_vitruvian_man.htm (Tom Pastorello died May 7, 2019).*

Reddy, Sarva Jagannadha (2015). The New Theory of the Oneness of Square and Circle. International Journal of Engineering Sciences & Research Technology, 4(8): August, 2015, *ISSN: 2277-9655, PP: 901-909.*

Reddy, Sarva Jagannadha (2015). Leonardo Da Vinci's Ingenious Way of Carving One-Fourth Area of A Segment in A Circle. International Journal of Engineering Sciences & Research Technology, 4(10): October, 2015, *ISSN: 2277-9655, PP: 39-47.*

Reynolds, Mark (2008). The Octagon in Leonardo's Drawings. Nexus Network Journal 10(1):51–76.

Richter. J., P., editor (1880). The Notebooks of Leonardo da Vinci. *http://www.fromoldbooks.org/Richter-NotebooksOfLeonardo/. Retrieved 9 Aug., 2019.*

Schröer, Klaus and Irle, Klaus (2017). Das Geheimnes der Proportionsstudie, Verlag: Books on Demand, Germany. *http://www.klaus-schroeer.com/leonardo/*

Schröer, Klaus (2018). Leonardo's Vitruvian Man and the Squaring of the Circle. YouTube Video. *https://www.bod.de/buchshop/ich-aber-quadriere-den-kreis-klaus-schroeer-9783743190870. Retrieved 9 Aug., 2019.*

Sinisgalli, Rocco (2010). Playing With Leonardo: The Vitruvian Man. Rome: Federighi Editori.

Ueshiba, Morihei (2013). The Heart of Aikido. The Philosophy of Takemusu Aiki, Kodansha America, Inc.

Vitruvius, Marcus Vitruvius Pollio. De Architectura, Book III. *penelope.uchicago.edu.* Retrieved 28 September 2018. *http://penelope.uchicago.edu/Thayer/E/Roman/Texts/Vitruvius/3*.html*

Voarino, Phillipe (2013). Aikido and the Vitruvian Man. Copyright TAI (Takemusu Aikido Intercontinental). *http://www.aikidotakemusu.org/en/articles/aikido-and-vitruvian-man-2*

Weller, Hubert (1999). Squaring the Circle and Leonardo's Vitruvian Man. *http://www.acdca.ac.at/kongress/1999goesing/g_weller.pdf. Retrieved 22 Sept., 2018.* Post not found on 8th Aug., 2019.

World Mysteries (2011). Vitruvian Man by Leonardo da Vinci. *http://blog.world-mysteries.com/science/vitruvian-man-by-leonardo-da-vinci/. Retrieved 9 Aug., 2019.*

12

SIGNATURE RHOMBICUBOCTAHEDRON & MEANINGFUL EYES

The Rhombicuboctahedron. Leonardo da Vinci's Pictorial Signature

No other symbol in the *Pacioli Portrait* better represents Leonardo da Vinci's hand and signature in the painting than the hanging, transparent rhombicuboctahedron (Fig. 12.1). It has been long acknowledged that Leonardo da Vinci was the first to publish an image of the rhombicuboctahedron structure, first as a hand-drawn painting in the manuscript of *De Divina Proportione* presented to Duke Ludovico Sforza in 1498 and then as a woodcarved print in the published printed version of *De Divina Proportione* in 1509 with all the 66 drawings attributed to him. How the amazingly subtle painting of the hanging rhombicuboctahedron crystal in the *Pacioli Portrait* could have been attributed to Jacopo de' Barbari is a total mystery, staggering beyond belief. Was it because of ignorance, malice, petty-politics or because of incompetent and bloody-minded art history scholarship? Possibly, it was part incompetence and ignorance and part financial politics and ownership rights at play. It also shows how flakey, opinionated, incorrect and fraudulent art history scholarship can be. Given these caveats, we can assume safely that the floating rhombicuboctahedron in the foreground of the *Pacioli Portrait* was beyond the technical skill and know-how of Jacopo de' Barbari and that the geometrical knowledge and the patience and skill required to paint the rhombicuboctahedron crystal required somebody of Leonardo's ability and innovativeness. Moreover, Jacopo de' Barbari had no documented meetings with Luca Pacioli, so why would he want to paint a portrait of him in the presence of a floating rhombicuboctahedron, anyway?

The hanging polyhedron in the *Pacioli Portrait* is Leonardo da Vinci's pictorial signature. It demonstrates his painting skills using *sfumato* (dark and smoky glazes), natural muted hues, and the contrasts of light and shadow and subtle tones of black and white with tinges of blue and green transparent glazes (*contrapposto*); together with complex perspectives, reflections, illusions, narrow tonal ranges, soft gentle lighting, contrasted by the triple reflections of the bright-blue light of the sky, and mysterious, dark, shady, figures lingering within the crystal (Fig. 12.2); all of this contained in one painted object, the rhombicuboctahedron (Fig. 12.1). The depiction of the pictorial and geometrical elements that are characteristic of the rhombicuboctahedron in the *Pacioli Portrait* undoubtedly were far beyond the skills, imagination and capabilities of most painters other than Leonardo during his lifetime. Even, if Jacopo de' Barbari or some other painter was capable of solving the geometry and creating a 3D image of the rhombicuboctahedron, given the context and the overall philosophy of the painting, you would have to believe that the floating polyhedron hanging in front of Luca Pacioli's eye line was all about Leonardo da Vinci and his painterly genius. In short, the rhombicuboctahedron is a symbolic portrayal of the eyes, brain and soul of the universe or an allegorical representation of Leonardo's creative third eye.

The crystal rhombicuboctahedron in the *Pacioli Portrait* is composed of 18 squares and 8 equilateral triangles with 24 identical vertices, and each vertex is shared by three squares and one triangle (Fig. 12.3). The transparent shell was constructed with 26 fused glass plates and filled with liquid up to its centroid. Leonardo da Vinci was the only one known to have drawn, painted and constructed models of the rhombicuboctahedron structure in his lifetime. Some others soon followed in his footsteps, especially Albrecht Durer with his treatise on geometry, *Underweysung der Messung*, published in 1525. Thus, the hanging polyhedron in the *Pacioli Portrait* is one of the earliest known images of an accurately constructed rhombicuboctahedron. It could only have been painted by Leonardo and not by any other painter, particularly not by Jacopo de' Barbari who had limited skill and knowledge on how to draw and paint this structure, although he did paint a transparent glass filled with water (Fig. 4.1.11).

Leonardo could have included himself in the *Pacioli Portrait*. After all, he was Luca Pacioli's mathematics student and he provided him with 60 geometric shapes to illustrate the *Divine Proportion's* manuscripts for Galeazzo Sanseverino and Ludovico Sforza. However, Leonardo probably refrained from embedding himself into the portrait because for a modest painter like himself it was the greatest sin of vanity to embed oneself uninvited into the portraits of others. In this regard, the rhombicuboctahedron symbolically replaces Leonardo and it hangs there in the context of the theme of the painting and in the presence of Pacioli and Sanseverino. It is his signature, his ghost telling us that, '*Here I am next to Luca Pacioli; he is looking at me while I am painting this picture.*'

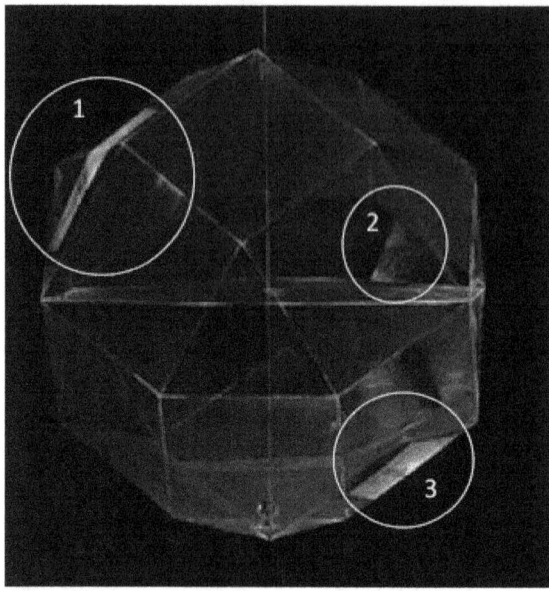

FIG. 12.1. *The hanging rhombicuboctahedron. Detail from the* Pacioli Portrait *at the Capodimonte Museum. Three reflected and refracted images of a window are circled and labelled 1 to 3. The polygon is half-filled with water with image 2 located just above the surface. A cord passes through the centre of the polygon and is attached to a ring shaped like an A or inverted V at the bottom vertex (see Fig. 12.14 for greater detail).*

The rhombicuboctahedron was of great interest to Leonardo da Vinci and Luca Pacioli and they referred to it in their handwritten manuscripts and printed publication of the *Divine Proportion* because the square and triangular faces represented four of the five regular Platonic solids. Leonardo emphasised this point by half filling the rhombicuboctahedron with Water and Air to evoke the four corresponding chemical elements described by Plato in the *Timaeus*; with the other two elements, Earth represented by the physical glass shell, and Fire depicted by the bright reflections of the light from the window(s).

The characteristics of the water in the hanging polyhedron are different to the air above it. The force of gravity keeps the water in the lower half of the polyhedron displacing most of the air to the upper half. The air and the water both assume the shape of the surface and the internal volume in their respective halves of the polyhedron. There is an atomic interplay between the water and the air at the surface where they meet and it is seen as a fuzzy horizontal ellipse illuminated and reflected by the light like a glassy lake in the mountains. Although not obvious from the picture itself, water is incompressible and its mass is always conserved. Leonardo saw water as the chief agent in the formation of the Earth's surface and he wrote:

CHAPTER 12

'Water wears away the mountains and fills up the valleys and if it could, it would like to reduce the Earth to a perfect sphere.'

FIG. 12.2. *Detail of the rhombicuboctahedron and the surface view of the liquid layer, light reflections and the submerged dark figure in the triangle.*

Many ancient cultures, including the Greeks, explained the nature and complexity of all matter in terms of the four simplest substances, Fire, Air, Water and Earth. Aristotle added a fifth element, Aether, also know as Space in Tibetan philosophy, and *Akasha* in Indian cosmology, and it is 'an element' that is beyond the material world. Aristotle reasoned that because Fire, Earth, Air, and Water were earthly and corruptible, the stars cannot be made out of any of these four elements, and he introduced Aether as a different, unchangeable, heavenly substance. According to Hinduism, *Akasha* (Aether) is beyond the sense of smell, taste, sight and touch, but is accessible to the sense of hearing. The other elements are perceived by two or more of the five senses of hearing, touch, sight, taste and smell; Earth is perceived by all five senses, Water by four senses except for smell, Fire by three senses except by taste and smell, and Air can only be heard and felt. The alchemists of the Renaissance used four triangular symbols and a square, with the square integrating all the four elements. Air is drawn as a standard triangle with a horizontal line through its middle, whereas Fire is the same triangle without the horizontal line. Earth is the inverted triangle with a horizontal line, and Water is the same inverted triangle without the horizontal line (Fig. 12.3C).

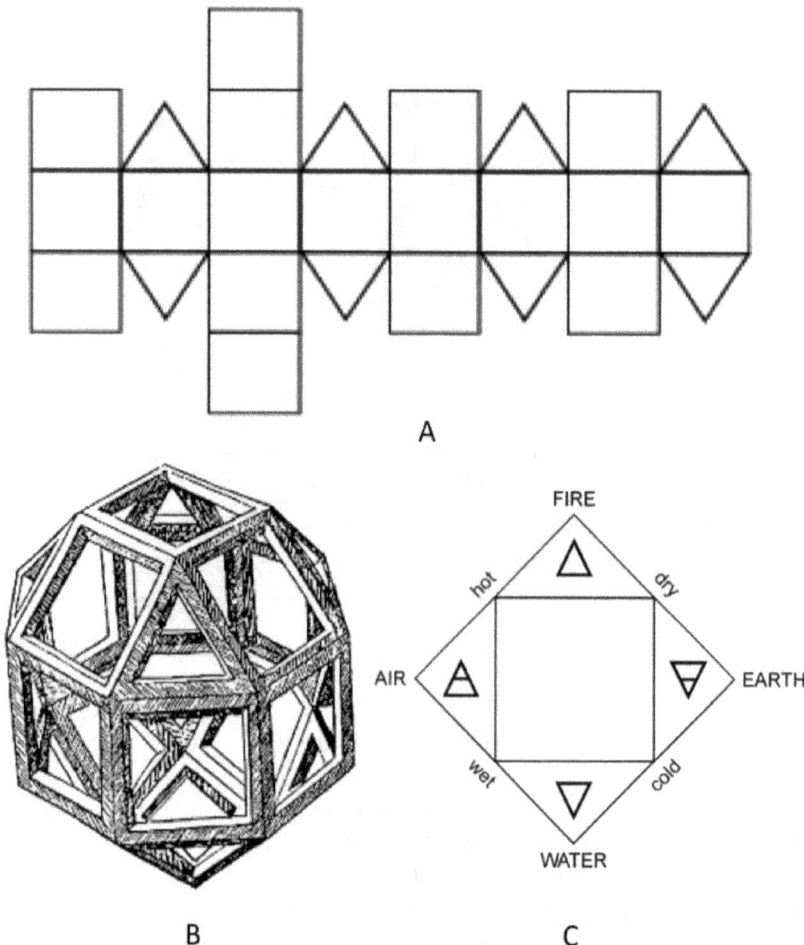

FIG. 12.3. *The 18 squares and 8 triangles as linear components (A, top) and 3D structure (B, lower left) of the rhombicuboctahedron, and the four basic Aristotelian elements and qualities of nature represented as triangles and squares (C, lower right).*

While the Water, Air, Fire and Earth are seen for what they are in the hanging rhombicuboctahedron, Leonardo represented Aether by the solid dodecahedron placed on top of Luca Pacioli's published red book, the *Summa Mathematica*. Leonardo also may have represented Aether either by the space in which the rhombicuboctahedron hangs or by the thin, red neural cord to which the rhombicuboctahedron is attached, that is, connecting the polyhedron to the mysterious element (Aether) or (GOD) that is outside the picture.

CHAPTER 12

Modern Criticism of Leonardo's Rhombicuboctahedron Drawing

Dirk Huylebrouck, in an article published in the *Scientific American* on March 29, 2011, presented a Dutch sculptor's criticism of the accuracy of the structure of the rhombicuboctahedron that Leonardo da Vinci had drawn and painted for Luca Pacioli's manuscript of the *Divine Proportion* for the Duke of Milan Ludovico Sforza. The Dutch artist Rinus Roelofs discovered an error in Leonardo da Vinci's drawing after he saw the painting of the rhombicuboctahedron in the *Pacioli Portrait*. According to the mathematician **Dirk Huylebrouck** the correct rhombicuboctahedron has a triangular pyramid surrounded by six quadrangular pyramids (Fig. 12.4):

'But in da Vinci's drawing (again reproduced, directly below) this isn't the case: The pyramid at the bottom of his rendering has four upright ribs, although it should have three. And the pyramids adjacent to it, at the bottom, along with the two above them that point directly left and right (at nine and three o'clock), are also doubtful: They appear to be triangular whereas they should in fact be quadrangular. The apexes of two triangular pyramids at the bottom left and right (eight and four o'clock) seem to be missing as well. The latter omission can be explained as a matter of interpretation from the observer's point of view. But the drawing of the pyramid pointing down is clearly wrong.'

Dirk Huylebrouck then provided the corrected version of Leonardo da Vinci's drawing that you can see in Fig. 12.4. After correcting Leonardo's mistake on the rhombicuboctahedron that had been drawn for one of Pacioli's manuscripts, **Dirk Huylebrouck** acknowledged that Leonardo de Vinci was the first person to draw the rhombicuboctahedron for a print version in 1509, presumably correctly, ten years after completing the first three hand-drawn manuscripts of 1498. He also made the following interesting observations and conclusions about Leonardo and the *Pacioli Portrait*:

'But big, solid models of polyhedrons, made by da Vinci, have never been found. It isn't even certain whether he had a model for the rhombicuboctahedron: the figure on Pacioli's portrait seems to be made out of glass and therefore had to be very heavy. Moreover, it was half filled with water. How could such a heavy model hang from a small string? And how could the glass side surfaces be attached to each other in a waterproof way, in a time when superglues didn't exist yet?
At the same time, the reflections of the light in and on the model are marvellously drawn. This seems practically impossible without models. Unfortunately, it's not even

certain who the painter of Pacioli's Portrait *was. The name of the Venetian Jacopo de' Barbari often comes up, but this allocation is controversial.*

Does this error alter the fact that da Vinci was a genius? "No," *Roelofs says,* "it goes without saying that da Vinci was a genius, probably even the greatest genius of all time. But he was also a human being, who had to think and reason, and who also committed an error every once in a while. And this only makes him an even greater genius.'*

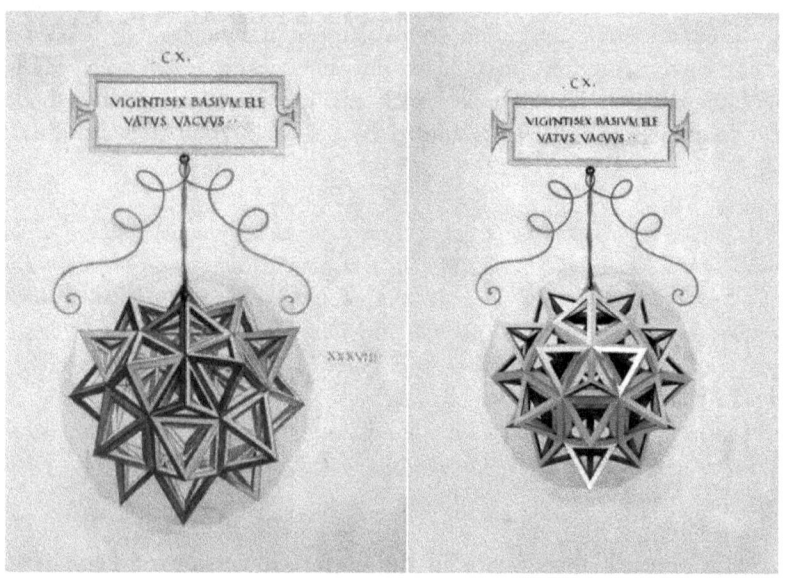

FIG. 12.4. *Dirk Huylebrouck's corrected (right) version of Leonardo da Vinci's painting and drawing of the incorrect structure (left) of the rhombicuboctahedron for the* Divine Proportion *manuscript. https://www.scientificamerican.com/article/davinci-mathematical-slip-up/*

This criticism of Leonardo da Vinci's *'minor mistake'* seems far too harsh considering that he had no computer modelling facilities in his day, more than five hundred years ago. To say that even geniuses make mistakes seems highly condescending considering that Leonardo da Vinci was self-taught to a large degree and he learnt by experimentation, life experiences, meditation and contemplation, and from his own mistakes along the way. We all know that he was human and not perfect, unlike some who consider a sculptor, a computer or Michelangelo to be perfect. It was possibly a slip of Leonardo's brush or the pen or a slight loss in concentration. He probably was depressed and disappointed with the Duke of Milan, Ludovico Sforza, who was not paying him for monies owned when he was busy with the completion of the *Last Supper*, the *Giant Horse* sculpture, and other major works. He and the citizens of Milan were still mourning the

death of the Duke's wife Beatrice, and the highly suspicious death of the previous Duke, Ludovico's nephew, Gian Galeazzo Sforza. And if Leonardo da Vinci made a few minor errors in calculating or depicting the rhombicuboctahedron incorrectly on the manuscript that was presented to the sinister black fly of Milan, Ludovico Il Moro Sforza, then it is surely even more unlikely that the correct model of the rhombicuboctahedron in *Pacioli's Portrait* was painted by the lesser painter Jacopo de' Barbari who probably had no idea what a rhombicuboctahedron looked like or cared much about how to construct one. For an alternative interpretation on Leonardo's drawing inconsistencies, see the following Internet address:
https://people.eecs.berkeley.edu/%7Esequin/X/Leonardo/leonardo.html

According to the encoded message on the notepaper in the *Pacioli Portrait*, the painting probably was finished by the end of 1496 (see Chapter 20 for details). However, if Leonardo da Vinci had corrected his drawing of the rhombicuboctahedron only after the completion of Luca Pacioli's manuscript of the *Divine Proportion*, then the correct version of the rhombicuboctahedron in the *Pacioli Portrait* might have been painted after the 9th day of February 1498. This is the date that the rhombicuboctahedron drawing was handed over to the Duke of Milan in an official ceremony at the impregnable citadel as reported by Luca Pacioli in the introduction to his manuscript. The correct printed version of the rhombicuboctahedron structure was first published in 1509 when Leonardo da Vinci had returned to Milan for the second time after having spent about six or seven years back in Florence. This was when the French king Louis XII was also the Duke of Milan, and it was soon after Ludovico Sforza had died in France (27 May 1508) after spending nine years in prison.

If Galeazzo Sanseverino was given the *Pacioli Portrait* because he had commissioned the painting and the manuscripts of the *Divine Proportion*, Leonardo and Luca lost touch with him after the French invaded and conquered Milan in October of 1499 and he was exiled in Innsbruck, Germany, supported by Ludovico Sforza's niece and his cousin Bianca Sforza, the Queen of Germany and the Empress of the Holy Roman Empire. If he had the painting in Milan then it was likely lost during the French occupation when his political opponents confiscated many of his Milanese properties and art treasures. On the other hand, he might not have received the painting from Leonardo because by 1498 he was overwhelmed with various government and administrative issues and busy trying to prevent the French and their allies from capturing Milan and Ludovico Sforza. Perhaps, Leonardo presented the portrait instead to Luca Pacioli to take with him to Florence when they left Milan in December of 1499. These are simple speculations that require proper historical investigation.

JERZY K. KULSKI

The Eyes Have It. How the Rhombicuboctahedron Glass Crystal Might Represent Leonardo's All-Seeing Third Eye

Although the rhombicuboctahedron appears slightly larger than the faces of Luca Pacioli and Galeazzo, its centre is positioned at a horizontal level slightly below the level of the mouths of Luca Pacioli and Galeazzo Sanseverino (Fig. 12.5). The rhombicuboctahedron possibly symbolises the universal 'third eye' or 'inspiration' positioned to the right of Luca Pacioli and Galeazzo Sanseverino and slightly below the horizontal level of their eyes. Lines drawn from the top and bottom of the rhombicuboctahedron to the top and bottom of Galeazzo's head represent Leonardo's pyramids of inspirational light shining onto the two figures' faces, although Luca's head might block Galeazzo's view of the hanging crystal (Fig. 12.5).

FIG. 12.5. *The position and size of the rhombicuboctahedron relative to the faces of Luca Pacioli and Galeazzo Sanseverino.*

Galeazzo's eyes stare out at us directly and follow us wherever we stand before the picture. Luca's eyes are slightly cross-eyed, with one eye focused on the rhombicuboctahedron and the other looking out towards us. On the other hand, the transparent rhombicuboctahedron is attached to a thin red nerve (line) and its surface reflects three images of an unseen window (Fig. 12.1). To look at the painting with only one eye opened slightly, the rhombicuboctahedron seem to float in space and reflect some lights or images from inside and outside the room. It seems to hang there as if it represented Leonardo's 'third eye', showing us how the creative genius in his brain has overseen the whole painting.

The rhombicuboctahedron reflects or refracts the same outside image onto at least three different triangles or squares of the hanging polyhedron as if it was part of a 3D *camera obscura* (Fig. 12.1). Luca's eyes are slightly wall-eyed with divergent *strabismus* or *exotropia* where one of his eyes is turned out, fixed on the hanging crystal, and the other eye is turned out towards us and enlarged by a revelation or intense inner concentration of the mind (Fig. 12.6). Meanwhile, Galeazzo Sanseverino's eyes stare at us arrogantly [or is it guiltily, accusingly, suspiciously or seductively?] from the corners of his eyes. If the eyes are the windows to the soul, Sanseverino has built a strong defensive wall around his soul. I find it almost impossible to guess why he stares out at us so intensely. He definitely demonstrates more interest in us than does Luca Pacioli. He follows us with his eyes, no matter where we stand in front of the painting (Fig. 12.5 and 12.6). Why? What is it that he is trying to convey to us? The 'muscle' between the eye and the *senso comune* in the brain that Leonardo called the *imprensiva* seems to be vibrating nervously in Sanseverino's brain. Why? We will never know for sure, we can only guess.

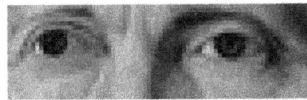 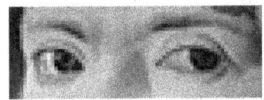

FIG. 12.6. The eyes have it. Luca Pacioli (left) and Galeazzo Sanseverino (right).

The rhombicuboctahedron hanging in the left foreground of the painting as we look at it parodies Leonardo's studies on the material workings of the brain and the eye. This hanging polyhedron suggests a *camera obscura* that Leonardo used to model the function of the eye. Luca Pacioli has one eye on the rhombicuboctahedron while drawing his model of an eye, adding measurements in the form of an equilateral triangle including two internal isosceles right triangles with 90-degree angles, while Galeazzo keeps both of his eyes on us, sizing us up and down. Luca Pacioli could easily be Leonardo da Vinci looking at and studying the model of an eye, drawing the elliptical shape of the eyeball with the light entering through the aperture of the eyeball and refracting or diverging to a single point on the retina before telling the brain (the misaligned rhombicuboctahedron) that it is looking upside down at Leonardo's portrait of Luca Pacioli and Galeazzo Sanseverino who look out at us and mock us that we are so stupid that we can see nothing of the hidden dimensions in this allegorical masterpiece. It seems that this painting is meant to disturb us, in keeping with the growing role of art in the Renaissance as a form of visual poetry - an allegorical conversation piece where the painting is an intellectual puzzle inviting the viewers to demonstrate their humanistic pedigree and cultural sophistication, and elucidate the hidden meaning and truth within the encrypted dimensions of pictorial symbolism, allegory and anagrams.

Leonardo's Anatomy of the Eye, the *Camera Obscura* and the Hanging Globe, Half-filled with Water

Leonardo believed that the eyes were the windows to the soul just as the rhombicuboctahedron might symbolically represent the window to the universe. He undertook many studies of the eye and investigated how light passes through lenses and pinholes to reflect from various objects and demonstrate their existence as an image. He also cut open a boiled bovine eyeball and studied its structure and anatomy. Leonardo used the *camera obscura,* a little box with a small hole (a pinhole or box camera), and a glass globe instead of the rhombicuboctahedron as his mechanical instruments and models to study the function of the eye and perform experiments on vision and the phenomena of light and shadow. He could have used the rhombicuboctahedron, but the *camera obscura* was a simpler instrument to construct and use. He never invented the *camera obscura,* which was known to the ancient Chinese, Greeks and Arabs, and he probably learnt about it when he was an apprentice in Verrocchio's workshop in Florence.

Before Leonardo was born, the great Florentine architect Filippo Brunelleschi demonstrated perspective with a *camera obscura* when he pointed the pinhole at the Baptistery of Florence, and with a mirror reflected a reconstruction of the Baptistery image in full perspective, done in part by perspective drawing and the reflected image itself. In 1475, after Filippo Brunelleschi erected the dome of Florence Duomo in 1461, the astronomer and geographer Paolo di Pozzo Toscanelli installed an astronomical *gnomon,* a round hole on a bronze plate at the top of the dome. It projected an image of the sun on to calculated markings on the cathedral's floor to track the movements of the sun and to show the exact time for midday of each day and the date of the summer solstice. That same year, Andrea del Verrocchio and Leonardo da Vinci hoisted a gilded copper sphere to the top of the lantern of the Duomo and, while they were on the lantern, they inspected the circular aperture of Toscanelli's *gnomon.* Leonardo da Vinci later used the smaller aperture of a *camera obscura* to learn that, *'no image, even of the smallest object, enters the eye without being turned upside down.'* He could not elucidate or explain how the human eye saw the image the right-way-up, although he did propose several ingenious models that he thought might be the correct solution. Even today, we do not know how the brain transforms the inverted image in the eye by way of the nerve cells, chemicals and electrical impulses so that the brain interprets the inverted image the right way up – it just does.

Leonardo's solution for seeing the right way up was that when the light rays entered the pupil, they exited the pupil turned upside down, and then they converged and crossed over again to enter the optic nerve the right way up. In most of his drawings, the paths of light rays behind the pupil cross over before they pass into the lens, and while there, they cross over again to impinge on the optic nerve (Fig. 12.7). Although technically incorrect, it was an ingenious proposal not too far from the actuality. This was his standard explanation for seeing the right way up that he had founded on a number of his observations and experiments. The two intersections of the light rays were governed by the necessity that the final image would be upright. It was inconceivable to Leonardo that the image carried by the optic nerve could be inverted anywhere else except at the start of the optic nerve. Yet, after all these years, we still do not know the correct answer for how the image is corrected and interpreted by the brain. It might be that the image correction occurs in Leonardo's *imprensiva*, a region in the brain located between the eye and the *senso comune*. If so, this would be a monumental discovery five hundred years after Leonardo's proposal for the existence of the *imprensiva* in the brain.

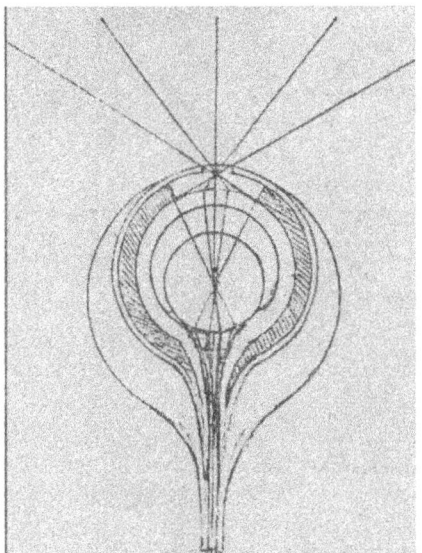 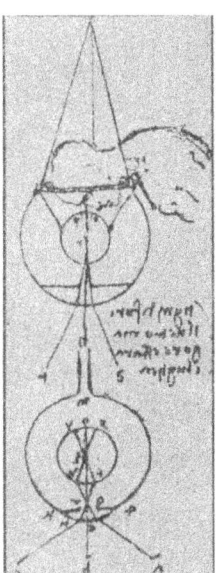

FIG. 12.7. Leonardo's drawing of a cross-section of the eye showing light rays entering through the pupil intersecting twice before impinging onto the optic nerve (left), and his artificial eye consisting of glass globe with a layer of water (right).

To experiment with the power of vision and to try to elucidate the location where the image is seen in the brain. Leonardo constructed an artificial eye consisting of a glass globe with a layer of water at the bottom. A lens hung from the top of the globe and the observer placed his head into the globe with his eyes located over the lens to observe an object placed outside the globe. The observer's eye was thus intended to be the optic nerve with the visual power. '*Such an instrument will bring the species to the eye, just as the eye brings them to the visual power*'. Leonardo drew the model of the artificial eye shown in Figure 12.7 and below the globe he drew the passage of the main light rays, noting that the power of vision lies in the optic nerve where the two rays intersected.

Leonardo used the *camera obscura* as an alternative to his hanging globe experiment (Fig. 12.8). This involved placing the eye in a square box with an aperture representing the pupil, behind which a glass ball was placed to represent the lens. Again, the human eye occupied the position of the optic nerve. He illustrated the *camera obscura* model in a page of a manuscript (D.8r) where the passage of light rays through the cornea, pupil and lens is represented at the top whilst below is the comparable scheme in a *camera obscura* with a sheet of paper inserted like a film to pick up the reversed image transmitted from outside. Leonardo described the *camera obscura* as follows:

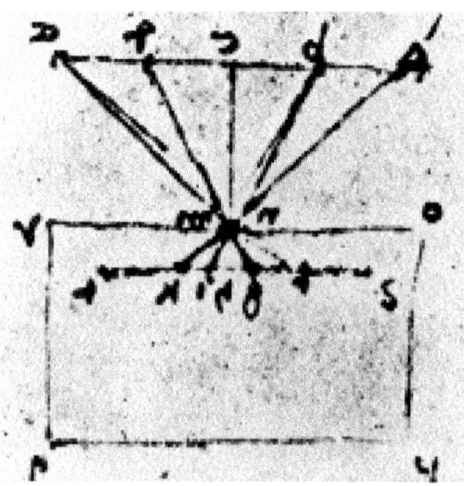

FIG 12.8. Leonardo da Vinci, Notebooks, drawing of camera obscura, Manuscript D, fol. 8r.

'*How the images of objects received by the eye intersect within the crystalline humour of the eye. An experiment, showing how objects transmit their images or pictures, intersecting within the eye in the crystalline humour, is seen when by some small round hole penetrate the images of illuminated objects into a very dark chamber. Then, receive these images on a white paper placed within this dark room and rather near to the hole and you will see all the objects on the paper in their proper forms and colours, but much smaller; and they will be upside down by reason of that very intersection. These images being transmitted from a place illuminated by the sun will seem actually painted on this paper which must be extremely thin and looked at from behind. And let the little perforation be made in a very thin plate of iron. Let a, b, c, d, e, be the object illuminated by the sun and 'o r' the front of the dark chamber in which is the said hole at 'n m'. Let 's t' be the sheet of paper intercepting the rays of the images of these objects upside down, because the rays being straight, 'a' on the right hand becomes 'k' on the left, and 'e' on the left becomes 'f' on the right; and the same takes place inside the pupil. (D.8r.)'*

Three Distinct Images of a Building Projected on the Hanging Rhombicuboctahedron

The painting of the hanging polyhedron addresses a few interesting attributes about the force of gravity and the transmission of light passing through transparent material and their effects as Leonardo saw them. First, the effect of gravity on water is why it is contained below the air in a glass vessel. Second, the physical property of transparency that allows light to pass through different transparent materials (glass, air and water) without being scattered. Third, the reflection of an image of a window that is seen at least three times on the surface of the polyhedron. Fourth, how the transmitted light highlights the joins of the square and triangular tiles that contribute to the structure of the rhombicuboctahedron. Leonardo never wrote about these four points directly, but he did approach them tangentially by way of his many experiments and investigations.

Nobody has provided a reasonable explanation as to why there are three distinct images of different sizes of a building and blue sky on the rhombicuboctahedron in the *Pacioli Portrait* (Fig. 12.1). In comparison to the *camera obscura*, the rhombicuboctahedron might act like the compound eye of a fly and project its images onto its various 'retinas'. Perhaps, the images of the window on the polyhedron are simple lessons about how light passes through transparent material or, in this case, through glass and air, and glass, air and water of the rhombicuboctahedron. When light hits the window, some of it goes through the window and some is reflected off the window. The viewer sees some of the light reflected from the window as an image of the building and the light. The largest and brightest image on the glass vessel is the one that is nearest to the window and the hanging vessel. The smallest and dullest reflected image is located across the surface of the water and therefore it is the greatest distance away from the viewer and the window and it is the smallest image. The third reflected image is brighter and larger than the second one, but not the first one, and it might be there because of the refraction of the image through the water.

The three images on the rhombicuboctahedron (Fig. 12.1) have confused modern scientists because they are unsure whether these are real images copied by the painter or whether the painter created them using his imagination. Carlo H. Sequin and Raymond Shiau wrote about this as a contemporary scientific problem in an academic paper entitled *Rendering Pacioli's Rhombicuboctahedron* (see reference section). Rendering in this context means the process that is involved in generating two-dimensional or three-dimensional images from a model using computer application programs. According to Sequin and Shiau, the reflection in the painting of an unseen window on the rhombicuboctahedron on two separate facets seems scientifically incorrect. The painted reflections show buildings and sky and indicate the directions from where they come from (an open window), either top left or bottom right of the Luca Pacioli picture. Because Sequin and Shiau believed that the three reflected images from the same window did not make sense according to the laws of optics, they set out to investigate what an actual glass rhombicuboctahedron half-filled with water really might look like by modelling; using computer graphics, a basic ray-tracing algorithm and computer programmes to render complex test models. On the basis of their computer simulations, they concluded that it was highly unlikely that the painter observed or tested a physical glass container half-filled with a clear liquid when painting the rhombicuboctahedron, and that the artist's objective was to create the most 'plausible' and 'convincing' depiction of such an object as an imagined representation for the appreciation of a broader public. At no stage during their rendition of the rhombicuboctahedron did Sequin and Shiau suggest that it was painted by Leonardo da Vinci, although they did indicate that there was a controversy about the attribution and that Leonardo was one of the possible candidates.

Carlo H. Sequin presented on his blog page the following additional comments about his analysis of the three images reflected on the rhombicuboctahedron (RCO):

My own intuition, when looking at this painting, tells me that my eyes are about at the height of Pacioli's nose or eyes, and that the person on the right is looking slightly down on me. This would place the view center properly above the water level. I also tried to find a horizon compatible with the objects on the table, and I found:

1.) A vanishing point on top of Pacioli's head for the slate tablet;

2.) A vanishing point somewhat above the middle of the RCO (but way out on the left) for the open book (with substantial error margins);

3.) A vanishing point about half a head-height above the top of Pacioli's head for the red box (also with substantial error margins).

All of these vanishing points are higher than the center of the RCO, and that explains why we see the water surface from above. But then, the bottom triangle must be slanted upwards towards the viewer, so that we can see its lower side. ==> Thus the red

CHAPTER 12

suspension line wins. The water surface is indeed horizontal.

So, did the painter indeed observe a water-filled glass polyhedron? -- I don't think so! The convincing clue is that there are no refractive effects visible in the "water-filled" bottom half. The edges on the backside of the polyhedron appear almost precisely in the locations to which the edges of my empty polyhedral frame are being projected. With water inside this object, those apparent edge positions would be moved dramatically because of refraction. Thus, it may be possible that this internal surface is an additional (irregular) octagonal plate, which may have been inserted into this glass shell to give it some stability, (if indeed this object was ever actually built from glass plates!). But it is more likely that this is an artistic rendering of an imagined water surface inside a real, or imagined glass model.

That reflection of that window is drawn like a "paper sticker" containing the view from the window, which has then been pasted onto two adjacent facets of the polyhedron. However, when the reflection of a rectangular window stretches across an edge with a substantial dihedral angle, the continuity of the reflection is broken, and it is split apart into two quite different, disconnected reflections. Thus this must be a beautifully drawn reflection -- as imagined by the artist!

The inside reflection on the lower right would also look quite different in the presence of water!

... more and more intriguing mysteries surround this painting!

Yes, *'more and more intriguing mysteries* [do] *surround this painting',* and this is typical of other Leonardo da Vinci paintings. There are few or no mysteries surrounding Jacopo de' Barbari's paintings. However, the intriguing factor is as true for Leonardo's painting of the *Pacioli Portrait* as it is true for all of his other paintings such as the *Last Supper* or the *Mona Lisa,* that, to this day, remain intriguing mysteries. It seems that this was always the Maestro's intention for most of his paintings, even the simple portraits, and even the different versions of *Madonna and Child* that he and his assistants painted. There is always an element of mystery and intrigue that is associated with them all. And yet, if you look at Jacopo de' Barbari paintings, most of them have little or no mystery or intrigue. They are stolid, impassive.

The water level is the equator of the rhombicuboctahedron in the *Pacioli Portrait.* The rhombicuboctahedron is an approximation of the sphere where the horizontal water level represents the equator with a vertical North Pole and South Pole at the top and bottom of the sphere, respectively. Should the light or image passing through the sphere provide a stereographic projection, that is, a map of the rhombicuboctahedron onto the table? No, because the sphere is transparent, it has no metal or wooden frames to create shadows as seen in Fig. 10.6.

Yet, metaphorically, the rhombicuboctahedron with its three images of the building provides a magnified stereographic projection of the contents of a room in the building. The contents of that room in the building are

Luca Pacioli and Galeazzo Sanseverino Sforza providing a lecture to a fly glued to the yellow notepaper positioned directly below Galeazzo Sanseverino Sforza's eye line (Fig. 12.9). What is the message on the paper from Leonardo da Vinci that he wants us to see, decode and analyse? See Chapter 20 for the message, decryption and solution.

Thus, one particular way to look at the projected rhombicuboctahedron images is to see them as the windows of light giving direction to the soul and intellect to look elsewhere for revelation as indicated in Fig. 12.9. The lines AC and BC are drawn from the reflected images of the rhombicuboctahedron to pass through directly to the coded yellow notepaper on the desk. A slight realignment to the line EF points to the fly on the notepaper. Line DP from the midpoint D between Galeazzo Sanseverino's eyes and along the bridge of his nose points directly to the pen and inkwell that is attached to the pen holder directing us back to the cartouche via Pacioli's left hand. The two lines AC and BC that begin with the reflected upper image on the rhombicuboctahedron are narrowed by the reflected lower image and connected at point C to draw attention to the note with the code and the black fly.

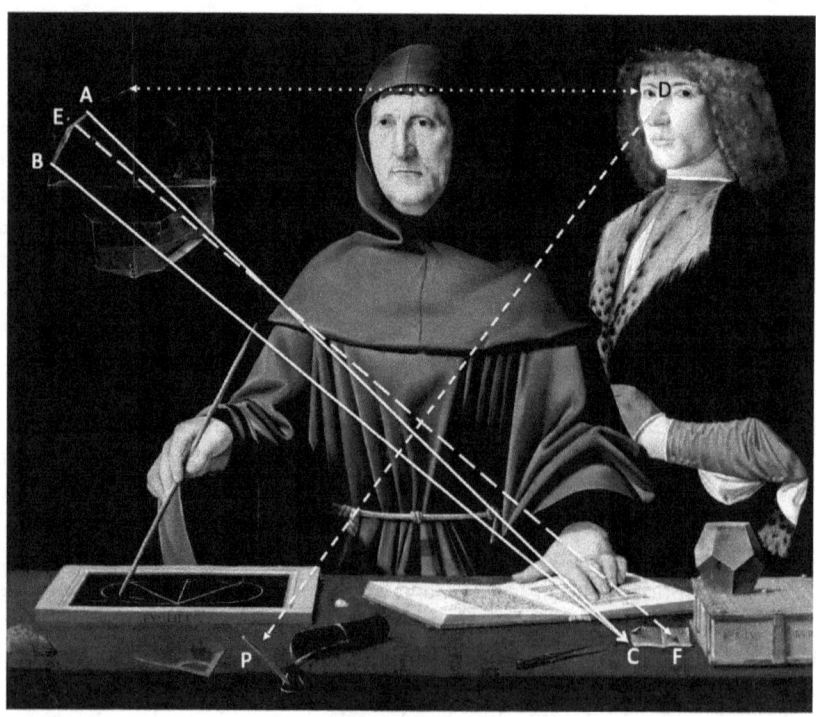

FIG. 12.9. *Aligning the light rays of the window images from the rhombicuboctahedron to the blackfly on the notepaper while Galeazzo's third eye ponders the pen in the inkwell.*

CHAPTER 12

The Rhombicuboctahedron as an Allegorical Symbol of Leonardo's Study of the Eye

The importance of optics, vision and the eye is one of the main themes of the *Pacioli Portrait*. This is seen in the way Leonardo has painted the mysterious rhombicuboctahedron and Luca Pacioli and Galeazzo Sanseverino's expressive eyes (Fig. 12.6). Leonardo da Vinci spent most of his adult life in the study of vision and in developing his theories about the anatomy, physiology and physics of the eye and vision. His views and theories changed and developed markedly from his early days in Milan in the late 1480s to his last years in Italy (1513 to 1516) before he left to live the last three years of his life in France. Essentially, there was nobody else of note in Leonardo's time who was as interested as he was in understanding the process of vision in the way that the ancient scholars Galen, Plato, Euclid and Ptolemy had investigated and described it. Most of the physicians and anatomists of his day stuck by the prevailing Galen theory of 'emissions' that the eye cast out rays or a spirit to touch the seen object either directly or by way of the intervening atmosphere that conducted the visual information. The scientists in Leonardo's time and throughout the sixteenth century made no substantial innovations in the theory of vision. Leonardo rejected the theory of emissions and supported the intromission theory, a theory that he worked on in complete isolation to investigate and further develop and understand. He said of his studies that, *'The eye which so clearly reveals its function, has been defined by an infinite number of authors up to my own time in one way, while I find by experiment that it is another.'* Leonardo's experimental and theoretical work remained mostly in his private notebooks and it had little or no impact on the future of optics except, through his disciples, in the area of the painters' perspective.

It seems that the rhombicuboctahedron in the *Pacioli Portrait* represents the passive eye and that the three images seen within the floating crystal are those transferred into the eye through a window from the outside world (Fig. 12.1). What we see appears to be Alhazen's intromission theory of visual perception (65 - c. 1040) that Leonardo and some other Renaissance scholars of optics and vision had supported. The following is what James S. Ackerman wrote in his 1978 paper about Alhazen's intromission theory:

'In his description, rays come from the object to the eye in a pyramid; they are received on the entire surface of the eye in such a way that any point on the eye can receive a light impulse from any point on the object. From here they pass on to the entire surface of the crystalline humour, the primary seat of sensation (without being refracted, since the two surfaces are concentric). The pupil or 'hole' apparently has no significant function, though it must at least have cut off the more peripheral rays. Innumerable impulses thus reach every point on the cornea and crystalline, but confusion is avoided because the latter

admits only those rays that are perpendicular to the points on its surface where they strike. The eyes constant scanning movements assure the complete registration of all the points on the object.

Behind the 'hole' the image is spread in precisely the form and proportions of the object viewed on the anterior surface of the crystalline humour, which is the effective sensory organ. Though Alhazen knew from experiments with the camera obscura *that the image would be inverted in passing through the hole, he could not bring himself to apply the analogy directly to the eye, because that would require the image sensed on the crystalline humour to be inverted – and Alhazen, followed by everyone prior to Kepler, could not accept the implication of an inverted image being transmitted to the brain. Even after penetrating the surface, the rays are not permitted to cross: they diverge again because, on the analogy of light passing from air into water, they are refracted into divergent paths by passing from the 'rarer" crystalline humour to the denser vitreous. Thus, the crystalline was prophetically defined as a lens; but, since it had also to serve as a sense organ, the implications of this concept could not be developed correctly.'*

Although not related directly to the *Pacioli Portrait*, this description by Ackerman could well describe the three images in the rhombicuboctahedron that Leonardo painted for us (Fig. 12.1). This could be the stimulus for Leonardo's expanded version of the intromission theory. Although Leonardo knew that the pupil would invert the image received by the crystalline humour (retina), like Alhazen, he chose not to illustrate this inconsistency, an inconvenience that he observed with the *camera obscura* (Fig. 12.8). Thus, all the images in the rhombicuboctahedron are left upright even the diminished bottom one that is closest to the symbolic region of the optic nerve (the hanging thread) holding up the polyhedron (Fig. 12.1). Presumably, the *Pacioli Portrait* was started about the time Leonardo was finishing off his painting of the *Last Supper* and before 1500 while Pacioli and Sanseverino were still together in Milan. If so, then at this time he was still in his early phase of understanding the physiology of the eye and the physics of vision. It seems highly likely that Leonardo added the three outside images of the buildings onto the rhombicuboctahedron in the *Pacioli Portrait* in order to demonstrate to the observers of his painting that he strictly supported the intromission theory of vision: that the light rays of an image enter the eye, are recorded in the crystalline humour, perceived in the optic nerve and transmitted for storage and interpretation in the *'sensus communis'* that is located in the anterior ventricle of the brain. Thus, the rhombicuboctahedron is like the *camera obscura* attached to the brain; that is, allegorically, it is attached to the eye and brain of the observer who looks at and sees (Fig. 12.7) the painting of the *Pacioli Portrait*.

CHAPTER 12

Philosphere Projections: Modern Rhombicuboctahedron Image-Display-Spheres

Surprisingly, Leonardo da Vinci displayed three separate images on to the rhombicuboctahedron, albeit in a painting, well ahead of anybody else by more than four hundred years. Today, the rhombicuboctahedron has been used to generate images and project them onto its surface as a 3-D image; to project panoramas and to display them as *'philospheres'* at trade shows. One such *'philosphere'* image is shown in Figure 12.10 that Philippe 'Philo' Hurbain created with his computer software (PTgui v1 and Panorama Tools) that can be downloaded from his web page, the *'Philosphere projection'*, on the Internet. The software was created to produce a rhombicuboctahedron or *'philosphere'* to display images and panoramas inside and/or outside the sphere as *'low cost virtually reality capsules'*. His web page also shows a few pictures of the larger *'philospheres'* or rhombicuboctahedrons that were featured at international trade shows.

Another rhombicuboctahedron structure that was built recently and often is used to display coloured lights and patterns is the National Library in the city of Minsk in Belarus (Fig. 12.10). Today, models of polyhedrons are easy to construct and Professor Carlo H. Sequin has provided a description on his webpage (referenced at the end of this chapter) on how to construct cardboard models of the augmented rhombicuboctahedron and augmented pseudo-rhombicuboctahedron.

FIG. 12.10. Philosphere: *(left), A rhombicuboctahedron projecting an 180x360° spherical panoramic image. (right), National Library in Minsk. Permissions obtained for image reproductions.*

It is not known if Leonardo actually built any image projections or *'philospheres'* that he might have displayed at the Leonardo Academy meetings at the Sforza Castle in Milan or elsewhere to impress his audience. It is likely that he produced various constructs of polyhedrons and even painted images on to them to create colourful displays as part of his various court entertainments. He could have constructed models of transparent rhombicuboctahedrons easily from his transparent unbreakable glass (*vetro assottigliato*) and films (*vetropannicolato infrangibile*) that he invented and kept highly secret for commercial reasons. Andrea Bernardoni wrote about these little known glass and transparent paper inventions by Leonardo in an academic paper in 2012 entitled "*Leonardo and Chemical Arts*" in volume 27 of *Nuncius* (pages 11 to 55). Leonardo mentioned these inventions obtusely in his notebooks.

> *'...and so one must take the membranous glass that I have invented, and with egg white or some other transparent and viscous liquor attach this glass. This very thin glass can be cut with scissors, and when placed over gilt or otherwise coloured bone inlay, you can cut it with a saw together with the bone and then fit the whole into place, and it will retain its lustre and not be scarred nor worn away when touched with the hand.'*

Leonardo da Vinci's Rhombicuboctahedron: An Intellectual and Humorous Parody of Piero della Francesca's Hanging Egg

Leonardo da Vinci's rhombicuboctahedron hanging by the thin red line in the *Pacioli Portrait* seems to have been inspired in part by the hanging pendant egg in Piero della Francesca's painting known as the *Brera Altarpiece* that was painted at least 24 years earlier in 1472 (Fig. 12.11). The symbol of the hanging egg has been used commonly in Islamic art and paintings of the Middle Ages and early Renaissance. Modern art historians have given the egg various meanings including the caducity of life, suspended by the imminent thin thread of destiny; a cosmic egg, or seed of life; the seed of life banally hanging down by a thread from a huge new Venus (the shell behind and above it); or the symbol of Mary's virginity. Alchemists believed that the shell and egg were the cosmic seeds or *Prima Materia*, not only to be born from the universe, but also from when the element Water turned into Earth.

Others say that the Philosophical Egg is an example of poetic and abstract symbolism. The shadow and light seems to be on the opposite side of the egg. While looking at the hanging pendant egg, the question also arises how do you attach a thread to the top of a hanging egg without breaking it? Is it a hard-boiled or soft-boiled egg? Piero della Francesca's hanging egg has inspired much debate about its enigmatic meaning.

CHAPTER 12

Here is a quote from the first four of eight paragraphs in a published letter about *Piero's Egg* by Laurence Homolka that he wrote in response to David W. Brisson's morphological analysis of Piero's egg.

'The solitary egg that Piero della Francesca depicted in his Montefeltro Altarpiece must be, by now, the most celebrated iconographical morsel in quattrocentro painting. Persistent uncertainties about its identity and meaning recently led David W. Brisson to undertake an enterprising morphological analysis in which the shape (not size) of Piero's egg was shown to resemble more nearly that of a chicken than any other natural species, such as an ostrich or a swan ("Piero della Francesca's Egg Again," Art Bulletin, LXII, 1989, 284-86). Brisson acknowledged that "This material does not 'prove' anything, particularly about what Piero della Francesca meant to imply by the egg, although it does seem fairly strong evidence that he used a chicken's egg as a model."

I would like to suggest, however, that Brisson's insightful distinction between elliptical and spherical profiles is more telling in a pictorial context: ... he depicted it with an elliptical profile largely for reasons for formal consonance; more specifically, he was aware of subtle but apparent modifications of three-dimensional form in light, as well as architectonic values that are implicit in the elliptical egg and are visible elsewhere in the picture. The "mysterious" egg should, I believe, be returned to its original pictorial context for scrutiny, and not be explicated simply as an iconographical item or a biological specimen; after all, it is a depicted egg.'

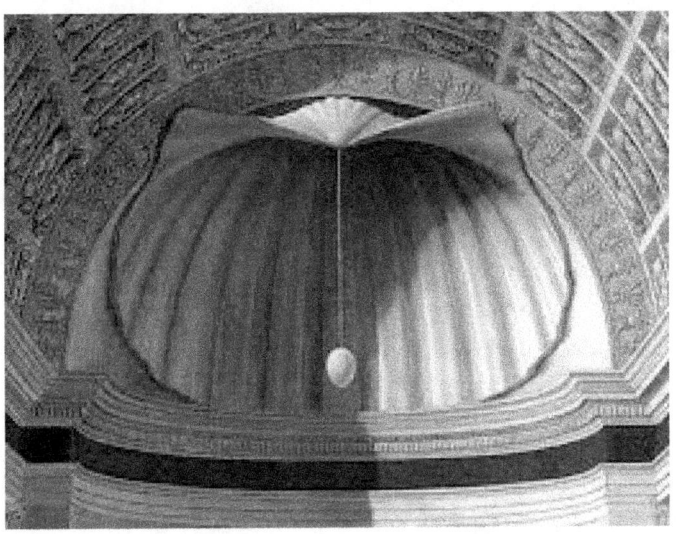

FIG. 12.11. *Egg suspended from a shell*. Detail in Madonna and Child with Saints *by Piero della Francesca (Montefeltro Altarpiece, 1472-1474).*

It should be remembered that Piero della Francesca's painting of the hanging egg has Luca Pacioli underneath it as one of the ten saints or apostles attending to the Virgin Mary and Infant with the Duke of Urbino down on his knees in his grey armour and in worship of the Holy Virgin and Child (Fig. 12.12). Undoubtedly, Leonardo da Vinci had seen the original or copies of Piero della Francesca's painting and received Luca Pacioli's opinions about it and what he believed the artist was attempting to achieve. None of the detailed information about the Francesca painting would have escaped Leonardo's acute and critical mind and he would have used all of his analytical faculties to compose his deeply contrasting portraiture of the Franciscan friar, the jouster, and the sinister black fly in the presence of the hanging glass polyhedron.

FIG. 12.12. *Detail of* Madonna and Child with Saints *by of Piero della Francesca, (Montefeltro Altarpiece, 1472-1474)*.

The different points of view about the various ways that Piero's egg is lit seem irrelevant when trying to interpret why Leonardo da Vinci has placed a hanging polyhedron next to or in front of *Luca Pacioli* because it contradicts or parodies the Francesca's painting of the hanging egg in at least two different ways. First, Leonardo has painted a hanging rhombicuboctahedron instead of a spherical egg hanging towards the right side of Luca Pacioli. Second, in stark contrast to Piero della Francesca's brightly lit hanging egg [instead of illuminating the hanging polyhedron with light from everywhere], Leonardo has left his hanging polyhedron as a dark, transparent and mysterious pseudosphere. If his hanging polyhedron represents the dark and mysterious universe, then that's the way it should be. After all, we now believe that the vast majority (85%) of the matter and a quarter of the total energy density of the expanding universe are made of a hypothetical 'dark matter' with many black holes that absorb light at the centre of galaxies. Could Leonardo have been so far ahead of his time that his allegorical dark hanging polyhedron symbolises and predicts the expanding universe, dark matter and black holes? Probably not; how could he have known anything about quantum mechanics in his time of interpreting the cosmos? It seems far too absurd to think that Leonardo da Vinci already had an intuitive, primitive understanding of quantum mechanics, the expanding universe, dark matter and black holes in the Renaissance simply because the hanging polyhedron reflects three images of a window scene that defies our understanding. However, the cliché since ancient times is that darkness is like death and that the light of everything is the natural way to meet the Creator. The main message in Leonardo's painting of *John the Baptist* is that the dark is light and that without the dark there cannot be the light of Heaven. When we look into John the Baptist's dark eyes we see that one of them looks at the viewer and the other looks away, up towards heaven, not unlike Luca Pacioli's divergent eyes in Leonardo's portrait (Fig. 12.6).

Before composing and preparing the *Pacioli Portrait*, Leonardo da Vinci undoubtedly had studied Francesca's use of light on the hanging egg and the saints before using his preferred scheme to paint light and shade on the rhombicuboctahedron, on the two standing figures and the 12 items in the foreground on the table. Perhaps, Leonardo used light and shade more for its three-dimensional effect than the symbolic, although one cannot deny the presence of the obvious symbolism of light and dark in the painting. There is a modern complexity that is easier to elucidate in the da Vinci painting than in the della Francesca's version, which is more symbolically archaic.

The Misalignment of the Rhombicuboctahedron with the Circle and the Sphere

For Nicholas of Cusa, the German philosopher, mathematician and author of the early Renaissance, God was pure mathematics and geometry; the perfect circle or sphere and He was the Centre, Area and Circumference of Everything.

> *'Moreover, it is no less false that the centre of the world is within than it is outside of the earth; nor does the earth, or any other sphere even have a centre (which is so true and precise) that a still truer and more precise centre could not be posited. Precise equidistance to different things cannot be found except in the case of God, because God alone is Infinite Equality. Therefore, He who is the centre of the world, viz., the Blessed God, is*

also the centre of the earth, of all spheres, and of all things in the world. Likewise, He is the infinite circumference of all things. (On Learned Ignorance, Book II, chap. XI).'

In the book entitled *Leonardo da Vinci: the Melzi Chronicles*, I considered whether Leonardo believed that the rhombicuboctahedron might have been a better representation of God and the Universe than the sphere:

'In 1496, while working with Luca Pacioli on his book De Divina Proportione, *Leonardo began to paint a portrait of the two men standing beside an image of a hanging rhombicuboctahedron, a distorted polyhedron half-filled with liquid. Here, Leonardo had some fun showing off the complexity of geometry using the symbols of spheres and polyhedrons. Luca Pacioli points to the Euclidian sphere, the flat circle, and the triangles contained within it. Euclidian geometry is simple, spherical, flat, and old school. The polyhedron hanging from the ceiling represents distortion and non-Euclidian geometry, a complex and three-dimensional shape holding together both the elements of air and water. Leonardo espoused the view that unity, whether social, spiritual, material or otherwise was more like a polyhedron than a sphere in that it lacks the simple and beautiful harmony and proportions of a sphere, but still retains the unity of a solid in its multifaceted complexity. While the sphere is homogenous, uniform, smooth, and equal in all its parts, the polyhedron consists of multiple forms, is multifaceted with flat faces, straight edges, sharp vertices, and has variable distances emanating from its centre that provide overall a complex unity within its diversity.'*

The polyhedron hangs over Pacioli's drawing of the Euclidian (Pythagorian) circle but not quite in full alignment with it (Fig. 12.13). This is Leonardo's lesson on Nicholas Cusa's revelation that the polygon can never fully coincide with the circle just as our reasoning (science) will never be able to grasp the totality of the Absolute [God]. Armed with this *docta ignorantia*, the Socratic knowledge of *'knowing that we do not know,'* Cusa evokes the image of the wall of Paradise. It is the wall of the coincidence of opposites, and only beyond it is revelation possible:

'O most wonderful God, who are neither singular in number nor plural in number but—beyond all plurality and singularity—are one-in-three and three-in-one! I see, then, my God, that plurality coincides with singularity at the wall of the Paradise in which You dwell; and I see that You dwell ever so remotely beyond [this wall]. . . . Hence, this distinction—which is inside the wall of coincidence, where the distinct and the indistinct coincide—precedes all comprehensible otherness and diversity. For the wall is the limit of the power of every intellect, although the eye looks beyond the wall into Paradise. But that which the eye sees, it can neither speak of nor understand. For it is the eye's secret love and hidden treasure, which, having been found, remains hidden. For it is found on the inner side of the wall of the coincidence of the hidden and the manifest. (Chap. XVII).'

Leonardo was well aware of the wall of the coincidence of opposites and he brought the phenomenon of opposites to our attention in his *Pacioli Portrait* by providing us with contrasts between the young and old, priest and layman, light and dark, polygon and circle, triangle and square, knowledge and ignorance, and ink and eraser. This is symbolised further by the misalignment seen between the rhombicuboctahedron, circle, sphere and differential geometry. And so, the rhombicuboctahedron hangs over Pacioli's drawing of the Euclidian circle, but not in full alignment with it (Fig. 12.13).

FIG. 12.13. The hanging polygon misaligned with the circle (and imaginary sphere) on the drawing tablet below it.

The Hanging Thin Red Line – a Neural Cord to Heaven

The cord attached to the rhombicuboctahedron might be an allegorical representation of the optic nerve to Heaven that is outside the view of the portrait.

'Having convinced himself that in such a science of vision, the geometric apex of the visual pyramid in the eye needs to be replaced by much more complex pathways of the sensory impressions, Leonardo then traced these pathways through the lens and the eyeball to the optic nerve, and from there all the way to the center of the brain where he believed he had found the seat of the soul.' (**Fritjof Capra**).

As part of the nature of things, we see a point at the end of the red line that threads through the polyhedron and is attached to an object shaped like an **A** (Fig. 12.1 & Fig. 12.14). Or is the **A** attached to the thin red cord hanging from somewhere above the polyhedron? There are some minor distortions seen below the surface of the liquid that is not seen in the air. Why is that? The cord from which the rhombicuboctahedron hangs seems to have been added to the painting almost as an after-thought, as if to create some sort of realism and not allow the polyhedron simply to be seen as an unsupported floating object in open space. Even so, the painting of the hanging red line looks unrealistic. It is so thin it seems unlikely to be able to hold up the polyhedron that is made of heavy glass and half-filled with water.

No estimate of the amount of water in the rhombicuboctahedron has been made that I know off, but if the polyhedron was the size of Pacioli's head and the water represented the size of his brain, then half the water content would be approximately 800 ml and weight about the same number in grams. This weight, together with the weight of the glass, seems much too heavy to be held up by the thin red cord, unless it was one of Leonardo's magical and unbreakable threads that he decided to advertise in the picture. Also, the cord seems to be attached at the bottom of the polyhedron to a brightly lit circle, O, attached to the top of an A, the symbol of a compass that is used by Leonardo for measuring proportions in his drawings. Furthermore, the hanging thread seems to enter the polyhedron slightly off centre at the top of the apex of the very top square and then finish at the centre of the vertex at the very bottom square. It creates an illusion that the polyhedron has turned or tilted slightly away from the straight line bisecting it at the top.

Although, with close inspection of the picture, the cord can be easily seen passing more or less through the centre of the rhombicuboctahedron, this would not be the case if the painting hung in a dimly lit corner of a room. Standing ten or more feet away from the picture, the red cord would not be seen and the rhombicuboctahedron would appear to be floating in the air with no attachment. Perhaps, the thinness and the colour of the cord was intentionally added to demonstrate how a straight red line that is seen up close can disappear from view in different light conditions and distances from the painting according to the inverse square law. In this regard, Leonardo knew that the intensity and clarity of seeing the light source (or object) with the eye was inversely proportional to the distance that the eye was away from the object. In other words, the further that you stand away from the painting the more likely the cord will diminish until it disappears. Maybe the hanging cord was a drawing aid for Leonardo to demonstrate his knowledge about the physics of light and how you can use this knowledge for various painting effects and cues, and how objects can be seen and disappear from a painting depending on the intensity of the light in the room and where you stand to look at it. The further that you stand away from an object the smaller it becomes and diminishes from view.

The All-seeing Rhombicuboctahedron of Providence

The hanging thread seems to be attached at the bottom of the polyhedron to a brightly lit circle, **O**, at the top of an **A**. Leonardo has drawn the same **A** shape on a page in his notebook (Fig. 12.14) essentially proving that the *Pacioli Portrait* was painted by him. Leonardo's drawings of the inverted **V** and compasses used for measuring distances and proportions are present on the pages of a number of his notebooks (Fig. 9.3). The hanging crystal can hear and see everything; it is the symbol of providence, the foreseeing care and guidance of God (or Nature) over the creatures of the earth. Leonardo's symbol of **V**, inverted as an **A** in the rhombicuboctahedron, is the universal symbol or logo of many public and secret organisations including the square and the compass of Freemasonry.

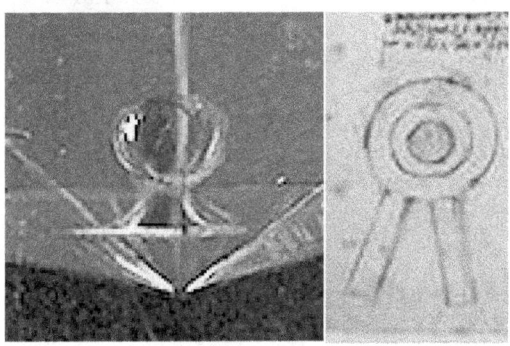

FIG. 12.14. The *A*-shaped attachment ring at the bottom of the rhombicuboctahedron in the Pacioli Portrait *(left)* and a similar shaped attachment ring drawn in Leonardo da Vinci's notebook *(right)*.

The Hanging Rope

The hanging rope in Leonardo's *Study of a Hanged Man* is a particular drawing of a hanging line that he never converted to a painting (Fig. 12.15). The hanged man was Bernardo Baroncelli who had assassinated Giuliano de Medici at the cathedral of Florence during an Easter Sunday service that was attended by more than a thousand people. Leonardo saw and drew the hanging in Florence in 1479 when Giuliano's brother Lorenzo de' Medici was away in Naples to negotiate a peace settlement with the king of Naples.

After escaping from Italy, Bernardo Baroncelli was captured in Constantinople and brought back to Florence to be charged and tried for murder and then hanged in the public square outside the cathedral where he had committed his murder. Leonardo's written notes alongside the drawing describe what Bernardo Baroncelli was wearing at his hanging. It is speculated that Leonardo had made the drawing in the hope that he would win the commission to paint a memorial for the assassination of Giuliano de Medici with the stark reminder and warning that the punishment for an assassin is death by hanging.

Maybe the thin red line in the *Pacioli Portrait* was a reminder for Leonardo of the live hangings that he saw and drew in Florence and so he attenuated it for the hanging rhombicuboctahedron – a hanging red cord that could come and go depending on where you stood to look at the painting. Moreover, the flickering red of the hanging thread compliments the red shirt of Galeazzo Sanseverino. Does matching the colour of the hanging thread with the colour of Galeazzo Sanseverino's red shirt imply that he was implicated in the assassination of the 6th duke of Milan Gian Galeazzo Sforza and that he deserved to be tried and hanged for treason?

FIG. 12.15. *Leonardo's Study of a Hanged Man. Musee Bonnat, Bayonne. Web Gallery of Art.*

References

Ackerman JS (1978). Leonardo's Eye. Journal of the Warburg and Courtauld Institutes 41:108-146.

Atalay, Bulent (2014). Math and the Mona Lisa: the art and science of Leonardo da Vinci. Smithsonian Books, Washington.

Bernardoni A (2012). Leonardo and Chemical Arts. Nuncius 27:11-55. Leonardo mentioned his 'glass' or 'plastic' inventions obtusely in his notebooks.

Bock S (2002). The "Egg" of the Pala Montefeltro and its symbolic meaning. University of Heideleberg Library website pdf link *(http://archiv.ub.uni-heidelberg.de/volltextserver/3123/1/PieroEgg.pdf).*

Brisson DW (1989). Piero della Francesca's Egg Again. Art Bulletin, LXII:284-86.

Homolka L (1982). Piero's Egg. The Art Bulletin, LXIV (1):138-140.

Hoy J, Millett KC (2015). A Mathematical Analysis of Knotting and Linking in Leonardo da Vinci's Cartelle of the Accademia Vinciana. Journal of Mathematics and the Arts.
   http://web.math.ucsb.edu/~millett/Papers/Millett2014Leonardov5.pdf

Hurbain, Phillipe (2001). 3-D Panorama Printing: enter physical reality. *www.philohome.com/rhombicuboctahedron/rhombicuboctahedron.htm*

Huylebrouck D (2012). Lost in Triangulation: Leonardo da Vinci's Mathematical

Slip-Up. Scientific American. *www.scientificamerican.com/article/davinci-mathematical-slip-up/*

Nicolaus of Cusa, The Catholic Concordance. Ed. by Paul E. Sigmund. Cambridge: Cambridge University Press, 1991.

Niyazi H (2013). Piero della Francesca's symbolic egg. 3 PipeProblem web site. *http://www.3pp.website/2013/03/piero-della-francescas-symbolic-egg.html.*

Sequin CH (2011). Constructing an Augmented Rhombicuboctahedron (RCO). *https://people.eecs.berkeley.edu/~sequin/PAPERS/2011_Augmented-RCO.pdf*
https://www.cosmosandhistory.org/index.php/journal/article/viewFile/594/1030

Sequin CH (2015). Misinterpretations and Mistakes in Pacioli's Rhombicuboctahedron.
http://www.cs.berkeley.edu/~sequin/X/Leonardo/pacioli_rco.html

Sequin CH, Shiau R (2015). Rendering Pacioli's Rhombicuboctahedron. Journal of Mathematics and the Arts 9:103-110.

Sequin CH, Shiau R (2018). The Best Writing on Mathematics 2017. Edited by Mircea Pitici. Princeton University Press, Princeton and Oxford, 2018.

Vereycken, Karel (2000). The Egg Without a Shadow of Piero della Francesca. Fidelio 9(1):48-77.

13

VISUAL PYRAMIDS OF LIGHT & SHADOW

Perspective of Light, Shade and Transparency

Probably no man in the Italian Renaissance gave up more time and effort to the study of light and vision than Leonardo da Vinci. He realised from an early age that to give his paintings a new and more natural 'illusion' (depiction) of reality he needed to widen the dimensions of contrasting light especially from the perspective of depicting objects more naturalistically and expressively with the contrasting quality of light and dark and the shadows on and/or around his objects. Thus, he embarked on a life long study of the nature of light.

This phenomenon of 'changing light quality' is visible in the *Pacioli Portrait*. The rhombicuboctahedron depicts transparency and reflection. This hanging glass container through which light travels shows off its inner contents of air and water and the reflections of blue sky and a building projected through an open window. The three images on the hanging polyhedron are lessons about light passing through transparent material and reflecting light from the window. *Luca Pacioli* and his friar's habit showcase his mastery of *chiaroscuro* as exemplified by the rippling effects of varying light and shadow on the grey garment and his aged face. *Chiaroscuro* is a technical term used by artists and art historians to describe the use of contrasts of light to achieve a sense of volume in modelling three-dimensional objects and figures. Leonardo's use of *chiaroscuro* in the *Pacioli Portrait* is deliberately subtle on two fronts, (1) to create illusions and lessons about light and dark and the use of realistic shadows, and (2) to provide a 3-D effect to his characters and the entire painting for added viewer experience.

CHAPTER 13

The younger Galeazzo Sanseverino stands gallantly behind Luca Pacioli in the glory of the bright light intensified by the black background and his dark blue coat and a darkening ghostly shadow creeping onto him from his left. His brightly lit face contrasts dramatically against the more subdued and tempered face of the friar. Each of the figures and the hanging polyhedron demonstrate the different effects of light on the subjects and objects. Luca Pacioli's grey habit, face and hands and some of the objects on the table such as the wooden slate, the pencil case, the open book and the dodecahedron create shadows that reveal the direction of the light that illuminates the painting. Throughout, we see the interconnectedness of light touching all the figures and objects inspired by Leonardo da Vinci's enhanced understanding of visual perception and the perspective of light.

Judging from the angle of the shadows on Pacioli, the light entering the room is coming from at least two sources. There is a strong light from the top left of the picture and slightly behind Pacioli as we look at the painting. Judging from the shadows on the solid dodecahedron positioned on the red book, Pacioli's right hand and the slate chalkboard, there also might be a weaker light from lower left interplaying with the stronger light from above and behind Pacioli. However, why is there no shadow on Galeazzo Sanseverino's green glove behind Pacioli? Is it because there is a light coming in from behind Pacioli as also indicated by the shadows on Sanseverino's face? There are other interpretations and/or criticisms about the light source in the painting. Renzo Baldasso, while a fellow at the John W. Kluge Center of the Library of Congress, wrote a paper about the portrait of Luca Pacioli and commented about the incongruous light source, saying:

'Finally, the unclear spatial relation of the two figures—which also assigns them a different source of light for which no shadow is cast on the gentleman's glove—offers additional evidence for considering this painting as dependent on and reworking a portrait featuring Pacioli with his book in a balanced and fully symmetrical composition.'

In note 12 of his paper, he wrote:

'The light source emanates from the upper left corner of the viewer's space, and the nobleman's glove, which is behind Pacioli, should be obscured by the shadow of the friar's body. While this might be intended, there are other problems with the painting's shadows. For instance, the two strings from which the ink container hangs should produce two shadow lines on the horizontal section of the green tablecloth, but only one is present. Another minor mistake concerns the binding of the closed book, which should include a part of the fourth clasp.'

Leonardo highlighted his two figures, Luca and Galeazzo, and the hanging polyhedron by illuminating them with light against the black of the background. Pacioli's face and his grey cloak show a greater gradation of light and shadow compared to Sanseverino's face that burns more brightly in light than shadow. Furthermore, Leonardo has varied the highlights and shadows, and he has rendered beautifully the contrast and differences in the wrinkles of the skin and the tightness or sagging of the muscles of the faces of the younger and older man. The transparency of the polyhedron hanging in front of a black background and the solid objects on the green tablecloth in *Pacioli Portrait* contrast spectacularly with the transparent glasses and other tableware items on a brilliant white tablecloth in his painting of the *Last Supper* on the wall of the Santa Maria della Grazie in Milan. This subtle play between the contrasts of the very black background and the well-balanced areas of light and dark and the grey of the friar's habit gives the painting its luminosity as well as its vibrant atmosphere and a variable depth of field or 3-D effect, especially if it is looked at with one eye only through an aperture of a few centimetres, as I will describe in more detail later on.

If you accept that the *Pacioli Portrait* depicts a masterful control of light and shadow by a master like Leonardo da Vinci, go and look at the Jacopo de' Barbari paintings and try to find at least one comparable painting of his dozen or more works where he has rendered light and shadow. Yes, Barbari used a daub of grey or black shadow here and there, but it is nothing like in the *Pacioli Portrait*. There is at least one painting by Jacopo de' Barbari that depicts a transparent object that he may have painted after 1500 when he was in Germany. Instead of a hanging glass rhombicuboctahedron, he chose to depict a glass of water containing a refracted stem of green mint that shows off his knowledge of the refraction of light when it changes passing from air to water (Fig. 4.1.11). The painting is called *Two Naked Lovers in a Room* and it is housed at the Gemäldegalerie der Staatlichen Museen zu Berlin in Germany. The reverse side (which is the front view of the panel) has a portrait of a German gentleman (Fig. 4.1.18) that looks like it was a copy of the painting known as the *Musician* by Leonardo (Fig. 6.1) or even a copy of Galeazzo Sanseverino in the *Pacioli Portrait*. This suggests that Jacopo de' Barbari had seen Leonardo's originals or at least some copies produced by painters other than Leonardo da Vinci.

Geometric Pyramids and the Nature of Light

The online *Physics Hypertextbook (2018)* defines the nature of light as a transverse, electromagnetic wave that can travel through a vacuum. It was first illustrated in the physical sciences by experiments on diffraction and interference. The transverse nature of light was demonstrated by polarisation using polarising filters and lenses. White light is produced as incandescence by a hot body like the sun or as luminescence by chemical or electrical radiation from an unheated body or living organism. It is polychromatic if it is composed of many different frequencies and relative intensities that can be separated by a prism into a visible colour spectrum ranging with a wavelength from 400 nanometres (nm) on the violet end to 700 nm on the red end of the spectrum. Ultraviolet (10 nm to 400 nm) and infrared (700 nm to 1000 nm) wavelengths are electromagnetic radiations that are mostly invisible to the human eye, but visible for a number of different animals. Our contemporary understanding of light to be a transverse, electromagnetic wave that also travels as a particle stems from the historical experiments on diffraction, interference and polarisation.

As the father of modern physics, Leonardo da Vinci made it very clear that the Lord is the light of all things:

'Among the studies of natural causes and reasons, light chiefly delights the observer. And among the great features of mathematics, the certainty of its demonstrations is what preeminently elevates the mind of the investigator. Perspective, therefore, must be preferred to all the discourses and systems of human learning. In this field, the radiating line of light is explained by those methods of demonstration which form the glory, not so much of mathematics, as of physics, and are graced with the flowers of both. But, its axioms being laid down at great length, I shall abridge them to a conclusive brevity, arranging them by the method both of their natural order and mathematical demonstration. Sometimes by deduction of the effects from the causes, and sometimes arguing the causes from the effects, adding also to my own conclusions, some of which, though not included in them, may nevertheless be inferred from them. Thus, if the Lord, who is the light of all things, vouchsafed to enlighten me, I will treat of light, wherefore, I will divide the present work into three parts, being a treatise on light.'

Perspective was a central issue in the Renaissance before Leonardo da Vinci arrived on the scene. The Florentine architect Filippo Brunelleschi (1377-1446) formulated a linear or orthogonal (perpendicular) perspective with a vanishing point, and a decade later the architect and philosopher Leon Battista Alberti (1404-1472) wrote a small book *On Painting* and showed how to construct a perspective drawing based on geometry, implying that the Universe was harmonic and ordered by harmonic principles. However, Leonardo da Vinci, while accepting the idea of linear and geometric abstraction, developed the concept of the perspective of light by studying and discovering the physical principles of the phenomena of light. This is what made him so different from the other geniuses and artists of his generation and era. He saw light as a physical phenomenon of Nature and he wanted to discover its true character and that of the

Universe in their transient forms. In contrast, Piero della Francesca, who preceded Leonardo da Vinci by 36 years, was not interested in the evolution of incongruities, exceptions and aberrations. He was more interested in the immutable, the unchanging laws of Nature. His most important work in geometry was devoted to the ordering of the five Platonic solids and he followed a long tradition of studies going back to Leonardo Fibonacci. The immutable physical and mathematical laws of Nature as an expression of God were also a major interest of Luca Pacioli.

The American art historian Dr. D. Stephen Pepper presented a lecture in Virginia in September 2000, a few months before his death, about Leonardo da Vinci's great interest in light and a mutable Nature that *Fidelio* published in 2001. Pepper said:

'Leonardo was interested in the fact that the immutable laws of Nature appear to us in a mutable, transient Nature. And therefore, we have to discover the relationship, using our senses, and using our experimental method, we have to establish the relationship between the transient Nature and the immutable laws. This became physics. This became the systematic study of physical phenomena, which reveal—which cannot be assumed, but reveal—immutable laws. And this, to my mind, is the birth of modern physics, and is one of the great changes in the history of culture. Certainly, the period of Brunelleschi to Piero is a great change, but the change from Leonardo to Raphael to eventually Kepler, and so on, is an even greater one, in my view. And this is the nature of it.'

The Austrian-American theoretical physicist Fritjof Capra, in his book *The Science of Leonardo*, recognised and acknowledged Leonardo da Vinci's particular contribution to the physics of perception in this way:

'Unencumbered by the mind-body split that Descartes would introduce 150 years later, Leonardo did not separate epistemology (the theory of knowledge) from ontology (the theory of what exists in the world), nor indeed philosophy from science and art. His wide-ranging examinations of the entire process of perception led him to formulate highly original ideas about the relationship between physical reality and cognitive processes—the "actions of the soul," in his language—which have reemerged only very recently with the development of a post-Cartesian science of cognition.'

Leonardo da Vinci in his *Treatise on Painting* highlighted three branches of perspective that he believed the painter ought to always consider:

'The first deals with the diminution of objects as they recede from the eye, and is known as diminishing perspective. The second contains the way in which colours vary, as they recede from the eye. The third and last, is concerned with the explanation of how the objects ought to be less-finished in proportion, as they are remote, and the names are: linear perspective, the perspective of colour, and the perspective of disappearance.'

CHAPTER 13

Leonardo attributed the causes of these three branches of perspective to physical effects, the first to the structure of the eye, and the other two to the atmosphere and the light that intervenes between the eye and the object seen; and he used geometry and basic mathematics to describe the physical principles of perspective and light.

Visual Pyramids as Geometric Light Particles and Waves

Starting with Alberti's definition of linear perspective Leonardo defined perspective as, *'nothing else than seeing a place behind a pane of glass, quite transparent, on the surface of which the objects behind that glass are to be drawn.'* Producing a series of geometric images of *'pyramid of lines,'* Leonardo explained, *'These [objects] can be traced through pyramids to the point of the eye, and the pyramids are intersected on the glass pane.'*

In one such drawing, Leonardo clearly showed the corresponding 'pyramids' (isosceles triangles) of light with the two different visual angles where the object is kept stationary and the observer's eye, together with the glass pane in front of it, is placed in two different locations (Fig. 13.1). In a series of experiments, Leonardo varied the following three variables—the height of the object, the distance from the eye, and the distance between the eye and the vertical glass pane in all possible combinations. From these experiments, he established conclusively that if the distance between the eye and the glass pane is kept constant then the height of the image on the glass pane is inversely proportional to the object's distance from the eye. He recorded this experiment in Manuscript A, *'I find by experience that, if the second object is as far from the first as the first is from the eye, although they are of the same size, the second will seem half the size of the first'* and he reached the conclusion that, *'As the space passed through doubles, the diminution doubles.'*

FIG. 13.1. *Visual pyramids. The geometry of linear perspective, Codex Atlanticus, folio 119r.*

Leonardo da Vinci wrote the following often-quoted poetic description about the nature of light:

'Every body in light and shade fills the surrounding air with infinite images of itself, and these, by infinite pyramids, infused in the air, represent this body, all in all, and all in each part. Each pyramid that is composed of a long converging course of rays, includes within itself, an infinite number of pyramids, and each has the same power as all, and all as each. The equidistant circle of converging rays of the pyramid gives to their object, angles of equal size. And, the eye will receive the thing from the object, as of equal size. The body of the air is full of infinite pyramids, composed of radiating straight lines, which are caused by the boundaries of the surfaces of the body, in light and shade, placed in the air. And the further they are from their cause, the more acute are the pyramids. And although in their concourse, they intersect and interweave, nevertheless, they never blend, but pass through all the surrounding air independently, converging, diverging, diffused. And they are all of equal power, all equal to each other, and each equal to all. By these images of bodies, are carried all in all, and all in each part, and each pyramid, by itself, receives, in each minutest part, the whole form of the body, which is the cause.'

This statement by Leonardo da Vinci so impressed Stephen Pepper that he concluded:

'Now, this is really one of the most beautiful statements of physics that you can ever come across. You can see, that what he is saying is, that, it is as if this luminous air, which we occupy, has the potential for all images. Everything that we see is potentially there in this luminous air, as a consequence of light and shade. Now, when you think about it, you can see that that's what we saw in the difference between Verrocchio and Leonardo. In Verrocchio, as in all other artists of the Fifteenth Century, the images are all closed and bounded, as if they were sealed into themselves. With Leonardo, none of these images are sealed or bounded. They are all interacting with the atmosphere. And that interaction, the active ingredient of that interaction, is light and shade.'

The theoretical physicist Fritjof Capra also referred to Leonardo's poetic statements about the nature of light as travelling waves and pyramids, and he wrote the following descriptions and statements about them:

'With this poetic description, Leonardo simply rephrased Alhazen's original insight, but he added the significant observation that the pyramids of light "intersect and interweave" without interfering with each other. In a remarkable display of systemic thinking, Leonardo used this observation as a key argument to speculate about the wave nature of light. Here is how he proceeded. First, he combines the fact that light is radiated equally in all directions, which he has tested repeatedly, with the image of visual pyramids. He draws a diagram that shows a spherical body radiating equal pyramids (represented by triangles) in different directions, and he notes in the accompanying text that their tips are enclosed by a circle: "The equidistant perimeter of converging rays of the pyramid will give to their objects angles of equal size." In other words, if observers were placed at the tips of these pyramids around the circle, their visual angles would be

the same (see Figure ...). In the same diagram, Leonardo extends one pyramid to show that the visual angle at its apex decreases as the pyramid becomes longer. From this exercise, he concludes that light spreads in circles, and he immediately associates this circular pattern with the circular spread of ripples of water and the spread of sound in air: "Just as the stone thrown into the water becomes the centre and cause of various circles, and the sound made in the air spreads out in circles, so every object placed within the luminous air diffuses itself in circles and fills the surroundings with an infinite number of images of itself."

Having linked the circular pattern of the spread of light to the similar spread of ripples in water, Leonardo then sets out to study the details of the phenomenon in a pond in order to learn something about the radiation of light. In doing so, he uses, at the very beginning of his scientific explorations, a technique that would become an integral part of the scientific method in subsequent centuries. Since he cannot actually see the circular (or, more correctly, spherical) propagation of light, he takes the similar pattern in water as a model, hoping that it will reveal to him something about the nature of light under close study. And he does indeed study it very closely.

In Manuscript A, the very same Notebook that contains his analysis of perspective and many of his optical diagrams, Leonardo records his detailed investigations of the circular spread of water waves:

"If you throw two small stones at the same time onto a sheet of motionless water at some distance from one another, you will see that around those two percussions two separate sets of circles are caused, which will meet as they increase in size and then interpenetrate and intersect one another, while always maintaining as their centers the places struck by the stones."

Leonardo illustrates this phenomenon with a diagram (Fig. 8-7), and to understand its exact nature, he focuses on the precise movement of the water particles, making it easier for the eye to follow them by throwing small pieces of straw into the pond and watching their movements. Here is what he observes.

"Although there seems to be some demonstration of movement, the water does not depart from its place, because the openings made by the stones are closed again immediately. And that motion, caused by the sudden opening and closing of the water, makes in it a certain shaking, which one could call a tremor rather than a movement. And so that what I say may be more evident to you, pay attention to those blades of straw which, because of their lightness, float on the water and are not moved from their original position by the wave that rolls underneath them as the circles arrive."

Leonardo accepted the idea of Alhazen's original insight of pyramids or cones of light from a radiating source and developed it in his amazing drawing (Manuscript A fol 86v) of concentric circles of radiations emanating from an object whereby the radiations diminish to varying degrees depending on the amount of shadow. This beautiful drawing of concentric circles of radiation shows without any doubt that he recognised that light travelled in a wave motion. This was an extraordinarily enlightened insight by Leonardo at that time of a scientific awakening that was not corroborated until about four hundred years later with the gradual development of electromagnetic wave theory of light from Newton to Einstein.

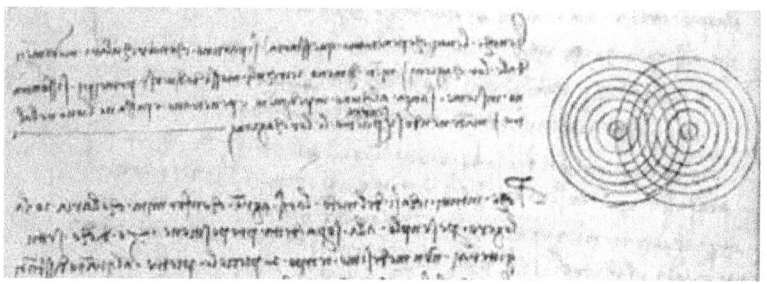

FIG. 13.2. Intersection of circular water waves, Ms. A, folio 61r. Reproduced from F. Capra (2008) Fig. 8-7.

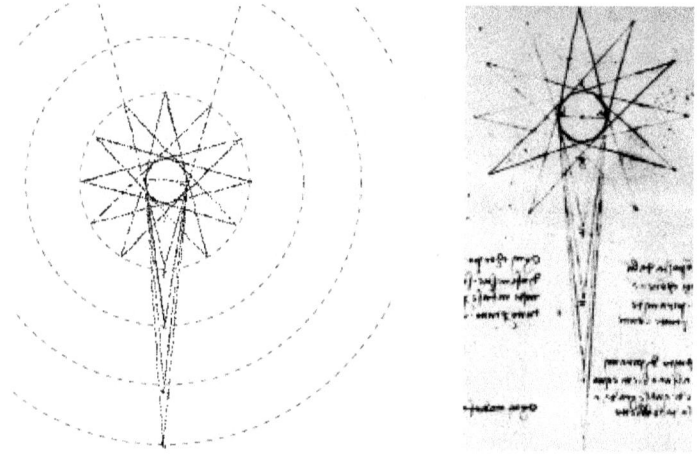

FIG. 13.3. Leonardo da Vinci, Notebooks, diagram of spherical radiation of light as spherical pyramids, redrawn from Manuscript A, fol. 86v. Taken from Dr Pepper's paper published by LaRouche. Detail, Leonardo da Vinci, Manuscript A, fol. 86.v.

In summary, Fritjof Capra reached the following points about Leonardo da Vinci and his experimental findings and drawings on the nature of light.

1. Leonardo recognised the essence of wave motion—that the water particles do not move along with the wave but merely move up and down as the wave passes by. He noted that the pyramids of light "intersect and interweave" without interfering with each other, and he applied the same reasoning to sound. The smooth intersection of water waves is the key property that suggested to Leonardo that light and sound, too, propagate in waves. From these observations, Leonardo concluded that both light and sound are waves. A few years later he extended his insight to elastic waves in the earth and concludes that wave motion, caused by initial vibrations (or "tremors"), is a universal form of propagation of physical effects.

2. The realization that wave motion is a universal phenomenon in all four elements—earth, water, air, and fire (or light)—was a revolutionary insight in Leonardo's time. It took another two hundred years before the wave-nature of light was rediscovered by Christian Huygens; the wave-nature of sound was first clearly articulated by Marin Marsenne during the first half of the seventeenth century, and earthquakes were associated with elastic waves only in the eighteenth century. In spite of Leonardo's impressive insights into the nature of wave motion and its widespread occurrence in nature, it would be an overstatement to say that he developed a wave theory of light similar to that presented by Huygens two hundred years later. To do so would have meant to understand the mathematical representation of a wave and relate its amplitude, frequency, and other characteristics to observed optical phenomena. These concepts were not used in science until the seventeenth century, when the mathematical theory of functions was developed.

3. Leonardo gave a correct description of transverse waves, in which the direction of energy transfer (the spreading of the circles) is at right angles to the direction of the vibration (the "tremor"), but he never considered longitudinal waves, in which the vibrations and energy transfer go in the same direction. He did not realise that sound waves are longitudinal. He appreciated that waves in different media travel at different velocities, but believed erroneously that the wave velocity is proportional to the power of the percussion that sets it off.

4. He marvelled at the swift velocity of light: "Look at the light of the candle and consider its beauty," he wrote. "Blink your eye and look at it again. What you see of it was not there before, and what was there before is not anymore." But he also realised that, however fast light moves, its velocity is not infinite. Even though Leonardo did not state explicitly that the velocity of light is finite, it is clear from his Notebooks that he held that view. Since antiquity, the traditional view was that the propagation of light is instantaneous. Even Huygens and Descartes subscribed to this view, and it was not until the end of the seventeenth century that the finite velocity of light was established.

Light and Shadow

The difference between Leonardo and the other artists in the way of seeing and drawing or painting light and shadow led him to develop *sfumato* (smokiness) and *chiaroscuro* (contrast) as two important methods to render drawings and paintings towards a natural realism because light and shade are continuous in nature, but can be measured and seen by the degrees of shading or by the use of colour differentiation. The starkest form of *sfumato* and contrasts can be seen in the *Pacioli Portrait* where there are no images sealed by single black outlines as you see in the Botticelli paintings like *The Birth of Venus* where each figure is closed and bounded by a black outline (Fig. 8.16). In the *Pacioli Portrait*, Leonardo da Vinci has achieved the same result by the use of a black background, light and shade, and colour to illuminate his two figures, *Pacioli* and *Sanseverino*, the green table and all the items on the green tablecloth. Many painters including de' Barbari quickly grasped the significance of this technique and they developed and used it to varying degrees for their portraiture paintings. Thus, a revolution was born with Leonardo's innovative painting and drawing methods and they became etched into stone after his death with their continued application by the Leonardeschi followers and Masters like Titian, Caravaggio, Rembrandt, Whistler and many thousands of others that followed in his footsteps over the centuries who used his painting methods of black (or dark coloured) backgrounds, *sfumato*, and the contrasts (*chiaroscuro*) of light and shade.

Stephen Pepper highlighted two of Leonardo da Vinci's drawings on light and shadow to emphasis the point further:

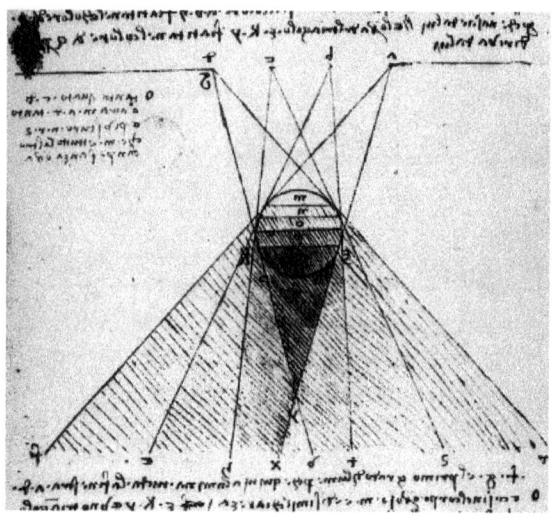

FIG. 13.4. Leonardo da Vinci, Notebooks, drawing of gradation of light and primary and derived shadows, Manuscript B.N. 2038, fol. 13v. [Ms. Ashburnham II, folio 13v].

'He has drawn the light so that it strikes this object. Just grasp the incredible precision of his eye and of his rendering. You see, he shows how the light on the surface turned to the light, how it gradually turns into shadow, and therefore, the area where no light reaches, has become perfectly dark. Where there are all of these gradients, this is where there is a mixture of light and shade. In other words, contrary to what most people believe, light and shade are continuous in nature. They don't cut off. They don't have boundaries. Of

course, this is the basis for his famous rendering of drawings in the method of sfumato, "smokiness." And he shows you that all of this can be measured, by degrees, not numerically, but by degrees of shading.'

Leonardo has drawn the light striking a sphere from different points 'a' to 'd' on an open aperture and has illustrated how the light on the surface of the sphere has gradually turned bright light into shadow and eventually to the area of perfect darkness where no light reaches. He has simply demonstrated all of the gradients (mixtures) of light and shadow falling on an opaque solid from a brightly lit light source.

Of this drawing, Fritjof Capra wrote:

> '... shows a diagram of a sphere illuminated by light falling through a window. Leonardo has traced light rays emanating from four points (labeled a, b, c, and d). He shows four gradations of primary shadows on the sphere (labeled n, o, p, and q), and the corresponding gradations of derived shadows, cast between the boundary lines of the eight light rays behind the sphere (labeled by the letters along the base of the diagram). ...
> He also introduces several lamps, studies how the gradations of the shadows change with each new lamp, and examines how the shadows move when the lamps and the object are moved. As Kenneth Clark has remarked, "The calculations are so complex and abstruse that we feel in them, almost for the first time, Leonardo's tendency to pursue research for its own sake, rather than as an aid to his art."'

Leonardo's Vision of the Eye

So why was Leonardo interested in pyramids, cones, points and lines (straight or curved) that he illustrated symbolically and practically throughout the *Pacioli Portrait*? They provide drawings lessons in perspective, which according to Leonardo, *'is nothing else than a thorough knowledge of the function of the eye.'*

Let us once again refer to Fritjof Capra's book *The Science of Leonardo* and see what he wrote about Leonardo's studies on vision and the eye.

> *To complete his science of perspective, Leonardo studied not only the external pathways of light rays, together with various optical phenomena, but also followed them right into the eye. Indeed, during the 1480s, he pursued his anatomical studies of the eye and the physiology of vision simultaneously with his investigations of perspective and the interplay of light and shadow. At that time there was a debate among Renaissance artists and philosophers about the exact location of the tip of the visual pyramid in the eye. Most artists followed Alberti, who paid little attention to the actual physiology of vision and located the apex of the visual pyramid in a geometric point at the centre of the pupil. Most philosophers, by contrast, took the position of Alhazen, who asserted that*

the eye's visual faculty must reside in a finite area rather than in an infinitely small point. In the beginning of his investigations of perspective and the anatomy of the eye, Leonardo adopted Alberti's view, but during the 1490s, as his research became more sophisticated, he came to embrace Alhazen's position, arguing that "if all the images that come to the eye converged in a mathematical point, which is proved to be indivisible, then all the things seen in the universe would appear as one, and that one would be indivisible." In his late optical writings in Manuscript D, finally, he asserted repeatedly and confidently that "every part of the pupil possesses the faculty of vision (virtù visiva), and…this faculty is not reduced to a point, as the perspectivists wish." In this Notebook, Leonardo offers three simple but very elegant experiments, involving the shadowy perception of small objects held near the eye, as persuasive proofs of Alhazen's position. From then on he distinguished between two kinds of perspective. The first, "perspective made by art," is a geometric technique for representing objects located in three-dimensional space on a flat surface, while the second, "perspective made by nature," needs a proper science of vision to be understood. Having convinced himself that in such a science of vision, the geometric apex of the visual pyramid in the eye needs to be replaced by much more complex pathways of the sensory impressions, Leonardo then traced these pathways through the lens and the eyeball to the optic nerve, and from there all the way to the centre of the brain where he believed he had found the seat of the soul.'

Leonardo provided many notes and comments on sight and linear perspective in his notebooks that were translated by Richter (1880) and are now available on the Internet (see References at the end of the chapter). Here are some of Leonardo's well-known judgements on light and vision.

The function of the eye as explained by the camera obscura [note 70 of the Richter translation). If the object in front of the eye sends its image to the eye, the eye, on the other hand, sends its image to the object, and no portion whatever of the object is lost in the images it throws off, for any reason either in the eye or the object. Therefore we may rather believe it to be the nature and potency of our luminous atmosphere, which absorbs the images of the objects existing in it, than the nature of the objects, to send their images through the air. If the object opposite to the eye were to send its image to the eye, the eye would have to do the same to the object, whence it might seem that these images were an emanation. But, if so, it would be necessary [to admit] that every object became rapidly smaller; because each object appears by its images in the surrounding atmosphere. That is: the whole object in the whole atmosphere, and in each part; and all the objects in the whole atmosphere and all of them in each part; speaking of that atmosphere which is able to contain in itself the straight and radiating lines of the images projected by the objects. From this it seems necessary to admit that it is in the nature of the atmosphere, which subsists between the objects, and which attracts the images of things to itself like a lodestone, being placed between them.

CHAPTER 13

PROVE HOW ALL OBJECTS, PLACED IN ONE POSITION, ARE ALL EVERYWHERE AND ALL IN EACH PART.

I say that if the front of a building—or any open piazza or field—which is illuminated by the sun has a dwelling opposite to it, and if, in the front which does not face the sun, you make a small round hole, all the illuminated objects will project their images through that hole and be visible inside the dwelling on the opposite wall which may be made white; and there, in fact, they will be upside down, and if you make similar openings in several places in the same wall you will have the same result from each. Hence the images of the illuminated objects are all everywhere on this wall and all in each minutest part of it. The reason, as we clearly know, is that this hole must admit some light to the said dwelling, and the light admitted by it is derived from one or many luminous bodies. If these bodies are of various colours and shapes the rays forming the images are of various colours and shapes, and so will the representations be on the wall.

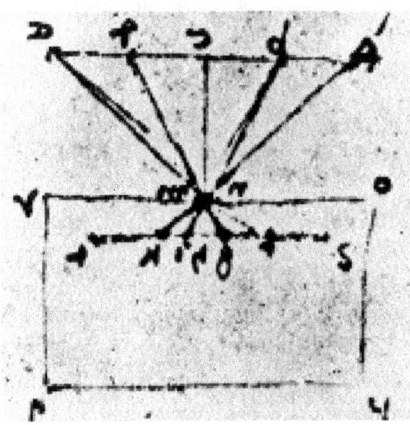

FIG. 13.5. *Leonardo da Vinci, Notebooks, drawing of camera obscura, Manuscript D, fol. 8r.*

The function of the eye as explained by the camera obscura. (71, Richter translation).
HOW THE IMAGES OF OBJECTS RECEIVED BY THE EYE INTERSECT WITHIN THE CRYSTALLINE HUMOUR OF THE EYE.

An experiment, showing how objects transmit their images or pictures, intersecting within the eye in the crystalline humour, is seen when by some small round hole penetrate the images of illuminated objects into a very dark chamber. Then, receive these images on a white paper placed within this dark room and rather near to the hole and you will see all the objects on the paper in their proper forms and colours, but much smaller; and they will be upside down by reason of that very intersection. These images being transmitted from a place illuminated by the sun will seem actually painted on this paper which must be extremely thin and looked at from behind. And let the little perforation be made in a very thin plate of iron. Let a b c d e be the object illuminated by the sun and o r the front of the dark chamber in which is the said hole at n m. Let s t be the sheet of paper *intercepting the rays of the images of these objects upside down, because the rays being straight, a on the right hand becomes k on the left, and e on the left becomes f on the right; and the same takes place inside the pupil. (D.8r.)*

By using a little *imaginatio* Leonardo's drawings of the light rays passing through the *camera obscura* also can be seen on the front of *Luca Pacioli's* grey monk's habit (Fig. 13.6).

FIG. 13.6. Detail. The shadow and light passing through Leonardo's Camera Obscura painted onto Pacioli's chest.

Leonardo painted rays of light onto the chest of *Luca Pacioli* as a simplified demonstration of the intersection of these rays as light and shadow. In the detailed figure of Luca's grey habit (Fig. 13.6), the horizontal line of his cape (cowl) is equivalent to the horizontal line D to A in Leonardo's Fig. 13.5 of the *camera obscura*. The horizontal white cord is the horizontal line L to O in Fig. 13.5.

The edge of the table is equivalent to the horizontal line T to S in Fig. 13.5. The diagonal lines from the line D to A to the midpoint (knot) of white cord L to O are like those running to the pinhole of the *camera obscura* in Fig 13.5. The lines run through the pinhole to the edge of the table that records their angles depending on the lens in the pinhole.

The shadows and light on the folds of Pacioli's chest (Fig. 13.6) provides an analogy also for another of Leonardo's hypothesis on the intersection of the rays (Fig. 13.7) in his notebooks as translated by Richter (1880).

AS TO WHETHER THE CENTRAL LINE OF THE IMAGE CAN BE INTERSECTED, OR NOT, WITHIN THE OPENING.

It is impossible that the line should intersect itself; that is, that its right should cross over to its left side, and so, its left side become its right side. Because such an intersection demands two lines, one from each side; for there can be no motion from right to left or from left to right in itself without such extension and thickness as admit of such motion. And if there is extension it is no longer a line but a surface, and we are investigating the properties of a line, and not of a surface. And as the line, having no centre of thickness cannot be divided, we must conclude that the line can have no sides to intersect each other. This is proved by the movement of the line a f to a b and of the line e b to e f, which are the sides of the surface a f e b. But if you move the line a b and the line e f, with the frontends a e, to the spot c, you will have moved the opposite ends f b towards each other at the point d. And from the two lines you will have drawn the straight line c d which cuts the middle of the intersection of these two lines at the point n without any intersection. For, you imagine these two lines as having breadth, it is evident that by this motion the first will entirely cover the other—being equal with it—without any intersection, in the position c d. And this is sufficient to prove our proposition.

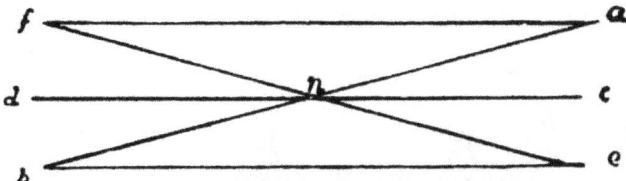

FIG. 13.7. *Diagram from Leonardo da Vinci's Notebooks showing that the central line of an image cannot intersect itself.*

Another analogy might be that the folds of the habit represent rays of light that hit the surface of a liquid (the horizontal white cord) and bend (refract) or reflect according to density of the liquid used in the study (Fig. 13.8).

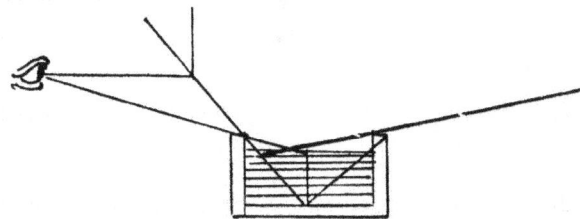

FIG. 13.8. *Diagram from Leonardo da Vinci's Notebooks showing refraction of the rays falling upon the eye.*

Refraction of the rays falling upon the eye (75, Richter translation). If the judgment of the eye is situated within it, the straight lines of the images are refracted on its surface because they pass through the rarer to the denser medium. If, when you are under water, you look at objects in the air you will see them out of their true place; and the same with objects under water seen from the air.

Anamorphosis: A Change in Perspective

Leonardo found anomalies with linear perspective and he illustrated one such visual problem with three equal spheres, or balls, and what happens at two linear intersections and then at a curvilinear intersection (Fig. 13.9). What he showed according to linear perspective was that the further an object is from the eye, the smaller it should appear. This is the great advantage of linear perspective because it provides a very precise, mathematical system for establishing the ratios of distance to size and height. But, if this intersection is very close, then the two objects (a and c) that are further away on the periphery, would project a broader, that is, a larger image, than the one in the center (b), which is closest to the eye—contrary to the presumption, and contrary to Nature. The three-sphere diagram operates contrary to natural vision.

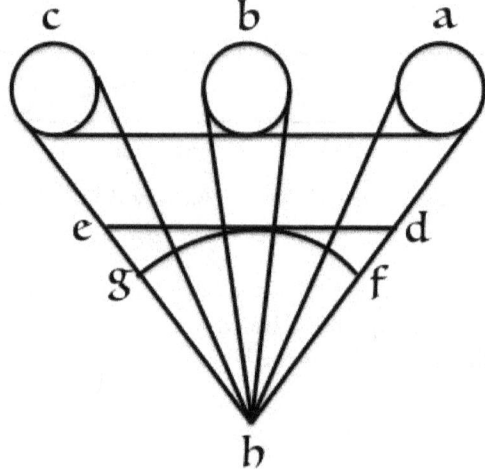

FIG. 13.9. Leonardo da Vinci, Notebooks, diagram showing flaws in linear perspective, redrawn from Manuscript E, fol. 16a.

However, if the intersection is curved as represented by the line 'gf' in Fig. 13.9 then that distortion would disappear. This analysis by Leonardo showed that there are flaws in the way linear perspective normally was understood. If you come very close, or you extend the angle of vision, and you approach the margins, you obtain unusual or abnormal phenomena, anomalies that do not correspond to immutable Nature. Since the leading thinkers of the Renaissance accepted that the principle of perspective is universal and true under all conditions, this anomaly created a difficulty in their thinking. Leonardo was determined to solve the problem geometrically with the study of curved intersections.

CHAPTER 13

The following are a series of Leonardo's pronouncements about the perspective of light as pyramids of lines (Fig. 13.10) taken from his Notebooks edited by Jean Paul Richter in 1880.

'*By natural perspective, I mean that the plane intersection on which this perspective is represented as a flat surface, and this intersection, although it is parallel, both in length and height, is forced to diminish the remoter parts more than its nearer parts. And this is proved by the first of what had been said above, and its diminution is natural. But artificial perspective, that is, that which is derived by art, does the contrary.*'

'*For objects equal in size increase on the intersection, where they are foreshortened in proportion, as the eye is more natural and nearer to the intersection, and as the part of the intersection on which it is figured, is further from the eye*'

'*The nature of the outline (item 50): Drawing is based upon perspective, which is nothing else than a thorough knowledge of the function of the eye. And this function simply consists in receiving in a pyramid the forms and colours of all the objects placed before it. I say in a pyramid, because there is no object so small that it will not be larger than the spot where these pyramids are received into the eye. Therefore, if you extend the lines from the edges of each body as they converge you will bring them to a single point, and necessarily the said lines must form a pyramid.*'

'*Perspective is nothing more than a rational demonstration applied to the consideration of how objects in front of the eye transmit their image to it, by means of a pyramid of lines. The Pyramid is the name I apply to the lines, which, starting from the surface and edges of each object, converge from a distance and meet in a single point.*'

'*Perspective is a rational demonstration, by which we may practically and clearly understand how objects transmit their own image, by lines forming a Pyramid (centred) in the eye.*'

'*Perspective is a rational demonstration by which experience confirms that every object sends its image to the eye by a pyramid of lines; and bodies of equal size will result in a pyramid of larger or smaller size, according to the difference in their distance, one from the other. By a pyramid of lines I mean those, which start from the surface and edges of bodies, and, converging from a distance meet in a single point. A point is said to be that which [having no dimensions] cannot be divided, and this point placed in the eye receives all the points of the cone.*'

'*Experimental proof of the existence of the pyramid of sight (item 53)*'

'*PERSPECTIVE. Perspective comes in where judgment fails [as to the distance] in objects, which diminish. The eye can never be a true judge for determining with exactitude how near one object is to another which is equal to it [in size], if the top of that other is on the level of the eye which sees them on that side, excepting by means of the vertical plane which is the standard and guide of perspective. Let n be the eye, e f the vertical plane above mentioned. Let a b c d be the three divisions, one below the other; if the lines a n and c n are of a given length and the eye n is in the centre, then a b will look as large as b c. c d is lower and farther off from n, therefore it will look smaller. And the same effect will appear in the three divisions of a face when the eye of the painter who is drawing it is on a level with the eye of the person he is painting.' (Fig. 13.10).*

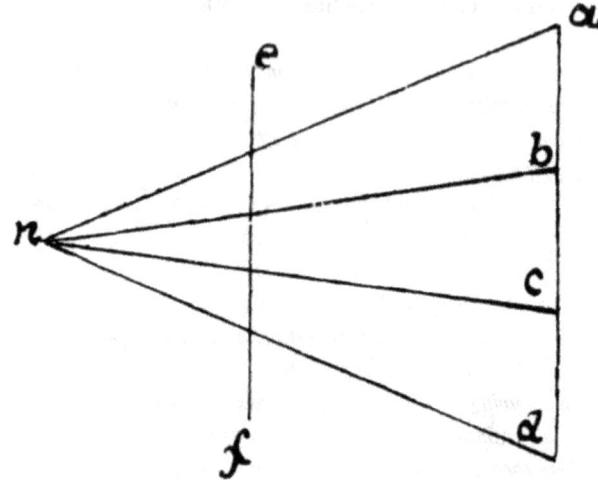

FIG. 13.10. *Recreation of Leonardo's figure illustrating the pyramid of sight.*

'*HOW WE MAY CONCLUDE THAT A SUPERFICIES TERMINATES IN A POINT? An angular surface is reduced to a point where it terminates in an angle. Or, if the sides of that angle are produced in a straight line, then—beyond that angle—another surface is generated, smaller, or equal to, or larger than the first.*'

This latter point is illustrated on Luca Pacioli's habit where the angular straight lines of light and shadow on his habit (angular surface) terminate in angles at a point on the white cord and then diverge at another angle on the other side of the horizontal white cord (Fig. 13.6 and Fig. 13.11).

The light and shadow on *Pacioli's* habit in part resembles the light and shadow painted on *Venus's* shell by Botticelli in 1486 (Fig. 13.12). Let the horizontal curved line at the heel and toe of Venus's feet correspond to the white rope around Pacioli's waist and then look at the vertical lines that slant in above the horizontal line and slant out below the same line. This seems to be another of Leonardo's parodies, a joke mimicking the curvilinear patterns of the inside of the open-shell in Botticelli's *Birth of Venus* (Fig. 13.12) and the rather insipid shadows on the shell of della Francesca's *Brera Altarpiece* painting of 1472 (Fig. 12.11). Nobody, other than Leonardo could come up with such a silly joke or parody of other painters in their own very serious painting about science, religion, relationships, history and art as contained within the *Pacioli Portrait*.

CHAPTER 13

FIG. 13.11. Detail. The change of angles and directions of shadow and light above and below the rope tied around Pacioli's waist.

FIG. 13.12. Detail of the angles and directions of shadows and light on the shell in Botticelli's Birth of Venus *relative to those on Pacioli's chest in Fig. 13.11.*

Also, the play of the light and shadows on *Luca Pacioli's* habit resembles the direction of light travelling through the apertures of a pinhole camera or the surface of a liquid and bending by refraction. It is the strange way that the folds of his habit have formed above and below the rope. Are the rays of light and shadow being reflected or refracted by the rope around Pacioli's waist? It resembles the movement of monochromatic light through a glass prism rather than through glass or a solution. Perhaps, he is showing us a pictorial analogy of the deviation (refraction) of monochromatic light through a minus double prism. Why this play of light and shadows on *Luca Pacioli's* tunic? Is it meant to ask a question or convey a message? Is there a plausible answer in hand?

Jacopo de' Barbari's Painting of Light and Shadow and his Depiction of Refraction in a Glass of Water

The painting known as *A Room with Lovers* by Jacopo de' Barbari at the Gemäldegalerie der Staatlichen Museen zu Berlin in Germany shows two nude lovers in a well-lit room with a glass of water on a ledge in the foreground (Fig. 13.13). The painting parodies the *Pacioli Portrait*, demonstrating de' Barbari's understanding and mastery of light and shadow and the phenomenon of refraction in water. *A Room with Lovers* is like a double portraiture, but instead of *Luca Pacioli* and *Galeazzo Sanseverino*, it has a man and a woman, both naked, with the man standing slightly behind and to the left of the woman fondling her left breast while she stands with a mirror in her right hand admiring her own and her lover's reflection. Light streams in over the two lovers from two windows, side by side, from their right and from a partially open door behind them. De' Barbari paints shadows of different shape and gradation on the nude bodies of the two lovers, on the floor and along the edge of the wall, as a long single streak behind the lovers, along the sides of the pillars and the bottom edge of the partly opened back door. The shadows lack the care, precision, mystery or *sfumato* seen in the *Pacioli Portrait*. Two very different painters have painted *A Room with Lovers* and the *Pacioli Portrait* using their own distinctive and different techniques. The glass of water with the leafy stem of a plant, perhaps a Tiger Lily, at the front and to one side of the painting of *A Room with Lovers*, is de' Barbari *coup de grace* on the subject of light, reflection and refraction. He seems to mock Leonardo da Vinci's hanging transparent rhombicuboctahedron half-filled with water by showing us what a glass of water should look like with light passing through the glass and reflecting brightly off the surface of the water. We see the bottom of the glass and the plant's stem distorted in the water highlighting for us that de' Barbari understood the physics of refraction. But this illustration of the refraction in water by de' Barbari is nothing new in the Renaissance because Plato had written about it in his *The Republic* in the times of the ancient Greeks:

> *'A stick will look bent if you put it in the water, straight when you take it out, and deceptive differences of shading can make the same surface seem to the eye concave or convex; and our minds are clearly liable to all sorts of confusions of this kind. It is this natural weakness that the scene-painter and conjuror and their fellows exploit with magical effect. Measuring, counting and weighing have happily been discovered to help us out of these difficulties, and these calculations are performed by the element of reason in the mind.'*

And yet, the overall painting style by de' Barbari still looks more like that created by Piero Francesca than by Leonardo da Vinci; it lacks inventiveness and that extra essence of refinement and subtlety that we see in a da Vinci painting. Nonetheless, we can acknowledge that Jacopo de' Barbari had a sense of the bizarre and seemed to know what Leonardo's scientific interests and painting theories were about. It's almost as if he had his own copy of Leonardo's *Treatise on Painting* and would follow up on a painting exercise now and then in an attempt to match or outdo the master.

FIG. 13.13. Jacopo de Barbari's painting of A Room with Lovers and a Glass with Water (bottom). Creative Commons. Public Domain. Retrieved from https://commons.wikimedia.org/w/index.php?title=File:Jacopo_de%27_Barbari_-_Una_stanza_con_gli_amanti.jpg&oldid=296341987

References

Capra, Fritjof (2008). The Science of Leonardo: Inside the Mind of the Great Genius of the Renaissance. Anchor Books Edition, New York. https://erenow.com/biographies/the-science-of-leonardo-inside-the-mind-of-the-great-genius-of-the-renaissance/

Baldasso, Renzo (2010). The Portrait of Luca Pacioli and Disciple: a new mathematical look. Art Bulletin. Vol. XCII, n°. 1-2, pp. 83-102.

Elert, Glenn (1998). The Physics Hypertextbook. *https://physics.info*

Kemp, Martin (2006). The Marvellous Works of Nature and Man. Oxford University Press. Oxford, New York.

Pepper, D. Stephen (2001). Leonardo da Vinci and the Perspective of Light. Fidelio 10 (1):33-53.

14

DA VINCI STEREOPSIS: DEPTH PERCEPTION, DISPARITY & SHADOWS

Da Vinci Stereopsis and Parallax

Apart from many other things, the *Pacioli Portrait* by Leonardo da Vinci is an experiment about depth perception and his ability to create a 3D effect in a painted 2D image. Depth perception is the visual ability to perceive the world in three dimensions (3D) and estimate the distance of an object using binocular and monocular cues. The binocular cues include stereopsis, eye convergence, disparity, and estimating parallax. Monocular cues include size, visual angles, texture, and motion parallax. Occlusion, interposition or blockage of objects can affect depth perceptions when near surfaces overlap far surfaces or closer objects partially block the view of more distant objects.

While conducting his numerous experiments on binocular vision in Milan, Leonardo discovered the phenomena of monocular occlusions – areas invisible (occluded) to one eye, but not the other. In conventional stereopsis (perception of depth and stereo [3D] vision), the depth perception between two objects is based on the retinal disparity in the position of matching points in the two eyes. When an object is occluded by another object in the scene, so that it is visible only by one eye, its retinal disparity cannot be perceived. In 1990, the Japanese scientists Nakayama and Shimojo named the occlusion-based depth phenomena as '*da Vinci stereopsis*' in honour of Leonardo da Vinci and as the basis of ongoing research to better understand the mechanisms of binocular vision and depth perception. They wrote: '*Thus, we have four separate findings which can be linked to rivalry, depth, subjective contours, and motion, respectively - all of which are related to occlusive conditions in the real world and require explicit eye-of-origin information. Because these phenomena are closely related to notions put forth by Leonardo da Vinci (Wheatstone, 1838), we group them under his name, thus making the distinction between da Vinci and Wheatstone stereopsis.*'

CHAPTER 14

They made another important distinction that Leonardo knew about.

'Classical stereopsis relies on the fact that two physical points in space, lying at different distances lead to differential retinal disparity of the two pairs of binocular image points. But just noting a difference in retinal disparity is not enough to identify depth. The sign of this difference is critical, determining whether one sees the one target in front or in back. The basis for this signed disparity, of course, is eye-of-origin information. Only by specifying which eye is which can it be determined whether disparity is crossed or uncrossed.'

In this regard, a marker point closer to the pair of eyes than an *horopter* (the set of points with zero disparity, that is, the fixation point and optical centres of the two eyes) is crossed disparity [+ sign], whereas a marker point further away has uncrossed disparity [- sign], that is, you have to uncross your eyes to fixate on the point.

After the publication of the Nakayama and Shimojo paper in 1990, there has been a relatively large and growing scientific literature on the study of *'da Vinci stereopsis'*, the name given by the two Japanese scientists to the study of occluded depth perception in honour of Leonardo's studies, observations and discovery of monocular occlusion zones, and perceived depth of field and parallax. The term *'da Vinci stereopsis'* as a monocular or occluded form of depth of vision is used to distinguish it from non-occluded Wheatstone stereopsis, which are both well-established principles in the scientific literature on vision and depth perception. A search of *PubMed* on the Internet using the term *'da Vinci stereopsis'* listed 50 different publications. In comparison, *Google Search* on the Internet found about 9,550 entries. A growing body of research suggests that monocular occlusions are an integral part of the mechanism of binocular depth perception and that forward-facing eyes in animals were advantaged and advanced in their evolution by the ability to see monocular occluded areas in cluttered environments. Many natural scenes contain zones that are visible to one eye only and that can be seen at a precise depth even though there are no binocular disparities that uniquely constrain their locations in depth. Whereas stereopsis is believed to be an innately hard-wired depth cue, occlusion (or interference) is acquired through visual experience. This implies a difference between physiological and cognitive cues to depth perception, although some researchers argue that both kinds of depth processing are neural inferences implemented early in the visual pathway and both exploit real-world geometry using the differences in the horizontal position of the two eyes. Disparity gives a reliability scale for evaluating depth perception in the distance dimension. In this regard, *'da Vinci stereopsis'* is regarded as a depth ambiguity seen in a monocular object occluded by a binocular one that the visual system must solve.

Leonardo da Vinci never used the terms stereopsis, disparity or parallax in his writings, but he showed in his drawings that binocular disparity, that is, the difference in image location of an object seen by the left and right eyes, results from the eyes' horizontal separation or what we now call parallax. Stellar parallax, the apparent shift of position of a nearby star against the background of distant objects, was observed and calculated by astronomers and astrologers since the ancient times of the Greeks and Egyptians for their measurements of the planets and the stars, but it became more important in 1600 after the Copernicus publication of the planetary heliocentric model for the movement of the heavenly spheres. Although Leonardo realised that there was binocular disparity between the right and left eye, and that this disparity was the difference in image location of an object seen by the left and right eye, he wanted to know how this disparity of images was brought together geometrically onto the optic nerve (retina). These observations arose in part from his interest and studies on the perspective of light and how he modelled the inversion of an image through the eyeball to the optic nerve. Furthermore, he wanted to know the reverse pathway, that is, how do you add stereoscopic vision to the 2D plane of paper or the canvas and make the drawing or painting standout like the depth of field achieved with binocular vision of natural scenes. It was a great geometrical problem that he never seemed able to solve completely, although there are claims that he succeeded to produce a stereoptic effect with the painting of the *Mona Lisa*. Leonardo wrote the following:

'*A Painting, though conducted with the greatest Art and finished to the last Perfection, both with regard to its contours, its lights, its shadows and its colours, can never show a* Relievo *equal to that of Natural Objects, unless these be view'd at a distance and with a single Eye.*'

That is, the perception of depth is incomplete in a painting, unlike that for a 3D natural scene viewed with two eyes. But, if painted perfectly, the subjects or objects in the painting might stand out from the surrounding background if '*view'd at a distance and with a single Eye*'.

Leonardo da Vinci used a sphere with a diameter less than the interocular separation to examine binocular vision and to compare it with monocular observation. According to the coauthors Wade, Ono and Lillakas in a paper that they published in 2001, Leonardo struggled long and hard with capturing on canvas the essence of 3D (depth of field) reality and to characterise the difference between monocular and binocular vision. At first, he used the concept of Alberti's window to provide a monocular match between a picture and a view of a scene from a single point. Alberti's perspective for conveying visual angles to a picture plane from a vanishing point simulate the monocular visual world on a canvas, but not that of the binocular visual world. Leonardo wanted to know what happens and what is seen from a binocular viewpoint. He examined this problem many times in the context of a small object lying in front of a background and found that vision with two eyes was optically and phenomenally different from that with one eye. Leonardo's drawings in Fig. 14.1 reproduced from the Wade et al., paper (2001) represent both binocular (left) and monocular (right) observations of a small sphere, and his accompanying text emphasises the differences between viewing a scene and painting it in terms of perceived depth and the amount of the background that is visible. He found that a sphere with a diameter smaller than the interocular distance will obscure a more distant one when viewed with one eye, but not when two are used:

'Why a Painting Can Never Appear Detached as Natural Objects Do. Painters often fall into despair of imitating nature when they see their pictures fail in that relief and vividness which objects have that are seen in a mirror; while they allege that they have colours which for brightness or depth far exceed the strength of light and shade in the reflections in the mirror, thus displaying their own ignorance rather than the real cause, because they do not know it. It is impossible that painted objects should appear in such relief as to resemble those reflected in the mirror, although sides of the central line, the eyes see the space G D behind the object; the eye A sees the whole space F D, and the eye B sees the whole space G E. Thus, the two eyes see the whole space F E behind the object C. The object C remains transparent, according to the definition of transparency, by which nothing is hidden. This cannot happen to him who looks with one eye at an object larger than his eye, as it could not happen when the eye looks at objects smaller than the pupil. This is shown in the second diagram. Because of what has been said, we can conclude our investigation, because the painted object covers all the space that is behind it, and it is in no way possible to see any part of the background behind it within the outlines of the object.'

The paper by Wade et al., (2001) provides an interesting account of Leonardo da Vinci experiments and findings in his attempt to understand the differences between the perception of a scene and painting it, which he reduced to the differences between binocular and monocular vision; and his observations were followed by the emergence of Wheatstone's stereoscope more than 350 years later, which has led to modern approaches that are now used to depict virtual reality. They conclude speculatively that, *'As a scientist, Leonardo would have been excited by Wheatstone's stereoscope; as a theorist, he would have appreciated the subtlety of Ames's concept of equivalent configurations.'* However at this stage you might wonder what has all this to do with the *Pacioli Portrait*?

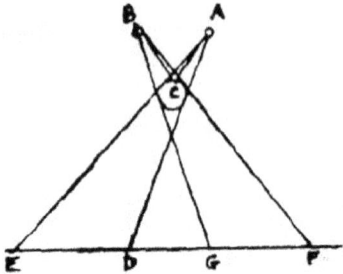

FIG. 14.1. *Leonardo da Vinci used a sphere C, with a diameter less than the interocular separation of AB, to examine binocular vision of eye A and eye B and to compare it with monocular observation, A or B. Taken with permission from Wade et al (2001).*

Luca Pacioli's Tunic: Diagonal lines of Light and Shadow, a Simple Demonstration of Binocular Vision and Parallax

Leonardo da Vinci's basic ideas of binocular vision are displayed on Pacioli's tunic with the converging parallel lines of light and shadow above the horizontal cord and the diverging parallel lines of light and shadow below the cord to guide the viewer's attention. If Pacioli could look down at the sphere (middle knot) of his belt made of rope that is smaller than the width between his two eyes it might produce a binocular and monocular blind spot somewhere beyond that sphere. Since Pacioli is not looking down, let us draw an eye on each of his shoulders and draw lines up to and past the small knot on the rope around his waist (imagined as a sphere drawn in front of the knot) then we can see that these lines resemble the lines that Leonardo drew for us in Fig.14.1. In this regard, we are using Pacioli's chest as Leonardo's blackboard to demonstrate his geometrical explanation of binocular and monocular vision. Moreover, poor Pacioli is straining intensely to focus on the hanging polyhedron with one eye while the other eye appears to stare past the polyhedron out to some fixated point of interest in outer space.

In Fig. 14.2, if both of the symbolic eyes on Pacioli's cloak fixate only on the opaque sphere then they will not see the region A to D behind the sphere, it will be occluded or constrained from view. However, if both eyes focus behind and slightly to the left or right of the sphere then both eyes will see what is directly behind the sphere. If the left eye is closed and the right eye kept open and focused on the sphere it easily will see the background behind the sphere except for the occluded blind spot CD. Similarly, if looking only with the left eye, there will be a constrained (blind) spot in the area AB behind the sphere. Opening both eyes will remove all the blind spots behind the sphere, unless both eyes focus only on the sphere. This is an example of parallax that Leonardo observed with his monocular and binocular experiments.

FIG. 14.2. The direction of the shadows on Luca Pacioli's habit illustrates Leonardo's light rays, occlusions and other propositions about vision and depth perception. Fig 10.1 has been recreated onto Luca Pacioli's habit with an added pair of eyes to illustrate Leonardo's concept of occlusion, parallax and shadows. In regard to the eyes in Luca Pacioli's head, one eye focuses on the suspended rhombicuboctahedron and the other stares somewhere out into space.

Leonardo's studies were more than just simple demonstrations of parallax. Various interesting physical phenomena and types of perception are at play with binocular and monocular disparity that Leonardo da Vinci grappled with all his life, and even today not much more is known about '*da Vinci stereopsis*' than what Leonardo had already discovered. There are four basic types of '*da Vinci stereopsis*' cues that are recognised and tested by the modern scientist: occlusion, aperture, camouflage and phantom. These four types are illustrated in Fig. 14.3. In the case of the first three types of *da Vinci stereopsis* cues (a to c), the boundaries of the background and foreground are rigid and independent of any angle of the scene that is viewed. However, in the phantom type (d) the presence of shadows as non-apparent luminance edges can cause phantom surfaces to generate monocular regions, which in turn can stimulate a depth perception. In this regard, the boundaries of the background and foreground become non-rigid and become dependent on the angle of viewing the scene.

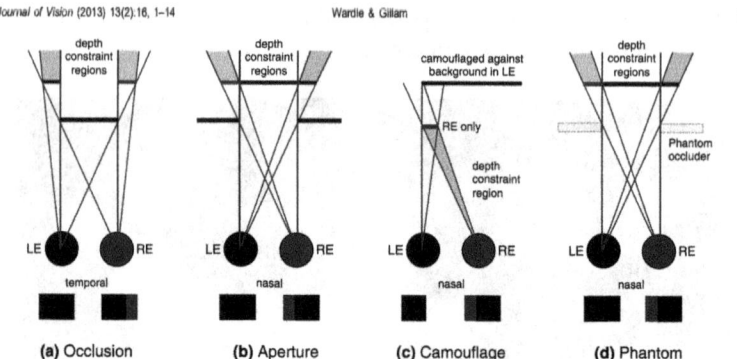

FIG. 14.3. *Four basic types of da Vinci stereopsis cues, presented by Wardle & Gillam (2013).*

Based on his experiments and observations, Leonardo knew that the location of monocular regions in binocularly viewed 3D scenes is determined by the occlusion relationships of near and far surfaces between the two eyes. With *occlusion*, the monocular regions arise because a near-surface occludes part of a more distant surface from the view of the other eye that is on the temporal side of the binocular surface as indicated in Fig. 14.3a. With an *aperture* type (Fig. 14.3b), the monocular regions result from viewing a background surface through an aperture and each eye sees more of the background surface on the nasal side of the binocular region. With *camouflaged* cues (Fig. 14.3c) the occlusion nearer to the observer, such as with the same colour and luminance as a binocular background surface, maybe invisible to one eye because it is camouflaged against the background surface in that eye's view. With the *phantom* cue (Fig. 14.3d), the depth of a monocular region with a phantom aperture is insufficiently constrained in the same way as it is for a physical aperture. If the border of the texture is taken to be the edge of the figure in each eye's half-image, the depth of the *phantom* surface itself is precisely determined by the lines of sight for the edge of the monocular region in one eye and the edge of the binocular region in the other eye. The *phantom* might be located at a greater depth (closer to the observer) if an arbitrary amount of white space is included in the temporal side of each eye's half-image. Leonardo da Vinci achieved this greater depth with the hanging polygon by bordering the structure with white lines of reflected light and the addition of the two bright images reflected from the 'imaginary' window located somewhere to the left of the painting as we look at it. Moreover, the *phantom* cue using shadows is an important technique for generating the illusion of a 3D image in paintings because shadows as non-apparent luminance edges cause *phantom* surfaces to generate monocular regions, which in turn stimulate a depth perception.

Does the *Pacioli Portrait* have any clues or indications about Leonardo da Vinci's studies and interest with binocular vision and disparity? This question is difficult to answer because there are no obvious clues or concrete indications other than it is a painting that has two human subjects, a hanging rhombicuboctahedron with three images of the view outside a window, a black background and a foreground of a green table with at least 12 objects related to measuring, drawing and geometry on it. On the other hand, we might speculate correctly that the whole painting is about monocular and binocular vision because Leonardo was obsessed for most of his painter's life with these problems and the question of whether the limited optical projections and the inadequacy of monocular painting could be overcome and developed by more than just adding a few strategically placed stereoptic cues into the painting. When looking at the *Pacioli Portrait* there are many questions that we can ask about depth of field and what occlusions Leonardo added to create the illusion of depth.

Let us begin here with a search for occlusions within the inner workings of the *Pacioli Portrait*. The occlusions we want to find within the painting are the objects or scenes hidden in part by nearer surfaces in the painter's attempt to create the illusion of different depths and overlapping. Barbara Gillam of the School of Psychology at the University of New South Wales in Sydney, Australia has written widely about the occlusion issues in the early Renaissance and has pointed out that painters often used occlusions to try and depict realistic 3D scenes on a picture plane. What important objects or surfaces are partially occluded from our view in the *Pacioli Portrait*, if any? What can Galeazzo Sanseverino see on the display table while standing behind Luca Pacioli? Is he tall enough to see over Pacioli's shoulders? Presumably, he cannot see any of the items in front of Pacioli except for a portion of the book to the left of Pacioli's left hand. Can he see the fly on the yellow paper directly beneath his eye line, and might it interest him? Is there anything that blocks his view of the fly or the cartouche written out on the yellow paper? Do the two subjects in the painting have monocular or binocular vision? Can we see any of the figures or items in the painting as if they were in 3D and do any of them stand out as if they were real? The last question is the one that occupied and frustrated Leonardo the most with what he believed were painting methods limited to a 2D rather than a 3D visual experience.

Seeing the *Pacioli Portrait* in 3D with One Open Eye

Leonardo da Vinci knew from experience and theory that it was always better to view a 2D painting with one eye than two. Although Leonardo could not produce on canvas an equivalent configuration of reality as a 3D image, he still managed to provide his paintings with dramatic punch by providing it with illusionary tricks that he learned from his studies and experiments of monocular and binocular vision and its disparity. He learnt from a young age that when a person looked at a conventional 2D picture of a 3D scene, they were able to conjure a form of virtual three-dimensional space with height, width and depth. His task was to find additional or new ways to improve perception of a conventional painting in 3D. He found that by looking at a picture of an appropriately painted 3-dimensional scene simply with one eye through a small aperture (a pea-sized hole), it induced the phenomenon of seeing it in 3D. Therefore, while 2-eye vision is important in many ways for depth perception, it is not necessary for experiencing 3D effects. Dhanraj Vishwanath and Paul B. Hibbard from the University of St. Andrews in Scotland proved this in 2013 when they published their experiments in a scientific paper entitled *'Seeing in 3-D with just one eye: Stereopsis without binocular vision*' in *Psychological Science*. They found from their experiments that a significant majority of subjects who looked at test images reported a change in perceived object size, distance, or both accompanying the impression of stereopsis. They concluded that, *'the explanation of monocular stereopsis based on picture-surface visibility, distance estimation, and scaling of absolute depth provides a plausible mechanistic basis for previous claims that changes in picture-surface visibility underlie shifts in perceived stereopsis in pictures'*, and that, *'contrary to long-held beliefs, stereopsis is not a simple by-product of binocular vision or visual parallax.'*

The ability to see a 2D picture in a limited 3D format with only one eye (Fig. 14.4) seems to be a message that Leonardo provided with his three images projected onto the rhombicuboctahedron in the *Pacioli Portrait* (Fig. 12.1). The two images above the water line are brought together as one image below the water line. How do you explain seeing a single image in the brain (or the visual nerve of the brain), from the two images on each eye (above the water) as opposed to seeing the three-dimensional image of the window that is totally out of his or our view? The three images on the polyhedron suggests that he is showing his frustration in not being able to reproduce on canvas the virtual 3D image of the window that he could see so easily out of the corner of his eye while painting the *Pacioli Portrait*. Leonardo might have envisaged some of the modern approaches to virtual reality that incorporate moving viewpoints and immersion spaces (e.g., images projected in and on the polyhedron), but he was defeated by the technical and engineering limitations of his day for creating a truly immersive virtual reality or layered holographic images. Many of the technical and performance issues that confronted Leonardo still are ongoing concerns for the virtual reality industry and developers to this day.

Leonardo's three images of the window on the rhombicuboctahedron perhaps parody the concept of looking through Alberti's window that provided a monocular match between a picture and a view of a scene from a single point. In this instance, we might speculate that vision with two eyes as depicted by the two images of the window above the waterline is optically and phenomenally different from that with one eye that is depicted by the single image of the window below the waterline. Leonardo's binocular images are placed in the air above the waterline, whereas Alberti's monocular image is drowned by water, but seen a lot clearer than the one above it in the air. Leonardo never solved the problem of being able to reproduce on canvas the virtual 3D image of the window that he could see so easily while painting the *Pacioli Portrait*. But, he determined that if you looked at his paintings with one eye through a spherical aperture such as using your thumb and forefinger shaped into a circle and closed the other eye, then observing the picture monocularly through an aperture results in seeing 3D shapes that can only be seen as 2D shapes with two eyes. Try it out and see if it works.

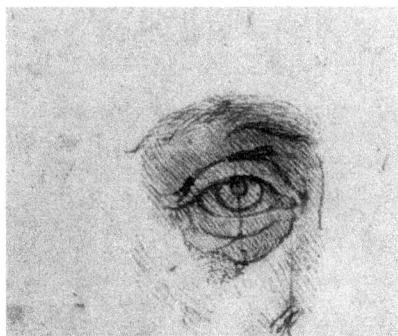

FIG. 14.4. One Eye Open Aperture Test. Using one eye to look at the Pacioli Portrait *reveals its 3-D effects.*

Stand about 3 to 6 feet directly in front of the *Pacioli Portrait* and use only the left eye (Fig. 14.4) to look through a small aperture (curl the thumb around the curled forefinger not much bigger than a large pea) at Pacioli in the centre of the painting. You will see a dramatic 3D effect bringing out the images of the hanging rhombicuboctahedron and Pacioli. On the other hand, if you use only the right eye (Fig. 14.4) to look through the same aperture at Pacioli, then you will see a dramatic 3D effect bringing out the images of Galeazzo Sanseverino, the dodecahedron and the closed red book as well as Luca Pacioli. Leonardo also used certain pictorial cues of contrast such as shadow and light and colour to enhance the 3D effect of visual depth in the phenomena that is now known in the scientific and clinical field of visual perception as *'da Vinci stereopsis'*.

If we look closely at the *Pacioli Portrait*, we can see occlusions of various kinds in the painting that psychologically stimulate our 3D perceptions.

These occlusions might not be recognised instantaneously and it might require a few minutes of concentrated viewing, but as the eye and the brain work together to identify the pictorial and *da Vinci stereoptic* cues the viewer will soon begin to see the overall painting in 3-dimensions without even realising that this has happened. The two dimensional rectangular plane of the *Pacioli Portrait* will transform into a 3D pictorial experience.

In 2015, two scientists in Sweden, Wei Wen and Siamak Khatibi, presented a paper at a scientific meeting on how depth perception was enhanced by monocular shadowing. They described a method using an array of interconnected cameras to capture images from a portrait and measured depth perception in human volunteers after they had looked at the changes in the shadow areas (shadow technique) of a classical Renaissance painting of a *Madonna Nativity* from the Kulenovic collection in Karlskrona Sweden. They analysed 100 points selected by volunteers on the photographed image of the portrait of the painting and used corner detection algorithms to measure the depth of perception associated with them (Fig. 14.5).

FIG. 14.5. One hundred depth perception points on the image of the portrait selected by human volunteers and corner detection algorithms as illustrated by Wen and Khatibi (2015).

Wen and Khatibi showed that the 3D effects of the classical painting could be measured as a perceptual and physical tangible phenomenon by measuring the depth perception of monocular shadows. They concluded that the shadow technique used in the portrait and the phantom type of *da Vinci stereopsis* could explain its 3D effect for viewers. Therefore, although a painted portrait is strongly limited to evoke any depth perception caused by its 2D physical shape and monocular pictorial cues, the implementation of the *da Vinci stereopsis* cues such as phantom ones (e.g., shadows) can stimulate real depth information.

They also produced an informative summary slide of the main depth perception cues incorporating the different binocular cues, monocular cues, pictorial and kinetic cues, and *da Vinci stereopsis* (Fig. 14.6).

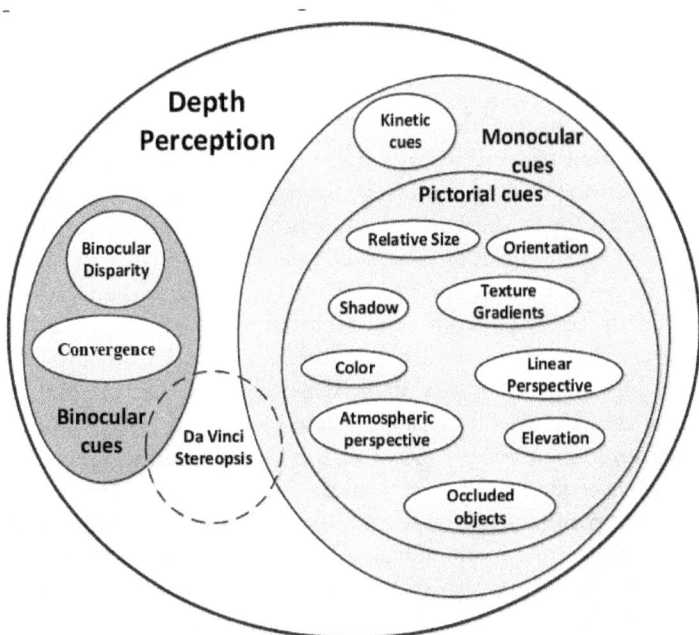

FIG. 14.6. *The cues involved in the depth perception as presented by Wen and Khatibi (2015).*

They described the relevance of the slide as follows (with their numbered citations removed from the text for ease of reading).

The depth cues in the single images can be pictorial cues or Da Vinci Stereopsis cues which are observed by two eyes. The binocular cues stimulate a depth perception by observing two images where each image is only seen by one eye. The binocular cues as presence of parallax disparities in the two observed retinal images cause the depth sensation. The parallax disparities refer to the objects, which are in overlapping region of a scene seen by the two eyes. They also refer to points within objects that are well defined, such as edge points. The binocular cues in absence of parallax disparities but presence of shadows in the two observed retinal images may also cause the depth perception. The shadows can be defined as regions in an image, which have abrupt luminance and/or color changes but are neither edges nor boundaries. The da Vinci stereopsis cues in single images, as a phenomenon, have a close relation to binocular cues of shadows stereopsis in two images. In binocular observation of the da Vinci Stereopsis cues, the entire observation region is not seen by two eyes. Assuming the observed region has a distinguishable background and foreground objects, when part of the background is occluded by the foreground objects, some regions are seen only by one eye which are called monocular regions. The monocular regions left out the use of parallax disparity cues in the related regions on the observed two images. However the monocular regions can contribute to stimulation of a depth perception if they are adjacent to e.g. a shading region, a texture area or a color differences area. The perceived depth is quantitative in nature. The perceived depth of a monocular point increases with increasing its separation from occluding edge.'

This explanation of the depth cues by Wei Wen and Siamak Khatibi provides us with a reasonable description of how to view and interpret the depth and pictorial cues in the *Pacioli Portrait*. Furthermore, they allow us to conclude that the subtle use of these depth and pictorial cues to enhance the 3D effect of the painting are additional signature clues in support of Leonardo da Vinci's attribution rather than Jacopo de Barbari or any other painter. These are the depth and pictorial cues of a scholar and an experimenter, the same or similar cues that Leonardo da Vinci used for his other paintings like the *Virgin of the Rocks* and the *Last Supper*, and his portraits of the *Musician*, the *Lady with the Ermine*, *La Belle Ferronnière*, the *Young Man with the Date 1494* (possibly the Duke of Milan, Gian Galeazzo Sforza) and *John the Baptist*. Many of the same cues are shared between these different paintings. Extrapolating from the Wen and Khatibi analysis of the classical painting by the unnamed artist in the Swedish collection, we might infer from their analysis that Leonardo da Vinci also knew a thing or two about how to create a 3D effect in his finished paintings.

Pictorial Space

Pictorial space is the illusory space in a two-dimensional painting that seems to recede backward into depth from the picture plane, giving the illusion of distance. The viewer can find at least sixteen areas of pictorial space in the *Pacioli Portrait*, counting the viewer's own location and then the space moving from the bottom of the panel and further back as the eye moves up and across the panel. The sixteen areas of pictorial space in the *Pacioli Portrait* are:

1) The viewer's space in front of the hanging inkwell.
2) The space of the hanging inkwell.
3) The space at the edge of the table with a small portion of the tip of the A-frame of the projector hanging over the edge of the green table.
4) The space on the front portion of the table containing the sponge, projector, pencil case, compass, folded yellow paper, and the polyhedron on top of the book.
5) The space at the back portion of the table containing the blackboard and slate, the chalk, the opened book and Luca Pacioli's left hand on the book.
6) The rhombicuboctahedron hanging above the blackboard and slate on the green table.
7) The space of the green table itself.
8) The space of the hands in front of Luca Pacioli.
9) The space of Luca Pacioli's head and hood.
10) The space of Luca Pacioli's robes, chest and shoulders.
11) The space between Luca Pacioli and Galeazzo Sanseverino.
12) The space of Galeazzo Sanseverino's bent left arm with the hand in the green glove.
13) The space of Galeazzo Sanseverino's chest and shoulders.
14) The space of Galeazzo Sanseverino's neck, face and head.
15) The space of the hair behind the face.
16) The black background. A mysterious psychological blackhole.

These 16 areas of pictorial space in the *Pacioli Portrait* provide a feeling of visual depth. This is a remarkable achievement for a double portraiture for its time and even today, more than five hundred years later; it still provides an effective illusion of distance and depth for the viewer.

Juan Carlos Meana in his published paper (2016) on the understanding of pictorial space listed ten space-building strategies of the Baroque. Many of them are seen in the *Pacioli Portrait*. As already mentioned above, there is the division of planes inside the painting so that several scenes are brought together. There is the use of dark backgrounds to leave an indeterminate mysterious space at the back of the scene and that enables the foregrounds to show up sharply contrasting the light and dark areas. The elements in the foreground appear to come out into the viewer's space: the table, inkwell, set-square, pen case, red book and dodecahedron. The gaze of the characters in the scene occupies the space of the viewer and attracts the observer into the space of the painting. The two characters' poses and expressions are theatrical (dramatic, contemplative, surprised). The gaze of Galeazzo Sanseverino follows the viewer everywhere even if the viewer observes the scene from outside the right or left edge of the painting. The

Renaissance notion of painting in a window is also in the *Pacioli Portrait* where a reflected window is incorporated three-times in the window-like, hanging rhombicuboctahedron. The reflected outdoor scene, although miniaturised, provides an awareness of what is outside the indoor scene. The painter also provides objects of wonder or confusion in the foreground on a green table. These objects across different pictorial spaces of the green table provide a rhetorical riddle with pictorial and spatial codes to encourage audience participation. What are all these different objects on the table and why are they there?

Pacioli's Wandering Eyes and Stereoblindness

Another important example of monocular depth cues in Leonardo da Vinci's painting is the use of aligned eyes and misaligned eyes as kinetic symbols of differences in depth perception. In 2006, Brenda Patoine interviewed Margaret Livingstone, a vision scientist, and obtained the following answers to her questions:

Q: Another interest of your laboratory is to use what you've learned about vision to explain some aspects of art. What do you think Leonardo da Vinci understood about color and light that neuroscience is just beginning to unravel?
A: Leonardo da Vinci produced an illusory dynamic quality in the Mona Lisa. People love this painting because her smile seems to come and go; her expression is so dynamic that she seems almost alive. When you look at a reproduction of this painting (or better still the original), look at her eyes and observe how much she seems to be smiling; then look directly at her mouth and see if she doesn't seem to be much less cheerful. Look back and forth between her eyes and her mouth and see if you don't see a systematic change in her expression.

The art historians said that her smile was blurry (sfumato) and therefore ambiguous, so her expression depended on the observer's imagination. But I find that her expression is systematically related to how far from her mouth my gaze is. Your central vision has much higher resolution than your peripheral vision; that's why you move your eyes when you read. You can see tiny detailed things much better than big blurry things with your central vision, but the reverse is true of your peripheral vision. Mona Lisa's smile is blurry, therefore it's much more apparent to your peripheral vision than to your central vision (see image). She seems to be smiling more when you're not looking directly at her mouth, and she stops smiling as soon as you look at her mouth. This gives the painting a dynamic, even coy, quality.

It is not clear to me whether Leonardo knew this explicitly. He wrote about a lot of his painting techniques and their scientific basis, but he never described this phenomenon explicitly. He was apparently very fond of this painting, and, as far as we know, he never did this again.
Q: You have suggested that stereoblindness, an impairment in one aspect of depth perception might actually be an asset for artists, enabling them to better render 3-D scenes on a flat surface. What evidence have you uncovered that many famous artists might have had deficits in depth perception?
A: We have two eyes that are horizontally displaced, so they see the world from two slightly different perspectives. As Leonardo da Vinci noted centuries ago, these viewpoints produce two distinct retinal images. Try this: hold your two index fingers up with one about ten inches from your nose and the other a dozen inches away, directly behind the first. Now look at your fingers

CHAPTER 14

out of one eye at a time and you will notice that the two "scenes" vary significantly. The brain uses these differences between the retinal images, in addition to other monocular depth cues, to estimate distance and generate a rich perception of depth.

This phenomenon, known as stereopsis, is just one important cue for depth perception; others include perspective, shading, occlusion, haze, and relative motion. Our visual system integrates all of these cues, enabling us to navigate through our environment. In paintings, though, only the monocular static cues can contribute to the illusion of depth; stereopsis and relative motion reveal that the canvas is actually flat. So the next time you find yourself looking at a painting rich in depth cues, stand at arm's length and try closing one eye; you may experience more of the illusion of depth that the painter was trying to achieve.

The ability of painters to translate the three-dimensional world into two dimensions is remarkable. Perhaps more astonishing, however, is the curious feat our visual systems perform in enabling us to perceive the visual world as three-dimensional in the first place. The brain's only visual input comes from a pair of two-dimensional images; the retinal images are, after all, flat. Our brains then convert these flat images into a vividly three-dimensional experience by using the same cues a painter employs, plus stereopsis and relative motion.

Our brains convert flat images into a vividly three-dimensional experience by using the same cues a painter employs, plus stereopsis and relative motion.

Just as stereopsis is a hindrance to the viewer who wants to see all the depth the artist put into the painting, it can also be a hindrance to the artist trying to depict three-dimensional scenes on canvas. Art teachers often instruct students to close one eye when viewing a scene in order to flatten it. I have therefore suggested that stereoblindness might prove an asset rather than a handicap to an artist. A person lacking stereopsis might become more sensitive to other (monocular) depth cues, such as shading, perspective, and occlusion—precisely those cues artists can render in paintings.

Stereoblindness is not a prerequisite for artistic talent. Yet the notion that stereoblindness might prove an asset for painters demonstrates the broader possibility that other aspects of brain organisation considered detrimental under some conditions might offer advantages under other circumstances. Indeed, many talented artists, musicians, mathematicians, and engineers are dyslexic. It is often thought that the over-representation of dyslexics among artists and musicians represents a compensation for failure in conventional academic fields. Yet growing evidence suggests that the correlation may be based, in part, on a positive correlation between dyslexia and extraordinary talent.

Bevil Conway, himself a stereoblind artist, and I have suggested that a number of very talented artists might have been stereoblind, a notion based on looking at photographs of them and finding that their eyes are misaligned. Stereopsis requires precise eye alignment; therefore, people whose eyes are misaligned usually have poor or no stereopsis; they have fine depth perception because they use other depth cues to gauge distance and depth. We recently suggested that Rembrandt was likely to have been stereoblind because he usually portrays himself as having divergent eyes. Misaligned eyes might seem like a stylism in a painting, except for the fact that the same eye is usually deviated in all Rembrandt's self portraits, and the opposite eye deviates in his etchings. Since an etching is reversed in the printing process, this mirror reversal of his eye deviation between the paintings and the etchings suggests that the deviating eye was something in his physiognomy that he accurately portrayed.'

Dr. Margaret Livingstone's following comment is worth re-emphasising: '*Stereopsis requires precise eye alignment; therefore, people whose eyes are misaligned*

usually have poor or no stereopsis; they have fine depth perception because they use other depth cues to gauge distance and depth.'

This is relevant to the *Pacioli Portrait* because Luca Pacioli also has misaligned divergent eyes staring towards the hanging polyhedron. In contrast, Galeazzo Sanseverino has perfectly precise alignment even while he stares out at us rather seriously with no evidence of a smile. Luca Pacioli's eye misalignment is intriguing because one of his eyes stares at the rhombicuboctahedron and the other eye stares at some undefined point in space. The meaning of this difference in eye alignment between the two main characters in the context of the painting is ambiguous. Does Leonardo imply that they have a different view of the world and that Luca Pacioli is more monocular than Galeazzo Sanseverino or vice versa because of stereopsis. My interpretation of the different eye alignments is that Leonardo has sent us the message that Pacioli's gaze is an important pointing device that he can point to an object in real space (the rhombicuboctahedron) with one eye and to an undefined point, off centre and in outer space with the other averted eye. Pacioli's gaze is saying, 'look at that hanging rhombicuboctahedron – it's such a marvellous symbol that has something important to do with the space in the universe and God. What could it be?' His double gaze to two different points in space is unintentionally non-mechanical compared to him intentionally pointing with a finger on an open page of a book or with a pointer on the blackboard, and it is nonintrusive and subtle. It is subtler than Galeazzo Sanseverino's gaze that is targeted directly at us and looks a lot more antisocial and aggressive and less contemplative than Pacioli's gaze.

Leonardo also created medical portraits so it might simply be that he is showing us that Luca Pacioli had divergent eyes. *Luca Pacioli* was not the only one that Leonardo provided with divergent or misaligned eyes because *John the Baptist* has divergent eyes. Even *Mona Lisa* has a hint of misalignment to suggest that she may have had poor depth perception, and *Mona Lisa*'s eye pathology is the subject of several medical and scientific publications (see the published paper by Kulski (2018) in the References at the end of the chapter). It seems that Leonardo pioneered divergent eyes to make his portraits more interesting. There is no evidence that Jacopo de Barbari or Albrecht Durer introduced divergent eyes into any of their portraits. Rembrandt likely used divergent eyes in his self-portraits as a stylistic nod to Leonardo da Vinci, even if in reality Leonardo's own eyes did not diverge.

Two Paintings of the *Mona Lisa*: a Hypothetical Stereogram

There are two versions of the *Mona Lisa* painting that were suggested to be an intentional stereogram. The better-known version is at the Louvre in

Paris and the lesser-known version is at the Prado museum in Madrid. Carbon and Hesslinger claimed in a 2013 scientific publication *Perception* that these two versions of Leonardo's *Mona Lisa* were parts of a stereogram. They scanned the Prado version in Madrid, and they found underlying preparatory sketches and layers of paint corrections that appeared highly similar to those on the version in the Louvre Museum. They proposed that an apprentice working alongside Leonardo produced the Prado version, resulting in two images of the subject from slightly different viewpoints. They claimed that the differences between the two perspectives were confirmed both by subjective human judgements and objective analysis by computer modelling; these images '*can be combined to an image of Mona Lisa that has obvious stereoscopic qualities.*' While stereoscopic versions (with colours altered to match more closely) were presented, no data on perceived depth were provided. However, in 2017, in a more recent scientific analysis of the two *Mona Lisa* images, Kevin R. Brooks reported in a paper for *Iperception* that, '*contrary to the claims of Carbon and Hesslinger, there is no evidence of stereoscopic depth in any version of the Mona Lisa figures. The single marginally significant result identified here refers to the coherence of perceived depth in an image lacking stereoscopic depth. As such this result is most sensibly interpreted as a Type I error*' [A type I error is also known as a false positive error].

Sanseverino Stares Out with a *Mona Lisa* Gaze

The *Mona Lisa* 'gaze-effect' is an established scientific phenomenon. When looking at a portrait such as the *Mona Lisa*, the portrait's eyes appear to 'follow' the viewer as they move around and change their viewing angle. A number of studies found strong evidence for the *Mona Lisa* gaze-effect using various picture and observer displacements, and that the gaze-effect holds for portraits with direct gaze and observer displacements in the horizontal, vertical, and diagonal planes. The effect persists to a lesser degree even if the portrait has an averted gaze. For example, if we look at *Galeazzo Sanserverino's* portrait with his straight-ahead gaze in *Pacioli Portrait*, he appears to look directly into our eyes even if we step to the side of the painting. If we change our position relative to the picture, his eyes still maintain contact with our eyes. This change in position or 'rotation effect' also applies to Luca Pacioli with his averted gaze: he always appears to be looking to the side, regardless of our viewing position.

In 2015, the scientist Evgenia Boyarshaya and her colleagues published the results of their research on how the brain interpreted the *Mona Lisa* gaze-effect as neural correlates of centred and off-centred gaze. They used functional magnetic resonance imaging to scan the brain regions involved in gaze direction of volunteers who looked at pictures of portraits with varying gaze directions ranging between direct eye contact (0 degrees), gaze at the edge of the gaze cone (5 degrees), and averted gaze (10 degrees). They found that the brain response to gaze at the edge of the gaze cone was similar to that produced by direct eye contact and different from that produced by averted gaze. Although the brain clearly distinguished averted from centred direct gaze, a substantial change of vantage point did not alter neural activity, thus providing a possible explanation as to why a 'feeling' of eye contact is perceived even in decentred stimulus positions.

The power of *Mona Lisa's* gaze that Leonardo has used deliberately in his paintings to capture the attention of the viewer is that the direction of the gaze not only attracts the attention of the observer, but it also can reveal information about the painted subject's psychological state, albeit emotional, neutral or indifferent. The painted sitter is looking out at us as objects of their interest rather than *vice versa*. As Boyarshaya and her colleagues pointed out in their paper, '*gaze direction is a powerful cue for implicit (nonverbal) communication. The direction of gaze expresses communication disposition or attendance, synchronises turn talking, regulates level of emotionality, intimacy or affiliation and dominance, signals liking, attraction, credibility, and even mental health.*'

So, we can thank Leonardo da Vinci for drawing our attention to the *Mona Lisa* gaze-effect in painting ambiguous and illusionary 2D images. Examples of the *Mona Lisa* gaze-effect outside of art schools are also plentiful, especially in respect to situational and multiparty interaction and in the developing field of personal and interactive robotics where the heads and faces of robots are built with eyes and mouths to interact with human customers. We know that infants establish purposeful eye contact as early as 7 months of age and that they quickly learn to use their gaze for nonverbal communication and social interaction to provide information, express intimacy and familiarity, exercise social control, and facilitate services for their needs. Modelling and delivering accurate gaze targets for social functions such as expressing and communicating attitudes and emotions in personal interacting robots and talking heads is crucial in modern development of robotics. Traditionally, systems communicating through talking heads have been displayed to people using 2D displays, such as flat monitors with a need to eliminate the fixed *Mona Lisa* gaze-effect that either looks everybody in the eye or at nobody. In some situations, there is a need to use 2D displays to establish eye contact with one particular observer without simultaneously establishing eye contact with all others that might lead to unintended miscommunication and unexpected results.

One simple way to eliminate the *Mona Lisa* gaze-effect from a talking head or robot is to use a 3D display instead of a 2D display. Might this be what Luca Pacioli is contemplating while staring at the hanging rhombicuboctahedron? *'For a more realistic effect of my face and eyes, Leonardo should have projected the image of my head on to the 3D polyhedron instead of onto this 2D canvas.'*

According to the Swedish computer scientist Samer Al Moubayed and his colleagues, when their experiments compared the accuracy of the perception of gaze direction and *the Mona Lisa* gaze-effect in 2D and 3D projection surfaces, the results confirmed that a 3D projection surface eliminates the *Mona Lisa* gaze-effect and delivers very accurate gaze direction that is independent of the observer's viewing angle. Essentially, their experiments showed the difference between looking at the *Mona Lisa* gaze-effect gaze of a 3D sculpted head and that of a painted head on a 2D canvas. With the 2D canvas, the observers perceived a painted head in a virtual space being displayed through a flat 'window' (the frame of a painting or edges of a monitor) and saw the gaze direction as if they were standing directly in front of the window, regardless of actual position in the room. Therefore, any gaze directed straight out of the picture at an angle perpendicular to its surface always will be perceived as being directed at the observer as is the case with the *Mona Lisa*. Observers of 2D renditions can judge gaze angle relative to the monitor or the frame and interpret this as gaze angle relative to their position. However, in the case of the sculpted head, regardless of viewing angle, any gaze directed to the left or right will be perceived as being directed at something to the left or right of the observer, respectively. Also, the observers of a 3D sculpture have more choices to establish their viewing angle to experience different views independent of each other; that is, if the observer moves around the sculpted head, then the observed perspective will change accordingly. This essentially is the same message that Leonardo has sent us more than 500 years ago within the *Pacioli Portrait*. That is, if you project an image of *Mona Lisa*'s head onto the 3D surface of an opaque hanging sphere like the rhombicuboctahedron or some other polyhedron then you will see her head or face without the *Mona Lisa* gaze-effect because it will be like a sculpted head that you can move around without her eyes following you, unless the sphere is transparent, and even then, her eyes will be hidden from your view at certain viewing angles.

The *Mona Lisa* Smile

The *Mona Lisa* painting by Leonardo da Vinci is famous for her smile. Various neuroscientists have tackled the question of how did Leonardo achieve her enigmatic smile. In general, the Margaret Livingstone opinion prevails that the ambiguity of the facial emotion resulted from the superimposition of two conflicting information cues in two different spatial frequency bands. A smile is visible when only the low spatial frequencies are considered, but a more neutral emotion is seen when all spatial frequencies are considered. The ambiguity of *Mona Lisa's* smile is most striking if the observer looks quickly from the mouth to the eyes and back to the mouth because then her mouth is seen slightly blurred in the visual periphery where only the low spatial frequency information is available and her emotion is interpreted to be a smile. '*She seems to be smiling more when you're not looking directly at her mouth, and she stops smiling as soon as you look at her mouth*'. To quantify whether the change of emotion came mostly from the mouth region, Leonid L. Kontsevich and Christopher W. Tyler of the Smith-Kettlewell Research Institute in San Francisco added random luminance noise to the lower region of *Mona Lisa's* face and they concluded that their survey and statistical analysis indicated that there were no potentially meaningful areas consistently related to the SAD–HAPPY change of facial expression other than the mouth corners. The perceived emotional expression in the eyes was solely attributable to a configurational effect projecting from the mouth region.

Pascal Mamassian provided an useful overview in Vision Research in 2008 on the ambiguities and conventions in the perception of visual art with a survey of the various works related to these ambiguities in composition, spatial scale, illumination and colour, three-dimensional layout, shape, and movement. He supported Margaret Livingstone's interpretation of the ambiguity of the facial emotion, but also provided an alternative view using an illusionary portrait of *Voltaire* by Dali for comparison with *Mona Lisa's* face and concluded that both *Mona Lisa's* enigmatic smile and the disappearing bust of *Voltaire* comes from the ambiguous interpretation of the shadows in the paintings.

> '*Leonardo da Vinci took great troubles to depict highly saturated shadows around the mouth thanks to the delicate sfumato technique which consists in overlaying multiple translucent layers of paint. (Elias & Cotte, 2008). The smile of Mona Lisa at low spatial frequencies comes from the large shadows of her cheekbones. If these shadows were properly interpreted, they could be discounted when the observer looks at the mouth, and thus the emotion of the mouth should not change when one considers different frequency bands. Similarly, the nuns in Dali's painting are defined from the shadows of the brow ridges and cheekbones of Voltaire, providing the hats and the dresses of the nuns. One sees Voltaire when the dark regions of the painting are interpreted as shadows and the two nuns when they are interpreted as dark surface material. By default, shadows tend to form large dark areas in a painting and as such contribute to the low spatial frequency information of the image. If these shadows are placed in specific areas (near the mouth in Mona Lisa and under the brow ridge in the disappearing bust of Voltaire), they can lose their role as shadows and offer an ambiguity to the interpretation of the painting.*'

Thus, Pascal Mamassian has provided a reasonable explanation for *Mona Lisa's* changing smile based on changes in both depth perception and the

CHAPTER 14

shadowy occlusions seen with the *'da Vinci stereopsis'* phantom type phenomenon that was discussed earlier in this chapter.

Where to Stand to Look at the *Pacioli Portrait*

Because Leonardo had studied the perspective of light rays and understood the pathway of light rays from the light source to the eyes and concepts such as incidence and reflective light, and he was a painter, he could provide sound advice where to stand to view a picture in a room:

'547. Where A Spectator Should Stand To Look At A Picture. Supposing _a b_ to be the picture and _d_ to be the light, I say that if you place yourself between _c_ and _e_ you will not understand the picture well and particularly if it is done in oils, or still more if it is varnished, because it will be lustrous and somewhat of the nature of a mirror. And for this reason the nearer you go towards the point _c_, the less you will see, because the rays of light falling from the window on the picture are reflected to that point. But if you place yourself between _e_ and _d_ you will get a good view of it, and the more so as you approach the point _d_, because that spot is least exposed to these reflected rays of light.'

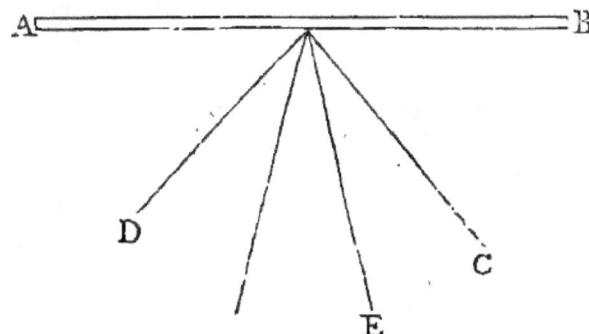

FIG. 14.7. *A scheme provide by Leonardo da Vinci for the spectator to know where to stand to look at a picture. Image adapted from* Treatise for Painting *by Leonardo da Vinci (The 1877 edition translated by JF Rigaud).*

Paragone: A Need for an In-depth Analysis of the *Pacioli Portrait*

Leonardo wrote in his *Treatise on Painting* that, *'A Painting, though conducted with the greatest Art and finished to the last Perfection, both with regard to its Contours, its Lights, its Shadows and its Colours, can never show a Relievo equal to that of Natural Objects, unless these be viewed at a Distance and with a single Eye.'* That is, he concluded that the perception of depth is incomplete in a painting, unlike that for a natural scene viewed with two eyes. He believed that a flat painting could never fully recreate the depth that is experienced when viewing real objects, unless it is viewed with one eye. According to Wade, Ono and Lillakas (2001), Leonardo struggled with representations of reality all his life because he could not depict 3D on a 2D canvas. In this regard, the hanging rhombicuboctahedron might show off both Leonardo da Vinci's frustration and solution for solving the depiction of 3D, not as flat painting, but as a 3D projection. He could have shown us his version of a 3D portrait using a sphere or polyhedron, but strangely chose not to. Perhaps, this was straying far too much towards sculpture than painting, and after all, he did condemn sculpture as an inferior art form when compared to painting. This was his *Paragone* (comparison) argument, the supremacy of painting over the arts of poetry, music, and sculpture. Painting required more mental ability than physical effort and the technical skill was important in the painters' attempts to elevate their art to the level of a learned, scholarly endeavour. However, Leonardo's *Paragone* has been argued variously for and against by the Leonardeschi and art scholars and historians, with some even suggesting that he never actually took a definite stand either way about the superiority of one form over another, but instead, that his argument was a rhetorical exercise to promote and discuss the arts, medicine and science in the context of dialectic conventions of the time. This latter view is Claire Farago's argument in her systematic study of 46 passages compiled from 18 of Leonardo's notebooks and their relationship to his writings on painting. The painter and art historian Giorgio Vasari, a generation or two after Leonardo, argued that drawing is the father of all arts, and as such, the most important one. Nevertheless, Leonardo agreed with the Florentine architect and sculptor Filarete (Antonio di Pietro Averlino) before him that painting has greater potential for naturalistic representation because of its ability to render colour and texture to create the illusion of any material or object. Possibly, that is why the hanging rhombicuboctahedron was painted transparent without adding the portrait of an opaque solid face and instead included three small images of a reflected window scene on the hanging structure. A sculptor or glassblower can make a transparent object, but he cannot easily include it in a complex scene like the *Pacioli Portrait*. In this regard, it is interesting to reiterate that a modern computer scientist questioned the realism of the painted hanging rhombicuboctahedron because such a structure could not be easily built of glass with a large volume of water and remain suspended by such a thin, unnatural thread without crashing to the floor. Thus, painting also has greater potential for an unnaturalistic or fantasy representation because of its ability to create the illusion of any material or object that might not be constructed easily.

We can look at the *Pacioli Portrait* and easily see that it is part of Leonardo da Vinci's *Paragone* debate showing us the strong connection between painting, drawing, mathematics, architecture, education (learned books) and sponsorship. Yes, without financial support, sponsorship and education, the art of painting could never have flourished in Leonardo's time. The rich (Galeazzo Sanseverino, Ludovico il Moro Sforza) and the Catholic Church (Luca Pacioli) were great educators, promoters and sponsors of the arts and the talented artists like Leonardo, Botticelli, Raphael and Michelangelo.

When I look at a reproduction of the *Pacioli Portrait* I think, yes, Leonardo has achieved a stunning depth of field on a 2D canvas. Was the *Pacioli Portrait* an experimental attempt to address the problem of depth perception and how to create a more satisfying pictorial representation of the potential reality of two contrasting subjects painted onto a rectangular 2D canvas? When I asked a small sample of people to view a reproduction of the painting through the One Eye Aperture Test, all my test viewers saw the painting in 3D as they slowly moved their eyes across the painting, briefly pausing at particular vantage points. Of course, my sample size was too small (less than ten) for reliable statistical conclusions and the results were based on subjective opinions of the viewers to my questions such as: Can you see a 3D effect? What stands out most? Why do you think the 3D effect works for you? Undoubtedly, it would be a much more reliable analysis if the professionals and academics assess the 3D effect in the *Pacioli Portrait* using their scientific instruments and analytical methods. I would like to know how does the 3D effect in *Pacioli Portrait* compare to Leonardo's other paintings and those of other painters before, during and after his life.

References

Alberti, LB (1966). On painting. (Trans. by J. R. Spencer), New Haven: Yale University Press. (Original work published (1435). Della pittura. Florence).

Al Moubayed S, Edlund J, Beskow J (2012). Taming Mona Lisa: Communicating gaze faithfully in 2D and 3D facial projections. ACM Trans. Interact. Intell. Syst. 1, 2, Article 11, 25 pages. *DOI = 10.1145/2070719.2070724.* http://doi.acm.org/10.1145/2070719.2070724

Azzolini, Monica (2005). In praise of art: text and context of Leonardo's Paragone and its critique of the arts and sciences. Renaissance Studies 19(4):487-510.

Boyarshaya E, Sebastian A, Bauermann T, Hecht H, Tuscher O (2015). The Mona Lisa effect: Neural correlates of centered and off-centered gaze. Human Brain Mapping 36:619–632.

Brooks KR (2017). Depth Perception and the History of Three-Dimensional Art: Who Produced the First Stereoscopic Images? Iperception8(1): 2041669516680114. *doi: 10.1177/2041669516680011.*

Carbon CC, Hesslinger VM (2013). DaVinci's Mona Lisa entering the next dimension. Perception 42(8):887-93.

Cavanagh P, Leclerc YG (1989). Shape from shadows. Journal of Experimental Psychology: Human Perception & Performance 15(1):3-27.

Cook M, Gillam B (2004). Depth of monocular elements in a binocular scene: The conditions for da Vinci stereopsis. Journal of Experimental Psychology 30:92–103.

da Vinci, Leonardo (1877). A treatise on painting (Trans. John F. Rigaud). London: George Bell and Sons. Original publication, 1651.

Elias M, Cotte P (2008). Multispectral camera and radiative transfer equation used to depict Leonardo's sfumato in Mona Lisa. Applied Optics 47:2146–2154.

Farago, Claire J (1992). Leonardo da Vinci's Paragone: A Critical Interpretation with a New Edition of the Text in the Codex Urbinas. (Leiden).

Gillam B (2011). Occlusion issues in early Renaissance art. i-Perception 2:1076-1097. *dx.doi.org/10.1068/i0468aap*

Gillam B, Borsting E (1988). The role of monocular regions in stereoscopic displays. Perception 17(5):603–608. *Doi: 10.1068/p170603. PMID 3249668.*

Gillam B, Nakayama K (1999). Quantitative depth for a phantom surface can be based on cyclopean occlusion cues alone. Vision Research 39:109–112.

Goldstein EB (2001). Pictorial perception and art. In E. B. Goldstein (Ed.), Blackwell handbook of perception. pp. 344–378. Oxford, UK: Blackwell.

Harris JM, Wilcox LM (2009). The role of monocularly visible regions in depth and surface perception. Vision Research 49:2666-2685.

Howard IP, Rogers BJ (2012). Perceiving in Depth, New York: Oxford University Press. *ISBN 978-0-199-76414-3, 2012.*

Iyer AV, Burge J (2018). Depth variation and stereo processing tasks in natural scenes. J Vis. 18(6):4. *doi: 10.1167/18.6.4.*

Kontsevich LL, Tyler CW (2004). What makes Mona Lisa smile? Vision Research 44:1493–1498.

Kulski JK (2018). The Mona Lisa portrait: Leonardo's personal and political tribute to Isabella Aragon Sforza, the Duchess of Milan. International Journal of Art and Art History 6(2):31-50. *DOI: 10.15640/ijaah.v6n2p5.*
  http://ijaahnet.com/journals/ijaah/Vol_6_No_2_December_2018/5.pdf

Liu L, Stevenson SB, Schor CM (1994) Quantitative stereoscopic depth without binocular correspondence. Nature 367:66–69.

Livingstone MS, Hubel DH (1987). Psychophysical evidence for separate channels for the perception of form, color, movement, and depth. The Journal of Neuroscience 7:3416–3468.

Livingstone MS (2002). Vision and art: The biology of seeing. New York: Harry N. Abrams.

Makino Y, Yano M (2006). Pictorial cues constrain depth in da Vinci stereopsis. Vision Research 46:91–105.

Mamassian P (2008). Ambiguities and conventions in the perception of visual art. Vision Research 48:2143–2153.

Meana JC (2016). An Approach to the Understanding of Pictorial Space: A Methodological Proposal Based on Three Case Studies. Creative Education 7: 1891-1898. *http://dx.doi.org/10.4236/ce.2016.714191*

Nakayama K, Shimojo S (1990). Da Vinci stereopsis: Depth and subjective occluding contours from unpaired image points. Vision Research 30(11):1811–1825.

Makino Y, Yano M (2005). Pictorial cues constrain depth in da Vinci stereopsis. Vision Res 46(1-2):91-105.

Patoine B (2006). Visual System Processing and Artistic Genius. An Interview with Margaret Livingstone, Ph.D.
http://www.dana.org/Publications/ReportDetails.aspx?id=44154

Santos-Bueso E, Vico-Ruiz E, García-Sánchez J (2012). Eye pathology in the paintings by Leonardo da Vinci (iii). Comparative study between the Mona Lisa and the copy in the Prado Museum in Madrid. Arch Soc Esp Oftalmol 87:381-3. DOI: 10.1016/j.oftal.2012.06.015

Sato T (2012). Mona Lisa effect of eyes and face. i-Perception 3:707. dx.doi.org/10.1068/if707

Tsirlin I, Wilcox LM, Allison RS (2012). Da Vinci decoded: Does da Vinci stereopsis rely on disparity? Journal of Vision 12(12):2.
http://www.journalofvision.org/12/12/2, doi:10.1167/12.12.2.

Tsirlin I, Wilcox LM, Allison RS (2014). A computational theory of da Vinci stereopsis. Journal of Vision 14(7):5,1–26.
https://jov.arvojournals.org/pdfaccess.ashx?url=/data/journals/jov/933548/on 08/31/2018, http://www.journalofvision.org/content/14/7/5

Vishwanath D, Hibbard PB (2013). Seeing in 3-D with just one eye: Stereopsis without binocular vision. Psychological Science 24(9):1673–1685. DOI: 10.1177/0956797613477867

Wade NJ, Ono H (2012). Early studies of binocular and stereoscopic vision. Review. Japanese Psychological Research 54:54-76. doi: 10.1111/j.1468-5884.2011.00505.x

Wade NJ, Ono H, Lillakas L (2001). Leonardo da Vinci's struggles with representations of reality. Leonardo 34:231–235.

Wardle SG, Gillam BJ (2013). Phantom surfaces in da Vinci stereopsis. Journal of Vision 13(2):16.

Wen W, Khatibi S (2015). Towards measuring of depth perception from monocular shadow technique with application in classical painting. Conference paper. https://www.researchgate.net/publication/285577969

Wijntjes MWA (2014). A New View Through Alberti's Window. Journal of Experimental Psychology Human Perception & Performance 40(2) DOI: 10.1037/a0035396

Zannoli M, Mamassian P (2011). The role of transparency in da Vinci stereopsis. Vision Research 51:2186–2197.

Zannoli M, Love GD, Narain R, Banks MS (2016). Blur and the perception of depth at occlusions. Journal of Vision 16(6):17, 1–25. doi:10.1167/16.6.17.

15

VINCI'S ALPHABETIC TYPE SETS

Leonardo da Vinci's Alphabetic Printing Style

The printing style of the Roman lettering and Arabic numbers painted in the *Pacioli Portrait* are strikingly similar to that seen in two of his other paintings, *Ginevra de' Benci* and *Young Man Aged 20* and in his design of the capital letters used in the *Divine Proportion*. This similarity between different paintings appears to further support Leonardo da Vinci's attribution of the *Pacioli Portrait* where the lettering style of **EUCLID** on the drawing tablet, **LI. R. LUC.BUR** on the spine of the red book, and **IACO.B AR. VIGEN NIS. P. 1495** printed on the notepaper with the black fly is essentially the same typeface that is used in the *Ginevra de' Benci* painting that has **VIRTUTEM FOREM** printed on a scroll inscribed on the back of the painting. The Italian art critic Giovanni Barca in his paper entitled *IACO. BAR. VIGENNIS P.1495. Enigma e Secretissima Scientia* highlighted the similarity of the use of the alphabetic types in a direct comparison between the *Ginevra de' Benci* painting of 1474, the *Pacioli Portrait* and the *Divine Proportion* of 1497. This comparison is reproduced in Fig. 15.1 and Fig. 15.2.

Another intriguing similarity in the use of Leonardo's alphabetic types can be seen in two portraits of a young man of Milan who is likely to be the young duke Gian Galeazzo Sforza who died in suspicious circumstances on the 20th/21st of October in 1494. The painters responsible for these two portraits are not known, but they are likely to have been Leonardo da Vinci and/or Marco d'Oggiono or Ambrogio de Predis. In the portrait of the *Young Man Aged 20* by Marco d'Oggiono/Leonardo da Vinci, the youngman holds a scroll in his fingers with the following printed message **1494. AAR. ANO.20** (Fig. 15.3). Look at the distinctive fusion of **AR (A/R)** on the notepaper in the *Pacioli Portrait* and the similar fusion of letters used again in the portrait of the *Young Man Aged 20* with the ticker tape (**1494. AAR** [or **MR** or **MP**] **ANO. 20**) held between the thumb and finger of the left hand. Is this an affectation or pictorial cue? ANO could mean anonymous or 'the other person', or it might be the last three letters of MILANO if it is the portrait of the Duke of Milan who died in 1494 under extraordinary suspicious circumstances. The number 20 also might be somewhat symbolic and provocative in the political circumstances of Milan at that time because Gian Galeazzo Maria Sforza was born on the 20th of June 1469 and he died, allegedly by poisoning, on the 20th/21st of October 1494. However, this is not the traditionally accepted interpretation of the painting. The cryptic monogram is believed by some to be composed of the letters AMPRF and taken to mean AM(brosius) Pr(eda) Fecit - Ambrogio de Predis made this, although others have opposed this interpretation because of Predis's different painting style (National Gallery, London). In general, the scroll is believed to record the age of the sitter in the portrait to be 20 years old.

FIG. 15.1. *Comparison of the alphabetical types used by Leonardo da Vinci in the Divine Proportion and on the back of his portrait of Ginevra de 'Benci. Reproduced from GA Barca's paper entitled 'IACO. BAR. VIGENNIS P.1495. Enigma e Secretissima Scientia'*

FIG. 15.2. *Comparison of the alphabetical types used by Leonardo da Vinci in the Portrait of Luca Pacioli and in The Divine Proportion. Reproduced from GA Barca's paper entitled 'IACO. BAR. VIGENNIS P.1495. Enigma e Secretissima Scientia'*

In Milan, the year of 1494 was an important year to remember and commemorate because it was when the Regent and Governor Ludovico Sforza organised the marriage between the Holy Roman Emperor Maximilian and his niece, Bianca Maria Sforza; when he encouraged the young French king Charles VIII to enter Lombardy on his way to invade Rome and Naples; and when he allegedly murdered his nephew, the young duke of Milan Gian Galeazzo Sforza; and then usurped the Duchy of Milan from Isabella of Aragon and her five year old son Francesco II Sforza, the Duke of Pavia. This was the year when Ludovico Sforza declared himself officially as the Duke of Milan immediately after the Gian Galeazzo Sforza's death because he had already secretly obtained the official investiture from the Holy Roman Emperor Maximilian I. In May of 1495, the French king Charles VIII had invaded and occupied Naples for a few weeks before Ludovico Sforza and the League of Venice turned against him. On the 20th of May in 1495, after the newly formed anti-French League of Venice threatening to cut off his return through northern Italy, Charles left Naples to return to France via Lombardy and a short intervening battle against Ludovico's mercenary forces.

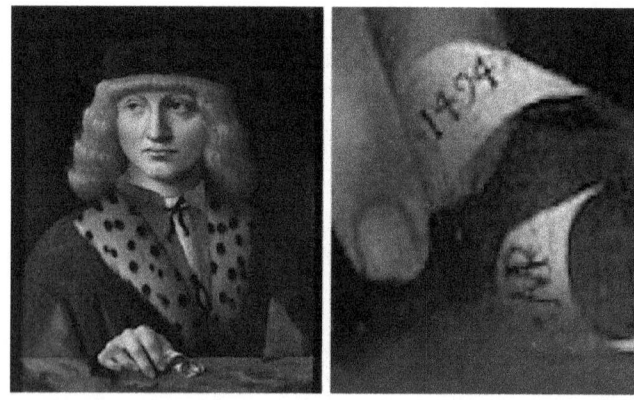

FIG. 15.3. *Portrait of the Young Man Aged 20 with ticker tape that reveals the print of 1494, ANO.20. VP or M° (morte) or MP.*

In the portrait of the *Young Man Aged 20* with ticker-tape (Fig. 15.3), Gian Galeazzo Sforza is dressed in blue and black, the colours of his uncle Ludovico Il Moro Sforza who usurped his crown and the Duchy of Milan. Gian Galeazzo Sforza looks forlorn and melancholic as if he has lost something that he knows that he will never retrieve. He holds a message in his right hand on which is written a partially visible message, 1494, AR, ANO, and 20; 1494 was the year that the French king Charles VIII visited him a few days before his death. AR is a Latin abbreviation for *Anno Regi* (Year of the King), ANO is Latin for 'the other person or party', and the number 20 was the day of the month that Gian Galeazzo Sforza was born and close to the day of his death. Many thought that he had died on the night of the 20th of October. The ANO can also be interpreted as the last three letters of Milano in Italian, that is, the portrait is of the Duke of Milano. Leonardo also added the same Vinci knotted bows to the young man's jacket that he and his assistants had presented in their earlier paintings of the young duke of Milan as St. Sebastian.

FIG. 15.4. *Portrait of a Young Man* by Leonardo da Vinci and/or Ambrogio de' Predis of a sad and dead Gian Galeazzo Sforza painted in his heraldic colours of red, green, and brown.

The other portrait of Gian Galeazzo Sforza that probably was produced by Leonardo and/or Ambrogio de' Predis is entitled as the *Portrait of a Young Man* and it portrays him in his heraldic colours of green and red and with his glistening golden hair (Fig. 15.4). A tinge of green is reflected in Gian Galeazzo's face and eyes, and green is the colour of arsenical dyes. The Latin inscription on the top, left hand side of the painting honours his life:

VITA, SI SCIAS UTI, LONGA EST, meaning *Life, if you know how to use it, is long enough.* It was a saying of Senaca the younger who was Gian Galeazzo Sforza's favourite Roman philosopher. Again, the alphabetic type mimics that seen in the *Pacioli Portrait*. The *Portrait of a Young Man* is held at the National Gallery and it is attributed traditionally to Giovanni Ambrogio de Predis rather than to Leonardo da Vinci, although de Predis painted mostly portraits in profile and rarely produced three-quarter poses. The extraordinary feature of the *Portrait of a Young Man* is that the young man wears the same red shirt with the same number of buttons and a similar coat as that worn by Galeazzo Sanseverino in the *Pacioli Portrait*. This identical red shirt cannot be a coincidence and it surely is further evidence that the *Pacioli Portrait* originated in Milan in the workshop of Leonardo da Vinci and not in Venice or Germany with the hand of Jacopo de' Barbari.

The Alphabetic Print of the *Divine Proportion*

The alphabetical characters used by Pacioli that he attached to the first printed edition of the *Divine Proportion* that was published in Venice in 1509 by the printer Paganino de' Paganini (Fig. 15.5) led to later scholars accusing him of plagiarising Leonardo da Vinci's alphabetic style. Pacioli is considered not to have had the practical and graphic sensibility to be the creator and executor of the elaborate alphabetic style used in the *Divine Proportion*. The French printer Geoffroy Tory accused Pacioli of plagiarism to the detriment of Leonardo in his 1529 treatise of printed letters *Champ Fleury*.

'Fra Luca Pacioli of Borgo San Sepolcro, of the Order of Friars Minor and theologian, who wrote in Italian vernacular a book titled Divine Proportion, and who intended to represent the aforementioned using Attic letters, has nothing at all to do with its descriptions or explanations; and I'm not surprised at all, because I have heard from some Italians that he has extracted his letters and taken them from Mr. Leonardo Vinci, who is deceased at Amboise and who was a very excellent person, philosopher and admirable painter and almost another Archimedes. It is said about Luca that he has printed his letters as if they were his own.'

Geoffroy Tory refers to the font that was used in the woodblocks for the capital letters at the beginning of the paragraphs in the printed version of the *Divine Proportion*. Luca Pacioli was known for his plagiarism or not to fully acknowledge the source of many of his ideas. This he did mainly in order not to interrupt his narrative by continually referencing a source; for the narrative and its message can readily become lost in the sources, notes, asides and their history. However, a reference list is often added at the end of the printed narrative or discourse to acknowledge the sources.

CHAPTER 15

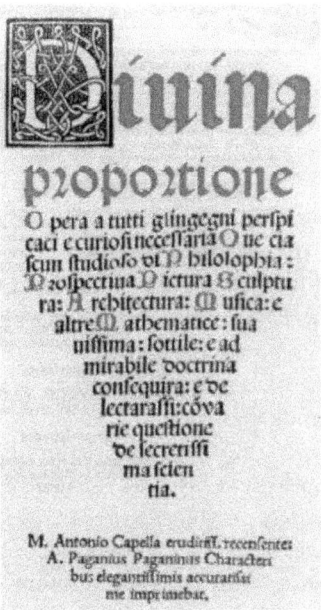

FIG. 15.5. Divine Proportion, written by Luca Pacioli with illustrations of geometric solids and decorated capital letters with the intertwining knots provided by Leonardo da Vinci and published in Venice in 1509 by the printer Paganino de' Paganini.

Leonardo da Vinci did not invent the alphabetic type sets used in his paintings or the printed version of the *Divine Proportion*. The alphabet that Leonardo used in his printing was based on the old Attic style of Greek capital letters used by the Romans, a type of alphabetic chiselling found on Roman monuments. The Roman Attic innovation was the application of a baseline - the imaginary line upon which most letters 'sit' and under which the descenders of certain letters extend. By introducing the baseline, the Romans ensured that their type, unlike the misaligned writing of the Greeks, was perfectly aligned in rows. This contributed greatly to the aesthetics of letters in handwritten manuscripts and then later for the letters used in the printing press methods. The alphabet used by the Romans consisted only of capital (upper case or majuscule) letters that were retained for formal inscriptions and emphasis in written documents. The languages that use the Latin alphabet generally use capital letters to begin paragraphs and sentences and for proper nouns. Many painters before or during the time of Leonardo da Vinci used the same or similar Roman Attic style. In 1460, Felice Feliciano produced his manuscript on the *Alphabetum Romanum* (*Roman Alphabet*), the first guide to the construction of antique letters using a scaffold of a circle and a square to form the shape of the letters. Leon Battista Alberti adapted Feliciano's circle and square method in 1467 to produce architectural inscriptions, but with slimmer and more elegant proportions. Leonardo's practice and design of the alphabetic letters also placed them within a circle and a square, but he often used the golden ratio in his distinctive way as beautifully illustrated in the printed version of the *Divine Proportion*. The Capital letter at the start of each paragraph in the *Divine Proportion* is intricately designed with Leonardo's intertwining Vinci knots (Fig. 15.5). Also, Leonardo exhibited a stylistic choice of greater originality than many of his contemporaries such as making the middle bar of E shorter than the others; and producing the R like the P within the intersections of the square except that the lower tail of the R passed beyond the intersections to the corner of the square. Also, the lower circle for the B was larger than the upper circle to provide a solid base. Albrecht Dürer also showed how to construct the letters of a Roman font in his 1525 publication the *Unterweysung*, using methods that were influenced by the *Divine Proportion*.

In comparing Jacopo de' Barbari's lettering, the clear difference between him and Leonardo was his preferred use of low case letters (such as in *Still-Life with Partridge and Iron Gloves*, 1504) instead of using the Leonardesque uppercase lettering. When Jacopo de' Barbari started copying Leonardo or Durer's upper case printing style, the capital letters became slightly more embellished than Leonardo's starker style. Barbari's alphabetic lettering was often uneven and varied between different paintings and wood engravings, whereas Leonardo remained largely consistent in form and style between different paintings. Leonardo had used the same alphabetic characters in his paintings since adding the printed cartouche to the rear of his portrait of *Ginevra de' Benci* in 1474, more than twenty years before he met Luca Pacioli in 1496 and well before Jacopo de' Barbari began to use them in his wood engravings to print aerial views such as *View of Venice* (1500) or in his mythological prints such as *The Guardian Angel* (1509).

References

Barca GA. IACO. BAR. VIGENNIS P.1495. Enigma e Secretissima Scientia. http://www.ritrattopacioli.it/Jacobarvigennis2.pdf

Magnaghi-Delfino, Paola and Norando, Tullia (2019). Luca Pacioli: A Friend of Leonardo da Vinci De Divina Proportione in Capital Letters. L. Cocchiarella (Ed.), ICGG 2018—Proceedings of the 18th International. Conference on Geometry and Graphics, Advances in Intelligent Systems and Computing 809:2205–2208. https://doi.org/10.1007/978-3-319-95588-9_203.

Magnaghi-Delfino, Paola and Norando, Tullia (2019). Luca Pacioli's *Alphabeto Dignissimo Antiquo*. A Geometrical Reconstruction.
https://www.academia.edu/14169739/Luca_Paciolis_alphabeto_dignissimo_antiquo_a_geometrical_reconstrstruction

Syson, Luke and Keith, Larry (2012). Leonardo da Vinci: painter at the Court of Milan. The National Gallery, London. *IBSN 9871857094909* (paperback).

PART 3

Colours, Dukes, Black Castle Rooms & Vinci's Academy

Black is like a broken vessel, which is deprived of the capacity to contain anything. ~ Leonardo da Vinci, (1452-1519)

16

LEONARDO'S COLOURS

The Essence of Colour

The essence of any painting including that of the *Pacioli Portrait* is its colour and form, which is the visible shape or configuration of something on the canvas. The colour in the painting can be the form itself as a natural thing or it can add to the form with various contrasts, functions and objectives. Leonardo da Vinci wrote a manuscript about colour (now lost) that he entitled a *Book on Colours* where he covered the theory, perspective and the preparation and use of colours for painting. Much of Leonardo's theory of colour was based on the writings of Aristotle who developed the first known theory of colour during the times of Ancient Greece. Aristotle postulated that God sent down colour from the heavens as celestial rays and he identified four colours corresponding to the four elements: yellow for earth, red for fire, blue for wind, and green for water. Leonardo da Vinci was probably the first to suggest an alternative hierarchy of colour beyond Aristotle's four colours. In his *Treatise on Painting*, he said that while philosophers viewed white as the 'cause, or the receiver' of colours and black as the absence of colour, both were essential to the painter, with white representing light, and black, darkness. The detailed understanding of the science of colour only really began in 1666, when Isaac Newton, using two prisms, observed that white light was composed of all the colours of the rainbow, and could be identified and ordered as a 'spectrum' of energies - or the proportional frequencies and inverse wavelengths. He assigned seven colours to the spectrum in an analogy to the musical scale. These were red (musical note C), orange (D), yellow (E), green (F), blue (G), indigo (A), and violet (B). The visible light spectrum ranges from about 400 nanometers for violet to 700 nanometers for red. Yet, **Leonardo also was aware that white light carried all the colours of the rainbow that he** described so beautifully in his *Treatise of Painting*. He saw the phenomenon of the visible colour spectrum as a rainbow projected on the floor by simply placing a glass full of water on the window sill and exposing it to the sun's rays.

287. Treatise of the rainbow in the last book on Painting, but first write the book on colours produced by the mixture of other colours, so as to be able to prove by those painters' colours how the colours of the rainbow are produced.

288. WHETHER THE COLOURS OF THE RAINBOW ARE PRODUCED BY THE SUN. The colours of the rainbow are not produced by the sun, for they occur in many ways without the sunshine; as may be seen by holding a glass of water up to the eye; when, in the glass--where there are those minute bubbles always seen in coarse glass--each bubble, even though the sun does not fall on it, will produce on one side all the colours of the rainbow; as you may see by placing the glass between the day light and your eye in such a way as that it is close to the eye, while on one side the glass admits the [diffused] light of the atmosphere, and on the other side the shadow of the wall on one side of the window; either left or right, it matters not which. Then, by turning the glass round you will see these colours all round the bubbles in the glass etc. And the rest shall be said in its place.

THAT THE EYE HAS NO PART IN PRODUCING THE COLOURS OF THE RAINBOW. In the experiment just described, the eye would seem to have some share in the colours of the rainbow, since these bubbles in the glass do not display the colours except through the medium of the eye. But, if you place the glass full of water on the window sill, in such a position as that the outer side is exposed to the sun's rays, you will see the same colours produced in the spot of light thrown through the glass and upon the floor, in a dark place, below the window; and as the eye is not here concerned in it, we may evidently, and with certainty pronounce that the eye has no share in producing them.

Leonardo's Colour Theory

About half of Leonardo's *Treatise on Painting* is about colour. However, by today's standards, most of it is mundane information. Most modern painters and designers would find little in the chapters that was of much use in their training at the art schools that would have covered it with greater thought, theory, practice, scientific theory and technical language. Leonardo provided little information for the painter about preparing or mixing colour pigments because it was the subject of a separate book and he also assumed that most painters would have received the basics as apprentices during training at their *Bottega* workshops. Instead, the colour in the *Treatise on Painting* was more about the physics of light, how colour is formed, the colour spectrum seen in a glass of water or a rainbow, why the sky is blue and usually not another colour (red sky at night). Much of his colour theory stemmed from and expanded on the writings of the ancient Greek, Aristotle. Leonardo's explanation for the blue colour of the sky is based on Aristotle's account that is surprisingly innovative and contemporary given the relatively poor understanding of physics in their time. In general, what Leonardo has written about colour in his *Treatise on Painting* has little direct relevance to the *Pacioli Portrait*. We can draw attention to a few chapters that are relevant to the painting. Since a significant amount of the *Pacioli Portrait* is its black background it is of interest to know what Leonardo told us about a black background in his *Notebooks* and *Treatise on Painting*.

'A painter should begin every canvas with a wash of black, because all things in nature are dark except where exposed by the light.'

On the other hand:

'For those colours which you wish to be beautiful, always first prepare a pure white ground.'

In his *Treatise*, he also wrote:

'(210) Of Backgrounds. To give a great effect to figures, you must oppose to a light one a dark ground, and to a dark figure a light ground, contrasting white with black, and black with white. In general, all contraries give a particular force and brilliancy of effect by their opposition.'

When contrasting white and black he wrote in item 222 of his *Treatise*:

'White is more capable of receiving all sorts of colour than the surface of any body whatever that is not transparent. To prove it, we shall say, that any void space is capable of receiving what another space, not void, cannot receive. In the same manner, a white surface, like a void space, being destitute of any colour, will be fittest to receive such as are conveyed to it from any other enlightened body, and will participate more of the colour than black can do; which latter, like a broken vessel, is not able to contain anything.
Black and white are not reckoned among colours; the one is the representative of darkness, the other of light: that is, one is a simple privation of light, the other is light itself. Yet I will not omit mentioning them, because there is nothing in painting more useful and necessary; since painting is but an effect produced by lights and shadows, viz., chiaro-scuo. After black and white come blue and yellow, then green and tawny or umber, and then purple and red. These eight colours are all that Nature produces. With these I begin my mixtures, first black and white, black and yellow, black and red; then yellow and red: but I shall treat more at length of these mixtures, in a separate work, which will be of great utility, nay very necessary.'

Following on, Leonardo writes:

'The first of all simple colours is white, though philosophers will not acknowledge either white or black to be a colour; because the first is the cause, or the receiver of colours, the other totally deprived of them. But as painters cannot do without either, we shall place them among the others; and according to this order of things, white will be the first, yellow the second, green the third, blue the fourth, red the fifth, and black the sixth. We shall set down white for the representative of light, without which no colour can be seen; yellow for the earth; green for water; blue for air; red for fire; and black for total darkness. If you wish to see by a short process the variety of all the mixed or composed colours, take some coloured glasses, and, through them, look at all the country round: you will find that the colour of each object will be altered and mixed with the colour of the glass through which it is seen. Observe which colour is made better, and which is hurt by the mixture.'

Leonardo seemed to write very little about the symbolism and psychology of colour and yet we know that he used colour skillfully for symbolic and psychological effect in the *Last Supper*, *Mona Lisa* and the *Lady with the Ermine*. Leonardo da Vinci probably understood the psychological effects of colour on the viewer more than any other painter in the Renaissance. In his *Treatise on Painting* (TP) and his *Notebooks*, he lists black, white, blue, yellow, green, ochre, purple and red as the eight colours with which a painter has to work. Ochre ranges in colour from yellow to deep orange or brown and he often used it as an undercoat in a number of his unfinished paintings such as *St. Jerome in the Wilderness* (1480), the *Adoration of the Magi* (1481), and the *Study for a Portrait of Isabella d'Este*.

He emphasised that *'nothing ever looks to be its real colour unless the light which illuminates it is entirely similar in colour'* (TP I 197). And this occurs very rarely because of other lights, shadows and the colour of the medium. Thus colour perspective supplements linear perspective. *'The eye can never arrive at perfect knowledge of the interval between the two objects at different distances by means of linear perspective alone unless assisted by colour perspective.'* Leonardo writes that black and white are not commonly included among colours because *'one is the absence of colour and the other is the source of colour'* (TP I 178). His combinations of these theories and techniques are the reasons why his painted artworks are so lifelike.

Colours in the *Pacioli Portrait*

The *Pacioli Portrait* has Leonardo's eight essential colours, black, white, grey, blue, red, green and varying degrees of brown or orange. The black background, green foreground, the grey of Pacioli's habit, and the dark blue of Sanseverino's coat dominate the picture. There is also black distributed as part of the blackboard, pencil case and inkwell, the blackfly, the black of the eyes and the shadows of Pacioli's habit. The white stands out brightly on Sanseverino's shirt, the cord around Pacioli's waist, the pages of the open book, the small lump of chalk between the open book and the chalkboard, and the circle and triangles drawn on the chalkboard. The various gradations of brown, yellow and orange are seen in the skin tones, Sanseverino and Pacioli's hair, the pointers, the wooden portion of the blackboard, the redbook holder and the octahedron, the sponge, set-square, the yellowed notepaper and the dotted fur linings of Sanseverino's coat. Sanseverino shirt underneath his coat is a bright red – perhaps to conjure up the thought that he has blood on his hands and body as a consequence of his political and financial intrigues. Then there is the bluish-green (cyan or turquoise) of Sanseverino's glove and a dab of sky blue in the images projected onto the rhombicuboctahedron. And that's pretty much the full range of a painter's colour palette. What's missing? Not much, perhaps a pink and violet.

Leonardo has used all of his eight essential colours in his *Pacioli Portrait* and added a ninth – the colour grey – the grey of the San Franciscan habit. He has not used grey often. It is rarely used in his other paintings. Grey is black mixed with white or white mixed with black, and like black or white, it is a neutral or achromatic colour, meaning that it is 'without colour'. Leonardo shows off his mastery as a painter by presenting us with an array of shades of grey ranging between black and white. It dominates the central portion of the painting. It dominates our eye over the black background and the blue coat of Galeazzo Sanseverino. We can easily see all the folds, pleats and shadows on Pacioli's grey habit, but we must strain our eyes to see them on Sanseverino's blue coat. The colour grey embodies Luca Pacioli as a celibate monk who has entered a mendicant religious order within the Catholic Church to adopt an ascetic lifestyle of poverty, travelling, and living in urban areas for purposes of preaching, evangelism, and ministry, especially to the poor. In comparison, the blue and red clothing on Galeazzo Sanseverino invoke a wealthy gentleman who is confident with his importance, significance, courage, leadership, vibrancy, libido, determination and energetic power.

Apart from using colour for establishing contrasts and a three-D effect in the *Pacioli Portrait*, Leonardo has used colour for mood, atmosphere, psychology and symbolism. The most obvious use of colour symbolism is the grey of Luca Pacioli's habit. It tells us that he is a member of the Franciscan order; a different colour, red, blue, green, orange, pinky-black would have implied a different order and something else to those in the know about Franciscan colours. In the following chapters we will see more about the less obvious colour symbolism, that the black and blue are used to convey the House colours of Ludovico il Moro Sforza, the green and brown convey the House colours of the young Duke of Milan Gian Galeazzo Sforza and that the red and white are the House colours of Galeazzo Sanseverino Sforza. The flag of the Ambrosian Republic of Milan in 1447 to 1450, like today, was the Cross of Ambrose, a red cross inside a white field. The Red Cross is also the flag of the Crusades and the symbol of victory over death. The Ambrosian Republic with its symbolic red cross replaced the Visconti flag and the Duchy of Milan for a few years after the death of the Duke of Milan Filippo Maria Visconti who had no male heir. It ended when Francesco Sforza overthrew the Republic and conquered Milan to establish the ruling House of Sforza. With the reestablishment of the Duchy of Milan, Francesco Sforza changed the flag from the red cross of Ambrose back to the one with the emblem of the House of Visconti, the *biscione* (a great serpent shown devouring a Saracen), and quartered with the imperial eagle of the Holy Roman Empire.

In the following chapters, I will highlight the symbolic nature of the colours green and black in the *Pacioli Portrait* and how they were used by Leonardo to represent the two dukes of Milan, Gian Galeazzo Sforza and Ludovico Moro Sforza, during his time in the Duchy of Milan from 1481 to 1499. However, to conclude this chapter and to better appreciate the psychological effect that the main colours in the *Pacioli Portrait* might have on the viewer I have included what the modern designer and colourist Jennifer Bourn has posted on her web page on the Internet about the impact of colour on emotions.

Color *has a huge impact on our emotions, our perceptions, and our spiritual and physical wellbeing. When choosing colors for your brand, color that will represent you, your business, and your message, are you choosing the right colors? Understanding the meaning behind color is important. When you understand the meaning and power a color holds you can leverage that to help you better communicate your message and connect with your clients and customers.*

Green*, the color of life, renewal, nature, and energy, is associated with meanings of growth, harmony, freshness, safety, fertility, and environment. Green is also traditionally associated with money, finances, banking, ambition, greed, jealousy, and Wall Street.* ***The color green*** *has healing power and is understood to be the most restful and relaxing color for the human eye to view. Green can help enhance vision, stability and endurance. It is a natural choice in interior design as an ideal background or backdrop because we as humans are so used to seeing it everywhere. With the color green's association with renewal, growth, and hope, often green stands for both a lack of experience and a need for growth. Green also stands for new growth and rebirth, common in the spring season when all of the plants are coming back to life with fresh growth and life after the cold winter months.*

CHAPTER 16

Bl**ack** is associated with power, fear, mystery, strength, authority, elegance, formality, death, evil, aggression, authority, rebellion, and sophistication. Black is required for all other colors to have depth and variation of hue. **The** black color is the absence of color. Black is a mysterious color that is typically associated with the unknown or the negative. The color black represents strength, seriousness, power, and authority. Black is a formal, elegant, and prestigious color. Authoritative and powerful, the color black can evoke strong emotions and too much black can be overwhelming. In heraldry, black is the symbol of grief. In western countries black is the color of mourning, death, and sadness. As the opposite of white, movies, books, print media, and television typically depict the good guy in white and the bad guy in black.

Gray is a cool, neutral, and balanced color. The color gray is an emotionless, moody color that is typically associated with meanings of dull, dirty, and dingy, as well as formal, conservative, and sophisticated. The color gray **is a** timeless and practical color that is often associated with loss or depression. Dark, charcoal gray communicates some of the strength and mystery of black. It is a sophisticated color that lack the negativity of the color black. **The** gray color affects the mind and body by causing unsettling feelings. Light grays are feminine in nature, while dark grays are masculine in nature.

Bl**ue** communicates significance, importance, heraldry and confidence without creating somber or sinister feelings. This is where the corporate blue power suit and the blue uniforms of police officers and firefighter came from. Considered a highly corporate color, blue is often associated with intelligence, stability, unity, and conservatism. Too much blue can create feelings of melancholy, negativity, sadness, self-righteousness, and self-centeredness.

Re**d**, the color of blood and fire, is associated with meanings of love, passion, desire, heat, longing, lust, sexuality, sensitivity, romance, joy, strength, leadership, courage, vigor, willpower, rage, anger, danger, malice, wrath, stress, action, vibrance, radiance, and determination. Red is assertive, daring, determined, energetic, powerful, enthusiastic, impulsive, exciting, and aggressive. Red represents physical energy, lust, passion, and desire. It symbolizes action, confidence, and courage. The color red is linked to the most primitive physical, emotional, and financial needs of survival and self-preservation. The color red is an intense color that is packed with emotion ranging from passionate, intense love to anger and violence — representing both cupid and the devil. The color red is a highly visible color that is able to focus attention quickly and get people to make quick decisions, which is one of the reasons fire trucks and fire engines are usually painted red. Flashing red lights mean danger or emergency, while stop signs and stop lights use the color red to alert drivers about the dangers of the intersection. Red represents power and courage.

References

Bell J (1993). Aristotle as a Source for Leonardo's Theory of Colour Perspective after 1500. Journal of the Warburg and Courtauld Institutes 56:100-118. *https://www.jstor.org/stable/751367, accessed 10-05-2019.*

Bourn, Jennifer (2011). Meaning of Color.
https://www.bourncreative.com/meaning-of-the-color-red/, 2-05-2018.

Douma M., curator. (2008). *Cause of Color*. Accessed 11-05-2019.
http://www.webexhibits.org/causesofcolor, accessed 10-05-2019.

Kandinsky W (2011). Concerning the Spiritual in Art. Empire Art Press.
http://www.gutenberg.org/ebooks/5321, accessed 11-05-2019.

17

IL MORO & THE ENIGMATIC BLACK FLY

The Black Room and the Enigmatic Black Fly

The *Pacioli Portrait* has an overwhelmingly black background and a depiction of an enigmatic black fly, hardly visible, resting on yellow notepaper on the green table beside the red book with the dodecahedron solid (Fig. 1.1). The black background together with the enigmatic black fly represent Ludovico il Moro Sforza known as il Moro – the Moor – black, sinister and evil just like the black fly spreading maggots and disease from rubbish tip to you.

Born in Vigevano in 1451, Ludovico Maria was the fourth son of Duke Francesco Sforza and Duchess Bianca Maria Visconti. He was known from childhood by the nickname of II Moro, which he perpetuated by adopting the mulberry and the Moor's black-head as his emblematic devices. Ludovico was called II Moro for the simple reason that his second name was originally Maurus that was misspelt as Mauro. When he was five years old, however, he became seriously ill, and his mother, wishing to place him under the protection of the Blessed Virgin, changed Mauro into Maria. Yet, his Moro (black) nickname was not easily lost and Ludovico became Il Moro for perpetuity, and forever a fertile theme for the artists and poets of Milan (Fig. 17.1). According to Simonetta, a contemporary Milanese historian, Ludovico had always been the clever boy of the family, and his father Duke Francesco prophesied that this particular son would make his mark in the world.

Leonardo thought Il Moro's mark in the world was best depicted by the sinister Black Fly of Milan sitting on a yellowed piece of notepaper with an obscure inscription – **IACO BAR. VIGENNIS 149-** and using his front left leg to partially cover over the last number of 149- (Fig. 17.2). What is the number after 9? Is the year meant to be 1496, supposedly when Luca Pacioli arrived in Milan to teach mathematics and work with Leonardo da

Vinci on the project of the *Divine Proportion*? The years 1494 to 1499 were often dark times for Leonardo da Vinci and many of the citizens of Milan.

FIG. 17.1. *Ludovico il Moro Sforza, Duke of Bari, Duke of Milan. Left, detail from a painting of Ludovico with his family and with the doctors of the church and the enthroned Virgin and Child by an unknown master at Pinacoteca di Brera in Milan. Picture sourced with permission from the Web Gallery of Art.* https://www.wga.hu. *Right, Detail of Ludovico in his blue armour painted by Giovanni Ambrogio de Predis and stored at castle Trivulzio Library (code 2167). Picture sourced from Wikimedia Commons as File: Ludovico Sforza by G. A. de Prefis (Donatus Grammatica).*

FIG. 17.2. *The enigmatic black fly shaped like a human, black, stick figure on the notepaper with the da Vinci code. A detail from the Luca Pacioli painting (Figure 1.1) from the collection of the National Museum of Capodimonte in Naples.*

CHAPTER 17

In his writings, Leonardo da Vinci seemed ambivalent about Ludovico Sforza and he possibly held some resentments and grudges against him. In 1500, when Leonardo heard that the French had captured Ludovico il Moro Sforza at Novara and taken him as a prisoner to France, he jotted in a notebook:

The Saletta above ... (left unfinished).
Bramante's buildings ... (left undone).
The duke has lost state, fortune, and liberty, and not one of his works has been completed.

Leonardo's note about the *Saletta* (left unfinished) probably refers to the *Saletta Negra*, a small Black Room in the Corte Ducale of the Sforza Castello which owes its name to the sad time in January of 1497 when Il Moro ordered all his apartments to be hung in black while he mourned his dead wife Beatrice.

Bramante's unfinished buildings probably refer to the cathedral of Pavia, the dome and vault of the Santa Maria delle Grazie, the piazza of Vigevano and various works at the Castle (*Castello*) of Milan and Pavia. The Florentine Donato Bramante left Milan for Rome in 1499 the same year that Leonardo da Vinci and Luca Pacioli left for Florence.

Many contemporary historians see Ludovico Sforza as a great sponsor of the arts and supporter of architecture. Yet, it seems clear from Leonardo's comments that he did not have the same positivity about Ludovico Sforza as these historians when he wrote '*... and not one of his works has been completed.*' Perhaps, he was thinking bitterly of his unfinished sculpture of the horse that was to meant to be a monument to Francesco, the first Sforza duke, the rushed job to finish the *Last Supper* so that he could move on to the opposite wall to paint the portrait of Ludovico and Beatrice with their children or the myriad of other projects that may have been commissioned by the young duke Gian Galeazzo Sforza, but were stymied by Ludovico because he didn't want the glory to be given to his nephew.

Leonardo's giant clay horse was finished and ready to be cast in bronze in 1494 four or five months before the death of Gian Sforza who had acquired the bronze for him. The people of Milan saw the horse when it was exhibited at the Piazza del Castello before and after the occasion of the marriage of Bianca Maria Sforza to the Emperor Maximilian in November of 1493. It stood twenty-three feet high and weighed nearly 80 tons and the people named it '*Colossus*'. Soon after Gian's death in October of 1494, Ludovico Sforza confiscated all of the bronze acquired for Leonardo's horse and he sent it down the River Po to his father-in-law Ercole d'Este in Ferrara to build and cast cannons instead. The confiscated bronze was never replaced and Leonardo was unable to complete his big project that he had researched, planned and sculpted for more than ten years. The young duke Gian Sforza was his friend and ally, but Ludovico was his stumbling block if not a direct enemy. The finished clay model stood neglected and exposed to wind and weather in the Sforza Castle's square and later at Leonardo's vineyard outside the gates of Porta Vercellina between the monasteries of San Vittore and Santa Maria delle Grazie, until the French invasion of 1499 when the French archers used it as target practice and damaged it beyond repair. '*Colossus*' was destroyed by Ludovico Sforza and his French enemies before it could be cast in bronze for posterity and Leonardo never saw it again.

Leonardo da Vinci and Ludovico Sforza were the same age, with only a few months difference between them. One was a genius and artisan and the other had the power and the privilege. Despite the many speculations about their relationship, it is not known how they really got on and what they thought of each other. Ludovico Sforza was tight with his money, and Leonardo on many occasions found the need to write to him and complain about the late payments owing him:

I am greatly vexed to be in necessity, but I still more regret that this should be the cause of the hindrance of my wish, which is always disposed to obey your Excellency. Perhaps your Excellency did not give further orders to Messer Gualtieri, believing that I had money enough.

I am greatly annoyed that you should have found me in necessity, and that my having to earn my living should have hindered me ...

It vexes me greatly that having to earn my living has forced me to interrupt the work and to attend to small matters, instead of following up the work which your Lordship entrusted to me. But I hope in a short time to have earned so much that I may carry it out quietly to the satisfaction of your Excellency, to whom I commend myself; and if your Lordship thought that I had money, your Lordship was deceived. I had to feed 6 men for 56 months, and have had 50 ducats.

The following few drafted and unfinished letters by Leonardo to Ludovico Sforza regarding stalled payments or work matters illustrate his constant frustration with the Duke.

My Lord, I know your Excellency's mind to be occupied ... to remind your Lordship of my small matters and the arts put to silence that my silence might be the cause of making your Lordship scorn ... my life in your service. I hold myself ever in readiness to obey ...

CHAPTER 17

Of the horse I will say nothing because I know the times [are bad] to your Lordship how I had still to receive two years' salary of the ... with the two skilled workmen who are constantly in my pay and at my cost that at last I found myself advanced the said sum about 15 lire ... works of fame by which I could show to those who shall see it that I have been everywhere, but I do not know where I could bestow my work [more] ...

I not having been informed what it is, I find myself ... [In April, 1498, Leonardo was engaged in painting the *Saletta Negra* (Black Room) of the Castello at Milan].

remember the commission to paint the rooms ...

I conveyed to your Lordship only requesting you ... [The paper on which this is written is torn down the middle; about half of each line remains.]

Leonardo also jotted down a few moralising comments about Ludovico Sforza next to a drawing of a labourer beating an ermine with a vine in his hand.

*Il Mora with the spectacles and Envy represented with lying Slander, and Justice **black for Il Mora**.*
Labour with the vine in her hand.
The ermine with mud.
Galeazzo between time of tranquillity and flight of fortune.

Leonardo drew a political allegory of Ludovico Sforza steering the Duchy of Milan to Maximilian's Roman Empire and the unknown – and possibly to political disaster for him and Milan.

The complaints were not only one-sided, for Il Moro also had a few of his own about Leonardo's tardiness or his inability to start or finish projects. In a note to Marchesino Stanga, dated 30th June of 1497, Ludovico wrote,

ask Leonardo the Florentine to finish his work on the wall of the Refectory, and to begin the painting on the other wall of the Refectory.

Leonardo da Vinci in the Service of the Young Duke of Milan and his Regent, 1481 to 1494

Exactly when and how Leonardo da Vinci came to Milan is still a matter of conjecture. An anonymous writer during his lifetime relates that Lorenzo de Medici of Florence sent the thirty-year old Leonardo to Milan as his emissary with a gift of a lyre for his godson Gian Galeazzo Sforza who was the 12-year old Duke of Milan under the care and regency of his uncle Ludovico il Moro Sforza, the Duke of Bari. This and other considerations point towards the end of 1481 as the most probable date of Leonardo's arrival in Lombardy. Il Moro may have influenced Leonardo's visit to Milan because Leonardo spoke of himself as *'the man whom my lord the Duke summoned from Florence to carry out his work'*. The legendary letter, in which Leonardo offered his services to *'my lord the Duke'* in which he so confidently proclaimed his powers as a military and hydraulic engineer, as architect, sculptor and painter, was probably written soon after his arrival in Milan, when the rumoured outbreak of the War of Ferrara would render his military talents especially valuable to the rulers of Milan. In the concluding words of the document Leonardo declared himself able *'to undertake the work of the horse, that will be to the immortal glory and eternal honour of my lord your father, of happy memory and of the illustrious House of Sforza'*. This refers to the equestrian statue in the memory of Duke Francesco Sforza, which formed Leonardo's chief work during the first years of his stay in Milan. The idea of such a statue was proposed first by Gian Galeazzo Sforza's father Galeazzo Maria Sforza who was the Duke of Milan, but he was assassinated at a church in the city of Milan the day after Christmas Day in 1476. Thereafter, all initial attempts to construct the equestrian statue had failed until Leonardo completed a full-sized model in 1493 that was placed under a triumphal arch in the Piazza of the Castello on the occasion of Bianca Maria Sforza's marriage to the Roman Emperor Maximilian I. All were loud in praise of the magnificent statue.

When Leonardo first arrived in Milan, Ludovico Sforza was not the duke of Milan, he was the duke of Bari. This difference in authority may have hindered Leonardo's initial attempts to be appointed as a court artist. Some of the decisions to employ Leonardo in the court may have fallen directly to Ludovico's advisers and the young duke Gian Galeazzo Sforza who at 12 years of age was the legitimate Duke of Milan, although supervised by regents, initially by his mother Bona of Savoy, and then by his uncle Ludovico Sforza. Gian had his own coin as well as one with Ludovico when Leonardo was first in Milan. Although Ludovico Il Moro Sforza was officially the Duke of Bari and not the Duke of Milan, he was the appointed regent and Governor of Milan for most of Gian's tenure. Thus, he is better remembered and acknowledged than Gian by historians as being the true guardian and ruler of Milan and the arbiter of Italy. On this basis, Ludovico il Moro Sforza also is usually credited for many of the great architectural works and historic buildings found in Milan and its surroundings. These days, we rarely read or hear much about the negative aspects of Ludovico Il Moro Sforza's management because the historians tended to look through their gilded filters at how marvellous and caring he was about the arts and architecture; often citing the Carthusian monastery and the Certosa of Pavia as examples of his greatness. In reality, he inherited all the great architecture of Milan and Pavia such as the churches, the Duomo, the Certosa, the grand Palaces and Houses, the Castello of Milan and Pavia and the Corte Ducale of Milan from the dukes before him starting from the very first of them – Gian Galeazzo Visconti.

Although *'none cared more for the Certosa than did Ludovico Il Moro'*, his achievements for the Certosa were relatively minor and he never managed to finish anything major. Most of the works were finished and in place by the time he came to rule Milan and its Duchy.

'Great as was the activity of Ludovico Il Moro in the sphere of architecture, he had inherited so vast a field in the monuments founded by his predecessors, that the buildings begun under his auspices form the least important part of his work. His chief function was to adorn and improve the foundations of his ancestors, notably the Castello of Milan and the Certosa of Pavia.' [Cecilia M. Ady, 1907].

Should we acknowledge that the Duomo of Pavia, the churches of S. Maria Presso Celso and S. Satiro, and the monasteries of S. Maria delle Grazie and S. Ambrogio in Milan were built during Il Moro's reign? I think not, because we must acknowledge the fact that the Duomo of Pavia (started in 1488), the churches of S. Maria Presso Celso (opened 1493) and S. Satiro in Milan (opened 1482) and the monastery of S. Maria delle Grazie (started 1463 and completed 1497) and S. Ambrogio (a new rectory 1492) were completed or started during the reign of the 6th Duke of Milan, Gian Galeazzo Sforza. All these works required Gian Galeazzo Sforza's approval and signature, and Ludovico Sforza could only sign off building projects on behalf of Gian Galeazzo Sforza and not in his own right. The Basilica of S. Ambrogio in Milan was consecrated in the year 379 and rebuilt in the Romanesque style by 1099, and the Benedictines commissioned Donato Bramante in 1492 to renovate only the new rectory. For some reason most historians choose to omit the fact that many of these building were constructed or renovated during Gian Galeazzo Sforza's reign, preferring instead to attribute them only to Ludovico Sforza. Yet, Gian Galeazzo Sforza was the legitimate Duke of Milan at the time and he should be honoured as much as Ludovico even if his uncle was the dictatorial regent and Governor of Milan during most of Gian Galeazzo Sforza's reign (1478 to 1494). Strangely, the historians continually neglect to give Gian Galeazzo any credit in helping to manage the art and architecture of his Duchy.

In 1488, Ludovico and Gian agreed to erect a cathedral at Pavia upon the site of the ancient basilica, which was rapidly becoming a ruin. This was intended to be a place of worship for Gian Galeazzo Sforza and his bride Isabella Sforza Aragon, the Duke and Duchess of Milan, during their permanency at the Castello of Pavia. In 1490, Leonardo da Vinci was sent to Pavia with Bramante and the Sienese architect Francesco di Giorgio to consult on rebuilding the cathedral. They furnished a plan for the cathedral with a nave and two aisles flanked by semicircular niches and a large central dome. The architect Cristoforo Rocchi was appointed to supervise the project, but was later replaced by Giovanni Antonio Amadeo and Gian Giacomo Dolcebuono. Initially, Ludovico Sforza insisted that Amadeo should not be involved with the Duomo for more than two or three times a month in order not to neglect his duties at the Certosa. Despite this stipulation, Amadeo's appointment as architect of the Duomo in 1498 paved the way for his resignation from his post at the Certosa, and the preliminary construction of the Cathedral of Pavia was in large measure due to him after Ludovico Sforza was gone from Milan in 1500. Although Amadeo carried the work several stages nearer completion, the altar area of Duomo of Pavia remained unfinished by the end of Il Moro's reign and was not finished until 1521.

Portrait painting was an important branch of art in Milan largely developed by rich merchants, patricians and ducal patronage. At a time when an interchange of portraits was the necessary accompaniment of a marriage contract, and when it was the custom to paint the portraits, the art had a semi-political and social value reflecting power and wealth. When Leonardo da Vinci first arrived in Milan, the painters Vincenzo Foppa, Alessandro Araldi, Borgognone, Bernardino Zenale and Ambrogio de Predis were among the most favoured by the Sforza court and Milanese rich merchants and patricians. Foppa enjoyed the patronage of Il Moro for a short time and he was painting at the Church of S. Maria del Brera in Milan in 1485. However, by 1489 Foppa returned to his native city of Brescia in the Republic of Venice, where he spent the remainder of his life. The new era that dawned under the auspices of Leonardo da Vinci did not favour Vincenzo Foppa who still was wedded to the traditions of the old Lombardian school, and who for a long time was regarded as its chief representative. Zenale was born in Treviglio in Lombardy in about 1460 and he collaborated on the decorations of the Certosa di Pavia, painted a room in the Sforza Castle and painted frescos in the old Lombardian traditions in the chapels of various churches in and around Milan. After 1500, he developed a new style that was influenced greatly by the paintings of Leonardo and Bernardino Luini as seen in his polytech that he painted for the Confraternity of the Immaculate Conception of Cantu (1502) in the province of Como.

The painter Ambrogio de Predis probably had the closest relationship with Il Moro and his Court. From the year 1482, he held the official post of portrait-painter to the reigning House, and despite his debt to Leonardo, he ranks both as a contemporary and a collaborator rather than Leonardo's pupil or assistant. He and his brother Evangelista probably helped

CHAPTER 17

Leonardo in 1483 to obtain the commission for the *Virgin of the Rocks* from the Confraternity of the Immaculate Conception for their chapel at S. Francesco. In 1493, Ambrogio de Predis travelled to Germany with the newly married Bianca Maria Sforza and her large group of escorts, attendants and courtiers in order to paint her portrait and that of her affianced husband Maximilian. The connections which Ambrogio de Predis formed with the German court during this visit stood him in good stead and in 1502 he crossed the Alps for the second time and settled permanently in Innsbruck among the Sforza exiles gathered at Maximilian's Court. Another popular portrait-painter of the day was Leonardo's pupil and assistant Boltraffio who mostly worked outside the Court of Milan, but painted a fine profile portrait of Ludovico II Moro that is in the Trivulzio collection.

Leonardo da Vinci and his assistants like Boltraffio, Marco d'Oggiono, Cesare da Sesto, Bernardino Luini, Salai, and Giovanni Antonio Bazzi (Sodoma) received many commissions for painting portraits when in Milan. Perhaps there are portraits by Leonardo da Vinci yet to be discovered or attributed to him, although some of Leonardo's 500-year-old portraits may have been lost or deteriorated beyond recognition. Surprisingly, there is no known portrait of Ludovico Sforza that has been attributed solely to Leonardo's hand, and yet there are many portraits of the young duke Gian Galeazzo Sforza that seem to have been painted by him and/or his assistants. Among the commissions given by Il Moro to Leonardo were portraits of the Duke's two mistresses, Cecilia Gallerani and Lucrezia Crivelli, a picture of Madonna and child for Matthias Corvinus of Hungary, and an altarpiece containing a Nativity, which was sent by the Duke to the Holy Roman Emperor Maximilian. None of these pictures have been satisfactorily identified, but it has been suggested that the altarpiece sent to Maximilian was the '*Virgin of the Rocks*' now in the Louvre. Leonardo originally undertook to paint this picture for the Church of S. Francesco in Milan, but because of a dispute about its price, the matter was referred to Ludovico Sforza. It seems that the monks of the Confraternity refused to pay the sum that Leonardo had asked for and he, therefore, reclaimed his picture. Leonardo and Ambrogio de Predis, who was engaged upon the side-panels of the altarpiece, executed a replica of the original for the Confraternity. The replica with the two side-panels remained at S. Francesco until they were taken to England and the National Gallery. According to one suggestion, the original was bought by Il Moro and sent to Maximilian at the time of his marriage to Bianca Maria Sforza, whence it passed into the French Royal Collection. Alternatively, the original was sold to King Louis XII of France when he and the French occupied and governed Milan and Lombardy.

Painting pictures was only one branch of Leonardo's manifold activities in service of the Sforza Court. He decorated the rooms of the *Castello*, he organised State pageants and wedding celebrations and costumes for the public jousts. The Sforza Court hung upon his fables and satires; his epigrams were on everybody's lips. He discussed pure mathematics with Luca Pacioli, Galeazzo Sanseverino consulted him on military questions and singing, and he joined in debates about science, philosophy and literature conducted by Il Moro and other kindred spirits of the Court at the so called Vinci Academy. He acted as the Duke's adviser on questions ranging from the designs suggested for the *tiburio* (a crossing tower) of the Cathedral to the most approved methods of irrigation for the farmlets bordering the walls of the city and the vegetable and fruit gardens on Ludovico's farms and property at Vigevano. Thus, the years that Leonardo spent in Milan were among the most fruitful in his career. Nowhere did his genius find so congenial an atmosphere or so wide a scope as at the Court which Isabella d'Este named *'the school of the master of those who know'*.

Leonardo flourished in Milan for three good reasons: One, the prosperity of the city and the duchy; two, the relative informality of the rulers and the nobility, despite the dictatorial presence of Ludovico Sforza; and three, because of his prodigious talent and uniqueness. The main industries that formed the basis of Milan's prosperity as a manufacturing centre were its armoury, wool and silk industries and also its propensity for trade and commerce. Milanese armour was famed throughout the world, and the city boasted some hundred armouries from whence goods were dispatched across the Alps to France, Switzerland and the Empire, or went eastward to be bought at high prices by the Saracens. The armoury included the whole equipment of a knight and his horse and the ancillary requirements for bouts and jousting. The wool industry was equally important and it supplied Venice with cloth to the annual value of 120,000 ducats. The manufacture of woollen and silken materials led to the production of the more costly fabrics necessary for the outfit of a courtier. The silk weaver, the goldsmith, the manufacturer of embroidery and gold and silver cloth found a ready market for their wares inside and outside of Milan. The artisans engaged in these numerous crafts worked, not just for the consumer, but also for the merchants for trade. The banking and transport industry grew in the wake of manufacturing and agriculture and the merchants and bankers from the great Milanese families rose to power, and many a noble house grew wealthy through trade. Almost all of the classes in Milan were concerned with commerce and industry, and so society and laws alike proclaimed the overwhelming importance of the trade and commercial interests. In this regard, the aristocracy of Milan was one of wealth and not of birth. Thus, social and political rivalries lay between capital and labour and in the ways to best protect the prosperity of

CHAPTER 17

the citizens. In Milan, there was no social stigmatism or discrimination against illegitimate children and they were given equal opportunity in most things, except to inheritance, where the legitimacy and primacy of primogeniture was still the family preference and the law.

Leonardo was reasonably successful in Milan because he possessed wide knowledge and understanding, wit and humour and he was talented, entertaining, handsome, athletic, honest and a foreigner who was willing to learn and accept the ways of the Lombardians and Insubrians. He made friends easily and was surrounded by many admirers who were ready to take his work on trust. He was given far greater opportunity for undertaking his scientific experiments and broadening his interests in Milan than he was among the more critical and competitive Florentines. His high conception of art prompted him to devote a great part of his time to its scientific and theoretical aspects, and Ludovico II Moro possessed the patience and the discernment to allow him to work in his own way. Leonardo was suited to II Moro's interests because they were the same age with a strong sense of wonder, curiosity, ambition and a love for beauty, science, language and literature. Although war was not necessarily Ludovico's preference as a political or territorial solution, he knew that the military aspect of the State could not be neglected, and he recognised the value of Leonardo da Vinci who could invent *'various and infinite means of offence and defence'*. Leonardo's knowledge of engineering was of great advantage to Ludovico in his plans for the material improvement of his dominions. Above all, Leonardo was recognised as a man of genius, and II Moro had the sensitivity and education to appreciate the genius and realised that Leonardo sought perfection in all he did, the nexus of art and science where beauty becomes the outward expression of truth.

During Leonardo da Vinci's time in Milan, he saw no lack of splendour in court life, particularly in the four years between 1489 and 1493. In January of 1489, the 19-year old Isabella of Aragon arrived in Milan from Naples to marry her cousin, the 20-year old duke of Milan, Gian Galeazzo Sforza. She was the daughter of Prince Alfonso II and the granddaughter of king Ferrante (Ferdinand) of Naples. Her mother Ippolita Maria Sforza who died in 1484 was the sister of Ludovico Sforza and the deceased Duke of Milan Galeazzo Sforza, who had already arranged their marriage a few years after their birth. Their marriage was remembered as a grand occasion with many of the great festivities and pageants organised by Leonardo.

'The festivities which attended their wedding were conspicuous even in the Renaissance for their magnificence and ingenuity. Ermes Sforza, the Duke's brother, went to Naples with a suite of some four hundred persons "clad like so many kings" from whence he escorted Isabella by sea to Genoa. The meeting between the bridal pair took place at Tortona, and was celebrated by a banquet at which each course was sensed

by mythological characters in appropriate costume. Fish was handed round by naiads. Jason bore in the Golden Fleece. Hebe produced wines which rivalled nectar and ambrosia in their preciousness. Orpheus offered birds which, he declared in elegant verse, had flocked around him to hear the melodies which, he had raised in praise of Isabella of Aragon.' [Cecilia M. Ady, 1907].

The wedding between Isabella and Gian took place in the Duomo of Milan to the accompaniment of fresh pageants. The festivities were crowned one year later by the performance of a masque called the *Paradiso*, written for the occasion by the Florentine poet Bernardo Bellincione and organised by Leonardo. Two years later there was another round of splendid festivities and display of wealth in honour of II Moro's wedding, which took place in the Castello of Pavia in January of 1491. The *piece de resistance* on this occasion was a tournament in which Galeazzo Sanseverino, as usual, remained the victor, and he received the pallium of gold brocade from the bride's hands in a costume, which Leonardo had designed for him. And then there was the grand occasion of the marriage between Bianca Maria Sforza and the Holy Roman Emperor Maximilian I held in proxy at the Duomo of Milan in 1493, when Leonardo da Vinci unveiled for the citizenry his colossal clay sculpture of the Francesco Sforza memorial horse.

Ludovico Sforza's Betrayal of the Young Duke of Milan Gian Galeazzo Sforza, 1492-1494

For many a student of Italian Renaissance history, the year 1492 was the beginning of the end of the independence of the native Italian States and the Sforza dynasty in Milan. By the start of 1492, Ludovico had exiled Gian and Isabella to Pavia, far away from his seat of power in Milan, and he quickly eroded all of their remaining power, profile and existence before murdering Gian Galeazzo Sforza in October of 1494. To consolidate his power over Gian Sforza and Isabella Aragon Sforza, Ludovico entered into an alliance with King Charles VIII of France in support of king's intention to invade Naples and overthrow Isabella's grandfather, the King of Naples. This was Ludovico's most treacherous act, to plot and usurp the title and Duchy of Milan from his nephew and niece, Gian Galeazzo Sforza and Isabella Aragon Sforza, the Duke and Duchess of Milan.

The Alps had long-served to protect Italy from the invasions of European armies and now Ludovico Sforza intended to break this barrier and plunge the Italian States into the vortex of European politics. Before 1492, he and his nephew and their forefathers and brothers maintained a strong Triple Alliance between Florence, Naples and Milan to prevent France from entering Italy. In 1490, the French king provided Gian

CHAPTER 17

Galeazzo Sforza with the investiture of Genoa for 8,000 ducats. Now, Ludovico Sforza was on the way to break up the Triple Alliance in favour of France so that he could usurp the Duchy of Milan from his nephew Gian Galeazzo Sforza with the support of the French. The quarrel between Charles VIII and Maximilian, King of the Romans, over Anne of Brittany was acceptable to Il Moro because he believed that a war between them would favour his scheming. Charles VIII had no wish to see Maximilian on the side of his enemies, and so, he formed an alliance in January of 1492 with the Milanese Government. This eventually was to realise his short-lived claim to Naples on behalf of the French crown using the armies of France.

The death of Lorenzo de Medici in April 1492, proved a further blow to the peace of Italy, to the Triple Alliance and to the safety of Gian Galeazzo Sforza who was Lorenzo's godson. So long as Lorenzo lived, he protected Gian Galeazzo Sforza from his enemies and his influence was always on the side of moderation. If Lorenzo had lived, he would have done his utmost to mend the rupture between Milan and Naples. Thus, the rise to power of Lorenzo's uninfluential eldest son Piero dei Medici at a time when the relations between the other two members of the Triple Alliance were growing daily more strained was unfortunate. The Sforza cardinal Ascanio added to the growing tension on the Italian peninsula by supporting the election of a Borgia for Pope who took the name of Alexander VI.

The birth of Il Moro's first son in January of 1493 proved too much for Duchess Isabella and her powers of endurance. For the sake of her son Francesco, she resolved to make a desperate bid for the supremacy, which was hers only in name. Hence her famous letter to her father Alfonso of Calabria in which she accuses Ludovico of acting in all things as if he and not Gian Galeazzo was the true Duke, while she and her husband were forced to live as private and influential persons in exile from the governing powers of Milan. The letter concludes with an appeal to her father Alfonso to come to the aid of his unhappy daughter. '*If you will not help us I would rather die by my own hands than bear this tyrannous yoke and suffer in a strange country under the eyes of a rival.*'

The Duchess Isabella received support from the Milanese noble and general Gian Glacomo Trivulzio who was at the Court of Naples and proclaimed the wrongdoings she suffered to her father Alfonso, whose enmity towards Ludovico dated from the War of Ferrara and he was ready to take arms against the usurper in his daughter's defence. Yet the King of Naples, Ferrante, thanked Ludovico for his good government of the Duchy during Gian Galeazzo's minority, and suggested that he should crown his virtues by retiring in his nephew's favour. Il Moro replied politely and pointed out to the king that he would stay on until all the secret enemies were rooted out from his State. Then, on behalf of Milan, he immediately formed an alliance between Venice, the Papacy, Siena, Mantua and Ferrara for the preservation of the States of the Church, and for the maintenance of the present Government in Milan. This new direction in Milanese foreign policy was the result of the friendly relations developed between Ludovico and the Venetian Signoria since the conclusion of the Peace of Bagnolo. The Pope, moreover, was incensed against Naples and Florence in that their rulers had facilitated the sale of some papal fiefs near Rome by the late Pope's son to Virginio Orsini, dismissing Alexander VI's rights. Hence in April of 1493, this novel alliance between five of the major Italian Powers was formed as the Pact of San Marco and essentially left Gian Galeazzo Sforza's only allies Naples and Florence politically isolated.

In May of 1493, Il Moro sent his ambassador Erasmo Brasca to Germany on a secret mission to purchase the investiture of the Duchy of Milan from the Emperor of the Roman Empire and overthrow the young Duke of Milan, Gian Galeazzo Sforza, and his son, Francesco II Sforza. The terms of agreement were that Ludovico would provide the Emperor with Gian Galeazzo's sister, Bianca, as his bride, as well as a dowry of 300,000 ducats and an extra 100,000 ducats to give the secret treaty and betrayal, *'more solemnity and lustre to the deed,'* as an extra incentive for the price of the Imperial Investiture. The Emperor accepted the terms of agreement and provided Il Moro with the investiture to Milan to be foredated and accepted in law in September of 1494. The Emperor's reasons for granting the investiture to Il Moro instead of to his nephew Gian Sforza were given at length in its preamble. Not only was Ludovico the eldest surviving son of Francesco Sforza (Ludovico's elder brothers Galeazzo, Sforza and Filippo were all dead by 1493), but after Milan lapsed into the hands of the Roman Empire with the death of Filippo Maria Visconti, it allowed Maximilian to bestow the fief on to whomever he favoured, and *'you we have judged to be the only person worthy of being raised to this high rank.'* In spite of this vile vindication of the deed, Maximilian stipulated that the investiture for the present time should be kept secret. Thus, Ludovico then pocketed the diploma until he was ready to play it as his trump-card; and that day finally arrived a year later when he murdered his nephew Gian Galeazzo Sforza and quickly disposed of his body in the last week of November of 1494.

While organising his investiture of Milan in 1493, Ludovico sent his child-bride Beatrice to pay a complimentary visit to the Venetian Signoria in recognition of their recent alliance and to seek their continued support. She was an instant success and stayed there a few weeks at the Signoria's expense. However, they informed her that they would not go to war against Naples if the French were involved; and before she was back in Milan,

CHAPTER 17

Ludovico received news from the French King Charles VIII that he was determined to invade Italy without further delay and that he appointed Ludovico the head and director of the Neapolitan expedition. On receiving the news from the French, Ludovico raised no objections and unreservedly supported the French King.

Ludovico expressed his policy during the years 1492-93 in a letter to his younger brother Ascanio, a cardinal, in March, 1494:

> *'It is not true that all this movement comes from me. It is the Christian King himself who took the initiative… At this time, I do not deny that, in view of the evil proceedings of the King of Naples towards the Holy Father, it did not displease me to find an occasion for coming to the aid of His Holiness. Hence, I ceased to dissuade the most Christian King from his enterprise, I even approved of his resolution, and since then he has persisted in it with so much warmth that here he is to-day at Lyons.'*

Although Ludovico had hoped that the much younger Charles VIII would be *'docile enough to serve his designs and powerful enough to ensure their success,'* Charles proved to be the authoritative and dominant partner of the French alliance, until Ludovico turned against him in 1495.

Pope Alexander VI on hearing that there was an alliance been Milan and France immediately left the Pact of San Marco and instead sided with Naples. He could not afford to remain neutral or side with Milan because he was afraid he would lose his Papal territories to the French if they attacked Rome. Thus, he reconciled with King Ferrante of Naples and sealed the marriage between his illegitimate son Don Gioffre Borgia and Alfonso's illegitimate daughter, Sancia Aragon. Thus, towards the end of 1493, the lines of war were determined, Charles VIII of France would come to Italy as the ally of Milan in opposition to Naples, the Papacy and Florence, while Venice would stand by as neutral until an advantage opened up for them and their interests. Ludovico's treacherous nature had come to the fore once more. He betrayed the Triple Alliance between Milan, Florence and Naples and sided with his two oldest enemies France and Venice and with the German Holy Empire to ingratiate himself with the Holy Roman Emperor in an attempt to gain for himself the investiture for the Duchy of Milan.

One year before the death of the young duke Gian Galeazzo Sforza on 30th November of 1493, his younger sister Bianca was married by proxy to the Imperial ambassadors in the Duomo of Milan. The French envoys whom Charles VIII had sent were there to honour the occasion. A few days later the new Empress of the Holy Empire and Queen of Germany set out for Innsbruck accompanied as far as Como by her mother Bona of Savoy and other members of the Milanese Court including her brother Gian and his wife Isabella, the Duke and Duchess of Milan. Maximilian was a tardy bridegroom, and it was not until the following March in 1494 that he and Bianca eventually met to remarry in a wedding ceremony held in Tyrol.

Early in 1494, the English diplomats had already stopped sending their official correspondence to Gian Galeazzo Sforza as the Duke of Milan and instead addressed their correspondence to Ludovico Sforza as the Duke of Milan, even though Gian Galeazzo Sforza was still alive and living in Pavia. Previously, the English had always addressed Ludovico Sforza as the Duke of Bari or Governor of Milan, Regent to the Duke of Milan. This premature change of diplomatic titles demonstrates that Maximilian's investiture to Ludovico had already leaked out in the diplomatic circles of Europe. Most European rulers already knew that Ludovico Sforza was about to usurp his nephew's title of Duke of Milan.

On the other hand, Rome and Naples made their last desperate efforts to avert the coming invasion and entreated Ludovico not to allow the passage of the French army through Lombardy. King Ferrante of Naples offered to meet with Ludovico in Genoa to persuade him not to side with France. Il Moro declined to meet and expressed much regret to the King of Naples at his inability to dissuade Charles VIII and explained that the ambitions of the Duke of Orleans for Milan rendered it impossible for him to quarrel with France. He no longer bothered to disguise his real intentions or that his enemies were now Naples and Rome and that his ally was France. He sent Galeazzo Sanseverino to France with instructions to push on with the Neapolitan expedition by every means in his power. With King Ferrante's untimely death in January of 1494, the last obstacle to the outbreak of war was removed. Alfonso succeeded his father on the throne of Naples and he and Pope Alexander VI became Il Moro's most bitter enemies in the ensuing invasion from France.

Ludovico had his wizards and astrologers conjure up the spirits of good fortune with the hope of a speedy arrival of the French to save him from the vengeance of Alfonso of Naples. The Archbishop Paolo Fregoso, the former doge of Genoa, encouraged the King of Naples to attack Genoa, and in June of 1494 Alfonso's brother Frederico sailed his fleet of warships to support the Fregosi family in their attempt to liberate the city from Milan's rule. Federico surprised the Milanese forces with an attack on Porto Venere near La Spezia about eighty kilometres southwest of Genoa, and he occupied Rapallo. In September, the Duke of Orleans launched his French fleet from Genoa, and with an army from Milan, he recaptured Rapallo, forcing Federico to retreat to Leghorn. Thus, the Duke of Orleans saved Genoa from occupation by the King of Naples. Meanwhile, Alfonso's son Ferrantino, the Duke of Calabria, promoted a rebellion in Romagna against Il Moro in the name of Gian Galeazzo Sforza, until Ludovico's French allies arrived and chased him out of the territory in August.

CHAPTER 17

Finally, in September, to save Ludovico from a possible invasion by Naples, King Charles VIII arrived at the town of Asti that is located about 100 km south-west of Pavia where Ludovico and his entourage greeted his arrival. After a short bout of illness, the French king made his way to Pavia in October to meet with his unfortunate cousin Gian Galeazzo Sforza, the Duke of Milan, who was seriously ill and bedridden. Their meeting was polite and avoided the topic of Ludovico and his plan to usurp the Duchy of Milan. Instead, it was Gian's wife Isabella of Aragon who fell to her knees before the French King and implored him to spare her father, brother, husband and son. King Charles replied that it was far too late for him to alter his purpose and he bade her to pray instead for herself and her husband. After the polite and friendly meeting, the king's personal physician Theodore Gnaynler declared to his king that he had detected signs of poison in Gian Galeazzo Sforza's system. Despite this revelation by Gnaynler, a few days later, Charles VIII and Ludovico Sforza travelled together to Piacenza as allies. Here, Ludovico received the news that his nephew was dying, and he quickly returned to Pavia to find that Gian Galeazzo had died on the morning of 21st October.

'Without a moment's delay, he hurried on to Milan to gather some of the leading citizens within the Castello. He proposed that Gian Galeazzo's infant son, Francesco, should be proclaimed Duke in his father's stead. Thereupon, the Treasurer, Antonio Landriano, at the instigation of Ludovico's supporters, if not of Il Moro himself, rose to protest against the election of a child-Duke during these troublous times [instigated by Ludovico], and to propose that Ludovico, who had for so long exercised the functions of Duke, should now assume the title. Baldassare Pusterla, Andrea Cagnola and other friends of Ludovico warmly seconded Landriano's proposal, and none daring to contradict them, Il Moro was proclaimed Duke of Milan without further delay. Ludovico only remained in Milan to provide for the funeral of the late Duke. After the body of Gian Galeazzo had been laid to rest in the Duomo on 27th October, he departed to rejoin Charles VIII, who was travelling by way of Pontrernoli to Florence.' [Cecilia M. Ady 1907].

YES, THE DEED IS DONE. The Green Duke is dead. Hurrah – Long live the new duke, Il Moro. This type of pronouncement was even heard before the green duke was buried.

'For all his eighteen years' reign, Gian Galeazzo Sforza remains but a shadowy figure in the history of Milan. Horses, dogs and the pleasures of the table appear to have been the chief delights of his feeble mind. He was occasionally rendered violent by drink; yet he showed signs of pathetic affection for the uncle who might well be considered his worst enemy. The night before his death he anxiously asked his attendant whether Ludovico loved him and was sorry to see him ill. Then, consoling himself with the

thought that Il Moro would have come to see him if he had not been obliged to attend Charles VIII the young Duke went peacefully to sleep. So died Gian Galeazzo. "It seemed an inhuman thing," says Corio, "that before he had reached the age of twenty-five this Immaculate Lamb should be taken from the number of the living." His death had occurred at such an exceedingly opportune moment that it appeared to many a clear case of poisoning.' [Cecilia M. Ady 1907].

When Ludovico Il Moro Sforza was the duke of Milan he had to contend with the common belief throughout Milan, Italy and Europe that he had murdered his nephew, the 6th Duke of Milan. This was the dark shadow that hung over his head during his remaining five years of rule as the 7th Duke of Milan. Leonardo depicted these dark times beautifully, but symbolically in his *Pacioli Portrait* with the troubling black background and the sinister black fly of Milan contrasted against the living green of the foreground. Contemporary chroniclers repeated the accusations of murder; the fact that Ludovico Sforza was his nephew's murderer should have been ingrained forever in history. Subsequent historians have been somewhat sceptical of Ludovico's guilt, even though there is no doubt that he usurped the right of Gian's son Francesco II, *il duchette*, to be the Duke in-waiting while still in the care of the Duchess Reagent of Milan, Isabella Aragon Sforza. That is documented historical fact and indefensible against most of the cynical interpretations by some historians.

There are those, however, who continue to lay the guilt at Il Moro's door, and who detect in the long delay, in the emphatic disavowals, and in the death of the young Duke when Ludovico had at length received the imperial diploma drawn up in his own name, the hand of a past master in the art of intrigue. In view of the existing state of evidence, they have at least a right to their opinion.' [Cecilia M. Ady, 1907].

For Cecilia M. Ady, a great admirer of Ludovico il Moro Sforza, it was difficult to accept that he had murdered his nephew and usurped his grand-nephew despite the overwhelming circumstantial and historical evidence. She preferred in her historical account to gush over how wonderful, tolerant, intelligent and romantic Il Moro's enlightened heart was and she refused to see him as the sinister blackfly spreading maggots and disease from rubbish tip to the innocent and righteous in his grasp for tyrannical power over the populace and rightful rulers of the Duchy of Milan. She even belittled and smeared Gian Galeazzo Sforza as a violent, immature, feebleminded, snivelling drunk in her support of his uncle, Ludovico Sforza. However, to Ludovico's credit, he did handover to Isabella Aragon Sforza his title to the Duchy of Bari in 1499 before she left Milan forever with her two daughters Bianca and Ippolita. In this sense, he did retain some semblance of sentimentality, decency and honour.

CHAPTER 17

Leonardo at Work with the Sinister Black Fly, 1495 to 1499

In 1495, soon after the death of Gian Galeazzo Sforza, Leonardo was still busy with the equestrian statue when he began to paint his *Last Supper* in the Refectory of the convent of S. Maria delle Grazie. Il Moro took credit and honour for having commissioned the greatest genius of the age to paint this masterpiece, although he generally made others pay Leonardo for his work. In his published stories entitled *Novelle*, Matteo Bandello, the bishop of Agen, described how as a boy in Milan he saw Leonardo sometimes paint from sunrise to dusk without so much as pausing to eat or drink. Then, for several days he would not touch the painting, instead he would spend an hour or two each day in contemplation and criticism of his own work. Sometimes, an idea about the painting of the *Last Supper* would spring to him while he was working on his equestrian statue, and then he would hurry off through the midday sun to S. Maria delle Grazie to paint two or three strokes and then depart again, back to the statue or somewhere else for conversation or contemplation. Matteo Bandello also tells how Matthias Lang, Cardinal of Gurk, once visited the Convent and questioned Leonardo about his salary. He expressed great surprise on learning that the artist received 2,000 ducats besides the liberal gifts that the Duke gave him from time to time. Leonardo was greatly indignant about the Cardinal's failure to appreciate what was involved in the high calling of art. Ludovico also commissioned Leonardo to paint his portrait with his wife Beatrice and their boys on the wall opposite to the *Last Supper*. The long wait for Leonardo to finish the painting of the *Last Supper* seemed completely justified and appreciated in the end because it was immediately hailed a triumph and a masterpiece. The *Last Supper* captured the jangling effect of the word '**betrayal**' upon his 12 disciples, men '*of various ages and temperaments. Fear, grief, astonishment, love, all find their expression among the Apostles when they learn that "one of you shall betray Me'* as well as on all those who saw it. Unfortunately, the painting deteriorated almost immediately. When Antonio de Beatis, the secretary/chaplain to Cardinal Luigi of Aragon, visited Milan in 1517, he wrote in his diary that the picture was already beginning to spoil, '*whether from the damp of the wall or from some other accident I do not know*'. Leonardo might have told Antonio de Beatis when they met in Amboise that the maggots of the sinister black fly of Milan had spoilt his masterpiece because of its political allegory.

Ludovico Il Moro made great efforts to obtain a complete and accurate history of Milan and he desired something that would weave the deeds of his own family into the general history of the Duchy. He chose Bernardino Corio to be his historian and provided him with a copyist and anything else that might render the book about Ludovico and his ancestors with real historical value. In 1497, he commended to the bishops, abbots and lay officials in the districts around Lake Como that his servant Bernardino Corio be allowed to *'explore the ancient writings pertaining to the history and deeds of our ancestors'* and that they aid the historian by *'freely opening all archives and libraries,'* and by giving him every facility for reading and making extracts. Although Corio's *Storia di Milano* remains the standard history of the period, the rough and lumbering style and frequent inaccuracies did not achieve the excellence that Ludovico Sforza had hoped for. Leonardo's name pops in and out occasionally in the letters of luminaries of the day, but nothing substantial or particularly informative. In his *Novelle*, Matteo Bandello described his experiences as a novice at S. Maria delle Grazie, when Leonardo was at work in the Refectory and when II Moro was constantly visiting the monks. Tales of the illustrious men whom Bandello saw there and stories which he heard from Leonardo's lips were woven into the *Novelle* and dedicated to Ippolita, the only member of the House of Sforza who remained in Milan. Baldassare Castiglione, who went to Milan for purposes of education during the last years of Ludovico's reign, filled his *Courtier (Cortegiano)* with allusions to the people whom he met there and to the beauty and splendour of his surroundings. Ludovico's wife Beatrice d'Este found her place among the noble ladies described in the *Courtier* who were known and admired for their beauty, their virtues and their talents. The company gathered around the Ludovico and Beatrice in the Castello of Milan including the splendid jouster Galeazzo Sanseverino seemed to Castiglione *'the flower of the human race'*.

In this regard, Ludovico II Moro, allowed his Court in Milan to become an informal Academy for artists, poets and scholars; a place where illustrious men of varied rank from all parts of Italy gathered to meet and dispute science, literature and the arts. There were Greeks, Venetians, Florentines, nobles, secretaries, lawyers, professors, and artists drawn together on equal terms by the Duke's patronage. Comparatively few of the Court circle were born in the Duchy. Gaspare Visconti, poet, soldier and courtier and the historian Bernardino Corio, were practically the only Milanese. Leonardo da Vinci from Florence and Bramante from Urbino stood foremost among the brilliant assembly drawn outside the Duchy. Bramante, although he described himself as *'a man without letters'*, was an acclaimed architect and engineer skilled in mathematics, and he also won fame at the Court as a poet of sonnets. In one of the literary disputes, in which II Moro loved to partake, Bramante joined with the Duke and his Duchess in upholding the supremacy of Dante against the more popular Petrarch of Arezzo. It was the very informality of these gatherings that gave the intellects of Milan a freshness and a spontaneity that were missing in the more fastidious and serious academic settings of universities and other courts of Italy. Because of Leonardo's celebrated contributions at these debates, these meetings soon became known as *Academia Leonardo da*

CHAPTER 17

Vinci. It was at one of these gatherings that Leonardo da Vinci maintained that the theory of painting should be nothing short of the *'universal science of the visible,'* and that the fully equipped artist must have studied not only perspective and anatomy, but also all forms of natural science. In every sphere of knowledge, authority and convention were pushed aside in the general quest for truth that was drawn from experience. Luca Pacioli attended these 'Academies' when he was in Milan between 1496 and 1499. His manuscript *On the Divine Proportion* begins with a dedication to the Duke of Milan, Ludovico II Sforza, describing a great gathering in the Duke's presence, in his illustrious city of Milan: *'an assembly dedicated to scientific debate, composed of people of all ranks, famous and most wise, both religious and secular, with whom your court continually abounds.'* He turns again to this great gathering at the conclusion of the book, alluding to the prominent participation of his own Franciscan Order, and others; and, although he states in both cases that it occurred in the year 1498, it might be a metaphorical description of the great scientific debates and arguments discussed at the Academy of Leonardo Da Vinci in one of the darkened rooms at the Sforza Castle.

The tragic death of Beatrice d'Este at the Sforza Castle on the 2nd of January in 1497 led to her husband's ruin, and quickly broke up the literary circle of the Court before the advent of the first French occupation in 1499. The camaraderie, which had been the essence of Il Moro's Court, was gone never to return, pleasing some and disappointing others. And so, *'after one more year of joy of complete supremacy in 1496 it all started to unravel about him and in three of four years the* **devious black duke of Milan** *would be attacked again by the French in 1499, captured in 1500, and imprisoned for five years in France until his ignoble death in 1507. While held in high regard by some, many saw him for what he really was – a devious self-serving dictator who murdered his own nephew to attain the golden crown of his destiny.'*

Ludovico's display of grief for Beatrice d'Este's death was self-imposed mourning with the walls and ceilings of many rooms of the Sforza castle blackened with paint or curtains. One of the rooms became known as the *Saletta Negra* (**Black Room**) and it might be the backdrop in the *Pacioli Portrait*.

Ludovico Il Moro Sforza was officially the Duke of Milan for only six years compared to eighteen years by Gian Galeazzo Sforza. Because Ludovico was the Regent and Governor of Milan for most of Gian's tenure, he is much better remembered than Gian and therefore acknowledged as being the true guardian and ruler of Milan and the arbiter of Italy. Machiavelli would see Ludovico Sforza's major failures as vacillation and the inability to honour his word, content his people, keep the allegiance of his nobles, and to maintain a strong and uniform military organisation. Ludovico also failed by spending too much time indulging himself and his vassals with social and political intrigues and relying far too much on his astrologers like Ambrogio Varesi who often led him down the wrong paths and into deadly *cul-de-sacs*. This is what Machiavelli had to say of the Sforza and their Castle in Milan in his classic account of the *Prince*:

> *'It can be put like this: the prince who is more afraid of his own people than of foreign interference should build fortresses; but the prince who fears foreign interference more than his own people should forget about them. The castle of Milan, built by Francesco Sforza, has caused and will cause more uprisings against the House of Sforza than any other source of disturbance. So the best fortress that exists is to avoid being hated by the people. If you have fortresses and yet the people hate you they will not save you; once the people have taken up arms they will never lack outside help.'*

According to Machiavelli, the misfortune that Leonardo and Ludovico shared was that both artist and patron were unsuited to the times in which they lived. In a less unsettled period, Ludovico may have been a more successful ruler and Leonardo might have been a more productive artist. The suspicious death of the young duke Gian Galeazzo Sforza and the French invasions were perhaps the greatest misfortunes in both their lives. Although Leonardo lived to be honoured by two French kings, to travel in the Marches with Cesare Borgia and to win further triumphs as a painter, the twenty years of unstable wandering that followed II Moro's fall was not kind to his genius nor his art. Ludovico's epitaph of *'The Duke lost State, possessions and liberty and no work was completed for him,'* reflects on Leonardo's own career no less than on one of his greatest patrons.

Leonardo returned to Milan in 1506, when he was summoned back by the French governor Charles d'Amboise whose admiration for his works made him eager to know the artist personally. After staying for some time in the Governor's house, Leonardo was commanded to await the arrival of Louis XII who wished to employ him *'for certain little pictures of Our Lady'* and possibly for his own portrait. Except for another short visit to Florence, Leonardo seems to have remained in Milan until 1512 again working on destabilised projects because of political intrigue, skirmishes and threats of renewed wars. Louis XII's entreaties could not induce him to renounce the man of science for the artist, and his passing years were chiefly spent in research and experimentation. After three years of relative instability in Rome, Leonardo visited Milan once again in 1516 when it was the property of the French king Francois I, shortly before he left Italy for Amboise, never to return. And so, Leonardo was lost to Milan, as was his *Pacioli Portrait*. Although we know how Leonardo left Milan for France, we know nothing about the origins of the *Pacioli Portrait* and can only speculate.

CHAPTER 17

References

Ady, Cecilia M (1907). A history of Milan, under the House of Sforza. Edward Armstrong (editor). New York: G. P. Putnam's Sons. London: Methuen & Co. 1907. *https://archive.org/stream/historyofmilanun017956mbp/historyofmilanun017956mbp_djvu.txt.*

Azzolini, Monica (2004). Anatomy of a Dispute: Leonardo, Pacioli, and Scientific Entertainment in Renaissance Milan, Early Science and Medicine, 9: 128–135, and notes.

Azzolini, Monica (2013). The duke and the stars: astrology and politics in Renaissance Milan, Cambridge, Mass., Harvard University Press.

Barca GA. IACO. BAR. VIGENNIS P.1495. Enigma e Secretissima Scientia. *http://www.ritrattopacioli.it/Jacobarvigennis2.pdf (site disconnected).*

Cartwright, Julia Mary (1908). Beatrice d'Este, Duchess of Milan, 1475-1479. J. M. Dent amp Co. *http://readcentral.com/massappealnews/chapters/Julia-Mary Cartwright/Beatrice-dEste-Duchess-of-Milan-1475-1497/003.*

Codex Trivulzianus. *https://en.wikipedia.org/wiki/Codex_Trivulzianus#/media/File:Codex_trivulzianus.jpg* Also see, Leonardo da Vinci at *http://www.universalleonardo.org*

Collison-Morley, Lacy (1933). The Story of the Sforzas. London, G. Routledge & sons, limited.

Glori, Carla (2010). Il cartiglio di Leonardo. La Ricerca – 2010. *http://www.carlaglori.com/cartiglio/luca-pacioli/*

Glori, Carla (2013). Il cartiglio di Leonardo. Decifrazioni e Soluzioni 2013.

Glori, Carla (2018). Il cartiglio di Leonardo. Il cartiglio. *http://www.carlaglori.com/mi-presento/, http://www.carlaglori.com/cartiglio/*

Kulski JK (2017). Leonardo da Vinci: The Melzi Chronicles. Published by Jerzy. K. Kulski. *ISBN: 978-0-6480653-1-9.*

Vaglienti FM (2004). Isabella d'Aragona, Dizionario biografico degli Italiani (Rome, 1960ff.), lxii. 609–615. *http://www.treccani.it/enciclopedia/isabella-d-aragona-duchessa-di-milano_(Dizionario-Biografico)/*

Vasari G (1550). The Lives Of The Most Excellent Painters, Sculptors, and Architects. de Vere GdC, trans. New York, NY: The Modern Library; 2006.

18

THE GREEN TABLE: IN MEMORY OF GIAN GALEAZZO SFORZA

The Green and Black Dukes of Milan

The black background and green foreground are two contrasting colours that add a dramatic tension to the overall picture of the *Pacioli Portrait*. Why had Leonardo chosen to paint his table in the foreground using a bright-green colour? Possibly, because it is the one colour that identifies Gian Galeazzo Sforza, the sixth Duke of Milan, and because it contrasts so dramatically to the dark blue and black of the treacherous uncle, Ludovico il Moro Sforza also known as the Moor (see Chapter 17).

And yet, the green foreground in the *Pacioli Portrait* could have a double meaning. It could be a shared colour that represents both Gian Galeazzo Sforza, the 6th Duke of Milan as well as Ludovico il Moro, the Duke of Bari, who became the 7th Duke of Milan after usurping the dukedom from Gian Galeazzo's young son, Francesco. Ludovico Sforza often represented himself as black, blue or green because he was both a dark-skinned Moor and a verdant mulberry tree (see Chapter 19). Thus, green could represent either Gian or Ludovico or both of them in the contradictory iconic symbolism of Milan in 1480s and 1490s. The green table, if it symbolises either or both of the Sforza dukes, nevertheless sets the scene of the painting in Lombardy either in Milan or Pavia, but most likely in the Sforza Castle in Milan where large windows either on the western or eastern sides of the room are reflected in the hanging rhombicuboctahedron.

The green foreground in the *Pacioli Portrait* most likely represents a burial cloth covering the casket of Gian Galeazzo Sforza, the 6th Duke of Milan. The Franciscan monk Luca Pacioli stands there symbolically administering the last rites over the green casket of the young duke of Milan whose life sadly ended in Pavia on 21 October 1494 aged 25 years before he could take over the Duchy of Milan in his own right, freed from the chains imposed on him by his uncle Ludovico. As soon as Gian Galeazzo Sforza was dead, his body was quickly transported from Pavia to Milan where the period of mourning was staged for seven days and he was buried at the cathedral of Milan on the 29th of October to remove him from the memory of the people as quickly as possible. The new black duke had replaced him and was waiting impatiently to be revered. Neither Gian's mother Bona of Savoy nor his wife and children were brought to Milan to attend his burial for fear that their heartbreaking mourning and accusations of murder might lead to an uprising against Ludovico's regime.

Where was Gian Galeazzo Sforza buried? There is no obvious memorial in Milan to this young duke, no grand mausoleum or crypt to visit and commemorate his death. He is supposedly buried in an unmarked grave in the Cathedral of Milan according to the *Find a Grave* database on the Internet (https://www.findagrave.com). However, a few 'anonymous' portraits remain of Gian Galeazzo Sforza, most of them painted by Leonardo and/or by his assistants (Figs. 15.2 and 15.3), and many of them feature him with long golden hair and wearing his symbolic green vest or tunic and occasionally with his Duke's chain around his neck and over his chest to distinguish him from other anonymous sitters (Fig. 18.1). The Leonardeschi painters also depicted him as Saint Sebastian riddled by the arrows of martyrdom (Fig. 18.2) and Leonardo produced many drawings of Saint Sebastian including a pen and ink drawing newly discovered in 2000 (Fig. 18.3).

Green Chest Armour and Rule of Gian Galeazzo Sforza

Gian Galeazzo Maria Sforza (1469-1494), the Sixth duke of Milan, is most likely the subject of the *'Portrait of a Youth as Saint Sebastian'* (Fig. 18.1) that dates to the mid-1480s when Leonardo da Vinci was in Milan engaged in collaboration with Giovanni Ambrogio de Predis on the painting of the *Virgin of the Rocks*. The youth in the portrait looks up contemplatively with angelic inner sanctity. His long golden locks fall to his shoulders, and he wears a green vest and undergarments with red sleeves. His face could be the angel in Leonardo's *Virgin of the Rocks*, but he holds an arrow as a reference to Saint Sebastian, an early martyr of the church who had been shot to death by the arrows of the Praetorian Guard when they discovered that he was a 'secret' Christian. Although the painting is often attributed to Giovanni Ambrogio de Predis, it reflects Leonardo da Vinci's hand or influence through its muted tones and smoky shadows (*sfumato*) that were characteristic of the great master's style. Note the expressive hands that are a landmark of Leonardo da Vinci. Also, note the ringed chains across his chest, demonstrating the youth's entitled position as the Duke of Milan. These ducal chains are highly visible on Gian and Ludovico Sforza in their emblematic portraiture as the co-rulers of Milan in the picture from an illumination by Birago of the *Sforziada Book of Hours* held in the French National Library in Paris (Fig. 18.4).

FIG. 18.1. Portrait of a Youth as Saint Sebastian, about 1483 Oil on wood panel, 18-11/16 × 16-1/8 inches, attributed (probably incorrectly) to Giovanni Ambrogio de Predis. The Cleveland Museum of Art. Image source: Web Gallery of Art. The youth is in heraldic red and green with his ducal chains over his chest and arrow of St. Sebastian in his hand.

CHAPTER 18

FIG. 18.2. *Gian Galeazzo Sforza painted as the martyr Saint Sebastian with Isabella of Aragon as St. Mary with Child and Leonardo da Vinci as St. Roch by Bernardino Luini. Left at Collection of The John and Mabel Ringling Museum of Art, The State Art Museum of Florida. Right at Parish of Santa María de la Mesa (Utrera). Public domain. Wikimedia commons. PD-Art.*

FIG. 18.3. *Leonardo's drawings of Gian Galeazzo Sforza in the image of St. Sebastian. Left, discovered in 2000, private collection. Right, Royal Collection Trust / © Her Majesty Queen Elizabeth II 2017.*

FIG. 18.4. The ducal chains around the neck of the duke of Milan, Gian Galeazzo Sforza, in green chest armour (left), and his uncle the Duke of Bari, Ludovico Il Moro Sforza, in the blue chest armour (right). The image is a detail from an illumination by Birago of the Sforziada Book of Hours held in the French National Library in Paris.

The painters of Milan often portrayed Gian as an angel and he was the likely model for the two angels playing the musical instruments in the panels (Fig. 18.5) that bordered Leonardo's *Virgin of the Rocks* painted in 1483/1484. Furthermore, a few years after Gian Galeazzo's death, it is likely that Leonardo depicted him as the blond apostle John (Gian) the Evangelist (Fig. 18.6) seated at Jesus's right hand side as a victim of the betrayal by Ludovico Sforza (Judas), the dark seated figure in Leonardo's painting of the *Last Supper* (Fig. 18.6). The apostle John's pretty and feminine face like that of Gian (Fig. 18.1) has confused many art aficionados to think that Leonardo's Apostle John was a woman, such as Mary Magdalene in Dan Brown's pulp fiction *The Da Vinci Code*.

FIG. 18.5. Panels of the angels (left dressed in green and right dressed in red) that bordered Leonardo da Vinci's Virgin of the Rocks.

CHAPTER 18

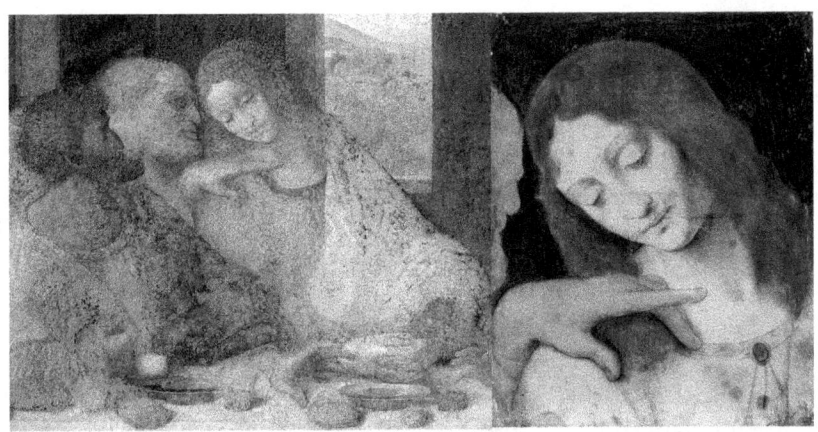

FIG. 18.6. *Leonardo's painting of Gian Galeazzo Sforza in the image of St. Gian (John) in the* Last Supper *(left) and a copy of the head of* St. John *by Boltraffio at the Musees de Strasbourg, Strasbourg. Public domain. Wikimedia commons. PD-Art.*

Leonardo's preparatory drawing for the *Last Supper* is very telling with St. John (Gian Galeazzo Sforza) slumped over the table as if he was dead while the betrayer and assassin Judas (Ludovico Sforza) sits opposite him pointing a forefinger or knife at him (Fig 18.7).

FIG. 18.7. *Leonardo's drawing for the* Last Supper *(left) with St. John (Gian) the Evangelist slumped over on the table with his arms crossed in the form of St. Andrew's cross. Study for the Last Supper.1494-95. Gallerie dell'Accademia, Venice. Web Gallery of Art. Public domain image. PD-Art.*

Like many of the artists of Milan who saw Gian Galeazzo Sforza as a gentle lamb and victim of Ludovico's greed for power, Leonardo would have been shocked by Gian's untimely death and he would have bestowed his sympathy to the young widow and her children. He probably tried, with possible danger to himself, to immortalise Gian Galeazzo Sforza as a lasting memorial for the widow and her children on the wall of the refectory of the Convent of Santa Maria delle Grazie. In this regard, the painting of the *Last Supper* is a pictorial statement of the betrayal and the unsavoury politics of Ludovico Sforza in Milan between 1493 and 1498. I am also of the strong opinion that Leonardo's *Mona Lisa* at the Louvre in Paris is his tribute to Gian Galeazzo Sforza's widowed wife, Isabella of Aragon, showing her as the dignified duchess of Milan, stripped of her entitlements and held in house arrest with her children by Ludovico Sforza.

Although blond, prettily handsome and decent (Fig. 18.1), nothing good has been published about Gian Galeazzo Sforza in his eighteen-year reign over Lombardy as the Duke of Milan from 1476 to 1494. After all, most of his reign was under the Regency of his uncle Ludovico Sforza, the guardian (prison warden) and the official governor of the city and Duchy of Milan. After the death of Gian Galeazzo Sforza, his uncle's reign resulted in a revisionist view, expunging from the records all the good things that Gian Galeazzo Sforza might have initiated or done for his Duchy. Ludovico and his two sons, Massimiliano (also known as Maximilian) and Francesco II, during their reign as the Dukes of Milan, contributed and led to the rewriting of Gian Galeazzo Sforza's history. The last of them, Francesco II Sforza, reigned from 1521 to 1535 and he made sure the legacy of his father Ludovico and his brother Massimiliano would be remembered in the records forever as innovative and caring leaders and that the Gian Galeazzo Sforza would be forgotten or remembered as an imbecilic weakling who had no initiative and was forever led by the nose by others, especially by his uncle Ludovico.

Gian Galeazzo Sforza is portrayed in the modern literature usually as having grown up weak both in mind and body, whereas Ludovico Sforza is represented both as the wise guardian of Milan and as the arbiter of Italy. However, Gian Galeazzo Sforza was not the imbecile and the derelict drunkard that some historians tried to make him out to have been. He was gentle, intelligent and immensely likeable and a great supporter of the arts, social justice and charities. He took the symbols of just and proper leadership that he inherited from his father extremely seriously, symbols such as the unchained dog, i.e., the unclasped collar of the dog attached to the tree [freedom from tyranny], the cheesecloth to filter out injustice, and the burning bush of justice and peace for the vulnerable. Ludovico Sforza and his ancestors probably destroyed the records of Gian's many charitable works to diminish his image as one who at a young age contributed much of his wealth and taxes for the good of his citizens. If historians are interested, they might still find evidence of such good works including his

CHAPTER 18

tireless diplomacy with the king of England to restore the rights of the Genoese merchants and for the English king to allow them access to the seaways around Great Britain and trade with them in wool to the advantage of his Milanese citizens.

Gian Galeazzo Sforza, Duke of Milan, to Francesco Pagnano, his Ambassador in England. We are advised by our community of Genoa that the Florentines are making efforts with that most serene king that no wool shall be taken out of England for Italy unless it is all discharged at Pisa. If this were allowed, it would not only seriously damage the trade and convenience of our city of Genoa, but it would also cause great detriment to our people of Milan and other towns of our dominions, which could not obtain from Pisa, except at great expense and inconvenience, the wool which is easily brought to them from Genoa, owing to its nearness. You will see the importance of the matter, and this has moved us to write to his Majesty and beg him not to show that he looks less kindly upon the Genoese than heretofore, since they have returned to our obedience. We are also writing to my Lord of Canterbury, the Lord Chancellor of the said king. For this reason we think it right to inform you also, because when you fully understand all about the matter from the Genoese merchants, who have the burden of the affair in that island, you will speak about it to his Majesty and commend to him most earnestly the interests of the Genoese, telling him how much they are bound up with the interests of our other towns and assuring his Majesty that it will afford us exceptional pleasure, besides the favour which he will obtain therefrom; it being understood that by the offer and ... which is proposed to him he will not choose to depart from his customary graciousness, in affording freely the use of this wool, according as he (cognoscendosi che per offerta e ... che li sii proposto non vogli manchare de la consueta benignitade ... ettendo liberamente l'uso de queste lane secundo ch'ella ...). Viglevano, the 10th December 1489. [Italian; draft, torn at the end.]

Henry VII, King of England, to Gian Galeazzo Sforza, Duke of Milan. Declaravit nobis Vestra Celsitudo immensam quandam ac prope inestimabilem amoris sui vim et conceptam erga nos benevolentiam nec eam quidem literis tantum ad nos suis iterum atque iterum ...etc ... (go to Reference source)... Superest ut diu et felix valeat ad vota Vestra Sublimitas et si qua in re sibi gratificare valeamus nostra opera uti confidanter velit. Ex Regia nostra juxta Westmonasterium, die xviii Februarii, MCCCCLXXXVIIII. [On parchment.]

Letters patent of Henry, King of England, to Gian Galeazzo Sforza, Duke of Milan, granting protection and safe conduct for seven years to all merchants and subjects of the Duke of Milan in England and other places of his dominions, with their ships, carracks and galleys and all their goods and merchandise, notwithstanding any letters of marque or reprisals issued against them, which letters of marque shall be of none effect against these presents, provided always that all customs and dues are faithfully paid. Dated at

Westminster, the 24th February in the 5th year of the reign. Per ipsum Regem. Cloc. B. (Latin; copy.)

Gian. Galeazzo Sforza, duke of Milan, to Bartholommeo Chalco, his Principal Secretary. Francesco Pagano has returned from England and presented letters from the king, telling us of his Majesty's great goodwill. As regards the league and the marriage alliance he has told us verbally the same as his letters related, and that his Majesty readily granted a safe conduct for seven years to all our subjects in his dominions. And as regards the fact that the wool exported from that island must be taken to no other place in Italy except Porto Pisano, his Majesty through some of his ministers gave him to understand that although this demonstration was made to gratify some Florentine merchants residing in London and some Londoners who have an understanding with them, the condition and respect of whom induced his Majesty to show them consideration, yet he declared that the matter shall stand in its original terms, and he admits that this cannot but offend the rest of Italy. We think, after this reply, that we must send again to his Majesty in response to the league which he proposed, and we have selected Benedetto Spinula who lives in London without sending any one from here except a courier with the necessary letters. We wish you to have the following letters written: one to the king announcing the return of Francesco Pagano, expressing our esteem and thanking him for his friendship and recommending Benedetto Spinula. Another to Benedetto telling him of the good report brought of him and that he must go and thank the king and be ready for further instructions, as we have decided to employ him with his Majesty, and tell him to ask from the king the confirmation of his stipulation. He will also thank the king for his friendly reply. As M. Francesco reports that his Majesty proposes to give the first of his sisters in law to the King of Portugal, he will discover the king's intentions but not to give up the plan, as we shall follow his Majesty's intent, and we may send a fresh councillor to show our esteem for his alliance. With regard to what we are informed that his Majesty does not intend to provide a dowry owing to the custom of the country, he will beg him to consider the custom here. He will thank the king for the safe conduct. The question of the wool requires circumspection, but he can point out the advantages to that kingdom that there be not too great a mart in Italy. [Translated from Italian]

Gian. Galeazzo Sforza, Duke of Milan, to Henry VII, King of England. Francesco Pagano has returned, whom we sent to your Majesty, bringing your most friendly letters, and in a long discourse has related your great kindness in all the matters he had to treat with you, especially your willingness to conclude a league and marriage alliance with us. We are greatly rejoiced and cannot adequately express our esteem for you. Our envoy, M. Joannes, informed us of your goodwill and now this is more than confirmed. We thank you with all our heart for the safe conduct granted to our subjects, as it also concerns our dignity. We have instructed Benedetto Spinula, citizen of Genoa trading in England, to express to your Majesty what we have written to him and he will also speak about the grievance of your subjects at Genoa, which we understand to be without reason. Pavia, the 9th June, 1490. [Latin; draft.]

CHAPTER 18

Gian. Galeazzo Sforza, Duke of Milan, to Benedicto Spinula, his Agent in England. Since the exposition of what we informed you by our other letters our ambassador, Francesco Pagnano, who has returned from that most illustrious king, has reported, he has given us to understand that certain Englishmen had complained bitterly to him that the merchants of that country were weighed down with very excessive gabelles and in addition to these they are forced to make other payments beyond what is usual. He has shown a note containing the particulars of their grievance, and said that his royal Majesty had charged him to speak to us about it so that provision might be made. As we do not wish to fail in our office and are very desirous that no one shall be able to complain with reason of unfair treatment at Genoa, especially in the case of the subjects of princes united with us by such ties of singular friendship as the said king, we have written on the subject to Genoa, so that a careful enquiry may be made into the matter, and if the representation is true that good and proper provision may be made. Accordingly an enquiry has been made by those who received our commission, and after carefully considering all the particulars of the complaint made by the English, the office of Saint George, to whom this pertains in particular, after pointing out that they have no reasonable cause for complaint, has made the reply which we enclose, with a copy of their letter and a note of the complaints made against them, so that you may possess all the facts and may inform the king of what we have done and the arguments which the Genoese adduce on their side. As a matter of fact, we do not consider these at all unreasonable, and we believe that they will be accepted by his Majesty. You will make every effort to persuade him with the strongest arguments you know, assuring him that he may be perfectly sure that his subjects and interests at Genoa and in all parts of our state will always have the attention demanded by the exalted dignity of his Majesty and the singular affection and esteem which we bear towards him. Pavia, the 9th June, 1490.

This diplomatic exchange between Gian Galeazzo Sforza when he was twenty years of age and the thirty-three-year-old King Henry VII of England in 1489/1490 shows Gian to be a sensitive and thoughtful ruler who cared deeply about the welfare of his citizens and dominions and was willing to act diplomatically on their behalf. If Gian Galeazzo Sforza had lived and ruled in his own right after 1494 as the Duke of Milan, he would have done so with the Duchess Isabella Aragon Sforza and his son Francesco Sforza, Count of Pavia, by his side. We may acquire some reasonable idea of how the Duchy would have been ruled by them from the history of the Duchess's rule of the Duchy of Bari. In 1499, Ludovico having a moment of remorse and guilt for his misdeeds against his nephew and the Duchess Isabella Aragon Sforza granted her his entitlements to the Duchy of Bari. This was confirmed and granted to her by the King of Spain in 1502 when he and the French controlled the Kingdom of Naples. She moved from Milan at the end of 1499 and settled in Bari in 1503 with her remaining child Bona Sforza. Her son Francesco was a captive of King Louis XII in France and her other daughter Ippolita died tragically of illness on the island of Ischia. By most accounts, Isabella Aragon Sforza the former Princess of Naples and Duchess of Milan ruled her Duchy of Bari kindly and astutely, sensitive to her people's needs and wishes. It is also evident from the letter that she wrote to her father in 1492 that she had a much different view of governing Milan than her jailer Ludovico Sforza, the Duke of Bari who long neglected the people of Bari because of his obsession with Milan. Moreover, Gian Galeazzo Sforza and Isabella Aragon Sforza's daughter Bona Sforza married the Polish king in 1518 and she ruled Poland for a time in her own right with a reasonable historical legacy. She abdicated the Polish throne in 1548 in favour of her son Sigismund II Augustus and returned to Bari where she ruled as the Duchess of Bari until her secretary Gian Lorenzo Pappacoda who, hoping to have all the power and wealth for himself, murdered her in 1557.

What if the Duke and Duchess of Milan Gian Galeazzo Sforza and Isabella Aragon Sforza had ruled the Duchy of Milan together after 1494 without interference and intrigue from their enemies?

1. They would have maintained the TRIPLE ALLIANCE between Milan, Naples and Florence together with an alliance with the Pope and there would not have been an invasion of Italy by their enemy France and then later by the Spanish.
2. They would have served their citizens with greater tolerance, generosity and kindness as became Gian Galeazzo's sweet nature and Isabella Aragon Sforza's example of benevolence as was seen later in her peaceful rule of the Duchy of Bari.
3. The arts, literature and science would have flourished even more so under their tutelage than that of Ludovico for both Gian Galeazzo Sforza and Isabella Aragon Sforza were well educated in the classics, arts, sciences and literature and they favoured diplomacy over war or sanctions.
4. And most importantly, Leonardo da Vinci would have stayed on in Milan and Lombardy for a much longer and stable time to create his magic, art and science without the interference of wars, and intolerable intrigues.

Of course these predictions are a fantasy and nobody has a crystal ball to say that the scenario predicted above would have happened for there may not have been anything or anybody to stop the ambitions of other men and kings who were the enemy of the Sforza and the Aragon Houses ready to disturb their peace and invade their Duchy or Kingdom. But, then again, the alternative to Ludovico Sforza's despotic rule is rarely contemplated or commented on by the historians who forever dismiss Gian Galeazzo

CHAPTER 18

Sforza as a simpleton and a debauched drunk rather than somebody who was a good person and able to rule his people fairly and properly. After all, his wife Isabella Aragon Sforza stood by him and indicated to her father that he would be an able and good leader. Besides, the painters of the time portrayed Gian Galeazzo Sforza as an angelic and saintly figure with musical instruments and books rather than *'carousing at a table laden with food'*. Therefore, it seems that the historians of today could look at Gian Galeazzo Sforza and his rule of the Duchy of Milan as a young boy and a man more positively and in a different light than they have in the past, possibly using a torchlight with a green filter rather than a blue, black or opaque one.

When Leonardo arrived in Milan he would have given Gian Galeazzo Sforza the respect expected for properly honouring the Duke of Milan whether or not a Regent or an appointed council governed the Duchy of Milan. Gian Galeazzo Sforza was the godson of Lorenzo de Medici of Florence who possibly sent Leonardo to Milan as his representative. So Leonardo would have been especially aware of the proper protocols for his own advancement in a Duke's court. The young Duke was the ruler of his dominions and the superior of all in his cities, counties and provinces, although the day-to-day administration was run by two Councils or Senates under the auspices of an elected governor or advisor and a constitution. Also, a Secret Council advised the young Duke on matters of State security and intrigue. The ducal revenues amounted to between six and seven hundred thousand ducats, and the increasing prosperity of Milan and the Duchy was largely due to the young duke and the wise economic policy of his two Councils and the continued irrigation works that enhanced the productive power of his dominions. With the rise to power of Ludovico, he rearranged the administration of the government and councils and made appointments to favour himself at the expense of the young duke. So he appointed Bartolomeo Calco as the Secretary for Foreign Affairs, who in turn had special clerks under him for France, Venice and other States, with which Milan was in frequent communication. Calco opened the diplomatic dispatches and determined their answers, submitting only the more important documents to Ludovico and/or to Gian - the duke of Milan, and arranged for the reception of foreign ambassadors in Milan, and acted as the conduit between the home Government and the Milanese ambassadors abroad. Jacopo Antiquario controlled the ecclesiastical affairs of Milan, Giovanni da Bellinzona was Secretary for Justice, and Jacopo Terafino was Secretary for Finance. This system of secretarial appointments concentrated the power to Ludovico and he filled the chief offices of State with men dependent on him alone, to the exclusion of all possible rivals. Thus, the two ruling Councils that were composed of men drawn from the leading families of Milan, whom Il Moro did not trust, gradually lost their share of influence in matters of State.

The last great rival to Ludovico's authority was removed in 1489 in the person of Filippo degli Eustachi who was the general of the military force in Milan. He was lured from the Rocchetta by a ruse and then seized by Galeazzo Sanseverino and imprisoned at Abbiategrasso on the charge of having agreed to cede the Castello of Milan to the Emperor of the Romans, Maximillian I. This false accusation of treachery disgraced Eustachi and left Il Moro in possession of the Rocchetta and in-charge of the citizen military. This act of treachery and *coup de grace* by Ludovico raised him to a new height of power that the young duke was not able or unwilling to rebel against.

Ludovico's cynicism to take over the ducal power from his nephew Gian Galeazzo Sforza was evident when it came to preparing his own sons as future Duke's of Milan. In preparing his will in 1498, he instructed the Ruling Council that they provide his sons with the privileges and an education on how to rule the State by proper administration, something that he never dared to allow for Gian Galeazzo Sforza. When Ludovico's eldest son Maximilian reached the age of twenty, he wanted the Council to instruct him on how to immediately apply to the King of the Romans for the same ducal privileges that had been granted to him. Furthermore, he specified in his will that his son Maximilian reside at the Castello and not travel further than his country houses in Abbiategrasso, Cussago, Monza, Dece, and Melegnano, not until he reached the age of fourteen; that he be educated in all branches of religious and secular learning, in good conduct and habits, and the knowledge of letters, and be entrusted to the best governors and teachers; that he take his place in the council from his earliest years and be gradually initiated into the management of affairs; and that he be taught to deliver speeches and know how to receive ambassadors graciously, and receive instruction in all that is necessary to make him a wise and good prince. In comparison, he neglected to provide such instruction and guidance to his nephew when he took over from Bona of Savoy as the Regent and the carer of Gian Galeazzo Sforza who was eleven years of age.

Gian Galeazzo Sforza in the British Archives and Collections of Milan 1477-1493

To get on with the wealthy and the influential in Lombardy and the city of Milan, Leonardo da Vinci like anybody else in his situation as a foreigner from Florence would have had to deal with the young duke of Milan, Gian Galeazzo Sforza, for it was he who had the official title and respect of his citizens and government and those outside Milan who wanted to deal formerly with the Duchy. And so it was that Leonardo organised the festivities and celebrations of the young duke's marriage to Isabella Aragon, renovated their rooms and bathrooms, and painted their portraits. He knew them well and he must have had great insight into their personalities, abilities, authority and their difficulties with their ambitious uncle, Ludovico Il Moro. It was good etiquette and protocol to meet with the young duke or his secretarial staff when doing business with the Duchy of Milan. There is a web site on the Internet entitled British History Online that reveals some of England's official correspondence with the Duchy of Milan and Gian Galeazzo Sforza as the Duke of Milan between 1477 and 1493.

Gian Galeazzo Sforza was seven-years-old when he inherited the title of the 6th Duke of Milan after the assassination of his father Galeazzo Maria Sforza in 1476. Because he was too young to rule and make sound and mature decisions his mother Bona of Savoy acted as regent on his behalf; the English addressed their official correspondence to Gian Galeazzo Sforza, Duke of Milan and/or Bona of Savoy Regent of Milan. This was the case from 1477 to 1479 until it all changed for Bona of Savoy when her devious brother-in-law Ludovico Moro Sforza, whom the English addressed in their correspondence as Duke of Bari, usurped her position as Regent. Gian Galeazzo Sforza was still addressed as the Duke of Milan in diplomatic dispatches at least until 1493.

Ludovico Moro Sforza became the Duke of Bari in 1480 when he convinced the King of Naples to present him with the title and deeds of the Duchy of Bari, a faraway community on the east coast of Italy, on the edge of the Adriatic Sea. Ludovico needed a Duchy and the title of Duke for his prestige and to have some sort of equivalency with his nephew the Duke of Milan. Ludovico's older brother Sforza Sforza was the previous Duke of Bari, a title that was bestowed on him by the King of Naples because he had married the King's daughter. When Sforza Sforza died of unknown (suspicious) causes in 1480, Ludovico grabbed the opportunity and the title for himself. So the English addressed their official diplomatic correspondence with the Duchy of Milan mainly to Gian Galeazzo Sforza, Duke of Milan between 1477 and 1491, but began to favour Ludovico Moro Sforza, Duke of Bari in 1493. In 1494, Ludovico Moro Sforza began to address himself in diplomatic dispatches as the Duke of Milan before the death of Gian Galeazzo Sforza in October 1494.

The diplomatic dispatches and exchanges between the English and Milan show that the young duke Gian Galeazzo Sforza was active and interested in foreign affairs from an early age in 1477 until Ludovico Sforza essentially imprisoned him Pavia in 1493 and then completely disposed of him in 1494. As the young Duke of Milan, Gian Galeazzo Sforza personally communicated with King Richard I and King Henry VII on various matters including on solving an English trade embargo against Genoan wool merchants; resolving a fraudulent 100-year-old debt supposedly incurred by Milan due to an unpaid dowry for Lucia Visconti, Duchess of Kent, by two devious Englishmen as the heirs of Richard Heron; finding marriage partners for the French, English and Scottish royalty and nobility; and negotiating various alliances and issues involving Genoa, the Pope, French king Louis XI, the Holy Roman Emperor Maximilian, the King of Naples and the Signoria of Venice and Florence. It is evident from these diplomatic exchanges that Ludovico Sforza did not assert himself over the young duke in foreign affairs until 1492, and then more strongly in 1493 until he eliminated the young duke by poison in October of 1494.

The last reference in the archives of British History on-line to Gian Galeazzo Sforza as Duke of Milan in diplomatic dispatches was in 1493.

'Carlo Barbiano, Milanese Ambassador in France, to Gian Galeazzo Sforza, Duke of Milan. The admiral tries to upset the peace in every way. He persuades the king that the emperor only wants peace in order to deceive him and set up Burgundy again. He says if the king gives back the daughter one of two evils will follow, either her father will never marry her, saying that she is the wife of his Majesty, and thus make out that the king's children are bastards, or they will try to make King of England the boy who calls himself the son of King Edward, who fled thither, and give him this daughter to wife, so as by his means to make perpetual war in France. These arguments have left the king very perplexed. Senlis, the 4th April, 1493.' [translated from Italian]

And then in July of 1494, three months before the death of Gian Galeazzo Sforza, Ludovico Sforza had referred to himself as the Duke of Milan.

'Ludovico Maria Sforza, Duke of Milan, to Bartholomeo Chalco, his Principal Secretary. M. Raymundo will come to you with an instruction which we have had drawn up for him. You will get it despatched for him, having the credentials made for him and a letter as a pass. Bernate, the 25th July, 1494.' [Translated from Italian]

*'Acostino Spinola to Ludovico Maria Sforza, Duke of Milan.
Has understood from Messer Raymondo that his Highness is content with his service. Thank God, this is so, as has no other desire in the world than to please him as is the nature of every good Spinola. Will give every advice and assistance to M. Raymondo on his return. London, the 20th September, 1494.' [Translated from Italian]*

Bloated with power and privilege, Ludovico Il Moro Sforza had no intention of losing it and so he usurped the title of Duke of Milan from his nephew even before he had killed him with poison. This was a vicious and dastardly action by Ludovico Il Moro Sforza that Leonardo da Vinci would

CHAPTER 18

have been aware of. Leonardo, secretly, would have sympathised and supported Gian Galeazzo Sforza and his young wife Isabella Aragon Sforza, the Duchess of Milan, and their young son, Francesco Maria Sforza, who was officially the next in line to become the new Duke of Milan. Thus, Ludovico Sforza, not only stole the Duchy of Milan from Gian Galeazzo Sforza, but he also stole it from Gian Galeazzo's wife and son. This tragic action is symbolised in the *Pacioli Portrait* with Ludovico Sforza represented by the black background, the black fly and the year 1495, whereas the dead young duke is represented by the green casket (burial) cloth and 1494, the year Gian Galeazzo Sforza was killed by intrigue and poison. Carla Glori deciphered the code **IACO. BAR. VIGENNIS P.1495** and the meaning of the symbol of the black fly to reveal the suppressed history of those tragic events that destroyed the lives and happiness of many good people (see Chapter 20 for the code's deciphering and solution).

With the greatest of apologies to Carla Glori for breaking her rules of decryption (based solely on the perfect anagrams) and her Latin translations (see Chapter 20), I have shuffled and translated the anagram loosely as follows to interpret Gian Galeazzo Sforza's death in 1494:

O **NIS** GIAN VI BAR P. C 1494 = O! The end [fiNIS] of GIAN, the 6th (VI) Duke of Milan, care of [c] the Duke of Bari (BAR), in Pavia (P), about (Circa). 1494/95.

O! The end (fiNIS) of GIAN, 6th (VI) Duke of Milan, care of the Duke of Bari (BAR), in Pavia (P) about (Circa). 1494/95.

$O = O!$
NIS = end
GIAN = Gian Galeazzo Sforza
VI = 6th Duke of Milan
BAR = Duke of Bari, Ludovico Moro Sforza
P. = killed (.) in Pavia (P)
C = Circa, about
1495 = 1494/95

The *Pacioli Portrait* shows the tiny black fly of death on the yellow notebook that lies on top of the green coffin that hides the secrets and the dead body of the Duke of Milan, Gian Galeazzo Sforza (aged 25 years) buried in his green chest armour. The complicity of Ludovico Sforza's son-in-law Galeazzo Sanseverino in the murder of Gian Galeazzo Sforza is symbolised by the green glove of his left hand; the green colour symbolises Gian's green armour and the colour of arsenic that killed him. Amen.

References

Ady, Cecilia M (1907). A history of Milan, under the House of Sforza. Edward Armstrong (editor). New York: G. P. Putnam's Sons. London: Methuen & Co. https://archive.org/stream/historyofmilanun017956mbp/historyofmilanun017956mbp_djvu.txt.

Azzolini, Monica (2004). Anatomy of a Dispute: Leonardo, Pacioli, and Scientific Entertainment in Renaissance Milan, Early Science and Medicine 9(2):128–135 and notes.

Azzolini, Monica (2013). The duke and the stars: astrology and politics in Renaissance Milan, Cambridge, Mass., Harvard University Press.

Barca GA. IACO. BAR. VIGENNIS P.1495. Enigma e Secretissima Scientia. http://www.ritrattopacioli.it/Jacobarvigennis2.pdf *(site disconnected)*.

Cartwright, Julia Mary (1908). Beatrice d'Este, Duchess of Milan, 1475-1479. J. M. Dent amp Co. Online:
http://readcentral.com/massappealnews/chapters/Julia-Mary Cartwright/Beatrice-dEste-Duchess-of-Milan-1475-1497/003.

Codex Trivulzianus.
https://en.wikipedia.org/wiki/Codex_Trivulzianus#/media/File:Codex_trivulzianus.jpg
Also see, Leonardo da Vinci at http://www.universalleonardo.org

Collison-Morley, Lacy (1933). The Story of the Sforzas. London, G. Routledge & sons, limited.

Glori, Carla (2010). Il cartiglio di Leonardo. La Ricerca – 2010.
http://www.carlaglori.com/cartiglio/luca-pacioli/

Glori, Carla (2013). Il cartiglio di Leonardo. Decifrazioni e Soluzioni 2013.

Glori, Carla (2018). Il cartiglio di Leonardo. Il cartiglio. http://www.carlaglori.com/mi-presento/, http://www.carlaglori.com/cartiglio/

Hinds, Allen B (1912). British History Online. Calendar of State Papers and Manuscripts in the Archives and Collections of Milan 1385-1618, Diplomatic dispatches of Gian Galeazzo Sforza in the archives of British History. Milan 1476 to 1495, pp. 220-293. https://www.british-history.ac.uk/cal-state-papers/milan/1385-1618 [accessed 22 May 2019].

Kulski JK (2017). Leonardo da Vinci: The Melzi Chronicles. Published by Jerzy. K. Kulski. *ISBN: 978-0-6480653-1-9*.

Kulski JK (2018). The Mona Lisa portrait: Leonardo's personal and political tribute to Isabella Aragon Sforza, the Duchess of Milan. International Journal of Art and Art History. 6 (2), 31-50. *DOI: 10.15640/ijaah.v6n2p5*.
http://ijaahnet.com/journals/ijaah/Vol_6_No_2_December_2018/5.pdf
https://www.researchgate.net/publication/331087584_5MonaLisa

Vaglienti FM (2004). Isabella d'Aragona, Dizionario biografico degli Italiani (Rome, 1960ff.), lxii. 609–615. http://www.treccani.it/enciclopedia/isabella-d-aragona-duchessa-di-milano_(Dizionario-Biografico)/

Vasari G (1550). The Lives Of The Most Excellent Painters, Sculptors, and Architects. de Vere GdC, trans. New York, NY: The Modern Library; 2006.

19

SFORZA CASTLE, BLACK ROOMS & LEONARDO'S ACADEMY

The Sforza Castle According to Luca Pacioli

When we look at the *Pacioli Portrait*, did Leonardo expect us to ponder where this lecture on Euclidian geometry was staged? Was it at the Sforza Castle or somewhere else? If Leonardo was living today how would he answer the question about the black background in the painting - was it just a simple prop that he had used in his other portrait paintings such as *Portrait of a Musician*, *Lady with an Ermine*, *La Belle Ferronniere* and *John the Baptist* or was it depicting an actual black room in the castle?

In the introduction to the *Divine Proportion*, Luca Pacioli told us that he presented a lecture at the Sforza Castle:

'Today, Eminent Duke, the 9th day of February, the year of our Lord 1498, we are gathered in the impregnable citadel of your illustrious city of Milan, the most worthy place of your usual residence, in the presence of your majesty, and an assembly [dedicated to] praiseworthy scientific debate, composed of people of all ranks, famous and most wise, both religious and secular, with whom your magnificent court constantly abounds. Among whom, besides most reverend Lord Bishops, Protonotaries, and Abbots, there are present from our sacred seraphic Order, the reverend father and sublime theologian, Maestro Gometius; the most worthy preacher of the Sacred Scripture, friar Dominico, surnamed Ponzone; the reverend father Maestro Francesco Busti, presently acting regent in our worthy convent of Milan. And among the laymen present, first my own illustrious patron Signor Galeazzo Sforza, the powerful Vicar of Sanseverino and a general officer in the service of your Excellency, a captain of arms second to none today, and a diligent practitioner of our disciplines.'

And just to remind ourselves that the man in black in the *Pacioli Portrait* is Galeazzo Sanseverino, we also can quote the words of Luca Pacioli that he provided for us at the end of the *Divine Proportion*:

'And truly, excellent Duke, not misleading your Excellence, I say that the speculation of the mathematicians can extend virtually no higher, whether the length of a work happens to be sometimes more and sometimes less... It is here in your illustrious, great city of Milan, with not ordinary efforts and long vigils, under the protective shade of your Excellency, and of your, as if son, **my**, *unworthy that I am,* ***personal and singular patron, his eminent lordship Galeazzo Sanseverino de Aragon****, second to none in the military arts, and a great lover of our disciplines, especially in the day's work of his assiduous studies, where he tastes of the most useful and sweet fruit.'*

Who is the sponsor of the *Divine Proportion* and perhaps the *Pacioli Portrait*? That's right, it is not Guidubaldo da Montefeltro, Duke of Urbino, as told to us by the Capodimonte Museum (Naples) and that provided us with a dubious attribution that lacks evidence. The patron and disciple of the portrait is most likely none other than '*his eminent lordship* **Galeazzo Sanseverino** *de Aragon, second to none in the military arts, and a great lover of our disciplines.*' Luca Pacioli says so in the *Divine Proportion*. It is the extant document that reveals to us who is in the painting, what it is about (at least at one level), where it is staged and who painted it. There is no mention of Jacopo de' Barbari in the *Divine Proportion*.

The effusive dedication by Fra Luca Pacioli to the Duke of Milan provides us with a reasonable assumption that the painted lecture in the presence of Signor Galeazzo Sanseverino Sforza was staged most probably in a room or a hall at the Sforza Castle, a walled fortress to keep out the riff-raff and the enemies of Ludovico Sforza. Here is what Machiavelli thought of the Sforza castle.

'It can be put like this: the prince who is more afraid of his own people than of foreign interference should build fortresses; but the prince who fears foreign interference more than his own people should forget about them. The castle of Milan, built by Francesco Sforza, has caused and will cause more uprisings against the House of Sforza than any other source of disturbance. So the best fortress that exists is to avoid being hated by the people. If you have fortresses and yet the people hate you they will not save you; once the people have taken up arms they will never lack outside help.'

In their introduction to their translation of Luca Pacioli's *Divine Proportion*, Johnathan Tennenbaum, John P. Scialdone, and Richard Sanders (2015) wrote:

'Luca Pacioli opened his manuscript on the Divine Proportion with a dedication to the Duke of Milan, Ludovico II Sforza, describing a great gathering in the Duke's presence, in his illustrious city of Milan: "an assembly dedicated to scientific debate, composed of people of all ranks, famous and most wise, both religious and secular, with whom your court continually abounds." He turns again to this great gathering at the conclusion of

the book, alluding to the prominent participation of his own Franciscan Order, and others; and, although he states in both cases that it occurred in the current year, 1498, it is not clear whether this gathering actually took place, or whether it is a metaphorical description of the great scientific ferment occurring over time at **the Academy of Leonardo Da Vinci at the Castle of the Duke.**'

History of the Sforza Castle

The Sforza Castle or *Castello* Sforza was the seat of power during the reign of Gian Galeazzo Sforza and his uncle Ludovico Sforza when Leonardo da Vinci was in Milan, and its reconstruction and renovations are worth considering in terms of the Sforza history. The original *Castello* was the *Rocca Viscontea* built at the *Porta Giovia* between 1360-1379 by Galeazzo II Visconti. The *Castello* that still stands today in Milan was built during Francesco Sforza's reign (1450 to 1466) from the ruins of the *Rocca Viscontea* after the citizens of the Ambrosian Republic (1447 to 1450) destroyed most of the original *Castello* in an attempt to wipe out all traces of the tyrannical rule by the Visconti. Francesco Sforza used the remaining *Castello* as early as August of 1451 to lodge his soldiers in a tower before he began to rebuild it. His architects for the rebuild were chosen for their military authority, devotion to the House of Sforza and their technical skill. The cost of rebuilding the *Castello* was derived from a monthly charge taken from the taxes, a special duty to meet the expenses of transport, and from a fee on mortar. In 1452, the building of the *Castello* was advanced enough to appoint a permanent castellan, and the Duke's kinsman Foschino Attendolo took command of the fortress. Francesco Sforza only used the *Castello* for military purposes, and it was his son and successor, Galeazzo Maria Sforza, who built the additional rooms within the main building and added other changes to render the *Castello* habitable. Beyond the main entrance a large courtyard, known as the *Piazza d'Armi*, spread out to the *Corte Ducale* that was the ducal residence. The *Rocchetta*, or inner fortress, that could be defended against hostiles from the rest of the *Castello*, could only be approached using a drawbridge from the *Piazza d'Armi*. The ducal treasure was kept in the lower room of the *Rocchetta* tower, while the Treasurer-General slept above, guarding the ducal wealth by day and by night. Beyond the main building lay an outer line of fortifications.

The *Castello* was too large and too open to the worst elements of the weather, too hot in summer and too cold and drafty for habitation in the winter months. So, Galeazzo Maria Sforza introduced further reconstruction of the *Castello* when he brought his wife Bianca of Savoy from France to Milan in 1468. The improvements that the Duke ordered before taking up his abode in the *Corte Ducale* were decorations for the rooms, stables for a hundred horses, and the provision of a room lined with wood (the *Sala delle Asse*) as insulation to keep out the cold from the *Castello's* draughty halls and large ill-fitting windows.

The years 1469-1474 saw the origin of the Sala Celeste, *with its sky-blue ceiling sprinkled with stars; of the* Sala delle Colombine, *adorned with Bona's favourite device of doves in the midst of flames; of the* Sala degli Scarlioni, *so called from the zigzag stripes in mulberry and white which covered its walls; of the* Sala delle Caccie, *decorated with hunting scenes; of the greater part of the rooms, in short, on both floors of the* Corte Ducale. *Galeazzo's chief architect in the* Castello *was Benedetto Ferrini, whose name figures with that of his master on the stairway of the* Corte Ducale. *Ferrini, moreover, was the moving spirit in the construction and decoration of the ducal chapel, which formed the most important part of Galeazzo's work for the* Castello. *The damaged remains of frescoes representing the* Resurrection *and the* Annunciation, *which can still be seen in the roof and on the walls give but a faint reflection of its former glories.' [Ady 1907]*

During the brief Regency of Bona, the further decoration of the *Castello* was abandoned in favour of enhancing the fortifications. Hence, the construction of the *Torre di Bona di Savoia* at the corner of the *Rocchetta* adjoining the *Corte Ducale* and opposite to the *Torre del Tesoro*.

'Under the auspices of II Moro, the decoration of the Castello *was carried, as, indeed, were all the artistic enterprises of the Duchy, to heights hitherto unknown. On the marriage of Gian Galeazzo to Isabella of Aragon elaborate preparations were made to do honour to the bride. A special suite of rooms was made ready in the* Corte Ducale, *while monasteries, nobles and merchants were alike called upon to lend their tapestries to decorate the* Castello *for the occasion. Ludovico's wedding in 1491 necessitated the formation of a separate household for Beatrice. Hence fresh improvements were introduced into the* Rocchetta *in order to provide her with suitable apartments there. At the same time, painters were summoned from all parts of the Duchy to adorn the walls and ceiling of the ballroom. Later again, Ludovico's elevation to the ducal throne was marked by the erection of that elegant addition to the* Corte Ducale *known as the* Ponticella of Bramante. *The arches of the* Ponticella *spanned the* Castello *trench and it thus formed a means of communication with the park and city, while a series of small rooms connected it on the other side with the* Corte Ducale. *Another feature of the* Castello, *which must have been executed by Bramante at about the same time, is the fresco of the thousand-eyed* Argos, *of which traces can still be seen upon the walls of the* Sala del Tesoro. *Between the years 1495-1498 Leonardo is known to have been at work in the* Castello. *Those among the recently discovered decorations which most distinctly bear the trace of his hand are in the lower room of the* Corte Ducale *tower, sometimes called the* Camera Grande delle Asse. *Round the walls are painted trees of which the foliage covers the ceiling with a green canopy while golden cords are entwined in the branches after a characteristically Leonardesque pattern. Woven into the design are the*

heraldry of the Duke and Duchess and inscriptions commemorating their various claims to renown. Leonardo is known to have assisted also in the decoration of the Saletta Negra, *a small room in the* Corte Ducale *which owes its name to the sad time when Il Moro ordered all his apartments to be hung in black while he mourned for Beatrice, It was at this juncture that Il Moro had his initials and those of his wife placed upon Filarete's tower, upon the* Torre di Bona *and upon various other parts of the* Castello. *The decorations in memory of his dead wife were the last which Ludovico undertook in the* Castello.' *[Ady 1907]*

Remarkably, a part of the Renaissance Sforza *Castello* and two of its cylindrical towers have survived intact to this day and now, after various renovations, it stands witness as a worthy Museum of Antiquities to the past glories of Sforza Milan (Fig. 19.1).

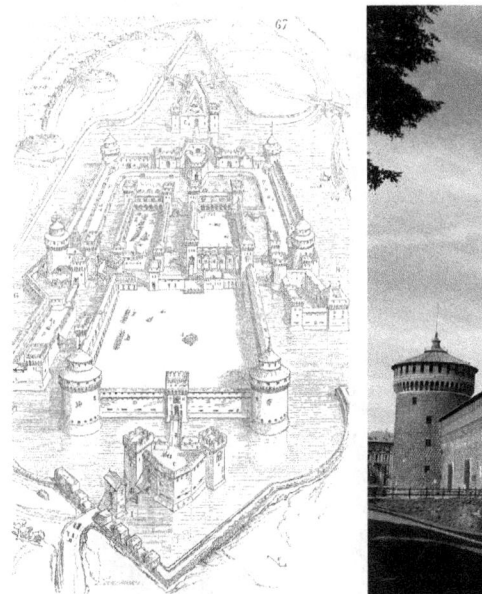 

FIG. 19.1. *The Sforza Castle in Milan. Left, 16 century,* File:Chateau.Milan.png. *(2014, December 9). Wikimedia Commons, the free media repository. Retrieved May 17, 2019*
 from https://commons.wikimedia.org/w/index.php?title=File:Chateau.Milan.png&oldid =142061349. Right, 21 century, Wikipedia contributors. (2019, April 15). Sforza Castle. In Wikipedia, The Free Encyclopedia. Retrieved May 17, 2019, from https://en.wikipedia.org/w/index.php?title=Sforza_Castle&oldid=892556713

The entire castle was planned to be demolished in the 1830s, but was saved from demolition by the architect Luca Beltrami (1854 to 1933) who restored and transformed it into the civic museum that it is today. The castle holds many exhibitions, and within its collections it has the

Trivulziano Code, a work by Leonardo da Vinci of 62 pages (only 55 remain) that deals especially with military and religious architecture and provides a long list of learned words that he had copied from authoritative lexical and grammatical sources. It also includes a drawing of an old man's head in profile with a distinctive protruding lower lip and jaw (Fig. 19.2). Some scholars believe that this is a profile of Leonardo's wealthy father Piero Fruosino di Antonio da Vinci, whereas others have suggested it is an exaggerated drawing of Gian Giacomo Trivulzio, a Milanese aristocrat, governor and *condottiere* who sponsored Leonardo at various times when they were together in Milan. The Trivulzio family members have the distinctive nose and jaw seen in many of Leonardo da Vinci's drawings of old men (Chapters 2 and 7).

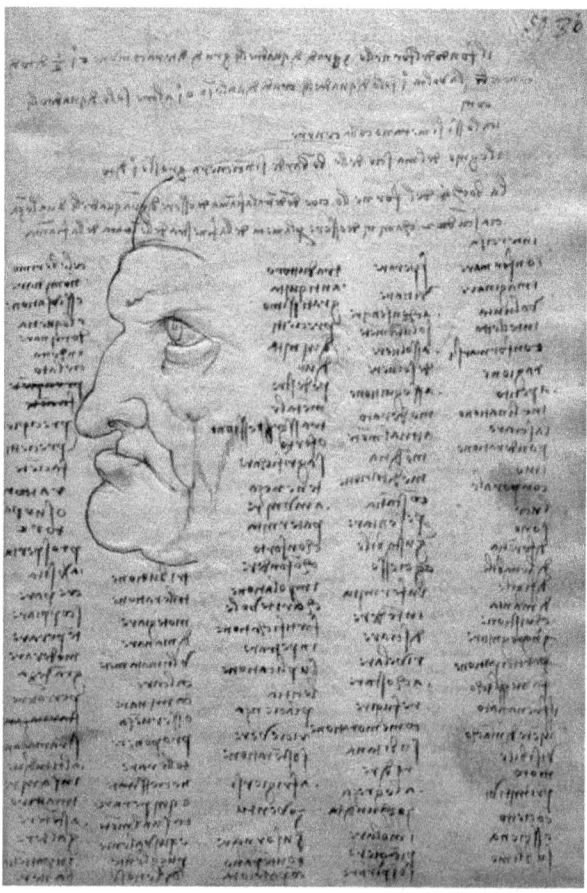

FIG. 19.2. A sheet from Leonardo's Trivulziano Codex *showing a drawing of an old man's face and a list of learned words. Public domain. File:Codex trivulzianus.jpg*

CHAPTER 19

Black and Green Rooms of the Sforza Castle

Given the black (background) and green (foreground) themes of the *Pacioli Portrait*, it is worth considering the purpose of the black room (*Saletta Negra*) and the green room (*Sala delle Asse*) in the Sforza castle that Leonardo da Vinci painted and decorated at about the same time as his portrait in 1497/8. In either context, the black and green is the obvious symbolism of Ludovico Sforza because he is both a dark-skinned Moor and a verdant mulberry. This may be true for the *Pacioli Portrait* as it is for the two rooms in the Sforza castle. Both rooms were dedicated to the memory of Ludovico's young wife Beatrice d'Este who had suffered a miscarriage and died two days after her supposedly uncontrollable dancing and drinking during the night of the 1497 New Year while her unfaithful husband was indulging himself with his new mistress Lucrezia Crivelli. The historians Muratori and Alessandro Giulini believe that Francesca dal Verme, the daughter of Count Pietro Dal Verme, had poisoned Beatrice d'Este in retaliation for the murder of her father in 1485 by Ludovico Sforza who confiscated the Dal Verme family properties including Voghera and the Valtrebbia properties, and the militarily strategic fort and village of Bobbio. The poisoning was kept secret to prevent unmanageable rebellions from breaking out in the Duchy. Nevertheless, to assuage his genuine grief for the sudden death of his wife, Ludovico il Moro Sforza urged Leonardo to complete the decorations in each of the rooms that had begun five years earlier by other artists. The decorations were never finished because of the French invasion in 1499.

Leonardo da Vinci made the following comments in his notebook after he heard that the French had captured Ludovico Sforza in Novara (once in Lombardy, but now in Piedmont) on April 10th 1500 and had imprisoned him at the castle of Lys-Saint-Georges in Berry:

The Saletta above ... (left unfinished).

The duke has lost state, fortune, and liberty, and not one of his works has been completed.

'*The Saletta above (left unfinished)*' probably refers to the *Saletta Negra*, a small room in the Sforza Castle that owes its name to the sad time when il Moro ordered all his apartments to be hung in black cloth, while he mourned for Beatrice. Leonardo was commissioned at about this same time to brighten up another room in the castle by painting green images of Ludovico's other emblem, the green mulberry tree. Leonardo tackled it with his usual fervour and alacrity. As usual, we are left with more speculation than concrete details. We can consider some of the academic hypotheses and facts put forward that might be relevant to the *Pacioli Portrait* that comply with our theme of contrasting the black with the green and contemplate why they might have been in Leonardo's subconscious and/or conscious mind.

The Saletta Negra (Black Room)

Paul Muller Walde described the room next to the staircase leading to the chancellery on the first floor as the *Saletta Negra* after the discovery in 1893 of its telltale frescoes. In 1914, new investigations by Luca Beltrami found that Ludovico il Moro reassigned the name *Saletta Negra* to a different room (today's rooms IX and X) and that previously Room V with the winged cherubs in the segments of the wall was erroneously called *Saletta Negra*. The decorations that Leonardo placed on the walls of Il Moro's private room, the *Saletta Negra*, after the death of Ludovico's bride Beatrice are no longer visible; it was where Ludovico went to find solitude with his grief.

Sala Verde (Green Room) or Sala della Balla (Ballroom)

Leonardo was employed at the Sforza Court to organise festivals, large entertainments and theatre with choreography and machinery, and provide spectaculars and cheerful parties to amaze court guests. The *Festa del Paradiso* was one of the most famous events organised in the *Sala Verde* (Green Room) of the ducal court when Leonardo created a spectacular theatrical representation of Dante's *Paradiso* on a semi-circular stage to celebrate one year of marriage between the young duke of Milan Gian Galeazzo Sforza and his wife Isabella of Aragon, the former Princess of Naples, and now the Duchess of Milan.

The *Paradiso* operetta was written and sang by the actors and choir in praise of Isabella Aragon Sforza and to depict her as being at the centre of the universe. In appearance, she had reddish copper-coloured dark hair, dark eyes and a feisty energetic personality. In contrast, her husband Gian Galeazzo was blond, pale, studious and melancholy. The Duchess fascinated Leonardo and she is one of the few women who he mentioned by name in his notebooks. He noted cheerfully that he had to prepare her bathroom and a pergola. It is most likely that he painted her portrait as the *Mona Lisa* when she was a widow four or five years after the death of Gian Galeazzo in October of 1494.

The *Festa del Paradiso* was held in the green room because this was the symbolic colour of Gian Galeazzo Sforza, the Duke of Milan's chest armour (Fig. 18.4). Thus, the green room was where audiences were held in the presence of the young duke. He also had a Green Reception Room in the Pavia Castle. It was his symbolic colour that he had inherited from the first duke of Milan, a Visconti who had the same Christian names, Gian

Galeazzo. The extraordinary event of the *Festa del Paradiso* was described in Latin by a witness whose full account was presented by Edmondo Solmi in a number of academic papers and by Patrizia Costa in her PhD thesis for the University of Pittsburgh (see References at the end of this chapter). In part she writes, *'Description of the Festa del Paradiso that took place on January 13, 1490 in honor of the Duchess Isabella of Aragon and Gian Galeazzo Maria. According to Edmondo Solmi, the feast was held in the* sala verde superiore.'

Vault of the Hall delle Asse (Room of Planks)

The Vault of the Hall *delle Asse*, also known as the *Sala delle Asse or* Hall of Planks, is a square shaped room located on the ground floor of the Folconiera Tower at the northeastern corner of the Sforza Castle. The 'asse' or planks in the room once lined the room's four walls from 1471 to 1498 to insulate the room and provide a surface for mounting tapestries or paintings. They were dismantled in 1498, but the name of the room *Sala delle Asse* remained.

The square room is vaulted in the Gothic style, fifteen metres on each side. It has four lunettes on each wall and two large windows in the northeast and northwest walls. In 1498, the Duke of Milan, Ludovico il Moro Sforza commissioned Leonardo to paint a pergola in the *Sala delle Asse*. Leonardo painted on the ceiling and walls a verdant covering of interlaced boughs stemming from eighteen massive mulberry tree trunks. These sturdy trunks grew upwards from a deeply rooted base high into the walls of the room to provide a rich and lush green covering and the illusion of many trees in a forest. This work of arboreal art by Leonardo was covered over with lime and whitewash at the end of the eighteenth-century when the hall was converted to a stable for French troops occupying Milan. It essentially disappeared from view until Luca Beltrami, the chief restorer of the castle more than a century ago rediscovered the remnants of these paintings in 1893. Since then, the surviving paintings that were in extremely bad condition and the hall were restored a number of different times in an attempt to recapture the style of Leonardo and Ludovico's era (Fig. 19.3).

Martin Kemp in his 2006 publication entitled *Leonardo da Vinci: The Marvellous Works of Nature and Man* (Cambridge MA) provides a clear diagram (his Fig. 44) of the vault and wall decorations and an explanation for some of Leonardo's motifs and emblems in his painting of the mulberry trees, the meaning of the intertwined golden rope and other notable elements of the arboreal pergola in the *Sala delle Asse*.

Symbolic Meaning of Leonardo's Arboreal Painting in the *Sala delle Asse*

Was there more to Leonardo's arboreal painting in the *Sala delle Asse* than just an exercise of a spectacular and intricate decoration? Why remove the planks from a closed room and replace them with a painting creating the illusion of being present in a natural pergola open to the elements and the sky? What was the purpose of this conceit? Given that there is no documentary evidence about the symbolic intention of the *Sala delle Asse*, the purpose of the original pictorial cycle by Leonardo da Vinci in Ludovico il Moro's *Sala delle Asse* is mostly speculative.

In the *Codex Altanticus*, Leonardo wrote: '*Many trees planted in such a way as to touch, by the second year will have learnt how to dispense with the bark which grows between them and become grafted together; and by this method you will make the walls of the gardens continuous, and in four years you will even have very wide boards.*' And also, '*The branches of plants are found in two different positions: either opposite to each other or not opposite. If they are opposite to each other the centre stem is not bent: if they are not opposite the centre stem is bent.*'

His study of botany illuminated his art. Perhaps, Leonardo's arboreal design tried to capture a verse from Dante's *Paradise XIV*, 127-120 that expressed Ludovico Sforza's love for his Beatrice who had recently lost her life while giving birth to his child:

> *I was so enamoured therewith*
> *That until then there had not been anything*
> *Which had fettered me with such sweet bonds.*

The Sforza tree emblem painted by Leonardo for the *Sala delle Asse* that included the roots penetrating a rocky ledge and the trees bound together by an intertwined golden cord that may have conjured a supposed Sforza emblem seen in the Piazza Ducale at Vigevano with a speculative motto that Martin Kemp imagined could have been '*to stand firm and united*'. Although an emblem of ducal power, the trees also reminded Kemp of the fable of the *Walnut and the Wall* that Leonardo had told the Sforza court in past entertainments, possibly even when Gian Galeazzo Sforza was still alive:

The Walnut and the Wall.

A nut, having been carried by a crow to the top of a tall campanile and released by falling into a chink from the mortal grip of its beak, it prayed the wall by the grace bestowed on it by God in allowing it to be so high and thick, and to own such fine bells and of so noble a tone, that it would succour it, and that, as it had not been able to fall under the verdurous boughs of its venerable father and lie in the fat earth covered up by his fallen leaves it would not abandon it; because, finding itself in the beak of the cruel crow, it had there made a vow that if it escaped from her it would end its life in a little hole. At these words the wall, moved to compassion, was content to shelter it in the spot where it had fallen; and after a short time the nut began to split open and put forth roots between the rifts of the stones and push them apart, and to throw out shoots from its hollow shell; and, to be brief, these rose above the building and the twisted roots, growing thicker, began to thrust the walls apart, and tear out the ancient stones from their old places. Then the wall too late and in vain bewailed the cause of its destruction and in a short time, it wrought the ruin of a great part of it.' [Leonardo da Vinci]

This fable meant different things to different people. For many, it was the history of Gian Galeazzo Sforza and how he might eventually wreak revenge on Ludovico Sforza and bring about his fall from grace. For others, it was political symbolism expressing the full energy of a vital natural force. For Leonardo it was about the life force that enables man's artifice and can also destroy it. '*O envious age! Thou dost destroy all things and devour all thing ...*', including his own art works.

Apart from fables, the decorations were refined demonstrations of courtly life and family. The boughs of the painted canopy were ordered according to the tastes of two men of distinct opposites, Leonardo and Ludovico. The trees and rope provided symbolism and puns encouraged by Ludovico, for the mulberry or Moro tree refers to Ludovico the Moor (il Moro). The oddity of mimicking Court symbolism began with the accumulation of black slaves or servants to compliment Ludovico II Moro for his darkness. Courtiers suddenly took possession of a black page because Ludovico Sforza, Duke of Milan, had the popular nickname of Il Moro. In contrast to black servants, the complex interlaced patterns of the rope that represent Moorish designs are also a pun on Leonardo's name of Vinci (knots) and the Moresque interlaces are known as *fantasia dei vinci*. The golden knots expressed Leonardo's fascination with the meaning, mathematics and symbolism of knots as a topological pursuit of repeating convergence, closure, separation, divergence and a coming together that result in repeatable and complex interlacing patterns.

The trunks of eight of the eighteen mulberry trees in the painting rose up to touch the Sforza crest at the apex of the vaulted ceiling to impress courtiers and honoured visitors and to flatter Ludovico il Moro. Among the painted trees, four inscribed plaques hung from the four sides of the vaulted room to herald the Sforza rule (Fig. 19.4). Three have survived and they feature inscriptions that record important political events such as battles and marriages in Ludovico Sforza's domination of his family and the Duchy of Milan.

FIG. 19.3. *Restoration of the Sala delle Asse in the Sforza Castle in Milan.* Copyright Comune di Milano. *http://saladelleassecastello.it/*

FIG. 19.4. Detail of Sala delle Asse *with commemorative plaque.* Copyright Comune di Milano. http://saladelleassecastello.it/

The first plaque commemorates the 1493 marriage between the Holy Roman Emperor Maximilian I and Ludovico's niece Bianca Maria Sforza. The second plaque shows Ludovico's imperial investiture as the Duke of Milan that was granted secretly to him by Maximilian in 1494, but officially in 1495. The third plaque highlights Ludovico's alliance with the Emperor and his battle against the French and victory over Charles VIII at the Battle of Fornovo. The inscription is missing from the fourth plaque and we do not known what it said. However, we can glean from the surviving plaques that Ludovico's alliance with the Emperor granted him the legal right to rule. The imperial investiture for the Duchy of Milan that was granted to Ludovico before the suspicious death of his nephew, the Duke of Milan, Gian Galeazzo Sforza, was the most coveted event of his power escalation and dominance. When he commissioned the paintings for the *Sala delle Asse*, Ludovico's unpopularity was growing among his courtiers and the citizens and he wanted to demonstrate his new gained power and legal status by way of the renovations and symbols in the castle. He no longer had to share the stage or portraits on coins, frescos and canvases with his pesky nephew, Gian Galeazzo Sforza. The green symbolism of Gian Galeazzo Sforza, the 6th Duke of Milan, in the *Sala delle Asse* was transferred now to the foliage of the mulberry trees and his murderer, Ludovico Sforza. It is not difficult to imagine the discontent within the *Castello* at that time, and the memory of the poisoned Gian Galeazzo's suddenly returning with a token remake of the image of him clinging to his uncle depicted as the powerful mulberry tree on the cover of a desecrated *Sforziada* (Fig. 19.5).

FIG. 19.5. *Gian and Ludovico Sforza as mulberry trees and protectors of the Duchy of Milan. Detail of the frontispiece to the Paris Edition of the Sforziada, c, 1493. Paris, Bibliotheque Nationale.*

The Painted Pergola: A Tribute to the Origins of Architecture

John F. Moffitt in his 1990 article for *Arte Lombarda* proposed a motive for Leonardo's *Sala delle Asse* that is markedly different from those of most other scholars before him. He cleverly argued that Leonardo's '*illustionistic arboreal decorations*' symbolised the primordial origins of architecture. It was a pictorial metaphor of the *'natural'* primitive hut, from whence all subsequent architecture sprang as described by Vitruvius in *De architecttura II*. Moffitt provided us with the following quote by Vitruvius about the origins of the primitive hut:

'The Origin of the Dwelling House
The men of old were born like the wild beasts, in woods, caves, and groves, and lived on savage fare. [...]. As they kept coming together in great numbers into one place, finding themselves naturally gifted beyond the other animals in not being obliged to walk with faces to the ground, but upright and gazing upon the splendour of the starry firmament, and also in being able to do with ease whatever they chose with their hands and fingers, they began in that first assembly to construct shelters. Some made them of breen, others dug caves on mountain sides, and some, in imitation of the nests of swallows and the way they built, made places of refuge out of mud and twigs. Next, by observing the shelters of others, and adding new details to their own inceptions, they constructed better and better kinds of huts as time went on.'

And soon they were using tree trunks to build walls, and wooden crossbeams for the roofs covered with leaves and mud.

'Then, taking courage, and looking forward from the standpoint of higher ideas, born of the multiplication of the arts, they gave up huts, and began to build houses with foundations, having brick or stone walls, and roofs of timber and tiles.'

From this Vitruvian passage and other documentary evidence, Moffitt concluded that Leonardo's pergola in the *Sala delle Asse* was a metaphorical tribute to the Vitruvian text and to the Sforza's dedication to sponsoring ongoing architectural constructions such as the Cathedrals of Milan and Pavia, and the *Piazza Ducale* in Vigevano.

Vinci Knots *(Fantasia Dei Vinci)*

Leonardo painted a golden rope that moved through the pergola twisting and curling its way among the branches and canopy of the ceiling and walls of the *Sala delle Asse* (Fig. 19.6). It was part decoration and part metaphor binding together the entwined branches of Ludovico Il Moro's mulberry trees. Moreover, parts of the knotted golden cord that entwined within the tree branches also formed the design of the Jerusalem Cross that Leonardo used to embroider the dress of *Mona Lisa* and some of the illustrations of Vinci knots (Fig. 19.7). On one level, the twisting golden rope probably commemorated the marriage between the Sforza and Este families and on another level the ornate rope patterns reminded courtiers of the six engravings of elaborate knots dedicated to the Academia Leonardo Vinci.

Many scholars have pointed out that the ornamental rope patterns are also known as *moreschi* or Moorish designs that provided a punning reference to the Duke's name. Both Leonardo's motifs and the mulberry trees of the *Sala delle Asse* were humorous puns served to flatter the Duke's name, Ludovico il Moro, the Moor.

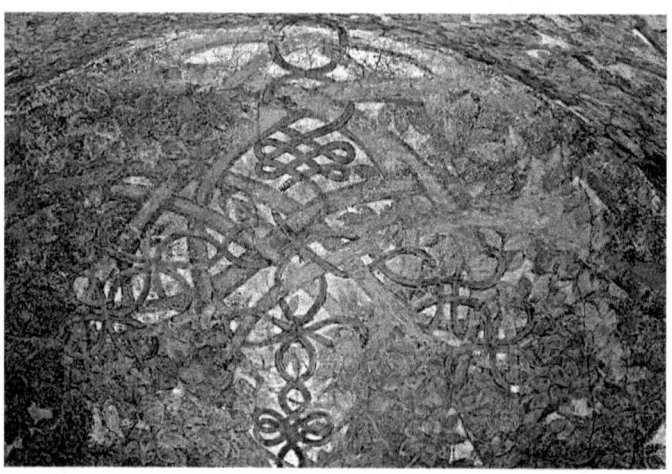

FIG. 19.6. Detail of Sala delle Asse *with golden cord hanging among the branches*.

The Leonardo da Vinci scholar Martin Kemp suggested that the knotted rope in the *Sala delle Asse* functioned as a memorial to Beatrice d'Este after she died in January of 1497. He provided visual and literary evidence to demonstrate that this was one of her favourite motifs that she had embroidered into the bodice or sleeve of her dresses and that were known as *fantasia dei vinci where the word 'vinci' means 'knot'*.

These *fantasia dei vinci* were not exclusive to Beatrice and Isabelle d'Este, and other women in the Sforza court, such as Isabella Sforza of Aragon, who married the young duke Gian Galeazzo Sforza, was from Naples and loved Spanish fashion, possibly also favoured these fantasia knots as patterns on their dresses.

Also, these knotted motifs can be found in the frontispiece of the mathematician Fra Luca Pacioli's *Summa de Arithmetica*, published in Venice in 1494. Variations of these Far Eastern motifs intertwine his capitalised letters at the start of each paragraph of his published book *Divine Proportion* that Leonardo da Vinci had illustrated. Moreover, these *fantasia dei vinci* are embroidered into the dresses of Leonardo da Vinci's portraits of the *Lady with an Ermine*, *La Belle Ferronniere* and even the *Mona Lisa*. The four-leaf-clover shape on *Mona Lisa's* dress (Fig. 19.7) symbolically ties her to the Sforza court and suggests that she is a Sforza, most likely the unfortunate Isabella Sforza Aragon, the Duchess of Milan, and widow of Gian

Galeazzo Sforza. Since the *Lady with an Ermine* was finished by 1489/1490, at least one year before Beatrice d'Este married Ludovico Sforza, the Vinci knots probably were not influenced originally by Beatrice d'Este, but more likely by Isabella of Aragon who was in Milan in February 1489 for her marriage to the young duke of Milan.

FIG. 19.7. *Leonardo's four-leaf-clover shape or Palestinian Cross design within the knots of his mulberry trees in the* Sala delle Asse *(left), the knot engravings of his circular Academia posters (middle) and the stitched embroidery of* Mona Lisa's *dress (right).* Figure taken from Carla Glori's article entitled '*Il ritratto della Signora Milanese in Blois, la testimonianza di de Beatis e la Gioconda.*' www.academia.edu.

Academy of Leonardo da Vinci

In his *Life of Leonardo*, Vasari writes:

'He wasted time in designing a series of knots in a cord, which can be followed from one end to the other, with the entire cord forming a circular field containing a very difficult and beautiful engraving with these words in the middle: Leonardus Vinci Accademia.'

The scholar Jill Pederson wrote about the reality of the Academy of Leonardo da Vinci in her paper entitled *Henrico Boscano's Isola beata: new evidence for the Academia Leonardi Vinci in Renaissance Milan* that was published in *Renaissance Studies* in 2008. The abstract of her paper says:

'The recent rediscovery of the early sixteenth-century vernacular text of the Isola beata (private collection, c.1513) by Henrico Boscano throws light on the Milanese intellectual circle of Leonardo da Vinci, and through the examination of this unpublished manuscript this article will put forth a new account in support of the existence of the Academia Leonardi Vinci. This Milanese text has gone virtually unseen by modern scholars and has never been specifically discussed in relation to the other literature, historical or modern, on the Academia Leonardi Vinci. The contents of the Isola beata *will allow us to reconstruct Leonardo's intellectual community with greater precision, and with this information we will be able to better define the nature of the academy centred in late fifteenth-century Milan.'*

In the Pederson account of Henrico Boscano's *Isola Beata (Blessed Island)*, the Academy was made up of a community of like-minded friends and intellectuals with the names of poets (Gaspare Visconti, Antonio Fileremo Fregoso, Bernardo Bellincioni, Lancino Curzio), historians and archivists (Bartolomeo Simoneta, Cornelio Balbo, Bernardino Corio), musicians (Joanne Maria Giudeo, Bagno, Janes da Legi, Pietro da Olline, Gasparo, Giovan Ciecho, Antonio Pagano Perino), and painters and engineers (Leonardo da Vinci, Donato Bramante, Cristoforo Foppa, known as Caradosso). Why was the Academy named after Leonardo da Vinci? Was it so-called because of the existence of the engravings of elaborate interlaced knots bearing the *Academia Leonardi Vinci* inscriptions (Fig. 8.3) such as ACADEMIA LEONARDI VIN (or VICI), ACA DE MIA LEO NAR DI VICI, and ACHDIA LEDI VICI?

Another engraving exists, *Profile of a Young Woman with Ivy in a Tondo*, with the inscription ACHA.LE.VI (Fig. 19.8) that is a Latin abbreviation of *Academia Leonardi Vinci*. It seems reasonable to conclude from the slope and angle of the lines of the hatchings on the engraving that they probably originated from the left hand of Leonardo da Vinci. Based on such clues and writings from the period, it seems that the Academy of Leonardo da Vinci was advertised and named so by Leonardo himself. Similar patterns painted by his hand appeared on the walls of the *Sala delle Asse* in Sforza *Castello*. In this sense, the word Academy probably was used simply to refer to the regular gathering of literary men who met to debate, argue and discuss various historical and contemporary philosophical, artistic and literary issues and topics of interest. Luca Pacioli's teachings of mathematics, Euclidean solids and the *Divine Proportion* depicted by Leonardo da Vinci in his portrait of the saintly mathematician were undoubtedly some of the topics discussed and argued at the Academy.

There is a similarity and an undoubted connection between the patterns of the golden rope intertwined among the painted boughs and branches in the *Sala delle Asse (Fig. 19.6)* and the design of a Vinci knot for the Academy of Leonardo da Vinci (Fig. 19.9). The *Academia Leonardi Vinci* motto is variously abbreviated on all six of the engraved copperplates of the intertwined knots. These engraved designs include the mathematical ratio known as the Golden Section and they provide the clues to the meaning of the knot motif in the *Sala delle Asse*. It is likely that these twisting, interlacing cords that loop through various branches of the walls of the *Sala delle Asse* contain within their pattern not only Luca Pacioli's divine proportion but also the geometric complexity and topology of interlacing and interconnecting shapes and networks.

FIG. 19.8. Leonardo's engraving of a Profile of a Young Woman with Ivy in a Tondo. *The inscription ACHA.LE.VI is an abbreviation for* Academia Leonardi Vinci.

FIG. 19.9. Leonardo's design of a Vinci knot for the Academy of Leonardo da Vinci. The measureable divine proportion (golden section) is contained within the patterns.

While Jill Pederson suggested that the *Academia Leonardi Vinci* is better understood by comparison to Ficino's Platonic Academy in Florence, the scholar Carlo Pedretti considered that the trees painted for the *Sala delle Asse* portrayed the sacred *Grove of Akademos* in reference to Plato's Academia that was established by Plato as the cradle of philosophic learning in Ancient Greece (the fourth century B.C). Thus, the emblems of the Leonardo Academy and the use of the Platonic rope motif interconnect Leonardo and Plato's Academia and bring together a group of like-minded intellectuals, artists, and musicians to debate and dispute issues of mutual interest with Ludovico Sforza as their royal patron in Milan. And so it is that Ludovico Sforza's court poet, Bernardo Bellincioni, has invited us to participate in the Academy, *'Come, I say, to today's Athens in Milan, for here is the Ludovican Parnassus.'*

The *'laudable scientific duel'* that Luca Pacioli and Leonardo da Vinci took part in at the Sforza castle to defend the nobility of geometry and mathematics is described briefly by Pacioli in the *Divine Proportion*. Luca Pacioli named Galeazzo Sanseverino among a number of the most illustrious members of Ludovico's court who attended the courtly disputation. The scholar Monica Azzolini provided us with an enlightening analysis of Pacioli's *'scientific duel'* in a paper entitled *Anatomy of a Dispute: Leonardo, Pacioli and Scientific Courtly Entertainment in Renaissance Milan*. This was a study of *'the dynamics of scientific patronage and social advancement ...in Renaissance courtly disputes.'* In her introduction, she wrote the following:

'From this passage we can evince that although Pacioli received the patronage of the Duke of Milan, his broker at the time was Gian Galeazzo Sanseverino, who had probably acted as intermediary with the Duke to procure Pacioli his teaching job in Milan. It seems plausible also to infer that Sanseverino had a professional interest in mathematics and geometry and that he had personally pursued the study of these disciplines, possibly under the guidance of Pacioli himself.'

This further supports my argument and those of Carla Glori and G. A. Barca that the patron and disciple in the *Pacioli Portrait* is none other than Galeazzio Sanseverino. Monica Azzolini goes on to assess the importance of the duel, the patronage and the possible courtly participants and the roles played by Pacioli and Leonardo. She suggests that the opponents were the mainstream courtly physicians and astrologers, such as Ambrogio Varesi da Rosate and Nicolo Cusano. Accordingly, Luca Pacioli defended the nobility of mathematics and geometry as superior to all other arts and sciences, including astrology and astronomy. On the other hand, Leonardo used the arguments that he developed for the *Paragone* to claim that painting is a *scientia* based on the principles of mathematics and geometry and uses the noblest sense of vision. He suggested that painting was superior to astrology, thereby questioning and challenging '*the traditional hierarchy of disciplines*' like astrology and poetry. Monica Azzolini made the following comment, demonstrating how Leonardo and Pacioli were brothers-in-arms.

'By participating in the duel, Leonardo and Pacioli challenged the traditional hierarchy of disciplines and, at the same time, the social, economical and intellectual status that indissolubly came with it. In arguing for a higher social position for themselves and their disciplines, they attempted to gain new prestige and status outside the strict boundaries of university training and traditional education.'

In this regard, the *Pacioli Portrait* challenges the traditional discipline or norms of portraiture, requiring the viewer to also consider the intrinsic science, narrative and history within the portrait, and not just admire the representation (likeness, personality or mood) of the person or people.

Luca Pacioli's Knot and the Golden Ratio

Since Leonardo da Vinci and Luca Pacioli undoubtedly spent time together in the rooms of the Sforza castle, including the *Sala delle Asse*, I leave the last two sections of this chapter to them, the portrait and the hanging rhombicuboctahedron. In the *Pacioli Portrait*, Leonardo has painted a realistic Franciscan white cord with knots tied around the waist of Luca Pacioli's habit. His cord has four knots tied in a bullion style. The Franciscans wear the knotted cord as a reminder of their commitment by showing that they are bound to Jesus. They display one to five knots where three knots represent their commitment to vows of poverty, chastity, and obedience, the fourth knot shows a commitment of enclosure, and a fifth knot for penance and detachment. As a teacher of mathematics, Luca Pacioli did not support detachment and therefore excluded the fifth knot.

As additional evidence of Leonardo's attribution in this story, he seems to have painted a golden section with the ratio of approximately 1:1.6 on a horizontal portion of Luca Pacioli's cord (Fig. 19.10). Also, the comparable lengths of the two cords hanging down vertically from his waistband are at an approximate ratio of 1:1.6 (Fig. 1.1). The golden proportion is displayed also on the pages of the open book of Euclid's *Elements* and can be easily measured using a compass to gauge the height and width of the page opposite the page on which the hand of Luca Pacioli rests. The height and width of the page is about 1:1.6 (Fig. 8.6): see Chapter 8.

It is noteworthy that the folds created by the light and shadows on Luca Pacioli's tunic stand upright and that they are tilted approximately at right angles to the cord that is around his waist. They appear like beams holding up Pacioli's collar and hood (Fig. 8.14 and Fig. 13.11). In this regard, if taken as an architectural metaphor, then it is similar to Leonardo's tree trunks supporting the *Sala delle Asse*'s vaulted ceiling (Fig. 19.3). Here, in the *Pacioli Portrait*, those pillars of light and shade essentially hold up the friar's head and shoulders like the tilted columns that are found in some of the vaulted structures of the Catalan architect Antoni Gaudi (1852-1926).

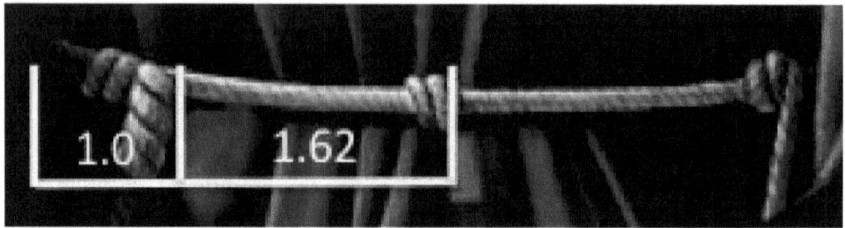

FIG. 19.10. The divine proportion on the Franciscan cord from the right side of Luca Pacioli's waist in Leonardo's portrait.

Sforza Castle Reflected on the Rhombicuboctahedron

Figure 12.1 in Chapter 12 highlights the three reflected images of the Sforza castle on the surface of the hanging rhombicuboctahedron in the *Pacioli Portrait*. These three images are reflected in the hanging glass polyhedron presumably through one or more of the open windows of the *Saletta Negra* or some other room of the castle. One of the three reflected images is shown in Fig. 19.11. A thin cord passing through the centre of the hanging polygon is attached to a ring O with a hanging A or inverted V at the vertex. As pointed out in Chapter 12, Leonardo's drawing of the attachment ring, the circle O and inverted V (Fig. 12.14), is part of his compass drawings found on a page of one of his notebooks (Fig. 9.3).

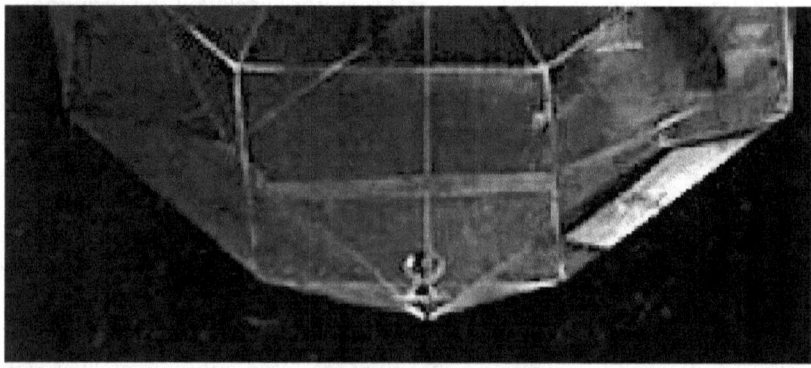

FIG. 19.11. Leonardo's Masonic emblem of the projector, the inverted V with the circle or O attached to the central cord at the bottom the rhombicuboctahedron with a reflected image of the grounds of the Sforza castle outside the darkened room.

References

Ady, Cecilia M (1907). A History of Milan, under the House of Sforza. Edward Armstrong (editor). NEW YORK: G. P. PUTNAM'S SONS. LONDON: METHUEN & CO. 1907.
https://archive.org/stream/historyofmilanun017956mbp/historyofmilanun017956mbp_djvu.txt

Azzolini, Monica (2004). Anatomy of a Dispute: Leonardo, Pacioli, and Scientific Entertainment in Renaissance Milan, Early Science and Medicine, 9. 128–135 and notes.

Azzolini, Monica (2013). The duke and the stars: astrology and politics in Renaissance Milan, Cambridge, Mass., Harvard University Press.

Bernini F, Scrollini C (2006). I Conti Dal Verme, Gianni Iuculano Editore, Pavia.

Cartwright, Julia Mary (1908). Beatrice d'Este, Duchess of Milan, 1475-1479. J. M. Dent amp Co. Online:
http://readcentral.com/massappealnews/chapters/Julia-Mary Cartwright/Beatrice-dEste-Duchess-of-Milan-1475-1497/003.

Codex Trivulzianus. In the public domain,
https://en.wikipedia.org/wiki/Codex_Trivulzianus#/media/File:Codex_trivulzianus.jpg
Also see, Leonardo da Vinci at http://www.universalleonardo.org

Collison-Morley, Lacy (1933). The Story of the Sforzas. London, G. Routledge & sons, limited.

Comune di Milano. Castello Sforzesco Sala delle Asse.
http://www.saladelleassecastello.it/background/?lang=en#

Comune di Milano. Milano. Castello Sforzesco Sala delle Asse. Sala delle Asse. The restoration. Leonardo da Vinci painter at the castle in Milan.
http://www.saladelleassecastello.it/wp-content/uploads/2013/11/The_restoration_25_05_2016.pdf

Costa, Patrizia (2006). PhD thesis: The Sala delle Asse in the Sforza Castle. The University of Pittsburgh. Pittsburgh. http://d-scholarship.pitt.edu/6590/
https://d-scholarship.pitt.edu/6590/1/Costa2006etd.pdf

Glori, Carla. Il ritratto della Signora Milanese in Blois, la testimonianza di de Beatis e la Gioconda. https://www.academia.edu/38366754/

Glori, Carla (2011). Enigma Leonardo: decipherments and discoveries - La Gioconda. In memory of Bianca, graphic section by Ugo Cappello, Cappello Editore, Savona 2011-2012
http://www.carlaglori.com/mi-presento/

Glori, Carla (2011). Ricerca sul cartiglio - Aggiornamento sulle novita 2017.
http://www.carlaglori.com/wp-content/uploads/2017/04/LE-NOVITA-2017-PER-LATTRIBUZIONE-VINCIANA-DEL-CARTIGLIO-E-DEL-QUADRO.pdf

Kemp, Martin (2006). The Marvellous Works of Nature and Man. Oxford University Press. Oxford, New York.

Kulski JK (2017). Leonardo da Vinci: The Melzi Chronicles. Published by Jerzy. K. Kulski. ISBN: 978-0-6480653-1-9

Kulski JK (2018). The Mona Lisa portrait: Leonardo's personal and political tribute to Isabella Aragon Sforza, the Duchess of Milan. International Journal of Art and Art History. 6 (2), 31-50. DOI: 10.15640/ijaah.v6n2p5. URL:

https://doi.org/10.15640/ijaah.v6n2p5.
Moffitt JF (1990). Leonardo's Sala delle Asse and the primordial origins of architecture. Arte Lombarda, Nuova serie. 92/93 (1-2) 76-90.
Muratori L (1717). Of the Estensi Antiquities. Modena Ducal Printing House.
Pacioli, Luca (1498). Divine Proportion (in English). 1498 edition. *Tennenbaum pacioli-divine-proportion.pdf.* Uploaded by Israel Monroy Muñoz on Oct 22, 2014. Full text of original edition (1498) in English.
https://www.scribd.com/document/244035060/tennenbaum-paciolidivine-proportion-pdf
Pederson, Jill (2008). The Academia Leonardi Vinci: Visualizing dialectic in Renaissance Milan, 1480–1499. Ph.D. Thesis, The Johns Hopkins University, 2008, 428; 3288613.
Pedretti, Carlo (1978). The Codex Atlanticus of Leonardo da Vinci: A catalogue of its newly restored sheets, 12 vols. New York: Johnson Reprint Corporation, 1978.
Pedretti, Carlo (1985). Leonardo Architect. New york: Rizzoli.
Pedretti, Carlo (1989). Achademia Leonardi Vinci. Journal of Leonardo Studies and Bibliography of Vinciana, Vol. 2. Wittenborn Art Books.
Richter JP, editor (1880). The Notebooks of Leonardo da Vinci.
http://www.fromoldbooks.org/Richter-NotebooksOfLeonardo/
Solmi E (1904). La festa del Paradiso di Leonardo da Vinci e Bernardo Bellincione (13 gennaio 1490), Archivio Storico Lombardo, ser. 4, vol. 1, pp. 75-89; in Scritti Vinciani, Florence, 1924.
Solmi E (1936). La resurrezione dell' opera di Leonardo, Leonardo, ed. Garzanti, Milan, pp. 3.
Zygulski, Jr., Zdzislaw (1991). Costume Style and Leonardo's Knots in the Lady with an Ermine, in Leonardo da Vinci: Lady with an Ermine, ed. Józef Grabski and Janusz Walek (Vienna: IRSA), 24-2
Vaglienti FM (2004). Isabella d'Aragona, Dizionario biografico degli Italiani (Rome, 1960ff.), lxii. 609–615. *http://www.treccani.it/enciclopedia/isabella-d-aragona-duchessa-di-milano_(Dizionario-Biografico)/*
Vasari, Giorgio (1550). The Lives Of The Most Excellent Painters, Sculptors, and Architects. de Vere GdC, trans. New York, NY: The Modern Library; 2006.

PART 4

Cracking the Pacioli Code: Leonardo da Vinci's tribute to art, science, mathematics, geometry and the divine proportion (Phi – 1.618…)

Th' hast spoken right, 'tis true.
The wheel is come full circle, I am here.
William Shakespeare. King Lear Act 5, scene 3, 171–175

20

CARLA GLORI'S DECRYPTION WITH A LITTLE HELP FROM A BLACK FLY

The Da Vinci Codes: Pictorial Puzzles, Rebuses and Cryptograms

Leonardo da Vinci loved fables, puns, puzzles, jokes, riddles (prophecies), magic tricks and secret codes to entertain himself and others. His notebooks are full of such writings as reminders and scripts for oral performances and declamations. He scribbled fantasies, jests, fables, riddles, prophecies, absurdities, and paradoxes on all manner of subjects; many that reflected his love of animals, plants and nature. Often, these jokes, puns and fables were told as morality tales or allegories about the hypocrisy and greed of the clergy and human foibles, especially condemning cruelty, violence, reckless wars, greed, theft, betrayal and deceit. He was a witness to many of these intolerable human behaviours during the Italian Renaissance, not least in the 1490s in the Duchy of Milan.

He wrote many of these tales in ink with his left hand in a mirror-image cursive from right to left because it was probably easier for him than from left to right. It exercised his brain and imagination, did not smudge his notes, and kept his writings a secret from others. But, this reverse style of writing made it difficult in later years for his secretary and heir Francesco Melzi to translate Leonardo's notes and publish his various treatises, such as the *Treatise on Painting*. It was unfathomable and just too difficult for the normal person to translate his mysterious style of writing. And so, his notebooks remained untranslated and a secret for hundreds of years.

There are many jokes, puns, fables, riddles and word-games, but few clear-cut anagrams or pictorial puzzles scattered throughout his notebooks. However, Leonardo did produce at least one fascinating page of pictorial puzzles (cryptograms or rebuses) in the late 1480s in Milan that is now part of the Windsor collection. There are 154 rebuses, that is, visual codes –

words, names or sentences expressed pictorially - on the two sides of the Windsor sheet (Fig. 20.1).

FIG. 20.1. Leonardo da Vinci. A. Sheet of rebuses, c. 1489. B. Detail. Pero se la fortuna mi fa felice tal viso asponero *pictogram. London, Windsor Castle collection.*

In rebus B of Fig. 20.1, Leonardo constructed the sentence '*Pero se la fortuna mi fa felice tal viso asponero*' that translates to '*If fortune will make me happy I will remove this [unhappy] face*'. Leonardo may have transitioned some of his cryptic pictographs, visuals puns and rebuses into drawings and paintings for courtly entertainments and debates. For example, Larry J. Feinberg in his book *The Young Leonardo: Art and Life in Fifteen-Century Florence*

(Cambridge University Press, 2011), pointed out how the word-image for *'asponero'* –*'I will show'* was merged from *'aspo'* and *'nero'* and transferred to Leonardo's painting *Madonna of the Yarnwinder*. Of this painting, Fienberg says:

> '... the Christ Child not only eagerly seizes the instrument, but, with his left hand, emphatically points heavenward – a gesture, often associated with John the Baptist, that indicates "I will show" the way to redemption. Further, the bold motion of the child's arm, proximate and parallel to the crosslike yarnwinder, suggests that this salvation will come through his sacrifice.'

Most of Leonardo da Vinci's well known paintings can be viewed as mysterious rebuses or pictorial codes. Also, the acronym and the black fly on the cartouche in the *Pacioli Portrait* can be regarded as a Vinci rebus, but, as shown by Carla Glori, it is an enigma that requires an extremely complex solution.

IACO.BAR.VIGENNIS.P.1495: Historical Mystery Within the Secretly Coded Diary

> *The research in art, with its 'interrupted paths' that aim at the 'heart of the forest', remains for me the way to recompose the shattered truth; and literature is the challenge to make the Phoenix reborn from its ashes.*
> On repairing 'broken paths' by Carla Glori

The ultimate glory for deciphering the correct attribution for the *Pacioli Portrait* must go to Carla Glori, the art cryptologist from Italy who decoded Leonardo da Vinci's cartouche and the mysterious inscription of **IACO.B AR.VIGEN NIS. P. 1495**: a cryptic epigram with a black fly (*musca*) pointing the way to the correct solutions (Fig. 20.2). She completed the marvellous decryption and self-published her results in Italian on the Internet in 2010 to reveal the real story of the painting and how its production was born out of the history and the politics of Milan, mostly between the years of 1489 and 1499. It particularly covers the period between 1494 to 1495 that involved the death of Gian Galeazzo Sforza and the usurpation of the Duchy of Milan by Ludovico Il Moro Sforza in October of 1494 and Ludovico's arrogant and callous celebrations in 1495 at the expense of Gian Galeazzo Sforza's widow, the former duchess of Milan, Isabella Aragon Sforza and her young son Francesco Sforza.

This penultimate chapter is a tribute to Carla Glori and it presents summarised extracts and an English translation of some of her decryptions of the mysterious code **IACO.B AR.VIGEN NIS. P. 1495**. She generated a credible list of at least 148 different phrases that illuminated the hidden history of the painting. As a prelude to revealing some of her translations and revelations, we already provided some of the historical context in the earlier chapters; the background into the history of the Sforza rule of the Duchy of Milan and what Leonardo da Vinci had to face when he was in the service of the Sforza Court from the time of his arrival in Milan in about 1481 until his departure in December of 1499, soon after the invasion by the French King Louis XII.

FIG. 20.2. Detail of the Pacioli Portrait: *enlargement of Leonardo da Vinci's cryptic epigram on the notepaper with the black fly.*

The Carla Glori discovery of 2010 presented the deciphering of the coded diary relating to the history of the Sforza family and to the personal vicissitudes of its members noting that it revolved around the death of Gian Galeazzo Sforza in 1494, in addition to the deciphered phrases relating to Luca Pacioli, the polyhedra and the painter of the portrait. Although it can be defined as an 'artificial linguistic construction' generated by the program of the 'alphabetical machine' of the cartouche and not of natural language, the set of sentences and the Sforzesca plots that are intertwined within the message give rise to a 'secret diary' made up of fragments or short phrases, historically documented and permeated with vitality and literary suggestions. The sharing of the knowledge of the private and public history of the Sforza family, which in this case refers to the idea of the code as an organic system of symbols and references that allows transmission of the message and its comprehension, is essential background information required for decipherment of the da Vinci code that is encoded in the message IACO.BAR.VIGEN/NIS P.1495 on the cartouche in the *Pacioli Portrait*. As in a theatrical drama, one or more clues present the secret direction of the protagonists' interactions, fixing them to their destiny. At the centre of the yellowing notebook is the hidden message about the death of Gian Galeazzo Sforza, scenes from his funeral and the characters of the Sforza family deeply 'imprinted' within the coded diary to make them recognisable or identifiable by their name.

CHAPTER 20

The Carla Glori Solutions: Decoding the Cartouche's Cryptic Message IACO BAR VIGENNIS MUSCA

Carla Glori took 15 letters (IACOBARVIGENNIS) from the cartouche, inserted the five letters of the keyword MUSCA (the Latin word describing the fly painted on the cartouche), and moved around the total of twenty letters as if it was an ancient Chinese Puzzle in order to find a meaningful sentence. By breaking the linear order and meaning of the twenty letters of IACO.B AR. VIGEN NIS – MUSCA, she revealed a story about the painting and the historic times in Milan when the portrait was conceived and painted at sometime in the years of 1495 and 1496.

Carla Glori focused her scientific research exclusively on decrypting perfect Latin anagrams as a particular linguistic problem and calculating the probabilities of finding meaningful phrases. She hypothesised that Leonardo chose the alphabetic letters IACOBARVIGENNIS P.1495, together with the keyword MUSCA from the pictogram, in order to form the names of all the characters involved in the Sforzesca plot against Gian Galeazzo, the 6th duke of Milan, and that he did this based on a calculation of probabilities. So, if Leonardo was not aware of all the possible solutions that were deciphered by Carla Glori, he undoubtedly foresaw many of them.

Before shuffling Leonardo's 20 letters and symbols, Carla Glori established two rules for herself. First, she fixed the word VINCI to the end of each phrase as a criterion for validating sentences. Second, it was an imperative for her to shuffle the 20 letters to find meaningful phrases. Amazingly, a pattern and story emerged out of the IACO BAR VIGENNIS MUSCA reshuffled sequence. In 2013, she had generated at least 148 different phrases by using the two basic rules and forming perfect anagrams with the 20 letters. The first clues to emerge to show Carla Glori that she was on the right track were the repetitions of the same initials and names of the main characters who were important in Leonardo da Vinci's life and work in the Duchy of Milan. Here is a list of the main players:

G.S. = Galeazzo Sanseverino.
B.S. or B.B.S = Bianca Sforza or Bianca Sforza Sanseverino.
VINCI (constantly present in every sentence) = Leonardo da Vinci, himself.
P = *Pictus* (picture) or *Pictor* (painter), Leonardo da Vinci.
ABACUS = Luca Pacioli (Pacioli was a master of the abacus).
BAR = Duke of Bari (Ludovico il Moro).
AR = Isabella Aragon or Aragon family.
AGNUS = Gian Galeazzo Sforza (called 'the immaculate lamb').
MORUS = Ludovico il Moro Sforza.

ISA = Isabella Sforza Aragon.
BEA = Beatrice d'Este.
AMBROSIUS = Ambrogio da Rosate (Gian Galeazzo's doctor, Ludovico il Moro's astrologer and court magician).
ROCA = the *Rocca Nuova*, the fortress property of Galeazzo Sanseverino in Vigevano.
ROGIA = the *Roggia Mora* in Vigevano.

The initials of the names were used only in cases where the phrases uniquely identified the persons involved and who were documented in a historical-biographical context. In the case of the commander of the ducal army Galeazzo Sanseverino – nicknamed also 'mas/male' - his initials G.S. distinguished him in the majority of the sentences. For Gian Galeazzo Sforza, the nickname *'agnus'* ('immaculate lamb', in B. Corio, History of Milan) was used constantly. For Bianca Sforza, the eldest daughter of the Moor, both B.S. (Bianca Sforza) and B.S.S. (Bianca Sanseverino Sforza) were indicated always in contexts related to her marriage with Galeazzo Sanseverino or a wedding portrait commissioned to the Painter (P). Ludovico il Moro Sforza was called with his nickname **Morus**, whereas Ambrogio da Rosate was **Ambrosius**. The abbreviations **Isa** and **Bea** were used for Isabella Sforza Aragon and Beatrice d'Este, respectively. The variants of place names ROCA and ROGIA (*Rocca Nuova, Roggia Mora,*) referred to Vigevano, incorporating VIG or VIGE.

The Starting Point: Interpretation of the Acronym

The acronym was interpreted by using problem solving and focusing on Pacioli's stay at the Sforza Court in Milan. The problem solving was based on scientific methodology and the critical method of trial and error elimination using the guidelines of Karl Popper. In this case, the hypothesis of the research was founded on the analytical study of the painting and on the Sforza history, starting from the historical and biographical reconstruction of Pacioli's stay in Milan when he and Leonardo worked in the service of Ludovico il Moro and were brought together by their patron of artists and scientists, Galeazzo Sanseverino.

1. IACO.B AR.VIGEN/NIS.+MUSCA+P (the wildcard letter) 1495.
Illustris Augustus Comes BAR. VIGievinENsis (or even VIGiEviNe *) / NIS., where NIS placed at the head stands for *Nominatio Imperialis Sfortiae* (or even *Nominatione Imperiale Sfortiae*), but that can be read also as *Nepotis Interrupti Successor. Pictu*s 1495. (NB * Vigievine: usually used by Leonardo for Vigevano). Duke Sforza is designated in documents with the titles of *Augustus* and *Augustissimus*, but also as '*Anglus*', in reference to the

CHAPTER 20

Visconti's title of Count of Angera or Angleria, as a descendant of Anglo, 'Son of the Trojan hero, Aeneas' (according to the tradition of Giangaleazzo Visconti). [Jerzy K. Kulski author's note. The letter P could also refer to Pavia, the place where Gian Galeazzo Sforza died and where Leonardo loved to visit him and his wife despite Ludovico's insistence not to do so. P might be for Pictor, Pacioli or Pavia].

2. IACO.B AR.
IACO.B AR = [I] Illustris [A] Augustus (or Anglus) [CO] Comes (Co-Regent or Commanding Officer), [BAR] Duke of Bari (who is Ludovico Sforza and the Uncle of the under-aged duke, Gian Galeazzo Sforza, ruling in his own right).

[B AR]. The 'AR' (joined together on the cartouche) refers to the Aragon family of Naples who were related to the Sforza by marriage. Ludovico Sforza's sister Ippolita was married to Prince Alfonso II of Naples who was the son of King Ferdinand of Naples, the very king who awarded Ludovico Sforza with the title of the Duke of Bari. Alfonso was King of Naples and Jerusalem from 25 January 1494 to 22 February 1495. His and Ippolita's daughter Princess Isabella Aragon of Naples was betrothed to Gian Galeazzo Sforza the son of the 5th Duke of Milan Galeazzo Sforza in the year 1476, and they were married in Milan in February of 1489, 13 years after the assassination of Galeazzo Sforza. Leonardo da Vinci was largely responsible for their wedding decorations and festivities and then later for arranging a spectacular entertainment and feast for them known as the Feast of Paradise in celebration for their one year of marriage as the Duke and Duchess of Milan. Leonardo put on a similar spectacle for the King of France in Amboise in 1518 just one year before his death in May of 1519.

3. VIGEN/NIS VIGEN. VIGEN = Vigevano; NIS = an acronym with a double interpretation.
Illustris Augustus Comes (Co-regent, i.e., general lieutenant and tutor) Duke of BARI, **VIGEvaNense** (or even **VIGEvaNo**)/**NIS**. Regarding **VIGEN**, Vigevano was the preferred residence of il Moro, and Galeazzo Sanseverino was the owner of the fortress *La Rocca Nuova* in Vigevano. However, **NIS** might mean *Nominatio Imperialis Sfortiae or Nominatione Imperiale Sfortiae*, (for the *Imperial investiture of Sforza*), interpreted alternatively as the '*Successor of the Killed Nephew*' (=*Nepotis Interrupti Successor*).

Gian Galeazzo Sforza, the sixth (VI) duke of Milan (murdered on October 21, 1494), P - poisoned by the fat black fly (Il Moro, Ludovico Sforza, the seventh duke of Milan, 1495). Carla Glori translated *NIS* from Latin to Italian to mean [N] *Nomina* [I] *Imperiale dello* [S] Sforza. According to my interpretation, *Nis* in Latin is a contraction for *nisi*, 'unless, if not', as a conjunction. A *nisi* decree in law means not yet final or absolute to indicate that a judgement or decree will become final on a particular date unless set aside or invalidated by certain specified contingencies. This is what happened to the 6th Duke of Milan, Gian Galeazzo Sforza. By formal decree he was due to become the absolute ruler of Milan in **1495**, but died suspiciously in October of **1494**. According to most historians and chroniclers of the time, his death was at the 'order' of his uncle Ludovico Sforza who then used his allies and a small number of supporters to become the Duke of Milan immediately after Gian's death to usurp his nephew's widow and son who rightfully were next in line for the title. I also see in the anagram that **NIS** is spelt backwards as SIN. Although, Sin in Latin is 'if however', it is mentioned in the bible in Exodus 16-17 as part of the *Wilderness of Sin*, and in Ezekiel 30: 30:15-16 there is a cursed city called Sin. In Hebrew, sin means 'a mistake.' Leonardo was painting the religious mural *Last Supper* of Jesus at the same time that he was involved with the portrait of Fra Luca Pacioli and he was very familiar with various passages from the Bible and always in search of symbols and hidden meanings in his painting. Could he have used **NIS** as a play on **SIN, meaning a curse placed on the city of Milan,** in the heart of the Sforza court?

4. 1495

The year 1495 is the official investiture of Ludovico il Moro as Duke of Milan by the Holy Roman Emperor Maximilian I. In the summer 1494 il Moro obtained from the Emperor Maximilian the investiture to the Duchy for himself and his heirs before the death of his nephew Gian Galeazzo Sforza, the Duke of Milan, with an agreement that he would make it public only in May of 1495 when there were three investiture ceremonies:
- the first was a private ceremony on 22 May in the chapel of the Sforza Castle.
- the second was a public ceremony at the Milan Cathedral on 26 May with representatives of the various Italian powers in attendance.
- the third was in the Cathedral of Pavia on May 28 where the Moor (il Moro) was invested with the title of Count of the city, stealing the title from his grandnephew Francesco Sforza, the son of Isabella Sforza Aragon.

On painting the date of '1495' onto the notepaper, an ambiguity is evident in writing the 5 (which seems to be hybridised with the 4), possibly as an explanation to the fact that the two years of 1494 and 1495, coincided with Moro enhancing his power. It was two years of transition and therefore 1494/5 assumes an emblematic value. The sacrality in the Renaissance of 4 and of 5 (a number having a 'divine' value for Pacioli) in this case is probably referring to the two-year period that is related to the death of Gian Galeazzo Sforza.

5. MUSCA – the FLY.
The symbolic fly MUSCA can be understood as a provocative confirmation of the identity of the Moor and his role in the secret history that the Painter had hidden in the scroll. The fly symbolises Moro's signature. The insertion of the word **MUSCA** as the keyword formed 148 perfect anagrams containing the word **VINCI** and helped Carla Glori to reveal the presence of Leonardo da Vinci and other components to the storytelling.

6. The First Shuffling of Letters and Decryption.
The first shuffling of IACO.BAR. VIGEN / NIS. P. 1495 (plus the keyword 'MUSCA') by Carla Glori became ROGAS ABACUM SINE VINCI - (P.1495) translatable as (you, Pacioli) ASK THE ABACUS FOR SOLUTIONS WITHOUT VINCI-(P.1495), or 'alone, without me - VINCI - while I'm doing the portrait.' This was the first decryption made by Carla Glori in 2010 that immediately rendered a meaningful interpretation, since the sentence could be interpreted at various levels (given also the complexity involved in the term '*ABACO*'). Pacioli was a master of the abacus and arithmetic and for the painter (Leonardo) this word assumes a plurality of meaning extended also to the artistic sphere and the idea of an 'enigma'. *ROGAS ABACUM* reveals an invitation that the painter makes to those who seek the solution to the enigma contained in the cartouche and theme of the painting. A logical explanation for the enigma in the *Pacioli Portrait* is permeated by its ambiguities and various hidden dimensions. One of the deciphered sentences illuminating the complexity and depth assigned by the Painter (Vinci) to this word ENIGMA is the following: AENIGMA SUB SACRO-VINCI (P.1495) translatable as ENIGMA BELOW (i.e., hidden under) THE SACRED - VINCI (P.1495). This phrase, fascinating and enigmatic in itself, is extrapolated from the group of phrases that refer to the Painter himself, together with the group of phrases related to the mathematician Pacioli and the rhombicuboctahedron hanging above a green table. It focuses the relevant sentences to Gian Galeazzo Sforza and family, that is essential for the multidimensional deciphering of the enigmatic cartouche.

Decoding Leonardo's Enigmatic Messages for Emerging Tales

Carla Glori took this first interpretation of the acronym as a hypothesis ready to be retested. After she decrypted the hidden Latin phrases (the perfect anagrams) that were formed with the actual alphabetic letters of the inscription, she validated the hypothesis. She found many more reproducible and revealing phrases and sentences that all together produced a known historical narrative that assisted in the interpretation of the acronym. The decryption of the Latin sentences is falsifiable at many levels including linguistically, textually, grammatically, structurally, historically, methodologically and artistically. The decryption of each perfect anagram is qualified by the requisites of repeatability and reproducibility. Any deciphered perfect Latin anagram and construct (the documented Sforza stories formed within these anagrams) are not expected to alter over time. By 2010, Carla Glori had produced at least 148 decrypted phrases that are summarised in the following list of solutions.

Solutions 1 to 14
The decoding began with the theme of the fly (*La Mosca*) that produced the first 14 solutions. As examples of the decryptions, I have shown here only the first set of 3 x 2 solutions. The other solutions, all consisting of perfect anagrams, can be found and downloaded from Carla Glori's webpages referenced at the end of this chapter. The solutions shown here are coupled with the original phrase of the cartouche plus the keyword to underline that they are all formed with the very same letters of IACO.BAR.VIGEN NIS (P.1495)+MUSCA.

ROGAS ABACUM SINE VINCI–(P.1495)
IACO BAR VIGENNIS MUSCA–(P.1495)
AENIGMA SUB SACRO–VINCI (P.1495)
IACO BAR VIGENNIS MUSCA–(P.1495)
OBESA MUSCA NIGRA–VINCI (P.1495)
IACO BAR VIGENNIS MUSCA–(P.1495)

The three main solutions translated from Latin:
ROGAS ABACUM SINE VINCI = (you Pacioli), ask the abacus for solutions without Vinci–(P.1495), or 'alone, without me'-Vinci –'while I'm doing the portrait'.
AENIGMA SUB SACRO–VINCI = Enigma below (i.e., hidden under) the sacred-Vinci (P.1495).
OBESA MUSCA NIGRA–VINCI = Fat black fly Vinci P.1495.

The total set of 148 deciphered sentences is divided into subsets that narrate the events of the Sforza family around the year 1495. Carla Glori numbers the remaining sentences from 15 to 148 and divides them into two parts: solutions from 15 to 72 and solutions from 73 to 148.

Solutions 15 to 72
The solutions of this part are focused on the plot and mystery of Gian Galeazzo Sforza's murder in October 1494, which historians testify to be attributed to the arsenic poisoning done by Ambrogio da Rosate on Moro's

order. The main scene is the funeral of the duke, and the members of the Sforza family are recognised by their name or nickname. A series of decoded sentences also reveal the location of the 'Double portrait' to be in Vigevano, where il Moro has his residence and Galeazzo Sanseverino owned the fortress, *La Rocca Nuova* (ROCA). In 1495, Leonardo worked in Vigevano on the hydraulic project called *la Roggia Mora* (ROGIA), a canal to irrigate the fields and crops.

The absent (dead) Gian Galeazzo Sforza (poisoned by il Moro with the complicity of Ambrogio da Rosate) is the victim nicknamed the 'Lamb' (AGNUS). The anagrams provide the following revelations:
1) Prologue for the reader (solution 15).
2) History of the immaculate lamb (solutions 16 to 34).
3) His connection to the house of Aragon (solutions 35 to 46).
4) Galeazzo Sanseverino (G.S), the Student – 1st history: the green gloved hand (solutions 47 to 53).
5) 2nd history: G.S is the accomplice of his alter ego, the Duke of Milan, il Moro (the Moor) (solutions 53 to 58).
6) 3rd history: G.S as jouster and military commander (solutions 59 to 64).
7) The painter has portrayed G.S at the new fortress (solution 65).
8) The places of Vigevano: The Duke Moro's castle and Sanseverino's *Rocca Nuova* (solutions 66 to 72).

Solutions 73 to 148
The sentences from 73 to 134 are focused on the dynastic rights of Gian Galeazzo Sforza and on the usurpation of il Moro. In particular, this part focuses on the hostile relationship, marked by conflictual episodes between the rivals Isabella d'Argona and Beatrice d'Este as follows:
1) Gian Galeazzo Sforza, the legitimate duke usurped (solutions 73 to 77).
2) The Sieve, called *Buratto*, was the personal heraldic device (the '*impresa*') of Gian Galeazzo and a sign of his destiny (solutions 78 to 85).
3) Isabella d'Aragona, Gian Galeazzo's widow at his funeral, while she was pregnant with her daughter born after the death of Gian Galeazzo (solutions 86 to 103).
4) Beatrice d'Este and Moro in the year of transition 1494/95 – Beatrice d'Este dressed in mourning (solutions 104 to 110).
5) Beatrice and Moro, the year of their succession (solutions 111 to 113).
6) Two bitter rivals, Isabella and Beatrice, in the shadow of the Moro. The mutual accusations between the two duchesses (solutions 114 to 116).
7) The widow openly accuses il Moro of murder (solutions 117 to 121).
8) Bianca and her father, the duke il Moro on the eve of the wedding with Galeazzo Sanseverino (G.S.). Bianca's forthcoming marriage to G.S. (solutions 122 to 127).
9) G.S. marries Bianca to advance his own status as the son-in-law of

Ludovico il Moro Sforza (solutions 128 to 131).
10) Bianca marries G.S. for love (solutions 132 to 134).

The final part (solutions 135 to 148) concerns the preparations for Bianca Sforza's wedding with G.S. (Galeazzo Sanseverino) and the wedding portrait commissioned to Leonardo. The following solutions 137 to 141 provide five examples that refer to the imminent marriage between Bianca and Galeazzo:
1) Solution 137. BIANCA MUSA REO G.S.–VINCI = Bianca as muse for the liable G.S.–VINCI
2) Solution 138*. A CURA G.S. **P**ONAM EI B.S.–VINCI = From G.S. I'll portray B.S. for him–VINCI **P**. 1495*
3) Solution 139*. BIANCA SUMO **P**RAE G.S.–VINCI = Oh Bianca, I assume (the assignment or task) before G.S.–VINCI **P**. 1495*
4) Solution 140*. **P**RAE BIANCA SUMO G.S.–VINCI = In front of Bianca I assume the (assignment or task) from G.S.–VINCI **P**. 1495*
5) Solution 141. BIANCA MUSA ORE G.S.–VINCI = Bianca as muse in her aspect (or appearance) for G.S.–VINCI
And so on, from solution 142 to 148. (*Explanatory note: The solutions 138* to 140* were chosen to exemplify the insertion of the wildcard letter **P**. [1495] that was rarely used in the decryption).

The da Vinci Latin Codes (Anagrams) in the Portraits of *Luca Pacioli* and *Ginevra de' Benci*

Experts in the ancient language of Latin at the Department of Latin, Philosophy and History at the University of Genoa have recognised that the decryption of the motto IACO.BAR. VIGEN/NIS P.1495 on the Pacioli notepaper by Carla Glori using at least 148 Latin anagrams is academically reliable. Obviously, it was considered that these are anagram texts, similar to epigrams, and with contractions, and not corresponding to classical Latin. Also, she had done a similar decryption once before using 50 Latin anagrams derived from the motto VIRTUTEM FORMA DECORAT that is written on the cartouche painted on the reverse side of the portrait of *Ginevra de' Benci* by Leonardo da Vinci (Fig. 15.1) at the National Gallery in Washington, D.C. In her research on the portrait of *Ginevra de' Benci*, she discovered fifty anagrams that are related to the biography of Ginevra by introducing the Latin keyword IUNIPERUS to the motto. The *Ginevra de' Benci* portrait is certainly by Leonardo and the presence of the Latin anagrams in the motto VIRTUTEM FORMA DECORAT all signed by VINCI specifically reveals the history of the sitter. Moreover, Ginevra's motto confirms a connection with the Capodimonte cartouche signed by VINCI that reveals the history of the

Gian Galeazzo and Sforza family. The decryption of the da Vinci Latin message attached to his portrait of *Ginevra de' Benci* is compelling evidence that reinforces the Carla Glori thesis that the *Pacioli Portrait* of Capodimonte should be attributed to Leonardo da Vinci.

In the portrait of *Ginevra de' Benci*, the juniper (taken as the Latin keyword IUNIPERUS) is painted near the motto VIRTUTEM FORMA DECORAT in the same way that the fly (taken as the Latin keyword MUSCA) is painted near the motto IACO.BAR. VIGEN/NIS P.1495 in the *Pacioli Portrait* of Capodimonte. Whereas Leonardo da Vinci provided at least 50 anagrams signed VINCI for his *Ginevra Portrait*, he provided at least 148 anagrams that Carla Glori discovered in his *Pacioli Portrait* of Capodimonte. By using the identical methodology, Carla Glori obtained similar results in the decryption of both cartouches. While the deciphered anagrams from the cartouche of the *Ginevra de Benci* portrait form a faithful biographical reconstruction of her unhappy love story with Bernardo Bembo, the decoded anagrams marked VINCI in the *Pacioli Portrait* coincide with the dramatic events of the Sforza family and the biographies of the characters named in the period in which the duke Gian Galeazzo died. Carla Glori's website and her publications on discovering and decoding the Latin anagrams provided by Leonardo da Vinci in his portraits of Ginevra de' Benci and Luca Pacioli are listed in the References.

Why the Anagram and Why the Secrecy?

Is the Latin anagram so complex that it borders believability? No. Was Leonardo aware of these possible solutions and was his motive to hide the true meaning by going to enormous lengths? The most likely answer is yes. Look at his rebuses (Fig. 20.1). Leonardo loved word games and anagrams. He was a master of them. Mathematicians are not able to explain adequately why he placed the calculation $(478+935+621=2034)$ on the chalkboard at the end of Luca Pacioli's pointer (Fig. 9.10), and we are unable to comprehend why he placed a mysterious cryptogram on a sheet of yellowed notepaper accompanied by an 'obese fly' (Fig. 20.2) amongst the enormous number of anagram solutions to reveal the names of all the characters in his Sforza/Pacioli pictorial story.

Who was the anagram intended for? Anybody who could decipher it. Why? To divulge the truth even if it was seditious and a danger to its author. Leonardo wrote anagrams and codes that conveyed hidden meanings and provided an insight into his own psychological torments to anybody who could decipher them. He intended that the anagrams in the *Pacioli Portrait* reveal the history of Milan in the period between 1494 and 1495 – the betrayal and murder of the 6th Duke of Milan, Gian Galeazzo Sforza, and the usurpation of the title of the Duchy of Milan from his wife,

Isabella Sforza Aragon, the Duchess of Milan, and their son, Francesco Sforza II, il Duchetto, the Count of Pavia (1491-1499). This betrayal of Gian Galeazzo was initiated and led by Ludovico il Moro Sforza, the Duke of Bari, and his son-in-law, Galeazzo Sforza Sanseverino. Leonardo had to keep this historical revelation as a coded message for his own safety; otherwise, he would have been seen as betraying Ludovico Sforza and Galeazzo Sanseverino and severely punished. Leonardo could see Ludovico was rewriting his own history and involvement in a *coup d' etat* with his own investiture as the Duke of Milan in 1495 at the expense of Gian Galeazzo's son, Francesco. An enormous injustice was committed against Gian Galeazzo Sforza and his wife and their children and Leonardo acknowledged their tragic history with his cryptogram that was symbolically soiled by the black fly.

The 'obese black fly' represents the black prince Ludovico il Moro Sforza and places the entire cryptogram in its true historical context. The Sforza black fly, like Beelzebub - the Lord of the Flies, is symbolic of sinister corruption, intrigues and death; the people and the historians of the Sforza court believed that he was guilty of killing his nephew Gian Galeazzo the 6th Duke of Milan and usurping his throne. He was characterised by astrologers with the number five (pentagon), associated with the fifth house Mars (Leo) and the fire sign; an extrovert, impatient, unreliable, adventurous, eclectic, charismatic, and competitive. In the portrait he also can be associated with the black background, the solid dodecahedron and his son-in-law Galeazzo Sanseverino dressed in red and black – the symbols of war - blood, fire, and ash.

Comments and Conclusions About the Glori Decryption and Revelations

Bianca Sforza was the illegitimate daughter of Ludovico Sforza and the wife of Galeazzo Sanseverino. Carla Glori believes that Bianca Sforza is Leonardo's *Mona Lisa*. However, it is noteworthy that Leonardo da Vinci provided no coded messages about two tragic events that occurred at the end of 1496 in Milan. The first was the suspicious death of Bianca Sforza on the 23rd November 1496 often described without adducing evidence by various writers as 'complications giving birth', but historically documented in a letter from her distressed father il Moro accusing Ambrogio da Rosate. About six-weeks later, the second tragedy was the death of the Duchess Beatrice d'Este a few hours after delivering her stillborn son on the 3rd January 1497. Leonardo da Vinci was still working on his great mural painting the *Last Supper* at the Church of *S. Maria delle Grazie* when the Duke's daughter Bianca and his wife Beatrice were entombed there as part of two separate State funerals. It seems likely that Leonardo would have commented on their deaths in the cartouche if those events had happened before he completed the *Pacioli Portrait*. Apart from displaying Luca Pacioli, Galeazzo Sanseverino, the rhombicuboctahedron and the other geometric shapes in the *Pacioli Portrait*, there are no overt references to Luca Pacioli's manuscript *De Divina Proportione* that was commissioned by the Duke Ludovico il Moro Sforza and his son-in-law Galeazzo Sanseverino. The first two copies of the finished manuscripts were presented to the Duke of Milan and his son-in-law on the 9th of February in 1498. Thus, it appears likely that the *Pacioli Portrait* was finished by Leonardo da Vinci before the 23rd November 1496, the date that Bianca Sforza died, otherwise he may have felt obliged to include Galeazzo Sanseverino in funeral attire instead of showing him wearing a red and white sartorial undershirt that vividly represents his jousting house colours. The black overcoat looks sombre enough, but it may have been overpainted onto a different colour sometime after its earlier completion. It seems to me that the fly is covering up the number 6 rather than 5 in the portrait to date its completion at the end of 1496, perhaps when Luca Pacioli first arrived in Milan.

Given that the painting is a portrait of Luca Pacioli and Galeazzo Sanseverino, it is likely to have been commissioned by either one of them or their supporter Ludovico Sforza, Duke of Milan. If so, then it is intriguing how the painting managed to find its way into the 1631 inventory of Francesco Maria II della Rovere, Duke of Urbino. It could have been transferred to Urbino by Luca Pacioli, Leonardo da Vinci or one of Leonardo's painting assistants, possibly by Antonio Baltroffio, after they all left Milan at the end of 1499 for Bologna, Venice, Mantua and Florence when Milan fell into the hands of the French and Ludovico Sforza and Galeazzo Sanseverino fled to the safety of the Swiss and German alps. The solution to the mystery of how it came into the possession of Francesco Maria II della Rovere awaits the discovery of some historic documents or letters revealing the original history and ownership. The painting possibly ended up in Venice in April of 1500 when Leonardo da Vinci and Luca Pacioli were both there as guests and advisors to the Senators of Venice who were greatly concerned about an invasion from the Turks who already had occupied the north-eastern region of the Republic of Venice. Leonardo advised the Venetians that they should build a mobile dam and flood the Isonzo River valley and drown the Turks. Guidobaldo da Montefeltro, the Duke of Urbino, also may have been in Venice at that time for he had been previously hired by the Republic of Venice to fight against the French troops of King Charles VIII in 1494. So, could it be that while Guidobaldo was in Venice that he inherited or bought the painting from Leonardo and Luca for some unrecorded favour? Luca Pacioli had already dedicated his *Summa* on mathematics and accounting to the Duke of Urbino when Paganini published it in Venice in 1494. Were Leonardo and Luca in

Venice in 1500 to discuss and organise the publication of the *Divine Proportion*? Paganini eventually published the *Divine Proportion* as a printed and illustrated book in June of 1509. Leonardo's drawings from woodcuts are believed to be the first published illustrations of skeletonic solids that allowed them to be easily seen with a 3D shape, that is, 3D structures with a front and back.

Leonardo was briefly in Urbino in the service of Cesare Borgia and his army when the latter invaded and captured the city in late July of 1502. Leonardo wrote in his notebook, *'30 July – the dove-cote at Urbino'* and next day *'1 August – in the library at Pesaro'*, a place that is about 36 km from Urbino. Guidobaldo da Montefeltro, the Duke of Urbino, escaped capture and waited a year before he returned to Urbino and remained there until his death due to gout at the age of 36 years in 1508. It is unlikely that Leonardo carried the *Pacioli Portrait* with him during his engineering service for Cesare Borgia and left it with him or Guidobaldo da Montefeltro in Urbino.

At the time of painting Luca Pacioli's portrait, Leonardo da Vinci seemed to be upset by the tragic outcome of Gian Galeazzo Sforza and his wife Isabella Sforza Aragon and their three children. He seemed to foresee that Ludovico Sforza and his propaganda machine would soon expunge them from the official history of Milan and Lombardy. Ludovico would trumpet the glories of his own achievements, but rarely, if ever, would he refer to or acknowledge any of the achievements of his nephew Gian Galeazzo Sforza, the 6th Duke of Milan, who reigned for 17 years from 1476 to 1494 with substantially diminished power, at first represented by his mother Bona of Savoy, the Duchess Regent, and then by his uncle Ludovico Sforza, the Duke of Bari. Ludovico spent little or no time at his Duchy of Bari that was located too far away from his position of greater power in Milan. Leonardo seemed to have decided that an enormous injustice was committed against Gian Galeazzo Sforza and his wife and their children and he acknowledged their tragic history in his cartouche that was symbolically soiled by the black fly. Leonardo's concern about the historical revisionism by Ludovico's powerful political faction was correct because little has been written about the glorious reign of Gian Galeazzo Sforza, his understated achievements and his tragic inglorious end. Carla Glori in deciphering Leonardo's cartouche has at least brought back an important reminder of those dramatic Milanese and Italian historical events that its people and other nations should remember and acknowledge.

In decoding the da Vinci code, Carla Glori has revealed that the cryptic epigraph *IACO.B AR. VIGENNIS* is not the signature of the Venetian painter Jacopo de' Barbari. It is Leonardo da Vinci's Milanese enigmatic coded message telling us about the history of the painting and the political intrigues of the Sforza court in Milan between the years of 1494 and 1496.

This involved the death of the Duke of Milan Gian Galeazzo Sforza and the usurpation of the Duchy of Milan from his son Francesco Sforza and his wife the Duchess of Milan Isabella Sforza by his evil uncle Ludovico Sforza, il Moro, as represented by the black fly.

In the final analysis, it is amazing that the 520-year-old secret of the cartouche contains so many often repeated words and names that historians would be familiar with in respect to Leonardo da Vinci's history in Milan working for the two Dukes of Milan, Gian Galeazzo Sforza and Ludovico il Moro. Carla Glori successfully deciphered Leonardo da Vinci's perfect anagrams hidden within the mysterious acronym **IACO.B AR. VIGENNIS. P. 1495,** and yet so few people know about her extraordinary achievement. By decoding the series of messages contained within the cryptic cartouche, Carla Glori confirms the known history of the relationships between Ludovico Sforza, Gian Galeazzo Sforza, Galeazzo Sanseverino, Isabella Sforza Aragon, Beatrice d'Este, Bianca Sforza and the wizard Ambrogio da Rosate, and the long-held suspicions that Ludovico Sforza and his allies murdered his nephew, the legitimate 6th Duke of Milan Gian Galeazzo Sforza, in 1494. Moreover, the decoded secret message proves beyond reasonable doubt that the setting of the *Pacioli Portrait* is in Lombardy and that it was painted by the Florentine genius Leonardo da Vinci and not by Jacopo de' Barbari of Venice and Germany.

The portraits of Luca Pacioli and Galeazzo Sanseverino added together in one painting is more than just a double portrait, it is a historical/pictorial puzzle to be solved by forensic decryption methodology and deductive reasoning based on historical facts and timelines. Leonardo da Vinci provided subtle clues about an entertaining and dramatic period of Italian history to be solved. There is the underlining tension between Ludovico and Gian Galeazzo Sforza and their wives in the choice of the painted stark, black background and the green foreground. There is the forensic presentation of items on the green table and they are clues for us to decipher their historical meaning. The items such as the eraser, pen and inkwell, the compass and pointer are bearers of opposite meanings: they are mathematician's tools, but at the same time, in the enigma of the painting, they are charged with a cryptic dimension. The symbolic black fly points to the hidden dark history of the Sforza family: the murder of the '*immacolato agnello*' Gian Galeazzo Sforza. The anagrams generated by the coded inscription spell out VINCI and they describe the history of Milan when Leonardo was there with Luca Pacioli who he immortalised by painting a portrait of him presenting a lecture on the golden ratio, an infinite divine proportion. The painting is about one of Leonardo's most favourite subjects, Euclidian geometric shapes and mathematics; and it is about two of his friends, the mathematics teacher Luca Pacioli and his rich and powerful sponsor Galeazzo Sanseverino, the son-in-law and favourite of Ludovico il Moro Sforza, the 7th duke of Milan. This rich and telling insight into the hidden meaning of the *Pacioli Portrait* at the National Museum of Capodimonte in Naples, Italy, can be attributed largely to Carla Glori and her remarkable achievement of decoding the mysterious acronym **IACO.B AR. VIGENNIS. P. 1495**.

Postscript: The author Jerzy K. Kulski thanks Carla Glori for her clarification on the complex decryption of the acronym *IACO.B AR. VIGENNIS. P. 1495* written on the cartouche within the *Pacioli Portrait*. He acknowledges her kind permission to reproduce some of her copyrighted discoveries about the code described in this chapter. However, any possible mistakes, misinterpretations or omissions made about the cryptic inscription are purely his and not those of Carla Glori.

References

Ady, Cecilia M (1907). A history of Milan, under the House of Sforza. Edward Armstrong (editor). New York: G. P. Putnam's Sons. London: Methuen & Co. 1907.
https://archive.org/stream/historyofmilanun017956mbp/historyofmilanun017956mbp_djvu.txt.

Barca GA. IACO. BAR. VIGENNIS P.1495. Enigma e Secretissima Scientia. *http://www.ritrattopacioli.it/Jacobarvigennis2.pdf (site disconnected)*.

Cartwright, Julia Mary (1908). Beatrice d'Este, Duchess of Milan, 1475-1479. J. M. Dent and Co.

Ferretti Daniela, Vervoordt Axel, et al (2015). PROPORTIO (Catalogo della mostra 2015, Palazzo Fortuny, Venezia), Fondazione Musei Civici Veneziae e Axel e May Verdoordt Foundation, "Omaggio a Luca Pacioli", pp.10-13.

Glori, Carla (2010). Il cartiglio di Leonardo. La Ricerca – 2010.
http://www.carlaglori.com/cartiglio/luca-pacioli/

Glori, Carla (2013). Il cartiglio di Leonardo. Decifrazioni e Soluzioni 2013.

Glori, Carla (2018). Il cartiglio di Leonardo. Il cartiglio. *http://www.carlaglori.com/mi-presento/, http://www.carlaglori.com/cartiglio/*

Glori, Carla. La storia di Ginevra Benci nelle cinquanta frasi anagrammate dal motto VIRTUTEM FORMA DECORAT + LA PAROLA-CHIAVE IUNIPERUS. Academia edu. *https://independent.academia.edu/CarlaGlori*

Feinberg, Larry J (2011). The Young Leonardo: Art and Life in Fifteen-Century Florence (Cambridge University Press).

Marinoni, Augusto (1983). Rebus by Leonardo da Vinci (Silvana Editoriale, Acardia edizioni, Milano). *https://bibdig.museogalileo.it/Teca/Viewer?an=1055565*

Vaglienti FM (2004). Isabella d'Aragona, Dizionario biografico degli Italiani (Rome, 1960ff.), lxii. 609–615. *http://www.treccani.it/enciclopedia/isabella-d-aragona-duchessa-di-milano_(Dizionario-Biografico)/*

Vasari, Giorgio (1550). The Lives of The Most Excellent Painters, Sculptors, and Architects. de Vere GdC, trans. New York, NY: The Modern Library; 2006.

Zuffi, Stefano (editor), Glori Carla, Ferrari Simone, Luca Pacioli tra Piero della Francesca e Leonardo, Marsilio, Venezia, 2017.

21

A LEONARDO MASTERPIECE? MISUNDERSTOOD & MISATTRIBUTED

Correcting the Misattribution

Many different scholars, philosophers, accountants, commentators and mathematicians have written about Luca Pacioli and that the Museum of Capodimonte in Naples attributed the *Pacioli Portrait* to the Venetian/German painter and engraver Jacopo de Barbari. Although their analyses and comments often highlight and acknowledge the long-term friendship between Leonardo da Vinci and Fra Luca Pacioli and their collaboration to publish the illustrated *De Divina Proportione*, the great majority of them still accept the Jacopo de' Barbari attribution rather than concede that it was created by Leonardo and possibly by one or other of his assistants. Apart from a few scholars like Carla Glori and Giovanni Barca who have provided considerable evidence and support for the Leonardo da Vinci's authorship, the vast majority of scholars continue to propagate the false claim that de Barbari is the author of the painting.

The simple message in this book is that only Leonardo da Vinci could have painted the *Pacioli Portrait* given its subject and narrative and all the visible and hidden objects, symbols and meanings attached to them. I have provided details and sensible reasons and arguments as to why it should be attributed to Leonardo, the giant of the Renaissance, and not to Jacopo de' Barbari, a comparatively minor player and painter, best remembered for his wood engravings of Greek and Roman myths, and the aerial view of Venice. The *Pacioli Portrait* is a work of true genius, an immense visual puzzle, a pictorial feast of metaphors, history and allegories, a painting to meditate on for enlightenment and for inspiration. It is a mixture of realism and abstraction, and it highlights the skills and huge ability of somebody profound and talented enough to translate the science of mathematical geometry and Plato and Aristotle's philosophies into a visual art form, as a double portraiture. This was an astonishing achievement for its time. It is the only painting and portraiture of the Renaissance (and for at least the next few hundred years) that is dedicated to the subject of mathematics and geometric shapes, Euclid's *Elements* and Luca Pacioli's *Summa*. Argante Ciocci, in his paper, *Il doppio ritratto del poliedrico Luca Pacioli* (The double portraiture of the polyhedral Luca Pacioli), published in the *Spanish Journal of Accounting History* in 2011 suggested that:

'*The Double portrait can be read as a metaphor of the multifaceted faces of Luca Pacioli: the master of abacus, as emerges from the Abacus Treatise written for the students of Perugia (1478); the tireless supporter of the universality of mathematics and the promoter of the meeting between learned mathematics and practical mathematics; the creator of a Summa encyclopedic of the Medieval and Renaissance mathematical disciplines; the codifier of the double-entry accounting entry in the Tractatus XI of the ninth distinction of Summa; the disseminator of Euclid and a lover of geometry and metaphysics of regular polyhedra, as appears in the Divina Proportione; the master of geometry of Leonardo; the theoretician of Vitruvian architecture, as it is in the Treatise of Architecture published in the printed edition of Divine Proportione of 1509; the publisher of the Elements of Euclid (1509); the player and writer of the De ludo schachorum; the compiler of mathematical games of the De viribus quantitatis; the creator of the alphabet built with a line and compass and the indefatigable collaborator of his typographer, as emerges from the editorial characteristics of Summa and Divina Proportione. The cultural glue that holds together the multiple and varied activities of Fra Luca is constituted by the profound conviction of the universal applicability of mathematics. "If you do well," says Pacioli, "in all the arts you will find the proportion of all being mother and queen, and without her, no one could exercise". The interest of Fra Luca for the use of proportions in every area of human knowledge is traceable in all his works and allows the historian, as the author of his portrait, to assemble the polyhedral faces of Pacioli in a single figure.*' (Translated from Italian to English).

Because of its connection to the *Divine Proportion*, the *Pacioli Portrait* with polyhedrons and other geometrical shapes could only represent the mind and vision and technical brilliance of one person, and that is Leonardo da Vinci. Given its context and the historical time that it was painted, this painting is a monumental work of art. It is unlikely to have been constructed by the mind or technical achievements of the Venetian Jacopo de' Barbari, a relatively minor painter who was no genius or visionary as can be ascertained from the underwhelming oeuvre of his works and legacy. Is the genius of the *Pacioli Portrait* with the geometric construction of the hanging rhombicuboctahedron and the intrinsic psychology of its characters and symbols attributable to Barbari's creative and technical capabilities? This seemingly is an improbable question given our knowledge of the history between Luca Pacioli and Leonardo da Vinci and the absence of any known connection between him and Jacopo de' Barbari. This absence of an historical connection between Jacopo de' Barbari and Luca Pacioli should have eliminated Barbari immediately from the equation and any consideration of attribution. What would have been his motive or reason to paint the portrait and polyhedrons even if he had attended a Luca Pacioli lecture on mathematics in Venice? Moreover, the painting has all the added symbolism of a lecture presented by Luca Pacioli on Euclid's geometry or the *Divine Proportion* to the Leonardo da Vinci Academy at the Sforza Castle in Milan, which is far away from Jacopo de' Barbari's geographical location and influence of Venice.

Leonardo loved puzzles, riddles, jests and metaphors and he collected a large number of them in his notebooks with his secret mirror writing to remember and recite or elaborate on to the gentlemen and ladies of the Sforza court. The Italian Renaissance painter and historian Giorgio Vasari told us that Leonardo was a great entertainer, raconteur, fabulist, humourist, joker and theatre producer. He was handsome, strong and athletic, and he could sing, play instruments, design sets, create theatre and produce magic. He was employed by the Sforza Court to entertain them by organising plays, festivals, celebrations, jests, and academic debates. This gave him less time for his inventions and court paintings or undertaking sculptures, fortifications, town planning and engineering, although he could do all those things almost simultaneously in his busy schedule. He was a scientist and a polymath extraordinaire and this is reflected in the slightly distorted way that he created his symbolic portraits of Luca Pacioli, Galeazzo Sanseverino, Gian and Ludovico Sforza, providing us with a coded reminder of their history that they brought with them during his stay in Milan. In this context, like the *Mona Lisa* and the *Last Supper*, the *Pacioli Portrait* is part history and part mystery, a puzzle to be solved. Moreover, it is an important part of the history of the Duchy of Milan that should be recognised and acknowledged as being intrinsic to many of Leonardo's paintings. Leonardo has provided subtle clues such as the eraser, pen and inkwell, the compass and pointer, all pointing to the cartouche and mysterious inscription outlining Ludovico Sforza's guilt and his history of murdering and usurping his nephew's duchy. The underlining tension between Ludovico Sforza and Gian Galeazzo Sforza is depicted further in the choice of the painted stark black background and the green foreground, emblematic of their family rivalry and the reserved coloured symbols of their privileged status.

Leonardo collaborated enthusiastically with Luca Pacioli in the publication of the *Divine Proportion* because from an early age he understood the importance of mathematics in geometry, perspective and proportions in painting, sculpture, engineering and architecture. Hence, they worked well together on several different projects as exemplified by the *Pacioli*

Portrait. Carla Glori, in decoding Leonardo's inscription IACO.B AR VIGEN/NIS (P.1495) with the fly on top, has provided us with convincing evidence that the painting entitled *Fra Luca Pacioli and Student* (accession number inv. Q 58) at the National Museum of Capodimonte in Naples only could have been painted and produced by Leonardo da Vinci and by nobody else.

Here are 33 reasons why the *Pacioli Portrait* is by Leonardo da Vinci and not by Jacopo de' Barbari.

1. The painting is a portrait of Leonardo da Vinci's friend and mathematics teacher, the Franciscan friar, Fra Luca Pacioli.
2. The painting is also a portrait of Galeazzo Sanseverino, one of Leonardo's friends and sponsors and the son-in-law of Ludovico Sforza, the Duke of Bari and Milan, and the sponsor of Luca Pacioli in Milan.
3. Galeazzo Sanseverino in the *Pacioli Portrait* looks similar to the young man that Leonardo had painted as a *Musician* in an earlier painting.
4. The painting is about five of Leonardo's favourite subjects - Euclidian geometric shapes, mathematics, science, dialectics and painting.
5. The year 1495/6 is written in the painting. Leonardo da Vinci and Luca Pacioli worked together on mathematics and geometry for at least four or five years while in Milan (1495/6 to 1499) and then later in Florence (1500 to 1507) and possibly in Rome (1514).
6. Galeazzo Sanseverino sponsored Luca Pacioli and Leonardo da Vinci to produce three copies of the manuscript on Euclidian geometry entitled the *Divine Proportion*.
7. Leonardo produced 30 painted drawings of Euclidian solids hanging from a string as an addition to Luca Pacioli's manuscript of the *Divine Proportion*.
8. Leonardo may have been the first person with a documented drawing and painting of the rhombicuboctahedron, and a printed book version of it (1509). No other artist before or during Leonardo's lifetime seems to have drawn or painted the rhombicuboctahedron.
9. The addition of air and water and the reflected images within the rhombicuboctahedron are typical Leonardo pictorial intrigues, tricks and inventions.
10. The hanging cord is tied to a da Vinci Freemason's symbol, the inverse V or A, located at the bottom of the rhombicuboctahedron.
11. The symbol of the circle O on top of an A at the bottom of the rhombicuboctahedron in the *Pacioli Portrait* (Fig. 12.14) is also found among Leonardo's drawings of drafting and measuring compasses on a page of one of his notebooks (Fig. 9.3).
12. Leonardo has many drawings of old men's faces that look similar to Luca Pacioli.

13. Leonardo has a precursor drawing of a 'look-alike' Luca Pacioli with the same facial warts (Fig. 2.4); and there are at least two other profiles of old men's faces by Leonardo that G. A. Barca had identified to look very much like the Luca Pacioli in his portrait with Galeazzo Sanseverino.

14. The *Pacioli Portrait* shows Luca with a slightly asymmetrical smile (comparable to *Mona Lisa*) that is a Leonardo da Vinci pictorial signature and it shows his fondness for asymmetry.

15. Luca Pacioli's eyes are divergent or misaligned, which is a pictorial oddity for a conventional portrait painter; but an unique anatomical and medical depiction for a science-minded specialist like Leonardo da Vinci.

16. The bands of shadows and light on Luca Pacioli's grey habit are typical pictorial signatures of Leonardo that in this case are comparable to the shadows and light on the cosmic birth shell of the *Birth of Venus* by Botticelli (Fig. 13.12) and the *Madonna and Child* by Piero della Francesca (Fig. 12.11).

17. Given the hypothesis that the *Pacioli Portrait* is connected to the Sforza castle, we could conceive a geometrical/architectural/symbolic connection between the painted rope in the *Sala delle Asse* and the cord around Pacioli's waist, and also between the column-like folds of his tunic and Leonardo's metaphor of painted mulberry trees supporting the structure of the vaulted ceiling in the *Sala delle Asse* of the Sforza castle.

18. The painting contains symbolism and codes that only Leonardo was capable of consideration and execution.

19. The striking similarity between the design of the *Pacioli Portrait* and Leonardo's *Last Supper* with the various symbolic items spread across the table in the immediate foreground and with the central triangular shaped figures of Pacioli and Christ with their dramatic hand gestures and facial expressions facing the viewer from behind the table (Fig. 2.1).

20. The painting contains symbolism and codes that depict betrayal and the antagonism between Ludovico Sforza (black background, the black fly Moro) and his nephew Gian Galeazzo Sforza (green table in the foreground with the cartouche).

21. The blackened room in the portrait could be the *Saletta Negra* at the Sforza castle in Milan.

22. The cryptic acronym IACO.B AR. VIGEN (NIS) P 1495 on the notepaper in the *Pacioli Portrait* contains within it the word VINCI and the alphabetic letters that form the names of all the people associated with the portrait (see Chapter 20, pages 391-398).

23. The perfect anagrams decoded by Carla Glori describe 148 phrases relevant to the history of Milan when Leonardo was residing and working there with Luca Pacioli and it undoubtedly reveals that he was the portrait painter of Luca Pacioli and Galeazzo Sanseverino.

24. Carla Glori revealed that the inscription with the coded messages also

contain Leonardo's secret 'stories' about mathematics and the thoughts and sayings of others by using his signature VINCI and words like ABACUS.

25. The Roman or Atica letters in the *Pacioli Portrait* are the same that Leonardo used in some of his other paintings including the phrase VIRTVTEM FORMA DECORAT that he printed on the reverse side of the *Ginevra de' Benci* portrait.

26. The character and style of the handwritten numbers 1 to 9 on the Pacioli blackboard are highly similar to the handwritten numbers in Leonardo's notebooks.

27. The painting is about perspective, geometric shapes and the golden ratio; subjects at the heart of Leonardo's interests and painting designs.

28. The use of light and shadow in the painting is unique to Leonardo da Vinci.

29. Painting portraits of people in three quarter pose looking out directly at the viewer or slightly to one side is quintessentially Leonardo da Vinci and a trend that he introduced with his painting of *Ginevra de' Benci* and carried on in his subsequent portraits and religious paintings (perhaps he adapted some of these ideas from Antonello da Messina and Sandro Botticelli).

30. The use of expressive hands and arms in his portraits and religious paintings are uniquely Leonardo da Vinci based on his theory that people, *'speak with the movements of the hands, eyes, eyelashes and the whole person, in wanting to express the concept of their soul'* and the left and right side of their brain, as in the *Pacioli Portrait*.

31. The style and complexity of the painting is from a unique mind like that of Leonardo da Vinci and not others.

32. The subjects of the painting are unique, educational and completely consistent with Leonardo da Vinci who was a master practitioner and teacher of painting and perspective. He drafted *The Treatise on Painting* that was published posthumously by his assistant and student Francesco Melzi.

33. The painting is a philosophical work about mathematics, science, cosmology, religion, politics and history, all subjects that Leonardo excelled at and promoted in his writings, drawings, paintings and teachings.

Most of these 33 points have little or no direct relevance to Jacopo de' Barbari because it seems that he did not know Luca Pacioli personally and so, we can dismiss him as the painter of this uniquely Italian Renaissance portrait set in Milan and Lombardy and not in Urbino as many scholars had claimed previously. These 33 reasons should be sufficient evidence to convince most people in a jury beyond reasonable doubt that the *Pacioli Portrait* at the National Museum of Capodimonte in Naples was executed by Leonardo da Vinci and not by Jacopo de' Barbari. The question remains, however, whether the evidence and arguments provided in this book and by others elsewhere can convince art historians and experts in the world and at the Capodimonte Museum in Naples to finally acknowledge that Leonardo da Vinci painted the *Pacioli Portrait*.

And what is the actual year that is printed beside the fly on the notepaper in the *Pacioli Portrait*? Is it 1494, 1495 or 1496? Many historians believe that the year 1494 was the beginning of the end of the Renaissance in Italy when the French invaded Italy in that year at the invitation of Ludovico il Moro Sforza. It was the beginning of a new era marked by war and political turmoil that led to great economic disruption and a significant reduction in the amount of patronage available to artists. This eventually resulted in a large decline in the sponsorship of the arts and sciences in Lombardian and Italian society in the decades after 1500. Thus, the portraits of Luca Pacioli and Galeazzo Sanseverino standing together in a castle room in Lombardy at some particular time in 1495/1496 places them together with the painter Leonardo da Vinci at the crossroads of the Italian Renaissance.

In the opening chapters of this book, I pointed out that the current 'natural belief' about the *Pacioli Portrait* is that Jacopo de Barbari was its author even though there is no evidence to suggest that he ever knew or met with his subjects Luca Pacioli and the Duke of Urbino. Throughout the remainder of the book, I tried to change this well-accepted 'natural belief' by providing evidence to show why Leonardo da Vinci is the only natural and correct candidate for the execution of this painting. The philosopher Edmund Husserl used phenomenological reduction or *'neutrality modification'* as he called it, to contemplate and clarify the ambiguity in philosophy or a work of art. As his example of an ambiguity in art, he chose Albrecht Durer's engraving *Knight, Death and the Devil* to clarify how neutrality modification in phenomenological reduction is used in the contemplation and redirection of belief in reinterpreting a work of art. In my analysis of the *Pacioli Portrait* I intuitively took a similar approach to neutrality modification by neutralising the standard or 'natural' belief and then attempted to redirect it by providing concrete evidence towards an alternative, unambiguous and correct explanation that Leonardo da Vinci was the real author of the portrait. I tried to *'bracket all incidental meaning and ask: what are some of the possible invariant aspects of this experience'*; are they closer to the experience and life of Leonardo da Vinci or Jacopo de' Barbari? This and all the previous chapters undoubtedly tip the scale of genuine authorship towards Leonardo da Vinci. But, without having Leonardo da Vinci's actual signature on the double portraiture or any officially validated documentation to convince the sceptics, a smidgen of ambiguity, indeterminacy and cognitive mystery remains that requires further enquiry into Leonardo da Vinci's genius and his mysterious masterpiece more than five-hundred years after its creation.

At about the same time that I was completing this last chapter, Carla Glori commenced her analysis of the infrared reflectography of the *Pacioli Portrait*. Perhaps, the results of this analysis will provide further evidence either in favour of Leonardo's attribution or contradict that possibility. Raman spectroscopy also could be used to compare the pigments of the *Pacioli Portrait* with those used by Leonardo or Barbari in their well-known paintings and help to resolve the attribution.

And so, let us ask ourselves what would happen if the Capodimonte Museum officially acknowledged, recognised and publicised that the *Pacioli Portrait* was painted and produced by Leonardo da Vinci? First, it might create enormous controversy, but probably less so than Leonardo's painting of the *Salvator Mundi* that was sold as Lot 9B at Christie's auction (Post-War and Contemporary Art Evening Sale) on the night of the 15th November of 2017 in New York for a record price of US $450,312,500 (including buyer's premium). Second, the general public suddenly might develop a much greater curiosity, interest and appreciation of the painting; after all, if it's a Leonardo then it must be good. Third, because it's a Leonardo, the painting might attract bigger crowds than usual to see it at the Capodimonte Museum. Fourth, with a greater interest in the painting, the insurance costs for the painting might sky-rocket; after all, if it's a Leonardo then it must be worth a fortune. Fifth, the costs for the security of the painting might rise and it would have to be displayed in a more secure location at a greater cost to the Museum and inconvenience to the public. These five reasons alone could make the Capodimonte Museum extremely cautious about changing the attribution of the painting from Jacopo de' Barbari to Leonardo da Vinci. Luca Pacioli with his slightly asymmetrical smile and stiff fingers might suggest to us that he has suffered an offense with the disbelief that his portrait is not yet attributed to Leonardo.

Leonardo's Hands as Expressions of the Soul

Leonardo da Vinci brought together five elements to many of his portraits that most other painters before him or during his time did not accomplish. These five elements were (1) the expressive or misaligned eyes, (2) the expressive hands often holding a symbolic, non-religious item, (3) the crooked mouth or cryptic smile, (4) the three-quarter or full-frontal pose with the bent or partly turned head, and (5) the occasional facial blemish or a revealing medical condition. The *Pacioli Portrait* has all 5 of these elements. If you examine any other painter's portraits of that time, including those of Barbari and Durer, only a few of the five elements were a part of their outputs and that one or more of the elements were always missing, for example, the expressive hands with or without an object, an uneven smile, or an odd blemish on the face such as a wart, pimple, fatty deposit or excessive wrinkles, as can be seen in the *Mona Lisa* and the *Pacioli Portrait*.

One of Leonardo's great artistic achievements and design innovations was to include the subject's hands in a portrait (Fig. 21.1). Up to that point, Italian portraiture, in general, only showed the upper chest and head, but Leonardo saw the expressiveness of hands as a gateway to the subject's state of mind.

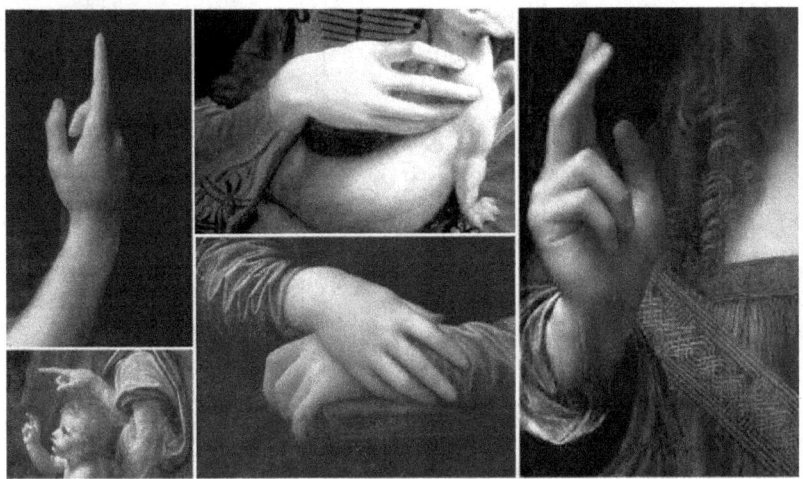

FIG. 21.1. *Leonardo's painted hands in* John the Baptist, Virgin of the Rocks *(left, top and bottom),* Lady with the Ermine, Mona Lisa *(middle, top and bottom) and* Salvator Mundi *(middle)*.

His psychological portraiture implicitly invalidated the mind-body split and he attempted to paint 'consciousness' itself. Some of the painters before him like the Early Netherlandish painters Robert Campin, Hans Memling, Jan van Eyck and Rogier van der Weyden occasionally added the hands to their portraits, but more in prayer or as ornaments rather than as expressions of a thought. For Leonardo, it was a key part of his portraiture. The hands and arms, like the eyes, express the right and left sides of the brain (Fig. 21.2A). You may be left-handed, right-handed or ambidextrous, but sometimes your hands betray you and reveal an emotion that you are attempting to hide. Many Renaissance painters, especially the Leonardeschi followed Leonardo's example and added the hands and arms as an extra expression of human life and tension in their portraits and narrative paintings. To reiterate point 30 on page 410: the use of expressive hands and arms in his portraits and religious paintings are uniquely Leonardo da Vinci based on his theory that people, '*speak with the movements of the hands, eyes, eyelashes and the whole person, in wanting to express the concept of their soul*'.

A. Pacioli hands, eyes & mouth

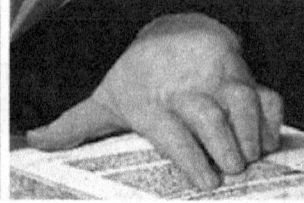
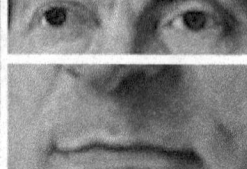

Pacioli's right hand (RH)   Pacioli's left hand (LH)   Pacioli's eyes & mouth

B. Hands of Judas, John & Christ in the Last Supper

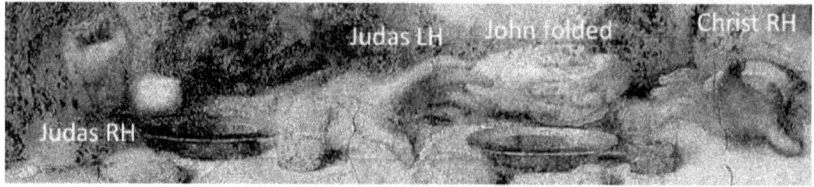

C. Annunciation & The Virgin of the Rocks

Annunciation   The Virgin of the Rocks

FIG. 21.2. Pacioli's hands, eyes and mouth in the Pacioli Portrait *(A), the right (RH) and left (LH) hands of Judas, folded hands of John, and right hand (RH) of Christ in the* Last Supper *(B), and the hands of the Archangel in the* Annunciation, *and hands of the Archangel, Christ Child and the Virgin Mary in* The Virgin of the Rocks *(C).*

Some friends and acquaintances of mine, including those who are painters, believe that Pacioli's hands and fingers are so distorted and ugly that Leonardo could not have painted them. Some say that Leonardo only drew and painted beautiful arms and hands, not ugly ones (Figs. 21.1 to 21.3). Possibly, Luca Pacioli's chunky bits of meat are meant to draw our attention and curiosity to the region of his hands, even if they are perceived to be ugly and poorly painted appendages (Fig. 21.2A). Luca Pacioli's hands and fingers look lumpy and arthritic, but they have purpose. They are like those of an artisan or painter busy at work; one hand holds a pointer or drawing implement, while the fingers of the other hand rest on a book with the forefinger pointing to a sentence that expresses a human instruction or thought. They are a dialectic contrast with Jesus's more refined hands in Leonardo's painting of the *Last Supper*. The comparison between Pacioli and Jesus's hands (Fig. 2.1) and those of the apostles was already investigated and discussed in Chapter 2 and will not be dwelt on here. The *Last Supper* was all about expressive hand gestures, with at least 20 hands visibly expressing the characters of the 12 disciples at the Supper during a climactic moment with the announcement of a betrayal (Fig. 2.2).

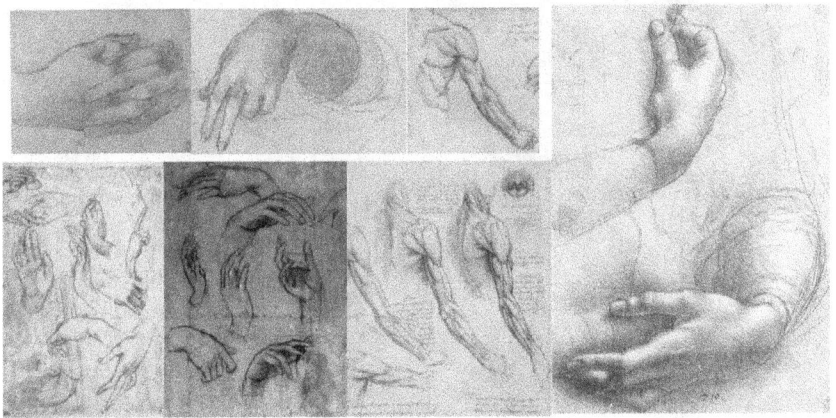

FIG. 21.3. Leonardo's studies of arms and hands. Most of these drawings belong to Royal Collection Trust of Her Majesty Queen Elizabeth II. Wikimedia Creative Commons. Public Domain.

In contrast to the questioning hands of Christ in the *Last Supper*, Pacioli's left hand expresses tremulous tension and distortion in his four fingers while his thumb and forefinger are spread in a wide V across a page of an open book (Fig. 21.2A). The same V shape is seen spread across the table with the V of the triangles drawn on the blackboard, the V shape of the bronze protractor, the V of the compass and the V shapes of the dodecahedron on the clasped book and the adjoining squares and triangles of the hanging rhombicuboctahedron (Fig. 21.4). The image of Luca Pacioli also is captured during a climactic moment, a moment of sudden understanding, inspiration or awareness that is represented by his facial expression and the visible tension in his left hand.

While Pacioli's left hand shows a certain degree of strain and tension resting on a book, his meaty right hand, although raised, is more relaxed and refined as he gently holds on to his pointer. While the V of the thumb and forefinger of his left hand is spread out like the open V of the protractor on the left side of the table, the V of the thumb and forefinger of the right hand looks more like the closed V of the measuring compass seen beneath his left hand. This difference between Pacioli's left and right hand also parallels the difference in his eyes where his right eye seems higher and looking in a different direction than his left eye. Similarly, the slant between Pacioli's left and right hand parallel that of Pacioli's mouth where the corner of the right side of the mouth is turned up and that of the left side turned down (Fig. 21.2A).

FIG. 21.4. *The golden ratio between points A and B along a line drawn between the thumb and forefinger of Pacioli's right and left hands and subdivided into the golden ratio by the knot tied near the middle of Pacioli's waist cord.*

The slant and the perspective of a line AB drawn between the V of the right hand and the V of the left hand pushes the viewer's eye away from the hanging rhombicuboctahedron and up towards Galeazzo Sanseverino looking out at us (Fig. 21.4). This connects Pacioli more closely to Sanseverino behind him and to the right of the picture, although Pacioli is looking intensely at the rhombicuboctahedron in the forefront to the left of the picture. This slanting perspective adds tension to a relatively static picture. Interestingly, the line AB passes through the middle of Pacioli's cord at point O and this creates another symmetrical and geometrical tension for the viewer's eye where the angled shadow lines on the front of his Franciscan habit meet along the length of the horizontal cord on the right side and left side of the O and then change direction. Moreover, the line AB between thumb and forefinger of Pacioli's left and right hands is subdivided into the golden ratio of 0.62 to 1 (=1.62) by the central knot of the cord tied around Pacioli's waist. This is another example of the use of the *Divine Proportion* in the *Pacioli Portrait* and Leonardo's experimental game of using perspective and contrasts to create a psychological tension (dialectic) within the limited boundaries of a 2D picture.

In comparison to Luca Pacioli, the hands of Galeazzo Sanseverino in the painting are mostly hidden from view. One hand is entirely hidden behind Pacioli's back. The other hand is partially hidden by Pacioli's left arm, and a puzzling green glove covers the hand that is partly in view. Why Leonardo has Galeazzo Sanseverino's hand and fingers hidden in a green glove is a mystery (Fig. 21.4). In this regard, Galeazzo's hands are somewhat reminiscent of Judas's hands in Leonardo's mural of the *Last Supper* where he clings on to his bag of silver pieces with his left hand while his right hand has a similar gesture as Jesus and grasps for something undefined (Fig. 21.2B). My interpretation of the green glove expressed in the book *Leonardo da Vinci: the Melzi Chronicles* was the following:

Galeazzo Sanseverino stands above the compass, the yellowed paper message, and the red book with his hand in a green glove (arsenic and Gian's heraldic colour) showing that he was complicit in the murder of the Illustrious 'Green' Duke Gian Galeazzo Sforza.

Pacioli's outstretched left hand also might be seen as a parody of the Virgin Mary's outstretched left hand in *The Virgin of the Rocks* and Judas and Christ's outstretched opposing hands in the *Last Supper* (Fig. 21.2). In this regard, Sanseverino's gloved hand and fingers even might satirise the Archangel's long-extended finger pointing towards John the Baptist on the left side of the painting in *The Virgin of the Rocks* that is at the Louvre. While the Archangel Gabriel points at St. John the Baptist, he looks out of the painting at the viewer in a similar, but less confronting way than Galeazzo Sanseverino does in the *Pacioli Portrait*. When Leonardo was obliged to create a new painting of *The Virgin of the Rocks* for the Confraternity of the Immaculate Conception at the basilica of San Francesco Grande and that is now at the London National Gallery, either he or Giovanni Ambrogio de Predis left out the Archangel's hand pointing towards St. John the Baptist that was in the original version. The obvious green and red house colours of the duke of Milan, Gian Galeazzo Sforza, worn by the Archangel were replaced with the brown and blue of Ludovico Sforza's house colours.

Also, halos were placed over the heads of the Virgin, Christ and St. John the Baptist, and St. John was given his symbolic staff and cross in order not to confuse him with Christ. Moreover, the Archangel no longer looks out at the viewer.

The analogy between *The Virgin of the Rocks* and the *Pacioli Portrait* can be pushed even further by pointing out that Pacioli's left hand hovers over the Circle and Triangle drawn on the blackboard and his left hand is placed on Euclid's *Elements* (Fig. 21.4) in much the same way that the Virgin Mary's right hand rests on the shoulder of the infant St. John the Baptist, while her extended left hand with an open palm hovers over the head of the Christ Child (Fig. 21.5.5). Whereas this coincidence of similarities between the *Pacioli Portrait* and *The Virgin of the Rocks* is a clear visual joke for the observant or informed insiders, it is difficult to judge whether or not he would have let Fra Luca Pacioli and Galeazzo Sanseverino in on the joke or whether he thought that if they cannot see the similarities themselves then it is best to say nothing. It probably depends on how well they knew each other and how well they could take a sacrilegious joke. There is a third version of *The Virgin of the Rocks* known as the *Borghetto Virgin* at the Church of San Michele del Dosso in Milan that is attributed to Francesco Melzi and that is almost an exact copy of the one at the Louvre. In this regard, I've often wondered if the *Pacioli Portrait* at the Capodimonte Museum is a repainted copy by Francesco Melzi. This possibility is worth considering, but remembering that the portrait is a Leonardo da Vinci concept and artwork even if it is a copy by Melzi or one of Leonardo's other assistants.

There are only two Leonardo da Vinci portraits that do not show the sitters' hands. One is *Ginevra de Benci* (Fig. 21.5.2) and the other is *La Belle Ferronnière* (Fig. 21.5.10). It is generally believed by the modern art experts that the lower third of the painting of *Ginevra de Benci* is missing because it was damaged. The reason for removing the lower portion of the painting is debatable. The awkward framing of the portrait indicates the removal of Ginerva Benci's hands from the painting—the space above her head is too wide in contrast to the narrow framing of her bodice and shoulders below. In other words, the lower part of the painting must have been cut off at some point after its completion. This is also evident on the reverse side of the panel, which contains an emblem in the form of a garland; with evidence that its bottom section is missing. Cropping a portrait or picture is a relatively common practice, particularly over a time frame of hundreds of years. Paintings often changed hands and, when they did, they sometimes were cut to fit a new frame or decoration scheme.

It seems Ginevra was holding something in her hand, possibly a flower that symbolised devotion, something like white lilies or laurel. Alternatively, she may have held something that became offensive to the sitter, owner, family member or viewer, and they had the painting cropped to remove the offence. Could Leonardo have had *Ginevra de Benci* holding an imaginary baby, his 'virtual' baby? Having a female sitter holding flowers as if they represented an infant was a theme that he and Francesco Melzi introduced in their painting of *Flora*, also known as *Colombina*. However, it is more likely that Leonardo da Vinci folded Ginevra's hands like those in Lorenzo di Credi's painting of *Ginevra de Benci* holding a wedding ring between her thumb and forefinger. (*Portrait of a Young Woman*, 1490 -1500, Oil on wood, 58.7 x 40 cm. Metropolitan Museum of Art, New York).

Leonardo used *Ginevra de Benci* as his first archetypal, beautiful, female model in several paintings including *Madonna with Baby* (*Benois Madonna*), and as the impregnated immaculate Madonna in the *Annunciation* (Fig. 21.5.1) where he also portrayed himself as the Angel Gabriel announcing her pregnancy. The presence of sexual symbolism and coded erotic dimensions in the painting of the *Annunciation* suggests that Leonardo may have been in love with Ginevra. She was pretty, classically educated and highly intelligent, a well-known poetess and the daughter of a wealthy Florentine banker. Leonardo was a close friend of her brother, which allowed him to access, entertain and paint her portraits. Frank Zollner saw the *Ginevra de Benci* painting as marking the point (1478-1480) when Leonardo broke away from *'the profile view traditionally employed in Florence for portraits of women'* in favour of the three-quarters view in order to impart *'a pyschological dimension to his sitter – something that would become the hallmark of Renaissance portraiture'*.

In the catalogue of essays written for the National Gallery of Art (Washington, DC) exhibition *Virtue and Beauty*, (2001 p. 145), David Alan Brown in his chapter showed a computer-reconstructed-figure made by the department of imaging and visual services of the *Ginevra de Benci* painting with her arms and hands digitally restored. The reconstruction used the hands drawn by Leonardo that is now part of the Windsor collection. This beautiful drawing of a woman's arms and hands was executed in metalpoint over charcoal with white highlights on buff paper (Fig. 21.3). It shows the hands in two positions: one with the hands in repose on one another, anticipating the composition of the *Mona Lisa*; and the other with the right hand high above the left, holding a flower. The digital restoration chose the former pose, similar to what Susan Dorothea White used in her painting of arms and hands reattached to the Ginevra de Benci portrait. The addition of the hands has an astonishing effect; the rather dour portrait suddenly comes alive.

The hands are missing also from Leonardo's *La Belle Ferronnière*, the portrait of a lady exhibited in the Louvre (Fig. 21.5.10). This appears to have been intentional because her hands are behind a barrier. On the other hand, most of Leonardo's other paintings show expressive hands. The use of expressive hands is best seen in his mural of the *Last Supper*. The hand gestures were in keeping with the growing role of art in the Renaissance as a form of visual poetry—an allegorical conversation piece. It reflects the urgent desire of many Renaissance artists to be recognised as creative masters and visionary poets, rather than mere artisans. Many Renaissance paintings like the *Pacioli Portrait* and the *Mona Lisa* were intellectual puzzles to invite the beholder to consider and demonstrate their humanistic pedigree and cultural sophistication in decoding the allegorical message.

Da Vinci's Soul

One of Leonardo's most subtly hidden dimensions in this painting is his philosophy of dialectics - the contrast of opposites, the contrast between light and dark, youth and old age, the crooked and straight smile, religion and science, good and evil, black and green, the circle and the square, the line and the point, etc., in relation to all things in the universe. This intellectual depth and breadth and curiosity expressed pictorially by Leonardo da Vinci is not at all evident in any of Jacopo de Barbari's known works. In the double portrait, Luca Pacioli's face expresses intense concentration and tight-lipped wonder about the rhombicuboctahedron and God's Universe while Galeazzo Sanseverino's presents a slightly bemused expression of arrogance knowing that he has the assured privilege of being Lord Ludovico's favourite. Or, perhaps, Luca Pacioli has had a revelation, an enlightenment, a startling realisation that 'I am who I am' through the nature of 'my experiences' and the awareness of the NonDual Self, knowing that the garden of unknowing is the hidden garden. If so, then Leonardo da Vinci's contemplation and painting of Luca Pacioli, Galeazzo Sanseverino, Euclid's geometry, the *Summa*, the divine proportion, the rhombicuboctahedron, the dodecahedron, the fly and the cartouche may have led him to better understand the mind-body connection between the spiritual and the physical world as the Soul, the One and Same Thing with no duality. In his notebooks, in his reverse writing, he has written the following about the phenomenology of painting and the nature of being as the *Soul of Life*:

We may justly call...painting...the grandson of nature and related to God.

Though human ingenuity by various inventions with different instruments yields the same end, it will never devise an invention either more beautiful... than does Nature because in her inventions nothing is lacking and nothing superfluous and she... puts there the soul, the composer of the body, that is the soul of the mother which first composes in the womb the shape of man and in due time awakens the soul which is to be its inhabitant.

CHAPTER 21

Behold here, O reader! A thing concerning which we cannot trust our forefathers, the ancients, who tried to define what the Soul and Life are--which are beyond proof, whereas those things, which can at any time be clearly known and proved by experience, remained for many ages unknown or falsely understood. The eye, whose function we so certainly know by experience, has, down to my own time, been defined by an infinite number of authors as one thing; but I find, by experience, that it is quite another.

The soul seems to reside in the judgment, and the judgment would seem to be seated in that part where all the senses meet; and this is called the Common Sense and is not all-pervading throughout the body, as many have thought.

And the Common Sense is the seat of the soul, and memory is its ammunition, and the impressibility is its referendary since the sense waits on the soul and not the soul on the sense. And where the sense that ministers to the soul is not at the service of the soul, all the functions of that sense are also wanting in that man's life, as is seen in those born mute and blind.

And you, O Man, who will discern in this work of mine the wonderful works of Nature, if you think it would be a criminal thing to destroy it, reflect how much more criminal it is to take the life of a man; and if this, his external form, appears to thee marvelously constructed, remember that it is nothing as compared with the soul that dwells in that structure; for that indeed, be it what it may, is a thing divine. Leave it then to dwell in His work at His goodwill and pleasure, and let not your rage or malice destroy a life--for indeed, he who does not value it, does not himself deserve it.

Now you see that the hope and the desire of returning home and to one's former state is like the moth to the light, and that the man who with constant longing awaits with joy each new springtime, each new summer, each new month and new year--deeming that the things he longs for are ever too late in coming--does not perceive that he is longing for his own destruction. But this desire is the very quintessence, the spirit of the elements, which finding itself imprisoned with the soul is ever longing to return from the human body to its giver. And you must know that this same longing is that quintessence, inseparable from nature, and that man is the image of the world.

The greatest deception men suffer is from their own opinions.

While Leonardo pondered and explored the nature of the soul and common sense, he was an avowed evolutionist four hundred years ahead of his time in the way that he saw and experienced the world and life. The historian and painter Giorgio Vasari wrote the following about Leonardo fifty years after his death. '*He had a very heretical state of mind. He could not be content with any kind of religion at all, considering himself in all things much more a philosopher than a Christian.*'

Leonardo understood that life was continuity in flux and he saw mutability everywhere. For him, everything seemed to be in the process of transformation. As Rebecca Stott wrote eloquently in her book *Darwin's Ghosts*, for Leonardo, *'patterns and shapes were all on the move, passing continually through ripeness to decay. Nothing, he knew, remained untouched by time. Even the apparently solid masses of mountain ranges were passing constantly through processes of putrefaction and regeneration, driven by water that was ever flooding, gushing, eroding, silting, slicing, levelling, blocking – destroying and remaking landscapes in an endless cycle.'* He spent much of his life studying fossils and pondering over the creation and origin of species. He rebutted the priests' explanation that fossils were washed to the tops of mountains by Noah's flood and he provided beds of shells as evidence that mountains were once seabeds. Like Aristotle two thousand years before him, Leonardo understood about the upheavals and geological processes that turned previous seabeds into mountains. Leonardo believed that *'all things are interconnected and this is relative or proportional depending on our perspective and movement and where we are when we observe these natural processes, but the laws of nature are constant and remain the same.'* For Leonardo, all powers are pyramidal, that is, they are perspectival, relative, and change in quantum amounts. This was his general theory of relativity. Leonardo deduced the pyramidal laws of perspective from his study of optics and light, and he carried them over to the four powers of nature: movement, force, weight, and percussion (impact) acting on the four elements, earth, water, air, and fire. With this came the four powers of man, with memory and intellect, desire and covetousness.

We will be telling the truth by affirming that it is possible to imagine all powers capable of infinite augmentation or diminution. Consequently, all powers are pyramidal (perspectival) because they can grow from nothing to infinite greatness by equal degrees. And by similar degrees they decrease to infinity by diminution ending in nothing. Therefore nothingness borders on infinity.

Amen to that!

More about Leonardo's studies and concepts of physical and metaphysical power as species of perspective in a qualitative science can be found in Fabio Frosini's 2016 essay on *Pyramids, Rays, Points, and 'Spiritual Powers': Leonardo's Research during the Last Decade of the Fifteenth Century*.

And so, O Patient Reader, let us conclude our exploration of Leonardo da Vinci and the *Pacioli Portrait* with the phenomenological and mystical words of Rupert Spira as written in his book *The Transparency of Things*, that, *'The abstract concepts of the mind cannot apprehend Reality, although they are an expression of it. Duality, the subject/object polarization, is inherent in the concepts of the mind. For* instance, when we speak of the "body" we refer to an object, which in turn implies a subject. If we expire this object we discover that it is non-existent as such and is in fact only a sensation.'

Leonardo da Vinci Picture Gallery: A Selected Collection

FIG. 21.5. *Leonardo da Vinci (1452-1519) picture gallery.*

1, Annunciation: 1472, oil on panel, 98 x 217 cm, Uffizi Gallery, Florence. **2,** Ginevra de' Benci: 1474-1478, oil on panel, 42 × 37 cm, National Gallery, Washington, D. C. **3,** Madonna of the Carnation: 1478, oil on panel, 67 x 42 cm,

Alte Pinakothek, Munich. **4**, Madonna Litta: 1476: oil on panel 42 x 33 cm, Hermitage, St. Petersburg. **5**, Virgin of the Rocks: 1483, oil on canvas, 199 x 122 cm, Louvre Museum, Paris. **6**, Virgin of the Rocks: 1504-1508, oil on poplar wood, 189 x 120 cm, National Gallery, London. **7**, The Virgin and Child with St. Anne: 1500-1513, oil on poplar wood, 168 x 130 cm, Louvre Museum, Paris. **8**, Portrait of a Musician: 1490, oil on panel, 43 x 31 cm, Pinacoteca Ambrosiana, Milan. **9**, Lady with an Ermine: 1490, oil and tempera on wood panel, 54.8 x 40.3 cm, Czartoryski Museum, Cracow. **10**, La Belle Ferronniere: 1495, oil on panel, 63 cm x 45 cm, Louvre Museum, Paris. **11**, John the Baptist: 1513-1516, oil on panel, 69 x 57 cm, Louvre Museum, Paris. **12**, Salvator Mundi: 1500, oil on panel, 65.6 x 45.4 cm, Private Collection. **13**, Mona Lisa: 1503-1519, oil on poplar wood, 77 cm x 53 cm, Louvre Museum, Paris. **14**, Last Supper: 1495-1497, fresco, 420 x 910 cm, Santa Maria della Grazie, Milan.

References

Baldasso R (2010). Portrait of Luca Pacioli and Disciple: A New, Mathematical Look. The Art Bulletin 92:83-102.
Barca GA. IACO. BAR. VIGENNIS P.1495. Enigma e Secretissima Scientia.
http://www.ritrattopacioli.it/Jacobarvigennis2.pdf (site disconnected)
Bogomolny, Alexander (1996). Golden Ratio in Geometry. https://www.cut-the-knot.org/do_you_know/GoldenRatio.shtml
Brown, David Alan [ed] (2001). Virtue and Beauty, Catalogue for the National Museum of Art (Washington, D.C), page 145. Princeton, N.J.; Chichester: Princeton University Press.
https://www.nga.gov/content/dam/ngaweb/research/publications/pdfs/virtue-and-beauty.pdf
Christie's (15th November 2017). Leonardo's Salvator Mundi makes auction history. *https://www.christies.com/features/Leonardo-and-Post-War-results-New-York-8729-3.aspx*
Ciocci, Agrante (2011), Il doppio ritratto del poliedrico Luca Pacioli (The double portraiture of the polyhedral Luca Pacioli). Spanish Journal of Accounting History 15:107-130.
Del Maestro, Rolando F (1998). Leonardo da Vinci: the search for the soul. The Journal of Neurosurgery 89:874–887.
Friedmann, Herbert (2019). Symbolic Goldfinch. Princeton University Press, Google Books.
Frosini, Fabio (2016). Pyramids, Rays, Points, and "Spiritual Powers": Leonardo's Research during the Last Decade of the Fifteenth Century. In Illuminating Leonardo. A Festschrift for Carlo Pedretti Celebrating His 70 Years of Scholarship (1944-2014). (Eds., Constance Moffatt, Sara Tagliagamba), Chpt 22, 315-328. Brill NV, Leiden/Boston.
Garrard MD (2006). Who was Ginevra de' Benci? Leonardo's portrait and its sitter recontextualized. Artibus et Historiae 27 (53):23-56.
Glori, Carla. Il cartiglio. *http://www.carlaglori.com/mi-presento/*
Kulski JK (2017). Leonardo da Vinci: The Melzi Chronicles. Published by Jerzy. K. Kulski. *ISBN: 978-0-6480653-1-9*
Kulski JK (2018). The Mona Lisa portrait: Leonardo's personal and political tribute

to Isabella Aragon Sforza, the Duchess of Milan. International Journal of Art and Art History 6 (2):31-50. DOI: 10.15640/ijaah.v6n2p5.
http://ijaahnet.com/journals/ijaah/Vol_6_No_2_December_2018/5.pdf
https://www.researchgate.net/publication/331087584_5MonaLisa

Mackinnon, Nick (1993). The Portrait of Fra Luca Pacioli. The Mathematical Gazette 77:130-219.

Museo di Capodimonte (2016). Il ritratto di Luca Pacioli a Capodimonte.
http://www.museocapodimonte.beniculturali.it/il-ritratto-di-luca-pacioli-acapodimonte/

Pacioli, Luca (1498). Divine Proportion (in English). 1498 edition.
tennenbaum pacioli-divine-proportion.pdf. Uploaded by Israel Monroy Muñoz on Oct 22, 2014. Full text of original edition (1498) in English.

Richter JP (1880). The Notebooks of Leonardo da Vinci.
http://www.fromoldbooks.org/RichterNotebooksOfLeonardo/
http://www.gutenberg.org/ebooks/5000

Stott, Rebecca (2012). Darwin's Ghosts. In Search of the First Evolutionists. Bloomsbury Publishing. London, Berlin, New York, Sydney.

Van Manen, Max (2011). Eidetic reduction. PhenomenologyOnline.
http://www.phenomenologyonline.com/inquiry/methodology/reductio/eidetic-reduction/

Wikipedia (2018). Ginevra de Benci. https://en.wikipedia.org/wiki/Ginevra_de%27_Benci

Wikipedia (2018). Jacopo de' Barbari.
https://en.wikipedia.org/wiki/Jacopo_de%27_Barbari#cite_note-NGA-2

Wikipedia (2018). Luca Pacioli. https://en.wikipedia.org/wiki/Luca_Pacioli

Wikipedia (2018). Leonardo da Vinci. *https://en.wikipedia.org/wiki/Leonardo_da_Vinci*

Wikipedia (2018). Portrait of Luca Pacioli.
https://en.wikipedia.org/wiki/Portrait_of_Luca_Pacioli

White, Susan Dorothea (2006). Draw like Da Vinci. Cassell Illustrated.
http://www.susandwhite.com.au/enlarge.php?workID=162

Zollner, Frank (2003). Leonardo da Vinci's portraits: Ginevra de' Benci, Cecilia Gallerani, la Belle Ferroniere, and Mona Lisa. In Dudzik, Sebastian (Hrsg.): *Rafael i jego spadkobiercy. Portret klasyczny w Sztuce nowozytnej Europy [Materialy sesji naukowej, 24 - 25 X 2002] (Sztuka i kultura, Bd. 4).* Torun 2003, S. 157-183.
http://archiv.ub.uniheidelberg.de/artdok/4220/1/Zoellner_Leonardo_da_Vincis_Portraits_2003.pdf

ABOUT THE AUTHOR

Jerzy (Yurek) K. Kulski is a retired scientist who lives in Perth, Western Australia. He is married with two sons and two grandchildren. Born in a displaced persons camp in Flensburg in Northern Germany in April of 1947, he immigrated with his Polish father and Russian mother to Perth in Western Australia in August of 1949 where he later attended Thomas Street Primary School, Perth Modern High School, and graduated from The University of Western Australia with Honours in Science, and a PhD for his research on the biochemical and endocrine changes in human milk composition during normal and abnormal lactation. He has published extensively in the medical and biological fields of lactation, virology, cancer, microbiology, genetics, genomics, and immunology, and has been a staff and freelance researcher at a number of universities, institutes and hospitals in Australia, the USA, and Japan. He is the author of the crime novel *China Heist*, and the historical novel *Leonardo da Vinci: The Melzi Chronicles*. He also guest edited and contributed chapters to two scientific books: *Next Generation Sequencing: Advances, Applications and Challenges* (InTech Publishing); and *The Major Histocompatibility Complex in Health and Disease* (MDPI Books). *Leonardo and the Pacioli Code* is his first non-fiction book on the science and art history of Leonardo da Vinci.

https://www.jerzykulski.com